Women of
MYSTERY

Women of MYSTERY

THE LIVES AND WORKS OF NOTABLE WOMEN CRIME NOVELISTS

Martha Hailey DuBose

WITH ADDITIONAL ESSAYS BY

Margaret Caldwell Thomas

THOMAS DUNNE BOOKS
ST. MARTIN'S MINOTAUR
NEW YORK

THOMAS DUNNE BOOKS.
An imprint of St. Martin's Press.

www.minotaurbooks.com

Production Editor: David Stanford Burr

Book design by Casey Hampton

Library of Congress Cataloging-in-Publication Data

Dubose, Martha Hailey.
  Women of mystery : the lives and works of notable women crime novelists/
Martha Hailey DuBose ; with additional essays by Margaret C. Thomas.—1st ed.
    p. cm.
  "Thomas Dunne books."
  Includes bibliographical references.
  ISBN 0-312-20942-8
  1. Detective and mystery stories, English—History and criticism. 2. Women novelists,
English—Biography. 3. Detective and mystery stories, English—Bio-bibliography.
4. Detective and mystery stories, American—History and criticism. 5. English
fiction—Women authors—History and criticism. 6. American fiction—Women
authors—History and criticism. 7. Women novelists, American—Biography. 8. Detective
and mystery stories, American—Bio-bibliography. 9. Women and literature—Great
Britain—History—20th century. 10. Women and literature—United States—History—20th
century.   I. Thomas, Margaret C.

PR830.D4 D83 2000
823'.0872099287—dc21

                                                                            00-040240

First Edition: December 2000

10 9 8 7 6 5 4 3 2 1

To Kate and Polly,
David and Kate

CONTENTS

FOREWORD
GUILTY PLEASURES

*Y*ou've picked up the latest hardback, hot off the presses. Or you waited, and now it's out in paperback. Or your name came to the top of the list at the library. Or the friend who knows exactly what you like just dropped off her well-thumbed copy with the coffee stain on page 64. However it came to you, you are about to plunge into your next novel of crime and detection. You are a mystery fan, a reader of detective fiction, a consumer of police procedurals, spy novels, imaginary murder and mayhem . . . an indulger in that guilty pleasure, *escapist reading.* If the first few pages of the book in your hands grab your attention, then it's going to be a long night. But don't worry. You're not alone.

People all over the world are doing it just as you are . . . popping a champagne cork with Nick and Nora Charles or a beer cap with Nero Wolfe. Cracking wise with Fletch or waxing poetic with Adam Dalgliesh. Chatting with Miss Marple over tea at the vicarage or cruising Southern California with Kinsey Millhone. Waiting, but not too long, for the first shoe to drop: the body in the library, the skeleton under the leaf mold, the missing business partner, the corpse on the sidewalk.

In opening his famous essay "The Guilty Vicarage," English poet W. H. Auden wrote, "For me, as for many others, the reading of detective stories is an addiction like tobacco or alcohol. The symptoms of this are: firstly, the intensity of the craving—if I have any work to do, I must be careful not to get hold of a detective story for, once I begin one, I cannot work or sleep till I have finished it. Secondly, its specificity—the story must conform to certain formulas . . . And, thirdly, its immediacy."

We know what you mean, Mr. Auden. Detective fiction is addictive, like potato chips, and we can't read just one. Having stumbled on, say, *Death on the Nile* or *The Nine Tailors,* we feel compelled to consume as much Christie or Sayers as we can, as quickly as possible. In our heart of hearts, we know that we read detective stories for one reason, pure and simple—to be entertained. A good crime writer will hook us as fast as Oreos. We're human. We're curious. We simply must find out who killed Roger Ackroyd or why so many people want to get their hands on the Maltese Falcon.

Women of Mystery is for mystery readers—the legions of intelligent and interested people who want to know more about the writers behind the crimes and the solutions. Without academic footnotes or feminist folderol, this book explores the private lives and public works of some of the most popular and important authors of mystery fiction—women who have rewarded their millions of readers with countless criminous acts, characters as comfortable as old friends, puzzles that test and tease our rational powers, and solutions that satisfy our deep-seated requirement that in books, if not always in life, justice will be done. Here you will discover the lives led by the women behind the bestsellers—their private adventures, their personal triumphs and tragedies, the real-life sources of their famous characters and curious plots. These life stories draw on the most reliable biographical sources available and, as far as possible, the subjects' own words.

Women of Mystery begins with a look at "The Mothers of Detection," women who wrote and published stories of mystery and detection throughout the pioneering days of the genre. With the notable exception of the prolific and engaging Mary Roberts Rinehart, none of these early authors are much read today, but some of their books can still be found, lurking on the shelves of libraries and used-book stores or perhaps hiding in Grandmother's attic. It's worth a look.

Then we turn to the headliners: from Golden Age writers to modern masters like P. D. James and Ruth Rendell who continue to shape the entire field of detective fiction and arguably of all fiction. In today's world of literary self-indulgence and psychobabble, who is doing more to keep the fires of narrative storytelling ablaze than the artists and artisans of crime writing? And in what other literary genre have women writers been, almost from the start, such powerful presences, so consistently on equal footing with their male counterparts?

This book has been planned for the reader's convenience. Taken cover to cover, it presents not only the lives of individual writers but also a rolling overview of the history of detective and crime fiction, with emphasis on the influence of its female practitioners. *Women of Mystery* can equally well be dipped into at any section; each stands on its own. Chronological listings of every writer's mystery novels and stories and other key writings, and notes on film and video adaptations, are especially helpful to anyone who enjoys reading series books—Dorothy Sayers's Peter Wimsey or Ruth Rendell's Inspector Wexford novels, for example—in the order of their writing. Resources are provided at the end for those who wish to investigate these writers in greater depth.

Conscientious efforts have been made not to reveal solutions to any mysteries because, as we know, everybody hates a stool pigeon.

One brief note before we begin: academics and practitioners alike have argued ad nauseam about the definitions of mystery fiction, debating the subtle and not-so-subtle differences between detective stories, crime novels, thrillers, tales of espionage, and novels of action-adventure. But in the name of simplicity, in this discussion, "detective," "mystery," and "crime" fiction will generally refer to any tale or story in which a mystery, most often involving crime, is investigated by professional and/or amateur sleuths using rational—not supernatural—means.

Part ONE

IN THE BEGINNING: THE MOTHERS OF DETECTION

"All goes to plan, both lying and confession,
Down to the thrilling final chase, the kill."
—from "The Detective Story" by W. H. Auden

In the 1800s, murder was decidedly *not* a proper topic for well-bred ladies and gentlemen. When the young Victoria became Queen of England and Great Britain in 1837, propriety ascended the throne, and the Queen's rigid standards of behavior dominated not only her own subjects but the upstart citizens of England's former colonies as well. Even at the raucous frontier fringes of the fledgling United States, Victorianism mixed well with the still-strong strains of Yankee Puritanism.

Luckily, more and more people were learning to read, and with literacy came a growing demand for literature in its broadest sense. Although fine books were beyond the financial reach of most people, newspapers, magazines, and cheap storybooks thrived in a market that clamored for entertainment and quick thrills, and even the most high-minded authors (and their publishers) discovered that they could actually make money and gain fame by feeding popular tastes. It was in this environment that the detective story was born.

The first true literary detective was a French gentleman named C. Auguste Dupin—the invention of America's foremost tortured genius, Edgar Allan Poe (1809–1849). With the publication of "The Murders in the Rue Morgue" in 1841, followed by "The Purloined Letter," "The Mystery of Marie Rogêt," " 'Thou Art the Man,' " and "The Gold Bug," Poe carved out the fundamentals of the genre. Dorothy L. Sayers credited Poe with the introduction of "the formula of the eccentric and brilliant private detective whose doings are chronicled by an admiring and thick-headed friend." Dupin was, according to mystery writer and critic Julian Symons, "what Poe often wished he could have been himself, an emotionless reasoning machine."

The brilliant-detective-and-dogged-sidekick formula was just one of the devices Poe innovated. From his fertile brain came the locked room murder, the innocent suspect, the most likely villain, the verbal clue, the cryptic clue, the in-plain-sight clue, the red herring, rudimentary ballistics evidence, armchair detection, fiction built on real-life facts—so many of what Dorothy Sayers called the "deceptions in the mystery-monger's bag of tricks. . . ." Sayers went on to declare that, "take it all round, 'The Murders in the Rue Morgue' constitutes in itself almost a complete manual of detective theory and practice."

The times were changing dramatically in mid-nineteenth-century England and France and in the United States. The story of the development of detective fiction is a record of relatively rapid cross-pollination among these three countries. The first seed was germinated by Poe. Seedlings were then transported from shore to shore, hybridized, and when conditions were propitious, a true genre emerged.

Howard Haycraft in *Murder for Pleasure* connected the development of civilian police forces to the rise of democratic states and the realization "that only by methodical apprehension and just punishment of *actual* offenders could crime be adequately curbed and controlled." The advent of professional police departments came in the early to mid-1800s in England, France, and the United States. With the acceptance of official detection, interest in fictional detection could prosper.

A second factor was the Industrial Revolution, which made the mass production of reading material a viable commercial activity. As Colin Watson demonstrated in his study of the rise of popular crime fiction, *Snobbery with Violence,* authors like Sir Walter Scott, Charles Dickens, and William Thackeray, who understood popular tastes, came along "at just the right moment to reap the benefit of cheap printing, big-scale serialization . . . and the direct marketing and wide distribution made possible by the growth of the railways."

A third critical factor was the spread of literacy. Throughout the nineteenth century, more and more of our foremothers and forefathers were learning to read, and what they wanted to read was sensationalism. Romanticism and, later, reaction against Victorian repression ignited a wildfire of lurid storytelling to satisfy the growing public demand. Even in polite British society, ladies and gentlemen wanted their excitement dished up hot and spicy—if not in their drawing rooms, at least between the covers of their books. Despite the condemnation of Victorian critics, nineteenth-century readers relished new tales of horror and sexual metaphor, snatching up Mary Shelley's* *Frankenstein* (1818) at the beginning of the century and Bram Stoker's *Dracula* (1897) at the end. Inbetween, they indulged in the soulful Gothic romances of the Brontë sisters, the stormy poetics of Byron and Shelley, the dark passions of Thomas Hardy.

The most successful writers of popular sensational stories were often women who spun feverish tales that revolved around dark secrets, dramatic revelations, and tragic consequences. What they delivered was truly sensational: overwrought tales of sex, betrayal, and death, usually justified by neatly high-minded conclusions. But readers knew that the sins along the road to the final moral—illicit love affairs, bastard children, hidden identities, bigamy, incest, and murder—were the real fun.

In 1860 and 1861, *East Lynne,* the first story by Mrs. Henry Wood (Ellen Price Wood, 1814–1887), appeared as a magazine serial and was later published as a complete novel. Although rejected by several cautious English publishers because of its controversial content, *East Lynne* eventually sold more than one million copies during Mrs. Wood's lifetime, making her a very wealthy woman. The story includes elements of detection (but no detective) and the legal prosecution of an old crime. Critics at the time were astounded by the author's presentation of courtroom procedures. The *Saturday Review* noted "an accuracy and method of legal knowledge which would do credit to many famous male novelists."†

An even more scandalous English novel, *Lady Audley's Secret,* was penned by young Mary Elizabeth Braddon. Wildly popular, this high melodrama was crammed with crime, from bigamy and blackmail to murder, leading to the unmasking of the charming Lady Audley's true nature. A lawyer's daughter, Miss Braddon (Mary Elizabeth Braddon Maxwell, 1837–1915) lived much closer to the edge of social acceptability than Mrs. Wood. By the time *Lady Audley's Secret* reached the British public in 1862, Miss Braddon had moved in with her publisher, John Maxwell. Because Maxwell's first wife was confined to a mental institution, the couple lived together without benefit of clergy until 1874, when they were at last able to marry. Together they had six children, two of whom became novelists, and Mary Elizabeth also raised her husband's five offspring.

Her writings, which reflected the influence of the French Realists,

---

* Mary Shelley's father, William Godwin, was the author of an early precursor of the detective novel, *Caleb Williams,* published in the last decade of the 1700s. Godwin employed several of the elements later associated with novels of detection, but the book is more correctly classified as political fiction.

† Quoted by A. E. Murch in *The Development of the Detective Novel.* 1968.

won the admiration of contemporaries including Charles Dickens, Robert Louis Stevenson, and Henry James, and she enjoyed a long and successful writing career. Like Mrs. Wood, Mary Elizabeth Braddon never dealt seriously with detection, but toward the end of her career, she included increasingly complex crimes in her books, and her influence on later generations of detective writers was substantial.

American readers in the early nineteenth century were drawn to the moody mysteries of Hawthorne and Poe and the novels of James Fenimore Cooper. Americans were still very much a part of a frontier culture and favored down-to-earth settings for their thrillers rather than the Gothic castles of their English cousins. Even Mark Twain dabbled with certain facets of the crime story, and he was one of the earliest writers to understand the importance of fingerprint evidence. It was an American woman, however, who took inspiration from Poe's short stories and expanded detection to novel proportions. The first detective novel by a woman is now recognized to be *The Dead Letter: An American Romance* (1867), written by Mrs. Metta Victoria Fuller Victor (1831–1885) under the pen name Seeley Regester. Mrs. Victor's novel—first serialized in *Beadle's Monthly* magazine in 1866—included a gentleman police detective named Mr. Burton, and through hundreds of pages, the novel mixed fevered sensationalism with detection and wild trans-American chases. The resilient Mr. Burton does his darnedest to solve the mystery rationally, but in the end, he must turn to his clairvoyant daughter for a resolution: a detective, yes, but hardly Poe's reasoning machine. While the Pennsylvania-born Mrs. Victor was a prolific writer, she was never a very good one, and *The Dead Letter* is now regarded as little more than a quaint historical footnote.

It was to be another American woman who would finally master the legacy of Poe in long form, eliminate the cheap sensationalism of Victorian romance, and write the first internationally successful detective novel—and she would earn her title as "The Mother of the Detective Novel" almost a decade before the birth of the great Sherlock Holmes.

ANNA KATHARINE GREEN

THE LADY AND THE INSPECTOR

"Have you any idea of the disadvantages under which a detective labors?"
　　　　　　　　　　　　　　　　　—The Leavenworth Case

*I*n 1853, Poe's concept of the reasoning detective had attracted no less a novelist than England's great Charles Dickens (1812–1870). His working-class Inspector Bucket of *Bleak House* has resonated through generations of police fiction, and Dickens's last, unfinished novel, *The Mystery of Edwin Drood,* is considered by many to have been a true detective story in the making. But with the possible exception of *Edwin Drood,* Dickens was never really interested in detection per se. Inspector Bucket was not a plodding crime-solver but a plot device, employed by Dickens to move his story forward with minimum complication.

It was Dickens's friend Wilkie Collins (1824–1889) who made the next real breakthrough in detective fiction after Poe. In 1868, Collins published *The Moonstone.* Although an earlier Collins mystery, *The Woman in White,* is more popular today, it was not true detection. *The Moonstone* was called by Dorothy L. Sayers "probably the very finest detective story ever written" and by poet T. S. Eliot the "first, the longest and the best"[*] of the English detective novels. It is a cunningly plotted tale of crime and misdirection into which Collins introduced his own working-class policeman, Sergeant Cuff, the prototype of so many ordinary men of inordinate rationality who populate fictional police departments even today. Cuff is described by Julian Symons as "a master of the apparently irrelevant remark, the unexpected observation. . ." that reveals his prodigious deductive powers. But Collins never followed up on *The Moonstone* and its detective, and although interest in the novel

---

[*] Although *The Moonstone* is often cited as the first English detective novel, that honor actually goes to *The Notting Hill Mystery,* written by Charles Felix and published in 1862.

was revived among writers in the 1920s, it never achieved broad public acceptance.

In the year of *The Moonstone*'s publication, a young American was scribbling away at her first novel, a secret project that took six years to complete. Anna Katharine Green's decision to become a professional writer of detective fiction was not so extraordinary as it might appear. She was already a boundary-breaker—a college graduate in a society that saw few rewards in the formal education of women. Born in 1846, Anna Catherine Green (she changed the spelling of her middle name when her first book was accepted for publication) was the product of hardy New England stock. Her father, James Wilson Green, was a lawyer who represented clients in the state and federal courts of Manhattan and raised his family across the river in Brooklyn Heights, New York. Anna was the fourth child born to James and his wife, Katherine Anne Whitney Green. Katherine gave birth to her fifth child in 1849, but neither she nor the infant survived. Left with four children to care for, James Green turned over the child-rearing duties to his elder daughter Sarah, whom Anna Katharine called "mother-sister."

In spite of his success as a lawyer, James Green had the soul of a wanderer and frequently moved his family from rented house to rented house, city to city. One of his many moves took the family to Buffalo, New York, where he met and married his second wife, "Mother Grace," a kind woman who encouraged her stepdaughter's education and burgeoning interest in writing.

As Anna Katharine was growing up, so was her country. Even with the Civil War looming, the United States was expanding economically and geographically, and a middle-class lawyer and his family were well positioned to benefit. The Greens were always devout Presbyterians, worshiping for many years at Brooklyn's Plymouth Church, whose firebrand pastor was Henry Ward Beecher, brother of *Uncle Tom's Cabin* author Harriet Beecher Stowe. It was probably this combination of factors—the family's relative affluence, their religion, and the influence of the powerful teachings of Henry Ward Beecher, a fervent supporter of women's rights—that prompted the extraordinary decision to send Anna Katharine to college. In 1863, she entered Ripley College in Poultney, Vermont, one of a gallant handful of women's institutions of higher education. At Ripley, Anna Katharine presided over the Washington Irving Association, made the acquaintance of Ralph Waldo Emerson, and determined to become a poet. She received her bachelor's degree in 1866 and returned to the family home—now back in Brooklyn Heights and filled to the rafters with brothers, sisters-in-law, and sundry extended family members.

Anna Katharine sent several of her poems to Emerson in 1868, but his response was not encouraging. She turned from writing poetry to a novel. Believing that her father would not approve of fiction, she kept her work secret from all but her stepmother until *The Leavenworth Case* was completed. In fact, James was enthusiastic about his daughter's first novel, perhaps because the story included extensive legal and courtroom knowledge that had to have been learned from him. Through a friend, James arranged for Anna Katharine to meet publisher George Putnam, a contact that proved highly profitable for both.

Published by Putnam in 1878, *The Leavenworth Case: A Lawyer's Story* was an immediate success at home and overseas. In England, Anna Katharine was praised in print by Wilkie Collins: "Her powers of invention are so remarkable—she has so much imagination and so much belief (a most important qualification for our art) in what she says. . . . "[*] In France, her work was promoted by Émile Gaboriau, and its international success opened the world of literary eminence to Anna Katharine. The novel eventually sold more than a million copies, became required reading at the Yale Law School, and was said to be a favorite of British prime minister Stanley Baldwin. In 1894, Anna Katharine was visited at her home by her friend and frequent correspondent Arthur Conan Doyle, who had brought Sherlock Holmes to the reading public seven years earlier.

In *The Leavenworth Case,* Anna Katharine created her version of the Bucket-Cuff working-class cop, Inspector Ebenezer Gryce of the New York Police. As the story opens, a wealthy merchant is found dead in the library of his home, and suspicion falls on two lovely sisters before Inspector Gryce unravels the mystery. The plot itself is clever and complex, but just as important were the new elements that Anna Katharine introduced into detective writing: the accurately observed coroner's inquest, expert testimony, scientific ballistics evidence, a schematic drawing of the crime scene, a reconstructed letter, and the first suspicious butler. In fact, according to historian Alma E. Murch, "in her work we can discern for the first time, in its entirety, the pattern that became characteristic of most English detective novels written during the following fifty years."

The success of *The Leavenworth Case* was the beginning of a long and rewarding career. Personal success also awaited Anna Katharine when she was introduced to a young actor named Charles Rholfs by their church pastor. Charles was twenty-nine, and Anna Katharine was thirty-seven. Naturally, her father had doubts about Charles's prospects, but the

---

[*] Quoted by Patricia D. Maida in *Mother of Detective Fiction: The Life and Works of Anna Katharine Green*. Bowling Green, Ohio: Bowling Green State University Press. 1989.

struggling actor quickly agreed to give up the stage for a more settled career. He entered the Cooper Union in New York, studying the design and crafting of iron stoves, and with his future apparently on track, he and Anna Katharine were married in November 1884. Charles soon switched from iron stoves to furniture design. He also continued to act, and in 1891 he appeared in the successful stage version of *The Leavenworth Case*. Furniture, however, proved to be his real forte, and his unique designs gained international recognition. His works have since been displayed internationally and are included in the collections of Princeton University and the Metropolitan Museum of New York.

The couple ultimately moved to Buffalo, the city Anna Katharine remembered so happily from her childhood. The girl who had known so much shifting and change now insisted on a home of her own and the settled lifestyle of a middle-class matron. The Rholfses and their three children—Rosamund, Sterling, and Roland—lived in a house designed and furnished by Charles. Sadly, Anna Katharine outlived two of her children: Sterling, a pilot, was killed in a mysterious air crash in Toluca, Mexico, in 1928, and Rosamund died in 1930. Roland, also an aviator, was an associate of the Wright brothers and later piloted for Franklin D. Roosevelt.

Though none of her subsequent books ever equaled the immense popularity of *The Leavenworth Case,* Anna Katharine was always able to support her family in comfort with her writing. But by 1923, when her last book, *The Step on the Stair,* was published, her somewhat dated style and Victorian mannerisms had already been overtaken by a new generation of crime writers—most of whom gladly acknowledged their debts to Anna Katharine Green. She died on April 11, 1935, at her home in Buffalo . . . a genuine pioneer.

There is a bit of Inspector Gryce in most of the fictional professional detectives that have followed. He was the first genuine series detective, featured in eleven novels and two short story collections, and solved his cases with hard investigative dedication. More than any of its predecessors, *The Leavenworth Case* set the standard for professional police work in detective fiction.

Twenty years after Inspector Gryce's first case, Anna Katharine Green created another detective convention by teaming the indomitable Gryce with a new character who was to inspire one of the most popular breeds of sleuth: the elderly spinster snoop. Miss Amelia Butterworth of Gramercy Park appeared first in *That Affair Next Door* (1897), and returned for *Lost Man's Lane* (1898) and *The Circular Study* (1900). Miss Butterworth, the amateur, is not a distaff Dr. Watson. There's nothing of the "stooge" (as Hercule Poirot once characterized his friend Captain Hastings) about her, and she is much respected by the good Gryce for her deductive and intuitive skills. In *The Circular Study,* the octogenarian inspector is constantly confounded by the intellectual powers of Miss Butterworth: "He was not often caught napping, but this woman exercised a species of fascination upon him at times, and it rather amused than offended him, when he was obliged to acknowledge himself defeated."

In the Gryce–Butterworth pairing, Anna Katharine found a workable solution for one of the most vexing problems of early detective fiction—the class difference. Police around the turn of the century were common folk. No matter how brilliant, the policeman was invariably a product of the working class and realistically subservient to the upper class—the wealthy in America and the titled in Britain. Yet detective stories about crimes committed by ordinary people (the natural milieu of most real-life police investigations) were not the stuff of popular and profitable fiction. Readers didn't want the pedestrian crimes and criminals that were part of their own everyday lives; they wanted to be privy to the excesses committed at the top of the social heap. They wanted entry to the ballrooms and boudoirs of the rich and powerful—lofty realms from which the average reader and policeman were excluded. By teaming Inspector Gryce with the well-bred and well-off Miss Butterworth, Anna Katharine provided her working-class detective with a polite introduction to the upper crust. Miss Butterworth knows how the wealthy think and behave. She understands high society and can guide the policeman into and through its arcane complexities.

(The class problem continued to plague detective writers, especially the English, until after World War Two, when the old class barriers began to crumble. Until then, the two most frequent approaches were to follow Anna Katharine Green's lead and pair an aristocratic amateur with a working cop, as Dorothy Sayers did with Lord Peter Wimsey and Detective-Inspector Parker of Scotland Yard, or to create an aristocrat who was also a law officer, such as Ngaio Marsh's hero, Roderick Alleyn. Agatha Christie, original as usual, overcame the class differential by making her most famous detective an outsider. A retired Belgian policeman, Hercule Poirot easily navigated between high and low society because, as his creator well understood, the British were simply too smug to care about his social status. When, in *Murder on the Orient Express,* the great detective is snubbed by a British Army officer, "Poirot reading the English mind correctly, knew that [Colonel Arbuthnot] had said to himself: 'Only some damned foreigner.'")

In addition to shaping the structure of the modern detective novel, Anna Katharine Green also gave it a uniquely American flavor. Unlike so many American writers at the time, who blithely copied class, character, and locations from the English, Anna Katharine wrote about the distinctly American people, places, and styles of life that she observed. Her court scenes are played out according to American legal rules. Society is separated by wealth rather than birth, and upper-class money is new and raw. Her New York has the gritty feel of a city on the grow, and there are no lords and ladies in her country villages. There is brashness in her characters, even the rigid Miss Butterworth, for who else in the 1890s but a snobbish American old maid would dare to attach herself to a police investigation for no higher motive than female curiosity?

> *"[Holmes] used to make merry over the cleverness of women. . . ."* —Dr. John Watson about Sherlock Holmes,
> "A Scandal in Bohemia"

In the mid-1880s, Arthur Conan Doyle (1859–1930), a young English physician who was having a difficult time attracting enough patients to make a living, used his idle hours to jot down ideas for a story about a detective named Sherrinford Holmes and his London housemate, Ormond Sacker. Sherrinford became Sherlock, and Sacker was transformed into Dr. John H. Watson. The rights to the finished story, which Doyle called *A Study in Scarlet,* were sold for a paltry £25, and the world's greatest detective made his first public appearance in the 1887 edition of *Beeton's Christmas Annual*—rousing little interest in his home country. It was the American editor of *Lippincott's Magazine* who boosted Doyle's career, contracting to publish *The Sign of Four* in 1890.

What Doyle achieved with his Sherlock Holmes stories was not a major literary revolution, even though he did impose the order of logic on the detective genre more rigorously than any writer to date. Doyle's everlasting contribution was the creation of a character so vivid that he single-handedly dragged detective fiction out of literary left field and toward the respectable mainstream. There's no way to downplay the impact of Holmes on all detective fiction. He was, and remains, the model of the totally rational, scientific problem-solver. Steeped in romance, he is the solitary hero, plagued by personal devils but dedicated to his quest for truth—an icon, the image of detection.

Arthur Conan Doyle was only the most successful detective writer of his time. Others were plowing the same field, and in some cases turning up new ideas. Women writers of popular fiction were enough of an oddity in the nineteenth and early twentieth centuries that they often adopted male pen names to encourage acceptance of their material for publication. Others simply published anonymously, abandoning all chance for recognition. Yet the fact remains that women were very much there from the beginning. Outside of academic circles, writers like Anna Katharine Green are hardly ever mentioned anymore. When their works do resurface, they are usually collected as Victoriana—nostalgic relics of a long-dead era. Even Arthur Conan Doyle is probably not so much read today as known through film and television versions of his Sherlock Holmes stories. But readers of contemporary crime fiction owe this turn-of-the-century generation more than a casual glance.

England's L. T. Meade (Elizabeth Thomasina Meade Smith, 1854–1914), after a long career writing children's stories and books for young people, collaborated in 1894 with "Dr. Clifford Halifax" to produce a series of stories generally believed to be England's earliest medical mysteries. Collaborating again, with "Robert Eustace" (a pseudonym of Dr. Eustace Robert Barton, who later assisted Dorothy Sayers), Meade introduced the first female master criminal in stories collected as *The Brotherhood of the Seven Kings*. Again with "Robert Eustace," she created the evil murderess Madame Sara in *The Sorceress of the Strand* (1903). The most memorable detective character imagined by Meade and "Robert Eustace" was Florence Cusack, who appeared in four stories published in *The Harmsworth Magazine* between 1899 and 1900. Accompanied by her friend Dr. Lonsdale, Miss Cusack, a handsome young woman of wealth and curious independence, briskly solves perplexing crimes with unerring common sense. She is described as "a power in the police courts, and highly respected by every detective in Scotland Yard"—a remarkable feat considering the status of women at the time.

Catherine Louisa (C. L.) Pirkis (18??–1910) added another common-sense female crime-solver to the lexicon in the 1890s. Her last short story collection, published in 1894, was *The Experiences of Loveday Brooke, Lady Detective,* featuring a poor, but determined, woman who deploys her considerable powers of observation ("I start on my work without theory of any sort—in fact, I may say, with my mind a perfect blank") in the service of a London detective agency.

A more influential female detective writer was Emmuska Magdalena Rosalia Maria Josefa Barbara Orczy Barstow—Baroness Orczy (1865–1947)—a native of Hungary who immigrated to England as a girl. Her first major success, the 1905 play *The Scarlet Pimpernel,* was a joint venture with her husband. Emmuska transformed the play into an equally popular series of Pimpernel books, but the adventurous Sir Percy Blakeney—"the demn'd elusive" Pimpernel—was not her only memorable character.

Inspired by the stories of Arthur Conan Doyle, Emmuska nevertheless determined to create a detective wholly unlike Sherlock Holmes, and she developed the grandfather of all armchair detectives, The Old Man in the Corner. His name is never known. He inhabits a table at the rear of an ABC luncheonette in London's Norfolk Street, drinking milk, eating cheesecake, and unfolding his ingenious solutions to seem-ingly insoluble crimes—all for the benefit of an amazed audience of one, a young newspaper reporter named Polly Burton:

> Polly thought to herself that she had never seen anyone so pale, so thin, with such funny light-colored hair, brushed very smoothly across the top of a very obviously bald crown. He looked so timid and nervous as he fidgeted incessantly with a piece of string; his long, lean, and trembling fingers tying and untying it into knots of wonderful and complicated proportions.
>
> —"The Fenchurch Street Mystery"

The Old Man first brings together all the frayed ends of a mystery, then neatly unties the complexities, just as he undoes the knots in his ever-present piece of string. His unmitigated self-regard and his arrogant disdain for time-wasting and unimaginative police officials (later to be hallmark traits of fiction's most famous sedentary detective, Nero Wolfe) are boundless. The Old Man starred in dozens of short stories collected in *The Case of Miss Elliot* (1905), *The Old Man in the Corner* (1909), and *Unravelled Knots* (1925). The stories themselves may seem stilted to to-day's readers, but many of Baroness Orczy's conceits still have real power. As Julian Symons has noted, "The misanthropic Old Man is con-cerned only with demonstrating his own cleverness. . . . and it is a pe-culiarity of the stories that in many of them the criminal goes free." This witty, almost malevolent disregard for the acceptable rules of con-duct and social order in the Old Man stories appears much later in the novels of writers like Patricia Highsmith and Ruth Rendell. In fact, the idea for switched-therefore-motiveless murders that ensured the popu-larity of Highsmith's 1950 debut novel, *Strangers on a Train* (subsequently filmed by Alfred Hitchcock), was first worked out in an Old Man case.

The Old Man was not the only detective created by the baroness, but he was by far the most successful. In 1910, Emmuska published *Lady Molly of Scotland Yard,* the adventures of the upper-class head of Scotland Yard's fictitious Female Department. Lady Molly has all the arrogance of the Old Man (hers born of social rather than intellectual snobbery), but lacks the hard-edged humor. Nor is the smarmy character of the lawyer-detective Patrick Mulligan in *Skin o' My Tooth* (1928) appealing.

There are many more names that can be included among the found-ing Mothers of Detection . . . women like Natalie Sumner Lincoln (1872–1935), a Washington, D. C.–born novelist who integrated politics with murder in *The Trevor Case* (1912) and other detective stories . . . England's Mrs. Belloc Lowndes (Marie Adelaide Belloc Lowndes, 1868–1947), sister of Hilaire Belloc and author of a number of popular, fact-based mysteries including *The Lodger* (1915), which revived the horror of Jack the Ripper . . . Isabel Egenton Ostrander (1885–1924), who wrote under pen names including Robert Orr Chipperfield and was one of the first to adopt the murderer's point of view in a detective story . . . Carolyn Wells (Mrs. Hadwin Houghton, 18??–1942), who penned more than sixty detective books and wrote the influential *The Technique of the Mystery Story* (1913), the first how-to-write guide for fledgling mystery-makers.

In 1841, Edgar Allan Poe wrote the blueprint for the detective story. Over the next seventy years, writers of varying talents assembled the building materials and dug the foundations. By the time of the First World War, the underpinnings of modern detective fiction had been firmly laid, and on both sides of the Atlantic, the mystery-reading public was ready for the structure to go up.

BIBLIOGRAPHY

THE MOTHERS OF DETECTION

" 'Mysteries!' he commented. 'There is no such thing as a mystery in connection with any crime, provided intelligence is brought to bear upon its investigation.'"   —The Old Man in the Corner

The following bibliography includes the detective/mystery novels and story collections of the best-known Mothers of Detection: Anna Katharine Green and Baroness Orczy. Recommended titles are noted with an asterisk. Books are listed chronologically by first publication title; alternate titles are noted. Featured detectives appear in ( ). US = United States. GB = Great Britain.

ANNA KATHARINE GREEN
1846–1935
American (born: Brooklyn, New York)

1878 *The Leavenworth Case* ★ (Inspector Gryce)
1880 *A Strange Disappearance* ★ (Gryce)
1881 *The Sword of Damocles* ★
1883 *Hand and Ring* ★ (Gryce)
1883 *XYZ* ★ (short stories)
1886 *The Mill Mystery*

1887   *Risifi's Daughter*
1887   *7 to 12*
1888   *Behind Closed Doors* ★ (Gryce)
1890   *The Forsaken Inn*
1890   *A Matter of Millions* ★ (Gryce)
1891   *The Old Stone House and Other Stories* (short stories)
1892   *Cynthia Wakeham's Money*
1893   *Marked "Personal"*
1894   *Miss Hurd: An Enigma*
1895   *The Doctor, His Wife and the Clock* (short stories; Gryce)
1895   *Doctor Izard* (Gryce)
1897   *That Affair Next Door* ★ (Gryce, Miss Butterworth)
1898   *Lost Man's Lane* ★ (Gryce, Miss Butterworth)
1899   *Agatha Webb*
1900   *The Circular Study* ★ (Gryce, Miss Butterworth)
1900   *A Difficult Problem and Other Stories* (short stories; one with Gryce)
1901   *One of My Sons* ★ (Gryce)
1903   *The Filigree Ball* ★
1905   *The Amethyst Box*
1905   *The House in the Mist* (title novel and two short stories)
1905   *The Millionaire Baby*
1906   *The Chief Legatee*/GB: *A Woman of Mystery*
1906   *The Woman in the Alcove*
1907   *The Mayor's Wife*
1910   *The House of the Whispering Pines* ★
1910   *Three Thousand Dollars*
1911   *Initials Only* (Gryce)
1913   *Masterpieces of Mystery* (also published in 1919 as *Room Number 3 and Other Stories*)
1914   *Dark Hollow*
1915   *The Golden Slipper and Other Problems* ★ (Violet Strange)
1916   *To the Minute and Scarlet and Black: Two of Life's Perplexities*
1917   *The Mystery of the Hasty Arrow* ★ (Gryce)
1923   *The Step on the Stair*

EMMUSKA, BARONESS ORCZY
1865–1947
British (born: Hungary)

1905   *The Case of Miss Elliott* ★ (short stories; Old Man in the Corner)
1909   *The Old Man in the Corner* ★/US: *The Man in the Corner* (short stories; Old Man in the Corner)

QUICK, CALL A BOBBY!

Bobbies are a fixture in British detective fiction. Lean and taciturn males and females in blue, they are generally the first officials at the scene, doing the hard work of evidence gathering, witness questioning, and crime scene protecting.

Ironically, the British police force traces its origin to a novelist, Henry Fielding, author of *Tom Jones*. In 1748, Fielding was made a magistrate in the Bow Street section of London, charged with adjudicating common criminal cases. But who would bring the miscreants to court? In Fielding's time, there was no organized force, so the magistrate recruited six volunteer "thief-takers" to pursue and apprehend petty thieves and troublemakers. These thief-takers soon became known as the Bow Street Runners, and the good citizens of London began to think that a regular force of civilian lawmen might be a good idea.

The Bow Street Runners—who received irregular compensation from the rewards, or "blood money," offered by crime victims—continued to police the streets until 1829. In that year Sir Robert Peel (1788–1850), the Home Secretary, established the Metropolitan Police of London. Peel had become a Member of Parliament in 1809. Three years later, he was appointed Secretary of Ireland, where one of his accomplishments was the establishment of the Irish Constabulary. In 1825, Peel undertook the monumental task of reforming England's entire criminal law system, one result of which was the founding of the Metropolitan Police.

Neither public nor politicians were initially thrilled with the idea; many feared that a government-supported police force would trample personal liberties and act as repressors for the powerful. Peel took every care to disassociate his police force from the military. The distinctive uniform of today's London bobby evolved from Peel's decision to dress the force in simple blue tailcoats and black top hats. First called "Blue Lobsters" by London's wary citizens, the police proved their worth by midcentury and were dubbed "bobbies"—a term of affection and gratitude to their founder, Sir "Bobby" Peel. (In Ireland, police constables are still referred to as "Peelers.")

The first home of Peel's Metropolitan Police was an office on White-hall Place that backed onto an alley called Scotland Yard. Wherever the offices have been located—today the police are headquartered on Victoria Street—the building is always called Scotland Yard. Although the British Home Secretary, a Cabinet minister, is responsible for the internal law and order of the nation, there is no British national police force akin to the FBI. Scotland Yard, now New Scotland Yard, remains home to the Metropolitan Police of London, who can, when requested, assist the country's more than fifty regional forces. Hence the frequent command in English detective novels to "call in the Yard!"

A STRANGE ENCOUNTER:
THE GENESIS OF THE FEMALE DETECTIVE

Female crime-busters emerged fairly early in the history of the detective story, created by male and female writers alike. The first was probably England's Mrs. Paschal, who appeared in W. S. Hayward's *The Revelations of a Lady Detective* in 1861, followed in 1864 by Andrew Forester, Jr.'s, unnamed "Female Detective." The problem for these early writers was to establish some remotely plausible reason for their lady sleuths to be in the business at all. There were several routes. Hayward's Mrs. Paschal finds herself widowed and poor, with only her mental resources to fall back on, and investigation becomes a legitimate avenue out of genteel poverty. Dorcas Dene solved mysteries in two volumes (1897–1898) by London journalist George R. Sims. A "brave and yet womanly" former actress, Dene takes up investigation "when her artist husband [is] stricken with blindness. . . . " Financial necessity again, and love for her man, made Dorcus Dene's sleuthing acceptable.

Then there was the chance encounter. Anna Katharine Green's Miss Butterworth just happens to be at the fringes of a murder case when she meets Inspector Gryce of the New York police, and it is natural that this contact should develop into a relationship (platonic, of course). There was also the desire to see justice done, almost always particularized for female detectives. Lady Molly, for example, gets into police work in order to prove the innocence of her husband, who languishes in prison until the end of Baroness Emmuska Orczy's 1910 book, *Lady Molly of Scotland Yard*. The baroness was not stymied by the fact that the real Yard had no women officers; she simply invented a Female Department for Lady Molly's convenience.

These early lady detectives were no Sherlocks. They might be bright, but the idea that they could solve crimes through sheer logic or scientific investigation was, as yet, unthinkable. Their tools were intimate knowledge of domestic interests, feminine intuition, and old-fashioned common sense. As often as not, they stumbled into solutions, and the crimes they uncovered were frequently felonious (theft, blackmail, kidnapping) but rarely gruesome or fatal.

But by the time Anna Katharine Green introduced Violet Strange in *The Golden Slipper and Other Problems* (1915), the status of women was changing. As the twentieth century reached its teens, female investigators could be young and single, where their predecessors had been mostly middle-aged spinsters, widows, or married women. They could be motivated by the mental and moral challenges of investigation. They worked at what they wanted to do and were less likely to retire at the wedding altar. Part socialite, part suffragette, Violet Strange is endowed with intelligence, a strong will, and a well-developed sense of social justice—plus the courage to venture where no fictional women had gone before.

MARY ROBERTS RINEHART

THE BURIED STORY

". . . I shall probably always be known as a writer of detective books, which I emphatically am not."
—Foreword to *The Mary Roberts Rinehart Crime Book*

The first female superstar of mystery writing is no forgotten tidbit of literary history, and Americans of a certain age can remember her still as a living presence, small, silver-haired, and usually swathed in plush furs and real pearls. She was born in the year of the nation's first centennial; in the year she died, the United States launched its first satellite into space. Her life spanned two world wars and the beginning of the Cold War. During her lifetime, too, crime writing evolved from an interesting sideline of sensationalist fiction to one of the most profitable segments of popular litera-

Mary Roberts Rinehart

ture, and Mary Roberts Rinehart was in the thick of it all.

She declared that she was not a writer of detective stories, and she wanted desperately to be taken seriously as a social commentator, journalist, and novelist. But of the mass of published writings she left behind, only her crime stories remain of interest. She developed a form of mystery that owes both to the Victorian sensationalists and, in lesser degree, to the rationalism of Anna Katharine Green and Arthur Conan Doyle. She produced a comfortable fusion of mystery and romance that is the direct ancestor of the works of writers such as Victoria Holt and Mary Higgins Clark; yet in most surveys of detective fiction, Mary

Roberts Rinehart rarely rates more than an embarrassed aside. To scholars of crime and detective fiction, she is problematic, for she never created a true detective. She employed scientific methods of crime-solving infrequently and self-consciously and made flamboyant use of coincidence, intuition, and even spiritualism. Yet she presented realistic crimes, concrete clues, and logical solutions.

She was without doubt a dedicated writer but a sometimes painfully undisciplined thinker. The occasional fine passages in her work demonstrate that she had the innate talent and imagination to become a very good novelist. But at some point early in her career, Mary Roberts Rinehart appears to have made a Faustian bargain: her talent in exchange for commercial popularity and its concomitant rewards and blessings. Popular she was—the first American mystery writer to enter the bestseller ranks; a household name that repeatedly appeared in the Most Admired lists favored by women's magazines; an associate of kings, queens, presidents, generals, and movie moguls; a Republican feminist who rated burial in Arlington National Cemetery.

There is no question that she could spin an intriguing tale, but to paraphrase Oscar Wilde, she put her art into her lifestyle. In her nonfiction and editorial writings and in the two versions of her autobiography, *My Story* (first published in 1931 and expanded in 1948), she created her own mystique, what biographer Jan Cohn calls "the Rinehart myth: the successful writer born out of financial need, family responsibility, and pure chance." But this carefully crafted public persona hid a real woman beset by internal devils and a lifelong series of external traumas that were, in nearly every particular, stranger than any mystery she wrote.

> *"I guess there are some curious stories hidden in these old houses."*
> —*The Case of Jennie Brice*

Mary Ella Roberts was born on August 12, 1876, in Allegheny, Pennsylvania, at that time a sister city to industrial Pittsburgh. The house into which she arrived, on West Diamond Street, was a multigenerational complex dominated by her widowed grandmother, Margaret Mawhinney Roberts. Baby "Mamie" was the first grandchild. Her parents, Tom and Cornelia Roberts, had been married for a year when Mary appeared, and they were to spend the next four years in the crowded home of his mother—together with his brother and sister-in-law, John and Sarah (Sade); his three younger sisters; and the assorted "sewing girls" who came and went daily to work the primitive sewing machines of Grandmother Roberts's home-based seamstress business.

The elder Mrs. Roberts had been widowed a dozen years earlier and raised her five children in as much middle-class comfort as she could provide by "falling back on her needle."* The Robertses were by no means impoverished, but money was tight, and it was certainly helpful when Tom and John reached the age to find employment and supplement the family coffers.

Tom was in his mid-twenties and working as a clerk when he met Cornelia Gilleland, an attractive young woman who had recently moved to Allegheny with her sister, Ella. Tom and Cornelia had at least one common bond—families steeped in the strict and dour theology of Covenanter Presbyterianism. Both the Roberts and the Gilleland families could trace their roots back to hard-scrabble Scotch-Irish farm people who had long ago pledged their loyalties to the humorless Calvinist God and the Protestant reforms of John Knox. Driven from Scotland to Ireland, many of these Covenanter Presbyterians had made their way to the New World in the eighteenth century. The Gillelands, like generations before them, stuck to the land and apparently prospered as farmers. The Robertses moved into the middle-class professions of teaching and preaching and became city-dwellers, but at least up to Grandmother Roberts's generation, they remained true to the stern precepts of their Presbyterian faith.

Perhaps it was their separate rebellions that drew Tom and Cornelia to one another. She had left her family's farm in Valencia, some twenty miles north of Pittsburgh, to escape a repressive stepmother. He had abandoned religion for a pugnacious agnosticism and proudly refused to honor his mother's Sabbath. Although Cornelia was in most other ways a conventional young woman of her times, Tom's individualism was constantly at war with the Victorian and religious restraints of his era and his family; it was a struggle that would eventually have tragic consequences for all.

But when their first daughter was born, Tom and Cornelia were housed in the second-floor front bedroom of his mother's house, just below the apartment of his brother and sister-in-law. They remained in these close quarters until the birth of their second daughter, Olive, in 1880. In that year Tom, chafing to be his own man, rented a row house for his family on Arch Street, just a short way from his mother's home. Tom was seemingly becoming a man of means. He had secured a sales

---

* Unless otherwise noted, quotations are from *My Story: A New Edition and Seventeen New Years,* Mary Roberts Rinehart's autobiography (1948), and from private writings, letters, and diaries cited by Jan Cohn in *Improbable Fiction: The Life of Mary Roberts Rinehart* (1980).

franchise from the Domestic Sewing Machine Company, and each morning he donned his carefully ironed black silk top hat and walked across the Sixth Street Bridge to his Pittsburgh office. In the front window of T. B. Roberts and Company, women employees pedaled away, demonstrating the remarkable capabilities of Domestic Sewing Machines.

Mary recalled her childhood as not especially happy. "I was frightfully impatient to grow up," she later wrote. "I hated being a child." But her early years were not haunted by the poverty or insecurity that later became part of the Rinehart mystique. Cornelia Roberts was a caring and capable mother who sewed beautifully and kept her young daughters outfitted in the latest fashions and her husband attired to spit-and-polish perfection. She was also an excellent cook and immaculate housekeeper. The Arch Street house, small but comfortable, was rigorously and regularly dusted and cleaned, as Cornelia fought an endless war with the black grime that drifted over Allegheny from the steel mills of Pittsburgh. On several occasions, Cornelia barred her family from the parlor and dedicated weeks to complete renovation, from carpets to slipcovers to discreetly draped nude statuary. Though simply educated, Cornelia was a lively and creative woman, possessed, Mary said, of "a sort of fierce driving energy." Cornelia sang constantly as she worked, and she bought herself an upright piano, over her husband's objections, on the installment plan.

For little Mary and Olive, the neighborhood in which they were born and reared constituted a busy universe, and elements of Arch Street life would provide Mary with inspiration for many years to come. The street was a microcosm of nineteenth-century city life, its inhabitants ranging from the solidly middle class to the genteel, and not so genteel, poor. Shopping was an everyday affair, and Cornelia often took her little girls to the farmers' market, where they might run into their country cousin Maggie Gilleland selling her vegetables, eggs, and butter. The German butcher on Federal Street had the neighborhood's only telephone, an emergency lifeline when illness struck—such as Cornelia's incapacitating headaches and Olive's near-fatal case of typhoid.

On warm days, all the Arch Street dwellers, save the snobbish family on the corner, sat on their front stoops and gossiped while the children played. Their neighbors included a landscape painter and a deaf and dumb Civil War veteran who communicated in writing. One of Mary's earliest playmates was Bessie Miller, the daughter of Professor Miller. Sadly, little Bessie, like so many children of the time, died of scarlet fever; she was only seven.

At their grandmother's house, where boarders now paid for the rooms once occupied by Tom, John, and their families, Mary and Olive often visited with their aunts Letitia ("Tish"), Anna Margaret ("Maggie"), and Matilda ("Tillie"), who was Mary's favorite.

The little Roberts girls were also frequent guests of their Uncle John and Aunt Sade, both of whom were to have special influences on Mary's career and adult behavior. John, three years younger than Mary's father, was the successful brother. The wholesale wallpaper business he opened in the late 1870s grew quickly, for John was a natural entrepreneur and salesman. He soon moved with his wife to a house with a stable that stood a stone's throw from Grandmother Roberts's place. Here—and at the grand suburban home in the fashionable suburb of Sewickley to which John and Sade moved in 1890—Mary learned to ride and became a more than competent horsewoman. She learned, too, her first real-life lessons in feminine manipulation from the lovely but "delicate" Sade. Sade's fragile health was, as Mary observed, like a "club . . . held over all our heads. She must never be worried, never do any labor." Although Mary later conceded that Sade was a neurotic sufferer and probably used the excuse of ill health to avoid motherhood, the sight of her lovely aunt, ensconced in luxury and never lifting a finger to maintain it, filled the little girl "with admiration and with awe." What a contrast Sade must have presented to her own hardworking mother.

Though Mary later complained of the restrictions imposed on her childhood and the lack of excitement, Allegheny was not always a placid place. The city sat at the convergence of the Allegheny and Monongahela Rivers and was routinely subjected to severe spring flooding when the rivers swelled with melting snow and ice. Although the Robertses' dwellings were on high ground, Mary clearly recalled the flood of 1884 when her father, wearing his omnipresent silk top hat, rowed the whole family through his flooded Sixth Street office building. When Mary was thirteen, she and her mother watched as bodies drifted through the city on the waters of the famous Johnstown Flood.

Years later, she set one of her early mysteries, *The Case of Jennie Brice*, in a flood-besieged Allegheny boardinghouse. As the book opens, the heroine-narrator, Bess Pitman, meets the oncoming waters by taking up her first-floor carpets and moving her piano to a higher level. What is so engaging about Mary's story is the sheer aplomb with which the inundation is greeted by the inhabitants of the Allegheny flood plain: neighbors row curious sightseers down city streets; the grocer on the corner lowers baskets of provisions to customers in boats; Mrs. Pitman ties her skiff to succeeding spindles of her front hall staircase as the water rises to the seventh step; a retired merchant (and amateur criminologist) poles his boat among the flooded houses and tosses slabs of raw liver to neglected cats and dogs. There is also a kind of flood etiquette regarding possession of dispossessed items. "It is not unusual to find one's household goods floating around during floodtime," Mrs. Pitman informs her audience. "More than once I've lost a chair, and seen it after the water had gone down, new scrubbed and painted, in Molly Maguire's kitchen next door."

Amid all the domestic details of *The Case of Jennie Brice,* there is a suspicion of murder, and the real Allegheny was not without its violent side during Mary's childhood. Mary never forgot the "terrible screams" of a young laundress who lost her hand to the hot rollers of an ironing machine appropriately called a "mangle." Then there was the gruesome Lizzie Borden–like ax murder of the butcher's wife by her daughter—an event Mary recalled in her 1933 novel *The Album.* Mary's own first brush with the law happened when she was about five. With the promise of candy, a strange woman tempted the child away from her grandmother's home, and Mary was recovered hours later by a policeman. The woman, she said, had shoved her inside a privy after taking her turquoise ring and brooch. Mary eventually identified a photograph of her alleged abductor but always wondered if it was the right woman.

Then there was the horrifying accident at the Pittsburgh Exposition, a commercial fair held in a temporary structure erected near the Allegheny River bank. Aunt Ella, Cornelia's sister, was baby-sitting Mary one evening, and the two visited the Exposition to see a display of Tom's sewing machines. They were browsing amid the pianos exhibited on the balcony of the crowded hall when the overburdened supports suddenly gave way and the whole balcony crashed to the floor below. Mary fell face-forward onto a spiked iron fence, and one of the spikes pierced her chin and jaw, emerging just below her lip. She also suffered a broken leg, and her Aunt Ella a badly fractured ankle. Mary's leg healed, her facial injury resulted in only a small scar, and she received $300 to compensate for her injuries. But her Aunt Ella was left with a permanent limp. Grandmother Roberts's Presbyterian judgment was that the accident was God's just punishment on Tom and Cornelia, who had gone out that night to attend a racy play entitled *The Black Crook.* (Little wonder that Mary grew up terrified of her family's harsh God and in adulthood switched her allegiance to the live-and-let-live Episcopalians.)

It's hard to imagine young Mary's life being as stultifying as she later claimed. Perhaps her school experiences colored her memory. She was never much of a scholar, and as a left-hander, she had a miserable time learning penmanship. In those days, the Second Ward School adopted the prevalent educational theory that left-handedness was a deviant condition to be cured. With the threat of a ruler to the knuckles or a full-fledged whipping, teachers forced their left-handed students to conform, and becoming right-handed was agony for Mary.

In high school, she opted for the academic English Course. She joined the debating society and wrote for the school paper, but "school work was sheer unenlivened drudgery," and she graduated with an unexceptional C average. Her best performance was in rhetoric and literature. She was an avid reader, and her literary tastes were catholic. No one—neither her parents nor Mr. Benny, the one-armed librarian—took much notice of her choice of reading matter. It was Tom who finally steered her to the classics, after he found her, at age eight, engrossed in the terrifying illustrations of Foxe's *The Book of Martyrs*. She read, she later said, strictly for the stories "and with no comprehension whatever of the human relations involved."

On summer visits to the Gillelands' Valencia farm, she uncovered a trove of reading of another type: the hired man's cheap penny dreadful books, which fired her romantic imagination. She was also well acquainted with the theater (once vomiting into the orchestra pit during an exciting performance of Mrs. Henry Wood's *East Lynne*) and the opera. Her earliest ambition was to become an actress—a girlish dream that she was to fulfill in a way, becoming one of the American theater's most successful writers in the 1920s.

"I had no mad itch to express myself, but I liked words. . . ."

Mary's literary abilities first surfaced publicly in 1892, when she submitted two short stories to a contest sponsored by the *Pittsburgh Press*. Both stories, under the name M. E. Roberts, were selected for publication, but neither received the $5 gold pieces awarded by the newspaper. This must have rankled, for Mary was attempting to meet a financial crisis that was threatening her family's security.

The problem was Tom Roberts, who was never able to reconcile his dreamer's soul with the responsibilities of a wife and children. In 1887, he had lost his sewing machine business and been forced into a series of sales jobs. In 1890, at Cornelia's insistence, the family moved from Arch Street to a larger house in the more prosperous Poplar Street neighborhood. The new house provided Mary and Olive their first separate bedrooms and a real bathroom, but as Tom's fortunes continued to decline, supporting the household became a terrible weight. For all her homemaking skills, Cornelia Roberts was not inclined to scrimp or count pennies (spendthrift traits her daughter inherited), and she struggled determinedly to keep up a middle-class front. Gradually, however, Mary and Olive saw the little luxuries of life disappear. No more maid. No more piano lessons. They were sharing a bedroom again, as Cornelia rented the other to roomers—a source of humiliation to an adolescent girl with visions of elegant "sub-deb" parties and a new level of interest in pretty clothes, popularity, and the opposite sex. Cornelia quietly began to take in sewing; Mary and Olive were drafted into housework; and Mary entered her two melodramatic short stories in the newspaper contest, hoping to improve the family's finances by a few dollars.

Tom had tried to establish a wallpaper showroom in his house, but when that didn't work, he took to the road, at different times peddling his brother's wallpaper, insurance, cash registers, and soft drinks. But he was never good at selling, in large measure because his heart lay elsewhere. Tom was an inventor in an age of American invention. His role models were the Edisons and Bells whose tinkerings were transforming society and amassing fortunes in the process. Tom, his lawyer and financial backer D. F. Patterson, and an inventor friend whom Mary called "the dreamer" would spend hours in the Robertses' Arch Street dining room, engrossed in plans for ideas that would change the world—an insulation material for telegraph wires, a method for transforming steel mill slag into cement. "They dreamed and talked in low voices and high figures, and in their dreams they were incredibly rich, incredibly successful."

Tom had one chance to hit it big and was defeated by his own grandiose visions. He invented and patented a rotary shuttle for sewing machines. The idea was a good one, and a manufacturer offered $10,000 for the patent. Tom could probably have bargained for a bit more cash plus royalties, but he turned the offer down flat. His reasoning is not clear, but pride more than greed was the likely motivator. At any rate, when Tom's patent expired, he didn't have the money to renew it, and he never earned a penny from an invention that became standard in the sewing machine industry. Mary always kept the prototype drawings made by her father, reminders of what might have been.

With his family, Tom—never demonstrative—was increasingly distant and preoccupied. There is no evidence that he was cruel or even uncaring. But clearly he was an absentee father, often gone on long road trips and rarely engaged even when he was at home. Mary recalled an incident when the girls and their mother had gone to the country for a visit. Tom had promised to care for Mary's canary, Dicky, while she was away. But Tom became absorbed in some new scheme, and when Mary returned, the bird had died of starvation.

From her mother, Mary received her notions of decorous womanhood and her desire for physical comforts, whatever the cost. But to her father, for all his faults, she owed her capacity to dream big dreams and perhaps her talent for self-justification.

Mary had always assumed she would go to college, and sometime during her school years, she had conceived a plan that was audacious for the time: to become a medical doctor. Perhaps it was triggered by the arrival in her Arch Street neighborhood of C. Jane Vincent, M.D., a somewhat forbidding woman who eventually built a practice treating children. But no one took Mary's ambition too seriously. Medical school was costly, and her parents had no savings. Besides, what medical school would accept a sixteen-year-old girl with a lackluster academic record?

Although the story of the lady novelist who had wanted to be a doctor became an important element in the Rinehart mystique, Mary in fact made no serious effort to follow this dream, even though her uncle John offered to pay for medical school. But after her high school graduation in 1893, she did decide to become a nurse. Nursing, at that time, was transforming into a legitimate profession for young women— though still suspect because of its association with bodies, illness, squalor, and death. Cornelia was vehemently opposed, but Mary insisted. As mystery writer Charlotte MacLeod noted in her 1994 biography, *Had She But Known,* "Mary had never been the most docile of daughters. She argued back." She also dressed herself in her most coquettish outfit and traipsed off to seek the advice of the family doctor. He, as she probably knew, was away for the summer; a younger and rather more attractive physician was taking his place.

"The hospital lured me . . . as an adventure, an experience, and as the solution of a practical difficulty."

Though just twenty-four and only recently graduated from Philadelphia's Hahnemann Hospital medical school, Dr. Stanley Marshall Rinehart, the summer stand-in for Mary's doctor, took a stern, fatherly tack with the young woman who wanted to be a nurse. It was not, he insisted, a romantic profession. The work was backbreaking, the hours were exhausting, and the conditions were dreary and depressing. The next day, he took her on a tour of the Pittsburgh Homeopathic Medical and Surgical Hospital, where his brother, Dr. C. C. Rinehart, was a director. But neither the young physician's dire warnings nor her first behind-the-scenes sight of hospital life dissuaded Mary; lying about her age, she applied to and was accepted by the Pittsburgh Training School for Nurses at the Homeopathic Hospital.

On August 18, 1893, just a few days after her seventeenth birthday, Mary was delivered by her father to the hospital that would be her home, school, and workplace for the two years and three months of her training. Those first three months were a probationary period in which she was assigned the worst possible chores—scrubbing a bloody operating theater on her second day—and endured grueling hours, terrible food, and her first direct contacts with the underside of city life. She survived and became a full-fledged student, entitled to $8.00 a month as well as her room and board. From that meager wage, she had to supply her own striped uniforms, tulle caps, and the appliances of her trade—thermometer, forceps, and scissors.

With the exception of the superintendent of nurses, Marguerite Wright (much admired by Mary as "a great lady, cultivated and of fine family"), and her assistant, the hospital's nursing staff consisted entirely of students. These young women worked twelve-hour shifts, rotating through every department of the hospital, and also took classes. Any fanciful schoolgirl notions of the healing profession were quickly banished by the "human wreckage" Mary encountered on every tour of duty: prostitutes who came in to have their babies and taught naive nurses the real facts of life; men horribly injured in the steel mills; children burned and mutilated by workplace accidents; suicides, homicides, alcoholics, and drug addicts; victims of the summer typhoid outbreaks and the ever-present plague of syphilis.

At the time, Mary said, she tried to write the drama of what she saw in the wards and emergency room, but she could not: "It was beyond me. It always has been beyond me." Years later, in her straight novels *"K"* and *The Doctor*, Mary would paint vivid images of the hospital as seen through the eyes of nursing novitiates, and nurses often feature in her stories. The one ongoing crime-solver Mary created is Hilda Adams, a nurse drafted into police work by a former patient. But it was always the romance of the professional healer, and not the reality of the suffering patient, that earned the writer's attention.

Inevitably, what Mary saw and heard in the hospital changed her. She became, if not truly empathetic, at least indignant at the circumstances of life in society's lower reaches. Though she was always conservative politically, she was stirred by the conditions of the workingmen she encountered. She was incensed by the callousness of great industrialists who would not pay for the care of workers injured, often beyond repair, in their mills, factories, and railroad yards. Though unable to fully analyze the injustices she saw, Mary understood that something was "wrong, rottenly wrong."

She was growing away from her family—cut off by "the unbridgeable gulf of differing interests"—and soon she did not even try to go home on her rare days off. Besides, she was increasingly involved with another interest, Stanley Rinehart, M.D. She hadn't seen much of the young doctor during her probationary period, but his reputation was well established among the nurses. Stan was a junior member of the surgical staff, notorious for his perfectionist techniques and his sharp temper in the operating theater. But Mary had encountered another side of his nature. During a smallpox outbreak in the men's surgical ward, Mary had been quarantined with staff and patients. Among the recuperating, there were fights and threats of mutiny; it was Christmastime, and the men wanted to go home. The staff created diversions, setting up a Christmas tree and providing gifts. They planned an evening of caroling, and while Mary played piano, Stan led the singing. Over refreshments, the doctor and the student nurse chatted. Later, Mary observed Stan in the pediatric ward, where, in contrast to his intimidating surgical persona, he was adored by the children.

It was strictly forbidden for doctors and nurses to fraternize, but Mary suddenly conceived an urgent desire to learn German, and she approached Stan, who spoke and read the language. Soon she was going to his home office for tutoring on her free afternoons. Whether she learned any German is doubtful, but romance blossomed, and Mary and Stan began meeting outside the hospital. By May of 1894, they were secretly engaged, but there are no secrets in hospitals. When word of the relationship got out, Stan was summoned to appear before the hospital's board of directors. Assuming that the best defense is a loud offense, Stan declared his intention to marry Nurse Roberts, and the hospital be damned. The hospital acquiesced. The engagement was on, though it could not be announced until Mary completed her training, and she could not wear her ring.

Not everyone thought this fairy-tale romance was so romantic. Some fellow students warned Mary about her future husband's terrible temper and told her that she could do better. Even Mary had some doubts: was she truly in love with Stan or would she, like Bess Pitman in *The Case of Jennie Brice,* "discover too late that she was only in love with love"? At the house on Poplar Street, however, Cornelia was elated by the engagement, largely because as a married woman, her daughter would not be allowed to continue in nursing.

That year, 1895, should have been filled with orange blossoms for Mary Roberts. She was now a senior nursing student, assigned to a variety of private cases that took her outside the hospital. She was engaged to a rising young physician with excellent professional credentials and family pedigree. But a series of events was about to take place—a pattern of tragic and grisly events that would recur throughout her life.

"A cloud seemed to have settled down on us. . . ."

Her father, ever dreaming of his great success, had hit the road as a traveling salesman of Nux–Phospho soft drinks and a line of cash registers: a dreary life of nameless hotels and too many whiskies in too many bars. Her mother was struggling to maintain the facade of middle-class com-

fort while taking in roomers and sewing. Mary was discovering that private nursing in the houses of the poor and ignorant was no less rigorous
or depressing than it was in the hospital wards. Then she received a letter from her father: Grandmother Roberts, who was living with Mary's
Aunt Tillie, had died of a broken neck after a fall down the cellar steps.
Mary could not even attend the funeral, for Tom's letter arrived too late.
Within days, however, she received more terrible news: her Aunt Tillie's
beloved little daughter had been struck by a train and killed.

The worst news was to come. Mary was nursing a dying woman—a
gentlewoman who had been banished by her wealthy family for refusing
to give up her illegitimate child—when a telegram arrived. It told Mary
simply that her father had died, and she must come home. On the train
ride back to Allegheny, she happened to see a newspaper headline:
"Pittsburgh Man Shoots Self in Buffalo Hotel Room."

No one knew why Tom had been in Buffalo, New York. Possibly he
was job-hunting. He had given up inventing, failed at several speculative
ventures, and just been fired by Nux–Phospho for his drinking and poor
sales record. He had left no explanation, no suicide's note for his family.
With just 37¢ in his pocket, Tom Roberts, not yet fifty years old, had
gone to his hotel room on the evening of November 14, 1895, wrapped
himself in quilts to muffle the sound, and shot himself through the
heart. (Mary later contended that she recognized the mark of a head
wound after the body had been prepared for burial.)

Mary, Olive, and their mother met the train that carried Tom's body
home and prepared for a family funeral. But the press, on the scent of a
dramatic story, gathered at the house until Mary had to beg them to
leave. She never forgot those intrusions, and in her novels, she often pictured vulturish pressmen at the scenes of tragedy. (In light of an obituary cited by Charlotte MacLeod in her biography, it is interesting to note
that virtually all we know of Tom Roberts came from his daughter. The
newspaper account said that Tom had been a well-known insurance
man and one of the city's best salesmen in his youth. The paper also recounted his success as a speculator in oil and his involvement in the
building-and-loan association business. Did the newspaper get the story
wrong? Or did Mary, who never received enough of what she wanted,
materially or emotionally, from her father, romanticize his failures?)

A week after Tom's funeral, Mary returned to the Homeopathic, and
she completed her nursing course that winter. Plans for the wedding
went forward, and it was arranged that the young couple would live in
the house that Stanley had shared with two of his half brothers. The
wedding preparations were probably the best gift Mary could have given
to her mother, an antidote to Tom's terrible death, and Cornelia threw
herself into the making of a magnificent trousseau and household linens

for her daughter. But Mary's wedding gown—the first dress she had ever owned that was not sewn by her mother or herself—was Uncle John's gift. An enormous affair of heavy white satin and lace ruffles, the dress had to be thickly padded to fill out Mary's tiny figure into a fashionable Victorian hourglass.

On the evening of April 21, 1896, family, friends, and most of the Homeopathic Hospital staff gathered in the Second United Presbyterian Church of Allegheny. Although Stan had six ushers, Mary's only attendant was her little sister, and Uncle John gave the bride away. The wedding and the reception at Mary's home were prominently reported in the Pittsburgh newspapers. For their honeymoon, Stan whisked Mary off to Bermuda, stopping on the way for her first visit to New York City. Although Stan enjoyed the island holiday tremendously, Mary became ill. Many years later, he recalled the trip as "halcyon days" for himself, but his bride "was sick practically all the time. . . . There were times when I had to give her a hypo of morphia before we went out. . . ." Mary wrote little about her wedding and nothing of the honeymoon in her autobiography, but she had achieved the one romantic dream that had been with her since childhood: she had lived out the girlish fantasy of "myself coming down a church aisle in a white satin dress with a long train and a veil, beside some youth who varied as time went on."

"I was enormously proud of my status as a wife."

On their return to Allegheny, the newlywed Rineharts set up their home and his private practice in the Western Avenue house. Though she never shirked her new duties as wife and homemaker, which included doing Stan's monthly accounts, Mary was often ill during the first six months of her marriage. Perhaps it was the inevitable emotional exhaustion brought on by the events of the preceding year; perhaps it was an early onset of the depression that dogged her adult life; perhaps it was the discovery that the intimacies of marriage were not the "great ecstasy"* of her dreams.

Whatever the cause, more serious illness was around the corner: before her first anniversary, Mary became pregnant, and with this and her next two pregnancies, she was constantly sick, racked by "pernicious vomiting" so severe that there were "consultations about terminating" the pregnancy. But on August 18, 1897, ninety-six-pound Mary deliv-

---

* From an unpublished autobiographical fragment written by Mary in the 1950s. Quoted by Jan Cohn in *Improbable Fiction*.

ered her first child, Stanley Marshall Rinehart, Jr., a healthy nine-pounder. Her second son, Alan Gillespie, was born in November of 1900, and her last child, Frederick Roberts (nicknamed Ted), arrived in September of 1902. Ted's birth was particularly difficult; Mary suffered severe hemorrhaging that brought her childbearing to an end and began years of gynecological problems and surgeries.

The year after Stan, Jr.'s, birth, the Rineharts moved to a larger house and office on Western Avenue. Stan's practice was growing, and they could now afford two maids and sometimes a houseboy. Mary was often ill, undergoing several surgeries and a case of diphtheria caught from her eldest son. Her little boys, though generally robust, were subject to their share of childhood diseases and accidents. Ted survived severe whooping cough in infancy, and was two when he swallowed carbolic acid found in his father's office. He was saved when Mary, remembering a lecture in nursing school, poured vinegar down his throat.

As biographer Jan Cohn found in her research into Mary's life, the myth began around this time. Although Mary later publicly described the first decade of her marriage as a whirlwind of devoted motherhood and housewifery, a private account of her life, written for her sons when she was in her eighties, reveals a woman, in Cohn's words, enduring "considerable unhappiness." In this autobiographical fragment, Mary called herself a "household drudge" and admitted her fierce jealousy of her husband's wealthy female patients—"their ease, their leisure, and most of all their clothes." (Among the first items she was to purchase with her own money was a tailored blue suit exactly like one worn by an attractive young patient.) Years later, these women were to echo in the archetypal Rinehart troublemaker: beautiful, vain, haughty, lazy, socially nouveau man-eaters like Juliette Ransom, the blonde seductress and blackmailer who meets a fitting end in *The Wall*.

It was difficult, of course, to raise three boisterous little boys so close in age, though the Rineharts could easily have afforded a nursemaid. Mary often found herself expected to assist Stan in his practice. (Once she helped her husband with the surgical removal of a sailor's tattoo. The name "Nellie" was emblazoned over the sailor's heart, but since he had moved on to a new love, the name had to go. Mary used this same operation as a critical clue to the identity of a murder victim in *The Case of Jennie Brice*.) Without question, Stan's chaotic schedule—hospital, office hours, duties as medical inspector for Allegheny County, and late-night house calls so frequent they were routine—made it difficult to run an orderly household or find time for an active social life.

But Mary was the author of much of her own discontent. She had married a doctor in some part for the social status of being a doctor's wife, but her public and private writings reveal a strong strain of resentment at the responsibilities of that life. She recalled young Stan's birth as the beginning of a transition "from a pair of happy children into a family group," but the reality of her own maturation is debatable. Whatever she had, Mary always wanted more, and she judged success by its material and social accessories. Was she, in her marriage, learning that even a good life was not good enough for her?

> *"I did not want a career. The word has never been used in the family and never will be."*

At some point, Mary Roberts Rinehart must have decided that if a fortune was to be made, she had to make it. When recuperating from her bout with diphtheria, she had, at the suggestion of her nurse, submitted two original poems to *Munsey's Magazine*. Both were accepted, and she received $22. Earlier that year, 1904, another poem had been published in the *Pittsburgh Sunday Gazette* and earned $2. Here, perhaps, lay the road to the kind of material success she dreamed of. She continued to write and submit throughout 1904 and 1905. Her first short fiction for *Munsey's* was "His Other Self," based on one of Stan's patients, a man who had sustained a head injury that caused him to recover memory lost many years before in a train wreck. Mary's story, complete with her trademark happy ending, brought in her largest payment to date. (She often returned to the theme of the recovered amnesiac; it became the basis of several plays and her 1921 novel *The Breaking Point*.)

She was earning money now—not much, but she was still testing the waters. At some point, she went on her own to New York, seeking a publisher for a book of children's poems; she was not successful, but she did visit the publishing firm of Bobbs-Merrill. She was learning her trade, too, trying virtually every kind of popular subject, from comic tales to romance and intrigue to sentimental human interest. As Charlotte MacLeod has noted, these early stories "could only be described as hack writing." But Mary was essentially a self-taught writer who initially copied the styles of the writers she read, and her reading was as undisciplined as her early writing. Her strength was always her plotting, which she later dismissed as "that crutch of the beginner, that vice of the experienced writer." Complex and often driven by wild coincidences and O. Henry–like twists of fate, her plots were always exciting. But she had never learned to edit or rewrite; she would dash off stories in the evening, then have them typed and mailed the next day. A young teacher and journalist named Willa Cather once told her that writing involved putting a work aside, then going back to it after some time and revising and revising. Mary hadn't paid much attention to the advice, but she should have listened.

However much Mary exaggerated the demands of family, she probably did have to snatch her writing time from the few free hours afforded by an active household and a continuing pattern of tragedies. Her mother moved in with the Rineharts for a brief time after Olive, who had trained as a teacher, married in 1903. Her Aunt Sade, after so many years of "delicacy," died painfully of cancer, and Uncle John was shattered. Soon after Sade's death, Olive's infant daughter died after accidentally taking poison, and the whole family was devastated.

But it was a loss of another sort that gave Mary the excuse to justify her writing as a necessity. Stan was doing well financially, so he had begun investing in the stock market. Unfortunately, he bought on margin, and on a day when he and Mary happened to be visiting the New York Stock Exchange, a panic occurred. It not only wiped out the Rineharts' investments but left them $12,000 in debt. Returning to Allegheny, Mary began to cut back on household expenses, and though the family could probably have recouped its losses quickly enough, she contended that the financial pinch "forced" her to write. Hence another key element of the Rinehart mystique: loyal wife and mother compelled by financial need to save her family from ruin by turning to her pen. (Shades of Mary Elizabeth Braddon and so many other Victorian women writers.) A small truth gave birth to a larger and more lasting fiction, in much the same way that many of Mary's most popular stories were born.

"I liked mystery, and it was easy for me."

At the urging of Robert Davis, the editor of *Munsey's*, Mary took on her first extended fiction. During a family vacation in the summer of 1905, after one of her many operations, she wrote a novel-length narrative—a serial mystery she titled *The Man in Lower Ten,* for which she was paid $400. With this sale, the writing career of Mary Roberts Rinehart was truly launched, and two more magazine serials followed quickly: *The Circular Staircase* and *The Mystery of 1122.*

Given the slapdash quality of her previous writings, *The Man in Lower Ten* was, in Jan Cohn's words, "nothing short of miraculous"—a piece of sustained writing that needed no excuses. Mary had created a fully developed and logical, if still frenetic, plot that neatly wove together two distinct and seemingly unrelated crimes—a forgery and bribery case and a murder. She had also written relatively rounded characters with histories and quirks and, in several cases, genuine humor. In *The Man in Lower*

Ten, the principal elements of the Rinehart mystery formula took shape. The narrator-hero is a youngish lawyer, Lawrence Blakeley, who is hurled into a mystery not of his making. With one exception, the main characters are, like Blakeley, upper-middle-class professionals or wealthy and socially prominent. The exception is a character who becomes standard in Rinehart mysteries: the man of common sense and rational abilities who focuses on real clues while everyone else dithers, seethes, turns pale, and clouds the mystery by hiding critical information. In *The Man in Lower Ten,* this down-to-earth character—Wilson Budd Hotchkiss, a low-level government employee, dogged "amateur detective," and devotee of the methods of Poe, Doyle, and Gaboriau— also provides comic relief as he uncovers crucial information, performs remarkable feats of induction, yet arrives again and again at the wrong conclusions. The police, on the other hand, are shadowy figures, literally in the case of a competent detective who follows Blakeley's trail throughout the novel, nabs the mysterious character who holds the clue to both mysteries, yet is given just a smattering of real dialog.

While other, greater mystery writers have always been troubled by the necessity of grafting love stories onto their tales, Mary gave romance a central role. The course of true love never runs smoothly, but in *The Man in Lower Ten,* it does run smack down the center of the mystery, providing vital motivation and endless opportunities for misunderstanding and secretiveness in the name of gallantry and propriety.

Although her three serials earned far more money than her stories and poems, Mary went back to her short writings and even tried her hand at a play. But a visit from her recently widowed Uncle John Roberts caused a change of direction. He knew about her little writing hobby and asked to read one of her stories. Mary handed him *The Circular Staircase,* and John, a fair critic, suggested that it should be published as a book. But who would want it? Mary wondered. An Anna Katharine Green novel on the bookshelf gave the answer. Mary copied down the address of Green's publisher, then posted her own book to Bobbs-Merrill headquarters in Indianapolis.

(In her autobiography, Mary spins a romantic version of this incident. Shyly, she meets her Uncle John's request to read her writing by dredging "the battered old carbon copy" of *The Circular Staircase* from her desk drawer. She is shocked when he says "book." Her selection of Bobbs-Merrill is mere chance. It takes the combined persuasive powers of her uncle and her husband to induce her to take the monumental step. But any good detective would quickly come up against the facts behind the excuses. How could the manuscript have become so old and tattered when it had been sent to *All-Story* magazine just months before? Why was the name Bobbs-Merrill such a revelation when Mary had once met with a representative of the firm in New York, remembering his name and his kindness? And why was the approval of Uncle John and Stan required when she had already sought a book publisher—for her children's poems—on her own? The Rinehart mystique was already being carefully plotted.)

Not many days later, Mary was at the butcher's when a call came from Stan. Fearing some terrible tragedy had warranted his resort to the telephone, Mary was first relieved, then thrilled to learn that a letter had arrived from Hewitt Howland, an editor at Bobbs-Merrill. Howland loved *The Circular Staircase,* wanted to publish it, and hoped to visit the Rineharts to discuss further books. The Rinehart household celebrated that night with cake and ice cream—the first of a lifetime of indulgences bought by the novels of Mary Roberts Rinehart.

Bobbs-Merrill brought out *The Circular Staircase* in 1908 and *The Man in Lower Ten* in 1909. At Howland's suggestion, the title of *The Mystery of 1122* was changed to *The Window at the White Cat,* and this novel was published in 1910. Whatever led Hewitt Howland to publish *The Circular Staircase* first, it was an astute decision. The book was an immediate success with critics and the reading public. But on the verge of publication day, Mary, frightened of bad reviews and of everyone knowing that she had authored what her own father would have deemed trash, had fled with the boys to a country retreat in Harmony, Pennsylvania. The reviews, however, were excellent, and everyone seemed to fall under the spell of Mary's inexhaustible spinster narrator-heroine, Miss Rachel Innes. Praise for *The Circular Staircase* was soon followed by money—*real* money, enough to pay for a grand Premier touring car, more servants for the Rineharts' newly rented house on Beech Street, and private school for her three sons. Her "trash" gained her, as well, entrée to the literary establishment: at Bobbs-Merrill's invitation, she joined James Witcomb Riley, Booth Tarkington, and Charles Ade in a box at the Indianapolis Speedway and was invited to dine with the Tarkingtons at their home.

The Man in Lower Ten, published late in 1909, roared up the 1910 best-seller lists and became the first American mystery ever to make the annual roster of bestselling books, coming in at fourth place. Mary's romantic novel, *When a Man Marries,* also made the list that year, in tenth place.

> *"There . . . in New York, was a new life indeed, that casual comfortable life of all people affiliated with the theater."*

Mary's fear of the critics may have dated to her first theatrical experience, going back to 1906. The first play she wrote was terrible and quickly discarded. But the second, a one-acter titled *The Double Life* (based on "His Other Self" with its recovered memory theme), sent her on another mission to New York. In an extraordinary act of naive self-confidence, she delivered the play to the Belasco Theater, where David Belasco, the most successful theatrical producer in the country, was staging *The Girl of the Golden West*. The angels must have been at Mary's side that day, for Belasco not only read her play; he liked it enough to arrange a meeting. He was interested in producing *The Double Life* if it could be rewritten and expanded to three acts. All that summer, Mary shuttled back and forth between Allegheny, where she wrote, and New York, where she conferred with the mighty producer.

Belasco took her under his wing, teaching her stagecraft and introducing her to the world of the theater and theater people. The lives of these glamorous actors and actresses surely tugged at her: "Religion, politics, even the usual responsibilities of family ties hardly existed for them. . . . They were free. To most of them their art was themselves, and they were dedicated to it." How Mary, who had early on nurtured the desire to be an actress, must have longed for the beautiful clothes, the romantic intrigues, the egocentric freedom of these gods of the stage. In a short fiction written later, her main character, a young wife and mother who writes a successful play, is torn by ambition and duty, seduced by New York yet bound to husband and children. But unlike Mary, the heroine of the fictional story does not scuttle her own boat.

Mary's big mistake was listening to an actor's advice and seeking an agent without consulting her powerful mentor. The agent, Beatrice deMille, condemned Mary's contract with Belasco (a simple buyout of rights to the play) as "wicked." At deMille's urging, Mary confronted Belasco with new demands, but he was infuriated and refused to see her again. It was a stupid move on Mary's part, as she later admitted, sacrificing so important a relationship for the hope of more money, but perhaps it was in her genes; Tom Roberts had once done very much the same, pridefully turning down the $10,000 offer for his rotary shuttle patent.

DeMille did secure L. S. Sire to produce the play, and Mary and sometimes Stan accompanied the cast and crew on their tryouts. But when *The Double Life* opened in New York on Christmas Eve of 1906, it was a disaster. The critics were cool, theatergoers stayed away, and the play was closed after just twelve performances. Mary did not attend the opening, and she later blamed the failure on the leading man, painting herself as the tragic author who disavows her "mutilated, emasculated, sick and tormented brain-child"★ rather than see it ruined by an intransigent actor.

★ "Up and Down with the Drama," *The Saturday Evening Post,* July 6, 1912.

But by 1909, with three successful mystery novels and one bestselling romance to her credit, she was ready to try Broadway again. *When a Man Marries* was extended from her serial novella *Seven Days.* Although the plot includes a small mystery, the book is more accurately a comic romance. The nugget of the plot came from Mary's experience during the smallpox quarantine in the Homeopathic Hospital in her student nursing days. Instead of working-class patients, the characters in the book are upper-class socialites trapped at a party when the Japanese butler falls ill and a quarantine is imposed. The story, with its limited setting and farcical plot, was a natural for the stage, and a young playwright named Avery Hopwood was recruited to develop the script. When "Hop" brought his finished script to Pittsburgh, Mary was less than amused— he had written a four-act comedy; she wanted a three-act farce. Farce won, but Mary and Hop found they could work well together, and their coauthored *Seven Days* opened at the Astor Theater on November 10, 1909, to strong reviews and public delight. The play ran for more than a year, and road company productions brought in additional royalties.

For all her ladylike manners, Mary was never squeamish about discussing her finances in public. In a 1912 article, published anonymously in *The Saturday Evening Post,* she said, "I write and make a little money." She went on to reveal, in the same paragraph, what "a little money" meant—"as high as fifty thousand dollars a year. . . ." In an interview with the *Pittsburgh Press* a year later, she confessed to earning $100,000 from her novels and an equal amount from her plays. For a suburban housewife merely supplementing the family income, she was doing exceedingly well.

The years between 1908 and the beginning of World War One were not without their dark days. In the year that *The Circular Staircase* was published, Mary's mother had a severe stroke, followed by the onset of a form of epilepsy. The stroke left Cornelia partially paralyzed and unable to speak. She suffered complete memory loss and had to be retaught the simplest tasks; the epilepsy brought the constant threat of seizures. Although she recovered her memory and some movement, Cornelia was never able to speak again, and her frustration was miserable. Eventually, the family developed a primitive means of communication, simple yes or no questions that could be answered with a nod or shake of the head. Cornelia, with her nurse, moved in with the Rineharts, and Mary, the dutiful daughter, found herself "with a fourth child."

At about the same time, Stan, still the bedrock of the family, developed a health problem that threatened his career. Rheumatic-like pain in his hands led Stan, now chief of surgery at the Homeopathic Hospital, to take morphine for relief. But the morphine—then a fairly common painkiller sold without a prescription—had the side effect of causing tremors. Clearly, Stan could not continue to perform surgery. His obvious option was to settle into general practice, but as America entered the second decade of the twentieth century, general medical practice was quickly becoming passé; the age of the specialist had arrived. In a move that will be familiar to many modern readers, Stan decided to retrain, and the Rineharts had sufficient resources for him to pursue a specialty in what was then the hub of the medical universe, Vienna, Austria.

After a brief stint refreshing his skills at Hahnemann Hospital in Philadelphia, Stan, with Mary and the boys, set off for Europe, sailing from New York on October 8, 1910. After several weeks of leisurely sight-seeing and shopping in London, Paris, Zurich, and Innsbruck, they arrived at their destination on the first of November. Stan quickly secured a German governess for the boys and an apartment in the Pension Columbia. While his family settled into a routine of sorts in their new and sometimes uncomfortable surroundings (huge and ornate rooms that seeped cold and damp, candlelight instead of electricity, the permeating odor of cooking onions), Stan attended lectures and began clinical studies in thoracic medicine at the nearby Allgemeine Krankenhaus, a public hospital. Like many American doctors seeking the cachet of European credentials, he studied with an Austrian "dozent" [sic] or medical mentor under the auspices of the American Medical Association of Vienna.

Meanwhile, Mary and her sons took full advantage of Viennese art, entertainment, and food. Museums, opera, intimate theater, concerts at the Prater, tea and pastries at Demel's, late evenings at the Bal Tabarin— they certainly weren't in Pittsburgh anymore. They all learned a little German, though nothing approximating Stan's command. Mary even started a new novel. Beneath the fashionable glitter and exotic decadence of prewar Vienna, she also managed to discern the appalling gulf between rich and poor in this sophisticated Hapsburg capital. She was too good an observer to miss the startling contrasts between the smug and frivolous nouveau riche of Vienna's café society and the hideous poverty of its lower classes. At the same time Mary Roberts Rinehart was getting her first peek at the dirty petticoats beneath the silken gowns of the European class system, a young man named Adolf Hitler, an untalented but aspiring artist who lived in Vienna from 1908 to 1913, was learning the same lessons. In *Mein Kampf,* his bible of hate, Hitler later wrote, "To me Vienna, the city which to so many is the epitome of innocent pleasure, a festive playground for merrymakers, represents, I am sorry to say, merely the living memory of the saddest period of my life." Though poles apart from Hitler politically, Mary had something of the same reaction. "I came back," she wrote, "afraid of the bourgeois point of view, the comfortable acceptance of things as they were, the emphasis on possessions, on comfort, on peace at any price."

"I wanted that home fiercely. It spelled peace, security."

When Stan's training came to its end in February 1911, the Rineharts
wended their way home via Munich, Berlin, and London (where Stan
spent a couple of weeks working at Guy's Hospital and Mary shopped
Bond Street for custom-tailored fashions). They arrived back on native
soil at the beginning of April. Mary claimed that she had "learned
something in Europe," learned to fear the ignorance inherent in lives
lived solely for material comfort. But in one of those remarkable twists
of logic at which she was so adept, Mary leapt almost immediately into
the ultimate bourgeois dream—the purchase and reclamation of a massive house on seven acres in the wealthy Pittsburgh suburb of Sewickley,
where her Uncle John and Aunt Sade had once lived.

"Cassella," a rambling, twenty-room wreck on a cliff that overlooked
the Ohio River, had been built after the Civil War by one of Pittsburgh's railroad czars. By the time Mary fell in love with it, the house
and grounds were in serious disrepair. Undaunted by her supposed fear
of bourgeois values, Mary bought the house and began pouring her
money into its renovation. Only half-joking, Stan suggested that they
rename the place "The Bluff" because of its location and because that
was what Mary was putting up. The name stuck.

Once again, Mary worked like a demon to pay for what she wanted.
She had already cracked *The Saturday Evening Post* and other well-paying
magazines. Her comic "Tish" stories were becoming a staple in the *Post*,
and Bobbs-Merrill had published the first Tish collection. In 1912 and
1913, while the workmen hammered and the decorators swarmed over
her house, Mary wrote dozens of new stories and articles, four new
novels (*Where There's a Will, The Case of Jennie Brice, The After House,* and
The Street of Seven Stars), her first Miss Pinkerton story, and a play, *Cheer
Up*. (Produced by Beatrice deMille's son Cecil, Jesse Lasky, and Samuel
Goldfish, later Goldwyn, Mary's farce died after a cheerless twenty-four
performances.) The quality of her output was decidedly uneven: *The
Case of Jennie Brice* is a tight and well-written little mystery, but *The After House* is disappointing. *Where There's a Will,* based on an unproduced
play, was a lightweight comic romance. *The Street of Seven Stars,* her Vienna experiences transformed into a fictional blend of serious social observation with romance and a conventional happy ending, was very well
received, and some critics expressed hope that Mary had found her genuine voice in a serious format. They were eventually disappointed.

Whatever their literary quality, Mary's writings made money, and she
needed lots of it. She had lost a bundle investing in several get-rich-
quick schemes: a nonproducing gold mine and a nonexistent oil development. She had purchased The Bluff for $50,000 and then plowed

almost that much again into the renovation. She had acquired a large staff of household servants and groundskeepers, as well as a full-time secretary. The Rineharts joined the exclusive Sewickley Country Club, the boys' private schools meant tuition payments, and Cornelia required round-the-clock home nursing. But whatever the costs, her new house and lifestyle meant more than a move up the social ladder for Mary: "It spelled peace, security. There was behind that desire, I think, all the insecurity of my girlhood, even my father's tragic and unnecessary death. I wanted safety and permanence, a sanctuary for me and mine."

Stan, who was increasingly drawn to the treatment of tuberculosis (much to Mary's horror), had opened his new practice in an office in downtown Pittsburgh. He donated office space to Mary, a former X-ray room painted black from ceiling to floor where she worked most days, writing by hand at her furious pace on sheets of yellow paper. Perhaps from overwork, combined with her ongoing gynecological problems, she again became ill in 1913, and another trip abroad was just what the doctor ordered. The whole family was packed off to England for a motoring holiday, during which Mary and Stan became acquainted with Douglas Fairbanks, who was to become Hollywood's leading leading man and a good friend of the Rineharts for many years to come. On returning home, Mary underwent another surgery, and in early 1914, she contracted diphtheria for the second time.

That summer, she began another serious novel—one that took her back to the streets where she had grown up and the hospital where she had first discovered life "at its rawest and hardest. . . ." She was sick throughout the writing of "K" and suffered hand cramping so severe that she had to dictate her copy. Her emotional state was undoubtedly strained by her own illness and by the slow death from cancer of her Aunt Ella, the cheerful onetime baby-sitter who had endured the deaths of two husbands and a child from tuberculosis.

About the time Mary was beginning "K," the family took another vacation, camping and fishing at an isolated site on the French River in Canada. With limited contact with the outside world, they were initially ignorant of the assassination of Archduke Ferdinand of Austria and the outbreak of war in Europe. But when the news arrived, Mary immediately conceived one of her most daring plots: she would go to the war. Her determination, she later admitted, did not come from higher motives, "only a great interest and a great curiosity." Just as she had once turned to nursing out of her enormous craving for romantic adventure, so she now sought a posting to the war zone.

As soon as the Rineharts returned to civilized Sewickley, she contacted George Horace Lorimer, editor of *The Saturday Evening Post*. Although the *Post* editorially opposed American involvement in the conflict, Lorimer had already sent several male correspondents to Europe and seemed at first to support Mary's proposal. Stan objected, for obvious reasons, and by September, the issue seemed to be settled. There was much to do at home: Stan, Jr., was leaving that fall for boarding school, and Mary was struggling to complete an old project, a play she called *Otto IX* that drew on her Vienna experiences. But the goal of seeing and reporting on the war never left her mind, and when word came that the *Post* had another woman writing from Europe, Mary must have been livid. Sometime during the Rineharts' family Christmas, Mary confronted Stan, and following what she euphemistically called "a grave conference with my husband," she got her way.

She sent a telegram to Lorimer at the *Post,* telling him that she planned to go to England anyway, to oversee the opening of the London production of *Seven Days.* Would the *Post* pay for her trip and provide letters of introduction? Lorimer agreed, so long as she would write exclusively for his magazine. Whatever Stan may have thought, he was somewhat mollified by the knowledge that the European allies were maintaining strict censorship of war news and not allowing reporters to visit the battle areas; Mary would not be in any real danger.

> *"It was one thing to plan the great adventure, and another*
> *to go through with it."*

On January 9, 1915, after charging an expensive fur coat to the *Post,* Mary boarded the liner *Franconia* in New York for the voyage to England. On the ship she met "a very eminent English barrister" whose Belgian wife later helped Mary secure important introductions. By January 20, she was in London and meeting with the great British press baron Lord Northcliffe, publisher of *The London Times.* Over lunch, Northcliffe agreed to write letters on her behalf to the commander of the Belgian army and to the Belgian premier. When Northcliffe suggested that Mary seek an interview with the exiled king and queen of Belgium, Mary upped the ante by asking for a meeting with Britain's Queen Mary.

But how to get across the English Channel and to the action? Seasoned war correspondents were being frustrated at every turn, but Mary, through the barrister's wife and the Belgian Red Cross, managed the impossible. Ostensibly, she would report on the conditions of hospitals in the war zone; in fact, she wrote in her diary of the trip, "I am to go to the firing line." Five days after her arrival in London, she departed for Calais on the French coast, though somehow her boat landed in Boulogne and she had to find her own way cross-country. After a cold night in a Calais hotel, she moved on to Dunkirk, where she experienced her first bombardment, then to La Panne, a French seaside town where the court of the King of Belgium had established temporary residence. She was housed at the Red Cross's L'Ambulance Océan hospital, and she began her tour of medical facilities, venturing again and again into the war-torn countryside and the trenches near the Belgian lines.

Her reports from the war zone would dominate *The Saturday Evening Post's* coverage of the early days of the conflict, but she was also gathering inspiration from the people and places she saw. In one camp she met a young American nurse, Glory Hancock, who was called "Morning Glory" by the soldiers: Hancock would provide the model for Sara Lee Kennedy, the heroine of Mary's war novel, *The Amazing Interlude*. Another real-life character, a mysterious German-speaking man, "so cultivated and yet so obscure," who often escorted Mary during her visits to battle areas and advised on her writings, resurfaced in *The Amazing Interlude* as the equally mysterious and romantic Henri.

Near the end of her stay, Mary was included among a group of journalists who were allowed to visit No Man's Land itself—the fragile battle line where Belgian and German troops hunkered in mud trenches just a thousand feet apart on opposite sides of a flooded strip of ground. The male correspondents were more than a little miffed at her presence, but Mary didn't care; she would be the first woman to report from the front line of the war. It was night when the little group approached the line. Rain and sleet pelted the visitors, and even for the hospital-trained nurse, the stench of battle and death was almost overwhelming. Carefully, their Belgian escort led them to a ruined church where a Capuchin monk manned his observation post just two hundred yards from the Germans. The Belgian officials had not intended for Mary to make this last, dangerous part of the tour, but she did, and returned safely.

Several days later, Mary conducted her interview with King Albert of Belgium, the first authorized interview with him to be published. She also interviewed his young wife, Queen Elisabeth, a surprisingly informal occasion during which the two women chatted and smoked cigarettes together. That night, February 9, 1915, Mary crossed the Channel again and returned to London.

The next ten days were busy: she had wangled interviews with Winston Churchill (who bored her) and with Britain's Queen Mary (who charmed her), and she was doing everything in her power to get back to the Front. With the help of the French ambassador, she acquired the proper passes and introductions, and again she took the Calais boat, sneaking aboard when told that the vessel was taking no passengers. This trip took her to the French and English lines, but between homesickness and illness, Mary found it much less an adventure than her time with the

Belgians. She did lunch with and interview the French commander, General Foch, and dine with Britain's Viscount Haldane. Her contacts with the British troops ("the very pick of Englishmen . . . tall, erect and confident") assured her that the war would be ended quickly. But the tour was far more organized and formal than she had expected, and by the end of February, she was ready to return to the United States and her home.

Her war articles appeared, as promised, in *The Saturday Evening Post* from April through July of 1915. With Lorimer's permission, they were reprinted in Lord Northcliffe's *Times* and subsequently collected and published as *Kings, Queens, and Pawns*. Mary was not particularly happy that her articles had to be heavily edited to obtain official approvals and satisfy the *Post*'s commitment to American neutrality; the deletion of all references to the use of chlorine gas particularly galled her. But the impact on the American public was significant. Lorimer told her that the *Post*'s circulation had increased by fifty thousand. Mary had brought home vivid and accurate reports on the realities of war and its consequences. In the process, her celebrity was firmly established, and men in high places became aware of Mrs. Rinehart's value as a propagandist. But coming down from the high of her front-line experience left her depressed and restless. She looked at her sons and realized that some day soon they might be called to the war whose terrors she now understood too well.

That summer, she lost Uncle John, her lifelong model of stability and success. In the end, even he had failed. After Sade's death, John Roberts had remarried and had the child he always wanted. Then he had done what Mary's father had done so many years before—dreamed. John gave up his business and "set to work to build a fortune in the stock market." Instead, he lost much of what he had. He pulled out before everything was gone and bought a farm, which was "life to him" but "death to his family." His wife and child left, and shortly after, he died suddenly. Once again, Mary saw the danger of depending on a man for her security. It must have been a terrible reminder of her own father's death, "another futile and tragic end."

Relief from her depression came in an invitation from Pittsburgh native Howard Eaton. Now a rancher in Wyoming, Eaton was planning a horseback trip through the newly opened Glacier National Park, and he asked Mary along to record the excursion. Mary accepted, and on her own, she made her first journey into the West. She turned the trip into a series of articles for *Collier's* magazine (later published in book form as *Through Glacier Park*) and also a new Tish story for the *Post*. On the long and often dangerous trek, she came to know the Blackfoot Indians of Montana. She was initiated into the tribe, given the name "Pitamakin" or Running Eagle, and became an advocate for the American Indian cause. (She was not above grandstanding either, telegraphing details of her exotic initiation to her editor at Houghton Mifflin on the virtual eve of the publication of *"K"* and just in time to boost the book's publicity.) On her return home, she took the Blackfoot issues straight to Secretary of the Interior Franklin Lane, who oversaw the government's Indian affairs. She had fallen in love with the West and arranged several more packing trips with her family. For years to come, she would routinely retreat to the comfort of Eaton's ranch when she needed respite from her harried life and career.

She was now writing more comedy for the *Post,* including her "Sub-Deb" series, based on reports from Stan, Jr., about his social life at Harvard. She was producing more travel articles, opinion pieces, and her special brand of quasi-journalism. In 1916, she reported on the national political conventions for the *Philadelphia Public Ledger* syndicate, and, scooping the professional journalists, she managed to interview Teddy Roosevelt about his possible candidacy, initiating a long friendship with the former president. She had turned forty; she was enjoying her wealth and newfound celebrity status. She was also beginning to craft a new facet of her public image and the Rinehart mystique: living symbol of successful American womanhood.

"And as I looked about me, I saw many other women confused and at a loss."

By today's standards, Mary Roberts Rinehart was a decidedly conflicted feminist. Although she marched with the suffragettes during the Democratic convention in Chicago, she didn't really think that getting the vote was particularly relevant or productive for her sex. She did, however, believe that women should attain their financial independence through real jobs and hard work. She looked down on women who gained wealth through their husbands, though she cultivated and often called on the favors of powerful men. She preached the virtues of home and motherhood; yet she sent her children to boarding school, and at least once in print, she referred to her family as her "chains." In one of her earliest autobiographical articles, "My Creed" (*American Magazine,* October 1917), she counted herself among the "pathfinders" of the "new" womanhood; yet she lamented that these new women might abandon their maternal responsibilities in pursuit of "gainful occupation." She prophesied that the American woman would, in the end, choose wisely and put family always ahead of career; yet as her eldest son wrote many years later, the Rinehart boys lived "quite remote" from their parents.

In her writing, too, Mary practiced a double standard compounded of desire and actuality. She truly wanted to be taken seriously as a writer. She worked at improving the quality of her prose: studying grammar, learning to revise and rewrite, taming her baroque plot lines, and adding depth to her characters. But she rejected the one option that might have led to the kind of acceptance she craved. Realism, together with its more deterministic offshoot, naturalism, was the road that the good and great fiction writers of the early 1900s were traveling, but Mary simply refused to go along for the ride. Realism demanded open-eyed acceptance and exploration of the gritty details of the lives of ordinary people, sex and violence included. Realism also abandoned the syrupy conventions of Romantic fiction and the de rigueur happy or at least morally uplifting conclusion. Mary couldn't do it. She, who was fashioning her image as the moral guardian of chaste love, marriage, and motherhood, just couldn't bring herself to go beneath the surface and face the dark underpinnings of human endeavor. (Although her mysteries included violent and often gruesome murders, Mary always kept the actual acts off-stage and distant from her readers.)

She had tried realism in *The Street of Seven Stars,* but this book had not been, as some critics hoped, the beginning of a new direction for the popular writer. *The Street of Seven Stars* had delved rather bravely into the social ills of prewar Vienna and the potential of a two-career marriage, but in the end, the heroine, not the hero, must choose between love and work. Marriage, and Mary's romanticism, inevitably won the day, and so it was to be in all her attempts at serious, straight fiction.

She blamed her refusal to write in the new style on several sources. There was her own desire to escape into a world of adventure and romance. There were her children, whom she tried to protect from "sordidness and ugliness"; she would not be the one, she promised, to introduce her boys to life as it is really lived. Then, in a telling passage in her autobiography, Mary said that she came to have the same protective, maternal attitude toward her audience: "I would amuse it, interest it, even thrill it if I could, but I would not pander to it. If it wanted its passions roused and its lower instincts appealed to, let it read elsewhere."

Unquestionably sincere in her concerns, Mary nonetheless failed to understand how patronizing her attitude—and her references to her readers as "it"—was. In her writing and her life, she consistently pursued a me-them strategy that allowed her to preach to others a philosophy that she herself had no intention of following. In a 1920 article in *The Bookman* magazine, she tried to express a personal relationship with her readers, but even switching, mid-course, from "it" to "they" when referring to her public, she could not escape the condescension of mother to child. Of her obligations to this mass of followers, she said, "To keep faith with my readers, to give them my best, to spread such happiness as I could, never to preach an evil thing nor to exalt a wicked one, that has been my literary creed."

Despite her commitment to keep her readers entertained, Mary tried to move beyond the mystery in the years during and immediately after World War One. She wrote only two mystery novellas between *The After House* in 1914 and *The Red Lamp* in 1925. Lorimer, her editor at the *Post,* turned down *The Confession* as "calculated to appeal to your women's magazine audience." *Sight Unseen* was a mystery but more concerned with the popular interest in ghosts and séances than with real detection. Mary's only genuine mystery created during this period was a stage play, and its eventual outcome should have told her once and for all where her true talents lay. For the time being, however, *The Bat* had to take second place to Mary's growing obsession with the war.

As the United States drifted closer and closer to entering the world war, Mary became increasingly determined to get back to Europe; Stan just as adamantly opposed her. Giving in to her husband's rational concerns for her safety, she instead turned her attention to a series of propaganda projects: an article on the underfunded and outmoded U.S. Navy, written at the request of Secretary of the Navy Josephus Daniels, and two articles based on her visits to army training camps. More telling of her state of mind was the fact that Mary began promoting the military careers of both Stan and Stan, Jr. (Luckily for Alan and Ted, they were as yet too young for military service, though before the war's end, Alan enlisted in the Marines, and Ted joined the National Guard.)

On April 3, 1917, three days before the United States declared war on Germany, Mary sent telegrams to the White House and to Secretary of War Newton D. Baker. At such a time of crisis, she offered neither hope nor encouragement; instead, her communications demanded that the ROTC unit at Harvard, in which Stan, Jr., was an eager trainee, be supplied immediately with the latest Springfield rifles. The White House cabled a conciliatory message, and Mary received other officially courteous letters, but nothing was ever done. New rifles were for soldiers in the field, not Harvard undergraduates.

Several days later, Mary responded to a request from the *Post* for an article supporting the war effort. Writing for twelve hours straight, she produced "The Altar of Freedom," a resounding cry to America's mothers to demonstrate their patriotism by sending their sons to war. Years later, with her own family safe and sound, she came to regret this gung-ho and ultimately callous call to arms. "Perhaps only God knows," she wrote in her autobiography, "what a terrible thing that was to do, or how it haunts me now." But no woman ever battled harder to put her son and husband in harm's way or presumed more on the time and patience of the country's leaders. Determined that Stan, Jr., should fight as a commissioned officer, she took her demands into a face-to-face meeting with President Woodrow Wilson and then contemplated seeking a Senate investigation of the Army's commissioning policy. She also hammered Secretary Baker with futile requests for a West Point appointment for her eldest son, until young Stan, following his own instincts, enlisted as an Army private.

At the same time, Mary was waging a campaign for Stan, who was serving on the draft registration and military exemption boards in Pittsburgh. He hoped for a medical commission, so Mary wrote more letters, pleading her husband's case to the assistant secretary of war and to the judge advocate general of the Army. Stan was commissioned as a captain (later promoted to major) in the medical section of the Officer Reserve Corps in August 1917, and sent to Fort Sherman in Ohio, where his oldest son would also be stationed.

Mary had worked herself into a patriotic frenzy that, in retrospect, was clearly out of kilter. When writing her army training camp articles, published in the *Post,* she also composed a fourteen-page confidential report to Secretary of War Baker; she rated the Army's training efforts and criticized everything from dirty kitchen sinks to low morale. She also began seeing spies behind every bush, claiming that her report was stolen during a train ride (in an incident that oddly echoed the details of a key scene in her first novel, *The Man in Lower Ten).* When her office was broken into, she assumed the thief was searching for government secrets. She ferreted out a turncoat at Fort McPherson in Georgia. She reported suspicious activities at a hotel near her home—a business owned by a German immigrant—to Military Intelligence. She never ceased her efforts to get herself back to Europe and was just as consistently rebuffed by American officials. Her increasing agitation became obvious when she broke down in tears during a reading of "The Altar of Freedom" at a women's club meeting in Sewickley.

It's impossible not to wonder if harassed government officials didn't take a hand in an adventure Mary had in March of 1918. She was invited to join a riding tour in the Southwest. Organized by her old friend Howard Eaton, the party was to include Teddy Roosevelt. Neither the former president nor Eaton actually went, but at the last moment, an intelligence officer from the War Department and a Treasury Department agent showed up, and the itinerary was rerouted to Mexico. The government officials were ostensibly along to investigate smuggling and espionage, and when the mounted group departed San Diego, Mary was loaded like Annie Oakley with a Winchester .33, a "small combination rifle and shot gun," a Smith & Wesson .38 revolver, and enough ammunition to blow her to bits.

The horseback ride was long and tiring, winding through mountains and desert to the Gulf of California. Mary, as usual, fancied herself as the first woman ever to make such a journey, but no spies or smugglers were bagged along the way, and the trip was generally uneventful. Official Washington, however, got a well-earned two-week rest from the demanding Mrs. Rinehart.

By this time, with Stan and Stan, Jr., at Camp Sherman and her two other boys away at school, Mary had closed the Sewickley house and moved her mother in with her sister, Olive. (Olive's husband had been in the fight since the outset, and Olive was now teaching school and raising two small children on her own.) Mary settled into the Langdon Hotel in New York, where Teddy Roosevelt also had an apartment. She had completed *The Amazing Interlude,* which became her most popular romance novel, and continued work on her *Otto* play, transformed earlier into the novel *Long Live the King!* She was working on a new mystery play when word came that Stan, Jr., was at last going overseas. Tearfully, Mary saw him off in New York, then applied to the American Red Cross for credentials as a nurse. She continued to pester Secretary Baker and eventually wrote directly to General "Black Jack" Pershing, commander of the U.S. forces in Europe. Pershing turned down her requests, citing government policy that the wives and mothers of soldiers at the Front could not serve as nurses overseas.

Mary was a mess, physically ill and emotionally depressed. Stan, unlike his son, had not received an overseas posting but was assigned to the surgeon general's staff in Washington, a position that involved frequent travel. Mary rented a summer house on Long Island, where she worked on a new book, *Dangerous Days,* encountered the ghost that later inspired *The Red Lamp,* and generally sank deeper into depression. By the time word came that she would, at last, be allowed to go to Europe, she was "almost suicidal." The War Department had given her just a few days' notice, so she sent off her partially completed mystery play to Avery Hopwood, went to Washington to tell Stan farewell and get her passport, and shipped out for France on November 1, 1918.

She arrived in Paris on November 10 and found accommodations, though not at the Ritz as French officials had promised. At eleven o'clock the next morning, she was on the Rue de la Paix when the signal guns roared. The war was over. And Mary had missed it.

She was to spend several more weeks in Europe, touring for the Red Cross and trying to catch up with her son. Mary saw firsthand the awful devastation of the bewildering conflict that was to become known as the

First World War. She was taken into the Argonne Forest, visited German and French hospitals, met several times with General Pershing, and longed to return home. She was able to spend Christmas with Stan, Jr., and in mid-January, mother and son shipped out on the same transport, heading back to an America now at peace and forever changed.

> *"For almost five years I had been obsessed by the war;*
> *I knew nothing else."*

While in Paris, Mary had received a telegram from her publisher, George Doran, offering her the editorship of the *Ladies' Home Journal* magazine. Publisher Cyrus Curtis was prepared to pay her $50,000 a year, to let her work from Pittsburgh, and even to change the magazine's name in order to secure her services. It was an astounding opportunity, and she considered it seriously but eventually said no. The war years had drained her, and the end of hostilities left her, like many of her fellow countrymen, depressed and at loose ends. With her family intact, she returned to Sewickley, reopened The Bluff, and tried to get back to her old routines. She started a new book, *A Poor Wise Man,* that was in effect a romantic spy novel based on a purported incident of thwarted anarchist rebellion that had occurred in Seattle.

Stan, too, was facing some difficult choices. He had been disappointed by his domestic war duty but was not prepared for the return to civilian life. He didn't want to go back into private practice or to return to the Pittsburgh tuberculosis clinic, which he had built into one of the best such facilities in the country. He tried writing and had a number of articles published in *The Saturday Evening Post*. He also took over the management of Mary's financial affairs. All her working life, Mary displayed a remarkable facility for making money and spending it unwisely. The Rineharts lived well, even lavishly, and Mary never hesitated to buy anything she wanted. She was also a prime target for con artists and schemers, naively dumping thousands of her hard-earned dollars into a series of pipe dreams and plainly felonious scams. Stan, however, was a conservative and organized investor, and although he made some mistakes, his management put Mary on something like an even keel.

As Mary fluctuated between illness and hectic activity, an offer came along that seemed, at first, like a godsend. Samuel Goldwyn was making his fortune in movie production in Hollywood, and he contacted Mary about a new project called Eminent Authors. Famous writers, he said, would come to California to transform their books into films, and he wanted Mary to be one of the first. So in July of 1919, Mary, Alan, and Ted found themselves in the Beverly Hills Hotel in Los Angeles. Mary was ready to work, but it became clear almost immediately that her presence was resented by the established studio writers and that her only value to Goldwyn was as a publicity magnet. Her first novel to be adapted was *Dangerous Days,* and two more films were eventually made from her stories, but the Eminent Authors experience proved to be eminently unsatisfactory.

She returned to Pittsburgh and a project she had left hanging during the war. It was the play she had shuffled off to Avery Hopwood when she had left for Europe. Originally conceived as a dramatization of *The Circular Staircase,* the play had taken on a new plot, a new character, and a new title—*The Bat.* Hop had not finished the play, but now he came to The Bluff to work with Mary. The difficulty lay in Mary's determination that the identity of the master criminal called "The Bat" would not be revealed until the very final moments of the play. She and Hop struggled with the ending and the attendant plot difficulties even after the play went into rehearsals and tryouts. They were also collaborating on an adaptation of the Spanish play *Maria del Carmen,* which they called *Spanish Love.* As it turned out, *Spanish Love* opened on Broadway just six days before *The Bat* and earned excellent box-office returns. But *The Bat,* as Hop crowed in an opening night telegram to Mary, who as usual did not attend the premiere, was "a Babe Ruth home run."

Mary was more than a writer of *The Bat;* she was a backer. She and Stan had invested $5,000 in the original production, giving them a combined 25 percent share. Their producers, Wagenhals and Kemper, held 50 percent, and Hop owned the remaining quarter. As well, Mary received up to 15 percent of all royalties. This investment was no phantom gold mine. *The Bat* was an enormous success. It ran for almost three years in New York, and six road companies were soon spreading out across the country. In the play's first three years, Mary and Stan earned almost a half-million dollars in profits and royalties, and it was later estimated that the play grossed a total of more than nine million dollars. (When Mary had first presented her idea for the play to Broadway producer Edgar Selwyn, he had remarked that it was worth a million dollars. Happily, his estimate was considerably short of the mark.)

Mary's celebrity status was greatly enhanced by the popularity of *The Bat.* Though exhausted, she rarely turned down highly visible appearance opportunities, joining Alice Roosevelt Longworth and a delegation to discuss women's issues with Republican presidential candidate Warren Harding, and becoming the first woman to speak at the prestigious New England Day Dinner in Philadelphia. She kept working, developing a novel called *The Breaking Point* that returned to the amnesia theme of her first short story. Her own physical symptoms, however, were becoming more severe, and the doses of morphine that controlled her pains also deprived her of sleep.

In June of 1921, Samuel Goldwyn invited her to a New York screening of the final film made under her Eminent Authors contract, and as they left the theater, Mary collapsed. Rushed to the hospital, she underwent emergency gallbladder surgery. For the first time in her life, she thought she might die, and during her recuperation, she made a short-lived resolution to slow down and devote more time to her personal life. After all, she was a grandmother now. Stan, Jr., had married Mary Doran, daughter of publisher George Doran, in 1919, and a year later, he and "Dorrie" had their first child, a girl named Mary Roberts Rinehart II and called "Bab" for the popular heroine of Mary's "Sub-Deb" story series. The birth of her grandchild had shocked Mary. The famous writer was forty-three years old, and although she claimed to have no attachment to her vanished youth, she admitted to passing "a psychological milestone" on the night little Bab was born: "Of all the queer things that life had done to me, this was the queerest."

"So we said good-bye to the white house, there on its hill overlooking the river. . . ."

As soon as she had recovered her strength, Mary's ego and drive overcame her good intentions, and she accepted an offer to report on the International Disarmament Convention in Washington, D.C., in the late fall of 1921. She used the occasion to promote her husband's interests, and not long after she returned to Sewickley, Stan was offered a position with the Veterans' Bureau. It meant closing The Bluff again and moving to the nation's capital, but Mary was ready for another adventure.

Washington seemed to be the perfect milieu for the restless author and her capable husband. Had it not been for the corrupt management of the Veterans' Bureau, Stan might have found a worthy home for his abilities. He was appointed to serve as a consultant in the treatment of tuberculosis, and he plunged enthusiastically into a project to train specialist staff for tuberculosis facilities. But the project was abandoned by the Bureau, and Stan could make no headway in the atmosphere of political intrigue and suspicion that was overwhelming all of Washington during the Harding administration. Angry and disgusted, Stan finally resigned his post in June 1923, and never again practiced medicine or public health.

Although she complained about combining work with gala dinners at the White House and embassy receptions, Mary enjoyed the hectic social pace of D.C.; hobnobbing with the powerful was always her cup of tea. Her literary output in 1921 and 1922 was uncharacteristically slim, but her social commitments were voluminous. More than the rounds of ritual visiting and formal affairs, she loved being an insider, the famous and chatty Mrs. Rinehart who was privy to the secrets and the backstairs gossip that greased Washington's wheels. Other good things were happening for her: an honorary doctorate degree from George Washington University, a place among America's twelve most respected women in a poll conducted by *The New York Times*. But perhaps as a consequence of her dark Presbyterian past, Mary never quite trusted the good times.

On a summer day in 1922, Mary had set out from her Washington apartment in the Wardman Park Hotel for a trip to the ranch in Wyoming, where she was to be joined later by her family. But word came that she must return home immediately. Her mother was dying in a Washington hospital. In an accident as bizarre as it was hideous, Cornelia had slipped away from her nurse and climbed into a bathtub filled with scalding water. Unable to scream or escape, she had suffered fatal burns and died soon after Mary reached her side. Was it really an accident? Mary wasn't so sure. Her mother had been very unhappy in Washington, and perhaps, just perhaps, she had taken control of her life one last time. Mary blamed herself, she said, "for it was the move to Washington which killed" her mother. Cornelia Roberts was buried beside her husband in a Pittsburgh graveyard filled with family members lost to strange and unnatural deaths.

Mary and Stan were never to live again in their hometown. In September, they bought a large, redbrick house at 2419 Massachusetts Avenue, cleared out their beloved white mansion in Sewickley, and began to prepare for their first Christmas as citizens of the nation's capital. They gave each other saddle horses that holiday, precipitating another near-fatal accident. Riding together one afternoon in a city park, Mary broke her horse into a canter at the same moment Stan had taken his foot from his stirrup. Stan's horse bolted and ran. Before Stan finally fell headfirst onto a concrete pavement, he was repeatedly struck in the head by the flapping stirrup. He suffered a broken leg and a serious concussion. His recovery was slow; he experienced memory loss; and by the summer of 1924, it was clear the family would have to forego their annual Wyoming holiday. Instead, Mary and Stan retreated to a quiet New England coastal house. They were joined by Ted, who had just graduated from Harvard, and Alan, who had flunked out of the prestigious university and spent a year as a cowboy at Eaton's Wyoming dude ranch.

Perhaps Mary was tired of cool reviews for her serious novels. *The Breaking Point* had been a bestseller for two years, but the critics had been hard on it. Worse, the play she had written from the book had been an embarrassing flop. So for the first time in more than a decade, she sat down that summer to write a full-fledged mystery novel, *The Red Lamp,* which depended heavily on her interest in spiritualism, séances, and the current voguish belief in "spirit return." Although not a bestseller, the mystery was graciously received by the critics, who seemed relieved that Mary had returned to her forte.

Again, Mary sank into her depression. Her hand cramps had returned full strength and been diagnosed as Dupuytren's contracture. She was approaching fifty and menopause ("when an inner bleakness of soul devastates every woman"); her writing output had declined; she had faced several professional disappointments and was demoralized by what she perceived as the "mediocrity" of her work. She was beset by suicidal thoughts, but once again, travel brought relief. She and Stan packed their bags and headed for the Middle East—Egypt, Iraq, and Lebanon. Although Mary was still deeply depressed during the ocean voyage to Cairo, the trip brought just the kind of adventure that she loved, and loved to complain about. Soon she was sleeping again and furiously gathering notes, later documenting her sand-plagued sojourn in the travel book *Nomad's Land.*

The Rineharts returned home to more good fortune: Alan had become engaged to Gratia Houghton, the debutante daughter of the cofounder of Corning Glass and niece of the American ambassador to Great Britain. Mary was beside herself; two of her three handsome sons had now made socially advantageous marriages. Even when Alan announced several months later that he was leaving George Doran's firm (Mary's publisher and employer of her three boys) to become a writer, Mary was not overly anxious. Gratia, after all, could keep the newlyweds in comfort.

Mary had started a new romance novel when she and Stan traveled to Wyoming in the summer of 1926. But something happened there—a terrible argument—and Stan rushed back to Washington. For several months, the couple were estranged, communicating only by letter, and Stan even offered to move out of their Washington house when Mary decided to return.

Whatever the quarrel had been about, the Rineharts reconciled by late fall. Mary returned to Washington and completed one of her most popular novels, *Lost Ecstasy.* (This rich girl–poor cowboy romance was adapted for the screen in 1931 and retitled *I Take This Woman;* the film starred Gary Cooper and Carole Lombard.) Mary also acquired a new secretary—a young graduate student named William Sladen who was valued as much for his social skills as his typing. Although Sladen received his master's degree from George Washington University, he remained with Mary, as employee and confidant, until the end of her life.

In 1927, while convalescing from a fall in a hotel bathroom during a vacation in Honolulu, Mary began her most autobiographical novel to date, *This Strange Adventure,* a serious romance that took her back to her childhood on Arch Street. The life of her main character, Missie Colfax, at many points parallels that of the young Mary Roberts, and Mary admitted that there was much of herself in the character: ". . . Missie thought much as I did. She was cursed with the ability to see both sides of everything, so that she seemed often to be a poor shilly-shallying sort of creature." Mary believed *This Strange Adventure* to be her best work, although it was one of her few major books not to become a bestseller. But writing this story so similar to her own, combined with a period of interest in Christian Science, encouraged her to begin her autobiography.

Mary and Stan seemed to be settling into a new and somewhat less frantic life. Stan, who had never fully recovered from his riding accident, was occupied with managing Mary's growing fortune and keeping her indulgent spending under control. Mary was again writing at a furious pace, working on her autobiography, developing a new mystery novel, publishing opinion pieces on subjects ranging from fashion to Marxism in *The Saturday Evening Post, McCall's,* the *Ladies' Home Journal,* and other popular magazines.

Although she continued to fight the label of "women's writer," her articles were often directed to women, as she voiced her deep concerns about the changing moral standards of postwar America: "an America I hardly knew, a jazzed America, drinking, dancing, spending; developing a cult of ugliness and calling it modernity, and throwing aside the simplicities and charms of living in pursuit of a new god called Smartness." Her own carefully crafted mystique—loyal wife and mother forced to work by financial necessity—was being tattered by a new generation of women who needed no excuses to do what they wanted, including the pursuit of careers and sex outside of marriage. In an article titled "If I Had a Daughter" (*Forum and Century* magazine, March 1932), Mary imagined herself dealing with a daughter and the "new morality." It is an affecting piece of writing, though not perhaps in the way Mary intended, for it reveals her own ambivalence. Clearly the lifestyle of the young worried her—its egocentrism, its insistence on "liberty of action" and experimentation, its rejection of chastity as a condition for marriage. She admitted that she had no answer for parents, though she counseled patience and understanding. But there is a hint of envy and regret, too, as Mary credited the younger generation with "a certain honesty and a facing of facts, economic and otherwise." Mary always portrayed herself as sacrificing her own freedom on the altar of family— a kind of martyrdom that was rapidly going out of style.

"This depression will end very soon."
—"A Woman Goes to Market," January 1931

As the decade of the twenties roared toward its tumultuous close, a new venture occupied all the Rineharts. Stan, Jr., and Ted were leaving Doubleday Doran to form their own publishing firm with partner John Farrar, and one of their major authors would be their mother. The new company's first publications were scheduled for release in the fall of 1929—eighteen books that ranged from serious biographies to a collection of Mary Roberts Rinehart stories titled *The Romantics.* Ironically, the fledgling house of Farrar and Rinehart built its publicity campaign around the launching of a new game, *Speculation: The Wall Street Gamebook.* Their timing could not have been worse. The handsomely packaged book and game hit the market in October 1929, within days of the stock market crash that signaled the end of the country's wild fling with unregulated buying and selling.

Mary and Stan had not seen the coming storm. They were spending extravagantly, purchasing a twenty-eight-foot motorized cabin boat and undertaking construction of a large addition to their Washington home. Mary had just sold the serial rights to her new mystery, *The Door,* to *The Saturday Evening Post* for $60,000, and she blithely dismissed the Wall Street cataclysm as "a temporary setback." But Stan knew better: he had invested on margin in wheat, and when the bottom fell out of the market, he still had those margins to cover. The Rineharts were by no means desperate, and Mary increased her output to keep the coffers filled. Farrar and Rinehart managed to survive, helped in large measure by the publication of *The Door* and *Mary Roberts Rinehart's Mystery Book* in 1930, followed the next year by her autobiography, *My Story,* and two story collections. Mary also agreed to take on her first regular assignment, writing monthly editorial columns for the *Ladies' Home Journal.*

These columns, published for a year, soon became a burden as she disagreed with the magazine's editor on content. Mary was not in the best of shape to accept such an assignment; she had recently undergone major surgery to remove her gallbladder. (In the hospital, a psychiatrist had questioned her about her extensive record of surgeries. He had asked Mary what she was "escaping from." Although Mary responded angrily, reminding the impertinent doctor that her gallstones were quite real, she recorded the entire incident in the 1948 update of *My Story.* Mary wondered if Dr. White had been right.)

Stan, meanwhile, was enduring worsening arthritic pain and fatigue. He was persuaded to visit a New York specialist, but the doctor's report was good enough for Mary to leave her husband and settle in at the Homestead in Hot Springs, Virginia. Here she wrote the bulk of a new mystery that returned to an old subject. *Miss Pinkerton* revived the career of nurse-detective Hilda Adams, for whom Mary had written two extended short stories in 1914. After her seventeen-year hiatus, Hilda returned to the pages of *The Saturday Evening Post* at the beginning of 1932, earning Mary a tidy $50,000.

Stan's health, however, continued to deteriorate, and his physical illness was exacerbated by worry over the country's deepening financial crisis. He had been covering Mary's losses with his own funds, until Mary stepped in with a Christmas gift—enough money to support his investments. Briefly, Stan seemed to improve, and Mary planned a trip to visit Alan and his family in California, but just before her scheduled departure, she was informed by Stan's doctor that her husband's heart was failing and his condition was hopeless. The Rineharts tried whatever seemed to offer hope, including an arduous, and ultimately useless, trip to Europe's famous spa city of Baden-Baden. The German doctors could offer no cure but recommended extensive rest and winters in the warm, dry climate of Egypt.

Still, the Rineharts were hopeful when they returned to Washington on July 6, 1932. They immediately went on to join the family at a vacation retreat in the Adirondack Mountains, but on the last day of July, Stan collapsed. Brought back to Washington in a chartered railroad car, he lingered for another three months. With his wife and his sons at his bedside, Stan died on October 28, 1932. With the full privileges of a major in the U.S. Army, he was buried in Arlington National Cemetery.

Mary and Stan had been married for thirty-six years, and he had been the rock of the relationship. But Mary implied, in her autobiographical writings, that only in losing him did she finally understand how much she had needed him. She spoke often of his strength, "his strong hand in trouble." In unpublished writings, she admitted that the marriage was, for herself at least, not passionate; her focus had always been on her children. In *The Door,* published two years before Stan's death, she had created a generally unlikeable character named Katherine Somers who did marry for passion and who put love of husband above love of child. Mary saw herself as the opposite—the loving, indulgent, protective mother of the Rinehart mystique. But now her boys were grown and building their own families. (Ted had married in 1930.) However much she continued to involve herself in their lives (and she surely must have been a difficult mother-in-law), Mary could no longer entirely control them. She had also been unable, or unwilling, to fulfill Stan's one great wish: to retire from her hectic public life and share a private one with him.

There seems little doubt that she loved her husband. She even understood, intellectually, the difficult position of a professional man overshadowed by his more successful and celebrated wife. Yet, although

Mary liked to say that their marriage had been built on compromise, it was not she who had made the sacrifices. By manipulation or sheer willfulness, she had always gotten her way, though she sometimes regretted the consequences.

In a revealing incident cited in *My Story,* Mary recalled how, sometime late in the 1920s, she became determined to buy a very expensive diamond necklace. Stan objected, warning her against squandering her carefully invested securities for "such nonsense." But Mary persisted, becoming obsessed with proving that "the money . . . was mine, after all." After much discussion and without changing Stan's opinion, she bought the necklace anyway, though she rarely wore it. When she told Stan, his only remark was a damning "I thought you had better sense." Five years after Stan's death, she finally sold her diamonds for a third their purchase price.

Beyond her grief, Stan's death left her with too many empty hours. During the next year, she traveled frequently, probably to escape the solitude of the Washington house. She visited Florida, where she had shared Stan's fishing holidays; Howard Eaton's Wyoming ranch, where she always found some form of solace; and California, where she spent her first Christmas alone. And she worked at a breakneck pace, publishing two new mystery novels in 1933—*The Album* and *The State Vs. Elinor Norton.* This latter book was as much dark romance as mystery, and presaged a format popular in current mystery fiction. The murderer is revealed on the first page, and the novel revolves around the slow uncovering of her motivations. *The State Vs. Elinor Norton,* a whydunit, was praised by the critics; *The New York Times* called it "realistic" and "a definite contribution to serious American literature."

Work and travel were Mary's panacea, but illness was her companion. In the fall of 1933, she was alone in her Washington house when she suffered chest pains and collapsed. She was discovered, near death, by her son Alan. Her recovery from this first heart attack went well, and by spring, she was off on another journey, a cruise to northern Europe and Russia. She was accompanied by one of her Washington friends, Mrs. Evelyn Walsh McLean, the proud owner of the famous and supposedly cursed Hope Diamond. After some initial mistrust, Soviet officials decided to welcome Mary as an honored guest, and in the Kremlin, amid the excessive splendors of the old czarist palaces, she experienced a sympathetic reaction to the original aims of the Russian Revolution, though she roundly condemned the outcome of the Communist experiment.

Without question, Mary could see poverty and describe its ravaging effects with a vivid compassion; what she was never capable of conveying was genuine empathy. Throughout the Great Depression, she displayed an incomprehensible inability to grasp the reality of the lives that so many of her readers were living. She could feel intense sympathy for select individuals, but her writings display a disregard for general suffering that is almost pathetic. In an article titled "A Woman Goes to Market" (*The Saturday Evening Post,* January 31, 1931), she promised that the people could end their economic woes by spending more and complaining less. She declared that the situation of the unemployed was "tragic but not fatal," and chastised the average American as the "victim of his own temperament" and as "given to mass psychology." She reckoned that the American farmer's situation was not really so bad because farmers could at least feed themselves. She then declared her own intention to spend the economy back to health by buying a few mortgages and "in larger living and more generous giving." Even the popular Mrs. Rinehart couldn't get away with this degree of blind insensitivity, and complaints poured into the *Post*.

As Jan Cohn so effectively demonstrates in her biography, Mary was a Social Darwinist through and through. Simply put, for Mary was ultimately a simplistic thinker, the rich novelist believed that hard work bought success and laziness bought failure. At the time of the 1929 Crash, she had characterized the many suicides that resulted from the financial devastation as "taking the easy way out, as so long ago my own father had done." In a 1930 article for the *Ladies' Home Journal,* she had the temerity to blame the excesses of the previous decade on "bad dressing" and to call for "a revival of romance in living, in literature, and in art." She hated the economic relief efforts undertaken by the new administration of Franklin Roosevelt, elected to his first term in 1932. To the end, Mary never seemed to grasp that hard work—her personal ticket to the good things in life and affirmation of her own worth— could be grinding, degrading, and unrewarding for others.

Work was Mary's salvation, and it became the new foundation for the Rinehart mystique. With her husband gone, her children grown, and her personal security firmly established, she could no longer claim family as the force behind her career. Her credo, she maintained now, had always been the drive to work. For her readers, the years between Stan's death and the end of World War Two produced a bonanza of books.

At the beginning of 1935, she sold the Washington house and moved to a large penthouse apartment on Park Avenue in New York. Freed from the social demands and personal memories of the capital, she completed a novel that was a tribute to her late husband. *The Doctor,* which tells the story of a young physician struggling to make his career, serve the poor, and find love, earned mixed reviews and the largest payment Mary ever received for magazine serial rights. The summer after its publication, she bought a house with an ocean view in the fashionable resort conclave of Bar Harbor, Maine. "Far View"—purchased cheap from its Depression-depleted owners—required extensive renovation, but Mary had been down this route before. She plunged in and was rewarded with an environment conducive to her writing and by the company of rich and famous neighbors. Multimillionaire Atwater Kent, observing the ragged condition of her old Rolls-Royce, presented her with a brand-new Cadillac, which her amused family dubbed "My Sin."

The year she turned sixty, she faced perhaps her most frightening personal challenge—breast cancer. Mary had a genuine horror of cancer. On a visit with Stan, Jr., and his second wife at Useppa Island in Florida, Mary discovered a lump and rushed back to seek specialist care in New York. A biopsy revealed the malignancy, and Mary immediately underwent a radical mastectomy. The surgery was successful, and Mary recovered, apparently with few serious aftereffects.

But if cancer was terrifying to her, a later action showed her courage: she went public with the story of her disease and recovery in a 1947 interview published by the *Ladies' Home Journal.* It must be remembered that at this time cancer was a taboo subject and admitting to cancer risked social ostracism. But speaking forthrightly to the *Journal* interviewer, Mary not only related her own experience; she issued a strong plea to women to become aware of the disease and to fight it. The article, "I Had Cancer," which effectively "outed" breast cancer as a matter for frank and open discussion, brought an overwhelming response and may have been, in the long run, Mary's single most significant service to her public.

By May of 1937 she was going almost full steam again, sailing to England to attend the coronation of King George VI, from which she drew inspiration for the last two Tish stories ever published by *The Saturday Evening Post.* From New York, she directed the extensive makeover of the Bar Harbor house. She also maintained a prolific stream of books, articles, and stories. For the next decade, her novel-length writings focused entirely on mystery: *The Wall* appeared in 1938, followed by *The Great Mistake* in 1940; *Haunted Lady,* her last Hilda Adams mystery, in 1942; *Episode of the Wandering Knife* in 1943; and *The Yellow Room* in 1945.

She had just completed *The Wall,* set in a Bar Harbor–like resort, and was preparing for a South American cruise with her sister. At the hairdresser's for a permanent wave, she collapsed. This second heart attack was far more serious than the first, and following doctor's orders, Mary did make concessions to her medical condition. She at last took bed rest seriously and no longer wrote in the long marathons that had always characterized her method. With a bottle of nitroglycerin tablets ever at her side, she entertained less and focused her attention more on the closed circle of family. Even so, she remained more active than most sixtyish coronary patients. During a 1939 fishing trip in Florida, she again collapsed while attempting to land a huge tarpon—a mild attack that, in her embarrassment, she kept to herself.

"I had no apprehensions, save for a disturbed world."

All this time, Mary was closely following the news from Europe. She had never trusted the Germans, and the rise of Adolf Hitler confirmed her worst suspicions. Though initially hesitant about American involvement in another world war, she was infuriated by reports of the Dunkirk evacuation, and her old "fighting spirit" was fully revived. Just as she had done in 1914, Mary launched a determined campaign to get herself to the action: "It was my form of self-assertion, that I was still young enough, still brave enough, still strong enough, to go to a war."

Proposing to report on the Blitz, the German airborne bombardment of London, she badgered the *Post*'s new editor for press credentials and charmed the State Department into issuing her visas. Her plan was to fly to Lisbon, Portugal, and from there to England. At this point, her family and her physician put their feet down; her heart condition made the trip, which included a long, high-altitude flight in a plane without oxygen equipment, impossible ("a nice way to commit suicide" in her doctor's blunt words). So Mary, like her three sons, remained safe at the home front throughout her second global war.

She was still an effective propagandist, however, and turned her attention to writing inspirational and polemical pieces for a variety of official and semiofficial government agencies and departments. She sat on the advisory council of the Writers' War Board, chaired by mystery novelist Rex Stout, and served as one of six members of the Authors' Division of the American Red Cross. (Her fellow members comprised Carl Van Doren, Carl Sandburg, Stephen Vincent Benét, Clifton Fadiman, and John Steinbeck.) She became an air warden "armed with a musette bag containing a police whistle, a screwdriver, a flashlight, and a pencil, and later with a helmet from the First World War. . . ." (Some years afterward, she shared this voluntary occupation with the heroine of her last full-length novel, *The Swimming Pool*.)

She also wrote for her own benefit, cranking out *The Yellow Room* during 1944 to satisfy her growing income tax obligations and to support her two households. She set *The Yellow Room* in her Bar Harbor house, which included a guest room of that color and an elevator like the one that plays a pivotal role in the mystery's plot. In her autobiography, she recounted how an alert reader caught her in a serious error of logic as *The Yellow Room* was making its serial debut in the *Post*. In the story, the electric elevator is employed to transport a vital object, but Mary had forgotten to turn on the power in her fictional house. Always meticulous about the logistical details in her mysteries, Mary scrambled to concoct a reasonable explanation. Although she managed to alter the magazine text before the next installment was published, the book version was already on the printing press, "so even now that elevator . . . rises in the book under its own power. Or is levitated!"

The Yellow Room had another unexpected consequence: because the story was publicized as set in Mary's Bar Harbor home, she suddenly found hordes of fans appearing on her doorstep. Many, including a group of twenty young priests, arrived unannounced and asked to see the yellow room itself, and Mary, despite her frequent claim to abhor personal publicity, usually complied graciously with these requests.

As the war came to its end and the world struggled to adjust to its new alignment of powers, Mary, too, was struggling to adapt her life to the new demands of age and potentially serious illness. She had suffered a mild thrombosis on completing *A Light in the Window,* her last romantic novel. She had also experienced a series of rejections from *The Saturday Evening Post,* so long the linchpin of her commercial success. Her old friends were gone: George Lorimer had died, and Adelaide Neall, Mary's longtime editor and supporter, had resigned when a new regime took over at the magazine in 1942. Younger editors had less regard for their most famous writer, and more and more, her projects were turned down. Throughout her career, Mary had fought like a tiger against the label of "women's writer," but now she found herself depending almost entirely on women's magazines for publication. Although *The Yellow Room* had been serialized in the *Post,* the magazine refused both *Episode of the Wandering Knife* and *The Light in the Window,* which appeared respectively in *Good Housekeeping* and the *Ladies' Home Journal.* After 1945, the *Post* accepted only three more short stories and her final novella, *The Frightened Wife.*

Despite her declining market, Mary might easily have lived out her years in comfort. She kept up a busy social schedule, though she traveled less and paid closer attention to her doctors. She had arrived at the last stage of the Rinehart mystique—grande dame of popular American culture. In regal fashion, she granted more interviews and received her just rewards. She was honored by the Mystery Writers of America in 1954 and offered an honorary doctorate from the University of Maine. (She had to decline because of ill health.) She saw a number of her stories adapted to the new medium of television, and shortly before her death, she herself became the main character in a TV drama, a dramatic retelling of *The After House.* The teleplay included Mary's role in freeing the man who had been wrongly convicted of the murder that inspired her book. It must have pleased her to see herself played by one of the most glamorous actresses of the time, Claudette Colbert.

But Mary Roberts Rinehart's life was not to play out without two more bizarre and tragic events.

Since the Rineharts had moved to Washington in the early 1920s, Mary had employed a cook named Reyes, a native of the Philippines who proved to be an excellent chef and generally obedient servant. When he married an Irish girl named Peggy, she too joined the Rinehart staff. There had been some slight rumbling in the relationship when Dr. Rinehart died: as Mary explained, "Reyes, the chef, had always regarded my husband as his real employer . . . and it took a long time for him to accept me. . . ." For a quarter century, Reyes reigned as the sovereign male in the household, but when Mary hired a butler in the spring of 1947, Reyes took the implied insult hard. Mary attempted to explain his subsequent behavior as the result of health problems and his "new emphasis on racial discrimination." Whatever the real cause, Reyes tendered his two weeks' notice, which Mary refused to take seriously.

The next day, at lunchtime, he approached Mary in her library and pulled a revolver. At point-blank range, he pulled the trigger, but the old gun failed to fire. He tried again, and again the gun jammed. Mary leaped from her chair and ran for help; "I knew then that I had a maniac on my hands," she said, "and that he still meant to kill me." The would-be murderer was brought down by the chauffeur and disarmed by Mary's personal maid. But while Mary was calling the police, Reyes escaped, grabbed two kitchen carving knives, and came after her once more. He was again caught and disarmed in a wild melee during which the chauffeur was badly cut. The police arrived soon after and took the now-calm cook away, but almost as if the script had been written by Mary herself, Reyes hanged himself in jail that night. In that strange mix of sympathy and insensitivity that so often characterized her reactions to the tragedies of others, Mary decided, "It was for the best, of course."

In the fall of that year, an event occurred for which Mary could find no justification. In October, a massive forest fire destroyed much of the Bar Harbor resort, the village, and surrounding farms and nurseries. More than seventy of the grand summer homes burned, including Mary's beloved Far View. In her autobiography, she recalled her anxiety on hearing the first reports of the fire. She was in New York, hoping that her beautiful house would be spared. It was not. "The fire," she wrote, "left me four chimneys standing stark above the rubble that had once been my house." In a life that had been so filled with strange and unexpected losses of people, Mary experienced for the first time the loss of her possessions—her real security. She never again owned a house.

"Not many of us can bear the truth, even about our-selves."

It was not long after the destruction of her Bar Harbor house that Mary completed her updating of *My Story*. It is an odd addendum, both reflective and self-justifying. She returned, for example, to the events following the 1929 stock market crash, painting a quite different version of her own financial situation than the blasé portrayal in "A Woman Goes to Market," the article that had so incensed her readers in 1931. In her 1948 retelling, she was no longer the hectoring little busybody, rallying her fellow citizens to buck up and spend, spend, spend. She had become a fellow sufferer, ravaged by her own monetary crisis and "with my world crumbling about me." In hindsight, she admitted that the Crash had been no mere panic, and she tried to shrug off that devastating *Post* article as "editorially inspired."

In long passages about her Washington years, she pictured herself as the political insider, intimate of presidents, and well versed in sensitive subjects that must be kept from the world at large. She repeated an incident recounted in her earlier book, of meeting the king of Egypt on her trip to Cairo in 1925 and being, for all intents and purposes, politely snubbed by His Majesty. But Mary had the ultimate revenge, for she possessed "a deadly secret" unknown to the monarch—that his niece, the wife of the Egyptian ambassador to the United States, did not live "the sequestered life of most royal and aristocratic [Egyptian] women. . . ." Petty and self-aggrandizing, yes. But also in keeping with the character of a woman who had to have more and know more than everyone else and who needed always to elevate herself above the hoi polloi.

It also had to be clear to Mary by 1948 that her public had never taken her serious novels deeply to heart and that her name would survive through the mysteries she wrote. She was loved for her trash rather than her treasures. So the woman who once said dismissively that writing mysteries was "easy" now claimed that "straight writing is easier than the complexities of the crime story" and that "a crime book properly done *is* a novel" (aligning herself with the serious critics of the time who were proclaiming the virtues of crime writing as literature). If she would never embrace realism, she would at least try to raise what she had always regarded as escapist writing to the level of art. The Rinehart mystique required that her work and her sacrifices have merit.

She fell back once more on her old personal fiction, that she had "never expected nor greatly desired" her career, that it had all been for the benefit of her family and others. She was a generous patron of her sons and their offspring and of many needier causes. But with her family well established and herself more than well-off, still she continued to write, though at a reduced pace. *A Light in the Window,* her last romance, appeared in 1948, and in 1952 her sons' firm released her final full-length mystery novel, *The Swimming Pool.* Unlike the products of other long-lived writers, *The Swimming Pool* showed no dimming of the novelist's powers at the end of her career. In fact, it offers all the best, and only some of the most annoying, elements of the Rinehart formula.

There's rarely an extraneous character in a Rinehart mystery—even pets play crucial roles—and *The Swimming Pool* is no exception: a socially prominent but down-on-her-luck heroine is drawn into a mystery not of her own making; a selfish blond beauty, who married for money, causes countless problems; the strong hero appears seemingly out of nowhere and harbors ulterior motives; the stalwart but shadowy police are hampered at every step by the secretiveness of the rest of the cast. Set at The Birches, a New York summer home gone to seed, the novel includes Mary's usual plethora of murders, mayhem, and menacing atmospherics. The plot is complex yet ultimately logical when all the strands are sorted out and every buried story is revealed. Though it was the only Rinehart mystery rejected for magazine serialization, the novel achieved bestseller status in 1952.

The Swimming Pool is notable not only for its strong story but also for what Mary revealed of herself in its pages. Two key characters, Lois Maynard's father and mother, have died long before the action begins. The father, a wealthy financier brought down by the Crash of 1929, committed suicide, leaving his family to pick up the pieces. The mother was a domineering and difficult woman who always favored her beautiful middle daughter over her other three children. These dark parental legacies still hang over the adult offspring, just as the portrait of Mrs. Maynard, painted by a famous artist, overlooks the library of The Birches.

The portrait itself is Mary's inside joke; it almost exactly represents a John Lavalle painting of Mary herself: a handsome but not beautiful woman in late middle age, silver haired and attired in black velvet and expensive pearls. Was Mary commenting on her own role as matriarch of the Rinehart clan? Or was it a joke of contrasts—the real novelist who secures her family's future through hard work versus the fictional mother whose snobbery and guile leave her children materially and emotionally crippled?

A second and more direct self-portrayal is the character of Lois Maynard, the hapless but far from helpless heroine and narrator who is a writer of mystery novels and of crime stories that she sells to magazines. Born into privilege, Lois was just eight when her father died, and she has, in the tradition of the genteel poor, fended for herself for most of her life. She and her bachelor brother keep up The Birches as best they can, with the help of an old family retainer and a silly young maid (two Rinehart perennials), and Lois pays for repairs with income from her writing. Like her creator, Lois works at a desk by a sunny window, makes notes in bed, and assumes her family incapable of taking her career seriously. But unlike so many of Mary's earlier heroines, Lois is both spunky and resourceful, and Mary paints her as a fictional ideal of the "new" woman. Lois is willing to work hard and take risks; devoted to her family yet ready to fly in the face of old-fashioned snobbery when it comes to romance; tough in a fight but soft and yielding in the arms of her hunky Irish cop; an astute realist, a charming romanticist, and a sexually aware virgin all rolled into one attractive package. Though Lois Maynard is too modern to be truly autobiographical, she may well be seen as a 1950s version of the Rinehart mystique—the kind of daughter Mary might have wanted.

Although her health continued to decline, Mary remained tough-minded and sharp-witted to the end. Always handsomely coifed and made up even when she was confined to her bed, she still entertained in her elegant Park Avenue apartment. Her most frequent guests were her sons and their wives (both Stan, Jr., and Alan had divorced and remarried) and her grandchildren and great-grandchildren. In 1956, via the national television program *Person to Person,* her millions of loyal fans were also invited into her penthouse for a visit with the eighty-year-old mistress of popular mystery.

Though her activity was limited, still she wrote, producing her last mystery, the novella *The Frightened Wife,* in 1953, and her last short story in 1954. At about this time she also undertook autobiography for the third time, writing an intimate and more forthright account intended only for her family. Though just a few pages were typed and distributed to her sons, the hundred or so handwritten and edited pages were preserved with her papers. Early in 1958, she had another severe heart attack, and on September 22, she died. Mary Roberts Rinehart was buried beside her husband in Arlington National Cemetery.

". . . virtue must always triumph . . ."
—"The Repute of the Crime Story" (1930)

The true legacy of Mary Roberts Rinehart remains debatable. Try as they might, critics find it hard to evaluate her work as more than popular fodder. Her serious romances are now just so much ephemera. Her nonfiction works, never journalistic because of her insistence on overblown and under-researched opinions, are forgotten. She was unfairly credited as the progenitor of the "Had-I-But-Known" school of cheap thrills writing, and sometimes cruelly satirized even in her own time. But her mysteries remain in print, and most dedicated readers of the genre have probably read at least one or two. A number of popular crime writers have readily admitted, like Charlotte MacLeod (pen name, Alisa Craig), to Mary's influence on their own early interests in mystery fiction, and even the most severe critics will grudgingly concede that Mary was singularly significant as a popularizer of the form.

In his important 1941 history of the development of the detective story, *Murder for Pleasure,* Howard Haycraft lauded Mary as "one of the great story-tellers of the age" and called her "the unquestioned dean of crime writing by and for women." In a later, harsher critique, Julian Symons nonetheless arrived at the same conclusion: "[Mrs. Rinehart's books] are the first crime stories which have the air of being written specifically for maiden aunts. . . ." The woman who hated being associated with "women's writing" nonetheless succeeded in making crime and investigation a fit subject for the vast market of female readers.

Some of the flaws in her writing are serious, particularly her reliance on irrational coincidence to draw dozens of unrelated characters together, her maddening habit of withholding crucial information, and her long and drawn-out expository conclusions, required to explain every character, every clue, and every coincidence. But what she did with the mystery—fusing it with romance, believable dialog, and homely humor—generated a new kind of popular fiction that resonates with readers today.

With greater craft than she ever applied to her writing, Mary created a life to satisfy her public, her times, and her own ultimate needs for recognition, love, and feminine power. As she became a celebrity, she formulated her mystique—a story not wholly false, not wholly true—in much the same way she plotted her novels. In a 1930 article on "The Repute of the Crime Story," Mary maintained that "two narratives comprise the properly-written detective or crime story, the surface one which is given to the reader, and the buried one hidden until the end, whose occasional emergences throughout the tale form the authentic clues to what is beneath."

Her public saw only the surface Mary Roberts Rinehart, the always elegantly dressed and socially adept authoress. Her public only heard about the devoted mother and wife who turned to writing in order to provide her family with their share of the American Dream. Her public was allowed to share only the romance of her adventures and her heartaches. On the surface, she exemplified virtue triumphant, but beneath the public image was a far more complex, difficult, and often troubled woman. Despite all the things she accumulated over her long life, all the adventures she had, all the famous and powerful people with whom she claimed intimacy, her many writings reveal, between the lines, a life of conflicts and self-doubt.

My Story was, as Jan Cohn has pointed out, "in part an act of fiction-making." Mary described herself as "headstrong and self-willed," driven by "an intense curiosity." She claimed independence; yet "womanlike" (one of her frequent asides) she repeatedly avoided positions—including the editorship of the *Ladies' Home Journal* and at least one offer of a foreign ambassadorship—that required accountability to others. Ruthlessly loyal to those she loved, she was also highly manipulative and volatile, directing their lives like a martinet. She constantly asserted the overarching importance of work; yet had she been more concerned with the quality rather than the rewards of her own writing, she might have achieved the literary status she so wanted. Was she the confident, competent, and accidentally successful woman of *My Story*? Or was she a woman driven to prove her worth, needing the spotlight, perhaps yearning all her life for the attention of a distant and distracted father, and perhaps plagued by the same dark internal forces that motivated his unexplained suicide?

Whatever the subconscious needs that motivated her life and her writing, Mary Roberts Rinehart certainly earned her earthly rewards. Her literary reputation may be slight, but her romantic mysteries, the best of them highly readable and enjoyable, formed a substantial bridge across the gap between the nineteenth-century Mothers of Detection and the modern age of detective fiction. She was, in her own word, a twentieth-century "pioneer" who helped pave the way for a new generation of Women of Mystery.

BIBLIOGRAPHY

MARY ROBERTS RINEHART
1876–1958
American (born: Allegheny, Pennsylvania)

"If I had only known how to read the purpose of that gaping aperture, what I might have saved in anxiety and mental strain!"
—The Circular Staircase

America's first "mistress of mystery" wrote hundreds of articles, stories, and novels during her long career. The following bibliography is limited to her mystery novels, story collections, plays, and nonfiction books. Her first six novels were published by Bobbs-Merrill. She then moved to Houghton Mifflin, and in 1917 to Doran (later Doubleday Doran).

After 1929, all her books were published by her sons' firm of Farrar and Rinehart/Rinehart. Books are listed chronologically by American publication dates. Alternate British (GB) titles are also given.

Mystery Novels and Story Collections
1908   *The Circular Staircase*
1909   *The Man in Lower Ten*
1910   *The Window at the White Cat*
1913   *The Case of Jennie Brice*
1914   *The After House*
1921   *Sight Unseen* and *The Confession* (two short novels)
1925   *The Red Lamp*/GB: *The Mystery Lamp*
1926   *The Bat* (novel adapted anonymously by Stephen Vincent Benét from the play by Rinehart and Avery Hopwood)
1926   *Two Flights Up*
1930   *The Door*
1932   *Miss Pinkerton*/GB: *The Double Alibi* (features Hilda Adams)
1933   *The Album*
1933   *Mary Roberts Rinehart's Crime Book* (includes novellas *The Buckled Bag* and *Locked Doors*, both featuring Hilda Adams, and three crime novels)
1933   *The State Vs. Elinor Norton*/GB: *The Case of Elinor Norton*
1938   *The Wall*
1940   *The Great Mistake*
1942   *Haunted Lady* (features Hilda Adams)
1945   *The Yellow Room*
1950   *Episode of the Wandering Knife*/GB: *The Wandering Knife* (three short novels: *Episode of the Wandering Knife, The Man Who Hid His Breakfast,* and *The Secret*)
1952   *The Swimming Pool*/GB: *The Pool*
1953   *The Frightened Wife and Other Murder Stories*

Nonfiction
1915   *Kings, Queens, and Pawns* (collection of war articles)
1916   *Through Glacier Park* (travel)
1917   *The Altar of Freedom*
1918   *Tenting Tonight* (travel)
1920   *Isn't That Just like a Man?* (combined with *Well, You Know How Women Are!* by Irwin S. Cobb)
1922   *The Out Trail* (travel)
1926   *Nomad's Land* (travel)
1939   *Writing Is Work,* published by The Writer, Inc.

Autobiography
1948   *My Story: A New Edition and Seventeen New Years* (The first version of *My Story* was published by Farrar and Rinehart in 1931.)

Plays   **Dates are for first major productions.**
1906   *A Double Life*
1909   *Seven Days* (based on the novel *When a Man Marries.* A musical version, *Tumble In,* was produced in 1919.)
1912   *Cheer Up*
1920   *Spanish Love* (adapted with Avery Hopwood)
1920   *The Bat* (with Avery Hopwood)
1920   *Tish* (adapted by Edward E. Rose)
1920   *Bab* (adapted by Edward Carpenter)
1923   *The Breaking Point* (based on the novel)

Film and Television Adaptations
A number of Rinehart's "straight" and mystery stories and novels were adapted into silent films, including *The Circular Staircase* in 1915.

Sound films of her mysteries include two versions of *Miss Pinkerton*: a 1932 production starring Joan Blondell, as nurse-detective Hilda Adams, and George Brent; and a 1941 remake titled *The Nurse's Secret*. A British version of *The Case of Elinor Norton* was produced in 1935.

The Bat was first released as a silent film in 1926 and remade in 1930 as *The Bat Whispers,* starring Chester Morris and Una Merkel. Both of these adaptations were written and directed by Roland West. An updated version of *The Bat,* starring Vincent Price and Agnes Morehead, was released in 1959.

Several of Rinehart's works were adapted for television during the early era of live drama. Television productions of her mysteries included a 1956 *Climax* production of *The Circular Staircase* with Judith Anderson, and a 1957 *Telephone Time* adaptation of *The After House*. This latter play was combined with the story of Mrs. Rinehart's real-life solution to the mystery that was the basis of the novel.

HAD SHE BUT KNOWN

> *Had I But Known-ers are quick to assume the prerogatives of the Deity. For they will suppress evidence that doesn't suit their theories with appalling spontaneity . . .*
> —from "Don't Guess, Let Me Tell You" by Ogden Nash

Humorist Ogden Nash gave the name to the Had-I-But-Known or H.I.B.K. mystery. It wasn't a school, just a narrative formula that generally involved dropping some naive and often foolish woman into an ocean of trouble and letting her dog-paddle to safety. The most successful H.I.B.K. writer was Mary Roberts Rinehart. It was she and her less gifted imitators who inspired Nash to pen his satirical poem "Don't Guess, Let Me Tell You" in 1940.

Because the H.I.B.K. approach owes heavily to the romantic-Gothic and sensational traditions, the stories tend to be melodramatic, propelled by outlandish coincidences, irrelevant love interests, and pure dumb luck. There may be a detective, but he is rarely more than window dressing, for the objective is to engage the senses rather than the mind. The H.I.B.K. is usually told by its heroine (or occasional hero) in retrospect. She looks back and recalls the mystery, diminishing suspense from the outset. The reader knows that whatever happens, the narrator has already survived it, so the H.I.B.K. relies for its excitement on the question of *how* the heroine will come through unscathed.

What so annoyed Ogden Nash and other critics of the H.I.B.K. is the narrator's habitual concealing of vital information that she would have, of course, revealed if only she had understood the consequences. For Mrs. Rinehart, who wrote all of her mysteries with an eye to lucrative serial publication in magazines, the H.I.B.K. was an essential foreshadowing device: it alerted the reader that more deadly action was coming in the next exciting installment. Foreshadowing and frequent plot recapitulations kept the magazine reader involved over a half-dozen weeks or months. Even Ogden Nash, so long associated with magazines like *The New Yorker,* would surely have sympathized with Rinehart's observation that writers are "merely the sugar coating to the advertising pill in any periodical." In order to get those fat checks from demanding publishers, Mary had to keep her readers coming back for more, and H.I.B.K. did the trick.

THE GHOSTS AND MRS. RINEHART

In spite of repeated protests that she did not believe in material manifestations of the dearly departed, Mary Roberts Rinehart's life was steeped in a remarkable amount of ectoplasm. Her childhood fear of ghosts was hardly unusual, but Mary was a grown woman when she was visited by her Aunt Ella every night for two weeks after that good woman's death.

Then there were the communications with her dead husband. Dr. and Mrs. Rinehart had made a pact to attempt postmorten contact, and her first session with a medium was, if not conclusive, at least unnerving.

Though no voice spoke in the darkened hotel room where the two women met, Mary suddenly felt "something roughly pushed down inside the open neck of my dress." When the same hand returned moments later, it left behind a fresh rosebud that Mary kept for years. In another session, with English medium Eileen Garrett, "Doctor Rinehart's very voice, his mannerisms, even his little chuckle" came to Mary and her sons. After this second episode, Mary let the matter rest.

But she had other, less intimate encounters, and a number of these experiences were recreated in her mysteries. A rented summer home on Long Island in 1918 produced several months of eerie activity: members of the Rinehart household repeatedly heard footsteps in the hallway and unexplained bumps and thumps in the night, saw the lid on a laundry hamper rise and fall under its own power, witnessed a "strange and shapeless figure" crawl through a doorway, and saw a white light float above the garden and disappear into the marshes. These events formed the basis of Mary's novel *The Red Lamp,* in which a man of reason, a university professor, confronts both superstition and the supernatural.

In 1921, the Rineharts moved into a Washington, D.C., apartment where Senator Boies Penrose had recently died. Dead but seemingly not departed. Again family and friends experienced a series of surreal happenings: ringing bells, "curious noises, stirrings," knocking at doors, the sounds of crashing flowerpots, furniture that moved under its own steam. Two of Mary's aunts once heard nocturnal typing but on investigation found the study with the typewriter "dark and empty." A tightly sealed bathroom was visited by "small creatures," including a bat. The bat incident was immortalized in Mary's last Hilda Adams novel, *Haunted Lady,* and the ringing of house bells—which Mary attributed to her special poltergeist—became an element of intrigue in *The Wall.*

For years, Mary and Stan Rinehart explored "all sorts of psychic phenomena." After one disappointing session, they began corresponding with Sir Arthur Conan Doyle, who had endorsed the rascally medium. Mary also had several encounters with fortune-tellers, one of whom accurately predicted the death by drowning of Mary's frequent theatrical cowriter, Avery Hopwood.

Was Mary a believer? She claimed skepticism but never disbelief: ". . . to say that nothing exists which we cannot see has always seemed to me to be nonsense. We do not see the wind."

MRS. RINEHART TO THE RESCUE

Like most mystery writers, Mary Roberts Rinehart often took her inspiration from real-life crime stories. Her 1917 novella, *The Confession,* was based on information brought to her attention by a Pittsburgh district attorney: a scrap of paper with a written confession of murder that had been found secreted in a telephone booth. The supposed murderer had been a brothel madam, and the victim one of her female employees. Though the woman who signed the confession was still alive, no evidence of a murder was found, so the case was dropped . . . by everyone except Mary Roberts Rinehart.

The fine line between fact and fiction was even more dramatically crossed several years earlier. Through a fellow member of the Sewickley Country Club, Mrs. Rinehart became interested in a twenty-year-old case: triple ax murders committed aboard a lumber schooner named the *Herbert Fuller.* The first mate had been convicted and was serving life in prison, but from her reading of eyewitness testimony given at the trial, Mary became convinced that he could not have committed the crimes. She also learned that another crew member had since been imprisoned in Sweden as a homicidal maniac. When *The After House,* the book she based on the case (changing the setting to a luxury yacht), was first serialized in *McClure's* magazine, the authorities reopened the case of the *Herbert Fuller* murders, and the convicted man was pardoned and freed. In 1957, a television drama based on Mary's investigation and the writing of *The After House* starred Claudette Colbert—an actress almost as glamorous as the famous novelist herself.

Part
TWO

A GOLDEN ERA:
THE GENTEEL PUZZLERS

"Do you promise that your detectives shall well and truly detect the crimes presented to them . . . not placing reliance on nor making use of Divine Revelation, Feminine Intuition, Mumbo-Jumbo, Jiggery-Pokery, Coincidence or the Act of God?"

—from the oath administered to new members
of the Detection Club of London

In 1920, Agatha Christie's first mystery novel was bought by a mere two thousand English readers—inauspicious, but at least a start. In the same year, Dorothy L. Sayers was dabbling with ideas for her first whodunit. Christie and Sayers were hardly exceptional. In the years immediately following World War One, people all over England were thinking about, scribbling at, and actually producing novels of crime and detection. None of them knew it at the time, but over the next two decades, they would create the Golden Age of detective fiction.

The Golden Age roughly spanned the years between the two World Wars and was primarily a British phenomenon. It evolved a relatively precise formula of genre writing and secured mass readership for *novels* of crime and detection, making a small number of writers rich and famous and a good many more very comfortable. It forced critics—many of them kicking and screaming in protest—to recognize detective and mystery stories as something more than frivolous, if not quite serious, literature.

Most important, the Golden Age marked the ascendancy of the detective novel as intellectual puzzle. The formula of crime, rational detection, and solution that Edgar Allan Poe had originated in the 1840s was taken to its limit by a dozen or so extremely crafty and ingenious writers, and pushed over the edge in the end by radical changes following World War Two.

Golden Age detective fiction achieved a level of popularity that no one has ever completely explained. It was read at all levels of society, but was, as Colin Watson has pointed out, driven by middle-class tastes: "Here was no passing fashion; the weekly ration of whodunnits [*sic*] came to be one of the staples of life for thousands of middle-class families. Housewives brought it home in the shopping basket as conscientiously as they remembered to renew the family supplies of bread and sugar."

This taste was fed by a publishing industry geared to quantity rather than quality, and under the deluge of books that hit the market after 1920 or so, it took some time to sort the great and good from the merely competent and the incompetent. Truly bad writers tended to disappear quickly enough, though almost anyone who could put together a decent formula tale got a shot at publication. But eventually the real cream—for example, Agatha Christie—rose to the top and demonstrated genuine staying power.

Who were the dominant writers of the Golden Age? Critics disagree about some of the lesser lights, but most will second Julian Symons's nominations of Christie, Dorothy L. Sayers, and Anthony Berkeley/Francis Isles (pen names of Anthony Berkeley Cox) in England, and S. S. Van Dine (pen name of Willard Huntington Wright) in the United States. All four began publishing detective fiction in the 1920s and became enormously popular on both sides of the Atlantic, and all are still read today, though Berkeley-Isles and Van Dine novels suffer more from quaintness than the works of their female contemporaries.

Not far below these leaders came a second wave that included Margery Allingham, Ngaio Marsh, John Dickson Carr (master of the locked-room mystery who also wrote under the name Carter Dickson), Ellery Queen (the pen name of cousins Frederic Dannay and Manfred B. Lee), Nicholas Blake (pseudonym of English poet and eventually poet laureate Cecil Day-Lewis), Rex Stout (creator of Nero Wolfe), and Josephine Tey (pen name of Elizabeth MacKintosh). Not all were from Great Britain—Carr, Queen, and Stout were American, and Marsh was a New Zealander—but their work, if not their passports, bore the distinctly British stamp.

A large company of less gifted but skilled practitioners can also be squeezed under the great Golden Age umbrella. British writers included Gladys Mitchell (mother of the Mrs. Adela Bradley mysteries), Patricia Wentworth (Dora Amy Elles Turnbull, creator of Miss Maud Silver), Michael Innes (pen name of Oxford professor James Innes Mackintosh Stewart), Freeman Wills Crofts, H. C. Bailey, Philip Macdonald, A. E. W. Mason, Arthur William Upfield (whose "Bony" mysteries added the exotic element of Australian settings), John Rhode (pen name of Major Cecil John Charles Street), husband-and-wife team G. D. H. and Margaret Cole, Josephine Bell (pen name of Dr. Doris Bell Ball), and Georgette Heyer. Americans included Mignon Eberhart, Elizabeth Daly,

Dorothy B. Hughes, Helen Reilly (whose Inspector McKee books impressed readers with accurate police procedures), Mabel Seeley, Phoebe Atwood Taylor (also known as "Alice Tilton," creator of Asey Moore of Cape Cod), and Richard and Frances Lockridge (originators of the Mr. and Mrs. North series). The list goes on, and many of these writers, from Agatha Christie down, continued writing well past the arbitrary end of the Golden Age.

What is obvious at a glance is the number of women in the list. Before 1920, only Anna Katharine Green and Mary Roberts Rinehart could have claimed rightful places in the ranks of leading mystery writers. It was the advent of the puzzle mystery that finally gave women their equal chance at success because the first requirement of a Golden Age writer was an agile mind, not a masculine temperament, education, or vocation.

The book that got the golden ball rolling was not of the period; it was published in 1913, just before the outbreak of World War One, by an editorial writer for London's *Daily Telegraph* newspaper: Oxford-educated foreign affairs specialist E. C. (Edward Clerihew) Bentley (1875–1956). What Bentley's *Trent's Last Case* accomplished was a lasting break with the deadpan seriousness and florid romanticism of the Sherlock Holmes school. In his deliberate rejection of the great Holmes, Bentley created Philip Trent, a journalist like himself who must nose out the murderer of a powerful Wall Street capitalist. Unlike the near-omniscient Holmes, Trent is a regular guy, given to good humor and mistakes in judgment and just as inclined as the next man to fall for a pretty face. Trent can be urbane and witty; he can be silly and obtuse. In other words, he is altogether human, and it was this characteristic, rather than the nature of the mystery or structure of the book, that earned for E. C. Bentley the title "father of the contemporary detective novel."*

The humanity that Bentley brought to detective fiction was perfectly suited to writers who generally had only the most casual knowledge of police procedures, forensics, or even real dead people outside silk-lined caskets. True Golden Age detection is never about bloodbaths and body parts, and the most genteel of *women,* sheltered as they might have been, could write as well as men about people and their bad deeds. It is characteristic of the best Golden Age mysteries that motivation—sex, greed, revenge—is of equal importance with method and opportunity in un-

---

* E. C. Bentley was never a serious detective novelist and regretted that he would be remembered for *Trent* rather than his nonfiction and humorous writings. He did return briefly to his detective with a novel titled *Trent's Own Case* (cowritten with H. Warner Allen) in 1936 and a volume of short stories, *Trent Intervenes,* in 1938. *Trent's Last Case,* though stylistically stiff compared to contemporary detective fiction, is still a worthwhile read, especially for dedicated fans of the Golden Age.

earthing criminals and bringing them to justice. (Motive, it should be noted, is not the same as criminal psychology, and the modern interest in the twisted mental processes of the pathological criminal did not emerge as a dominant theme until after World War Two, though individual psychology was increasingly central in the works of transitional writers such as Josephine Tey.) Even if most female writers—and many a fastidious male, if the truth be told—either couldn't or wouldn't delve into the ghoulish details of how a murder was committed, they could with gusto lay out the whys and wherefores that led to the guilty "who."

> *"The detective story . . . is a sporting event."*
> —"Twenty Rules for Writing
> Detective Stories," S. S. Van Dine

By today's standards, Golden Age mysteries can seem stylized, but in a novel such as Christie's *The Murder of Roger Ackroyd* or Allingham's *Death of a Ghost,* the form may be predictable though the conclusion is not. The Golden Age puzzle mystery was distinguished from its predecessors by a shift in tone that led to a new structure. No longer was the author an all-knowing, all-powerful voice who revealed what he wanted, when he wanted, and was free to manipulate the story in any way he chose. The puzzle mystery is a game of logic between writer and reader, and the first rule followed by successful Golden Age writers was to "play fair." Anything else was just not cricket.

People who enjoy Golden Age mysteries are likely to enjoy chess and bridge, crosswords, anagrams, acrostics, Scrabble, charades—mind games with clearly defined rules. If the writer plays fair and the reader knows the rules, then the puzzle mystery becomes just such a contest. The challenge is for the reader, equipped with reason and close observation, to arrive at the correct conclusion—whodunit—before the author unmasks the killer. In this game, however, only the writer is in a position to cheat; if he or she doesn't play fair, then the contest is rigged. Under Golden Age rules, Arthur Conan Doyle would have been a cheat because his Holmes routinely solves the mystery using obscure and unexplained bits of real or imaginary science that the reader could not be expected to know, discover, or even guess.

Setting out the rules for concocting a proper detective story became a minor cottage industry in the 1920s and 1930s. The most famous set of regulations was the product of Monsignor Ronald A. Knox (1888–1957), Catholic essayist and mystery writer, whose famous "A Detective Story Decalogue" was published in 1929. True to his biblical roots, Father Knox laid down ten commandments. Some are facetious: "No Chinaman must figure in the story"; "The stupid friend of the detective, the Watson," must be "slightly, but very slightly" less intelligent than the average reader. But others—"The criminal must be someone mentioned in the early part of the story"; "All supernatural or preternatural agencies are ruled out as a matter of course"—were plainly designed to remedy the worst failings of earlier mystery and thriller writing. It was wrong, the priest declared, to put a secret room or hidden passage in a modern house. It was wrong, he admonished, to suddenly thrust "twin brothers, and doubles generally" upon an unsuspecting reader.

S. S. Van Dine (1889–1939), the creator of Philo Vance, published his own set of rules a year before Father Knox and insisted even more strenuously on logic, reason, and fairness. "The reader must have equal opportunity with the detective for solving the mystery. All clues must be plainly stated and described," reads rule 1 of Van Dine's creed. Rule 5 warns, "The culprit must be determined by logical deductions—not by accident or coincidence or unmotivated confession." In rule 20, Van Dine abjures a catalog of tricks and devices familiar from the Holmesian era, including the dog that doesn't bark.

Rules, of course, are made to be broken, and no Golden Age writer took all of Van Dine's or the good priest's commandments completely to heart. In her Peter Wimsey–Harriet Vane saga, Dorothy L. Sayers made mincemeat of Van Dine's rule 3: "There must be no love interest. The business in hand is to bring a criminal to the bar of justice, not to bring a lovelorn couple to the hymeneal altar." Earl Derr Biggers flouted Father Knox's "no Chinaman" rule by creating the inordinately popular Chinese-American detective Charlie Chan. And Agatha Christie . . . well, the Queen of Crime broke nearly every rule at one time or another, yet was one of the fairest of all Golden Age writers.

> *"It is the ladies and gentlemen of . . . the Golden Age of detective fiction that really get me down."*
> —"The Simple Art of Murder," Raymond Chandler

Golden Age detective fiction and its conventions are easy targets for contemporary critics, and even in its time, the puzzle mystery was not universally loved. In a notoriously angry essay published in the *Atlantic Monthly* in December 1944, English-educated American crime writer Raymond Chandler (1888–1959) launched some particularly explosive torpedoes against his British and Anglicized American peers. Though conceding that for puzzle detection he preferred the real British product to the more pretentious American variety, Chandler proceeded to dissect A. A. Milne's *The Red House Mystery*★ clue by clue, belittle *Trent's Last Case,* and assail Freeman Wills Crofts and Agatha Christie. His chief complaint was that the Golden Age classics failed the realism test: "They are too contrived, and too little aware of what goes on in the world. They try to be honest, but honesty is an art." He savaged Dorothy L. Sayers: "[Her kind of detective story] was second-grade literature because it was not about the things that could make first-grade literature."

Even though Sayers (who had already given up detective fiction for nobler pursuits) might have agreed, Chandler was really expressing the deep frustration of a uniquely American group of detective writers—the "hard-boiled" school—who were struggling for public recognition and financial reward under the gargantuan weight of Golden Age domination. Chandler's essay seethes with bitterness over the fact that the public preferred the puzzle to his brand of realism.

Chandler was a follower of Dashiell Hammett (1894–1961), one of the first and still the most memorable of the hard-boiled writers. Hammett was a former detective for the Pinkerton private investigation agency and a veteran writer for the pulp fiction magazine *Black Mask.*† He produced only five novels—*Red Harvest, The Dain Curse, The Maltese Falcon, The Glass Key,* and *The Thin Man*—all published between 1929 and 1934 and all superb examples of the tough-talking, hard-hitting, sexually explicit (for their time), violence-ridden, gutsy and gritty "realism" that characterized the new American approach. Hammett's detectives (the Continental Op, Sam Spade, Ned Beaumont, and even Nick Charles) walked the moral dark side. They represented a new breed of investigator, never much better, and sometimes worse, than the criminals they pursued. They were not white knights of rationality and legal justice. They were brutish and vulgar, drank bootleg whiskey instead of cocktails, liked their women oversexed and easy, hung out comfortably with lowlife and petty crooks, and fought more often with fists

---

★ A. A. Milne, poet and playwright now best known as the creator of Winnie the Pooh, wrote only one detective novel, *The Red House Mystery,* published in 1922, and one mystery play. *The Red House Mystery* was influential in its day not for its logical construction (which Chandler so efficiently mocked), but its lighthearted humor. Like *Trent's Last Case,* Milne's novel reminded writers at the beginning of the Golden Age to loosen up, give the reader some fun, and not take themselves or their mysteries too seriously.

† Appearing first during World War One, cheap magazines printed on wood pulp paper were the birthing room of the "hard-boiled dick" action story. *Black Mask* was one of the best, surviving until 1953 when it was overtaken by television.

than brains. Their environments were sleazy, their language crude, and their modus operandi even cruder.

But for all that, their stories had the chance of rising to the level of art, according to Chandler, because in them lay "the quality of redemption." The hard-boiled detective, in Chandler's words, "is the hero, he is everything. He must be a complete man and a common man and yet an unusual man. He must be, to use a rather weathered phrase, a man of honor, by instinct, by inevitability, without thought of it, and certainly without saying it. He must be the best man in his world and a good enough man for any world."

In other words, innovative American crime writers between the World Wars elevated the character of the detective above the plot and logic of the story. In the hard-boiled tales of Hammett, Chandler, Ross Macdonald (pen name of Kenneth Millar, the creator of Lew Archer), and their confreres, the raison d'être was not a solution to a complex puzzle, but the redemption of the hero through adherence to an individualistic moral code that elevated him, in spirit if not body, above the "mean streets" of everyday corruption. He was a man among men, a lonely figure in a world where other men had no moral center and where women were either room decoration or bad news.

Evolving from what Julian Symons called the "blue-collar workers' version of the crime story" in the pulp magazines of the twenties, these detective heroes translated brilliantly from book page to Hollywood, particularly in the film noir of the 1930s through the 1950s. The best of this potent film genre—*The Maltese Falcon, The Thin Man, Little Caesar* (from the novel by W. R. Burnett), *The Postman Always Rings Twice* and *Double Indemnity* (from works by James M. Cain), *The Big Sleep* (from Chandler's first Philip Marlowe book)—drew their intensity, moodiness, and moral sense from their central characters. Accents aside, it is impossible to imagine Humphrey Bogart, Edward G. Robinson, Robert Ryan, or John Garfield playing Hercule Poirot or Lord Peter Wimsey or Inspector Roderick Alleyn. Yet how smoothly they slipped into the movie skins of the hard-boiled heroes.★

Critics have long argued about why British and American crime writing took such opposite roads in the 1920s and 1930s. Any number of explanations (including national temperaments) are plausible, but

---

★ One Hollywood actor played on both sides. Leading man Robert Montgomery portrayed Lord Peter Wimsey in the 1940 British version of Dorothy L. Sayers's *Busman's Honeymoon* (*Haunted Honeymoon* in the United States) and six years later directed himself as Philip Marlowe in an odd, first-person film of Raymond Chandler's *The Lady in the Lake.*

since all writers are prisoners of their times, the social conditions on either side of the ocean must be taken into account.

World War One had affected Britain and the United States dramatically but differently. The United States was active in the war for barely a year, took far fewer losses relative to population, and emerged from the conflict a much stronger power, its territory unscathed by battle. Great Britain and the rest of the Allied nations were physically, economically, and spiritually devastated. The cost in lives was horrendous: approximately 115,000 Americans were lost, compared to nearly a million British dead. A whole generation of Englishmen was decimated; hundreds of thousands who returned from the Front alive were physically and mentally damaged almost beyond repair. The war—in Colin Watson's words "an experience so appalling that it rendered millions emotionally emasculated"—made little distinction among social castes.★ It also signaled the beginning of the ends of Britain's global empire and its rigid internal class system.

One unintended consequence of the human devastation was that Britain's young women, who would normally have married and been supported by husbands, found eligible, healthy men in short supply and were often forced to make their own livings or to support their families alone. A related result was the opening of many traditionally male occupations to women. These two factors, combined with the ravenous hunger of publishers for ever more popular novels, may help to explain the emergence of so many female mystery writers in England.

Victorious in war but battered and scarred, diminished as a world power, and facing the first shock waves of cataclysmic social upheaval—is it surprising that the British public sought comfort in a well-regulated form of popular literature that promised to deliver sensible solutions to the most senseless of human acts? Isn't it perfectly logical that in a new, postwar world that seemed beyond anyone's control, average British readers found solace in entertainments that enabled them to use their wits and solve problems (or at least to see problems solved) in a couple of nights' reading? Mysteries of the Golden Age are often criticized for lacking socially relevant content, failing to address the pressing political and economic problems of their day, and buttressing the old upstairs-downstairs stereotypes of a dying era. But what they gave readers was a few hours of retreat from reality into perfectly ordered fictions where

---

★ It was common for Golden Age detectives to have had affecting experiences in the war, and even Dorothy L. Sayers's fatuous Lord Peter Wimsey suffers frightening, recurrent bouts of shell shock. In *The Unpleasantness at the Bellona Club,* Sayers included a sensitive portrait of war veteran and murder suspect George Fentiman and his wife, reduced to poverty and despair by his debilitating neurasthenia, the result of nerve gas.

Right always triumphed over Wrong, where people knew their places, where the silver service was always polished and the strawberries always sweet.

The popularity of Golden Age novels in the United States indicates that a good many Americans were likewise seeking stability and moral clarity in their entertainments. But other factors were at work under the Stars and Stripes that gave rise to the machismo of hard-boiled realism. Where Europeans were seeing their social structure flatten out (Dorothy Sayers's *Murder Must Advertise,* set in an ad agency, and Margery Allingham's *The Fashion in Shrouds* both offer lively portrayals of the new social egalitarianism at work in postwar London), Americans, particularly the working classes at the onset of the Great Depression, watched helplessly as the nation's wealth and power were gathered into fewer and fewer hands. American faith in hard work as the means to success and happiness was shaken; it seemed to many ordinary folks that corruption in business, politics, and law enforcement—graft, bribery, profiteering, and low-level palm-greasing—had become the rule rather than the exception. Over its thirteen-year life span, Prohibition (1920–1933) decreased the consumption of alcohol but turned lawbreaking into a national pastime and transformed small-time punks and bullies like Al Capone into princes of organized crime.

The hard-boiled novel was a response to this environment. Hammett, Chandler, et al. provided their readers not escape, but a good nose-rubbing in the dirty realities of gangster-ridden cities, venal politicians, nasty capitalists, and violent cops on the take. In a country where men were still very firmly in charge of everything, the tough new literature was a man's province, and it was not until the 1960s that women began to bang loudly at its door.

The difference between Golden Age and hard-boiled detective writing was as day to night. But there was one point at which they came together—what novelist and critic H. R. F. Keating terms "the happy ending." Hard-boiled writers liked to think of themselves as groundbreakers, but when it came to the final act, they were as conventional as any Golden Ager. In puzzle mysteries, even when the hero is a village spinster like Miss Marple or a "silly ass" aristocrat like Albert Campion, she or he defeats Evil by bringing it to heel. In hard-boiled fiction, the hero, usually a seedy shamus, triumphs over evil by keeping his own cockeyed sense of honor intact, whether or not he solves the crime to everyone's satisfaction. Either way, good wins out, and the reader is satisfied.

In hindsight, the odd but inescapable conclusion is that, between Golden Age and hard-boiled fiction, the latter was the less inventive. In hard-boiled stories, the settings are certainly truer to life, there is more action, and no investigator kowtows to people with ancient titles and royal blood. But it was the "realists" who romanticized, imagining their tough private eyes as latter-day Lancelots. Hammett and his followers took the detective straight back to Sherlock Holmes and the era of the troubled but superior man searching for some internally satisfying moral resolution. At their best, hard-boiled mysteries reached for something mythic, Arthurian. But contrary to Raymond Chandler's contentions, in the hands of a genuine Golden Age master like Agatha Christie, truths closer to everyday reality—how and why people kill from greed or lust, for example—were just as likely to be uncovered amid the teacups and mannerly conversation of the English drawing room as in all the steamy bars and satin boudoirs of the rawest American metropolis. As the foremost female practitioners of the Golden Age puzzlers proved again and again, when crime is the subject, a soft touch is sometimes preferable to a knuckle sandwich.

IF IT'S FISHY . . . IT COULD BE A RED HERRING

> " 'Aren't you clever?' said Tuppence. 'Especially at drawing red herrings across the track.' "
>
> —Agatha Christie's *Partners in Crime*

Red herrings were stock-in-trade for the writers of Golden Age detective fiction—false clues deliberately designed to tempt incautious investigators (and astute readers) down dead-end roads and up blind alleys. Agatha Christie, for one, had a genius for diversionary clue-making, planting her trails with all manner of misleading and immaterial information, from fresh blood evidence to entire subplots, to waylay the reader. In Margery Allingham's first Albert Campion mystery, *The Murder at Black Dudley,* Campion himself is a big red herring. Under the rules of fair play, red herrings are always legitimate so long as they are logical and the writer includes the real clues necessary to solve the mystery.

But just what is a red herring? According to *Brewer's Dictionary of Phrase and Fable,* it's a smoked and salted fish once popular with the English lower classes. The modern meaning derives from fox hunting practice: a red herring "drawn across a fox's path destroys the scent and sets the hounds at fault. . . ." thus ending the hunt. So a red herring is a false and distracting scent. Follow it, and you'll wind up chasing a wild goose!

BIG, BAD BERTHA

Professional female private eyes were still rare wine in detective fiction of the 1920s–1940s. Mary Roberts Rinehart's Hilda Adams, also known as "Miss Pinkerton," combines nursing with sleuthing, and Mignon Eberhart picked up the same thread with her Nurse Sarah Keate mysteries. Hildegarde Withers is an old maid schoolteacher turned "private investigator without portfolio" in a series by Stuart Palmer. Rex Stout created a paid female investigator, Theodolinda "Dol" Bonner, who got one solo book, *Hand in the Glove* in 1937, and appeared in several Nero Wolfe novels. Then there was Dorothy L. Sayers's Miss Kitty Climpson, proprietress of a stenographic agency that doubles as an investigation service for Lord Peter Wimsey. Agatha Christie's Mrs. Ariadne Oliver, writer of detective novels, takes on cases at the behest of her good friend Hercule Poirot. But the real queen of the "she-dicks" was one tough broad named Bertha Louise Cool who costarred in twenty-nine novels written by Erle Stanley Gardner (1889–1970) under the pen name A. A. Fair—a series many connoisseurs prefer to Gardner's Perry Mason mysteries.

Bertha had a husband, a two-timing rat who died a couple of years before her debut in *The Bigger They Come* (1939). When the reader first meets her, she has set up Bertha Cool—Confidential Investigations in downtown Los Angeles. Until she hires a disbarred lawyer named Donald Lam, Bertha can just cover the rent with divorce cases. Lam pretty much takes over the investigative functions, letting Bertha deal with what she loves best—the money that she ruthlessly screws out of clients with the zeal of Torquemada at the Inquisition. Some say, based on her 275-pound bulk, that Bertha's first love is food, and she never passes up a pecan waffle, even after a bout with pneumonia cuts her down to a svelte 165 pounds. But what goes in her mouth is nothing compared to what comes out—a constant stream of profanity, wisecracks, and hard-as-rock cynicism.

Bertha gets one case of her own, *Cats Prowl at Night* (1943), which she fouls up, but she's no dope and is quick to nail the pompous and preposterous. She's also a canny investor and a tough negotiator when a dollar is at stake. With her "freight locomotive" figure and small, "diamond-hard" eyes, her cigarettes and outsized capacity for liquor, and her aggressive distrust of men, Bertha can easily be seen as a caricature, but an appealing one.

Erle Stanley Gardner is often lumped with the followers of Dashiell Hammett and like Hammett got his start with *Black Mask* magazine. But he disavowed the "hard-boiled" label, preferring "action type detective story" and demanding a level of fairness to his readers that was in sync with the best work of the Golden Age. He produced his eighty-two Perry Mason mysteries with the regularity of a baker making bread, but even a baker likes his cake once in a while. Perhaps that is what the Cool-Lam adventures provided. Bertha was never abandoned by her author; her last appearance came in 1970—the year of Gardner's death.

CRAIG RICE

The roundtable at the Algonquin had Dorothy Parker. Hard-boiled mystery had Craig Rice—a funny, bawdy, whiskey-and-soda voice that spoke loudly in its day. True, the hard-boiled school didn't welcome women writers, but Craig Rice (born Georgiana Anne Rudolph Craig) stuck her nose under the tent in the 1940s and stole a place in the limelight.

She wrote what might be called "soft-boiled" fiction—mysteries whose tough, boozy, screwball comic veneer covered a sentimental core. Her best books featured a dizzy trio of ersatz detectives: John J. Malone, the brawling but brilliant criminal defense lawyer; Jake Justus, newsman turned publicist turned nightclub owner; and Helene Brand Justus, rich, deliciously beautiful, and a quick-draw quip artist. The three made their debut in *Eight Faces at Three* in 1939 and appeared in thirteen more novels. A second detecting team, Bingo Riggs and Handsome Kusak, were featured in three novels. Craig's best work, *Home Sweet Homicide* (1944), was a domestic murder mystery modeled on herself and her kids. (Lynn Bari played the mystery-writing mom in the very popular 1946 film of the book.) Rice's output was decidedly uneven. She wrote under several pen names including Daphne Saunders and Michael Venning and ghostwrote for a couple of popular celebrities, penning Gypsy Rose Lee's *The G-String Murders* and *Mother Finds a Body* and actor George Sanders's *Crime on My Hands*.

Chicago-born in 1908, Craig was effectively abandoned by her globe-trotting parents and sent away to her grandmother and an aunt and uncle, the Eldon Rices. Her education, like her family, was eccentric, and at age eighteen, she headed back to Chicago and spent the Roaring Twenties and Depressing Thirties knocking about local Bohemian circles of artists and writers and making a modest living as a journalist and radio producer. Prone to wild exaggerations, she claimed three or four marriages. (The third was supposedly the result of a coin toss; the fourth was to writer Lawrence Lipton.) She produced three nice children, Nancy, Iris, and David, and took her fifth and final husband, the much younger Henry DeMott, in 1948. (At the wedding, she carried a copy of her mystery *The Lucky Stiff* and cut a wedding cake decorated with skulls.)

Despite her long affair with the bottle, she wrote consistently and profitably throughout the 1940s and managed to support children, various family members, and husbands on the income from her books and screenwriting. She was the first mystery writer to make the cover of *Time* magazine, and President Franklin D. Roosevelt was among the appreciative readers who wrote her fan mail. In 1946, the editor of Chicago's *Herald-American* newspaper rushed her in from her California home to put her exclusive spin on the notorious real-life murder trial of William Heirens; she guessed wrong, deciding the accused college student was "the kind of boy you could trust your teen-age daughter with" shortly before the jury convicted him of murdering and dismembering a six-year-old girl.

The drinking and pressure took their toll, however, and Craig, who was hospitalized for alcoholism in 1949, wrote nothing for eight years. She then returned to her typewriter and hammered out several more books before her death, at age forty-nine, in 1957. Her last novel, *The April Robin Murders,* was completed by newcomer Ed McBain.

Her books—so heavily laced with whiskey and rye, drunken driving, and intemperate behavior—are unlikely candidates for revival in today's politically correct culture. But the booze-free *Home Sweet Homicide* remains a little treasure of domestic malice, included among the ten best humorous mysteries in the Top 100 Mystery Novels of All Time poll of the members of the Mystery Writers of America in the mid-1990s. The Justus-Malone novels are quick, fun reads, steeped in 1940s carpe diem attitude and tough-is-tender dialog. Craig Rice was never a rival to Dashiell Hammett and company except in sales. She didn't struggle for depth and darker meaning (at three or four books a year in her heyday, who had the time?), and the streets her amateur detectives navigate are more goofy than mean. But the lady had a gutsy style that suited its era, and she deserves a toast for the road.

AGATHA CHRISTIE

THE QUEEN OF CRIME

"The most blessed thing about being an author is that you can do it in private. . . ."[*]

*H*er father called her Agatha-Pagatha; her sister's father-in-law dubbed her "the dream child." One country gentleman addressed her as "Pinkling," the pretty girl who wore pink to all the fancy dress balls. A few brave friends called her "Aggie," despite her objections. Her first husband called her "Angel." To her publicists and legions of fans, she was the Queen of Crime, the Mistress of Mystery, the Duchess of Death. She was most proud to be "Lady Mallowan," though near the end of her life she earned her own title: "Dame Agatha."

From *An Autobiography* by Agatha Christie (Dodd, Mead)

To the world at large she was—is—Agatha Christie, and beginning in the late 1920s her name became synonymous with a certain kind of tightly crafted, ingeniously plotted, classically trim novel of detection. For almost a half-century, British readers counted on their "Christie for Christmas," a new puzzler each year from her inventive mind. Her books continue to be read by mil-

---

[*] Unless noted, quotations are from *An Autobiography* by Agatha Christie, completed in 1965 and published posthumously in 1977, and from letters, diaries, and notes quoted in Janet Morgan's 1985 *Agatha Christie, A Biography*. Titles of novels and stories appear in their original published form.

lions, and even those who have not savored her mysteries firsthand know her name from scores of stage, film, and television adaptations.

But behind the famous name, there was a gentle, funny, self-effacing woman who ran from publicity like a fox from the hounds. Once in her life, in her mid-thirties, she was the object of sustained press and public scrutiny, suffering wounds that never fully healed. Though hardly a full-fledged recluse, she protected her private life and private thoughts against all comers. Until quite late in her career, her face was virtually unknown to her large public; she could move as freely about the streets of London as through the bazaars of Baghdad. Once she was even turned away from a party given in her honor: a hotel guard could not reconcile the somewhat lumpish old lady before his eyes with the famous Mrs. Christie, and he shooed the bothersome woman into the street.

Knowing "the real Agatha Christie" is not essential to enjoyment of her stories. She was a professional; she wrote to entertain. But in her life there are clues to her fiction, and even Agatha herself, who appreciated the social value of gossip and backyard chat, might not entirely disapprove of our curiosity.

"I had a very happy childhood."

The Queen of Crime was born on September 15, 1890, in the resort town of Torquay on England's Devonshire coast. She was christened Agatha Mary Clarissa Miller: Mary for her maternal grandmother, Clarissa for her mother, and Agatha at the last-minute suggestion of a family friend. She was the third child of Fred and Clara Miller—the much-loved "afterthought" who arrived when her sister, Madge, was eleven, and her brother, Monty, was ten.

The Miller family was typically Victorian and well-to-do, but by no means wealthy. Frederick Alvah Miller (Fred to his family and "Joe" to his friends) was an American, reared by his grandparents in New England after the death of his mother. Before his marriage, he had been a popular member of the New York social scene. In his daughter's words, he was "a very agreeable man" by nature, a man who brought to those around him "a great measure of happiness." He was also "a lazy man" who supported his family on income from his inheritance. Fred Miller never held a paying job, but his life was full. He loved the daily whist games at his club, was an ardent cricket fan, delighted in staging amateur theatricals, had an excellent eye for antique furniture, attended church regularly, and was notoriously generous with friends. Blessed with good humor and a steady temperament, he doted on his children and was devoted to his wife. Among his papers, Agatha found a letter written to her mother just days before his death. "You have made all the difference in my life," Fred declared. "No man ever had a wife like you. Every year I have been married to you I love you more."

Perhaps more than anything external to her own nature, the quality of her parents' relationship influenced the course of Agatha's life. She said that "they achieved that very rare production, a happy marriage." The Millers were conventional; the lines of demarcation between husbandly and wifely duties were distinctly drawn and carefully observed. But by all accounts, theirs was a true partnership grounded in love, goodwill, and mutual respect. Had her funny, charming, affectionate father lived longer, it's likely Agatha would have come to a more circumspect view of her parents' union. As it was, her perception of their marriage provided the ideal that would shape her future relationships and key themes in her fiction.

Fred Miller was eight years older than his wife, and the story of their courtship and tangled family lineage had all the complexity of an Agatha Christie plot. Clarissa (Clara) Boehmer was the daughter of Fred's stepmother's sister. Fred's widowed father, a successful Massachusetts businessman named Nathaniel Frary Miller, had met and married his second wife, Margaret West, in Portsmouth, England, in 1863 and settled in Cheshire. At about the same time, Margaret's sister, Mary Ann West Boehmer, lost her husband, a captain in the Argyll Highlanders, and was left to raise three sons and a daughter on a small pension and the earnings from her needlework. Anxious to provide for her only daughter, Mary Ann sent young Clara to live with Margaret and her wealthy American husband. While in their care, Clara first met her handsome, devil-may-care American step-cousin, Fred. What began as a schoolgirl crush survived both Clara's adolescence and Fred's wild oats, and they were married in 1878.

As the result of this convoluted kinship, Agatha's maternal great-aunt—Margaret West Miller—was also her paternal step-grandmother, called "Auntie-Grannie." Her maternal grandmother, Mary Ann Boehmer, became "Granny B."

Auntie-Grannie was a flamboyant dowager—physically large, imaginative, and always ready to play fanciful games. Her home in the Ealing section of London was filled with friends and fresh gossip; her cupboards and chests overflowed with clothing, fabrics, and preserved foods, all put aside for some dreaded rainy-day disaster. Resolute Granny B kept a small place in London's Bayswater where she quietly reared her sons, shopped for bargains at the Army and Navy Store, and was "always the old soldier." Although neither grandmother was replicated in Miss Jane Marple, ace old maid sleuth, they were to provide the blueprint, and Agatha later conceded her special debt to Auntie-Grannie: ". . . I endowed my Miss Marple with something of Grannie's powers of prophecy." As with Auntie-Grannie, "There was no unkindness in Miss Marple, she just did not trust people."

In spite of her devotion to her father and grandmothers, the central personality in Agatha's early life was her mother. Clara Boehmer Miller was a bright, curious, creative woman who flitted from idea to idea with the caprice of a butterfly on the herbaceous border. "Sameness bored her," Agatha recalled, "and she would jump from one subject to another in a way that sometimes made her conversation bewildering." Within the confines of proper Victorian manners and morals, Clara could be daringly experimental. In matters spiritual, she tried Roman Catholicism, Unitarianism, Theosophy, Zoroastrianism, Christian Science, and a brief flirtation with Quakerism before returning, much to her husband's relief, to the Church of England. She had what Agatha called "curious flashes of intuition" that hinted at psychic abilities. She lacked, the entire family agreed, a sense of humor. She could be strong-willed when necessary, but in Agatha's estimation, Clara was basically "shy and miserably diffident about herself, and at bottom, I think, with a natural melancholy."

The bond between Clara and her third child grew in intensity after Fred's death from double pneumonia in November 1901. For reasons never wholly explained, Fred's income had been drastically reduced in the years before his death. His family always attributed his health problems and early demise, at age fifty-five, in part to the strain of his financial worries. His inheritance was handled in New York, and there is some indication of poor management by his American trustees.

While not poverty-stricken, the newly widowed Clara had to make major adjustments to her lifestyle. There would be no return to the days of lavish dinner parties with guests that had included Henry James and Rudyard Kipling. Clara determined to reduce her household staff, though Jane Rowe, the Millers' magnificent cook, chose to accept lower wages rather than relinquish the kitchen where she reigned "with the calm superiority of a queen" for forty years. Clara apparently succeeded in her economies because Agatha hardly noticed the changes: "Luxury or economy mean little when you are young. If you buy boiled sweets instead of chocolates the difference is not noticeable."

Still, with her sister and brother grown and gone, Agatha and her mother were alone: "We were no longer the Millers—a family. We were now just two people living together: a middle-aged woman, and an untried, naive girl. Things *seemed* the same, but the atmosphere was different." Agatha experienced "terrible fits of anxiety." Fearful of losing her mother, too, she would spend sleepless nights crouched outside Clara's bedroom door, listening for the reassuring sound of her mother's snoring.

"Truly I believe there was a blessing upon the house."

If the Miller marriage was the foundation of Agatha's childhood, Ashfield provided the structure. Ashfield was a large, comfortable house located at the end of Barton Road in Tor Mohun, at the opposite side of Torquay from the truly fashionable section. Using a small inheritance, Clara purchased the house during a visit to Torquay in 1880. Fred, at the time on a business trip to New York, had planned to establish permanent residence in his native United States, but Clara's instinct for Ashfield, bought from a Quaker family, changed his mind.

The house and grounds bordered on the lush Devon countryside. The garden itself had three distinct areas: the kitchen garden, the garden proper with its grassy lawn and monkey puzzle tree for climbing, and the wood where Agatha found all the elements required to spark her imagination: "mystery, terror, secret delight, inaccessibility and distance. . . ." Under the watchful eye of Nursie, the caretaker who was the pivot point of her first four years, Agatha played for endless solitary hours in the gardens or the upstairs nursery. It was in the nursery that she acquired her earliest religious training. Far more doctrinaire than either parent, Nursie imbued Agatha with her own strict moral and religious code. Like the main character in her autobiographical novel, *Unfinished Portrait,*★ Agatha "was a serious little girl. She thought a great deal about God and being good and holy. . . . At times she had a horrible fear that she was 'worldly.' . . . But on the whole she was complacently satisfied with herself. She was of the elect. She was *saved*." Her parents were another matter; in *Unfinished Portrait,* the young heroine has a long discussion with her mother about Heaven and "God's love and goodness. . . . But Celia [Agatha's fictional alter ego] was not in the least convinced. There was Hell and there was Heaven, and there were sheep and goats. If only—if only she were *quite* sure Daddy was not a goat!"

A slim, pretty child with thick golden hair, Agatha had few nearby playmates, yet what she lacked of human peers, she compensated for with richness of imagination. Barely more than a toddler, she created "The Kittens," a make-believe family with whom she shared many vivid

---

★ *Unfinished Portrait* was the second of the six romance novels Agatha wrote under the carefully guarded pseudonym Mary Westmacott. Published in 1934, it coincides closely with the details of Agatha's first thirty-nine years, through the end of her first marriage.

adventures. Later, there was Mrs. Green, who "had a hundred children . . . not quite children and not quite dogs, but indeterminate kinds of creatures between the two." A pet canary named Goldie inspired a "secret Saga" of gallant steeds and marauding robbers. With a simple wood hoop as her train, Agatha envisioned a vast Tubular Railroad around house and garden.

When she was eight or nine, Agatha invented a new set of friends, The School, which initially included seven girls "of varying ages and appearances." There were Ethel Smith, "clever, good at games" and shy Annie Grey, the "worldly" Isabella Sullivan and Elsie Green, Isabella's poor but affable cousin. Agatha included two younger girls, Ella White and Sue de Verte, both aged six, and Sue's stepsister, Vera de Verte. Only Sue de Verte, as Agatha remembered, was "curiously colourless, not only in appearance . . . but also in character. . . . I think this is probably because Sue was really *myself*. . . . Sue and Agatha became two facets of the same person, and Sue was an observer, not really one of the *dramatis personae*." The girls of The School remained with Agatha into adulthood, mirroring her own growth and change. She added four new characters over time, and all but two she married off. "Even now," Agatha wrote when she was in her sixties, "sometimes, as I put away a dress in a cupboard, I say to myself: 'Yes, that would do well for Elsie, green was always her colour.' 'Ella would look very nice indeed in that three-piece jersey suit.' It makes me laugh when I do it, but there 'the girls' *are* still, though, unlike me, they have not grown old."

For Agatha herself, school was a catch-as-catch-can affair at home. Her mother had decided that early education was damaging for children, but when Agatha taught herself to read at age five, her father ordained that she should begin her instruction. He undertook her math training himself, and Agatha soon graduated from simple sums to a book of "Problems"; she loved these prose exercises and was quite good at deducing the correct answers. Throughout her career, Agatha struggled with spelling and writing, and she never enjoyed the actual composition of her novels. It was the working out of the puzzle that intrigued her. Many decades later, archeologist Max Mallowan, her second husband, wrote that she "had a natural mathematical brain. I think that this capacity appears in her books and in the neat solution of the most complex tangles, an ability in analysis as well as synthesis."

Despite her obvious intelligence, Agatha sensed that within the family circle, she was considered "the slow one," perhaps because her mother and older sister were both so verbally agile and articulate. "It was not until I was over twenty," she recalled, "that I realized that my home standard had been unusually high and that actually I was quite as quick or quicker than the average." Another habit of her childhood—

secrecy—prevented her from discussing her supposed "slowness" with anyone. Her tendency to hold her thoughts inside became a family joke: "Agatha doesn't like parting with information," they'd say. "It was true enough," Agatha explained. "Unless they struck me as apposite or interesting, I tucked away any scraps of information that came to me, locked them up, as it were, in a file inside my head." On more than one occasion, this instinctive reticence caused the little girl needless emotional distress, but it was the pattern of a lifetime.

Until she was six, Agatha's entire world was defined by Ashfield, but by the mid-1890s the Millers were already feeling the pinch of Fred's declining inheritance, and Fred and Clara decided to rent out the family home. Torquay—the "Queen of the English Riviera," known for its mild climate, clean beaches, sea air, and brisk social life—attracted visitors year-round, and Fred calculated that the rental would support his family during a lengthy holiday and produce a profit to boot. So Agatha, Madge, and their parents decamped for the south of France, where life in a good, middle-class hotel was less expensive, and far more exciting, than home.

The Millers settled first into the Hotel Beausejour in Pau, at the feet of the snowcapped Pyrenees. There, Agatha went through several governesses and discovered the sheer fun of friends her own age, particularly two little English girls, Dorothy and Mary Selwyn. "Left to myself," she said, "I was a good, well-behaved and obedient child, but in company with other children I was only too ready to engage in any mischief that was going." Agatha and the Selwyn girls must have sorely tried the patience of the friendly French waiters and unsuspecting hotel guests with their pranks. On one occasion, they scared their mothers speechless by walking the narrow ledge of the hotel's fourth-floor parapet. It was also in Pau that Clara finally found a successor to Agatha's beloved Nursie—a young woman named Marie Sije. Marie spoke no English, had no experience as a governess, and was a poor disciplinarian, but Agatha took to her immediately, and Marie stayed with the family for three years.

After Pau, the family moved on to the small town of Cauterets in the mountains, where Agatha made more friends, including an American girl named Marguerite Prestley, who became her constant companion. The Millers also visited Paris, of which Agatha remembered little more than the ferocious mosquitoes and her first glimpse of automobiles; Brittany, where she learned to swim; and Guernsey in the Channel Islands. Yet Agatha's most vivid memories were always of Cauterets and "one of the happiest summers I have ever known." Though she later revisited the south of France, Agatha never returned to Cauterets. This was another life pattern, her ability to enjoy people and experiences while they lasted and then to move on. In her autobiography, she advised, "Never go back to a place where you have been happy. Until you do it remains alive for you. If you go back it will be destroyed." This sentiment is echoed by Miss Marple in *At Bertram's Hotel*: "I learned (what I suppose I really knew already) that one can never go back, that one should not ever try to go back—that the essence of life is going forward. Life is really a one way street, isn't it?"

After the family's Continental adventure, Agatha at last began to widen her circle of friends and activities at home. There were dance classes and piano lessons. She accompanied Madge and Monty to the local theater, nurturing her fascination with the stage. Though she never attended school regularly, she took classes in algebra and grammar at Miss Guyer's Girls' School in Torquay. Agatha enjoyed the twice-a-week lessons but did not take to the intellectual discipline of the classroom.

At Madge's wedding to James Watts in September 1902, Agatha was introduced to Nan Watts, James's little sister. For Agatha, who normally preferred male to female companionship, Nan was to be a lifelong exception. There were more new friends—Dr. Huxley, his wife, and their five vivacious daughters, who tried to shock local society by going into Torquay proper without wearing their gloves! With the Huxley girls, Agatha loved to sing, play music, and perform in homemade productions of Gilbert and Sullivan. Still so shy she could "hardly bring herself to enter a shop," Agatha discovered that she could sing in public without any hint of stage fright. The Lucys, another large family who befriended Agatha after her father's death, taught her the art of roller-skating on the Torquay pier and included her in their notoriously disorganized family activities.

There were summer days spent swimming from the gender-segregated beaches, picnics in the countryside, the Torquay Regatta and garden parties in the coolish August evenings. There were visits to Auntie-Grannie's and Christmas holidays with Madge and her husband's family at Abney Hall near Cheshire. Best of all was the thrill of becoming aunt to Madge's son, Jack. But most important for Agatha, there was always Ashfield. After her husband's death, Clara had determined to sell the family home and find less expensive living quarters, but her children's protests were loud and insistent until Clara capitulated and Ashfield was preserved. For almost four decades more, the house was to be shelter and haven for all the Millers. When Auntie-Grannie's sight became so poor that she could no longer keep her London place, Ashfield became her home. Agatha's only child was born at Ashfield, and in Agatha's greatest desperation, it was her refuge. Her "Second Spring" —forty-five happy years of marriage to Max Mallowan—began there. Although she owned many other houses in her life, as many as eight at one time, she said, "I go back to that always in my mind. Ashfield."

Ashfield, which she finally sold in 1938, was razed in the early 1960s to make way for a housing development. Several years later, Agatha finally summoned the courage to revisit Barton Road, finding that everything except the struggling monkey puzzle tree had been obliterated: "But I minded less after I had seen what had happened. Ashfield had existed once but its day was over. And because whatever has existed still *does* exist in eternity, Ashfield is still Ashfield. To think of it causes me no more pain."

> *"I was always prepared to like the next thing that came along."*

When Agatha was fifteen, her mother decided that the time had come to finish her off. In 1905, this meant a finishing school to complete a girl's education and prepare her to face the world as a marriageable young lady. Clara rented out Ashfield yet again, moved into a Paris hotel, and enrolled Agatha in Miss Cabernet's, the same French boarding school that Madge had attended a decade earlier. Agatha studied French grammar and history, geography, dancing, and deportment, and continued her piano lessons. Initially homesick, she soon came to enjoy the school and her new companions—especially the American girls who were so like her childhood friend at Cauterets, Marguerite Prestley. (In her 1952 Miss Marple novel, *They Do It with Mirrors,* Agatha commemorated these American friends in the characters of Ruth Martin Van Rydock and Carrie Louise Martin Serrocold, American sisters with whom Miss Marple had attended finishing school in Italy: "The two Martin girls, Americans, exciting to the English girl because of their quaint ways of speech and their forthright manner and vitality.")

In the spring, Clara switched her daughter to an English-style school in Auteuil, and in the autumn of 1906, Agatha was shifted to Miss Dryden's, a small Parisian *pensionnat* located on the Avenue du Bois, near the Arc de Triomphe. Miss Dryden's, Agatha said, "suited me down to the ground." She approved of the school's "serious attitude" and emphasis on the arts and music. Students were taken to the Louvre and the theater, and classes regularly included exposure to professional artists from the Comédie Française and the Conservatoire. She studied piano with a demanding Austrian teacher and had voice training with one of the leading teachers in Paris, Monsieur Boué, who complimented her chest ("splendid expansion"), railed against her inexpressive "English face," and urged her to eat plenty of beefsteak. Agatha's devotion to music prompted her first thoughts for a career beyond a proper English marriage. Sadly, her ambitions were not to be realized. At Miss Dryden's, she was one of several girls selected to perform for the Countess of Limerick, "a very fine pianist." Agatha participated in the informal concert, but stage fright overwhelmed her, and the performance was a disaster: "I played wrong notes, my tempo went, my phrasing was amateur and hamhanded—I was just a mess." (The hope of a career in opera died several years later when an American acquaintance associated with the Metropolitan Opera in New York judged Agatha's voice perfectly suited for concert singing but too weak for opera.)

When Agatha was properly finished, she was ready to flirt with the goal of every well-bred English rose—a suitable marriage. Years before, her sister had been treated to a full-scale "coming out" in New York, but Clara couldn't afford the same luxury for her younger daughter. A happy alternative was a winter season in Cairo.★ The Egyptian climate would be good for Clara's health; they could gain financially by leasing Ashfield again; and Cairo was at that time awash in attractive, eligible young Englishmen. For Agatha, Cairo was "a dream of delight. We spent three months there, and I went to five dances every week. . . . I was passionately fond of dancing and I danced well. Also I liked young men, and I soon found they liked me. . . ."

Agatha's Cairo season resulted in no permanent relationships, though one suitor did approach Clara about proposing to her daughter. Agatha used the season to sharpen her social skills and come to terms with her shyness.† A very attractive young woman, she loved to dress well and was particularly fond of the fashionable evening gowns of the day. With her thick reddish-gold hair—so long she could sit on it—artfully dressed high on her head, her slim figure, and fresh good looks, it's little wonder her dance card was always filled. Under the wing of her protective mother, she found Cairo to be a thrilling, yet safe, introduction to adult romance: "Those were still great days for the purity of young girls. I do not think we felt in the least repressed because of it. Romantic friendships, tinged certainly with sex or the possibility of sex, satisfied us completely."

★ There's some confusion about Agatha's age. She states that she was seventeen when she went to Cairo, but Janet Morgan and others place the trip in 1910, when Agatha was twenty. The discrepancy is probably related to the fact that in 1930, when Agatha married Max Mallowan, she reduced her age by four years on the marriage license.

† In the mid-1930s, Agatha gave her own daughter, Rosalind Christie, a splendid London debut including Rosalind's presentation at Court—an event from which Agatha, a divorcée, was excluded. Still Agatha, then approaching the apex of her writing career, found inspiration in the gay round of parties: a gruesome entry in one of her notebooks reads, "Debutante teas etc. Mothers killed off in rapid succession."

After their return to Torquay, social activities, if not so hectic, continued to occupy much of Agatha's time, and she was a frequent guest at country house parties. After one such event, Agatha received an unwelcome marriage proposal from an ardent soldier whom she actively detested: "I am sure he was a good man—perhaps that was what made him so dull." At another country weekend, she began what appears to have been her first "high romance," with a handsome officer of the 17th Lancers, Boulton Fletcher. (Agatha identified him only as "Charles" in her autobiography.) Introduced at a riding event, they met again that evening at a costume ball that Agatha attended in the guise of the legendary Lady Elaine, dressed in white brocade and a pearl cap. Boulton pursued Agatha with presents, flowers, beautiful letters, frequent visits to Ashfield, and a marriage proposal. At thirty-five, he was an experienced courtier and when they were together, Agatha found herself captivated. Apart, she wasn't so sure. Her mother approved of Boulton but worried that Agatha was still too young to know her own mind, so she suggested a six-month hiatus in the relationship. Time was the tonic Agatha needed to say no.

Her next serious suitor was the son of family friends, Wilfred Pirie, whom Agatha had first met in childhood. He reentered her life as a sub-lieutenant in the Royal Navy, serving submarine duty that included shore leave in Torquay. "Wilfred was such a relief after [Boulton Fletcher]," she remembered. "With him there was no excitement, no doubt, no misery. Here was just a dear friend, somebody I knew well." When their friendship became an unofficial engagement, both Clara and Wilfred's mother were thrilled. Agatha loved Wilfred like a brother, and a marriage would have pleased their families, but that was no basis for a life together. At Agatha's instigation, she and Wilfred parted as friends.

The next man in her life was Reggie Lucy. In all the years Agatha had known the Lucy family, she had never met Reggie, the eldest son, who was away in the military. During an extended home leave, Reggie finally became acquainted with his family's young friend and offered help with her golf game. On the links they discovered mutual interests. They felt supremely at ease in one another's company, for Reggie, like Agatha, was constitutionally shy, and before his return to the Far East, they reached an understanding: Reggie would be gone for two years, and he wanted Agatha to use the time to test the depth of her feelings. Agatha would have preferred a more romantic and less conscientious proposal, but she agreed to postpone any wedding plans until Reggie's return.

There was one more flirtation, with a young man named Amyas (identified by Agatha's official biographer as Amyas Boston, who later became a vice marshal of the Royal Air Corps). Amyas played *Bluebeard* to Agatha's Sister Anne in an amateur theatrical in Torquay, and Agatha developed a serious but unrequited crush. Though they had mutual friends, she later avoided all opportunities to meet Boston again, preferring into her sixties "to be an illusion still to somebody." In 1943, however, she saluted him by giving his name to the charismatic victim in *Five Little Pigs*. The fictional Amyas Crale is a first-rate artist, and deadly attractive to women.

Convinced by her mother that Reggie Lucy did not want his unofficial fiancée to sit at home and mope, Agatha continued to accept social invitations, including one to a dance hosted by Lord and Lady Clifford at their home in Chudleigh. A number of young officers from the military garrison at nearby Exeter were also on the guest list, and before the party, Agatha received a letter from her friend Arthur Griffiths, a gunner stationed at the garrison. Griffiths would not be able to attend the party but asked her to look out for a fellow officer, a "good dancer" by the name of Christie.

"I loved a stranger. . . ."

Archibald Christie—Archie—was born in India in 1889, the first of two sons of an English judge in the Indian civil service. After his father's death, Archie's mother married William Hemsley, a housemaster and teacher at Clifton College preparatory school in Bristol. Archie attended Clifton, where he excelled, then entered Woolwich Military Academy. In June 1909, he was commissioned as a second lieutenant in the Royal Field Artillery. In 1912, his brigade was stationed at Exeter, and Archie took a month off from his duties to learn the new and dangerous art of flying. In July, he became the 245th person to qualify for the Royal Aero Club Aviator's Certificate—his passport into the new Royal Flying Corps.

On the evening of October 12, 1912, Archie attended the dance hosted by the Cliffords, and in the best fairy-tale tradition, the dashing young aviator danced the night away with an attractive stranger, Miss Miller of Torquay. A week or so later, as Agatha was enjoying afternoon tea with neighbors, she received an exasperated phone call from her mother. One of her "young men" had turned up unexpectedly at Ashfield, and he seemed determined to stay. Hurrying home, Agatha rushed into the drawing room to confront Archie Christie, who was "rather pink in the face and clearly embarrassed. . . ." He stayed for dinner, and after making plans to see Agatha again, he rode off into the autumn night on his motorcycle. The courtship was under way.

It's not hard to understand Agatha's initial attraction. Archie was very good-looking, confident, socially adroit, and an excellent dancer. And

he was one of a new breed, "those daring young men in their flying machines" who would soon test their bravery in the skies above France.
Over all the highs and lows of memory, Agatha attempted to explain her
powerful feelings: "I loved a stranger; mainly because he *was* a stranger,
because I never knew how he would react to a word or a phrase and
everything he said was fascinating and new. He felt the same. He said
once to me, 'I feel I can't get *at* you. I don't know what you're *like.*'"
Agatha was now almost twenty-three; Archie, a year older. They were a
handsome pair, full of passion and seriousness. They were, as well, sexual naïfs. In *Unfinished Portrait,* Agatha described the Archie character,
Dermot, as "eternally boyish," attracting the "child" in her fictionalized
self: "Their aims, their minds, their characters were poles apart, but they
each wanted a playfellow and found that playfellow in the other."

Just after the New Year in 1913, Archie proposed. He was scheduled
to begin his Royal Air Corps training and wanted to marry Agatha immediately, but Clara quickly brought him back to earth. Money, she reminded him, was critical, and Archie and Agatha had almost none.
Besides, neither the Army nor the Air Corps encouraged their young
officers to marry. Agatha and Archie were determined but not stupid;
they agreed to wait, and Agatha finally wrote to Reggie Lucy, canceling
their "understanding."

The engagement was a stormy, on-again-off-again affair. Clara had
serious doubts about Archie's ability to support her daughter. Archie's
mother, Peg, worried that Agatha was "one of those go-ahead girls
who, in 1912, wore a Peter Pan collar." In between breaking up and
making up, Archie continued to progress in the Flying Corps, and
Agatha took courses in first aid and home nursing. Oddly, since all of
Britain seemed to be engaged in some form of war preparation in 1913
and 1914, Agatha remembered that the actual outbreak of World War
One came as a surprise. She, like everyone else, sincerely believed that
the conflict might be over in a few months—not the four grueling years
that would sap the strength of all Europe, devastate a generation of
young Englishmen, and change society forever.

Archie's corps was among the first to be mobilized and was deployed
to France in August 1914. At home, Agatha took up duties as a member
of the Volunteer Aid Detachment (VAD), working as a nurses' helper in
the Torquay town hall, which had been converted to a hospital. When
Archie got his first home leave just before Christmas, Agatha and her
mother met him in London. The reunion did not begin well, and the
couple argued heatedly over a Christmas present. Still angry, they sent
Clara home to Ashfield and proceeded to Bristol to stay with the
Hemsleys at Clifton. There they finally made up and decided to go

ahead with their wedding on the following day. After a morning of frantic maneuvering—encouraged only by Archie's stepfather (his mother having retired to "a darkened room with a handkerchief soaked in eau-de-cologne on her forehead")—they at last got the correct license and were married by the local vicar on Christmas Eve. In Agatha's words, "Just as the ceremony was about to start, I thought for one sad moment that no bride could have taken less trouble about her appearance. No white dress, no veil, not even a smart frock. I was wearing an ordinary coat and skirt with a small purple velvet hat, and I had not even had time to wash my hands or face. It made us both laugh."

They spent their wedding night at the Grand Hotel in Torquay and Christmas with Clara. The following day, Agatha saw her new husband leave for France, and she returned, alone, to Ashfield. Their next meeting was for three days in the summer of 1915. Until they were reunited in London in September 1918, when Colonel Christie was posted to the Air Ministry, they would spend a total of just a few weeks together during their first three years as man and wife.

Agatha passed the war years mainly at the hospital. Early in the conflict, before field hospitals were established at the French front, the Torquay hospital received the seriously wounded directly from the battlefields. Agatha worked exhausting hours and discovered that she was suited for nursing. She handled a variety of tasks, from cleaning the bloody operating room and delousing soldiers straight from the trenches to writing love letters for her often illiterate patients. Later she was transferred to the pharmaceutical dispensary, a new department ably managed by Mrs. Ellis, a local doctor's wife, and by Agatha's friend Eileen Morris. Agatha worked as a paid assistant and studied for the Apothecaries Hall Examination, which would qualify her to prepare medicines for physicians and pharmacists. Although she found this work less interesting than nursing, she enjoyed her dispensary companions immensely and applied herself diligently to the work.

The dispensary would have significant influence: as an author of detective fiction, Agatha was to become well-known for her expert employment of poisons and toxins. She learned, too, about the behind-the-scenes practices of doctors and chemists, and eventually brought these insights to her fiction. An incident with the pharmacist who tutored her for the apothecary exam (identified in her autobiography as "Mr. P.") stood out. One day in his shop, Mr. P. pulled a lump of curare from his pocket. With obvious pleasure, he described its lethal properties, its almost instantaneous capacity to paralyze and kill when injected directly into the bloodstream. "Do you know why I carry it in my pocket?" he asked. "Well, you know, it makes me feel powerful." Agatha never forgot this strange, "possibly rather . . . dangerous man" and resurrected him in her 1961 novel, *The Pale Horse.*

Within two months of Archie's 1918 transfer to the Air Ministry in London, the war ended. Armistice Day was literally a new beginning for the Christies, the real start of their marriage. They had rented a small apartment in St. John's Wood in London. Archie was determined to leave government service; he had served his country with distinction but was forced to give up flying because of severe sinus problems. Unable to pursue aviation, he turned to the City, London's Wall Street. Success was important to him; he was attracted to the practical rewards of a financial career; and there was now an urgent need for money. Agatha was going to have a baby.

Pregnancy was nine months of constant sickness, but to her surprise, Archie, who habitually avoided people in bad health and emotional pain, proved uncharacteristically solicitous. They argued playfully about baby names, but Archie was unyielding in his desire for a daughter. Born at Ashfield on August 5, 1919, Rosalind Margaret Clarissa Christie weighed a healthy eight-and-a-half pounds and was, in her mother's eyes, "a *nice-looking* baby" blessed with lots of dark hair and a genial disposition.

Though Agatha suffered the loss of her beloved Auntie-Grannie that year, 1919 was good for Mr. and Mrs. Christie, newly moved into a large apartment at No. 96, Addison Mansions—and it would soon get better. Agatha Miller Christie, wife and mother, was about to become Agatha Christie, published author.

> "*. . . if you can write like this now you might go far.*"
> —letter from novelist Eden Phillpotts, February 6, 1909

Writing stories was a natural extension of two vital facets of Agatha's youth: reading and imaginative play. From the age of five, when she taught herself to read *The Angel of Love,* Agatha was a voracious consumer of books. As a child she favored fairy tales, Old Testament stories, and moralistic Victorian novels. As her tastes expanded, she discovered romantic adventure in Sir Anthony Hope Hawkins's *The Prisoner of Zenda* (to which she paid tribute in the plotting of her 1925 thriller, *The Secret of Chimneys*). She was devoted to historical fiction, and she read Alexandre Dumas and Jules Verne's fantastic fictions in French. Somewhat guiltily, she also read the popular girls' fiction of L. T. Meade, books that Clara disdained as "vulgar."

As a little girl, Agatha loved her mother's inventive bedtime stories;

after Fred's death, mother and daughter cultivated the habit of reading aloud to one another. Both Agatha and Clara favored Charles Dickens. Reading *Nicholas Nickelby,* Agatha developed a fondness for "the old gentleman who courted Mrs. Nickelby by throwing vegetable marrows over the wall" (a clue, she hinted, to the retirement plans of Hercule Poirot). In *Bleak House,* which she revisited many times during her life, she perhaps discerned the basics of mystery writing. At age twelve, she was introduced to the works of Arthur Conan Doyle by her sister, Madge,★ who would act out the popular adventures of Sherlock Holmes. Madge adored disguises, playacting, and games of confused identity. One of her favorites was "the Elder Sister"—the story of an older Miller sister who lived in a cave and was completely insane. In this game (echoed in the climactic scene of Agatha's 1927 Poirot adventure, *The Big Four*), the lunatic sister "was indistinguishable in appearance from [Madge], except for her voice . . . a frightening voice, a soft oily voice." On occasion, the Elder Sister would come to Ashfield, looking for all the world like Madge. Agatha never forgot the excruciating thrill: "I used to feel indescribable terror. Of course I knew really it was only Madge pretending—but was it?"

In her imaginary childhood adventures, Agatha was comfortable as either the active participant or the observer. As a player, she took the roles of hero, knight, rescuer—the very model of a moral detective. As observer (Sue de Verte of The School, for example), she was the shadowy creator who gave life to her characters and then watched their progress. These two distinct personae, activist hero and passive watcher, were key to her evolution as a writer.

She began writing fiction as a teenager. Her first serious attempt was undertaken to alleviate the boredom of being confined to bed with flu. Instead of playing cards to pass the time, she followed her mother's advice to write a short story and "finally found myself thoroughly interested and going along at a great rate. It was exhausting, and did not assist my convalescence, but it was exciting, too." She called her finished work "The House of Beauty," and whatever its flaws, this story opened the door to a new interest. Agatha was clearly not "called" to write. She had no technical training and copied the styles of her favorite authors, but once started, she continued to work on stories. She also wrote poems,

---

★ Madge Miller Watts was the first published writer in the family. Before her 1902 marriage, a number of her short stories, under the pen name Mostyn Miller, were accepted by *Vanity Fair* magazine. Later she turned to theatrical writing, and in September 1924, her play *The Claimant* was produced by Basil Dean at St. Martin's Theatre in London. The play's run was brief, but the experience thrilled her entire family.

experimented with music and operetta, and sometime after her return from Egypt decided to embark on a novel, which she set in Cairo. Her problem was that she immediately imagined two plots. She developed one and then the other, and finally combined the two: "Heavily encumbered by too much plot, I dashed madly from one set of characters to the other, occasionally forcing them to mix with each other in a way which they did not seem to wish to do." She titled the finished book *Snow Upon the Desert*.★

Again at Clara's suggestion, Agatha prevailed on a neighbor, the novelist Eden Phillpotts, to read her effort. Few young authors are lucky enough to encounter a mentor as thoughtful and honest as Eden Phillpotts. He not only read *Snow Upon the Desert*; he provided invaluable criticisms without dampening Agatha's enthusiasm, advising her to curb her taste for moralizing and to "leave your characters *alone,* so that *they* can speak for *themselves.* . . ." Gently, he warned her that getting a first novel published would be extremely difficult; graciously, he also provided an introduction to his own literary agent, Hughes Massie. (Agatha never forgot Phillpotts's kindness, and in 1932 she dedicated *Peril at End House* to him.)

Agatha met with Hughes Massie, one of the leading agents of his day, and although the old man rejected *Snow Upon the Desert,* Massie encouraged her to begin a new novel. Agatha was strongly inclined to abandon any hope of publication, just as she had abandoned her musical ambitions. But she continued to write stories, inspired by the vogue for "psychic" writing (ghost stories and other tales of the supernatural) and by her reading of the fiction of May Sinclair. Although she failed to be published, writing became "a habit" for her. But it was thanks to a chance conversation with Madge that her course was finally set.

Sometime probably in 1912 or 1913, the Miller sisters found themselves discussing their favorite detective fiction, including the especially baffling French novel *The Mystery of the Yellow Room* by Gaston Leroux. Agatha remarked that she would like to try writing a detective story herself. Madge said she couldn't do it. Agatha insisted that she could. Madge then raised the ante, and Agatha accepted: "It was never a definite bet; we never set out the terms—but the words had been said. From that moment I was fired by the determination that I would write a detective story."

She was delayed by the arrival of Archie Christie in her life and the

---

★ Agatha always filled her notebooks with cryptic observations, scraps of plot, and descriptive details that she would return to, often years later. Never one to waste an idea, in her 1937 novel *Death on the Nile,* Agatha included a dipsomaniacal romance novelist named Salome Otterbourne, whose work in progress is titled *Snow on the Desert's Face.*

beginning of World War One, but she never forgot Madge's challenge. After her 1915 transfer to the Torquay hospital dispensary, she found her work marked by periods of feverish activity and hours of tedious idleness. To occupy herself during the slow spells, she turned to the problem of crafting a detective story. She began with the crime: "Since I was surrounded by poisons, perhaps it was natural that death by poisoning should be the method I selected." Having arrived at the means, she then had to decide whom to dispatch. Victim and suspects slowly gathered in her mind. She discovered that she could not comfortably base her characters on people she knew but finally found inspiration among a trio of strangers she observed on a Torquay tram. She decided that her book would turn on "an *intime* murder . . . all in the family, so to speak." In her autobiography, Agatha explained her initial concept of the whodunit and its perpetrator: "The whole point of a *good* detective story was that it must be somebody obvious but at the same time, for some reason, you would then find that it was *not* obvious, that he could not possibly have done it. Though really, of course, he *had* done it."

The Mysterious Affair at Styles is notable as the exemplar for many of the elements that would characterize all her work: the closed circle of possible murderers, and the victim, a forceful personality who is done in before the reader can develop any personal attachment. The stock players in the Christie repertory company are there: domineering parent firmly clutching the purse strings of the family fortune; adult children chafing under the yoke of parental control; stalwart paid companion; poor relation; mysterious stranger; chatty servants. The liberal salting of physical clues is there, including Agatha's inevitable red herrings. (The reader who wishes to beat Christie to the solution should pay close attention to spoken and written clues; they are often more revealing than the physical evidence.)

And in the second chapter of *The Mysterious Affair at Styles* comes that most formidable of detectives—"an extraordinary looking little man. He was hardly more than five feet, four inches, but carried himself with great dignity. His head was exactly the shape of an egg, and he always perched it a little on one side. His moustache was very stiff and military. The neatness of his attire was almost incredible." Hercule Poirot . . . the strange little Belgian with the powerful "grey cells."

Dedicated readers love to speculate about Poirot's origins, his age, his family tree, his experiences, his love life or lack thereof. He has attained worldwide recognition second only to that of Sherlock Holmes, but his beginnings were humble. Agatha needed a detective. Logically, she looked to Arthur Conan Doyle for inspiration. Holmes and Watson: the great detective and his pedestrian sidekick. She considered other models. Maurice Leblanc's rogue adventurer Arsène Lupin? No, "not my kind." What about Joseph Rouletabille, the young journalist hero of Leroux's *The Mystery of the Yellow Room*? "[That] was the *sort* of person whom I would like to invent: someone who hadn't been used before." As Agatha explored various identities for her sleuth, she remembered the Belgian war refugees who were living at that time in her parish: "Why not make my detective a Belgian? I thought. There were all types of refugees. How about a refugee police officer? A retired police officer. Not too young a one."

Poirot was taking shape. He would be a retired police inspector, therefore familiar with crime and criminals. He would be a fastidious man, "always arranging things, liking things in pairs, liking things square instead of round." And he must be very smart. Originally she called him "Hercules," a clever play on his slight stature and large intellect. (She was to come back, in a way, to this name choice in *The Labours of Hercules,* in which Poirot sets himself the task of solving twelve mythically inspired mysteries before retreating into retirement.) And he should have his own Watson, a young war veteran whom Agatha named Hastings.

Styles proved more difficult to write than Agatha had anticipated, and she bogged down at the halfway point. Once more, Clara came to the rescue, suggesting a quiet holiday at Dartmoor. Alone in a "large, dreary hotel" at Hay Tor, Agatha had nothing to do but think and write. She spent solitary afternoons walking the windy moors, talking out each part of her story, chapter by chapter. In the mornings, she would write furiously, and by the end of her two weeks' retreat, the book was virtually complete.

Home again at Ashfield, she made revisions, especially trying to enliven the romance between her characters John and Mary Cavendish*—an inclusion dictated by popular tastes. Agatha's own instinct rebelled: "I myself always found the love interest a terrible bore in detective stories. . . . To force a love motif into what should be a scientific process went much against the grain." When she had done as much as she could, she packed up the manuscript and shipped it off to publishers Hodder and Stoughton, who promptly returned it. For once, Agatha refused to accept rejection. Following several more turndowns, she sent the book to John Lane at The Bodley Head, where it was nearly forgotten for almost two years.

---

* As her writing matured, her fictional romances improved, largely because Agatha abandoned beautiful but simpering females like Mary Cavendish for spirited modern girls like Tuppence Beresford in the Tommy and Tuppence stories and Lady Frances Derwent of *Why Didn't They Ask Evans?*—bold and bright go-getters who relished entering into the action. Agatha's romantic young males, however, remained in the mold of Poirot's sidekick, Captain Arthur Hastings: handsome, earnest, and a little dim.

The Christies were preparing to move to Addison Mansions when Agatha finally received a note from John Lane. He wanted to discuss publication of *The Mysterious Affair at Styles*. In their meeting, Lane asked for numerous changes, including the elimination of a lengthy trial sequence, and Agatha readily agreed. He also presented a contract, which she signed, much to her later regret. To celebrate her new status as an almost-published author, Agatha and Archie treated themselves to an evening of dancing. Looking back on that happy night, she later said with a hint of bitterness, "There was a third party with us, though I did not know it. Hercule Poirot, my Belgian invention, was hanging round my neck, firmly attached there like the old man of the sea."

"We had never been people who played safe."

Agatha had no real ambition to work at writing after the 1920 publication of *Styles*. She earned no money from book sales and a meager £25 from the serial rights, but Archie encouraged her to start a new novel on the assumption that more money would be forthcoming. Clara was in financial trouble, and there was still Ashfield to be maintained. If his wife could earn from her writing, Archie reasoned, the money would be put to good use. Neither of the Christies realized that Agatha's contract with John Lane obligated her to five more books under the same stringent financial terms.

Her second novel was a thriller, a high-speed tale of Bolshevist spies, stolen documents, kidnapping, amnesia, false identities, and the potential collapse of British civilization. In *The Secret Adversary*, Agatha introduced Lieutenant Tommy Beresford and Miss Prudence Cowley, "known to her intimate friends for some mysterious reason as 'Tuppence.'" These two naive charmers team up as Young Adventurers, Ltd., and set off on a wholly preposterous quest to find a missing girl and thwart an evil genius known only as "Mr. Brown." Agatha's five Tommy and Tuppence books (including the last novel she wrote, *Postern of Fate*) never achieved the popularity of her Poirot and Miss Marple stories, but Agatha was very fond of the Beresfords. They were her contemporaries, and she allowed them to age over the years as she did. They married, had children, matured into middle age, survived another world war, and entered old age together.

Agatha returned to Poirot for her third novel, *The Murder on the Links*. She was still making very little money, until she was approached by the *Sketch* magazine to write a series of twelve Poirot stories. As she rushed to complete this well-paid commission, she finally began to understand her professional position: ". . . not only was I now tied to the detective story, I was also tied to two people: Hercule Poirot and his Watson, Captain Hastings." This thought led to a second realization: "Now I saw what a terrible mistake I had made in starting with Hercule Poirot so *old*—I ought to have abandoned him after the first three or four books, and begun again with someone much younger."

She couldn't rid herself of Poirot, but in *The Murder on the Links,* she did eliminate for the time being the pleasant, honest, and romantic Captain Hastings. She liked Hastings (who, with his military background, bureaucratic career, banal charm and literal-mindedness, and passions for golf and cars, may remind some of Archie Christie), so she let him find love, marry, and move to Argentina. She never forgot him entirely, though, bringing him back in numerous short stories and several more novels, including her final Poirot mystery.

She was gaining confidence and became more aggressive with her publisher. There had been a lengthy argument over the spelling of "cocoa" in *The Mysterious Affair at Styles*: The Bodley Head's obstinate copy editor had won, filling cups with "coco," to Agatha's everlasting embarrassment. Now she obstinately challenged the book jacket design for *The Murder on the Links*; the cover was changed, and Agatha secured the right of approval in the future, although her battle for book jackets that satisfied her taste continued throughout her career, and she refused to allow either Poirot or Miss Marple to be pictured on jacket covers.

Life was good for the Christies: Archie's career was going well, and Agatha was on the brink of professional success. Then an extraordinary thing happened: Archie was invited to join a ten-month, round-the-world trade mission to promote the Empire Exhibition, a kind of World's Fair for the British Empire scheduled to take place in 1924. By sharing expenses and stretching Archie's £1,000 travel allowance, they could just afford for Agatha to go alone. It meant chucking Archie's job with no guarantee of reinstatement and leaving two-year-old Rosalind in the care of Clara and Madge. But the Christies were only a little hesitant, and even Clara supported their decision, in large measure because she believed it would be a mistake for Agatha to jeopardize her marriage by sending Archie off alone. Like Tommy and Tuppence, the Christies leaped at the opportunity for adventure. "We had never been people who played safe," Agatha recalled. "We had persisted in marrying against all opposition, and now we were determined to see the world and risk what would happen on our return."

She described the trip at length in her autobiography as well as letters home and her diaries. At times, it reads like low comedy. The British Empire Exhibition Mission set sail for South Africa aboard the RMS *Kildonan Castle* on January 10, 1922. The happy party of seven, whose picture appeared in *The Times,* was led by Major E. A. Belcher, a former schoolmaster of Archie's, who had secured for himself the position of assistant general manager of the Exhibition. Their itinerary comprised South Africa and Rhodesia, India and Ceylon, Australia, New Zealand, a month's holiday for Agatha and Archie alone in Hawaii, then Canada and home by way of New York. For Agatha, "It was so exciting that I could not believe it was true." But she hadn't counted on seasickness, a tendency she would share with her little Belgian detective. For days, she lay in her cabin, unable to eat or even move. She never became a seasoned sailor, but did recover sufficiently to enjoy the rest of the voyage.

Major Belcher—a pompous, garrulous glad-hander with a great gift for self-promotion—proved to be a man of manic highs and lows. A bright, amusing raconteur, he was also excitable, quick to anger, and a constant complainer. No bed was ever comfortable enough; no meal ever good enough. He abused his secretary, harassed Archie, who served as financial adviser, and irritated everyone. Still, there was so much to see and do that Archie and Agatha held their tongues and pursued their own interests at every possible opportunity. In Cape province, they discovered surfing in the waves off Muizenberg. From Cape Town, they traveled by train to Kimberley and its fabled diamond mines, Salisbury and the Victoria Falls, Johannesburg, and Pretoria, where they were stranded for several days by a violent labor strike.

Bypassing India, they next landed at Adelaide on the South Australian coast and traveled northeast to Melbourne for a strained reunion with Major Belcher, who had traveled ahead. He was suffering from an infected foot, and his mood was predictably foul: Agatha dubbed him the "Wild Man." Belcher's imperiousness did not sit well with the egalitarian Aussies, but Archie and the others did their best to smooth ruffled feathers. They visited the southern island of Tasmania, then proceeded to Sydney. After a rigorous Australian schedule, the group moved on to New Zealand, which Agatha called "the most beautiful country I have ever seen." By this time, everyone was thoroughly sick and tired of Major Belcher, but in the land of the kiwi, where he had once served as headmaster of a private school, Belcher's mood improved. Besides, Agatha and Archie were about to begin their long-anticipated private holiday in Hawaii.

In Honolulu, they were drawn immediately to the ocean: they rediscovered surfing, a much more arduous sport in Pacific waters, and spent virtually all their month's break swimming and roasting in the powerful sun. Hawaii proved to be far more expensive than they had expected, and by the time they rejoined the Mission in Canada, the Christies were short on funds. To save money, Agatha gorged on cheap Canadian breakfasts and took maximum advantage of the food served at official functions. Agatha left the party at Montreal to visit with her godmother,

Cassie Sullivan, in New York City, where she received royal treatment, visiting with Cassie's wealthy sister-in-law, Mrs. Pierpont Morgan, and dining at the finest restaurants. Yet the months of travel had been wearing, and Agatha was anxious to return to her home and her daughter. The members of the Mission shared one more sea voyage and landed back on English soil on December 1, 1922. To everyone's surprise, the Mission had been a great success in spite of the Wild Man.

Interestingly, once they were out from under Major Belcher's thumb, the Christies found that they enjoyed his company again, and he was a frequent guest in their home. He also became one of the few real-life friends whom Agatha featured in a book. Belcher called his place in Dorney "The Mill House," and he had often suggested that Agatha write a mystery about it. He nagged her to put him in the mystery too, and when she said in frustration that she would make him the victim, Belcher insisted that he should be the villain. Agatha did write the book, developing the plot during the Mission's visit to South Africa, and she granted Belcher's wish in the character of Sir Eustace Pedler. *The Man in the Brown Suit,* published in 1924, is dedicated "To E. A. B. In memory of a journey, some lion stories and a request that I should some day write the 'Mystery of the Mill House.' "

About the time she was finishing *The Man in the Brown Suit,* Agatha received shocking affirmation that her writing was serious business. The Inland Revenue, Britain's tax authority, requested details about her literary earnings. In spite of Agatha's protests that her earnings were merely "casual profit," the tax officials contended that, to their way of thinking, she was "an established author" who should henceforth keep her accounts more carefully. This was her first run-in with the tax authorities, and though quickly resolved, it foreshadowed more costly difficulties to come. The encounter with Inland Revenue convinced Agatha that she needed a professional agent, and back she went to find Hughes Massie, who had rejected her first novel years earlier. Massie had died, and Agatha was directed to his successor, Edmund Cork. In their first meeting, Cork reviewed her contract with John Lane. The discussion was an eye-opener, and Agatha confidently placed herself in Cork's hands. It was the beginning of an extraordinary relationship; until Agatha's death in 1976, Cork was to be friend, mediator, trusted counselor, and even errand-runner for the most successful literary figure of the century. Cork discussed his new client with Geoffrey Collins at William Collins Sons publishers, and when her commitment to John Lane was fulfilled, Agatha was ready to move. Her first novel for Collins was *The Murder of Roger Ackroyd*—a mystery with a twist that is still controversial. This book finally boosted her career into high gear, making her unquestionably the most talked-about mystery writer of 1926. But for Agatha Christie, professional success and fame were to provide little compensation for the devastation of her private life.

". . . after illness, came sorrow, despair and heartbreak."

The years 1922–1926 had been, on their face, happy and prosperous. Archie's position had indeed vanished when he returned from the Mission trip, but after one false start, he finally found the job of his dreams with a City firm. The position offered exactly what he longed for: the chance to make his way in the world of high finance. The Christies soon moved to a new apartment in the Berkshire suburb of Sunningdale, southwest of London. Agatha had always wanted a house in the country with plenty of room for Rosalind to play, and Archie, a fanatic golfer, wanted a convenient playing course. Sunningdale was something of a compromise for Agatha, but it was the site of Archie's new golfing club, and several years after the move, they bought a house—a grandiose place they named "Styles." Despite its many amenities, the house had a local reputation for being unlucky. Previous owners had suffered various reverses—financial ruin, divorce—and the rumor of bad luck possibly explains why it was affordable. Their household staff included a cook, butler, and housemaid. Agatha had also employed Charlotte (Carlo) Fisher to care for Rosalind and provide secretarial help. Carlo and her sister, Mary, became Agatha's close friends, the kind of friends whose loyalty would withstand the most difficult test.

Agatha was still providing assistance to her mother, who often stayed in Sunningdale. Agatha and Madge had also become financially responsible for their brother, Monty. Monty was, in every respect, the black sheep of the family. Blessed with dazzling charm, his father's wit, and a taste for the good life, he was also an amoral schemer, capable of bleeding his family dry without a backward glance. "In every family," Agatha later wrote, "there is usually one member who is a source of trouble and worry. My brother Monty was ours. Until the day of his death he was always causing someone a headache."

After leaving the Army in the early 1900s, Monty became an adventurer, wild game hunter, and entrepreneur, knocking about India, the Middle East, and Africa for years. He returned to England for medical treatment just before the departure of the Empire Exhibition Mission in 1922. Terribly ill from an old wound that had become reinfected, Monty was given less than six months to live, but he improved sufficiently to return to his mother at Ashfield, where he quickly became restless and bored. Always impulsive, he "took to shooting out of his window with a revolver" and frightening the locals. (Agatha was to re-create this incident several times in her fiction.) The strain on Clara was tremendous, so Agatha and Madge took over the support of their brother until his death in France in 1929.

While she was still under contract to The Bodley Head, most of Agatha's earnings came not from her books but from the sale of serial rights, and in 1924, "an almost unbelievable thing" happened—the *Evening News* offered £500 for *The Man in the Brown Suit.* Following Archie's advice, Agatha used her windfall to buy her own automobile, a "grey bottle-nosed Morris Cowley" that was one of the great joys of her life, comparable, she said, to "dining with the Queen at Bucking-ham Palace. . . ." The Christies' growing incomes now enabled them to live comfortably in a spacious suburban house, operate two cars, and va-cation in the south of France. But beneath the calm surface, real trouble was brewing.

Agatha felt increasingly constrained; she made few friends in Sun-ningdale, and Archie was spending more and more time with his golfing pals. He had already dashed her hopes for a second child (suggesting that they purchase another new auto instead), and the distance between them was growing. Agatha's handsome young aviator had become Mr. Christie of the City, a conventional man with conventional tastes. In *Unfinished Portrait,* Agatha would describe Dermot, the Archie-like hus-band, as a man uncomfortable with other people's feelings and any dis-play of adult affection, who "hated being touched at all unless he was in a recognizably amorous mood."

The beginning of the end came in the spring of 1926 when Agatha's mother died. Clara was seventy-two and had been ill with bronchitis, but her death was a terrible shock. Summoned to her mother's bedside, Agatha was on a train when Clara actually passed away, so she was never able to say good-bye to the woman who had always been the touchstone of her life. Archie, in Spain on business, came home a week after the fu-neral, but he returned almost immediately to the Continent. Agatha chose not to accompany him—a decision she regretted deeply later on—but stayed in Torquay in help settle Clara's estate and begin the process of clearing out Ashfield, her mother's bequest to her. In her autobiography, Agatha blamed herself for focusing on her private grief and failing to realize, as her mother surely would have, that "life with Archie lay ahead of me."

With Rosalind in tow, Agatha moved into Ashfield. The job of clean-ing and restoring the old house was daunting. Carlo Fisher had been called home to Edinburgh, and Madge could not come down to Torquay until August, so by herself, Agatha worked day and night throughout the summer. Trying to sublimate her grief and worry in ex-hausting physical labor, she made herself ill. She stopped eating, slept badly, and suffered frightening moments of memory loss, forgetting her name on one occasion and signing a check as "Blanche Amory," a character from the Thackeray novel *Pendinnis*. Presumably, she did not share her problems with Archie, who was always so averse to sickness and unhappiness. Throughout that summer of 1926, he lived at his club in London and spent weekends golfing at Sunningdale while Agatha remained at Ashfield. Archie, she said, "hated the feeling of sorrow in the house [Ashfield], and it left him open to other influences." The only light in her depression was the anticipated August reunion with her husband and sister to celebrate Rosalind's seventh birthday. But when the day arrived, Archie was not what she expected: "He went through the motions of ordinary greetings, but he was, quite simply, *not Archie*." When he finally explained his strange behavior, it was a bombshell: Archie Christie had fallen in love with someone else, and he wanted a divorce.

The other woman was a young, pretty girl named Nancy Neele. Agatha had met her several times and even entertained her at Styles, but the relationship between Archie and Nancy had bloomed during his long summer of separation from his wife. Although Agatha's biographers tend to agree that it was not an adulterous affair, Nancy Neele was a lively young woman who shared many of Archie's interests, including golf. (In his memoirs Max Mallowan discussed the failure of his wife's first marriage and the part Archie's obsession with golf had played. Before her second marriage, Agatha made Max promise not to take up the game.)

Except for gleanings from *Unfinished Portrait,* there would be no way of knowing Agatha's deepest feelings. She devoted only four pages of her autobiography to this painful time—the most argued-over period of her life. Her words speak of self-recrimination and her dwindling hope that the marriage could be saved, and finally she concludes, "There is no need to dwell on it. I stood it for a year, hoping he would change. But he did not. . . . So ended my first married life." But it was not to be so simple.

> "*Mental misery and physical misery are too much to have together. . . .*"

Agatha, already in a bad state, returned with Rosalind to Styles, where they were soon joined by Carlo Fisher. Archie came home for a few weeks during the fall, then moved back to his London club. Agatha was initially convinced that her marriage was basically sound and that Archie would come to his senses. She flatly refused to divorce him. Archie, however, was determined to end the marriage; Agatha called him "ruthless." But as Christmas approached, it had to be obvious that reconciliation was impossible, and Agatha was desperate. Some have theorized that she was suicidal. She was certainly at sea. She tried to work on her next book but couldn't. She was still getting little sleep and eating poorly. On December 3, 1926, at Agatha's urging, Carlo Fisher took an evening off to dine with friends in London. When Carlo arrived back at Styles late that night, she found Agatha's car gone. The maids told her that Mrs. Christie had left at about eleven o'clock and not said where she was going.

Sometime the next morning a policeman arrived at the house with word that Mrs. Christie's Morris car had been found in a ditch at a place called Newlands Corner, near the town of Guildford in Surrey. One witness had reported helping a lady start the car soon after six that morning. A fur coat and overnight bag were left in the abandoned car, but there was no sign of Mrs. Christie. Carlo Fisher later documented her account of the events of Agatha's disappearance in a letter to Rosalind, but the full text has not been published. Newspaper stories, which quickly became lurid, are conflicting, as are later accounts from police sources and others who participated in the search for Agatha. Interviewed by reporters at the time, Archie seemed to know as little as anybody.

Archie and Nancy Neele were both spending the weekend at the home of Mr. and Mrs. Sam James (who had introduced the couple) at Hurtmore in Surrey, not far from the spot where Agatha's car was found. Archie, notified of what had happened, rushed to Styles. Taken by police to the location of the car, Archie and Carlo found themselves amid a large crowd of sightseers and vendors hawking ice cream and drinks. Press and police were everywhere. The investigation was complicated by the fact that two police districts were involved, Berkshire and Surrey, and official jealousies abounded. As the days passed, the pitch of public interest heightened, and Archie approached Scotland Yard for help. There were searches that included law officers and volunteers. Witnesses came forward, telling a number of conflicting stories. The *Daily Sketch* called on a clairvoyant who described a log house where the missing body of Agatha Christie would be found. Rewards were offered, and the press enjoyed an eleven-day national sensation.

Word soon got round about the state of the Christie marriage and Agatha's depression, and inevitably Archie came under suspicion. A servant described a blazing fight on the morning before her disappearance, but Archie denied arguing with his wife. His mother, who now lived not far from Guildford, had been visited by her daughter-in-law on the same day, and Mrs. Hemsley told a *Daily Mail* reporter that Agatha was "in a fit of depression" and had "planned her end. . . ." Agatha also left several letters behind—one to Carlo instructing her to cancel upcoming engagements, another to Archie's brother, Campbell—but these have since been lost or destroyed. Every possible theory was explored: murder, suicide, amnesia, publicity stunt. On Sunday, December 12, a massive public search was carried out; dogs were brought in, and a place called the Silent Pool in Surrey was dragged for the second time. Two days later, Agatha was found at the Hydropathic Hotel in the spa city of Harrogate, far to the north of the search area. Piecing together her movements and motivations during the eleven-day absence has preoccupied Christie-philes for decades, and there will never be an answer to satisfy everyone.

What is known is that Agatha left her car in the ditch at Newlands Corner sometime on the night of December 3 or early morning of December 4. She made her way to London, probably on the milk train from Guildford to Waterloo Station, where she saw a poster advertising Harrogate. Later, under a psychiatrist's treatment, she would remember having blood on her face. In London she bought a coat, a small suitcase, and some night clothes at Whiteley's department store. She then took a train to Harrogate and checked into the Hydropathic Hotel—the Hydro—registering as "Teresa Neele" of Cape Town, South Africa. She was a quiet, pleasant guest who seemed to enjoy the pre-Christmas lull at Harrogate's oldest spa, although a maid who served her breakfast in bed each morning noticed that Agatha would cover her face as if to hide marks or bruises. On Saturday, December 11, a notice appeared in *The Times*: "Friends and relatives of Mrs. Theresa Neele, late of South Africa, please communicate." The ad had been placed by Agatha, though no one at the time connected it with the case.

As the publicity about the disappearance grew, various hotel employees began to suspect that their "Mrs. Neele" was, in fact, Agatha Christie. Finally, the wives of two members of the hotel orchestra took these suspicions to the police, forgoing the large rewards offered by the London newspapers. (Archie Christie later sent gifts of engraved silver pens to the musicians in appreciation for their discretion.)

On December 14, 1926, Archie and police officials went to the Hydro, and Archie approached his wife. According to reports, it was a low-key, gentle reunion. Avoiding the press as best he could, Archie escorted Agatha out of the hotel and to the train station. He then accompanied her to their final stop in Manchester, leaving her with Madge and Jimmy Watts, who took her to their home at Abney. Two doctors were immediately summoned—Madge's personal physician and a well-known neurologist—and their diagnosis was memory loss. Agatha could remember nothing of the past eleven days; she did not even recognize Rosalind at first. The doctors recommended psychiatric consultation. Although Agatha protested, Madge insisted on the treatment, and Agatha moved with Rosalind and Carlo to a small apartment in London near the office of a respected Harley Street psychiatrist. Under his care, much of her memory returned, although she was never to recall exactly what happened between the time she left Styles and her train trip to London.

The psychiatrist believed this memory loss was due to concussion, and certainly there is circumstantial evidence that Agatha had struck her head when she ran her little Morris into the ditch at Newlands Corner. Years later, after World War Two, she consulted an eminent psychiatrist at Oxford, hoping still to recover her memory of the crucial missing hours. The psychiatrist was unable to reconstruct the specific events; he did, however, try to help her overcome her feelings of guilt.

A reasonable case is made by biographer Janet Morgan that Agatha suffered a sudden memory loss known as an "hysterical fugue," a psychiatric condition in which an individual under severe stress escapes the emotional pain by forgetting his or her identity for a time. Gillian Gill, in her literary biography *Agatha Christie: The Woman and Her Mysteries,* relies more on the evidence of *Unfinished Portrait* to hypothesize that Agatha may, indeed, have planned to kill herself. Based on this novel alone, the evidence is strong. But in her first Mary Westmacott novel, *Giant's Bread,* Agatha drew an equally convincing portrayal of a character with traumatic amnesia. Taken together, the two books seem to represent not the actual circumstances, but Agatha's own attempts to work out the motives for her disappearance.

The suicide theory was supported with the publication in 1980 of a book of recollections by Shakespeare scholar A. L. Rowse, a friend of Agatha and Max Mallowan in their later years. Rowse claimed to have heard "the truth" from "Mrs. X"—"an old friend of Agatha's." This woman said that Agatha had suffered a breakdown and been prevented from "throwing herself over the balcony" before her disappearance. Rowse also used a supposed misprint in Max Mallowan's memoirs to confirm the tale told by "Mrs. X," but his detective work is tenuous at best.

Whatever the cause, the effect was to end Agatha's first marriage. Her divorce from Archie was granted in April 1928 on the grounds of his adultery with an unknown woman. (Nancy Neele was not named in the action. Under the legal restrictions of the time, it was the custom to hire a woman solely for the purpose of being publicly observed with the husband in order to establish grounds for divorce.)

The idea that Agatha's disappearance was a publicity stunt has remained popular, but there is little evidence to support the theory, and Agatha's subsequent behavior is not consistent with publicity-seeking.

She had never wholly defeated the shyness of her youth, and after the disappearance she retreated into her privacy and rarely emerged. She granted few interviews, and when she did talk with the press, it was always with the stipulation that there be no questions about the events of 1926. There was also the consultation with the Oxford psychiatrist some twenty years after the disappearance. If it had all been a publicity gambit or even a calculated revenge against Archie, why would she have sought to recover her memory at that late date?

Interest in Agatha's disappearance was revived after her death, particularly with the publication of *Agatha* by Kathleen Tynan. The novel, a mishmash of fact and romantic fiction, posited a theory of Agatha Christie holed up in the Hydro Hotel and planning a diabolically self-destructive revenge against her rival, Nancy Neele. A film based on Tynan's book, released in 1979, reinforced the image of Agatha Christie as a deeply disturbed, conniving, and self-loathing woman bent on lethal vengeance.

Another theory gained currency immediately after Agatha's death when Lord Ritchie-Calder, a distinguished member of the House of Commons, told the *New Statesman* that as cub reporter for the *Daily News* in 1926, he had "met" with Agatha at the Hydro Hotel shortly before her reunion with Archie Christie. His implication was that Agatha planned to take her own life in a fashion that would lead to Archie's arrest for her murder. This story was also cited by Gwen Robyns in her 1978 biography, *The Mystery of Agatha Christie*. Certainly Agatha, in normal times, was intellectually capable of devising so complex a plot. The question is whether, in a state of deep depression and mental turmoil, she would have been able to carry it out.

Agatha the conniver, Agatha the publicity hound, Agatha the suicidal nutcase: conjectures are certainly exciting. But more logical is the theory of a thirty-six-year-old wife—emotionally traumatized by her mother's death and the breakup of her marriage, possibly determined to confront her straying husband and his new love at a site not far from her home—who runs her little car into a ditch, bangs her head on the steering wheel, and suffers a short-term disconnection with the painful realities of her life.

In searching for an explanation, it is essential to remember how important the ideal of a good marriage was to Agatha. To a woman of her time, a career was virtually meaningless. Recalling the goals of every Victorian girlhood, Agatha said, "You were waiting for The Man, and when the man came, he would change your entire life!" With "Mr. Right," a girl like Agatha dreamed of creating the perfect union: "That, I think, is what a woman needs. She wants to feel that in her mate there is integrity, that she can depend on him and respect his judgment, and that when there is a difficult decision to be made it can safely lie in his hands." Agatha was also her mother's daughter, and Clara did not trust men on their own. At the time of the Empire Exhibition Mission, Clara had encouraged Agatha to accompany Archie. "A wife's duty is to go with her husband," Clara had advised. "A husband must come first, even before your children. . . . Remember, if you're not with your husband, if you leave him too much, *you'll lose him.*"

When the Christies' marriage came apart, it was natural for Agatha to blame herself. Had she not violated her mother's first rule and abandoned her husband to his own devices during her time of personal grief? In her autobiography, Agatha treated Archie with kindness (though she was less circumspect in *Unfinished Portrait*). Except for the remark about his "ruthless" determination—a characteristic later ascribed as a positive to Miss Jane Marple—there is none of the vitriol naturally expected from a woman scorned. Archie Christie was neither a monster nor a philanderer, and he was probably no more selfish than most men of his era, though he did seem excessively squeamish when confronted with domestic conflict or unhappiness. There are indications that he loved Agatha even after he had fallen out of love with her, and that his "ruthless" efforts to secure his wife's assent to a divorce may in fact have been his naive attempt to get Agatha's approval of his actions.

After the divorce, Archie married Nancy Neele. They had one son and by all accounts enjoyed a very happy life until she died of cancer in 1958. Archie's relationship with Rosalind, whom he adored, was somewhat more difficult, and he never saw his grandson, Mathew Prichard, although Mathew had arranged to meet with his grandfather in December of 1962. Sadly, Archie collapsed suddenly and died before that meeting could take place. After the divorce, Agatha wrote to Archie only once, at the time of Nancy's death, to express her sympathy.

But in 1926, Agatha's rock was shattered. She was approaching middle age and was no longer the pretty young thing whose dance card was always filled. She was about to become a divorcée, an implicit state of shame and failure. And she had to face a terrible fact; the one belief that was the underpinning of her life to that point—her faith in the transcendent integrity of marriage—was gone.

"I was scared of marriage."

Recovering from the events of 1926 was difficult. Agatha had Rosalind, her family, and her dear friends Carlo and Mary Fisher. She had her work. But she was alone all the same, and "in serious financial trouble again." Unable to write since her mother's death, she packed up her daughter and Carlo and headed to the Canary Islands, where she hoped to finish her next book. With the help of her brother-in-law, Campbell Christie, she had already created another Poirot novel, *The Big Four,* from a series of short stories, but that, she realized, was only "a stop-gap."

With Carlo's assistance, she managed to complete the bulk of her novel during the trip, and her publishers and her public were delighted with *The Mystery of the Blue Train,* a story that ironically centers on a high-profile divorce. Although Agatha maintained that she "always hated" the book, its completion marked a critical new phase in her self-perception: "That was the moment when I changed from an amateur to a professional. I assumed the burden of a profession, which is to write even when you don't want to, don't much like what you are writing, and aren't writing particularly well."

Returning to London, she set up housekeeping in a flat in Chelsea. Rosalind, who seems to have inherited all of her father's practicality as well as his good looks and almost none of her mother's creative flair, requested to be sent to boarding school, and Agatha found several possibilities. Rosalind chose Caledonia at Bexhill, a large girls' school that—together with Rosalind's next school, Benenden—would later provide much of the background for the 1959 Poirot mystery *Cat among the Pigeons.*

With the divorce behind her and Rosalind settled, Agatha decided to take a holiday on her own. She booked a tour to the West Indies and Jamaica for the fall of 1928, but two days before her scheduled departure, she happened to dine with a young couple just back from Baghdad in Iraq. Listening to their glowing praise of the ancient city and learning that she could reach Baghdad, not by sea, but overland via the Simplon Orient Express, Agatha immediately changed her plans. It was, in the best sense, a fateful decision.

The legendary Orient Express was all that she had dreamed, replete with exotic people, exotic views, and nipping bedbugs. In transit, Agatha was befriended by a resident of Baghdad's English colony. "Mrs. C." was a classic example of a certain type of British colonial—arrogant, demanding, and very efficient at getting her way. Agatha tried to shake the persistent woman, but when she reached Baghdad, Mrs. C. took over. The pushy "mem-sahib" orchestrated each step of Agatha's stay in Baghdad★ and also arranged a memorable side trip. Agatha wanted to visit the biblical city of Ur on the Euphrates River near the Persian

---

★ For a fictional account of Agatha's cross-desert trek from Damascus to Baghdad, read the short story "The Gate of Baghdad" in *Parker Pyne Investigates.*

Gulf, and through Mrs. C.'s contacts, she was invited to the archeological dig of Leonard Woolley. Woolley was perhaps the best-known archeologist working in the Middle East at that time, and much to the dismay of his team, the Ur excavations attracted many unwelcome tourists. But Katharine Woolley, Leonard's wife, had just read *The Murder of Roger Ackroyd* and took an instant liking to its shy author. Not only did Agatha receive VIP treatment during her visit; she was invited to return the following year.

On her second trip to the Ur dig, early in 1930, Agatha was introduced to a young man who had been absent during her previous visit. Max Mallowan, a classics graduate of New College, Oxford, had been a valued member of Woolley's team for some five years. He was a dedicated scholar and excellent organizer. Most important, he was a favorite of Katharine Woolley. Although Agatha and Katharine were to become good friends, Katharine was not a woman's woman. Autocratic and self-centered, she was subject to extreme mood shifts that no one, least of all her husband, could predict. It is evidence of Max Mallowan's judicious character that he had mastered the art of taming Katharine: "He knew when to keep quiet; he knew when to speak."

As the excavation team prepared for their return to England, Katharine assigned Max the duty of showing Agatha the local sites. This special treatment embarrassed Agatha, and initially she felt nervous with Max, but their sight-seeing venture proved to be highly successful. At Kerbala, they slept in bedrolls on the floor of cells in the police station. Near Ukhaidir, they swam in a desert salt lake—Agatha dressed in "a pink silk vest and a double pair of knickers. . . ." When their vehicle bogged down in the sand, Agatha chose to await rescue by going to sleep in the shadow of the stranded car. It was at that moment, Max told her later, that he decided she would make a good wife. "You didn't complain or say that it was my fault, or that we never should have stopped there," he said. "You seemed not to care whether we went on or not. Really it was at that moment I began to think you were wonderful."

Rescued in the desert, Max and Agatha continued back to Baghdad, where they met Katharine and Leonard for the long trip home. Despite Katharine's chaotic moods and outrageous demands. Agatha and Max found time to be alone, visiting a Crusader's castle near Aleppo in Turkey, swimming and picnicking in a field of yellow marigolds at Mersin. But on reaching her hotel in Athens, Agatha was handed a stack of telegrams from her sister: Rosalind was very ill with pneumonia and had been taken to Abney. In the days before antibiotics, pneumonia always carried the implicit threat of death, so Agatha made hurried arrangements to return to England. In the rush, she fell in a pothole in an Athens street, badly spraining her ankle.

It was Max to the rescue once more. Canceling his planned trip to Bassae, he instead accompanied Agatha as far as Paris, and again, he was the perfect companion. In Paris, Agatha had to borrow money from Max's mother in order to complete her trip, a decidedly inauspicious first encounter with her future in-law. But when she finally reached Madge's home in Cheshire, Agatha found Rosalind very weak but recuperating nicely, and some weeks later, Agatha returned to her London mews house. Max was also back in London, working at the British Museum, and Agatha invited her new friend to breakfast. Seeing each other again was a little awkward, but they soon overcame their shyness and even made plans for Max to visit Torquay.

On his first trip to Ashfield, in April 1930, Max met Rosalind and the rest of Agatha's household. They all spent a rainy day on the moor and generally enjoyed a happy weekend. But late on the second evening, after everyone had gone to bed, someone knocked at Agatha's door, and ". . . Max came in. He had a book in his hand which I had lent him," she recalled. "He put it down beside me. Then he sat down on the end of my bed, looked at me thoughtfully, and said that he wanted to marry me."

Agatha remembered the proposal as a complete surprise. She knew that their friendship was special, but the pain of her break-up with Archie was still very fresh, and marriage was not on her agenda. She had already rejected one proposal from an old friend and even contemplated the prospect of taking a lover someday. She enjoyed being courted by men after her divorce, though on one occasion, she had thwarted the erotic advances of a persistent Italian with the assurance that she was English "and therefore frigid by nature." But marriage, especially to a man fourteen years her junior? "I was scared of marriage," she confessed. "I realized, as I suppose many women realize sooner or later, that the only person who can really hurt you in life is a husband. Nobody else is close enough. On nobody else are you so dependent for the everyday companionship, affection, and all that makes up marriage. Never again, I decided, would I put myself at *anyone's* mercy."

That night and for several weeks, she peppered Max with a barrage of reasons not to marry. There was the age difference, of course. Max was Roman Catholic; Agatha was Church of England and a divorcée. He was an educated man and a scholar; she was a "lowbrow." Agatha thought of every possible objection but one: it never occurred to her that she didn't love him. By May or June, they were agreed. They would marry in September. They received the wholehearted support of Carlo and Mary Fisher. Rosalind was happy. (Agatha wrote to Max that "[Rosie] will give her consent if you send her by return 2 dozen toffee lollipops from Selfridges. . . .") Madge, on the other hand, was deeply opposed. She argued with Max, who was impressed by her concern for Agatha's well-being, and refused to attend the wedding, saying "I shall only cry and upset everyone."

Fearful of the reporters who had pursued her like "yelping hounds" after her disappearance, Agatha, with Carlo, Mary, and Rosalind, went north to the island of Skye, where the banns could be read without attracting the attention of the press. The wedding took place on September 11, 1930, at St. Columba's Church in Edinburgh, where the Fisher sisters' father had been rector. Three days later, Mr. and Mrs. Max Mallowan left on the Orient Express for their honeymoon in southern Europe. From their final stop in Athens, Max would go on to Baghdad and Ur to prepare for the Woolleys' next expedition season, and Agatha would return to England. In Athens, however, Agatha was hit with a terrible case of food poisoning, but she revived sufficiently to send her new husband off on schedule and, over the local doctor's emotional objections, to make her way home alone.

"There is a great deal of wickedness in village life."

Agatha Christie's private life was so full that it is hard to imagine when she found time for work. Yet she was prolific, publishing at least one new mystery and several short stories every year. In 1929, she had turned to a new fictional genre, writing her first "straight" novel, *Giant's Bread,* a complex study that revealed more of Agatha's own state of mind than anything she had written to date. For self-protection, she insisted that the novel be published under a pseudonym. This was the birth of Mary Westmacott, the pen name she used for six romantic novels published between 1930 and 1956.

She continued to develop new characters, introducing Mr. Parker Pyne, retired government statistician and professional problem-solver, in a series of short stories. She also produced a number of Harley Quin stories, which were collected in *The Mysterious Mr. Quin* in 1930. Fantasy confections deriving from Agatha's long-held interest in Harlequin and other players of the Italian commedia dell'arte, these stories, she said, were her favorites. In them, the magical Mr. Harley Quin is "a catalyst, no more," appearing out of nowhere to affect the lives of people in love and people in pain, often through the ministrations of his emissary, the very human Mr. Satterthwaite. Agatha's real magic act, however, was the creation of the one detective who could rival the popularity of Hercule Poirot. She made her debut in a series of six short stories:

Miss Marple wore a black brocade dress, very much pinched in round the waist. Mechlin lace was arranged in a cascade down the front of the bodice. She had on black lace mittens, and a black lace cap surmounted the piled-up masses of her snowy hair. She was knitting—something white and soft and fleecy. Her faded blue eyes, benignant and kindly, surveyed her nephew and her nephew's guests with gentle pleasure.

By the end of the first story, it is clear that Jane Marple is not just any old lady; she is gifted with a steel-trap mind and a genius for analogy. The direct inspiration was the character of Caroline Sheppard, the doctor's sister in *The Murder of Roger Ackroyd*: "an acidulated spinster, full of curiosity, knowing everything, hearing everything: the complete detective service in the home." In crafting Miss Marple, however, Agatha looked back into her childhood and the gatherings of elderly ladies at her Auntie-Grannie's house in Ealing. Miss Marple was not based directly on Agatha's grandmother, but they did have one critical common trait—"though a cheerful person, [Auntie-Grannie] always expected the worst of everyone and everything, and was, with almost frightening accuracy, usually proved right."

In the early Miss Marple stories, there is also something strongly suggestive of Baroness Emmuska Orczy's Old Man in the Corner, and it is quite possible that Agatha, who had parodied Orczy's Old Man in one of her *Partners in Crime*★ episodes, intended to create her own armchair detective. The elderly Miss Marple sits in a straight-backed grandfather chair in her drawing room, and like the Old Man who continually tied and untied complex knots in a piece of string, she unravels mysteries as she knits. The guests in her home, all friends of her novelist nephew, Raymond West, gather each Tuesday night to share tales of unresolved mysteries and attempt to divine the solutions. To everyone's immense surprise, it is the quiet old lady at her ceaseless knitting who invariably arrives at the right conclusions. The armchair detection was continued in a second series, and only in "Death by Drowning," the final story of this set, does Miss Marple actively involve herself in a contemporary crime.

★ *Partners in Crime* is a Tommy and Tuppence book in which the couple solve a number of mysteries using methods that parody those of the best-known fictional sleuths of the time, including Sir Arthur Conan Doyle's Sherlock Holmes, G. K. Chesterton's Father Brown, Baroness Orczy's Old Man in the Corner, Anthony Berkeley Cox's Roger Sheringham, Freeman Wills Crofts's Inspector French, and Agatha's own Poirot. For fans of Golden Age detective fiction, *Partners in Crime* is a delightful treasure hunt.

Agatha's first full-length novel starring Miss Marple, *Murder at the Vicarage,* was published in 1930. It is set in St. Mary Mead, the quiet English country village whose denizens and doings provide the basis for Miss Marple's worldview. Agatha was attracted not only to the character of the village spinster but also to the quality of village life in general. The country village, christened "Mayhem Parva" by critic Colin Watson in *Snobbery with Violence,* has always intrigued English writers, particularly detective fiction writers of the twentieth century. Watson defined Mayhem Parva as "a mythical kingdom, a fly-in-amber land" offering readers an "inward escape" into a sort of museum of nostalgia. Writer Robert Barnard, in *A Talent to Deceive: An Appreciation of Agatha Christie,* described the village milieu as a place where "the old outnumber the young, and tradition wins small victories over innovation. The inhabitants of Mayhem Parva play bridge, and garden, and go to church. They approve of self-help, self-control and capital punishment. They disapprove of Socialism, the modern woman and contemporary literature. . . . They are *very* aware of their proper stations."

Like a pyramid, Agatha's mythical St. Mary Mead rises on a base of faceless and often nameless servants—cooks and parlor maids, charwomen, gardeners, and housekeepers. At the next level come the shopkeepers, innkeepers, seamstresses, salesmen, and local constabulary, followed by the professionals (doctors, lawyers, bankers), then the retired colonels, the well-to-do widowed, the never-wed daughters of good families, and the rest of the upper middle class. At the top, the squire keeps the village under earthly control, while the vicar tends to its spiritual needs. On its face, the village is a place of benign order and unity, but beneath the placid surface. . . .

In *Murder at the Vicarage,* Griselda Clement, the vicar's young wife, introduces readers to "that terrible Miss Marple" and the rest of St. Mary Mead's aging gossips. To Griselda, they are the "cats," quick to spread rumor and pronounce judgment. But Mrs. Clement's older and wiser husband, Len, knows that Miss Marple is different. "Miss Marple is not the type of elderly lady who makes mistakes," he says. "She has got an uncanny knack of being always right."

There is precious little in St. Mary Mead that escapes Miss Marple's quick eye, but it is *how* she interprets what she sees that sets her apart. She understands that evil is not an aberration from the established order but intrinsic to it. She sees connections. She knows that the impulse to steal a bit of thread from the draper is the same impulse that can lead to murder for gain. Miss Marple possesses an almost superhuman capacity for discovering what scientist Jacob Bronowski called, in the context of artistic and scientific method, the "hidden likeness." Miss Marple herself draws the comparison to science in *Murder at the Vicarage*: ". . . my hobby is—and always has been—Human Nature. So varied—and so very fascinating. And, of course, in a small village, with nothing to distract one, one has such ample opportunity for becoming what I might call proficient in one's study. One begins to class people, quite definitely, just as though they were birds or flowers, group so-and-so, genus this, species that. Sometimes, of course, one makes mistakes, but less and less as time goes on."

In the early novels and stories, Jane Marple is an old harpy—nosy, caustic, arrogant with servants, and condescending to the working classes. But as Agatha developed the character and allowed her to range wider than St. Mary Mead, Miss Marple definitely softened. She aged little over the years—Agatha said that she was "born at the age of sixty-five to seventy"—but Jane Marple definitely mellowed. She never failed to demand the harshest sentences for murderers; like Agatha, Miss Marple had no doubts about capital punishment. But over time, she also gained tolerance for the less fortunate, the weak, and the slow.

"... so free of outside shadows ..."

The years between her marriage and the outbreak of World War Two were happy, busy ones for the new Mrs. Mallowan. She threw herself fully into the cultivation of her marriage and her young husband's career, without letting up on her own obligations.

By the spring of 1931, she was ready to join Max and the Woolleys as they wrapped up another season at the Ur site. This was to be Max's last expedition with the Woolleys. Agatha and Max then journeyed home by way of Persia, visiting Hamadan, Teheran, and Shiraz, where they discovered an elaborately decorated house, once the home of a shah, which Agatha memorialized in the Parker Pyne story "The House at Shiraz." In Isfahan ("the *most* beautiful city in the world"), Agatha and Max decided to attempt a trip to Russia. The ways of the new Communist state were alien, but they found the Russian people generally friendly and discovered that a few rubles in the right hands could work wonders.

It was also in 1931 that Agatha became pregnant. When she suffered a miscarriage, Agatha decided that she and Max should not try again for children. She was now forty-one (though she had falsified her marriage license, lowering her age by four years). The cause of her miscarriage isn't known, but Agatha ever afterward advised the wives of Max's young archeology colleagues to remain safely at home during their pregnancies—the one exception to her own mother's admonition that wives should always stick close to husbands.

Max's next mentor was Dr. Campbell (C. T.) Thompson, a noted specialist in engraved inscriptions who was mounting his last expedition to Nineveh, near Mosul in Iraq. Agatha, having passed C.T.'s endurance test for wives, joined Max at the site in late October 1931. While Max was occupied in digging a deep trench around the great mound of Nineveh, Agatha worked on *Lord Edgware Dies.* A skeleton unearthed at the mound was immediately christened "Lord Edgware." In December, she left the dig in advance of Max, traveling home alone via the Orient Express—a trip that quickly degenerated into a Keystone Kops comedy of mishaps, which was to inspire one of her most popular novels.

Immediately on her arrival back in London, she wrote Max a lengthy letter describing her trip, her fellow passengers, and their misadventures. Departing Istanbul in a thunderstorm, the train had become stranded near the Greek-Turkish border, where flooding had washed out the tracks. In a spirit of shared suffering, the passengers soon became acquainted, and Agatha detailed the group with a quick and observant brush: ". . . an elderly American lady. . . . a funny little Englishman from Smyrna—a little fussy man but very interested in archeology—an old gentleman of 85 with a *most* amusing wife of 70 with a hideous but very attractive face . . . a Hungarian Minister and his wife . . . two Danish lady missionaries. . . . There was also, most fortunately, a director of the Wagons Lits Company. But for his presence I think we should be there still!"

In the tradition of any good Christie story, the stranded travelers were joined by passengers from another train, including "a large jocose Italian, a little German with a bald head, a Bulgarian lady, a thin and *terrible* man from Chicago—a Turk by extraction dressed in an orange suit, lots of gold chains and things and a royal blue satin tie with horse shoes on it." For all his sinister appearance, the "Terrible Chicago Man" turned out to be "devastatingly friendly," though he did give Agatha a sleepless night by continually opening the door that connected their sleeping compartments: "not, let us hope, for the worst reasons but I think because he thought it was the wash place!!" After two days of multilingual mix-ups, on-and-off heating, food and water shortages, lost baggage, a muddy trudge to a new train, an hysterical weeping fit by the American lady, and a snowstorm outside Sofia, Agatha was on her way home. But there was one last adventure when royalty came on board at Belgrade: ". . . immediately the train swarmed with detectives looking exactly like they do on Cinemas and in plays." Two years later, Agatha would combine the essentials of this trip (the train marooned in a storm, the international cast of travelers, the stolid railway officials) with grisly murder, a high-profile kidnapping similar to the Lindbergh case, and the presence of Hercule Poirot. Eh, voilà! *Murder on the Orient Express.*

With Agatha's ardent encouragement, Max was now ready to take the giant step of mounting his own dig. In the spring of 1933, sponsored by the British Museum and the British School of Archaeology in Iraq, the Mallowans began scouting for promising locations near Nimrud, finally selecting the small mound of Arpachiyah. Agatha continued her habit of working out the plots of her novels while on site, trudging over sand dunes as she had once walked Dartmoor. She was writing *Murder on the Orient Express,* which she eventually dedicated to Max, and also began work on *Why Didn't They Ask Evans?,* a novel that is rumored to have been inspired by a question Agatha overheard during a luncheon with friends. Indicative of her new state of happiness and security with Max, she began the development of her second, and most revealing, Mary Westmacott novel, *Unfinished Portrait.* In this book she did what she had been unable to do with even her closest friends: verbalize the dark realities of her marriage to Archie Christie. Through fictionalized characters and under a pseudonym, she took a hard look at her youth, her romantic idealism, her mistakes, and the internal sources of discord that destroyed her marriage. She also explored the effects of divorce on Judy,* the child of her fictional Celia and Dermot.

The most interesting aspect of the book is Agatha's choice of narrator—an established portrait painter unable to pursue his art because of a devastating war injury. In the novel, the crippled artist, to whom Celia tells her story, believes that in their final moments together, when he reveals his injury, he becomes her Gun Man, a childhood nightmare figure and symbol of her fears. But what he provides, by enabling Celia to pour our her misery and grief, is *"Deliverance."* From her earliest childhood, Agatha had constructed fantasies with herself in the role of either active participant or shadowy observer who manipulates the action. In *Unfinished Portrait,* she played both parts: she is both Celia and the narrator. *Unfinished Portrait* is about confrontation, and it is the observing narrator who passively impels Celia, or Agatha, to confront her life, fears, guilt, and self-pity. It is logical to assume, given the extreme autobiographical nature of the novel, that Agatha was at last forcing herself to confront her own realities. In essence, she was conducting her own psychotherapy, and, as the detective of her own soul, assembling the evidence, sorting through the facts, discarding the irrelevancies, and making her judgment.

---

* Judy was the name of the daughter of Nan Watts, Agatha's dear friend from childhood and herself a divorcée. Agatha's 1952 Mary Westmacott novel, *A Daughter's a Daughter,* concerns the relationship between a sacrificing mother and her child and is said to have reminded those who knew them of Nan Watts and her Judy.

Unfinished Portrait is by no means a great book. Without foreknowledge of Agatha's life, it is not even particularly interesting. But with knowledge, it becomes a wonderfully hopeful book. In the end, the narrator tells the reader, "It is my fixed belief that Celia went back into the world to begin a new life. . . . She went back at thirty-nine—to grow up. . . . And she left her story and her fear—with me. . . ." Surely this was Agatha speaking. Through confrontation, she had found release. She could love Max. She could make a new peace with Rosalind. There is also clear evidence in her detective fiction that she had reached a new level of maturity in her work. With the exception of *The Murder of Roger Ackroyd* and *Murder on the Orient Express,* all her classic mysteries—*The ABC Murders; Appointment with Death; Ten Little Niggers; One, Two, Buckle My Shoe; Mrs. McGinty's Dead; The Pale Horse; Witness for the Prosecution; Curtain*—were written after the cathartic rendering of *Unfinished Portrait.*

The Mallowans had settled into a comfortable routine. The late autumn and spring of each year were spent in the Middle East. Rosalind joined them for her summer holidays at Ashfield. At Christmas, they gathered with Madge and Jimmy Watts at Abney. The rest of their time was divided between their houses in London and Winterbrook House in Wallingford, south of Oxford. Agatha acquired Winterbrook in 1934: a gracious, Queen Anne–style house with panoramic views of gardens and meadows that stretched to the bank of the Thames. Shortly before purchasing Winterbrook, Agatha bought yet another London house, at 48 Sheffield Terrace, Kensington—the only one of her homes in which she allocated a specific office for herself, a room no one was allowed to enter while she was writing. To its severe furnishings, she added a Steinway grand piano at which she could indulge her love of music in privacy.

Max's career was progressing well; he was gaining a reputation for his fieldwork and his archeological writings. Agatha was now a working member of his team when on site, particularly involved in cleaning and photographing their finds. When the political situation in Iraq became dangerous, Max decided to move on to Syria, where he worked at several sites until the beginning of World War Two. The Mallowans gathered an exceptional team of bright young scholars, and Agatha later recorded the lighter side of their Syrian adventures in a delightful nonfiction book titled *Come, Tell Me How You Live.*

In 1938, Agatha bought her "dream house," an expansive Georgian estate that dated to the late eighteenth century. Greenway House sat on thirty-five acres located not far from Torquay; it overlooked the river Dart and had always been admired by Agatha's mother. The sale price of £6,000 was steep, and the house required extensive renovation, so Agatha at last decided to part with her childhood home on Barton

Road. In a way, this decision was like closing the chapter on the first half of her life. She knew that Max had never liked Ashfield: "I think in some way he was jealous of it because it was a part of my life that I hadn't shared with him. . . ."

"Those years, between 1930 and 1938, were particularly satisfying," Agatha said, "because they were so free of outside shadows. . . . I wrote detective stories, Max wrote archaeological books, reports and articles. We were busy but we were not under intense strain." But even at idyllic Greenway, it was impossible not to see the dark clouds gathering.

"In England we had too much war in too short a time."

Agatha described the sensation of waiting for another war. It was different, she recalled from the First World War, which had come as such a shock. The British were not taken unawares by Hitler. The real surprise when war was declared in September 1939 was that "nothing happened": the expected bombardment did not immediately come to England. Unable to secure a government post, Max joined the Brixham branch of the Home Guard—a Gilbert and Sullivan–like corps of locals who shared two rifles among ten men—and Agatha refreshed her dispensary skills at the Torquay Hospital. Early in 1940, Max moved back to London to assist with the relief effort that followed a devastating earthquake in eastern Turkey. A year later, he joined the Intelligence branch of the Royal Air Force. With his expertise in Middle Eastern history, customs, and Arabic languages, he was posted to Cairo in 1942 to serve as a liaison between the Royal Air Force and the other Allied air forces. In 1943, he volunteered for a civil affairs post and moved to Tripoli, where he remained until the war's end, earning the rank of wing commander. Although the Mallowans conducted a lively, loving correspondence, they did not see one another until Max's return in May 1945.

On the home front, Agatha maintained her usual pace, somewhat breathtaking considering that she was now in her early fifties. She had moved to the Sheffield Terrace house (Greenway was rented out as a nursery for child evacuees and later requisitioned by the British Admiralty as headquarters for an American naval flotilla), and she took up duties as a part-time dispenser at University College Hospital in London. Rosalind contemplated several wartime jobs, but in September of 1940, she married Hubert Prichard, a major in the Royal Welsh Fusiliers. Agatha attended the tiny wedding, even though she knew Rosalind would have preferred an elopement. Three years later, Rosalind gave birth to Agatha's only grandchild, Mathew Prichard, upon whom

Agatha doted from the beginning. After staying awhile with Agatha in London, Rosalind and her baby moved to her husband's family home in Pwllywrach, Wales. It was there, in August 1944, that Rosalind was informed of Major Prichard's death in combat. Faced with her daughter's stoic acceptance of this terrible loss, Agatha struggled to know what to do. "The saddest thing in life," she later wrote, "and the hardest to live through is the knowledge that there is someone you love very much whom you cannot save from suffering."

Agatha's biographers have attempted to explain the relationship between Agatha and her daughter. The two were close, but they were very different types. Agatha realized this quite early: ". . . by the time that [Rosalind] was five years old, I was conscious that she was much more efficient than I was. On the other hand, she had no imagination." Rosalind never saw the point of make-believe and hated fairy tales. "But they're not *real,*" she would complain. Agatha's relationship with her own mother hadn't prepared her to raise a pragmatist.

There were also, as pointed out by literary biographer Gillian Gill, indications of other, more potent areas of conflict, particularly related to Agatha and Archie's divorce. Gill, citing the portrayal of the young daughter in *Unfinished Portrait,* says, "Christie presents little Judy as a stranger and rival . . . a miniature version of her husband's cool, judgmental common sense and resistance to intimacy. United by temperament and interests, Dermot and Judy are 'puzzles' to Celia, who feels an outsider in her own home." In the novel, Judy blames her mother: "It was *you* Daddy didn't like. He was fond of *me.*" Today, divorcing parents are taught to expect such outbursts, but Agatha had no counseling services, no relationship gurus. It seems only natural that mother and daughter would have had a difficult adjustment, possibly reflected in Rosalind's preference, at age nine, for boarding school over her mother's company. Whatever passed between them, Max appears to have been an ameliorating influence. He proved to be a sensitive stepfather and always respectful of Rosalind's loyalty to Archie.

Agatha admired her daughter's intelligence and resilience, and Rosalind was also one of the few critics whose judgment Agatha trusted. Late in Agatha's life, Rosalind was intimately involved in the management of her mother's affairs and fiercely protective of her literary reputation. But in so many ways, Rosalind Christie was her father's child, and that, perhaps as much as anything, may explain any element of psychological distance between mother and daughter.

Agatha continued to live in London throughout the worst years of the war. Though the Sheffield Terrace house was partly destroyed by an explosion, she refused to retreat to shelters during the German air raids and trained herself to sleep through the bombings. But neither she nor her publishers were oblivious to the danger. In 1940 Agatha began two novels that would not see the light of day for another thirty-five years: the Hercule Poirot swan song, *Curtain,* and a Miss Marple mystery, *Sleeping Murder.* On completion, both books were delivered to Collins, heavily insured, and stored in a bank vault, as Agatha remembered, "in anticipation of my being killed in the raids. . . ." Agatha survived the war in fine shape, but both books continued to be held for future release. Her publishers were naturally anxious that Poirot, then at the height of public favor, should not suffer a premature demise.

In 1965, Agatha wrote, "It is only now that I fully realize, looking back over my wartime output, that I produced an *incredible* amount of stuff during those years. . . ." Her writing had grown steadily better. Her plotting had always been brilliant, and her pacing was superb, so that even the recapitulation of clues (a standard device at or near the end of most Golden Age novels) is never tedious. While she preferred stereotypes to the end, her characters showed greater depth and honesty. Her grammar improved. She at last gained control over dialog, and she dropped the idiosyncratic tics and linguistic mannerisms that once threatened Poirot and Miss Marple.

But by the war years, Hercule Poirot had become a millstone, and he dragged her down. Her publishers and her public clamored for more just at the time when Agatha would have quite happily sent Poirot straight to detective heaven. Writing *Curtain,* the story of his final case, must have provided some relief, and Agatha deliberately gave more attention to Miss Marple with *The Body in the Library* and *The Moving Finger.* She also experimented with a detective story set in ancient Egypt, *Death Comes as the End,* and it was this book that inspired a famously malicious series of *New Yorker* magazine essays by American critic Edmund Wilson. In the first essay, "Why Do People Read Detective Stories?" Wilson concluded, on the reading of one book alone, that Agatha's "writing is of a mawkishness and banality which seem literally impossible to read." He went on to declare that the detective story generally had been in steady decline since Edgar Allan Poe, and attributed the popularity of detective fiction to pervasive public paranoia. Needless to say, Wilson's readers were not happy, and two additional essays did not redeem him.

Unlike the acerbic Mr. Wilson, theatrical producers and filmmakers were always attracted to Agatha's books. Her second novel, *The Secret Adversary,* had been translated to film by a German company as early as 1928, the same year that *The Coming of Mr. Quinn (sic)* was filmed in England. In the early 1930s, three Hercule Poirot movies were produced. The first play from one of her works was *Alibi;* adapted from *The Murder of Roger Ackroyd* in 1928, it starred a very young Charles Laughton as

Poirot. (More than thirty years later, Laughton was to appear in the best of all the Christie screen adaptations, American director Billy Wilder's version of *Witness for the Prosecution*.) Several more novels and stories, including "Philomel Cottage" and *Peril at End House,* were produced for stage and film, and by the beginning of World War Two, requests to adapt other Christie works were coming in constantly.

Although Agatha never became involved in movie adaptations (and refused later requests to transfer her works to television), by the late 1930s she was more and more determined to control the writing and staging of her stories for theater. She had already written the plays *Black Coffee,* a Poirot mystery, and *Akhnaton,* a lavish drama of dynastic Egypt, which has never been produced. But plays by other writers almost always disappointed her: "It seemed to me that the adaptations of my books to the stage failed mainly because they stuck far too closely to the original book. A detective story is particularly unlike a play, and so is far more difficult to adapt than an ordinary book."

When she contemplated doing her own adaptations, her first choice was *Ten Little Niggers*. With one significant change—a new, more upbeat ending based on an alternate version of the traditional English nursery rhyme—she was convinced it would make good theater, and eventually Bertie Meyer, who had produced *Alibi,* took on the project. After several frustrating delays, the play opened at the St. James Theatre in London in 1943. A Hollywood film treatment, *And Then There Were None,* directed by René Clair, was released in 1945. Although Agatha didn't much like it, this is by far the best of the four film versions made to date.

Between 1945 and 1952, she adapted four more novels—*Appointment with Death, Death on the Nile* (titled *Hidden Horizon* in London and *Murder on the Nile* in New York), *Towards Zero,* and *The Hollow*—and assisted with the writing and staging of *Murder at the Vicarage.* Agatha believed she had "ruined" *The Hollow* by including Poirot, but the stage play was her chance to correct her mistake; she left him out. *The Hollow* was produced by Peter Saunders, a young man with a great flair for promotion. Agatha got on well with Saunders during their first collaboration, but little did they know, on the opening night of *The Hollow* in June 1951, that together they would soon make theatrical history.

"Gone was that innocent simplicity. . . ."

With Max back at home and Europe beginning its recovery, the Mallowans were free to resume their normal lives, but like most of their countrymen, they were war weary and at loose ends. Many old friends and loved ones were gone. Carlo Fisher, severely afflicted with arthritis, had retired. Agatha's sister, Madge, in her late sixties, spent most of her time at Abney. Greenway had been relinquished by the Navy in December 1944. The visiting Americans left the house in good condition, but there was much repair to be done, including removal of fourteen lavatories from the pantry and the reclamation of the gardens, and Agatha found herself in tiresome battles with the Admiralty to cover the costs.

On another bureaucratic front, Agatha's escalating rows with the tax authorities were literally driving her to distraction. The problem involved taxes on her overseas income, especially her lucrative earnings from the United States. The American tax people had begun questioning her income in the late 1930s, and in 1940, her U.S. payments were stopped by the Internal Revenue Service, which threatened to withhold all her U.S. earnings against some future tax settlement. The British Inland Revenue, in the meantime proposed to tax her American income even though she had never received a penny. The situation became so tangled that Edmund Cork wrote in 1941 to Harold Ober, Agatha's New York agent, "It does not take much imagination to see what a nightmare it has produced for our most valuable client. . . ." At war's end, there were indications British officials might reach some sort of conclusion, until they decided that the whole case should be transferred from their Torquay office to London and negotiations started over virtually from scratch. In a September 1948 letter to Ober,★ Cork seriously suggested the possibility of bankruptcy for Agatha. The strain, he believed, was affecting her work, and indeed, she wrote nothing new that year.

A partial resolution was reached in 1948, but a final settlement of her American debt was not achieved for several more years. Still subject to horrendously high British taxation, she finally gained some relief with the formation of the Christie Settlement Trust and a separate company, Agatha Christie Ltd., from which she received a salary. But Agatha was never personally to reap the hard-earned financial rewards of her labor, and later in her life, she enjoyed the dubious honor of being hailed as a "martyr" to the British tax system. She did find one ray of hope: when informed about the duties that her relatives would owe at her death, she concluded that "their only hope was to keep me alive as long as possible!"†

★ Cork's letters are quoted by Janet Morgan in her biography.

† Taxing problems cropped up regularly in Agatha's books from the 1940s onward, and in *4.50 from Paddington* (1957), the British system came in for a cover-to-cover beating. Miss Marple blames taxation for the shortage of first-class train passengers. Old Mr. Crackenthorpe holds taxation and the Labour party accountable for virtually every human ill. Worst insult of all, the prospect of inheritance taxes provides the motive for three murders. Greed and taxes—to Miss Marple, they make a lethal combination.

Despite her problems, Agatha always had plenty of work on her plate. Early in 1947, for instance, she was approached by the British Broadcasting Corporation for a unique assignment. England's beloved Queen Mary would celebrate her eightieth birthday in May, and when contacted by the BBC, the mother of King George requested a radio play by one of her favorite writers, Agatha Christie. The half-hour mystery that Agatha developed was inspired by a true case of child abuse then in the news. Titled "Three Blind Mice," the play aired on May 26, 1947.

Both Mallowans were now itching to return to the Middle East. Following Max's appointment to the first Chair of Western Asiatic Archaeology at the University of London, he set about planning an expedition to Iraq. To finance her part of the trip, Agatha arranged with Collins for a business allowance to write a new book, tentatively titled *The House in Baghdad*. The 1948 expedition lasted five months and was mainly a scouting trip; the serious work began the next year. Max's old dream of digging at Nimrud, a great, grassy mound located two miles east of the river Tigris, was coming true.

The Nimrud digs were to continue for a decade. The going was slow at first, but during the 1951 season, exciting new results began to surface. The expeditions attracted scholars from Great Britain, Europe, and the United States, and with justifiable pride, Max noted in his memoirs how many successful archeologists got their "initiation" at Nimrud. One particularly welcome addition to the team was a Danish professor who brought "financial support from the Carlsberg Foundation as well as cans of beer." Another was Barbara Parker, who officially served as secretary but was especially valued for her willingness to take the blame for anything that went wrong.

Agatha's life took another upturn in 1948 when Rosalind remarried. Agatha's new son-in-law was Anthony Hicks. Qualified as a barrister, Anthony had no interest in law. He read Tibetan and Sanskrit and was a student of Oriental philosophies, especially Buddhism. Max, in his memoirs, characterized Anthony as "a born scholar . . . but his natural brilliance was unaccompanied by a particle of personal ambition." With Agatha, Anthony shared a love of gardening, travel, and the occasional bet on the horses. "Not only is he one of the kindest people I know," she said, "he is a most remarkable and interesting character. He has ideas."

There were two sad losses. Madge Miller Watts, the adored "Punkie," who had introduced Agatha to detective fiction, died at her Abney home in August 1950. (Strangely, Agatha didn't mention her sister's death in her autobiography.) The next year, Max's mother, Marguerite, died while Max and Agatha were at Nimrud. Otherwise, the family flourished, and Agatha took special pleasure in the activities of her grandson, Mathew, and Max's nephews and their friends. Whichever house the Mallowans lived in, it would often be filled with family and guests. Agatha was a gracious and somewhat restrained hostess, always listening more than she talked. In his *Memories of Men and Women,* A. L. Rowse included this diary entry from a day spent at Wallingford in January 1971: "The house was always warm and cosy, with a nice wood fire, sun coming cheerfully into the back drawing-room from the side. There's always good food, they both like their food and have second helpings. . . . Max likes his wine, face a bit flushed. She's an apple-juice drinker, like me."★

Agatha's books were coming once again, much to her publisher's relief. *They Came to Baghdad,* the novel she had promised Collins in exchange for funding her first season at Nimrud, was published in 1951 and generated more American sales than any of her previous works. She was subsequently honored as one of the ten greatest "active" mystery writers by *Ellery Queen's Mystery Magazine.* In 1951 she began two new mysteries and completed *A Daughter's a Daughter,* her next-to-last Mary Westmacott novel. (Agatha's final Mary Westmacott book, *The Burden,* which included a main character reminiscent of her mother, was published in 1956. The author's true identity had been uncovered by an enterprising American reporter and revealed in a 1946 review of *Absent in the Spring,* but the news took a while to spread. Agatha lamented the loss of her anonymity, telling Edmund Cork that "it spoilt my fun." She also worried that her friends would too easily recognize the autobiographical and biographical elements. So Mary Westmacott was laid to rest with *The Burden.*)

With *The Hollow* already running successfully, Peter Saunders was anxious to start production of Agatha's next play, an expanded version of the radio story she had written for Queen Mary's birthday. There was one problem, however: the title, "Three Blind Mice," was already taken. Anthony Hicks provided the solution—*The Mousetrap.* Script in hand, Peter Saunders began transforming Agatha's play into reality, and he attracted Richard Attenborough and his wife, Sheila Sim, to play the lead roles. Agatha had a wonderful time attending rehearsals. She had faith in the play; she considered it "well constructed," with broad-based appeal. But when she first saw *The Mousetrap* during its provincial tryout, she

---

★ Agatha had a lifelong love affair with good food. One of her passions from childhood was butter-thick Devonshire cream, eaten with a spoon or mixed with milk for drinking: "There is no doubt about it, my favorite thing has been, is, and probably always will be, *cream.*" She often celebrated her birthdays with a lobster dinner, and though she rarely touched alcohol, she indulged her taste for caviar at every opportunity. Her fondness for fresh apples was legendary, and she is said to have come up with some of her best ideas while soaking in a hot tub and eating apples.

worried about its flaws: "I had put in too many humorous situations; there was too much laughter in it; and that must take away from the thrill."

With minor adjustments, *The Mousetrap* reached London, opening at the Ambassadors Theatre on November 25, 1952. Peter Saunders happily predicted a year's run at least. Agatha was more conservative; she gave it six to eight months.

The Mousetrap celebrated its silver anniversary in 1977, the year after Agatha's death. It has changed theaters several times and gone through scores of actors, but barring disaster, it will reach its half-century in the year 2002. It is the longest-running play in modern theater history, probably in all history. Today it is as much an English landmark as the Tower of London and Westminster Abbey, a neon beacon for tourists worldwide. Agatha herself could never fully explain its popularity, assigning it finally to the realm of "miracles." The producers fought to protect the play's typically Christie surprise ending, and Agatha insistently refused to have the short story version of "Three Blind Mice" reprinted for fear it would spoil the impact of the play for theatergoers. She was abetted in this conspiracy of silence by her fans, and for many years it was considered a gross social faux pas to reveal the ending to anyone who had not yet seen *The Mousetrap.*

Agatha was now established as a playwright of both skill and box office appeal. Her next project with Peter Saunders was an adaptation of her short story "The Witness for the Prosecution." The first draft was written by Saunders himself; then Agatha stepped in, revising and dramatically altering the original conclusion by heaping surprise on surprise. She had to fight for her ending: "Some people said it was a double cross, or dragged in, but I knew it wasn't; it was logical." When *Witness for the Prosecution* opened at London's Winter Garden theater on October 28, 1953, it was an instant success, and Agatha experienced "the only first night I have enjoyed." She remembered standing on the sidewalk after the play and being "surrounded by crowds of friendly people, quite ordinary members of the audience, who recognized me, patted me on the back, and encouraged me. . . . Autograph books were produced and I signed cheerfully and happily. My self-consciousness and nervousness, just for once, were not with me."

In the autumn of 1953, while tryouts of *Witness* were under way, Agatha was approached to write a play for actress Margaret Lockwood. The actress and the mystery writer met over lunch, and a month later, Agatha delivered her script for *The Spider's Web,* which included, at Miss Lockwood's request, a role for her friend Wilfred Hyde–White and, unrequested, a part for the actress's teenage daughter. The play opened in September 1954 and ran for nearly two years. With *The Mousetrap, Wit-*

ness for the Prosecution, and *The Spider's Web,* Agatha Christie became the brightest light in the West End (London's Broadway)—her name blazing on the marquees of three theaters at once.

At the Nimrud dig that year, she completed a spy thriller, *Destination Unknown.* She also returned to Poirot and his crime novelist pal, Mrs. Ariadne Oliver, in *Dead Man's Folly,* set in a country estate called Nasse House in Devon—a thinly veiled portrait of Agatha's own Greenway. The popularity of her books and plays was now unassailable, and honors streamed in. The Mystery Writers of America presented her their first Grand Master Award, honoring the entire body of her work. The American production of *Witness* won the coveted New York Drama Critics Circle award. And in 1955, Agatha was named Commander of the British Empire (C.B.E.) in the Queen's New Year's Honours List.

She experienced one painful failure during this period: her play *The Verdict* was critically panned and ran only a month. But another play, *The Unexpected Guest,* opened in London in August 1958 to good notices and enjoyed a successful eighteen-month run. Earlier that year, Peter Saunders had thrown one of his famous publicity parties for *The Mousetrap.* Agatha, at Saunders's instruction, arrived early at the Savoy Hotel for a round of photographs but was turned away at the door by a guard who failed to recognize the elderly writer. Instead of telling him who she was, Agatha simply "retreated," recalling the incident as another example of her "miserable, horrible, inevitable shyness."

The annual expeditions to Nimrud were at last coming to an end. In 1958, the rulers of Iraq had been overthrown, and King Feisal, with whom the Mallowans were acquainted, was killed. The archeologists at Nimrud were not threatened by the new revolutionary government, but the political unrest and rising tide of Iraqi nationalism did create a sense of unease. The Nimrud site and Agatha herself had also become the objects of international attention, and increasingly the serious work was interrupted by hordes of tourists who arrived in buses and swarmed over the site, anxious for a glimpse of their favorite mystery writer. The Mallowans made their last working visit to Nimrud in the early spring of 1960, Agatha's seventieth year. Max's work was completed: the great stepped mound of Nimrud as well as the adjacent Fort Shalmaneser palace had been uncovered and explored, and Max was ready to finish his two-volume masterwork, *Nimrud and Its Remains.*

With characteristic aplomb, Agatha was ready to move on: "They were good days. Every year had its fun, though in a sense, every year life became more complicated, more sophisticated, more urban. . . . Gone was that innocent simplicity, with the stone heads poking up out of the green grass, studded with red ranunculus. . . . We have scarred it with our bulldozers. Its yawning pits have been filled in with raw earth. One day its wounds will have healed, and it will bloom once more with early spring flowers."

"Thank God for my good life. . . ."

Life after Nimrud was hardly placid for the Mallowans. Their spirit of adventure was alive and well, and Max now had time to devote to a new project—establishing British schools of archeology throughout the East. Soon after their last dig, Max and Agatha set off for a strenuous tour of India, Pakistan, and Iran, and everywhere they went, Agatha was besieged by press and fans. In September 1960 she celebrated her seventieth birthday with her family and a hot lobster dinner. She was working on a new novel, *The Pale Horse,* in which she drew on her experience as a trainee hospital dispenser some forty-five years earlier. (The exotic murder method described in this Christie mystery eventually inspired one unsuccessful real-life murder attempt and enabled police to foil another.) She was also working on several new theater ideas, though she took no active part in the Miss Marple films then in production for MGM. These movies, made in England, starred Margaret Rutherford, an extremely popular character actress just two years younger than Agatha. The Miss Marple films were crafted around Rutherford's unique personality and played broadly for humor—bearing faint resemblance to Agatha's spinster detective or her intricate plots. Yet in spite of her misgivings about the films, Agatha became friends with Margaret Rutherford and dedicated her 1962 novel, *The Mirror Crack'd from Side to Side,* to the engaging, elderly actress.

Max had become a Fellow at All Souls College, Oxford—a position that allowed more time for writing and research. He was also a trustee of the British Museum and of the British Academy. Despite a slight stroke suffered in the summer of 1962, he was sufficiently recovered to undertake a three-month trip with Agatha to Iran and India that fall.

When in London, Agatha often invited friends and family members to events sponsored by the Detection Club. Agatha was among the club's twenty-six original members, and in 1957, after the death of Dorothy L. Sayers, she had reluctantly agreed to take on the presidency, a life position, provided that she have a co-president to conduct all public business. There had been serious dissatisfaction among some club members when Agatha was named president—not out of antagonism to her, but because many felt it was time to honor the club's founder, Anthony Berkeley Cox. Younger members, however, knew that Agatha's reputation would strengthen the club and attract new membership, and in spite of her distaste for most social gatherings, Agatha seems always to have enjoyed association with her Detection Club peers.

She was not, however, at all pleased about the licenses MGM was taking with their Miss Marple films. Her frustrations finally erupted in 1964 when MGM announced that a fourth film, *Murder Ahoy,* would be produced from an original screenplay using her Miss Marple character. Agatha and Rosalind protested forcefully that this violated her integrity as author, but MGM went ahead. When word came that MGM was planning an adaptation of *The ABC Murders* that would transform Hercule Poirot into a modern buffoonish gumshoe (comic actor Zero Mostel had been tentatively cast), Agatha took her stand. She communicated her indignation to Edmund Cork, who warned MGM that his client was ready for a fight. MGM retreated, and the film version of *The ABC Murders,* with American actor Tony Randall as Poirot, was somewhat closer to Agatha's conception of her Belgian detective. Still, the contract with MGM was ended, and so was Agatha's interest in movies. "Don't talk to me about film rights!!" she wrote to Cork. "I have suffered enough!"

Back at her typewriter, she finished a new Miss Marple book, *A Caribbean Mystery*—set on an island much like Barbados, where she and Max had once vacationed—and went to work on *At Bertram's Hotel,* a complex story in which Miss Marple must navigate between what is real and what is contrived to seem real. When the book was published in 1965, readers and reviewers were quick to speculate about the hotel's real identity. For many years, it was said to be Brown's Hotel in Mayfair, but Agatha's letters to Edmund Cork clearly identify her inspiration as Fleming's Hotel in London.

The pace of Agatha's life in the mid-1960s was only somewhat slowed. She was generally in good health, though she had some trouble with her sight and her hearing was deteriorating. Her weight, a constant source of embarrassment, may have contributed to back problems. She continued to enjoy her favorite pleasures: jaunting back and forth between her homes, entertaining in her warm and casual style, puttering in her gardens, reading, traveling abroad whenever possible, and planning new projects. Both she and Max were now receiving the honors due their long careers. In the summer of 1966, they visited the new Hercule Poirot museum in Belgium, and that fall paid their second visit together to the United States, where Max delivered a series of university lectures. It was during this trip that Agatha visited the grave of her American grandfather, Nathaniel Frary Miller. She enjoyed much of what she experienced in the United States—central heating, the taste of Vermont butter, the Cleveland Symphony. In Texas, she found Austin to be "quite unexpectedly civilized" but was less impressed by the nouveau riche of

Dallas. During the New England phase of the trip, she observed the uniquely American customs celebrating All Hallows' Eve, and two years later she incorporated these details in the Poirot mystery *Hallowe'en Party.*

In 1967 Max received his knighthood, and Agatha became Lady Mallowan. That spring, her adored grandson married, and she and Max took their own second honeymoon in Yugoslavia. But in the autumn, Max was ill again. He had suffered another stroke while delivering a lecture in Persia; he completed the lecture but was hospitalized before being flown back to England to recuperate at Winterbrook House.

As she approached her eightieth birthday, Agatha continued to write at a pace that would stagger people half her age. Her birthday gift to her readers in 1970 was *Passenger to Frankfurt.* This book, a political thriller that her publishers and her family (with the exception of Anthony Hicks) feared would be a disaster, was a hit in England and America. Amid all the publicity surrounding the book and her birthday celebration, Agatha received her highest honor when she was named Dame Commander of the British Empire—Dame Agatha—in the Queen's New Year's Honours List of 1971. That spring she developed a new novel, *Nemesis,* in which Miss Marple becomes the avenging force for an old friend. It was to be the final adventure for the redoubtable old maid, and the beginning of Agatha's own decline.

In June, after a fall at Winterbrook, Agatha underwent surgery for a broken hip. Although she was walking again by Christmas, it was more and more difficult to do what she wanted. She worked at revising another play and in the summer of 1972 completed her manuscript for *Elephants Can Remember,* her last Poirot novel and a pale, confused reminder of her old powers. For nearly half a century, Agatha had consistently delivered at least a book a year (fudging on rare occasions with a collection of stories), and in England it had become a matter of faith that there would always be a new "Christie for Christmas." Now in her eighties, Agatha and her books were plainly suffering from the strain of this productivity. She had once likened herself to a "sausage-machine," but the machinery was at last giving way.

Agatha was still full of ideas, and there would be one more book for publication. For *Postern of Fate,* she turned a final time to Tommy and Tuppence Beresford. The Beresfords, now retired and elderly themselves, move into a new home, and discover an old mystery, but *Postern of Fate* is less concerned with crime than reminiscence. The opening chapters are a librarian's catalog of Agatha's childhood reading as Tuppence explores a cache of books left in the house by the previous owners. The house itself is a verbal re-creation of Ashfield. In the greenhouse, called the Kai-Kai as the greenhouse at Ashfield had been, Tuppence discovers Mathilde the rocking horse and Truelove the riding wagon—

both cherished toys from Agatha's childhood. The garden hosts a mon-key puzzle tree for climbing. Even the mystery is a pastiche of her tried-and-true themes including political conspiracy, the death of a child, the failures of memory, and the clearing of an innocent name.

Rosalind was now seriously concerned about her mother's health, and with good reason. In October 1974 Agatha had suffered a heart at-tack, and two months later she fell again, resulting in a bad head wound. As her health failed, she became increasingly difficult and erratic, al-though she still saw friends, read, and ventured out occasionally. One of her last appearances was at the London premiere of *Murder on the Orient Express.* Despite her disappointment with past attempts to film her nov-els (only *Witness for the Prosecution* had earned her approval), she agreed to the adaptation of *Murder on the Orient Express* at the request of her old acquaintance Lord Louis Mountbatten on behalf of his son-in-law, pro-ducer John Brabourne. The production was lush—the most expensive British film made to that time—and featured a large all-star cast. Al-though Agatha enjoyed the opening night activities, photos taken at the premiere clearly showed the ravages of age and illness. The once tall and robust woman, who complained endlessly about her O-S (out-size) fig-ure, now seemed tiny and achingly frail.

Collins had published a collection of Poirot stories in 1974, and the following year the decision was made to release *Curtain,* one of the two books Agatha had written during the 1940s as insurance against her early demise in the Blitz. When it appeared in bookstores in November 1975, *Curtain* was an instant success—and Agatha enjoyed the satisfac-tion of outliving her irritating little Belgian detective.

On January 12, 1976, at Winterbrook, as Max was wheeling her into the drawing room after luncheon, Agatha Miller Christie Mallowan quietly died. On the evening that her death was reported, the theaters of London's West End dimmed their lights in tribute. She was buried in a private family service at the little parish church of St. Mary's, Cholsey, in Berkshire. She had selected the site of her grave and the inscriptions for her tombstone. The epitaph she chose is from *Faerie Queene* by Ed-mund Spenser:

> *Sleep after Toyle,*
> *Port after Stormie Seas.*
> *Ease after Warre,*
> *Death after Life,*
> *Doth greatly please.*

Max was just completing his memoirs when Agatha died. Though her death was not unexpected, Mac wrote in his Epilogue that "it has left me with a feeling of emptiness after forty-five years of a loving and merry companionship. Few men know what it is to live in harmony beside an imaginative, creative mind which inspires life with zest." Bereft without her and in failing health himself, Max married their old friend from the Nimrud days, Barbara Parker, in September 1977. He died in August 1978.

"A writer's work . . . is . . . her offering to the world. . . ."

The world was to receive two more Agatha Christies: *Sleeping Murder,* with Miss Jane Marple, was published in 1976 and *An Autobiography* in 1977. As Agatha had hoped, her own charming memoir largely foiled other attempts, both serious and sensational, to capitalize on her life. It did not, however, answer the tantalizing questions surrounding her 1926 disappearance and its aftermath. Whether from her natural embarrassment and sense of privacy or for motives that were more perverse, Agatha Christie never recorded what she knew of the one great mystery of her life.

Despite reports at the time about Agatha's great wealth, her actual estate amounted to just a little over £100,000. She left carefully selected bequests to friends, employees, and family members, but most of her earnings had long been controlled by various trusts and corporate entities set up to protect her from onerous taxation. The truth is that Agatha had been quietly generous all her life. To her grandson, Mathew, she had given the rights to *The Mousetrap* and *Curtain* and to Rosalind her share of the film rights for *Witness for the Prosecution.* Max received the rights to *Sleeping Murder.* With the royalties from *Hickory, Dickory, Dock,* she had established a trust for her nephews, Peter and John Mallowan, and other book rights had been assigned to various individuals and charitable organizations during her life.

She had been a notorious shopper, with a special fondness for shoes, but gave away much of what she bought. She was never an easy touch but responded quickly whenever a demonstrable need arose. One of the real delights of her later years was Mathew Prichard's decision, in 1969, to endow the Agatha Christie Trust for Children, a charity to help poor and handicapped youngsters and to support pediatric medical research.

But her ultimate bequest and memorial is the work she left behind. Though she wrote nothing for publication after 1972 (and her best works date from the 1930s and 1940s), Agatha Christie remains the most popular writer of detective fiction in the world. Estimates put the number of Christie books sold worldwide at over 2 billion. Her works are read in more than one hundred languages, ahead of Shakespeare and just shy of the Bible. The universality of her appeal is simply undeniable, and her own name has entered the vocabulary as a synonym for "mystery."

No one has ever claimed that Agatha Christie produced great literature, but she was an exceptionally clever writer in a particularly difficult popular genre. Her first published novel, *The Mysterious Affair at Styles*, is often credited as the starting point of the Golden Age of British detective fiction, and she remains the acknowledged master of the detective story as puzzle. She created mysteries of labyrinthine complexity—plots that twist and turn, turn again, double back on themselves, seem to vanish down blind alleys, and breathlessly arrive at the only logical conclusion. She did not delve into academic psychology, relying instead on her own innate and astute understanding of human behavior. Even her most complete characterizations are mere sketches, and she wasted little time on scene-setting. Although she adjusted to changes in social mores over her career, she never addressed social issues in depth. Politically conservative, she kept her stories virtually apolitical.

That Agatha Christie's books are still read with enthusiasm and relish is due, in part, to the fact that she was not a self-consciously literary writer. She has often been compared to a magician whose feats of legerdemain are so audacious and skillful that they fool and delight even the most cynical of readers. She never cheated; her clues are always available, though deftly obscured. When the cry of "foul" went up with the publication of *The Murder of Roger Ackroyd*, Dorothy L. Sayers came succinctly to the defense. "Some critics . . . consider the solution illegitimate," Sayers wrote. "I fancy, however, that this opinion merely represents a natural resentment at having been ingeniously bamboozled."

Agatha Miller Christie Mallowan was a woman cursed with shyness but blessed with natural intelligence and good humor, a woman who felt deeply but acted with Victorian restraint, a woman who hated her notoriety but rather shamelessly exercised the nicer privileges of fame. Even in her lengthy autobiography, she kept her secrets, and at the end of her life there was no final revelation, no neat tying up of the disparate strands. The mystery of her 1926 disappearance will continue to tease; the sources of her professional success will provoke more volumes of academic analysis.

But what she left behind for her readers are her "children"—the dapper Monsieur Poirot with his mustaches, his "little grey cells," and his weakness for "large, flamboyant women"; the ever-faithful and ever-dim Captain Hastings; Miss Jane Marple with her balls of yarn and village analogies; evanescent Mr. Harley Quin and the all-too-human Mr. Satterthwaite; Tommy and Tuppence, always ready for adventure; Mr.

Parker Pyne and his statistical solutions for the lovelorn; the quixotic Mrs. Ariadne Oliver; stalwarts like Race and Battle, Spence and Japp; the courageous heroines, small and gay, and their bronzed heroes; and the villains, some outrageously evil but most of them pathologically prosaic.

And Agatha Christie bequeathed us their homes: sixty-seven novels of detection, more than 130 short stories, and more than a dozen plays, in each of which we are invited to stop for awhile and enjoy an evening's diversion. Our hostess never intrudes herself upon our pleasure and makes few demands beyond our careful attention. She is clever and quick-witted and anticipates the same of us. If our taste runs to puzzles, conundrums, ruses, and riddles, she will feed us a hearty meal with a finely crafted denouement for dessert. And if we enjoy ourselves, she will always welcome us when we come again.

BIBLIOGRAPHY

AGATHA CHRISTIE
1890–1976
English (born: Torquay)

"Murder isn't—it really isn't—a thing to tamper with light-heartedly."   —Miss Marple in *Sleeping Murder*

Agatha Christie's first six mystery books were published in England by John Lane and The Bodley Head. Her second English publisher—beginning with *The Murder of Roger Ackroyd* in 1926 and through *An Autobiography*, published posthumously in 1977—was William Collins Sons/ Collins. Her mysteries were first published in the United States by Dodd Mead & Company. In this chronology of her detective fiction, dates are for first publication in England, unless noted otherwise. Featured detectives appear in ( ). US = United States. GB = Great Britain.

Mystery Novels and Story Collections
1920   *The Mysterious Affair at Styles* (Poirot)
1922   *The Secret Adversary* (Tommy and Tuppence)
1923   *The Murder on the Links* (Poirot)
1924   *The Man in the Brown Suit*
1924   *Poirot Investigates* (Poirot short stories)
1925   *The Secret of Chimneys*
1926   *The Murder of Roger Ackroyd* (Poirot)

1927 *The Big Four* (Poirot)

1928 *The Mystery of the Blue Train* (Poirot)

1929 *The Seven Dials Mystery*

1929 *Partners in Crime* (Tommy and Tuppence)

1930 *The Mysterious Mr. Quin*/US: *The Passing of Mr. Quin* (short stories)

1930 *Murder at the Vicarage* (Miss Marple)

1931 *The Sittaford Mystery*/US: *Murder at Hazelmoor*

1932 *Peril at End House* (Poirot)

1932 *The Thirteen Problems* (Miss Marple short stories)

1933 *Lord Edgware Dies*/US: *Thirteen at Dinner* (Poirot)

1933 *The Hound of Death and Other Stories* (short stories; GB only)

1934 *Murder on the Orient Express*/US: *Murder on the Calais Coach* (Poirot)

1934 *The Listerdale Mystery* (short stories; GB only)

1934 *Why Didn't They Ask Evans?*/US: *The Boomerang Mystery*

1934 *Parker Pyne Investigates*/US: *Mr. Parker Pyne, Detective* (short stories)

1935 *Three-Act Tragedy*/US: *Murder in Three Acts* (Poirot)

1935 *The ABC Murders* (Poirot)

1935 *Death in the Clouds*/US: *Death in the Air* (Poirot)

1936 *Murder in Mesopotamia* (Poirot)

1936 *Cards on the Table* (Poirot)

1937 *Dumb Witness*/US: *Poirot Loses a Client* (Poirot)

1937 *Death on the Nile* (Poirot)

1937 *Murder in the Mews and Three Other Poirot Cases*/US: *Dead Man's Mirror and Other Stories* (four Poirot novellas)

1938 *Appointment with Death* (Poirot)

1938 *Hercule Poirot's Christmas*/US: *Murder for Christmas* (Poirot)

1939 *Murder Is Easy*/US: *Easy to Kill*

1939 *Ten Little Niggers*/US: *Ten Little Indians*/*And Then There Were None*

1939 *The Regatta Mystery and Other Stories* (short stories: US only)

1940 *Sad Cypress* (Poirot)

1940 *One, Two, Buckle My Shoe*/US: *The Patriotic Murders* (Poirot)

1941 *Evil under the Sun* (Poirot)

1941 *N or M?* (Tommy and Tuppence)

1942 *The Body in the Library* (Miss Marple)

1943 *Five Little Pigs*/US: *Murder in Retrospect* (Poirot)

1943 *The Moving Finger* (Miss Marple; first published in US in 1942)

1944 *Towards Zero*/US: *Come and Be Hanged*

1944 *Death Comes as the End*

1945 *Sparkling Cyanide*/US: *Remembered Death*

1946 *The Hollow*/US: *Murder after Hours* (Poirot)

1947 *The Labours of Hercules* (Poirot short stories)

1948 *Taken at the Flood*/US: *There Is a Tide* (Poirot)

1948   *The Witness for the Prosecution and Other Stories* (short stories; US only)

1949   *Crooked House*

1950   *A Murder Is Announced* (Miss Marple)

1950   *Three Blind Mice and Other Stories*/US: *The Mousetrap and Other Stories* (short stories)

1951   *They Came to Baghdad*

1951   *The Under Dog and Other Stories* (short stories; US only)

1952   *Mrs. McGinty's Dead*/US: *Blood Will Tell* (Poirot)

1952   *They Do It with Mirrors*/US: *Murder with Mirrors* (Miss Marple)

1953   *After the Funeral*/US: *Funerals Are Fatal* (Poirot)

1953   *A Pocket Full of Rye* (Miss Marple)

1954   *Destination Unknown*/US: *So Many Steps to Death*

1955   *Hickory, Dickory, Dock*/US: *Hickory, Dickory, Death* (Poirot)

1956   *Dead Man's Folly* (Poirot)

1957   *4.50 from Paddington*/US: *What Mrs. McGillicuddy Saw!* (Miss Marple)

1958   *Ordeal by Innocence*

1959   *Cat among the Pigeons* (Poirot)

1960   *The Adventures of the Christmas Pudding and a Selection of Entrees* (short stories, GB only)

1961   *The Pale Horse*

1961   *Double Sin and Other Stories* (short stories; GB only)

1962   *The Mirror Crack'd from Side to Side*/US: *The Mirror Crack'd* (Miss Marple)

1963   *The Clock* (Poirot)

1964   *A Caribbean Mystery* (Miss Marple)

1965   *At Bertram's Hotel* (Miss Marple)

1966   *Third Girl* (Poirot)

1967   *Endless Night*

1968   *By the Pricking of My Thumbs* (Tommy and Tuppence)

1969   *Hallowe'en Party* (Poirot)

1970   *Passenger to Frankfurt*

1971   *Nemesis* (Miss Marple)

1971   *The Golden Ball and Other Stories* (short stories; US only)

1972   *Elephants Can Remember* (Poirot)

1973   *Postern of Fate* (Tommy and Tuppence)

1974   *Poirot's Early Cases*/US: *Hercule Poirot's Early Cases* (Poirot short stories)

1975   *Curtain* (Poirot) (written in the early 1940s)

1976   *Sleeping Murder* (Miss Marple) (This novel was written in the early 1940s. To read the Miss Marple books in chronological order, read *Sleeping Murder* after *Murder at the Vicarage*).

[1998   A novelized version by Charles Osborne of Agatha's 1930 play *Black Coffee*, featuring Hercule Poirot, achieved bestseller status, demonstrating the enduring demand for more Agatha Christies. Charles Osborne's novelization of *The Unexpected Guest* was published in 1999. Collins (GB); St. Martin's Press (US).]

Mary Westmacott Novels
1930   *Giant's Bread*
1934   *Unfinished Portrait*
1944   *Absent in the Spring*
1948   *The Rose and the Yew Tree*
1952   *A Daughter's a Daughter*
1956   *The Burden*

Other Books
1924   *The Road to Dreams* (poetry, published by Agatha Christie under the Geoffrey Bles imprimatur; revised and republished by Collins as *Poems* in 1973)
1946   *Come, Tell Me How You Live* (memoirs, published under Agatha Christie Mallowan)
1965   *Star over Bethlehem* (children's stories and poems)
1977   *An Autobiography*

Plays   Dates are for first major production.
1930   *Black Coffee* (original)
1937   *Akhnaton* (original; never produced)
1945   *Appointment with Death* (adapted from the novel)
1945   GB: *Ten Little Niggers*/US: *Ten Little Indians* (adapted from the novel)
1946   GB: *Murder on the Nile*/US: *Hidden Horizon* (adaptation of *Death on the Nile*)
1951   *The Hollow* (adapted from the novel)
1952   *The Mousetrap* (developed from the radio play "Three Blind Mice")
1953   *Witness for the Prosecution* (developed, with help from Peter Saunders, from the short story)
1954   *The Spider's Web* (original)
1956   *Towards Zero* (adapted from the novel)
1957   *Verdict* (original)
1958   *The Unexpected Guest* (original)
1960   *Go Back for Murder* (adaptation of *Five Little Pigs*)
1962   *Rule of Three* (three one-act plays: *Afternoon at the Seaside, The Rats, The Patient*)

Plays Adapted by Others:

1928   *Alibi,* adapted by Michael Morton from *The Murder of Roger Ack-royd*

1940   *Peril at End House,* adapted by Arnold Ridley

1949   *The Murder at the Vicarage,* adapted by Moie Charles and Barbara Toy

1977   *A Murder Is Announced,* adapted by Leslie Darbon

1981   *Cards on the Table,* adapted by Leslie Darbon

Film and Television Adaptations

Agatha Christie enjoyed films and even tried her hand at a screenplay of Dickens's *Bleak House.* But she was rarely happy with cinematic treatments of her own works and was appalled by the few early attempts to translate her mysteries to television. Yet with the possible exceptions of Arthur Conan Doyle and Erle Stanley Gardner, Agatha Christie is the most often adapted of all mystery writers. Between 1928 and 1990, at least twenty-five films were based on her stories and characters. Television adaptations have been even more numerous, and a series of British productions in period style, beginning with *The Seven Dials Mystery* and *Why Didn't They Ask Evans?* in 1981, launched a wave of new interest in Christie that continues today. The full list of film and TV adaptations is too lengthy for inclusion, but the following titles are recommended:

Films

1945   *And Then There Were None:* US/Twentieth Century Fox, adapted by Dudley Nichols from Christie's stage play. Directed by René Clair and starring an Anglo-American cast including Judith Anderson, Louis Hayward, and Walter Houston. First and best of the four screen versions to date.

1947   *Love from a Stranger* (UK: *A Stranger Passes*): US/Eagle Lion, remake of 1937 British film based on "Pilomel Cottage." Featuring Silvia Sidney and John Hodiak.

1957   *Witness for the Prosecution:* US/United Artists, adapted by Billy Wilder and Harry Kurnitz from the stage play. Directed by Wilder and starring Marlene Dietrch, Charles Laughton, and Tyrone Power.

1960   *The Spider's Web:* British/Danziger, from the stage play. Featuring Glynis Johns and Cicely Courtneidge.

1966   *The Alphabet Murders:* British/MGM, from *The ABC Murders,* with Tony Randall as Poirot.

1971   *Endless Night:* British/United Artists, adapted and directed by Sidney Gilliat and starring Hayley Mills and Hywel Bennett.

1974   *Murder on the Orient Express:* British/EMI/Paramount, from the novel. Directed by Sidney Lumet, with Albert Finney as Poirot and an all-star cast including Lauren Bacall, Ingrid Bergman. Sean Connery, and John Gielgud.

1978   *Death on the Nile:* British/EMI-Paramount, adapted by Anthony Shaffer, directed by John Guillermin, and starring Peter Ustinov as Poirot.

1938   *The Mirror Crack'd:* British/EMI, from *The Mirror Crack'd from Side to Side.* Directed by Guy Hamilton, with Angela Lansbury as Miss Marple.

1982   *Evil under the Sun:* British/Universal, adapted by Anthony Shaffer. With Peter Ustinov as Poirot, James Mason, Diana Rigg, and Maggie Smith.

1984   *Ordeal by Innocence:* British/Cannon, from the novel, with Donald Sutherland and Faye Dunaway.

1988   *Appointment with Death:* British/Cannon (Golan-Globus), adapted by Anthony Shaffer, Peter Buckman, and Michael Winner. With Peter Ustinov as Poirot, Lauren Bacall, and Piper Laurie.

Television

1982–1989   Warner Brothers Television produced a number of two-hour dramas drawn from Christie novels and featuring her most famous detectives. Among the best are *A Caribbean Mystery,* adapted by Sue Grafton and Steve Humphrey and starring Helen Hayes as Miss Marple; *Murder with Mirrors* with Hayes and Bette Davis; *Dead Man's Folly* with Peter Ustinov as Poirot and Jean Stapleton as Ariadne Oliver; and *The Man in the Brown Suit* with Stephanie Zimbalist and Edward Woodward.

1982   A United Artists production for the Hallmark Hall of Fame of *Witness for the Prosecution* starring Beau Bridges, Donald Pleasance, Deborah Kerr, and Diana Rigg.

1982–1985   Thames Television productions of ten short stories under the series title *The Agatha Christie Hour.*

1983   Adaptations by London Weekend Television of the Tommy and Tuppence novel *The Secret Adversary* and ten stories from *Partners in Crime.* Starring Francesca Annis and James Warwick.

1984–1992   British adaptations of the Miss Marple novels, featuring Joan Hickson as the village detective, beginning with *The Body in the Library* and concluding with *The Mirror Crack'd from Side to Side.*

1989   First of an ongoing series of short story adaptations for London Weekend Television entitled *Agatha Christie's Poirot,* introducing David Suchet in what many believe to be the definitive portrayal of Hercule Poirot.

1991   *One, Two, Buckle My Shoe* and *The ABC Murders* launched a series of London Weekend Television productions of Poirot novels, which starred David Suchet as the Belgian detective. The series was revived in 2000 with British productions made in conjunction with America's Arts and Entertainment Network.

ACTING POIROT

To date, seven actors have portrayed Hercule Poirot in major stage, film, and television productions. The first was Charles Laughton in *Alibi* on the London stage in 1928 and briefly in New York. Next was Francis L. Sullivan, at 6'2" probably the tallest Poirot, who appeared in stage productions of *Black Coffee* (1930) and *Peril at End House* (1940). Austin Trevor—young, lean and, mon Dieu!, clean-shaven—introduced Poirot to the British cinema in the early 1930s in *Alibi, Black Coffee,* and *Lord Edgware Dies.* More than three decades later, Tony Randall took the role in *The Alphabet Murders.* The only Poirot who came close to satisfying his creator was Albert Finney in the star-studded 1974 film *Murder on the Orient Express*: Agatha enjoyed his performance but not his mustache. Peter Ustinov was the last big-screen Poirot, appearing in *Death on the Nile* (1979), *Evil under the Sun* (1982), and *Appointment with Death* (1988). Ustinov also starred in three television movies—*Thirteen at Dinner, Dead Man's Folly* with Jean Stapleton as Ariadne Olivier, and *Murder in Three Acts.* English actor David Suchet created what many believe to be the most accurate Poirot portrayal in British television productions beginning in 1989.

Miss Marple's part, however, has fallen to only three major actresses. Dame Margaret Rutherford played the part for comedy in four films made by MGM in the 1960s. Helen Hayes, the "first lady of American theater," portrayed the most British of lady sleuths in a series of television dramas made by Warner Brothers in the 1980s. But Joan Hickson took the teacake in the BBC's adaptations of the Miss Marple mysteries made between 1984 and 1992.

AGATHA'S BLUE-EYED NIGHTMARE

By her own account, little Agatha Miller had an almost perfect childhood; adored by her family, she wanted for nothing. But perfect pictures can cast dark shadows. As a toddler, Agatha was terrified by a recurring nightmare that followed her into adulthood. The dream initially focused on a character she called the Gun Man—"a Frenchman in grey-blue uniform, powdered hair in a queue and a kind of three-cornered hat.

The gun was some kind of old-fashioned musket"—who would appear in some ordinary situation. "His pale blue eyes would meet mine," she explained, "and I would wake up shrieking." As the dream evolved, the Gun Man lost his exotic costuming and weapon. Instead, he would simply emerge out of someone she loved. Even her mother might be the Gun Man, revealed only by the strange blue eyes. Freudians can analyze the meaning of the gun, but Agatha was never afraid of it or the prospect of being shot. It was not sex that frightened her: it was betrayal. What haunted her was the stranger who lurked behind the facade of trusted friend or lover.

One of the more persistent themes in her mystery novels became the character who is not what he or she seems to be. Agatha dwelt on the theme far beyond its usefulness as a plot device. Rarely did she present villains in real disguise. It was the appearance of normality that fascinated her—the seemingly gentle soul who could callously plot murder, and worse, allow an innocent to be blamed for the crime. This theme was the foundation for her breakthrough bestseller, *The Murder of Roger Ackroyd*.

In her Mary Westmacott novel *Unfinished Portrait*—a thinly veiled portrayal of the collapse of her marriage to Archie Christie—the Gun Man dream is shared with her main character, Celia, a young wife who becomes suicidal on learning of her husband's infidelity. In her agony, Celia realizes that "all the time Dermot had really been the Gun Man. . . ." Was Archie the embodiment of Agatha's dream? She never said so directly, but she remembered the day when Archie announced his love for another woman: "I think the nearest I can get to describing what I felt at that moment is to recall an old nightmare of mine—the horror of sitting at a tea table, looking across at my best-loved friend, and suddenly realizing that the person sitting there *was a stranger.* . . ."

THE POIROT FILE

NAME: Hercule Poirot ("Papa Poirot")
NATIONALITY: Belgian (never French!)
OCCUPATION: "Consulting detective"
PHYSICAL DESCRIPTION: Height: 5'4"; "delicately plump"; black hair and mustache (maintained with a tonic, not dye); green eyes with a tendency to shine brightly catlike when Poirot is on the trail of a killer.
DISTINGUISHING CHARACTERISTICS: Egg-shaped head; "cherubic" face; military-style mustache, waxed or pomaded to points (the best mustache in London following the death of Mr. Shaitana in *Cards on the Table*); scar on upper lip (acquired during the pursuit of *The Big*

Four; more or less pronounced limp, attributed first to a war wound and later to the tightness of his pointed, patent leather shoes. Never seen outdoors without a hat. Always impeccably dressed. Smokes tiny Russian cigarettes. Frequently carries a large "turnip" watch, later replaced by a more modern design.

ADDRESS: After refugee period at Leastways Cottage in the village of Styles St. Mary, Essex, Poirot shared rooms with his friend Captain Arthur Hastings at 14 Farraway Street, London. Later residence in apartment No. 203 of the modern Whitefriars Mansions, Eaton Terrace, "a large, luxury flat with impeccable chromium fittings, square armchairs, and severely rectangular ornaments. There could truly be said not to be a curve in the place." Brief, unsuccessful retirement to The Larches, King's Abbot. Weekend cottage, Resthaven, "a box with a roof, severely modern and a little dull." Last known residence: Styles Court, Styles St. Mary.

BIRTH DATE: Probably in the mid-1800s. Monsieur Poirot retired as chief of the Belgian police sometime between 1908 and the outbreak of war in 1914, but his age at retirement is unknown. Those who have nothing better to do have estimated his life span at between 120 and 160 years.

BIRTHPLACE: Probably near Spa in the Belgian Ardennes forest.

FAMILY: Unlike Mycroft Holmes, Poirot's twin brother, Achille, is pure fiction. Intellectually gifted but indolent, Achille appears just once, in *The Big Four,* before going home "to the land of myths."

RELIGION: "bon Catholique"

LOVE LIFE: None that we know of, although there is speculation about his relationship with Madame Vera Rossakoff ("a sumptuous creature—a Bird of Paradise—a Venus" and the only woman to inspire Poirot to contemplate marriage). Some have questioned the paternity of Vera's only son, Niki.

BANK BALANCE: "Four hundred and forty-four pounds, four and fourpence," and never a pence less. Only one speculative holding: fourteen thousand shares in Burma Mines, Ltd.

HEALTH: Generally good despite a tendency to hypochondria. Sips a healthy "tisane" or chamomile tea to refresh the little grey cells. Suffers dreadfully from the "mal de mer" when traveling by sea or air, relieved by practicing the Laverguier method. ("You breathe in—and out—slowly, so—turning the head from left to right and counting six between each breath.") Late in life, Poirot is crippled by arthritis.

ASSOCIATES: Captain Arthur Hastings; Mrs. Pearson, landlady at Farraway Street; trusted valet George ("an extremely English-looking person. Tall, cadaverous and unemotional" and "a social snob"); personal assistant Miss Felicity Lemon ("a woman without imagination . . . a born secretary"); Chief Inspector James Japp ("jaunty and dapper"); mystery novelist Mrs. Ariadne Oliver; private investigator Mr. Goby; attorneys McNeil and Hodgson; assorted police types, including Superintendents Spence and Battle and Colonel Race; various high government officials, prime ministers, and European royalty. Well-known to readers of *Society Gossip* as "our own pet society detective."

FAVORITE FOODS AND DRINK: Croissants or brioche and thick hot chocolate for breakfast; French and Belgian haute cuisine; sweet desserts, especially cream cakes; fine wines, dark coffee, "sirop de cassis," Benedictine, and green crème de Menthe.

FAVORITE PASTIMES: Crosswords, jigsaw puzzles, and other games of order; building houses of cards and structures of wooden blocks; reading; sorting his wardrobe.

MAGNUM OPUS: In *Third Girl,* we learn that Poirot has completed for publication a major "analysis of great writers of detective fiction." (Hates Edgar Allan Poe.)

MOTTO: "Be prepared" and "suspect everybody"

MODUS OPERANDI: "Order and Method"

FAVORITE CASE: *Cards on the Table*

ONLY FAILED CASE: "The Chocolate Box" (also the only mystery set in his native Belgium)

FAVORITE EXPRESSIONS: "Sapristi!"; "Mon Dieu!"; "Sacre!"; "Epatant!"; "thirty-six times an idiot!"; "Nom d'un nom d'un nom!"

A MISS MARPLE QUESTIONNAIRE

• *How old is Miss Marple?*
Agatha Christie said that Miss Marple was born at about age sixty-five or seventy and never really aged. But in *At Bertram's Hotel* (1965) Agatha seems to pin down Miss Marple's year of birth. Early in the book, Miss Marple says that she "stayed" at Bertrams' once before, "when I was fourteen," with her aunt and her Uncle Thomas, Canon of Ely. Twenty pages on, a perfect Bertram's breakfast takes her "back to 1909." If Miss Marple was fourteen years old at the time of her only other visit to Bertram's in 1909, then she was born in 1895.

• *Where was she born?*
In *They Do It with Mirrors,* we learn that she grew up in "a Cathedral Close," which eliminates St. Mary Mead. In England, a "close" is an area in the precinct of a cathedral. This reference has led to the supposition that Miss Marple's father was possibly a vicar or a canon of the Church of England.

• *What was her mother's name?*

Just like Agatha's, Miss Marple's mother was named Clara.

• *Does she have siblings?*

We know of one sister, who married a West and became the mother
of Raymond. (West was the maiden name of Agatha's grandmother.)
There were possibly other siblings. In "The Thumbmark of St. Peter,"
Miss Marple tells about her niece Mabel, who is at least a quarter-
century older than Raymond West, and there are numerous references
to various nieces and nephews, great-nieces and great-nephews.

• *How was she educated?*

Like her creator, Jane Marple and her sister received their early education at home. In "The Four Suspects," Jane recalls "a German
governess" who taught the girls the language of flowers. Another governess, Miss Ledbury, is mentioned in *At Bertram's Hotel.* Jane attended
finishing school in Florence, where her closest friends were Ruth and
Carrie Louise Martin, sisters from the United States with whom Miss
Marple is reunited in *They Do It with Mirrors.* Though she admits that
she doesn't know "very much Latin," she was "well educated for the
standard of [her] day." Her schoolgirl ambition, by the way, was "to
nurse lepers. . . ."

• *What is her home address?*

Her small house, "Danemead," is located on the High Street, next
door to Dr. Haydock, and adjoining the vicarage at the rear. Address
letters to Miss Jane Marple, Danemead, St. Mary Mead, Radfordshire.

• *What is her source of income?*

Miss Marple must watch every penny because her income is limited.
She seems to have inherited her house, but all the extras (vacations,
home nursing when she's ill, the latest books and plays) are supplied by
her nephew Raymond. Her prized possessions include "the plate and
the King Charles tankard" and her "old Worcester tea set." In her last
case, she earns the enormous sum of £20,000 for completing a task
for her friend Jason Rafiel, deposited in Middleton's Bank, 132 High
Street, St. Mary Mead.

• *Does she have a lawyer?*

Mr. Petherick, a "very shrewd man and a really clever solicitor," handled
her legal matters for years. At his death, his son takes over, though Miss
Marple never feels quite so confident with the younger Petherick.

• *Who is her closest relative?*

Unquestionably, her nephew Raymond West, a successful novelist and poet, although Miss Marple doesn't altogether approve of his modern books "about rather unpleasant young men and women." Raymond and his wife, artist Joyce (or Joan) Lempriere West, are devoted to his aunt. In "Greenshaw's Folly," Raymond tells a visitor, "Some commit murder, some get mixed up in murders, others have murder thrust upon them. My Aunt Jane comes into the third category."

• *Does she have many friends?*

Miss Marple seems to have friends in every corner of England. Among her closest St. Mary Mead pals are Dolly and Colonel Arthur Bantry, who live at Gossington Hall; Dr. Pender, the parish clergyman, who is succeeded by Vicar Leonard (Len) Clement and his young wife, Griselda; Dr. Haydock, the "broad, big-shouldered" parish doctor and police surgeon; and the three village gossips, Miss Caroline Wetherby ("a mixture of vinegar and gush"), Miss Amanda Hartnell ("weather-beaten and jolly and much dreaded by the poor"), and Mrs. Martha Price Ridley ("a rich and dictatorial widow"). Outside her village, Miss Marple keeps company with Maud Dane Calthrop and her husband, the Reverend Caleb Dane Calthrop, vicar of Much Deeping; Lady Selina Hazy of Leicestershire; "dear Robbie," the Bishop of Westchester, who may also be a nephew or godson; Mrs. Elspeth McGillicuddy, who lives in Scotland; wealthy Jason Rafiel, her ally and benefactor; Sir Henry Clithering, former commissioner of Scotland Yard and his godson; Detective Inspector Dermot Craddock; and so on and so forth. When in Chipping Cleghorn, she is a most welcome guest in the child-cluttered home of her "favorite godchild," Diana Harmon, called "Bunch," and her husband, the Reverend Julian Harmon.

• *What does she look like?*

When Gwenda Reed is first introduced to Miss Marple in *Sleeping Murder,* she sees "an attractive old lady, tall and thin, with pink cheeks and blue eyes, and a gentle, rather fussy manner." In *A Murder Is Announced,* Dermot Craddock's first impression is of a lady who "seemed very old. She had snow-white hair and a pink, crinkled face and very soft, innocent blue eyes, and she was heavily enmeshed in fleecy wool." She dresses in black lace at first meeting, later in simple black dresses and tweed suits with her ever-present knitted woolen shawls. For dinner at a Caribbean resort, she prefers grey lace "in the best traditions of the provincial gentlewomen of England. . . ." In *A Pocket Full of Rye,* we learn that her excellent posture is the result of using a backboard as a girl. Her voice is described as "fluting." She is a regular customer of Mrs. Jameson, also known as "DIANE, Hair Stylist," who caters to St. Mary Mead's "solid, stick-in-the mud, middle-aged ladies. . . ."

• *How is her health?*
Generally better than she lets on. She is a little deaf, but her eyesight is sharp. She had a broken wrist once, and her rheumatism can be bothersome. An "uncertain" left knee may slow her down, but she can move swiftly when confronting a killer, as in *Sleeping Murder* and *Nemesis.* She recovers from bronchitis and pneumonia. Sometimes she colludes with Dr. Haydock to " 'create' a little condition that might necessitate a trip to the shore." The good doctor's professional opinion is that for a woman her age "and in spite of that misleading frail appearance," Miss Marple is "in remarkably good fettle." Mistrustful of modern-day medications, she relies on homemade herbal mixtures, Easton's syrup, and a little glass of sherry for medicinal purposes.

• *Where does she find all those housemaids?*
Most of Miss Marple's maids come from St. Faith's Orphanage, where she serves on the board and helps with the fund-raising. In her home, an endless parade of Amys and Claras and Alices are trained in domestic service, deportment, and household management. Miss Marple is a taskmaster, but not unkind. She maintains contacts with the best of her "girls" and can rely on them when help is needed—like dear Gladys, who does a bit of investigating in "Sanctuary," and the faithful Florence, who opens her home to Miss Marple in *4.50 from Paddington.* Her last live-in helpers come from the Development that crops up in postwar St. Mary Mead. Cherry Baker is hired to help Miss Marple with cleaning, but winds up staying, with her husband, Jim: "Cherry . . . had qualities that to Miss Marple at this moment seemed of supreme importance: Warm-heartedness, vitality, and a deep interest in everything that was going on."

• *What does she like for breakfast?*
In a perfect world with perfect cooks and maids, Miss Marple would wake each day to one egg "boiled exactly three and three-quarter minutes," toast "evenly browned," served with a pat of butter and a little jar of honey, and tea "properly made with boiling water."

• *Does she follow the news?*
Two newspapers arrive at Danemead in the morning, but Miss Marple gives her attention first to the *Daily Newsgiver,* which she has nick-

named "The Daily All-Sorts." After lunch, she settles down in her "specially purchased, upright armchair" to peruse *The Times.* She reads the front page, skims the table of contents, then on to the births, marriages, and deaths. "It's sad really, but nowadays one is only interested in the deaths!"

• **Does she have a favorite book?**
Like Agatha Christie and her mother before her, Miss Marple keeps one book by her always, a well-thumbed copy of *Imitation of Christ* by the German theologian Thomas à Kempis.

• **What was her last mystery?**
There are two possible answers. *Sleeping Murder* was released posthumously in 1976 but was actually written in 1940–1941 and stored away by Agatha's publisher in case their popular author should meet an early end in World War Two. In order of writing, *Sleeping Murder* comes between *Murder at the Vicarage* and *The Body in the Library.* The last Miss Marple book that Agatha wrote was *Nemesis* (1971).

WHERE IN THE WORLD IS ST. MARY MEAD?

Home of Jane Marple and one of the best known of all quaint English hamlets, St. Mary Mead was first visited in *The Mystery of the Blue Train* (1928), before readers were introduced to the remarkable Miss Marple. It was located in the county of Kent, and as the local doctor's wife says, ". . . things don't happen in St. Mary Mead."

The same year *Blue Train* appeared, Agatha Christie returned to St. Mary Mead in her first series of Miss Marple short stories, but its actual location became more problematic. Readers learned, in *Murder at the Vicarage,* that St. Mary Mead is close to the town of Much Benham. In *The Body in the Library,* Colonel Melchett, chief constable of the county of Radfordshire, tells us that Much Benham is about eighteen miles from Danemouth, "a large and fashionable watering place on the coast."

After World War Two, modern housing developments (inspired by the new construction Agatha saw around Oxford) nearly span the distance between St. Mary Mead and Much Benham, to Miss Marple's dismay. A movie studio "towards Market Basing" attracts various cinema types to the quiet village. But even in the 1950s and 1960s—when frequent sonic booms from jets based at a nearby airfield shatter the glass in Miss Marple's greenhouse—"the old-world core" of St. Mary Mead persists, and The Blue Boar pub (an occasional inquest site) still serves "a first-rate meal of the joint and two vegetable type."

But where is St. Mary Mead? Definitely not in the Cotswolds or near Agatha's hometown of Torquay in Devon. Nor is it the real town of Marple, on the outskirts of Manchester in Cheshire, which was the site of a now-destroyed manor house, Marple Hall. Agatha happily admitted that Marple Hall provided the name of her spinster sleuth, but not the location of her village.

Repeatedly, Agatha describes St. Mary Mead as lying south of London. In the last Miss Marple novel, *Nemesis,* St. Mary Mead is "only about twenty-five miles" from Alton, Hants (a real place), and "only twelve miles from the coast at Loomouth." Miss Marple further describes her village as a "very small place halfway between Loomouth and Market Basing. About twenty-five miles from London."

Since Danemouth, Loomouth, Much Benham, and Market Basing are imaginary, we are left with educated guesses. In a Poirot novel, we learn that Market Basing is found in Berkshire. If Danemouth and Loomouth could be Brighton (one of England's most popular coastal resort cities) and Eastbourne . . . if the airfield from which those bothersome jets fly could be Gatwick . . . and if Alton, Hants is just what it seems, then St. Mary Mead should be found in an area between the counties of Sussex and Surrey. Possibly south of Crawley, through which Agatha may have wandered in her little gray auto during her years as a suburban housewife married to Archie Christie. Possibly amid real-life villages with names like Cowfold and Pease Pottage.

Does it matter? No. But it is a mystery, and in *The Murder at the Vicarage* Vicar Leonard Clement warns us never to "underestimate the detective instinct of village life."

MRS. ARIADNE OLIVER: DOPPELGANGER

As a rule, Agatha Christie kept herself out of her detective writing. But every rule has its exception, and Agatha's was Mrs. Ariadne Oliver. No less an authority than Max Mallowan, Agatha's second husband, recognized Mrs. Oliver as "lightly sketched, but a portrayal of Agatha herself. . . ."

We first meet Ariadne in a Parker Pyne story, "The Case of the Discontented Soldier." In a room cluttered with "notebooks, a general confusion of loose manuscripts and a large bag of apples," she hammers out fanciful scenarios for Pyne's wish-fulfillment business. She is described as a "sensational novelist," the author of forty-six bestsellers translated into "French, German, Italian, Hungarian, Finnish, Japanese and Abyssinian." In 1937, Agatha elevated Mrs. Oliver to a leading role. In *Cards on the Table,* she is one of four sleuths invited to a macabre party with four successful murderers. She is soon off on the trail of a killer—her ditzy detection based on unconditional faith in "Woman's Intuition."

At home in her Harley Street flat, Mrs. Oliver dithers and tears at her hair as she voices her latest plot twists aloud and wrestles with her fictional detective. Sven Hjerson—"the revolting man. . . . Why a Finn when I know nothing about Finland? Why a vegetarian? Why all the idiotic mannerisms he's got?" Writing drives her crazy, but Mrs. Oliver likes the income: "Some days I can only keep going by repeating over and over to myself the amount of money I might get for my next serial rights." Her books have a familiar ring: *The Affair of the Second Goldfish, Death of a Debutante,* even *The Body in the Library.* But their popularity is agony for the publicity-shy Mrs. Oliver, who avoids public events because she can't cope with fawning fans. On the whole she thinks that "trees are much nicer than people, more restful."

In appearance, she is a large, disheveled, fiftyish woman with "an agreeable, engaging smile rather like that of an impudent small child." Hercule Poirot notes her "rather noble face, the massive brow, the untidy billows of grey hair. . . ." A nonsmoking teetotaler, she consumes quantities of strong black coffee and buttered toast and leaves a trail of apple cores wherever she goes. She loves redecorating, has a mania for shopping, is loyal to her friends, and adores her many godchildren.

Of Mr. Oliver we know nothing, and there's no hint of romance in Ariadne's hectic life. She is called "a hot-headed feminist" but prefers the company of men. Her friendship with Poirot deepens over the years: "On occasion she maddened him. At the same time he was really very attached to her." The two have six adventures—*Cards on the Table, Mrs. McGinty's Dead, Dead Man's Folly, Third Girl, Hallowe'en Party,* and *Elephants Can Remember.* Only in *The Pale Horse* is she left mostly to her own devices. It's possible that in Ariadne, Agatha had at last found a satisfactory "stooge" to replace Arthur Hastings, and Mrs. Oliver is at the old Belgian's side in the last three Poirot novels Christie wrote. All in all, Ariadne Oliver is a formidable woman and a merry mirror for the creator—a comic doppelganger who provides a glimpse into the reality of Agatha Christie and her quirks.

INNOCENCE AND JUSTICE

Agatha Christie maintained that in her books, as in life, "It is *innocence* that matters; not *guilt.*" Protection of the innocent is her single most persistent theme, and her concept of innocence was biblical: "The more passionately alive the victim, the more glorious indignation I have on his behalf, and am full of a delighted triumph when I have delivered a near-victim out of the valley of the shadow of death."

She defined "victim" to include those wrongly suspected of crime as well as the bystanders affected, even tangentially, by wrongdoing. In her autobiography, she pleaded, "The *innocent* must be protected; they must be able to live at peace and charity with their neighbours." And if the innocent cannot live in peace, they may—in books like *Five Little Pigs, Sleeping Murder,* and *Postern of Fate*—be exonerated and avenged after death.

More than any of her other detectives, Miss Jane Marple was the keeper of Agatha's conscience. When, in *The Body in the Library,* a young blond woman is found strangled at Gossington Hall, Miss Marple's friend Colonel Bantry becomes the immediate subject of village innuendo. Of course no one thinks the retired colonel killed the girl, but you know how the old man flirts and . . . Ugly suspicion is the crime that engages Miss Marple; she knows that unfounded gossip and unchecked speculation will destroy the spirit of this proud, if somewhat foolish, old soldier if she fails to take on the case. In *A Caribbean Mystery,* Agatha came straight out and named her old spinster "Nemesis"—the Greek goddess of righteous anger. Then in *Nemesis,* Agatha delved into the most ancient themes of human emotion, pitting Miss Marple against three women whose very names—Clotilde, Lavinia, and Anthea—recall the Greek goddesses Clotho, Lachesis, and Atropos—the Fates who control human destiny.

Perhaps what always attracted Agatha to the detective genre was its clear-cut delineation of good and evil. "The detective story," she wrote, "was the story of the chase; it was also very much a story with a moral; in fact it was the old Everyman Morality Tale, the hunting down of Evil and the triumph of Good. . . ." Max Mallowan agreed: "The task of Hercule Poirot, of Miss Marple and all the others . . . is the relentless and fearless pursuit of the wicked. Here there is no room for any relaxation of moral standards. Evil must be pursued to the end."

THE MYSTERY OF THE PICKLED SHRIMPS

They make their debut in the very first Miss Marple story, "The Tuesday Night Club":

"I know just the sort of thing you mean, dear," said Miss Marple. "For instance Mrs. Carruthers had a very strange experience yesterday morning. She bought two gills of pickled shrimps at Elliot's.

She called at two other shops and when she got home she found she had not got the shrimps with her. She went back to the two shops she had visited but these shrimps had completely disappeared. Now that seems to me very remarkable."

They're back in "A Christmas Tragedy"—pickled (or picked) shrimps "that disappeared so incomprehensibly. . . ." Apparently the solution has been found, for Miss Marple declares that "it all turned out to be so trivial, though throwing a considerable light on human nature." In *Murder at the Vicarage,* Miss Marple's first novel, the old lady teases curiosity with her mention of "the gill of picked shrimps that amused dear Griselda so much—a quite unimportant mystery but absolutely incomprehensible unless one solves it right." Griselda Clement later tells us that Miss Marple's solution had something to do with an analogy to "a sack of coals." And in *Sleeping Murder,* Miss Marple's nephew Raymond West brings the whole issue up yet again: "Why a gill of pickled shrimp was found where it was. . . . All grist to my Aunt Jane's mill." So what did become of the missing gill of shrimp? That's for Miss Marple to know.

AGATHA SPEAKS . . . THE MOST LIKELY SUSPECT

Rarely in her detective fiction did Agatha Christie directly address her readers, but for *Cards on the Table,* a Poirot mystery published in 1936, she wrote a unique "Foreword by the Author." Agatha, who had taken substantial critical heat for following a least-likely-suspect strategy in her books, warned her readers that they were about to begin something different: "There are only *four* starters, and any one of them, *given the right circumstances,* might have committed the crime." The list of potential perpetrators—all of whom have apparently committed murder in the past—is divulged in Chapter 2, and the author remained true to her promise.

In fact, Agatha always advocated the most-likely-suspect approach. In explaining the process that she followed to develop her first novel, *The Mysterious Affair at Styles,* she said, "The whole point of a *good* detective story was that [the murderer] must be somebody obvious but at the same time, for some reason, you would then find that it was *not* obvious. . . ." Unlike Mary Roberts Rinehart, for example, Agatha would never drag a new suspect in at the last minute. She didn't toy with readers by concealing clues or introducing some unknown quantity to get her detectives to the right solution. It was Agatha's special genius for plot construction and details that enabled her to divert attention from the most likely suspect until the end. The careful reader might be flummoxed, but never cheated.

Cards on the Table is, in its deviousness, nearly on a par with *The Murder of Roger Ackroyd*. In the latter, the final revelation comes as a shock. In the former, the possible murderer is clearly identified from the start. But in both cases, when Monsieur Poirot unmasks the villain, it is the person most likely, by motive and opportunity, to have done the deed. The reader who feels tricked is the one who hasn't paid attention.

WHOSE IDEA WAS IT TO KILL ROGER ACKROYD?

In 1926, *The Murder of Roger Ackroyd* delighted many, angered some, and just plain annoyed a few. Not that the story was lurid or violent; the source of the uproar was the ending. It was so totally unexpected! *Roger Ackroyd* was an audacious exercise in a genre that followed rigid rules, and what Agatha did in this book, no one had done before (although her daring plot device was anticipated in *The Man in the Brown Suit*). Readers naturally wondered where she got the idea.

The inspiration came from two sources: an offhand remark by her brother-in-law, James Watts, and a more specific suggestion from a devoted reader (and later admiral of the British Fleet), Lord Louis Mountbatten. Jimmy Watts planted the seed. "Almost everybody turns out to be a criminal nowadays in detective stories," he complained, "even the detective." He went on to express his particular take on the whodunit, and Agatha found in his words "a remarkably original thought." Then in March 1924, she received a letter from Mountbatten, who had read her Poirot stories in the *Sketch* magazine. A writer himself, he volunteered a plot line for her consideration. Writing to Lord Louis in 1969, Agatha said, "I thought it a most attractive idea—one which had never been done—but I had great doubts if I could ever do it. But it was a great challenge! It stayed at the back of my mind and I gnawed at it— rather like a dog with a bone."

Agatha repaid her debt to Mountbatten by entrusting one of her favorite novels, *Murder on the Orient Express,* to his son-in-law, film producer John Brabourne. To Jimmy Watts, she'd said her thanks many years earlier, dedicating *Hercule Poirot's Christmas* (1938) to her adored brother-in-law, "the most faithful and kindly of my readers. . . ."

DOROTHY L. SAYERS

THE PASSIONATE MIND

*"I dramatised myself, and have at all periods of my life continued
to dramatise myself . . . but at all times with a perfect realisation
that I was the creator, not the subject, of these fantasies."*
— *My Edwardian Childhood*

Dorothy L. Sayers

Dorothy L. Sayers requested that no
biography be written of her life until
at least fifty years after her passing. A
half-century was enough time, she
reasoned, to determine if her works
were still valued and, by implication, if
she would be worth remembering. By
the early 1970s—a mere decade and a
half after her death—it appeared that
her caution had been prophetic:
Dorothy L. Sayers seemed doomed to
become one of the marginal names in
detective fiction. The twelve novels
that had made her one of the giants of
the British Golden Age were in
eclipse, and relatively few (though
fiercely loyal) readers were acquainted with her masterful sleuth, the noble Lord Peter Wimsey.

But the fates conspired to save Sayers's name from limbo. Buoyed by
the new wave of feminism, women looking for literary role models rediscovered her work and her life. Then, beginning in 1973, a television
series produced by the British Broadcasting Corporation and adapted
from the Wimsey books introduced a new generation to the charming
and capricious Lord Peter and by extension, his creator.

One of the first to tackle Sayers as biographical subject was British writer Janet Hitchman. In her research for *Such a Strange Lady,* Hitchman performed a feat of detection worthy of Lord Peter himself. Curious about the origins of Dorothy Sayers's "adopted" son, the biographer turned to Somerset House, England's archive of birth and death; there she uncovered a secret to which only a half-dozen or so people had been privy during Dorothy's life—the secret that in many ways shaped the course of her adult life, colored her work, and belied the public image of this most complex woman.

Those who had encountered the public Dorothy L. Sayers at the height of her career remembered a large, mannish, boisterous woman with a prodigious intellect, a love of intense argument, and a loud and often vulgar mouth. The public Dorothy Sayers of the 1930s and 1940s seemed confident to the point of combativeness. Undoubtedly those closest to her sensed the depths of her passions, uncertainties, and fears, though even her dearest friends were denied access to her secrets. But Dorothy deliberately manufactured her fiction out of personal experience, ideas, and beliefs—consciously and unconsciously littering her novels, plays, and even her nonfiction writings with a trail of clues to her life. Thanks to her published work, her private fragments, and most important, her extraordinary gift for letter-writing, we can now become acquainted with the real woman of mystery who was Dorothy L. Sayers.

*"I am a citizen of no mean city."** *

Dorothy Leigh Sayers was born in a small, seventeenth-century house at 1 Brewer Street in the university city of Oxford on June 13, 1893. She was the one and only offspring of parents somewhat past their prime childbearing years and, consequently, was pampered and indulged from the start.

Her mother, Helen Mary Leigh Sayers—called Nell or Nellie—had come from the town of Shirley, near the southern coastal cities of Bournemouth and Southampton; she was the daughter of a lawyer and niece of the well-known literary humorist Percival Leigh. The Leighs traced their lineage to the reign of Henry III and had a history as landed gentry on the Isle of Wight. Nell was, according to her daughter, "a woman of exceptional intellect, which unfortunately never got the ed-

---

* This quotation of St. Paul (Acts 21:39) is the opening line of *My Edwardian Childhood,* an unpublished autobiographical fragment written in the 1930s. Unless otherwise noted, quotations are from Dorothy L. Sayers's letters and unpublished autobiographical writings. The reference to "no mean city" also appears in *Gaudy Night,* Dorothy's Oxford mystery.

ucation it deserved." A "vivacious and attractive woman," though by no means a beauty, Nell is most frequently described as lively and spirited with a well-developed sense of humor, though she also had a darker side that later manifested itself in frightening episodes of nervous prostration.

Dorothy's father, the Reverend Henry Sayers, was the more strait-laced of the pair: tall, bald, and properly subdued. The son of a minister of Irish descent, Henry had taken his degree in divinity at Magdalen College of Oxford University. Ordained a priest of the Church of England in 1880, Henry took a position as headmaster of a school for boys in Tenbury. Four years later, he returned to Oxford as headmaster of the Christ Church Choir School and chaplain of Christ Church Cathedral. This post neatly combined his musical talents (Henry was an accomplished singer, composer of hymns, and violinist) with his scholarly interests, especially in Latin studies, and he remained at the school for thirteen years.

Henry and Nell were married when he was thirty-nine and she was thirty-six, and Dorothy arrived a year later. With her coming, the Old Choir House in Brewer Street was jammed to its historic rafters with Henry, Nell, and their daughter, Dorothy's maiden aunts Mabel Leigh and Gertrude Sayers, her Grannie Sayers, a nursemaid, and sundry servants. Soon after Dorothy's birth, the whole kit and caboodle moved on to a newer, more spacious Choir House on the same street.

Although she spent only the first few years of her childhood in Oxford, Dorothy retained bright memories of the city of her birth. In her unpublished autobiographical fragment, *My Edwardian Childhood,* she vividly recalled excursions to the Christ Church meadow and games with her nurse among the elm trees of Oxford's Broad Walk; the mechanical false teeth that chattered in the window of a dentist's High Street office; the Choir School's English sheepdog, "Scruggs" (immortalized in *The Five Red Herrings*); the ringing of the Tom Tower clock, which struck 101 times every night at five minutes past nine. Dorothy was inordinately proud of her Oxford birth and her baptism in the Christ Church Cathedral (with her father officiating), and she returned to the great university center many times, both in body and in spirit.

A precocious child, she was blessed with a quick mind. Encouraged by her proud parents, she was totally at ease in the company of adults. She also possessed a quick temper, which would plague her later years. Her earliest memory, she claimed, was of throwing a tantrum that involved screaming at the top of her strong lungs and rolling about on the floor.

As a result of being frequently read to by her parents, she had taught herself to read by age four and was enchanted by the stories of Uncle

Remus and the Brothers Grimm and by Lewis Carroll's Alice tales. This early exposure nurtured a love of the magic of words and language that endured for a lifetime. She had few playmates, with the exception of her cousin Margaret Leigh, so her earliest imaginative adventures involved her favorite toys: two monkey dolls named Jacko and Jocko—the former "puckish, mischievous . . . always in disgrace"; the latter "utterly virtuous and amiable"—and a villainous rag doll named Frenchman.

In 1897, Henry Sayers took the offer of the rectorship at Bluntisham-cum-Earith in East Anglia. Bluntisham and Earith are neighboring villages in a Fen country farming community near Huntingdon (Cambridgeshire). Perhaps because of the isolation of the parish, the Church provided well for its rector; his living included a large house with two acres of gardens at Bluntisham. Dorothy later surmised that her father was tired of teaching and welcomed the change. For her mother, however, the relocation to Bluntisham meant abandoning the social life of Oxford and the close company of friends and relatives.

Little "Dossie" was four and a half when the family moved, and she never forgot the golden winter aconites that lined the rectory's drive when she arrived, accompanied by her nurse and the family's parrot. The new rector brought a large entourage, including his mother, Aunt Mabel (Nell's sister), and the Oxford servants, all of whom had elected to remain with the family. Aunt Gertrude Sayers was also provided for; while not a permanent resident, she enjoyed frequent, extended stays at Bluntisham.

The Victorian manse—repaired and handsomely refurbished by a firm of Oxford decorators hired and directed by Nell—offered a wealth of possibilities for an imaginative child. There were spaces for everyone, including day and night nurseries for Dorothy, two drawing rooms, and her father's study with its American organ. The house lacked electricity and running water, and the servants were forever climbing the backstairs with pails of water for washing and bathing. For Dorothy, the grounds provided lawns and gardens where she could run and play, fruit trees and plantings from which she could gorge on fresh berries, peaches, and plums (saving her from the Leigh family curse of constipation), and a paddock for a pony named Jenny who carted the family from place to place before the acquisition of a Model T Ford. The flat, fertile countryside was wildly beautiful and ominously dangerous. The Fens—thirty square miles of peat marsh that had been drained and diked in the mid-seventeenth century—held the constant threat of flooding, and the man-made system of drainage canals and earthen dams required constant care. Even at the opening of the twentieth century, the farmers and villagers of Bluntisham and Earith were acutely mindful of the disastrous flood of 1713; Dorothy must have heard many accounts of this landmark event from which she drew inspiration for the climactic Fen flood in *The Nine Tailors*.

The whole Sayers family tended to the parish. Henry was a conscientious and caring shepherd to his conservative flock, and Nell was particularly attentive to the needs of the poor. But Grannie Sayers, herself a pastor's widow, often took too much interest in the affairs of others and was frequently present where she was not wanted. Though Dorothy was never very fond of her grandmother (or any of her Sayers relatives), she was to paint gentle portraits of dedicated country parsons and their wives in *The Nine Tailors* and also *Busman's Honeymoon*.

Dorothy's childhood was in many ways idyllic. She was educated at home by her parents and a series of governesses. Her day nursery was converted to a schoolroom, and the yearly calendar was divided into proper semesters and vacations. Her father began her Latin studies when she was six, and she was to learn excellent French and passable German from her governesses and au pairs. Dorothy's academic training concentrated on literature, languages, and music, with only passing attention to mathematics and science—a failing that was to cost her dearly when she was sent to boarding school. She had inherited her father's musical talents; he began her violin instruction when she was six or seven, and she also studied piano and singing. From time to time, other children joined her classroom, including Betty Osborne, who became one of Dorothy's few childhood friends, and a young boarder named Guy Cooke, of whom Dorothy, the pampered only child, was viciously jealous. (Even after his death in World War One, she maintained her petulant dislike of him.) Over the years, the Sayerses took in a number of male boarders, youngsters like Guy and older students who were tutored by Henry.

The whole family loved reading aloud, and Dorothy especially enjoyed her grandmother's renderings of the works of Sir Walter Scott and Aunt Mabel's vivid readings of Dickens. Dorothy's taste for literary blood and thunder translated into her role-playing. She was soon writing poetry and creating heroic plays in which she invariably was the hero and family and staff were enlisted as supporting cast members. Her parents stoked this love of drama by providing the costuming and props for her plays and serving as enthusiastic audience. Henry and Nell also took her to London at least once a year to see grown-up productions.

In the rough country environment of Bluntisham, Dorothy grew strong and tall. Through the indulgence of her parents and teachers, she was nurtured on the classics and the robust literature of epic adventure and romance. Her talents—poetry, music, love of learning and disputation—were nourished and encouraged. Perhaps too much encouraged.

"She was self-absorbed, egotistical, timid, priggish, and in
a mild sort of way, disobedient."   —Cat o'Mary

In her late thirties, Dorothy wrote two autobiographical pieces: the
memoir *My Edwardian Childhood* and the opening section of a novel titled *Cat o'Mary.* Both works were abandoned, and neither has ever been
published. Dorothy's biographers, including James Brabazon, whose
1981 book was "authorized" by Dorothy's son, are generally agreed that
these fragments from the 1930s were, in fact, psychological exorcisms.
As Brabazon comments, "Dorothy, for some reason, seems to have
needed to go back over [her childhood] and lay it bare in some detail. . . ." From the plateau of middle age, Dorothy looked down on the
child she had been, and she did *not* like what she saw. When, in the character of Katherine Lammas—the heroine of *Cat o'Mary* and a thinly
veiled incarnation of herself—Dorothy examined an only child raised
with every whim indulged, learning to manipulate adults at an early age,
convinced of her own intellectual superiority, ". . . it was with a hatred
of anything so lacking in those common human virtues which were to
be attained in after years at so much cost and with such desperate difficulty. . . . Strangers rightly considered her a prig."

Priggish she probably was. Naturally bright and clever, Dorothy was
prompted by her elders to show off at every opportunity. In *Cat o'Mary*
she told the story of a song that Katherine-Dorothy sang before bed
every night. The last line of the ditty ran, "I must love dolly best," but
the child learned to substitute for "dolly" the name of a family member,
rewarding or punishing the adults as the mood struck her. The grown-
ups played into this spiteful little game, waiting each evening to hear
which of them had won the child's affection that day.

Dorothy's cousins Margaret Leigh and Gerald and Raymond Sayers
occasionally came to stay at the rectory, but in a time of rigid adherence
to class divisions, the communities of Bluntisham and Earith offered virtually no middle class from which to draw acceptable playmates for the
rector's daughter. Although local children were sometimes included in
her schoolroom, except for Betty Osborne, Dorothy had no consistent
exposure to her peers until she was well into her teens. She was never
forced to compete for attention, and outside of rigidly structured settings
such as dancing class, she was rarely exposed to the rough-and-tumble
of socialization. Spoiled by adults without the balancing competition
with and companionship of other children, Dorothy learned to trust her
own knowledge and judgment above those of all others. In modern
parlance, she was steeped in self-esteem. In *Cat o'Mary,* she wrote of her
alter ego, Katherine Lammas, "She liked correcting other people, but
didn't like being corrected herself, and would argue a point with obsti-

nacy. She had a great opinion of her own cleverness, and to be proved wrong was humiliating."

Dorothy, who always had a low tolerance for children, was perhaps excessively hard in her evaluation of her young self, for she doesn't appear to have been a particularly troublesome child. What discipline she required was "imposed from inside and not outside" as she was expected to learn and follow the moral proscriptions of "duty, self-control, contentment with one's lot, obedience,"[*] and so forth. But the manner of her upbringing had telling consequences.

As an adult, she complained bitterly about her "cosseted" childhood. Sheltered from real emotional trials, she instinctively turned to literature for her concepts of feelings, weighing her own responses against those in books, and often finding herself wanting. As James Brabazon points out, Dorothy did not confuse reality and fantasy, "but she did expect that the feelings and behaviour of people in books would correspond with those of real people—including herself. She was puzzled that she was unable to experience some of the emotions described so convincingly in books. . . ." So Dorothy's play-making was more than a clever child's fun. It was a means to experience the emotional array that was effectively denied to her by her carefully circumscribed existence and her own generally sanguine temperament.

> *"What long talks we shall have together in the red firelight . . . long talks, with nobody to be bored by our conversation. . . ."*
>
> —letter to Ivy Shrimpton, November 1908

Dorothy's first real friend was her cousin Ivy Shrimpton. Ivy, the daughter of one of Nell's sisters, was born in California but had moved back to Oxford with her parents. Eight years older than Dorothy, Ivy was gifted with an ability to deal with children and treat them with genuine respect. The friendship between the two girls blossomed during one of Ivy's frequent visits to Bluntisham, when she was sixteen and Dorothy was eight. The cousins shared a love of reading, and Ivy introduced Dorothy to *Little Women* and *Ingoldby's Legends.* Ivy was also ready to discuss ideas and debate seriously and to play active roles in her younger cousin's extravagant fantasies.

When she was thirteen, Dorothy read Alexandre Dumas's *The Three Musketeers* in French and was so taken with the romantic adventure that

---

[*] From a 1948 letter to Barbara Reynolds, quoted in Dr. Reynolds's 1993 biography, *Dorothy L. Sayers: Her Life and Soul.*

she cast her entire household as characters from the novel. Her father became King Louis XIII, her mother was Cardinal Richelieu, and Aunt Gertrude became Madame de Bois-Tracy. Betty Osborne played Aramis; the French au pair of the moment was Porthos; and the governess, Miss Hamilton, was d'Artagnan. Ivy became the beautiful Duchess of Chevreuse, and Dorothy took the part of the lovesick hero Athos. Even the household and gardening staff were drafted into bit parts when Dorothy staged her re-creation of the swashbuckling novel in the schoolroom of the Bluntisham rectory, rechristened the Château de Bragelonne. She was to play at being Athos for years, and at least until she was seventeen, she continued to address family members by their fictional names and titles.

She wrote frequent, chatty letters to Ivy—addressed from "Bragelonne"—recounting family gossip and activities, discussing books and music, and revealing details of various crushes. One object of her affections was a dark-eyed visitor who was code-named "Dull Red" by the girls for his color choice when playing croquet. At Christmas in 1908, Dorothy's parents took her to see a London production of *Henry V,* and Dorothy immediately wrote to Ivy (already expressing herself in the exuberant style that will be familiar to readers of the Wimsey mysteries), ". . . I have fallen madly, hopelessly, desperately in love. . . ." The object of this outpouring was a popular, middle-aged actor named Lewis Waller, and if Dorothy's confession of love was histrionic, her grip on reality was secure: "Unfortunately I fear that my passion is totally unrequited."

It was around this time that Dorothy experienced a kind of intellectual revelation that ignited her: she discovered that Ahasuerus, about whom she read in the Bible, was also Xerxes, whom she had studied in history. People, things, ideas suddenly connected, "like fitting together two pieces of a puzzle and hearing all the other pieces fall into place one after the other, locking and clicking." Using geometry, she located an overgrown tennis court in the garden. Again she made the connection: ". . . the lovely satisfying unity of things—the wedding of the thing learnt and the thing done—the great intellectual fulfillment." The quick child had, on her own, grasped the concept that centuries of good teachers have tried to pound into young minds, that learning is not an isolated endeavor and that "lessons . . . were part of everything else." Whatever befell her, she knew that it was somehow part of a greater pattern.

*"She would be either the school star or the school butt.
Which? She had not imagined that it was perfectly
possible to be both."*
                                                        —Cat o'Mary

In June 1908, when she had just turned fifteen, Dorothy donned the
mask of Athos to announce that she was to be sent to boarding school.
"I am leaving the Court," she wrote to Ivy. "Out and alas! for our noble
company. The grand bond will be broken forever after Christmas! for
ever and ever. And now, no more shall the Four Musketeers walk side by
side in the garden, or fight together for the King."

Her parents had determined that she was destined for university education, and they may also have finally realized how much she needed the
company of peers. The decision to send her to boarding school may
have been difficult, but given the poverty of advanced education in their
area, Henry and Nell had no real choice. They settled on the Godolphin
School, to the south in Salisbury, where Dorothy would join some two
hundred other girls under the tutelage of Miss Alice Mary Douglas, her
sister Lucy, and their staff of teachers. For some reason, Dorothy was to
enter at midyear, so on January 17, 1909, she arrived at Godolphin for
her first extended stay away from home and family and her first experience of competitive academics among girls of her own station.

Her biographers disagree about her reactions to boarding school. Her
first days could not have been comfortable; Miss Douglas had mistakenly
classified Dorothy as an eight-year-old entering student. Then, because
of her poor mathematics skills, she was placed in the lower fifth form,
behind most girls of her age. Certainly she was well-read and accomplished in languages, surprising her French mistress with her knowledge
of Molière and her command of subjunctive forms. But she was an odd
and gawky girl, "a fish out of water" in the company of social equals,
physically awkward, argumentative, and bossy. She was not especially
popular with her schoolmates;* nor, to her astonishment, with her
teachers. Early on, the Godolphin staff judged her to be gifted but superficial and unable to accept criticism. At the beginning of her second
term, Dorothy wrote her parents that "Fanny M. [Florence Mildred
White, the French teacher for whom Dorothy had great respect] read
me a little lecture on Friday, saying that I'd had wonderful advantages,
and must not be too exalted!"

---

* Mystery writer Josephine Bell was almost thirteen when she was sent to board at
Godolphin and met Dorothy, then eighteen. She remembered Dorothy as not pretty
but "strikingly different." Bell recalled that Dorothy was lively and excessively talkative, but she "made little stir in the school." ("A Face-to-Face Encounter with Sayers" by Josephine Bell. In *Murderess Ink,* edited by Dilys Winn. 1979.)

Going strictly by Dorothy's letters home—letters that effervesce with excitement about activities and gossip about pupils and teachers—she would seem to have adjusted well to Godolphin. But her later comments and occasional off-key remarks in her letters paint another picture.

Dorothy certainly threw herself into activities at the school. She continued her violin and piano lessons and played first violin in the school orchestra. She attended and participated in theatricals, at one point considering a stage career for herself, though her teachers opined that she was better suited to be a dramatist than an actor. She excelled in the subjects she liked and continued to slough off those that bored her, notably history and mathematics. (She once wrote home in fury about a teacher who had accused her of "[spending] more time than I ought over my French and [slacking] over all my other work. . . .") She participated in organized debates with faculty members (". . . you can argufy with your revered form mistress till all's blue if you like, and pour out your sarcasm . . . with crushing force.")

She found a few friends, particularly Violet Christy, who shared her interests in playacting and literature, and Molly Edmondson, a girl whom Dorothy described as being, like herself, "considered a 'weird freak' by the conventional portion of this establishment." She continued to nourish her "pash" for the unattainable actor Lewis Waller. She developed other crushes, one on the handsome Antarctic explorer Sir Ernest Shackleton, whose lecture at Godolphin inspired Dorothy to write a sonnet in his honor. On more solid ground, she practiced her flirting on her cousin Raymond Sayers, who treated her to an evening in London on her sixteenth birthday. She also experienced the inevitable, chaste, girls' school crush on her favorite teacher, Miss White.

In 1910, Henry and Nell determined that their daughter should be confirmed with other Godolphin girls in a mass ceremony at Salisbury Cathedral. To a letter describing the ceremony to her parents—the setting, her dress and white veil, her first communion, the sermon—she added a poignant postscript: "I never can write about my *feelings*—that's why I haven't." But years later, she recalled, "Being baptized without one's will is certainly not so harmful as being confirmed against one's will, which is what happened to me and gave me a resentment against religion in general which lasted a long time. . . ." What Dorothy resented was the lack of an intellectual underpinning to this great rite of passage in her church; she wanted religion to be an adventure of the mind, not a set of time-encrusted rituals. She must also have felt keenly the absence of her parents, who stayed at home for the dedication of a new set of church bells.

In her schoolgirl letters to her parents and to Ivy, Dorothy proved herself to be a capable dissembler. Her unhappiness was buried like tiny nuggets in these letters—the "weird freak" comment, for instance. Another time she lamented, "One gets sick of school sometimes and being 'Dorothy' to everyone, and blown up by everybody, from Miss Douglas to one's Games Representative." At the opening of her spring 1911 semester, she reported, "The people who usually scowl at me or ignore me received me with open arms and wreathed smiles . . . ," possibly because everyone loves a winner and Dorothy had just come first in the nation in the Cambridge Higher Local Examinations, with distinctions in French and spoken German.

That semester she nearly died when a measles epidemic swept the school and she developed double pneumonia accompanied by dangerously high fever and delirium. The crisis passed, but her recovery was slow—first in a nursing home near Salisbury, then back at the rectory in Bluntisham—and James Brabazon speculates that it was during her convalescence that Dorothy finally confided her misery to her parents. She also experienced a humiliation that would have prostrated weaker women: her hair fell out as the result of her illness. Her thin, lank, straight hair was never her crowning glory, but to lose it—just when she was about to turn eighteen—was surely devastating. It is a mark of her strength in genuine crisis (seen again and again in her life) that she returned to Godolphin in the fall of 1911, sporting a wig and her usual jolly facade.

In her last letter from Godolphin, she mentions a "scarlet-fever scare" at the school, which possibly prompted her parents to keep her at home the following semester. Some have suggested that she suffered a nervous breakdown, but that seems unlikely in view of her continued academic performance during this hiatus. Tutored by mail, she prepared for the Gilchrist Scholarship competition to Somerville College, one of the two women's colleges at Oxford University. She won her scholarship, and by the summer of 1912 she was happily assembling a new wardrobe for her first term.

There's little doubt that, for all her academic success, Godolphin had been a painful experience and one that shaped her responses to other people and other difficulties. She learned, like Athos, to mask her unwavering conviction of intellectual superiority behind a jovial, boisterous, and often buffoonish facade. She learned to reveal and make fun of her own enthusiasms before anyone else had the chance, to play the clown who was the butt of her own jokes. She learned to keep her secrets close and let the rest of the world be damned.

In *The Nine Tailors*, written in 1933, Dorothy included a character strongly reminiscent of her own adolescent self—Hilary Thorpe, a precocious fifteen-year-old who gains the attention of Lord Peter Wimsey. Discovering Hilary's ambition to be a writer, Wimsey explains that she has "the creative imagination, which works outwards, till finally you will be able to stand outside your own experience and see it as something you have made, existing independently of yourself. You're lucky. . . . but your luck will come more at the end of life than at the beginning, because the other sort of people won't understand the way your mind works. They will start by thinking you dreamy and romantic, and then they'll be surprised to discover that you are really hard and heartless. They'll be quite wrong both times—but they won't ever know it, and *you* won't know it at first, and it'll worry you."

It did worry Dorothy. At Godolphin, she discovered that not only was she unlike other girls of her class; she was not especially liked by them. She was smarter than most, but certainly not all, of her schoolmates, but neither teachers nor students appreciated her self-possessed assertiveness. In two years at Godolphin, she cemented her ability to compartmentalize her life—crafting a public self that accounted well enough for her brash and often boorish behavior; maintaining her intellectual integrity; hiding her fear and secrets from all but herself; and learning, in Wimsey's words, "to stand outside [her] own experience."

"*Dear old Oxford! . . . I wonder why I love it so—I always feel when I go there as if I were going home. . . .*"

Dorothy entered Somerville College in the fall of 1912, going joyfully back to Oxford, the place of her birth. There were relatives and family friends who took a not-always-welcome interest in her welfare. There were famous thinkers and dedicated scholars to fire her mind, as well as young men who enjoyed flirtation as much as she. And as she quickly discovered inside the walls of Somerville, there were young women like herself: bright, intellectual, creative, curious, and odd in their own ways.

Her experience at Godolphin seems not to have diminished Dorothy's instinctive sociability, and she threw herself into university life with her usual enthusiasm. One of the first things she did was to audition for the Oxford Bach Choir. A strong contralto, she had been taking singing lessons at home in Bluntisham, and membership in the choir provided a deeply satisfying aesthetic outlet for her. It also brought her into close contact with Dr. Hugh Percy Allen, organist at Christ Church and conductor of the Bach Choir. Now she could expend her passion, not on a distant actor or adventurer, but on a living, breathing, and receptive presence. Dr. Allen (later to be Oxford Professor of Music and Director of the Royal College of Music) was the perfect object for one of Dorothy's exuberant crushes. Fortyish and married, he apparently made flirtation with female students something of an avocation; as Dorothy wrote with stunning openness to her parents, she was but one of "a long procession of little tame cats who have adorned his organ loft in succession. . . ." In Dorothy's case, the trips into the organ loft seem to have been harmless enough—a testing, perhaps, of her ability to vamp an older and more sophisticated man.

Dorothy had no illusions about her physical appeal. She was tall and thin with lovely arms and hands, and a long neck that had earned her the nickname "Swanny" at Godolphin. She had her father's clear blue eyes, smallish and often hidden behind spectacles for reading, and her mother's turned-up nose, narrow mouth accented with dimples, and long upper lip. She often wore her sparse dark hair with an old-maidish middle part (her Mona Lisa pose). Hardly the kind of looks to launch a thousand ships, but a face with "character," as she described Katherine Lammas in *Cat o'Mary*: "It could not help being an interesting face—could it?—when it belonged to such an interesting person." In fact, in the rare photographs that picture her smiling open-mouthed, Dorothy has an almost gamine attractiveness.

Shrewdly she chose to dress for dramatic effect, and she loved striking outfits: bold colors, dashing cloaks and hats, scooped necklines and shallow sleeves that displayed her shoulders and arms, exotic dangling earrings to accentuate her graceful neck. Though hardly extreme, her Bohemian style at Somerville echoed her childhood love of swashbuckling costuming.

Dr. Allen continued to fascinate even after she left Somerville, but he was not the only object of her attentions. She flirted with her German teacher and had a relationship that bordered on serious with Giles Dixey, an Oxford student and the son of family friends. She enjoyed the company of another Bach Choir member, Arthur Forrest, and when he was killed in World War One, she wrote a poem in his honor for publication in a university magazine. But far more important than these flutterings after the men of Oxford were the friendships she established with a group of gifted Somerville women—the girls of the Mutual Admiration Society.

At Godolphin, Dorothy had been the bumptious pariah, but at Somerville, she found her place. Actually, she made her first friend, Dorothy Rowe, when both were at Somerville to take the scholarship exam. As the two girls sat together in a waiting room, Dorothy Sayers ostentatiously began to recite a passage from *Cyrano de Bergerac* in French, and Dorothy Rowe quickly took up the quote. It was the beginning of the kind of friendship Dorothy Sayers had longed for.

Just a month into her first term at Somerville, Dorothy and another first-year student named Amphy Middlemore started an informal group—the Mutual Admiration Society, or M.A.S.—for a small group of girls who shared their interests in writing and creative scholarship. The girls supported and encouraged one another's efforts and provided what Dorothy craved, the companionship of like minds. Other M.A.S. members were Muriel Jaeger, called "Jim" (to whom Dorothy was to dedicate her first novel, *Whose Body?*); Catherine Godfrey, known as "Tony"; Charis Barnett; and Dorothy Rowe. Muriel St. Clare Byrne, two years younger than the original M.A.S. six, submitted the requisite example of original writing and was admitted into the chosen circle in 1914. The friendships forged among these girls were to be both lasting and productive.

In the cloistered world of a women's college, Dorothy had found friends who enjoyed her outgoing nature and shared her love of literature, music, poetry, and the power of words and ideas—young women who could debate the relative merits of G. K. Chesterton and George Bernard Shaw (both of whom had spoken at Oxford) in one breath and the latest fashions in the next. Despite her emotional reserve, with the M.A.S. girls Dorothy could share her ideas, her interests, even her anxieties about the future, and expect to be taken seriously.

She could freely indulge her intellectual fascination with classical and medieval languages in tutorials with Miss Mildred Pope, who would later become the model for the charmingly diffuse character of Miss Lydgate in *Gaudy Night*. As at Godolphin, some of the faculty at Somerville initially complained that Dorothy sloughed off what did not interest her, and in one report, a professor noted that she was "still lacking in self restraint."★ Dorothy herself recalled doing little actual academic work, but the work somehow got done, and she completed her baccalaureate program with First Class honors in medieval French in 1915. (For reasons of history rather than individual performance, Dorothy was not to receive her diploma until 1920, when Oxford at last chose to legitimate degrees for women, some forty-one years after the founding of Somerville.)

World War One began in August 1914, when Dorothy was on holiday in France with a school friend and a chaperon. The three women returned home safely, but even this firsthand experience of the war had little impact on Dorothy. Returning to Oxford in the fall, she initially involved herself as a volunteer helping to find housing for the influx of Belgian refugees, but she seems not to have felt the war's effects in any deeper sense. Though she must have worried about the young Oxford men fighting and often dying at the Front, her prayers were reserved for

---

★ Quoted by James Brabazon in *Dorothy L. Sayers: A Biography*.

Oxford itself, that the ancient city that had so captured her heart would be saved from the German bombs.

Her father offered to pay for a year of postgraduate study at Somerville, but Dorothy refused. She was concerned about the additional financial burden on her parents, but it seems likely that she was also tired of the academic rigor. She had long since determined to become a professional poet, and she probably felt the time had come to get on with it. Nevertheless, it wasn't easy to separate from her beloved Oxford and her coterie of friends.

The summer she "went down" (completed her studies), she returned to Bluntisham and toyed with the idea of becoming a Red Cross nurse in France. Nothing came of that plan, but she continued working at her poetry. A lay, comprising twelve poems celebrating Oxford and mostly composed while she was in college, was published in December of 1915, and a year later, her first solo volume, *Op. I,* was put out in an edition of 350 copies. *Op. I* was part of the *Adventurers All* series, the brainchild of Oxford publisher Basil Blackwell, who envisioned the books as launching pads for young poets. (Blackwell succeeded too well and eventually had to abandon the series when many of his young finds, including Aldous Huxley and the Sitwell brothers, moved on to more lucrative publishing contracts.) Other poems were accepted by other publications, but if Dorothy was to live somewhere other than her parents' home, she had to find a more profitable occupation. After some foot-dragging, she finally got on with the business of hunting for a job and secured a teaching position at a girls' high school in Hull, a port city in England's industrial north.

Apart from the ever-present grime of industry, Hull was better than Dorothy had expected, with cinemas and several nice shops and eating places. Dorothy enjoyed the company of her fellow teachers and sharpened her flirting skills on a local curate. She proved to be an energetic and inspiring teacher who not only taught her girls French but also organized a school choir and reluctantly took on a German class. But she learned in Hull that she did not enjoy teaching. In Hull she also discovered the reality of warfare as she had never imagined it in sacrosanct Oxford.

When the Germans began their zeppelin raids on England, Hull's port was a prime target, and Dorothy frequently found herself huddled in damp cellars as the bombs dropped. Here, her intellect was helpless, and her joking and high spirits were pointless. All around she saw genuine physical fear—"brutal, bestial and utterly degrading"—and she didn't like it. For a twenty-two-year-old girl with little more experience of the primal emotions than could be gleaned from novels and poetry, war was hell. Though she attributed cringing fear to others, she was far from immune, and once again she began to lose her hair. (Dorothy was admittedly a physical coward, notoriously so in later years, preferring battles that could be waged with mind and mouth.)

She taught at Hull for two terms, until her father intervened. Henry Sayers had been offered a new position as rector of Christchurch on the Isle of Ely (Cambridgeshire). The parish was even more isolated than Bluntisham-cum-Earith, but the annual stipend was larger, so Henry and Nell prepared to move. The extra money also allowed Henry to approach Basil Blackwell with an offer: if Blackwell would take Dorothy on as a publisher's apprentice, Henry would pay £100 for her support. Blackwell, who met Dorothy for the first time in February 1917, agreed, and Dorothy must have been ecstatic; the new job rescued her from teaching and from Hull and brought her back to Oxford.

By May, she was settled into rooms at 17 Long Wall Street and busily learning the publishing trade. Her M.A.S. buddies Muriel "Jim" Jaeger and Muriel St. Clare Byrne were still at Somerville, and others of the old society were in and out of Oxford. There were new friends, including Doreen Wallace, who remembered Dorothy in those days: "long and slim . . . small head alert on slender neck, she loped round Oxford looking for fun."*

Dorothy was in her twenties and full of juice. Her letters show a kind of giddiness that is charming in its way but clearly wore thin on some of her acquaintances. Her emotional remoteness could be infuriating, and her insensitivity shocking. When the 1918 pandemic outbreak of Spanish influenza (which claimed more lives than the war before it ran its deadly course) swept Oxford, Dorothy caught a mild case and quickly recovered. Her chief complaint, expressed in a letter to her mother, was that she had been forced to cancel her Halloween soiree: ". . . one can't give hilarious parties with people dropping dead all round one!" Apparently, her primary interest in the killer flu was its resemblance to the medieval Black Plague.

Though some of her biographers tend to skirt this issue, she was also, in the language of the times, man-crazy. However emotionally blocked she may have been, Dorothy was a physically passionate woman, strongly curious about, yet frightened by, sex. Flirting and crushes on unattainables such as Hugh Allen brought her close to the dangerous edge, but when she received her first marriage proposal, from Leonard Hodgson, "a perfectly delightful padre" and Vice-Principal of St. Edmund Hall, she bolted like a frightened rabbit. When Hodgson contin-

---

* Doreen Wallace later became a novelist. She is quoted by Barbara Reynolds in *Dorothy L. Sayers: Her Life and Soul.*

ued to pursue her, even joining the Bach Choir though he was not much of a singer, Dorothy was appalled. She wrote home, "To have someone devoted to me arouses all my worst feelings. I loathe being deferred to. I ABOMINATE being waited on. It infuriates me to feel that my words are numbered and my actions watched. I want somebody to fight with!" The unfortunately besotted Hodgson, who went on to have a distinguished career as a theologian, was too much the compliant lapdog. He also represented actual sexual as well as emotional commitment, and Dorothy was worried that she might be afraid of the physical side of marriage. With Hodgson firmly denied, she continued to enjoy her flirtations, one with the surgeon who removed her appendix in the summer of 1917.

Somehow, betwixt work and friends and countless activities, she continued to write seriously, and her second volume of poems, *Catholic Tales and Christian Songs,* was published by Basil Blackwell in the fall of 1918. To promote interest in her work, which was much influenced by both the style and theological ideas of G. K. Chesterton, Dorothy and a friend connived at a publicity scheme that they called "the Maynard controversy." When well-known Catholic poet Theodore Maynard reviewed *Catholic Tales* unfavorably in Chesterton's magazine, *The New Witness,* "Jim" Jaeger began a spirited correspondence, writing under various pseudonyms to the magazine. Other, genuine writers soon joined the fray, and the verbal sparring continued for several months, until Dorothy tired of it.

Her mind was on other things. Tossed out of her flat because the landlady preferred renting to young men, Dorothy moved into an apartment in a house on Bath Place, where she planned to launch a Thursday night "salon" in her sitting room. There were musical evenings and gatherings of the Rhyme Club (Dorothy, Doreen Wallace, and Eleanor Geitch) attended at least once by the poetic Osbert and Sacheverell Sitwell and Siegfried Sassoon.

In May 1918, Dorothy left Blackwell's (Basil Blackwell was converting from poetry to textbook publication and possibly let her go), and was supporting herself with freelance editing, some journalism, and tutoring. Money was tight, but Dorothy had no intention of moving on, not when Captain Eric Whelpton lived in the same house. Tall and handsome, Whelpton had been invalided out of the Army after contracting polio, which left him weak and subject to fainting attacks. He returned to his studies at Oxford and was soon a frequent presence at Dorothy's gatherings. Though Doreen Wallace had spotted him first, Dorothy quickly moved in. Part smitten schoolgirl, part teacher, and part mother, she devoted herself to his needs.

In fact, Whelpton had a romantic interest elsewhere, but he enjoyed

Dorothy's company, and they had a good deal in common, especially French language and literature. Raised in France, he was a sophisticate in her eyes, though, he readily admitted, her intellectual inferior. When he moved to France to take a teaching job at a private boys' school in 1919, Dorothy boldly wrote him to ask about a possible position there. It turned out that Whelpton needed an assistant. In addition to teaching English at L'Ecole des Roches at Verneuil in Normandy, he was establishing an exchange program for British and French students. He needed help, someone fluent in French and English, and he offered the post to Dorothy. Whelpton even agreed to present himself for inspection by Dorothy's parents and enjoyed a pleasant visit at the Christchurch rectory.

So Dorothy, her bicycle in tow, arrived in Verneuil by train to begin working for the man she had nicknamed "Snark." She was efficiency itself, tending to the exchange bureau's office affairs and occasionally shepherding groups of young scholars to and from England. She was also on hand to nurse Whelpton through his attacks, teaching his classes when he was ill and pampering him at all times.

She involved herself in school activities and enjoyed the company of the teachers and staff—excepting an Englishman named Charles Crichton, an Eton graduate and ex-cavalry officer who had lost his money during the war. Though down on his luck, Crichton could still tell spirited tales of the good old days when he maintained a bachelor flat in Jermyn Street (one street away from Peter Wimsey's fictional flat on Piccadilly), frequented his London clubs, partied lavishly in town and country, and was served by an eccentric valet named Bates who became his military batman. Though Dorothy and Crichton shared a mutual dislike, biographer Barbara Reynolds makes a good case that Crichton's stories supplied the details of life in the upper reaches of British society that later surfaced in Lord Peter Wimsey, and that Wimsey's man Bunter was modeled on Bates the batman. Eric Whelpton later contended, probably correctly, that Lord Peter's distinctive characteristics were an amalgam of his own and Crichton's.

Dorothy had detection on her mind in Verneuil. She was reading detective stories. With several of her friends back in Oxford (including G. D. H. Cole and his wife, Margaret, who were to become a successful mystery-writing team), Dorothy had discussed a plan to form a writing syndicate that would produce profitable detective books. The idea was obviously based on the extremely popular Sexton Blake series—formula mysteries cranked out by dozens of writers and published in magazines and as penny-dreadful novels. When she contracted mumps, which required three weeks' isolation, Dorothy requested that "Jim" Jaeger send as many Sexton Blake books as she could discreetly mail. Dorothy and

"Jim" then entered into one of their intellectual games, creating a satirical analysis of Sexton Blake that connected the hack detective to ancient myths and legends. This Sexton Blake escapade may have helped her turn her mind away from her failure with Eric Whelpton.

Oddly for a man of the world, Whelpton hadn't grasped the true nature of Dorothy's feelings for him until well into their tenure at Verneuil. Then they were caught up in the affairs of a young staff member named Adele. The unmarried Adele found herself pregnant and abandoned. When Dorothy discovered that the girl planned to have an abortion, she jumped into the situation, pulling Whelpton with her. Dorothy first convinced the girl that abortion would be an irredeemable sin. She and Eric then arranged for Adele to go to Paris, and he used his family connections to secure employment and shelter for the mother-to-be. Hard as it is to imagine today, the situation was extremely difficult and emotional, demanding both delicacy and secrecy. As Dorothy and Eric worked closely to rescue Adele, he finally realized that his flirtatious assistant was in love with him.

Eric was already in love with someone else, a married woman whom he had met during a recent visit to London. When he told Dorothy, she was torn with jealousy, and the atmosphere in their small office became tense and uncomfortable for both. But Whelpton was already job-hunting and also thinking about a move to Italy, and he was anxious to leave the school as soon as possible. He offered to sell Dorothy his interest in the student exchange venture so she could stay on in France.

Dorothy must have been distraught. She admitted to occasional "black times," and after her bout of mumps, she suffered another round of hair loss. She seriously considered buying the business but finally decided against it. She would fulfill her responsibilities in France, taking over Whelpton's teaching duties and the running of the bureau when he left. She wrote her parents the happy news of the birth of Adele's baby boy in June 1920, and by the end of September, she was ready to return home. But this time it was London, not Oxford, that called her.

There was, however, one stop in Oxford that she could not miss. On October 14, 1920, the great university at last formalized the education of its women by granting them degrees. It was an historic occasion, and Dorothy wouldn't have missed it for the world. Twice within a matter of minutes, she passed through the ceremonial line, first to receive her bachelor's degree and then her master of arts. The immediate problem was that her grand new degrees did very little to help her find a job. She might have returned to Somerville as a postgraduate student, but that would have required her parents to pay her fees, and besides, she always said she never wanted an academic career. She definitely didn't want to teach. When an offer came along to write a screenplay for a movie producer she had once met in London, she jumped at it. The screenplay, on which she collaborated with Dorothy Rowe, was accepted by the producer but apparently never paid for. This was the last time Dorothy was to be conned by a glittering financial promise. But her short-lived vision of a career in the cinema had at least provided the incentive she needed to pack up and head for London.

Relying on a monthly allowance from her father and what little else she could scrape together, she took an unfurnished room at 36 St. George's Square in Pimlico (where she would later house Peter Wimsey's spinster investigator, Miss Climpson). Reverend Sayers also found work for her, translating French documents for a Polish employer. She applied, unsuccessfully, for a series of full-time jobs and was eventually forced to take a temporary post teaching English. Students at Clapham High School were astonished by her teaching methods and her intense personality. No longer the bright, bustling mistress she had been at Hull, she nevertheless made a lasting impression on her Clapham pupils.

She had moved to a new room at 44 Mecklenburg Square (later to become Harriet Vane's address in *Gaudy Night*), and since the rent did not include board, Dorothy was teaching herself to cook. In the Bohemian circles of Bloomsbury, she enjoyed the company of a number of young men who would sometimes treat her to a good meal. Her most frequent escort was Norman Davey, a writer who encouraged Dorothy's ambitions. Davey's first novel, *The Pilgrim of a Smile,* was published in 1921. (Dorothy admired the book, which included a character named Major Bunter.)

She continued her translation work, took on more substitute teaching, and on Saturdays hied herself off to the Reading Room of the British Museum, where she had embarked on a study of criminology. In January 1921, she informed her mother of her latest activity: "My detective story begins brightly, with a fat lady found dead in her bath with nothing on but her pince-nez."

That fat lady never got to sing, but readers of Dorothy's first novel, *Whose Body?,* will easily recognize the fundamentals of its plot. The idea of the body in the bathtub had originated during an evening of intellectual party games played several years before in Oxford. She worked at the book throughout the spring, pushed on by Muriel Jaeger, and finished it during a visit with her parents at Christchurch in the summer of 1921. Lord Peter Wimsey had been born, though it would be three more years before he was presented to the world at large. Dorothy struggled to create her fictional detective and his first case, but he was no trouble at all when compared to the real man in her life. She was in love again, and the object of her passion was no noble gentleman.

*"If I could have found a man to my measure, I could
have put a torch to the world."*
—letter to John Cournos, October 1924

When Dorothy was preparing for her summer visit home, she wrote to
her parents that she would like to bring a friend along. He didn't make
the trip after all, but Dorothy told her family about him and even in-
duced them to read one of his books.

His name was John Cournos, born Johann Gregorievitch Korshoon
in Kiev, Russia, in 1881. His parents had divorced, and when John was
five, his mother married a man named Cournos, a member of the strict
Jewish Hasid sect. Faced with the turbulent anti-Semitism of czarist
Russia, they immigrated to the United States when John was ten, and
settled in Philadelphia. The family was poor, and at age twelve, Cournos
quit school to work in a factory. Two years later, he approached the publisher of the *Philadelphia Record* and so impressed the man that he was
immediately hired as an office boy. Cournos had risen through the
newspaper's ranks in classic journalistic tradition before he decided, in
1912, to move to England and freelance his writing. He proved to be an
adept interviewer, tackling the likes of G. K. Chesterton, H. G. Wells, D.
H. Lawrence, and poets John Masefield and William Butler Yeats. When
the war came, Cournos went to work as a translator for the Russians,
and in 1917 he joined a group of foreign correspondents on a mission
to Petrograd. Returning to London, he worked for the British Foreign
Office and the Ministry of Information.

He was, Dorothy said, the kind of man who "spells Art with a capital A." His art was Imagist poetry and dense fiction. His first novel, the
one read by Reverend and Mrs. Sayers, was *The Mask*. Published in
1919, the book was well received in literary circles and picked up a major writing prize. When Dorothy met Cournos, he was one of the
loftier members of the Bloomsbury crowd that so attracted her romantic soul. He was working on his second novel and a volume of poetry.
She was struggling to support herself, hammering out her second "Lord
Peter" novel and trying to sell the first, and facing the not-too-distant
prospect of turning thirty still unwed and a virgin. She fell like a bag of
bricks for the dark Jewish intellectual with the distinctive Slavic hand-
someness and Russian-tinted voice.

Their affair—reconstructed from a set of Dorothy's letters that
Cournos gave to Harvard University and from the later public writings
of both—was passionate, volatile, and all but consummated. As she had
done with Eric Whelpton, Dorothy turned earth mother, pampering
Cournos's physical and emotional needs, nursing his inflated ego, en-

during his moods and constant demeaning of her own literary ambitions, dreaming of wedding her hero and bearing his children, preferably peasant style in a field. When his second book, *The Wall,* failed to do well, she was sympathetic. She lent him her flat when she was away from London. When she at last landed a permanent job as a copywriter with the S. H. Benson advertising and publicity agency and then sold her "Lord Peter," she celebrated her success by preparing a sumptuous meal for Cournos. She also mentioned him frequently in her letters home.

Cournos's one generosity to her seems to have been an introduction to literary agent Andrew Dakers. Dakers took on her first novel, and by July of 1922 he had placed it with an American publisher, Boni and Liveright, which had also published a book of Cournos's poems. The Americans gave Dorothy's novel its title, *Whose Body?*

Then on September 18, 1922, Dorothy wrote to her parents that Cournos was returning to the United States. Though they had quarreled, she clearly expected to hear from him again, but by November, there had been not so much as a postcard. She had no idea that Cournos would soon marry someone else.

When all the excuses and rationalizations are cleared away, the catalyst that doomed the relationship was sex. Cournos, predictably, was dedicated to the new religion of free love. He did not believe in marriage; he did not want children. Dorothy was a peasant at heart, but a rector's daughter in her soul. She wanted sex that led naturally to marriage and children. She and Cournos disagreed mightily about contraception: he believed in it and she didn't. She refused to accept sexual intercourse that came with the "taint of the 'rubber-shop,' " and though they apparently did everything but, they did not have intercourse.

When Dorothy fictionalized Cournos as Philip Boyes in her 1930 novel *Strong Poison,* she presented a man who used sex as a test of a woman's willingness to submit to his control. Philip Boyes, the character whose death lands Harriet Vane in the Old Bailey on trial for her life, is described by the trial judge as an author of "literary works . . . of what is sometimes called an 'advanced' type. They preached doctrines which may seem to some of us immoral or seditious, such as atheism, and anarchy, and what is known as free love. His private life appears to have been conducted, for some time at least, in accordance with these doctrines." It is in that little aside—"for some time at least"—that Dorothy demonstrates Boyes-Cournos's ultimate betrayal.

Cournos's sin was not that he believed in "advanced" ideas; Dorothy was relatively advanced herself and certainly more than ready for premarital sex. Cournos failed her (as Philip Boyes fails Harriet Vane) by *not* believing in the ideas he professed. He wanted Dorothy to submit to sex without consequences to himself. When she wouldn't, he left, and within two years, he had married a twice-divorced American detective story writer, Helen Kestner Satterthwaite (pen name, Sybil Norton). Later he confessed to Dorothy that he would have willingly married her and settled down if she had submitted to him first.

Despite her acidic portrait of Cournos as Boyes in *Strong Poison,* Dorothy did not fictionalize intimate details of the affair. Cournos did, in his 1932 novel *The Devil Is an English Gentleman,* even lifting bits of dialog from Dorothy's letters to him. A cad to the end.

Emotionally battered and sexually frustrated when Cournos left, Dorothy did the obvious thing. She found an agreeable man and re-bounded. Bill White was as unlike Cournos as day to night. Though well educated, he was a sometime car salesman, a mechanic, and a motorcycle enthusiast without a trace of literary pretension. A man's man, he provided Dorothy the natural, healthy masculine sexuality so lacking in John Cournos. They were not in love, but they had wonderful times together, and she took Bill to Christchurch for Christmas in 1922, ar-riving on his motorcycle. She had written to her mother that "he's the last person you'd expect me to bring home, but he's really quite amiable, and will be desperately grateful for a roof over his head."

Dorothy was doing very well at her job with Benson's; her boss told her that she had "every quality which makes for success in advertis-ing. . . ." *Whose Body?* had been sold in England to Fisher Unwin, and *People's Magazine* had bought the American serial rights. She was still working on her second "Lord Peter" (as she referred to her Wimsey novels) and beginning to sample the financial fruits of her own labor.

With Bill White, Dorothy could let her hair down and get her hands dirty. He taught her about motorcycle mechanics and helped her with improvements to her apartment. They went to pubs and movies and dance halls; he told her dirty jokes, which she loved, and they made up obscene limericks together. It was a comfortable, no-demands relation-ship, and at some point Dorothy finally lost her virginity, ironically agreeing to use contraception. In fact, this interlude with Bill White might have been the perfect transition for her—except that, just two months before her thirtieth birthday, the contraceptives failed and Dorothy became pregnant. What she did next may be regarded as an act of supreme self-sacrifice or as sheer pigheaded stupidity, but for a woman of her genteel parentage and Victorian upbringing, it was noth-ing short of remarkable.

"To carry it through one needs two things: a) guts,
b) iron health."

By June 1923, Dorothy knew she was in a fix. She consulted a friend
from Oxford, Dr. Alice Chance, who confirmed the pregnancy and discussed Dorothy's options, including abortion. Whether Dorothy seriously considered ending the pregnancy is unknown, but given her
religious scruples, it is unlikely. She took a two-week holiday from Benson's near the end of the month and retreated to a country cottage at
Bovingdon in Hertfordshire, telling her parents that she wanted a place
to write in solitude. What she really did there was to think through her
situation.

Today, we can only begin to imagine the agonies of conscience she
must have suffered. England after the war was a profoundly changed
place; moral standards and behavioral rules had shifted dramatically in a
relatively short time. In London, just as in New York and Chicago, the
1920s roared with sex, drugs, and jazz. But some things remained ver-
boten, and for women of Dorothy's class and religion, unwed pregnancy
was still at the top of the forbidden list. For Dorothy to have her baby
openly and without a husband would have caused repercussions much
more profound than the two-day sensation we might expect now. It
would have meant lifelong shame for herself, her child, and her entire
family. Her parents, in their seventies, would be humiliated. Dorothy
would likely lose her job and all hope of financial independence. Her
child would be a bastard, and she would be branded a sinner in the eyes
of man as well as God.

What she decided, in that cottage in Bovingdon, was to stick it out
on her own, hide the pregnancy, and tell no one. More than anything,
she wanted to keep the secret from her parents, and that meant telling
no one who might, by the remotest chance, let the story out. None of
her closest friends from Oxford, no one at Benson's, no family member.
(Biographer Barbara Reynolds has uncovered evidence that Dorothy received assistance from an unexpected source: Bill White's wife. Dorothy
apparently didn't know of White's marriage until she told him about the
pregnancy.)

There was, however, one possible avenue out. Her cousin Ivy
Shrimpton and Ivy's recently widowed mother, Amy, were supporting
themselves by raising foster children in their Cowley home near Oxford.
Dorothy had grown away from Ivy, but they were still friends, and
Dorothy had received glowing reports from her own mother of Ivy's excellent care of the children. Here was a ray of hope for the child. Although Dorothy delayed writing to Ivy until the last possible moment,

the knowledge that she could place her baby in a loving home must have helped her through the long months ahead.

Bill White greeted the news with "helpless rage and misery." He drifted in and out of Dorothy's life until several months after the child's birth, when she finally told him to "go to hell." Dorothy may have considered marriage to White as an option, but the discovery that he was already married *and* a philanderer quickly closed that door.

Having decided to go it alone, Dorothy returned to Benson's, apparently her old lively self, and no one suspected what was happening beneath her billowing clothes. Thanks to her improved finances and her excellent cooking, she had been gaining weight for awhile before becoming pregnant, and her height also helped her carry the baby unobtrusively. She remained in good health throughout and experienced none of the typical symptoms that might have revealed her condition. Dorothy managed to hold off visits with her parents during the fall of 1923 and begged off Christmas by claiming that she was too busy with her new book: she told her parents to expect to see her at Easter. She remained at Benson's until her seventh month, then took two months' sick leave.

She had arranged to enter Tuckton Lodge, a maternity home in Southbourne, where Bill White's wife and young daughter lived. There on January 3, 1924, after a long and difficult labor, she gave birth to John Anthony. She registered her son in her own name, leaving the father's name officially blank although the baby was known by the surname White. She stayed at the hospital for three weeks, finally writing to Ivy two days before the baby's arrival. In this first letter, she pretended that the child was a friend's, but by the end of January, after Ivy had agreed to take the baby, Dorothy finally wrote the whole truth, asking Ivy to honor her confidence and leaving it up to her cousin whether or not to tell Aunt Amy.★

★ It is eerie to read a letter that fourteen-year-old Dorothy wrote to Ivy Shrimpton in February 1908. Dorothy hesitantly but strongly criticized her cousin for judging others too harshly. She feared that people would become afraid of Ivy. She wrote, "I shouldn't like to feel, Ivy, that supposing sometime I sinned a great sin that I should be afraid to come to you for help, only, unless you would try to make allowances for me, I'm afraid I should." Ivy, however, was more than willing to make allowances when the time of need arrived.

"I have a careless rage for life. . . ."

When she had delivered her child to her cousin, Dorothy went back to London and to work. Her colleagues at Benson's, assuming that she had recovered from her illness, assured her that she looked fit and well. She had lost her hair again and took to wearing a striking silver wig that went well with her exotic style of dress. Benson's must have been a life-saver, and she flourished in the bustling, creative atmosphere of the ad agency—free to indulge her love of words and verbal cleverness and getting paid for it.

Over the years she impressed more than a few of her working colleagues with her wit and style, both on and off the page. She was intimately involved in several of Benson's most successful advertising ventures, particularly the long-running Mustard Club campaign for Coleman's mustard and the ubiquitous Zoo ads for Guinness. One of her best friends at Benson's was a young artist named John Gilroy, who later received his knighthood as one of England's most-admired portrait artists. (It was Gilroy who accompanied Dorothy to Surrey on a dreary December day in 1926 when volunteers were called out to search for the missing detective writer Agatha Christie.) Gilroy remembered her as wonderfully funny, a superb copywriter, and to his artist's eye, attractive in spite of her increasing girth. Gilroy painted and sketched her several times: "terrific size—lovely fat fingers—lovely snub nose—lovely curly lips—a baby's face in a way."★

Dorothy worked at Benson's for nine years, and Gilroy believed she might have become a company director had she stayed. But for Dorothy, advertising eventually lost its edge, and she developed serious concerns about the ethics of the profession. Benson's was a means to her end: the support of the "fine little chap" whom she had consigned to the care of her cousin.

In 1924, Dorothy made one exception to her rule of absolute secrecy about John Anthony's existence. She wrote to John Cournos, who had returned to London, initiating a series of letters of which only her side remains. She wished Cournos well in his marriage and told him about her baby: "Both of us did what we swore we'd never do, you see—I do hope your experiment turned out better than mine." When Cournos pursued the correspondence and asked to meet, she agreed, but told him, "It's going to hurt me like hell to see you, because Judah with all thy faults I love thee still. . . ."

The letters to Cournos—so unlike the perky, gossipy, witty letters she

---

★ Quoted by James Brabazon in *Dorothy L. Sayers: A Biography.*

wrote to family and friends—are dark and anguished. She still loved Cournos but blamed him for her circumstances: "You broke your own image in my heart, you see. You stood to me for beauty and truth—and you demanded ugliness, barrenness—and it seems now that even in doing so, you were just lying." She confessed her loneliness and the fearsome responsibility she felt for her son. "It frightens me to be so unhappy," she wrote. "I thought it would get better, but I think every day is worse than the last, and I'm always afraid they'll chuck me out of the office because I'm working so badly. And I haven't even the last resort of doing away with myself, because what would poor Anthony do then, poor thing?"

Dorothy wanted both to share her pain and to make Cournos appreciate his loss: "I swear that if you had offered me love—or even asked for love—you should have had everything." She demeaned him, as he had demeaned her: "You were a rotten companion for a poor girl." She rejected him: "*As a companion* you aren't my choice." Dorothy ranted and raved, ". . . my dear, you stripped love down to its merest and most brutal physical contact. . . ."

She and Cournos met, perhaps several times, and he apparently suggested finding her a husband or lover. She entered into a mocking game, naming this phantom man "Troilus." She lectured Cournos about the difference between the married and unmarried states. She taunted him about his wife's age and future childbearing capability. (Sybil Norton already had two children before marrying Cournos.) She called Bill White the "Beast" but would not allow Cournos to criticize him. In her letters, Dorothy is a tornado of agony and anger: "I have a careless rage for life, and secrecy tends to make me bad-tempered. . . . I like to die spitting and swearing, you know, and I'm no mean wrestler."

(Dorothy's letters to Cournos should not be taken entirely at face value. The anger and pain were undeniably real, but there was more than a little overdramatizing and self-conscious intellectualizing. She wanted to hurt Cournos: she used every verbal weapon in her arsenal; and her harangues can be heartbreaking. But they can also be peevish and adolescent.)

As it must, the violence finally played itself out, and Dorothy's last extant letter to Cournos is almost collegial. He had sent her an article on detective fiction written by G. K. Chesterton. "Many thanks," she replied. ". . . I am indebted to you for saving me six useful pennies." We do not know if they ever met again.

Since the story of her son's existence was made public in the 1970s, biographers and critics have speculated about Dorothy's sense of guilt. It is only speculation because Dorothy left no record on the issue except what can be interpreted from her letters to Cournos and Ivy Shrimpton.

She did believe in the reality of sin and its consequences, and biographer Barbara Reynolds, a close friend of Dorothy's near the end of her life, makes the case that, as an Anglo-Catholic, Dorothy had recourse to confession, absolution, and compensation. The "bitter sin" of premarital sex could be forgiven and purged. "In practical terms," Dr. Reynolds has written, "this meant supporting and educating John Anthony and providing him, as best she could, with maternal love and concern for his welfare. This responsibility she amply fulfilled and continued to fulfill, for the rest of his life." Whether or not Dorothy was truly capable of a mother's love for her son, she felt absolutely responsible for him. When he was small, she visited him frequently, took pride in his progress, and wrote to Ivy, "Whoever suffers over this business . . . it mustn't be John Anthony. If the poor little soul has to be fatherless, at least he mustn't be motherless."

> *"Give me a man that's human and careless and loves*
> *life, and one who can enjoy the rough-and-tumble of*
> *passion."*   —letter to John Cournos, January 1925

Returning to London after John Anthony's birth, Dorothy completed her second "Lord Peter"—*Clouds of Witness.* She struggled with and never liked this novel because it reminded her too vividly of her own state of mind during the tumult of 1922–1924. In a letter to Cournos, she described it as the "cursed book—associated with every sort of humiliation and misery. . . ." By the time of her last letter to Cournos, however, she was already at work on *Unnatural Death.*

She and her son weathered one near-catastrophe, the death of Aunt Amy Shrimpton in April 1925 and the possibility that Ivy would have to give up her foster home for children. Worse, Dorothy's mother, who stayed with Ivy to help with the funeral arrangements, had met John Anthony,* and Dorothy again agonized over telling her parents the truth. But, no; she wrote Ivy, "If we told Mother, she'd want to help, and I don't want to be helped. J's my look-out entirely, and it's feeble if I can't manage without help—financially that, I mean—" The issue was mooted when Ivy decided to keep her home and the children, and Dorothy's parents never learned that the sturdy little one-year-old among the foster children at Cowley was their only grandson.

When Anthony was born, Dorothy thought that she might someday

---

* Dorothy usually referred to her son as "John" or "J.A.," but after coming of age, he always used "Anthony."

wish to reclaim him, but considered marriage an unlikely prospect for herself. On April 13, 1926, she reversed course—wedding a journalist and war veteran named Oswald Arthur Fleming in a London registrar's office. He had adopted the name "Atherton Fleming" for publication, but everyone knew him as "Mac," the voluble, hearty Scot.

Mac was just the kind of husband Dorothy thought she wanted: interesting, experienced, a manly man, but seemingly up to her intellectual standards—although he carried the baggage of an unhappy divorce and two adolescent daughters whom he had effectively abandoned after the war. When Dorothy met him, he was reporting for the *News of the World* (his beats were crime and motor racing), freelancing for other publications, and writing some advertising copy for extra income. Dorothy was now almost thirty-three, and Mac was forty-four (the same age as John Cournos). They had a great deal in common. Mac had published one book and was a dab hand at painting and photography (a hobby of Dorothy's that Cournos had mocked). He shared Dorothy's lusty approach to sex, food and drink, and conversation. Dorothy was open with him about her affair with Bill White and her illegitimate son; far from being horrified, Mac didn't care. He even expressed interest in taking on the father role and bringing John Anthony into the fold.

Dorothy worried how her parents would take the news of her union with a divorced man, a marriage that the Church of England would not recognize, and she delayed contacting them until a week before the wedding. Perhaps another family scandal—Reverend Sayers's elderly brother Cecil had recently separated from his second wife after he had been caught in flagrante with a much younger woman in the potting shed—took the sting out of Dorothy's announcement. Her parents, initially shaken, took the news well on the whole. They did not attend the registry office ceremony, but on Dorothy's wedding night, Henry and Nell Sayers toasted with champagne. Aunt Mabel, however, abstained.

Dorothy and Mac's first visit to Christchurch went beautifully; everyone got along, and Mac, a serious gourmet, was particularly impressed by Nell's table and household management. The new son-in-law was soon addressing Reverend Sayers as "guv'nor" and Nell as "Mother" and making himself thoroughly liked among the citizens of Christchurch. (The locals had never taken a fancy to their rector's aloof and unconventional daughter.) Mac even made a convert of Aunt Mabel, who rarely approved of any husbands.

Mac moved into Dorothy's Great James Street flat in London, and Dorothy at last was able to enjoy a satisfying relationship with a man who was a charming and interesting companion, a gifted raconteur, an experienced and caring lover, and a cook "capable of turning out a perfect dinner for any number of people." Although Dorothy kept her mar-

riage separate from her work at Benson's—John Gilroy was never introduced to Mac—she delighted in accompanying her husband to the auto
races at Brooklands, where he reported on and sometimes organized
events. In the early spring of 1927, they traveled to France: he was covering two crimes that were then being sensationalized in the British
press. Dorothy, like Lord Peter Wimsey, enjoyed the riotous company of
Mac's Fleet Street friends, the hard-living crowd of journalists who had
toasted the Flemings' marriage by getting "incapably drunk" at their favored pub, the Falstaff. The newlyweds frequented the cinema, theater,
and pubs, and they entertained friends at home, with Mac as head chef.

Marriage seemed to suit both partners well, and for the time, plans to
bring home John Anthony, whom Mac had met in May of 1926, were
put on hold. Dorothy and Mac were both working overtime, and the
Great James Street apartment was cramped for just two people. Even
with Mac's help (he contributed recipes and ideas for the Mustard Club
campaign, helped with her editing projects, handled her public relations, and kept track of her press clippings), Dorothy was busy day and
night with her job at Benson's and her writing. She had no time to
tackle motherhood if she was to continue to earn the wherewithal to
ensure her son's future.

Whether Dorothy really wanted to mother her small son is another
question. In 1928, Ivy moved her foster brood to a small cottage in the
village of Westcott Parton, northeast of Oxford. That same year,
Dorothy and Mac substantially enlarged the Great James Street flat by
taking the apartment above and combining the two into a comfortable
maisonette. There surely would have been room for a four-year-old boy
and a nursemaid, but Dorothy had decided that men generally do not
enjoy the company of small children, though her own experience had
certainly been the opposite. It was she who seemed frightened of nurturing. Despite the earth mother fantasies she had expressed to John
Cournos, she plainly did not have any inherent fondness for young children. When she learned that John Anthony, who had been taught to call
her "Cousin Dorothy," had broken his collarbone at age two and a half,
there was no rushing off to be at his side; instead, she wrote to Ivy ap-
proving of his "pluck," and noting "maternal affection is by no means
my strong point, I must say, but if there must be children, it is preferable
that they should have some guts."

Although Dorothy and Mac informally "adopted" John Anthony
later on and the child took Mac's surname, he never lived with them,
and Ivy was always his mother figure. In her 1928 novel, *The Unpleasantness at the Bellona Club,* Dorothy gave Lord Peter a sarcastic little
speech that perhaps reflected her own view: "I'm determined never to
be a parent. Modern manners and the break-up of the fine old traditions

have simply ruined the business. I shall devote my life and fortune to the endowment of research on the best method of producin' human beings decorously and unobtrusively from eggs. All parental responsibility to devolve upon the incubator." Dorothy herself took every precaution to avoid another pregnancy.

To be fair, Dorothy's interest in John Anthony's education, religious training, and intellectual development was sincere, and she never shunted off her financial duties. But even in the private letters she wrote to her son and signed "Mother," there is the sterile quality of schoolmistress to pupil. It would have been inhuman if she had not, at some time or other, resented the fact of him, resented perhaps that there is little romance or glory in the realities of parenthood. And it is helpful to remember Dorothy as a child, so unsure of her own feelings because they never seemed to measure up to the emotional content of literature. In a letter she wrote not long after she had left her son in Ivy Shrimpton's care, Dorothy expressed this ambivalence: "Poor little J.A.—I hardly know whether I love him or hate him. . . ." Perhaps she was never willing to test her feelings, never courageous enough to risk her son's seeming happiness by exposing him to her own conflicted emotions. It was easier, always, to lay off her own reluctance on work or Mac or the pressures of her busy schedule.

Nineteen twenty-eight and 1929 were watershed years for Dorothy and Mac. During the war, Mac had been gassed and suffered shell shock. Although the effects were not immediate (and he had given up the medical pension to which he was entitled), in 1928 his health began to decline, and with it, his earning ability. He no longer had his full-time position with the *News of the World*; his freelance income was unreliable; and he was in arrears on his taxes. There were some food writing assignments, including a cookbook for Crosse and Blackwell, but nothing steady. The Flemings were increasingly reliant on Dorothy's income, which paid for the renovation of the Great James Street apartments and a holiday in Scotland, in addition to John Anthony's support.

Then in September, Dorothy's father—the endlessly patient "Tootles," who had supported her every dream and plan—was gone. At age seventy-four, Reverend Sayers died unexpectedly of pneumonia, "very suddenly, peacefully and mercifully." His death shocked Dorothy, who had never before experienced the loss of a close loved one. She was also confronted with the problem of what to do for her mother and Aunt Mabel Leigh, who would no longer have the Christchurch rectory as a home.

Mac came to the rescue, locating a house called "Sunnyside" at 24 Newland Street in the country town of Witham in Essex. Using money from a legacy, supplemented by a loan from Nell, Dorothy purchased the house, and Mac managed the move from Christchurch. Dorothy's mother, depressed by the death of her husband, had not been particularly grateful. Dorothy was not especially sympathetic: "He bored her to death for nearly 40 years and she always grumbled that he was no companion for her—and now she misses him dreadfully." Nell's gloominess in turn depressed Mac, but her dark cloud lifted as they settled into Witham, and by Christmas, everyone seemed content with the new accommodations.

Dorothy and Mac continued to find peace on their Scottish holidays amid the artists and fishermen of the towns of Gatehouse on Fleet and Kirkcudbright in Galloway. (Dorothy would set her 1931 Wimsey mystery, *Five Red Herrings,* in these towns and dedicate the novel to Joe Digham, landlord of the Anworth Hotel, where the Flemings stayed.) Dorothy and Mac were in Scotland in July of 1929 when Nell Sayers became ill. She died of complications from a ruptured bowel on July 27. She had survived her husband by less than a year and was buried beside him in the cemetery at Christchurch. For some reason, Dorothy never commissioned stones to mark her parents' graves, though years later, the Reverend Sayers's parishioners placed a memorial plaque to the couple in the church.

Only Aunt Mabel was left, and Ivy quite sensibly wrote to Dorothy with the suggestion that she and her foster children move into Sunnyside to care for the now-octogenarian Mabel. Dorothy demurred; Aunt Mabel, she said, would be upset by the presence of youngsters in the house. In fact, Dorothy and Mac had decided to move permanently to Witham and keep the apartment in London. When Mabel died a year later, Dorothy still made no effort to bring John Anthony into her home.

> *"But if only there were 48 hours in the day or fewer exciting things to do in the 24! More time, O God, more time!"*

By the late 1920s and early 1930s, Dorothy L. Sayers had become a firmly established name in detective fiction. By 1929 she had published four Lord Peter novels and also found a publisher, Victor Gollancz, who suited her extremely well. He had been an employee of Ernest Benn (who had bought out Fisher Unwin), and when Gollancz left to form his own company, Dorothy wanted to join him. She had to wait for a while because Benn would not release her from her contract and continued to publish her novels through *The Documents in the Case* in 1930. Dorothy did, however, pull together *Lord Peter Views the Body,* a collection of twelve short stories, for Gollancz, and also undertook (with

Mac's assistance) the compilation of an anthology titled *Great Short Stories of Detection, Mystery and Horror*, released as *Omnibus of Crime* in the United States. Her introduction to the anthology has become a classic and is, to this day, one of the best and most readable short critical histories of the genre ever written.

She was working on what became her only non-Wimsey mystery, *The Documents in the Case*, coauthored with Dr. Robert Eustace Barton (pseudonym: Robert Eustace). Dr. Barton had provided scientific expertise for and cowritten mysteries and thrillers with Mrs. L. T. Meade and Edgar Jepson, both of whose works Dorothy included in her *Great Short Stories* collection. Dorothy wrote to Barton, suggesting a collaborative effort for which she would "invent a new detective." The method of the murder and its novel detection were Barton's major contribution, and Dorothy was fascinated by the science that Barton carefully assembled for her. "The religious-scientific aspect of the thing will require careful handling," she wrote to her collaborator, "but ought, I think, to be very interesting to people. . . ." Dorothy did not invent a new detective for *Documents*; she did not include Wimsey or any of his crowd except Sir James Lubbock, the distinguished fictional forensic chemist. She drew her plot from a real-life case—the Thompson-Bywaters murder—and constructed the novel as a series of letters that present the mystery from different first-person perspectives, in homage to Wilkie Collins.

It was around this time that she became involved in the formation of the Detection Club, a group of writers of detective fiction brought together in a confederation of collegial conviviality by Anthony Berkeley Cox. The club was formally launched in 1932, and Dorothy was one of its most enthusiastic members: the creator, or at least the moving hand, behind its semiserious rituals and routines. The club's activities put her in direct contact with a thinker whose theology she had long admired, G. K. Chesterton. In addition to his poetry and a large body of social, literary, and religious criticism, Chesterton was the author of the popular and influential Father Brown mysteries. He was elected first president of the Detection Club and served until his death in 1936. Among the original members were E. C. Bentley (author of *Trent's Last Case*, which Dorothy said greatly influenced her creation of Lord Peter), Agatha Christie, G. D. H. and Margaret Cole (who had once schemed with Dorothy to put together a detective fiction syndicate), Freeman Wills Crofts, R. Austin Freeman, Father Ronald Knox, A. E. W. Mason, Arthur Morrison, Baroness Emmuska Orczy, and John Rhode. Helen Simpson, who was to become one of Dorothy's close friends, was an associate member.

Probably at Victor Gollancz's suggestion, Dorothy also began a pro-

ject that was to occupy her off and on till she died—a biography of
Wilkie Collins. In 1929 Benn published her translation of *Tristan in Brit-*
tany, a twelfth-century narrative poem by the Anglo-Norman poet
Thomas. (Dorothy had begun the translation after leaving Oxford, under the guidance of her old tutor, Miss Pope. It had been published in
the journal of the Modern Language Association, which Dorothy
joined in 1919. She would serve as president of this organization in
1939.) Dorothy had never abandoned her scholarly interests and her ambitions to write works of serious import, but detective fiction was her
bread and butter, and Lord Peter Wimsey was her meal ticket.

Also at Victor Gollancz's suggestion, Dorothy had engaged a new literary agent, David Higham. Higham worked a small miracle, negotiat-
ing a contract with Dorothy's American publisher, Brewer and Warren,
that guaranteed her a steady income. She was no longer dependent on
advances and royalties. And she could quit Benson's. It was doubtless
hard to leave the camaraderie of the agency, but Dorothy had burned
out on advertising.

It is remarkable to look at the volume of writings she produced between 1921 and 1930 and realize that, through all this time, she was also
working full nine-hour days at Benson's. She learned a great deal during
her tenure there, particularly how to read the public mind and public
taste. A word lover always, she had also learned, through the daily grind
of practical application, the power of persuasive words as weapons for
good or ill. Three years later, she would memorialize Benson's and its
infamous spiral iron staircase in one of her best mysteries, *Murder Must
Advertise.*

Financially, Dorothy was now on her own, although Mac was still
working sporadically. He authored, anonymously, a volume of food and
dining stories and recipes, *Gourmet's Book of Food and Drink,* published by
The Bodley Head in 1933 and dedicated "To my wife, Who can make
an Omelette." He wrote another book that was published in 1936 under the pen name Donald Maconochie. (Maconochie was his mother's
maiden name.) Though from what little evidence exists, Mac himself
wrote dreadful fiction, this book was a guide to novice writers called
The Craft of the Short Story. The only book Mac published under his own
name was *How to See the Battlefields,* a combination of field guide and reportage of his own experiences in the Great War. Published by Cassell
and Company in 1919, this book is rare, but those who have seen the
text say that it is the work of a very capable journalist.

All of Dorothy's biographers agree that by the early 1930s, Dorothy
and Mac's relationship had changed, but exactly how and why is debatable. In *Such a Strange Lady,* Janet Hitchman portrays Mac as a truly de-
spicable character—"a liar, a pretender, a lazy . . . schoolboy who would

never be [Dorothy's] intellectual companion." Hitchman described him as "charming, goodlooking in a slightly decadent way," and "superficially gifted," but lacking even the character to be "an utter rogue . . ."—"just a weak, 'Bonnie Prince Charlie' type, looking for a cushy billet."

When Hitchman's book was published in 1975, a number of people came to Mac's defense. One of his daughters even claimed that Mac, not Dorothy, had masterminded the Wimsey novels—a ridiculous assumption. But cooler heads recognized that Mac Fleming, while he was no Prince Charming, was far from the feeble parasite of the Hitchman study. And a number of his failures may have been directly attributable to his wife's behavior.

Mac suffered a constant cough, a legacy from being gassed in the war, as well as high blood pressure, liver problems, and painful arthritis that caused him to limp slightly. As his health worsened, he became increasingly irascible and temperamental. He was a regular at his local pub in Witham and often relied on whiskey for companionship. He spent hours in his studio, painting his rather-good landscapes, or puttered about at home. Soon after Aunt Mabel's death, Dorothy brought another aunt into the Sunnyside household—Alice Maud Bayliss Leigh, the widow of Nell Sayers's brother and mother of Dorothy's childhood companion Margaret Leigh. Aunt Maud, like Aunt Mabel, was very fond of Mac, and during her frequent visits, she often acted as a peacekeeper between the Flemings. Mac enjoyed Aunt Maud's company, and she seemed to have a soothing influence on him. But Mac was becoming forgetful and would go "into such a frightful fit of rage" when reminded of something. Dorothy became concerned. "The doctors," she wrote to Ivy, "say that he *is* getting definitely queer—but there doesn't seem to be much that one can do about it." The doctors diagnosed most of Mac's ailments as war related, which put Mac in the company of hundreds of thousands of Britons who had been damaged by their service to the nation.

As Mac grew more erratic, Dorothy responded with a curious mixture of solicitude and annoyance. Late in 1933, during a holiday with Muriel St. Clare Byrne, she seriously considered leaving Mac, but for a variety of reasons—among which her religious principles must have ranked high—she decided against a separation. She had made the marriage; she would hold it together. Dorothy always felt great affection for her husband, but she may not have grasped the unique psychological difficulties facing a moderately talented and intelligent man married to a gifted, famous, and self-assertive woman. She seems to have compartmentalized Mac, as she so often compartmentalized troublesome things in her life. She usually left him behind when she went to London on business or for her own pleasure, and kept him away from her business associates, as she had excluded him from contact with her Benson's friends. In the house at Witham, they often passed like ships at night, eating lunch and dinner together but otherwise occupying their time in separate pursuits. People who did not know Mac well often blamed his drinking for the troubles; reliable observers who were familiar with the Witham household were not so sure.

Close friends later expressed their belief that Mac and Dorothy had simply reached the point of getting on one another's nerves. In Witham, they shared the same house day and night and could not help but get in each other's way. It has been reported that they had separate bedrooms, as if that were clear evidence of estrangement, but in *Busman's Honeymoon,* Dorothy gave Peter and Harriet Wimsey separate bedrooms even in the midst of their erotic honeymoon. It has also been said that the Flemings were not physically affectionate, but Dorothy always avoided touching and public displays like the plague.

She repeatedly implied that Mac was the cause of her failure to claim John Anthony as her own, but there is at least circumstantial evidence that *she* was the stumbling block. Adoption had become legal in England in 1926, but in order to adopt, Dorothy would be required to produce her child's birth certificate in court, revealing the secret of his birth. This she would not do, even after the deaths of her parents and when she had attained sufficient public stature to weather a scandal. (She did make some kind of formal arrangement, for she later told John Anthony that her lawyers had copies of his "adoption papers.") Was Mac the problem, as she repeatedly hinted in her letters to Ivy Shrimpton? Or was she?

Today, Mac might well be right to complain of mixed signals from his wife. In a 1976 interview, Muriel Byrne remembered Mac once asking, "What can I do to please her? She doesn't think I love her, but I do. Nothing I do seems to make any difference."* Did Dorothy want him in or out of her life? As James Brabazon writes, "Mac . . . was all very well up to a point, but he was not the man she really wanted to marry." But whom had she wanted? John Cournos? Eric Whelpton? Her old Bach Choir conductor, Hugh Allen? They all, sooner or later, failed to meet her standards. Could any man of flesh and bone have satisfied Dorothy's fiction-bred longing for an all-consuming passion that also left her free to pursue her own interests and goals without interference?

There was one such man, of course: he belonged wholly to Dorothy, and she could make him do exactly as she desired.

---

* From notes taken in an interview conducted by Lt. Col. R. C. Clarke, August 22, 1976. Quoted by Trevor H. Hall in *Dorothy L. Sayers: Nine Literary Studies.*

"Fair and Mayfair"

In 1936, Dorothy wrote an article explaining the origin of Lord Peter Death Bredon Wimsey. She said that when she needed a detective, he quite simply walked into her imagination and applied for the job. But rigorous literary sleuths have uncovered a more complicated story.

Lord Peter seems to have been forming himself in Dorothy's mind for some time before she sat down to craft her first novel. Probably in 1920, he made his first appearance in an outline she developed for a Sexton Blake short story: he is already listed in *Who's Who,* and a character describes him thus: "Younger son of the Duke of Peterborough. . . . Distinguished himself in the war. Rides his own horse in the Grand National. Authority on first editions. . . . Fair-haired, big nose, aristocratic sort of man whose socks match his tie. No politics." Dorothy had already located him in Piccadilly and at the center of a murder, though Peter was only a secondary character. As Barbara Reynolds points out, Dorothy may well have sketched out this story while she was still living in France, drawing on the characteristics of Eric Whelpton and the anecdotes of London high life told by Charles Crichton. Not long after, Dorothy wrote several pages of ideas for a play she entitled *The Mousehole: A Detective Fantasia in Three Flats,* and here he is again: "Lord Peter Wimsey. Thirty-two, unmarried; no occupation; residence, first floor; hobby, other people's business."

When Dorothy got her idea for the plot of a mystery novel that became *Whose Body?,* she had already put in a good deal of time on her highborn detective. She drew on a variety of sources, both real and literary. Lord Peter was part Eric Whelpton: young man of the world, speaks French like a native, war veteran, attractive to women. He shared some of the experiences of Charles Crichton: London bachelor flat, fast-lane lifestyle, loyal batman-valet. In attitude, he owed mightily to Philip Trent, the hero of E. C. Bentley's *Trent's Last Case,* the groundbreaking 1913 novel that is generally credited as the first to successfully humanize and "humorize" the fictional detective. He acquired not a few of his original "silly ass" mannerisms from Bertie Wooster, the popular upper-class nitwit of P. G. Wodehouse's beloved comic novels. There is even something of Baroness Orczy's Scarlet Pimpernel about him.

Lord Peter inherited his distinctive physiognomy from a real young man whom Dorothy had never met but had seen once during an Oxford degree ceremony she attended during her college days: he was the recipient of the Newgate Prize and read a poem on Oxford. She had written immediately to a friend that "Charis [Barnett] and I fell head over ears in love with him on the spot. His name is Maurice Roy Ridley—isn't it a killing name, like the hero of a six-penny novelette? He has just gone down from Balliol, so I shall see him no more. My loves are always unsatisfactory, as you know." Whether she remembered this exact occasion or not, Roy Ridley had taken up lodging in her mind, to reappear in the physical person of Lord Peter. Dorothy did, in fact, encounter Ridley again, when she was giving a lecture at Oxford in 1935. Afterward, she wrote to Muriel Byrne, with whom she was then plotting the play of *Busman's Honeymoon,* "I have seen the *perfect* Peter Wimsey. Height, voice, charm, smile, manner, outline of features, *everything*—and he is—THE CHAPLAIN OF BALLIOL!!!" (Ridley later became John Anthony Fleming's tutor at Balliol College and irritated Dorothy with his frequent claims to be the model of Lord Peter.)

But Lord Peter is most indebted to his creator; underlying all else is a fictional hero very much like herself in character and personality. Perhaps that is why he survives, and why Dorothy survives through him. Author and hero are like two sides of the same coin—intelligent, well educated, lovers of language and music, superficially rebellious and coarse but intensely loyal to tradition and duty, secretive, lusty, arrogant yet also self-doubting, and capable to a remarkable degree of separating their lives into convenient compartments. They are both, to use a phrase from Dorothy's schoolgirl days, "weird freaks" within conventional settings.

Peter Wimsey is an unusual serial detective because he not only ages on lines parallel to his creator; he develops and matures with age. When Peter made his first public appearance in 1923, he was thirty-two; Dorothy was thirty. In his last fictional outing, the 1942 short story "Talboys," Peter is fifty-two; Dorothy was almost fifty. He began his fictional life as a prattling and somewhat effete man of noble birth and seemingly unlimited resources,★ "Fair and Mayfair," full of nervous energy and facile interests. In his last appearance, he is happily and faithfully married after a long and emotionally exhausting courtship, his pleasures now focused on his wife and three young sons. Few Golden Age writers tried, much less succeeded as Dorothy did, in creating central characters whose personal development is fully as interesting as any of the crimes they solve.

Though she later claimed that Lord Peter's first outing was written "with the avowed intention of producing something 'less like a conventional detective story and more like a novel,' " Dorothy wrote her detective fiction primarily to make money; she regarded Lord Peter as first and foremost a means to meet her obligations until she earned the fi-

---

★ Dorothy said that she endowed Peter with great wealth in part because she had none of her own and could enjoy his free-spending lifestyle vicariously.

nancial security to write the serious works that were her prime objective. But it was impossible for her to divorce the creation from the creator. She simply was incapable of inventing a Lord Peter who was solely her breadwinner. He had to be real to her first, then to the people who bought her books. He could not remain static: the Peter Wimsey who interested her when she was thirty could not have held her attention two decades later.

In fact, by 1930, when she wrote *Documents in the Case* with Dr. Barton and deliberately left Wimsey out, she was losing interest in her chief character. In her next book, *Strong Poison,* she introduced Peter to the love of his life, Harriet Vane (her most autobiographical female character). Harriet is only sketchily developed in this book, largely because she was intended as nothing more than a device to free Dorothy from her attachment to Lord Peter. Dorothy didn't want to kill her profitable detective; she wanted to put him aside by marrying him off. Marriage, she reasoned, would logically bring Lord Peter's private investigation to a halt and also allow the author to revive him, if need be, at some future time. But when she came to the end of *Strong Poison,* Dorothy discovered that the curious relationship she had created between Harriet and Peter could not end happily ever after in this book. Almost in spite of herself, Dorothy had raised Peter to a new level of interest; her old bon vivant sleuth, once so footloose and fancy-free, had become a man in love, stricken with a new purpose and the stirrings of a new seriousness. Such is real life.

Some critics, pointing to the four Peter-and-Harriet novels and particularly to the perceived failures of *Gaudy Night,* her next-to-last, have accused Dorothy of ruining the Wimsey books by falling in love with her hero. It is sometimes suggested that what she failed to find in Mac Fleming, she fantasized in Peter Wimsey, and there may be some truth in this carping. Certainly Peter in the later novels comes closer to the type of man she envisioned for herself than any of her real-life loves. But as psychology has been telling us for some time, romantic fantasy is a perfectly normal adjunct to love and sex—and to fiction.

It was not long after *Strong Poison* that Dorothy got the itch to write her memoirs, and she began *My Edwardian Childhood.* She didn't work at it for too long before returning to a new Lord Peter project and her Wilkie Collins biography. Two years later, however, she transformed the work she had done on the memoir into the opening chapters of a proposed "straight"—and autobiographical—novel that she titled *Cat o'Mary: The Biography of a Prig,* to be published under the pen name Johanna Leigh. She eventually completed two hundred pages of revealing and self-flagellating writing, and in 1934 her publishers announced the forthcoming publication in the trade press. Then she dropped it.

In the process of developing the story of Katherine Lammas—Dorothy's alter ego in *Cat o'Mary*—the author had learned something about herself and what she valued in life. *My Edwardian Childhood* and *Cat o'Mary* had been cathartic exercises. Through them, she discovered both what, at age forty-one, she wanted to say and how to say it. There was no longer any need for memoir or autobiographical fiction. She had already invented a character who could express her ideas about love and work and the complicated business of remaining true to one's self. It was not Peter Wimsey.

Harriet Vane—a character conceived to serve a specific, onetime purpose and based, more for convenience than any deeper motive, on the author herself—would be Dorothy's voice. Her vehicle would be the dense, difficult, often self-indulgent and annoying, sometimes soaring, intellectually challenging, erotically charged *Gaudy Night*.

> *"On the intellectual platform, alone of all others, Harriet could stand free and equal with Peter. . . ."*
>
> —"Gaudy Night," a 1937 essay

Between *Strong Poison* and *Gaudy Night,* Dorothy was hardly idle. She wrote three Wimsey novels—*The Five Red Herrings, Murder Must Advertise,* and the work that many readers regard as her finest mystery, *The Nine Tailors*—that feature Peter alone. (Harriet is referred to, though not by name, in one sentence in *Murder Must Advertise.*) In 1932, Dorothy had returned to Peter and Harriet in *Have His Carcase,* expanding on their relationship but getting them no nearer to the marriage bed than at the end of *Strong Poison.*

The Nine Tailors was a difficult and time-intensive project; in order to meet her contractual obligations, Dorothy interrupted her work on it to write *Murder Must Advertise.* To prepare for *Tailors,* Dorothy immersed herself in the study of the arcane art of bell ringing, which forms one of the core events of the story. There is much of Bluntisham and more of Christchurch, her father's two parishes, in the novel's country village of Fenchurch St. Paul, its inhabitants, and its environs. She created, with the assistance of architect W. J. Redhead, an entire church that is, in Lord Peter's words, "like a young cathedral." Dorothy also delved into the engineering of the intricate system of dams and drainage canals, whose fictitious failure precipitates the book's final, dramatic flood sequence. Her attention to detail was meticulous, and she was "sinfully proud" that bell-ringing experts could find only "three small technical errors" in the finished novel.

The book ranged farther and wider than any of her previous novels and was more subtly layered than anything else she had written. It works as murder mystery; it works as serious novel of manners. Wimsey, who is involved in the criminal action by sheer chance, displayed a new depth and purpose. Gone was much of the giddy flippancy that previously characterized his behavior. He had settled more comfortably into the role of mature man of conscience. But Dorothy's ultimate achievement in *The Nine Tailors* was the creation of a character who overshadowed even Wimsey: the Reverend Theodore Venables. Though Dorothy said that the country rector and his wife were not directly based on Henry and Nell Sayers, they stand as a fitting tribute paid by a willful daughter to her good and patient parents. Dorothy called this book a "labour of love," and in it she perhaps made some kind of peace with her childhood.

The Nine Tailors—which owes its inspiration to a 1903 novel, *The Nebuly Coat* by John Meade Falkner, and its broad concept to Dorothy's study of Wilkie Collins—was an immediate success with critics and readers and pushed its author into celebrityhood. Her opinions were solicited by the press. She was hired by *The Sunday Times* to review detective fiction. She was elected as a charter member of the Sherlock Holmes Society. She became a sought-after speaker. The effects of this new public status on her marriage were predictable: kept out of his wife's limelight, Mac became more difficult, at times deliberately sabotaging Dorothy's schedule and plans. He was now the shadowy appendage of a famous wife, and it hurt. On one occasion, he stormed out of Witham's Red Lion pub, usually so welcome a retreat, when someone pointed him out as "Dorothy Sayers's husband." Dorothy persevered, humoring his whims and moods, yet all the while creating an increasingly separate life for herself.

In June of 1934, six months after the publication of *The Nine Tailors,* Dorothy was invited back to Somerville College to participate in a gaudy dinner honoring Mildred Pope. (In Britain, "gaudy" refers to a celebratory occasion, especially college reunions.) In her academic robes, Dorothy toasted not only her old French tutor but Oxford itself and "some of the noblest things for which this University stands: the integrity of judgment that gain cannot corrupt; the humility in the face of the facts that self-esteem cannot blind; the generosity of a great mind that is eager to give praise to others; the singleness of purpose that pursues knowledge as some men pursue glory and that will not be contented with the second-hand or the second-best."

The gaudy was pivotal: it gave her the answer to the problem of Peter Wimsey and Harriet Vane. In *Strong Poison,* Peter had met and fallen in love with Harriet when she was on trial for the murder of her ex-lover. In *Have His Carcase,* Harriet had called him in to solve a murder, and amid the sleuthing, their relationship had become more believable and complex. But Dorothy had loaded Harriet with an immense weight of self-doubt and guilt. (She was, after all, a sullied woman, having lived in sin and been publicly humiliated in the dock of the Old Bailey.) Though drawn to Peter, Harriet resists his endless proposals, fearing that to accept him will be an act of gratitude rather than love, fearing that he will be unable to put aside the memory of her love affair, and fearing that she will damage his social position and alienate his family. In fact, by the conclusion of *Have His Carcase,* Harriet seems intractably mired in her neurotic love-fear relationship with her ardent suitor. As Dorothy wrote in a 1937 essay about *Gaudy Night,* "[Harriet's] inferiority complex was making her steadily more brutal to him and his newly developed psychology was making him steadily more sensitive to her inhibitions."

To dig Harriet out of her passive-aggressive hole and move the affair forward, Dorothy needed a catalytic event that would suit the two human natures she had concocted. A simple homicide was not sufficient. What Dorothy did was send Harriet back to Oxford, to a reunion at Shrewsbury College (an invented version of Somerville, which she "built," as she had the church in *The Nine Tailors,* with the help of an architect and located on the cricket field of Balliol College). There is a mystery, nasty but not fatal, that serves to get Peter and Harriet together and throw suspicion on the faculty of the college. But *Gaudy Night* is really an intellectual romance in which the detection is only a means to push the plot along. The focus of the story is Harriet, as she comes to terms with herself so she can come to terms with Peter.

Gaudy Night was, and remains, Dorothy's most argued-about novel. When published in 1936, it won both praise and searing criticism, most particularly in a review by Q. D. Leavis. Mrs. Leavis attacked Dorothy's book basically for its phony literariness and its false picture of university life as intellectually pure. She accused Dorothy of writing "rationalized nostalgia" for her own college days, and Dorothy felt the full sting of that slap. Readers who were used to clever plotting and criminality in their Lord Peter stories were inevitably disappointed. In his study of detective fiction, *Bloody Murder,* critic Julian Symons said that "*Gaudy Night* is essentially a 'woman's novel' full of the most tedious pseudo-serious chat. . . ." At least one female reader wrote to the author that Lord Peter had lost his "elfin charm," to which Dorothy replied "that any man who retained elfin charm at the age of forty-five should be put in a lethal chamber." To others, Dorothy seemed to have plummeted, finally, over the edge of her superiority complex. (The book requires of the reader a more-than-passing familiarity with English and French literature and Latin construction. Dorothy also had a habit of writing her sexiest passages in French, and not providing translations. And in order to comprehend the novel's closing, and crucial, passage, the reader must know Latin *and* the rituals of the Oxford University degree awarding ceremony.★) Even latterday feminists, who have adopted Dorothy as a kind of minor saint, see the book as a sellout of the principles of independent womanhood.

Regardless, the book did very well, and it satisfied its author. Dorothy was notorious for the funks she fell into following the completion of her novels. Once done with a book of detection, she invariably hated it and bemoaned her failure to achieve her literary objectives. But when she turned *Gaudy Night* over to Victor Gollancz in September 1934, she said that "it's the book I wanted to write and I've written it. . . ." She understood that *Gaudy Night* would be difficult to market (leaving it up to Gollancz whether to promote it "as a love-story, or as educational propaganda, or as a lunatic freak"). It might flop, but she was satisfied.

While working on her Oxford love story, Dorothy also undertook what was to be her final full-blown Lord Peter project. It started with a totally unrelated incident at home in Witham. A chimney sweep was called into Sunnyside, and he arrived wearing layer upon layer of colorful knitted sweaters. As he worked, the heavy layers were successively peeled away. When Dorothy visited her friends Muriel Byrne and Marjorie Barber a few days later in London, she regaled them with the story of the stripping sweep and remarked what a fine stage character he would make. Muriel took her up on the idea.

For several years, Muriel had helped Dorothy sift through proposals to put Lord Peter on stage, but no one else's ideas had ever been acceptable. The time had come, Muriel argued, for Dorothy to do the job herself. Dorothy agreed, so long as Muriel, an experienced producer of amateur theater who was then teaching at the Royal Academy of Dramatic Art, would coauthor. So while Dorothy was knee-deep in *Gaudy Night,* she and Muriel began the comedy of detection that takes up near the point at which *Gaudy Night* ends, with the newly married Lord and Lady Peter on their wedding trip. As Dorothy was getting her novel couple engaged, she was also plotting their stage marriage, and at times the marriage ran well ahead of the courtship.

The play was accepted by producer Anmer Hall, and rehearsals began

---

★ For those who are not Latinists or Oxford graduates, Peter and Harriet's final *Gaudy Night* dialog is taken from the traditional degree confirmation at Oxford. An official of the university asks, "Placetne?" (Does it please?), to which the graduate responds, "Placet." (It pleases.) Another tradition—echoed in the final line of the book—is that as degrees are presented, proctors walk among those attending the ceremony so that anyone who objects to a particular degree candidate can register his complaint by pulling at the sleeve of the proctor's academic robe.

in November 1936, with Dennis Arundell and Veronica Turleigh cast as Peter and Harriet. Dorothy was at last in the real world of the theater, and just as she had thrown herself heart and soul into her backyard productions of *The Three Musketeers* so many years before at the Bluntisham rectory, she jumped into the production of *Busman's Honeymoon,* traveling to the tryouts, mothering the cast, refining and improving the dialog. Her dedication was rewarded on December 16, 1936, when the play opened at the Comedy Theatre in London's West End. *Busman's Honeymoon* was generally well reviewed and enjoyed a successful nine-month run. The novel that Dorothy developed from the play was published the following year.

Dorothy planned at least one more "Lord Peter," leaving behind the opening chapters and plot outline for a book she called *Thrones, Dominations* (completed some sixty years later by Jill Paton Walsh and published in 1998). But there would be no more full-length adventures for her "Fair and Mayfair" detective. She wrote two more Wimsey short stories: "The Haunted Policeman," which is set on the night of the birth of Peter and Harriet's first son, and "Talboys," which takes place seven years and three children into the Wimsey marriage. During World War Two, Dorothy put together a series of patriotic Wimsey family letters that were published in the *Spectator* magazine. But to all intents and purposes, the 1937 appearance of *Busman's Honeymoon* under hardcover was the end of the saga.

In her late forties, Dorothy was literally fat and happier than she had been in years. For all its many flaws, *Gaudy Night* had been an act of personal exploration and expiation, allowing her to determine where her true purpose—her "proper work"—lay, and *Busman's Honeymoon* had provided a kind of joyful denouement to the first quarter-century of her public career. There was much more work ahead, but work of a very different sort.

". . . their salvation is in themselves and in each separate man and woman among them. . . ."

In October of 1936, an offer came Dorothy's way that was to redirect her career and her life. Margaret Babington, organizer of the Canterbury Festival of Canterbury Cathedral, contacted Dorothy to ask if the mystery novelist would be interested in writing a play for the annual event. Dorothy must have been stunned. Her one play, *Busman's Honeymoon,* had not even reached the stage, yet here she was being offered what every playwright dreams of: a commission to do a play that was guaranteed performance. She would be in excellent company. The previous two Canterbury Festival plays had been T. S. Eliot's *Murder in the Cathedral* and Charles Williams's *Thomas Cranmer of Canterbury*. Dorothy had been recommended to the Festival Committee by Charles Williams, but still, the choice of a popular detective fiction writer seemed odd, even to Dorothy. There were plenty of experienced stage writers in England, but, as James Brabazon points out, the number of playwrights who were "competent, distinguished and Christian" was limited.

Dorothy was no theologian, but she was as firmly grounded in theology as anyone. She believed in the traditional Christian church—the Catholic church of history—and its doctrines, particularly the doctrine of the Incarnation. She also related human creativity to doctrine, believing that God created man to be creative.

The theme of the 1937 Canterbury Festival—a celebration of artists and craftsmen—naturally attracted her, and after some initial hesitation, Dorothy agreed to the project. She was soon deep into her new play, which she built on the story of twelfth-century architect William of Sens, who had rebuilt the Cathedral choir after a disastrous fire. The theme and her choice of subject allowed her to expand on ideas about the nature of work and creativity that she had already explored in *Gaudy Night*. The title of the play, *The Zeal of Thy House,* was taken from a verse in the book of Psalms.

Colorfully staged in the Canterbury chapel, *Zeal* was first performed on June 12, 1937, and reaction was excellent. Dorothy was joined by a trainload of friends,★ including Muriel Byrne, Dorothy Rowe, Helen Simpson and her husband, Marjorie Barber, and Aunt Maud Leigh. Mac Fleming did not attend, perhaps for health reasons.

The Zeal of Thy House was Dorothy's first move into a new and not altogether comfortable role as Christian apologist. For the next decade, her published output consisted almost exclusively of plays, essays, and theologically based books. She was engaged to write a second Festival play for Canterbury, a uniquely Sayers variation on the Faust legend titled *The Devil to Pay* that debuted in June 1939. In 1938, she was commissioned to write a nativity play for the BBC's "Children's Hour" radio

---

★ Dorothy had lost contact with her good friend Muriel Jaeger by this time, though "Jim" had been instrumental in getting Dorothy to complete her first novel. An explanation may be inferred from a letter that Dorothy wrote to Dr. Eustace Barton in 1928, while she was working on *The Documents in the Case*. Dorothy had asked the scientist about the subject of homosexuality, and he supplied some information and recommended reading. In her reply, Dorothy wrote of a friend who "won't see, speak or write to me now I'm married, because marriage revolts her." Dr. Barbara Reynolds, who has collected and edited Dorothy's letters, speculates that this friend was Muriel Jaeger.

program, a venture that set the stage for one of her most powerful achievements two years later.

She wrote a light romantic comedy, *Love All,* in 1940, but this play never reached the London stage. Dorothy, however, was already submersed in the war effort. She had volunteered her services to the War Office and been appointed to the Authors' Planning Committee of the Ministry of Information. But Dorothy Sayers and government bureaucrats mixed like fire and ice, and she was deemed "difficult and loquacious"* and dropped from the Ministry's list of authors. Although she was eventually invited back by the committee, Dorothy was not one to take any criticism lightly, and she refused.

Her eleven Wimsey letters appeared in the *Spectator* between November 1939 and January 1940. These letters purported to be from various members of the Wimsey family to Lord Peter, who was serving "somewhere in Europe." Although most of the letters were lighthearted morale boosters for the folks on the home front, the final letter, from Peter to Harriet, expressed Dorothy's deep concern about the nature of individual freedom and individual responsibility. In Peter's voice, she exhorted:

> Tell them [the British people], this is a battle of a new kind, and it is they who have to fight it, and they must do it themselves and alone. They must not continually ask for leadership—they must lead themselves. This is a war against submission to leadership, and we might quite easily win it in the field and yet lose it in our own country. . . .
>
> It's not enough to rouse up the Government to do this and that. You must rouse the people. You must make them understand that their salvation is in themselves and in each separate man and woman among them. . . .   —Wimsey Papers XI, January 26, 1940

Dorothy, like all her countrymen, worried about the progress of the war. She and Mac took a young evacuee from London into their Witham home for two years. (That the child enjoyed his long stay must in some way be a credit to Mac.) She sheltered her friends' cats as well as her own, and worried about a possible bombardment. She knitted endless pairs of woolen socks for sailors. She was gentle with Mac, whose moods and outbursts were still unpredictable.

But Dorothy could be a harridan, venting her temper in truly obnoxious and irrational ways. The most flagrant example came when she

---

* An internal memorandum quoted by James Brabazon.

was commissioned by Reverend Dr. J. W. Welch, director of Religious Broadcasting, to develop and write a series of half-hour radio plays on the life of Christ for the BBC's *Children's Hour*. Dorothy agreed but was immediately on her guard against any interference in her work by the BBC bureaucrats. She was unhappy when production of the plays was assigned to Derek McCulloch, the director of the Children's Hour Department; she wanted Val Gielgud, with whom she had worked very well on her earlier radio program, the 1938 nativity play. Regardless, she met McCulloch and seemed satisfied. When she submitted her first script in the series, she received a generally glowing response, not from McCulloch, who was unavailable, but from his assistant director, May Jenkin. Miss Jenkin's letter was in all ways civil and laudatory but contained some concerns about language that might be too sophisticated for an audience of children and discreetly asked permission to edit the script.

Dorothy L. Sayers hit the roof. She fired off letters to Dr. Welch and Derek McCulloch. She threatened, she hectored, she insulted with condescension. Dr. Welch, an apparent master of diplomacy, finally managed to calm the situation. But Miss Jenkin, an experienced radio producer, chose to defend herself against Dorothy's personal attacks. (Dorothy had accused her, among other things, of impertinence, tactlessness and literary ignorance.) She wrote directly to Dorothy and received in return an envelope containing a terse note and the torn-up pieces of Dorothy's contract.

The impasse was eventually resolved by Dr. Welch. The series of plays, given the overall title *The Man Born to Be King*, was moved out of the Children's Hour Department, and Val Gielgud was assigned to produce. But May Jenkin, who had behaved professionally throughout, was to be avenged in a way, when the tables were turned on Dorothy.

Shortly before the finished series was set to air, Dorothy participated in a press conference and read a statement to the assembled journalists that addressed two key issues: the use of an actor to play the role of Jesus and the adoption of modern-day idiomatic speech. She also read a short passage from one of the plays. The next day's headline in the *Daily Mail* shouted, "BBC 'Life of Christ' Play in US Slang." Religious conservatives—particularly the Protestant Truth Society and The Lord's Day Observance Society—were incensed. Public protest rained down; there were questions in Parliament; some even blamed the Japanese capture of Singapore on the BBC's blasphemies.

Dorothy, who had spent so many years in advertising, appreciated the value of publicity, but this uproar had quickly gotten out of control, and the situation depressed her. It was now *her* work being unfairly judged, and she bemoaned the stupidity of willfully ignorant people. Still, she was prepared to fight, especially when the Bishop of Winchester expressed concerns again about her choice of language. But when the series finally aired, the tide turned, and *The Man Born to Be King* was greeted as a major achievement. Letters of gratitude and congratulations poured in. Dorothy was gracious in success and paid tribute to Dr. Welch, Val Gielgud, and all the cast and crew she worked with on the final production. She now jokingly referred to her earlier temper tantrum as "the Battle of the Scripts" and refrained from referring to Miss Jenkin at all.

Some time afterward, Dr. Welch recommended Dorothy for an extraordinary honor, the Lambeth Degree of Doctor of Divinity. When the degree was offered by the Archbishop of Canterbury, Dorothy was deeply torn. Certainly it was a prestigious recognition of her work and her intellectual achievements, and if she accepted, she would be the first woman to receive a Lambeth Degree. But she worried that a degree in divinity did not suit: ". . . I should feel better about it if I were a more convincing kind of Christian," she wrote to the Archbishop in a rare mood of humility. "I am never quite sure whether I really am one, or whether I have only fallen in love with an intellectual pattern." She may also have been troubled, as James Brabazon speculates, by the awareness of her own secret sin and by the prospect of discovery of her son's existence. Dorothy was an intellectual Christian, but she admitted that the only truth she knew and accepted through personal experience was the existence of sin. After some soul-searching, she declined the Lambeth Degree.

Still, Dorothy and her opinions were in great demand, especially in the religious and scholarly communities. In 1941, she published what many believe to be her masterwork, *The Mind of the Maker,* the first in a proposed series of books by different authors. This "Bridgeheads" series was abandoned after only three books were published, but *The Mind of the Maker* remains a powerful and challenging essay on the creative process. Scholars of her work tend to agree that this book, which links the three broad phases of artistic creation to the doctrine of the Trinity, is her most original work and most important contribution to literary and theological criticism.

Dorothy had become identified with a small group of influential lay Christian apologists that included C. S. Lewis, T. S. Eliot, and Charles Williams. She corresponded with all three (leading Lewis to proclaim her one of the great letter-writers of the century), but she established a special relationship with Williams. It was Williams who helped to change the course of her career with his recommendation to the Canterbury Festival Committee in 1936. He may also have influenced her personal life by challenging her sense of intellectual superiority. He certainly introduced her to her last great love.

As illustrated by the altercation with May Jenkin and the BBC, Dorothy could be monstrously hostile and unjust to those who questioned her God-given right to be right. It was a lifelong pattern, perhaps exacerbated by the onset of menopause, but few dared to risk her wrath with confrontation. One who did was the gentle Charles Williams, a writer and lay scholar who, in James Brabazon's words, "seemed . . . to understand in his blood and bones the [spiritual] truths of which the laws were merely man-made formulations." Writing to Dorothy in 1943 and 1944, Williams raised the troubling issue of the separation of intellectual Christianity from real-world application. "I darkly suspected," he wrote, "that you and I were both dangerously near coming under judgement. The temptation of thinking that the business of writing frees one from everything else is very profound. . . ."* In his subtle and generous way, Williams had put his finger on Dorothy's weak spot: her belief that her "proper job" was the intellectual explication of Christian dogma. Was she using, as he suggested in another letter, "the byways of the literary mind" as an "excuse" to avoid personal responsibility? Brabazon speculates that her contact with Charles Williams had a powerful impact, possibly allowing her own doubts to surface. Her behavior did change at about this time, as the seething intolerance of others receded and a gentler Dorothy began to emerge.

Her second debt to Williams was her introduction to the *Divine Comedy* of Dante Alighieri, whom she often quoted but had never read. It was Williams's critical work *The Figure of Beatrice* that opened Dorothy's eyes and mind to the great Italian poet. It was a German air raid that launched her on the project that would occupy her until her death. Retreating to a shelter during a bombardment of London, she took a copy of Dante's *Inferno* with her. Though she had to stumble her way through the original Italian, the encounter was life-altering. As she said later, "I can remember nothing like it since I first read *The Three Musketeers* at the age of thirteen. . . ." She soon contracted with Penguin Classics to do a new translation (after teaching herself medieval Italian) of the entire *Commedia,* and though she continued other projects, Dante was to be her most constant companion for the next dozen years. Here was the final intellectual romance—a man centuries dead whom she could "fight with," battling every step of the way to bring to life in modern English the rich, earthy, exuberant brilliance she discovered in his words.

---

*Quoted by James Brabazon in *Dorothy L. Sayers: A Biography*.

"He seems to be turning out a good sort of kid, and I'm disposed to like him. . . ."

For all her professional activity, Dorothy's dedication to her son's welfare was unwavering. In 1935 she and Mac had made some kind of adoption arrangement, and John Anthony was instructed that he should address Dorothy as "Mother" and Mac as "Father." Henceforth his surname would be Fleming.

Dorothy knew that the time had come to prepare her son for formal education, and with Ivy, she arranged for him to attend a small boy's school that would provide the tutoring he needed to be accepted by a good secondary school (as her father had so often tutored boys at his rectory in Bluntisham). At twelve, John Anthony was sent off to a rectory school in Somerset. When the headmaster died, the boy was transferred briefly to a school in Devon, then to a school in Broadstairs, Kent, that passed Dorothy's rigorous inspection.

They corresponded fairly often, and sometimes Dorothy met her son when he changed trains in London, treating him to shopping and sightseeing. Her letters are punctuated with congratulations and encouragement, for John Anthony was an able student, and she was always solicitous of his needs, stretching her budget to see that he could take piano and riding lessons. John Anthony won a scholarship to Malvern College (prep school), where he began to show a serious interest in writing and also an aptitude for mathematics. When the boy had difficulty with history, perhaps from an inherited lack of interest, Dorothy wrote with understanding that "it is a difficult subject to make much of, or take much interest in, until one grows up—and then it suddenly becomes enthralling, and one wishes one had done more about it in one's school-days."* Early in 1939, John Anthony sought her advice about his future academic course: writing and the humanities or math and science. Dorothy was reassuring, offering the advice that she believed in so intensely for herself: "Of one thing you can be sure: if you are a creator in any particular medium, you will end by discovering the fact. Nothing can prevent the genuine creator from creating or from creating in his own proper medium."

In 1941, John Anthony won a scholarship to Balliol College at Oxford, but he wrote to his mother about the possibility of deferring his

---

* Dorothy retained her girlhood bias against the teachers of history well into adulthood. In *Gaudy Night,* the only objectionable scholar is the history don, Miss Hillyard, who hates Harriet Vane with a distorted passion that has nothing to do with scholarship.

education to take up some kind of war work. Her response was as even-handed as possible, and she left the decision to him. John Anthony opted to postpone Oxford, and he joined the Technical Branch of the Royal Air Force. He did not "go up" to Balliol until 1945 and completed his studies in 1948, taking, as his mother had, a First Class degree. In her congratulatory note to him, she enclosed money for a holiday.

She had done it. She had seen to it that her son was reared to full adulthood, given every opportunity that he deserved, and sheltered always from the public shame of his birth. Dorothy never directly admitted to him that she was his real mother. She had denied herself all the potential joys of parenthood, and avoided most of its messes and terrors and disappointments. She had purged her great sin, and it was time to move on with her "proper job."

Following his graduation, Dorothy and her son grew apart, which is hardly unusual in any parent-child relationship when the child is in his twenties. John Anthony White had matured into Anthony Fleming and was ready for the responsibilities of adulthood. It is likely, too, that Dorothy wanted to avoid the questions that every grown man has a right to ask about his paternity and his heritage. Anthony had suspected that Dorothy was his mother at least since his early adolescence; his suspicions were later confirmed when he got his birth certificate in order to apply for a passport. But there is no indication that he ever confronted Dorothy with his knowledge of the truth.

The first volume of Dorothy's Dante translation, *Hell,* was published in 1949. A year later, she lost her husband of twenty-four years. Mac had been in and out of the hospital several times for coronary artery disease, and on June 9, 1950, he suffered a stroke that was instantly fatal. He was sixty-nine. He was cremated, and following his wishes, his remains were taken to rest in his family's ancestral homeland. His attending physician scattered Mac's ashes in the churchyard of the town of Biggar in Scotland. Appropriately, the church was located next door to a pub, The Fleming Arms. Dorothy did not accompany Mac on his final journey, but perhaps to her own surprise, she missed his presence in her life. She wrote to Muriel Byrne, "It will seem very queer without Mac. I shall miss having him to look after, and there will be no one to curse me and keep me up to the mark!" To another friend, Dorothy lamented, "It seems impossible that there should be so many uninterrupted hours in the day."

Nine months later, there was another loss, one that drew Dorothy together with her son once more. Ivy Shrimpton died, leaving her worldly goods to Dorothy—about £4,000, which Dorothy gave to Anthony. He handled the funeral arrangements and purchased the burial plot in Banbury for the woman who was always the closest he had to a real mother.

Dorothy went on with her life, filling it with old friends and new. She was now president of the Detection Club and ran it, some complained, like a drill sergeant. She also became involved in establishing St. Anne's House in London, an often contentious but worthy project designed to provide common ground for the expression and discussion of Christian and secular ideas. St. Anne's was in part an action taken to address the serious concerns Dorothy had long held about the nature and organization of postwar society and the proper role of the Church. It was through St. Anne's that she became friends with James Brabazon. Her relationship with Barbara Reynolds, a lecturer in Italian at Cambridge University, began when Reynolds arranged for Dorothy to deliver a talk on Dante—a meeting that ultimately led to a close personal and professional friendship. (Dr. Reynolds was to complete Dorothy's translation of Dante.) Some of her old crowd were gone—Helen Simpson and Charles Williams—but others were as close as ever: Muriel Byrne, Marjorie Barber, Dorothy Rowe. She had long been friends with Norah Lambourne, a set and costume designer whom Dorothy worked with on several of her plays, including her last, *The Emperor Constantine,* staged at the Colchester Festival in 1951.

Dorothy could still rise to a good fight and did so with some regularity, taking on scholars, critics, and the occasional unfortunate politician or bureaucrat. She could still shock with her costuming, adopting a mannish style of dress that led to wholly wrong suppositions about her sexuality. She still took enormous pleasure in her physical appetites: good foods, good wines, and endless cigarettes. And there was also her Dante. The second book, *Purgatory,* was published in 1955, and by the end of 1956, she was well into the final volume, *Paradise.*

On December 11, 1956, she received a most welcome visitor, her old radio producer Val Gielgud, who had come to Witham to interview her for a newspaper article. On Friday, December 13, she traveled to Cambridge, where she joined Barbara Reynolds, her husband, and children for an unusual ceremony. Barbara was to be baptized, and Dorothy stood as her godmother. The next day, Saturday, Norah Lambourne was an overnight guest at Sunnyside. On Sunday, Val Gielgud's interview was published, and it surely must have pleased Dorothy because, instead of focusing on the fate of Lord Peter, as the newspaper hoped, Gielgud reported on her recently published translation of *The Song of Roland.* Two days later, Dorothy went to London to Christmas shop and to see her portrait, painted by Sir William Hutchinson, which was on show in the Royal Society of Portrait Painters exhibition. After canceling another London engagement, she took the train back to Witham and was driven home late. It was the 17th of December. Her body was found by the cleaner the next morning, at the foot of the stairway. Dorothy had died of a stroke and heart failure. She was sixty-three years old.

Muriel Byrne rushed to her friend's home. She was soon joined there by Anthony Fleming and learned, for the first time, that he was Dorothy's child. Dorothy left her entire estate, valued at around £34,000, to her son and appointed Muriel as her literary executor. Even with his mother gone, Anthony maintained her secret against public disclosure, telling the curious press that he was her "adopted" child.

Dorothy was cremated, and her ashes were placed in the chapel being constructed in the bombed-out tower of St. Anne's Church in Soho, her London parish. The resting place was supposed to be temporary, but in 1978, a commemorative plaque was placed there by the Dorothy L. Sayers Historical and Literary Society. The epitaph reads, "The only Christian work is good work well done."

"When we go to Heaven all I ask is that we shall be given some interesting job and allowed to get on with it."

At the end of her life, the questions remained. Who was this woman? A bold thinker in both fiction and Christian theology or merely a gifted pseudo-intellectual? A genuine original in the field of detective writing or a prosy and snobbish pretender? A loud and aggressive vulgarian or a softer soul who hid her genuine emotions behind a well-crafted facade? A caring mother who did everything in her power to provide for her illegitimate son or a singularly selfish woman who denied her child genuine parental love?

There is some truth in all these characterizations. In the late 1920s, after the birth of her son, Dorothy sat for several portrait studies done by her friend and colleague John Gilroy. In charcoal sketches and oils, Gilroy captured something of her nature—the earthy, deep-bosomed body and peasant-style dress contrasted to the graceful swan's neck and haughty tilt of the chin; the theatrical silver wig, long cigarette holder, and Mona Lisa smile contrasted with the eyes, alert, cast sideways, hinting at some deeper experience. Charcoal was a good medium for Dorothy, a woman and a writer who is best imagined in the shadings of gray.

Like her most famous creation, Lord Peter Wimsey, there was always more to Dorothy than she cared to reveal, and perhaps less than she dared to contemplate. She was not a woman of contrasts so much as of complexities. Convinced of her own intellectual abilities very early in life, she could, without a seeming twinge of conscience, reduce those she considered less gifted—less bright—to dust. But she was also smart enough to recognize her limitations, fighting off all attempts, for example, to cast her in the role of the Christian evangelist and refusing to proselytize for the faith whose dogmas she so ably defended.

She was a woman of powerful physical appetites and raucous humor, but emotionally handicapped and aloof. She was a gifted excuse-maker, always able to blame someone or something else for her perceived failures. Whether she was capable of any deeply committed love for another is open to debate, but she had an unusual aptitude for friendship, forging relationships that spanned decades. She loved her son, her husband, and her parents as best she could; yet she cut them off, one and all, from the truest part of herself.

But once she had decided where her deepest obligation lay, she gave herself heart and soul to her work—the work of a passionate mind that first showed itself to her readers in *Gaudy Night.* In her religion, she discovered the source of the divine pattern and the connectedness of things that had attracted her since childhood, and through her work— particularly *The Mind of the Maker, The Man Born to Be King,* and her monumental translation of Dante—she tried to reveal and invigorate this intellectual pattern for all minds. Her weapons were words, and her great adventures were imaginative and intellectual. (Unlike her contemporary Agatha Christie, Dorothy was not a traveler, apart from holidays to Scotland with her husband and Venice with her friends. She never visited the United States, where her novels were generally more popular than in England.)

She is often cast as a social rebel, but her rebellions were superficial at best. To the end of her life, she dressed to shock and attract attention. She argued loudly, joked bawdily (one of her final projects was a series of comic sketches on secular sainthood, published in the humor magazine *Punch*), ate and drank with gusto, and never backed off from a verbal fight even when she was demonstrably in the wrong—all behaviors that conveyed the image of a "tough broad" in a culture that still worshiped at the pedestal of femininity.

But when it came to genuinely antisocial thoughts and actions, she was utterly conventional and even judgmental. She hated socialism and communism; her political and economic views were conservative, and her belief in individual rights and responsibilities was virtually libertarian. She championed Christian dogma against all attempts to soften and sugarcoat the teachings of the Church.

Even her place in the ranks of detective fiction is hotly debated. Dorothy's supporters maintain that she was the most erudite and novelistic of Golden Age mystery writers and that her hero, Lord Peter Wimsey, is a masterpiece of originality. To her detractors, her erudition is offensively exhibitionist, her attempt to blend detective and serious fiction was forced and false, and her Lord Peter is no better than the trite confection of a literary social-climber.

Again, simplistic evaluations are not adequate. What seems contrived and snobbish in her fiction was in fact natural to Dorothy. She was well-read; she loved intense disputation and flamboyant literary quotation. (In her last novel, *Busman's Honeymoon,* she mocked herself by including the running joke of a quotation contest between Lord Peter and the stolid and often ungrammatical Inspector Kirk.) She did believe that detective fiction could be serious fiction, and she wrote to this objective. (Most readers agree that her worst book is *The Five Red Herrings,* her last attempt to write a pure puzzle mystery.) If she didn't succeed, she set the stage well for writers like Patricia Highsmith, P. D. James, and Ruth Rendell, who have truly linked mystery and literature.

As for Lord Peter, he is what he is. Love him or hate him—readers and critics are rarely neutral—it's hard to ignore his presence. Dorothy was not a snob because she made her detective a wealthy aristocrat; plenty of writers did it before and after her (witness Ngaio Marsh's Roderick Alleyn and Margery Allingham's noble Campion). Wealth gave him the leisure to detect, and high birth gave him access to the most interesting people and cases. Lord Peter was not the first "humanized" detective; both E. C. Bentley and G. K. Chesterton had humanized the rational model handed down from Edgar Allan Poe and Arthur Conan Doyle. But Dorothy made her sleuth not merely love-struck, like Bentley's Philip Trent, or contemplative like Chesterton's Father Brown.

Lord Peter is complicated, like Dorothy herself. He is loquacious and giddy. "A buffoon, that's what I am," he declares in *Strong Poison.* He is also a man of sincere and often-troubled conscience who suffers deep depressions at the end of every case. He is a gay blade, dead attractive to women. He is also a loyal friend, unwilling to exploit a woman to whom he is not attracted or to abuse the vulnerability of the one woman he truly loves. He is intellectually fearless; he avoids physical confrontation. He is vain; he is self-effacing. He is pompous; he is kind. He is well-bred· he is rude. He retains, through eleven books and dozens of short stories, an almost adolescent curiosity and romanticism combined with rock-solid fidelity to his own moral code. Though small in stature, he is always a little larger-than-life. Dorothy gave her Lord Peter many of her own strengths and a substantial measure of her weaknesses. He is, like his creator, a character of many moods and shadings. If we like him, with all his many flaws and foibles, chances are we would also have enjoyed the company of his all-too-human maker.

What Dorothy Sayers contributed to detective fiction—as well as Christian theology of the mid-twentieth century—was a vigor and robustness that defied refinement. She approached every project, even the lowest work for hire, with integrity and rarely gave less than she was capable of. The emotional commitment she could not give to other people or even to her God, she poured into her work. Like almost everything about her, her faults and failings were large, but that is consistent with a woman who was always willing to live and to think in grand scale.

BIBLIOGRAPHY

DOROTHY L. SAYERS
1893–1956
English (born: Oxford)

". . . in detective stories virtue is always triumphant. They're the purest literature we have." —Lord Peter Wimsey in *Strong Poison*

Dorothy Sayers wrote so extensively that full bibliographies of her original works and translations are lengthy. This chronological listing includes only her major writings and focuses on her detective novels, story collections, plays, and criticism. The first publisher of her first mystery was Boni & Liveright in the United States. Her British publishers to 1930 were Fisher Unwin and Ernest Benn. Her novels were then published by Victor Gollancz. Dates are for first publication. Alternative U.S. titles are given. US = United States. GB = Great Britain. Main characters appear in ( ).

Mystery Novels and Story Collections
1923   *Whose Body?* (Wimsey)
1926   *Clouds of Witness* (Wimsey)
1927   *Unnatural Death*/US: *The Dawson Pedigree* (Wimsey)
1928   *The Unpleasantness at the Bellona Club* (Wimsey)
1929   *Lord Peter Views the Body* (collection of Wimsey short stories)
1930   *The Documents in the Case,* written with Robert Eustace Barton
1930   *Strong Poison* (Wimsey, Harriet Vane)
1931   *The Five Red Herrings*/US: *Suspicious Characters* (Wimsey)
1932   *Have His Carcase* (Wimsey, Harriet Vane)
1933   *Murder Must Advertise* (Wimsey)
1933   US: *Hangman's Holiday* (collection of short stories featuring Wimsey and Montague Egg)
1934   *The Nine Tailors* (Wimsey)

1935   *Gaudy Night* (Wimsey, Harriet Vane)

1937   *Busman's Honeymoon* (Wimsey, Harriet Vane)

1939   *In the Teeth of the Evidence* (short stories with Wimsey, Montague Egg)

1973   *Striding Folly* (three Wimsey short stories, including the posthumously published "Talboys," published by the New English Library)

1998   *Thrones, Dominations* (novel fragment featuring Peter Wimsey and Harriet Vane; written in 1936; completed by Jill Paton Walsh. GB: Hodder and Stoughton/US: St. Martin's Press)

Selected Essays and Criticism

1928   Introduction to *Great Short Stories of Detection, Mystery and Horror/* US: *The Omnibus of Crime*

1931   Introduction to *Great Short Stories of Detection, Mystery and Horror, Second Series/*US: *The Second Omnibus of Crime*

1934   Introduction to *Great Short Stories of Detection, Mystery and Horror, Third Series/*US: *The Third Omnibus of Crime*

1936   Introduction to *Tales of Detection*

1941   *The Mind of the Maker*

1944   Introduction to *The Moonstone* by Wilkie Collins

1946   *Unpopular Opinions* (collection of essays and speeches)

1963   *The Poetry of Search and the Poetry of Statement* (collection of twelve essays)

1977   *Wilkie Collins* (uncompleted literary biography, edited by E. R. Gregory and published by Friends of the University of Toledo Libraries)

Detection Club Collaborations

1930   "Behind the Screen" radio serial (part three), BBC

1931   "The Scoop" radio serial (parts one and twelve), BBC

1931   *The Floating Admiral* (Introduction, Chapter Six, and Solution)

1933   "The Conclusions of Roger Sheringham" in *Ask a Policeman*

1936   "The Murder of Julia Wallace" in *The Anatomy of Murder*

1939   *Double Death: A Murder Story*

Plays   Dates are for first production.

1937   *Busman's Honeymoon,* cowritten with Muriel St. Clare Byrne (Lord Peter Wimsey, Harriet Vane)

1937   *The Zeal of Thy House* (religious festival play for Canterbury Cathedral)

1939   *The Devil to Pay* (religious festival play for Canterbury Cathedral)

1939   *He That Should Come* (religious radio play, BBC)

1940   *Love All* (romantic comedy)
1941   *The Man Born to Be King* (religious radio play series, BBC)
1946   *The Just Vengeance* (religious play for Litchfield Festival)
1951   *The Emperor Constantine* (religious play for Colchester Festival)

Translations

1929   *Tristan in Brittany*
1949   *The Comedy of Dante Alighieri the Florentine, Cantica I: Hell*
1955   *The Comedy of Dante Alighieri the Florentine, Cantica II: Purgatory*
1957   *The Song of Roland*
1962   *The Comedy of Dante Alighieri the Florentine, Cantica III: Paradise*
        (translation completed by Dr. Barbara Reynolds after Dorothy
        Sayers's death)

Film and Video Adaptations

1935   *The Silent Passenger* British/Phoenix—original story by Basil Ma-
        son based on the character of Lord Peter Wimsey. (Sayers ini-
        tially cooperated with the project but eventually disavowed it.)
1940   *Busman's Honeymoon* (US: *Haunted Honeymoon*) British/MGM—
        adapted from the stage play by Monckton Hoffe, Angus Macphail,
        and Harold Goldman. Starred Robert Montgomery as Lord
        Peter and Constance Cummings as Harriet.
1973–1977   The BBC produced its first series of full-length Peter
        Wimsey adaptations. Ian Carmichael starred, and though some-
        what long in the tooth for the young Lord Peter, his perfor-
        mance catches the detective's fey qualities admirably. Productions
        include *Clouds of Witness, The Unpleasantness at the Bellona Club,
        Murder Must Advertise, The Nine Tailors,* and *Five Red Herrings.*
1987   A second BBC series focused on the Lord Peter–Harriet Vane
        relationship in *Strong Poison, Have His Carcase,* and *Gaudy Night.*
        Edward Petherbridge portrayed a nervy Wimsey in love.

THE LORD PETER FILE

NAME: Peter Death Bredon Wimsey (Lord Peter)
BIRTH DATE: 1890
NATIONALITY: English (with the saving grace of $\frac{1}{16}$ French blood)
WIFE: Harriet Deborah Vane Wimsey (Lady Peter), mystery novelist
CHILDREN: Bredon Delagardie Peter (born 1936), Roger (born 1938),
    and Paul (born, probably, 1940)
FAMILY: Parents: Mortimer Gerald Bredon Wimsey, fifteenth Duke of

Denver (deceased) and Honoria Lucasta Delagardie Wimsey, the dowager duchess (known to good friends as "Lucy"). Elder brother: Gerald Wimsey, sixteenth Duke of Denver ("Jerry"), married to Helen and father of Saint-George (the heir apparent, known as "Pickled Gherkins") and Winifred. Younger sister, Lady Mary Wimsey ("Polly"), wife of Charles Parker and mother of Charles Peter and Mary Lucasta. (Chief-Inspector Parker of Scotland Yard—"the one who really does the work"—is Wimsey's best friend.)

ADDRESS: Ancestral home: Bredon Hall/Denver Castle, Duke's Denver, Norfolk; London flat at 110A Piccadilly (second floor, "directly opposite the Green Park"). Marital home in Audley Square, Mayfair. Country home, Talboys.

PHYSICAL DESCRIPTION: "Physically, he should ideally be five feet nine and a half inches, clean shaven, fair hair brushed straight back, hawk nosed, fine hands, nervously energetic and with a rather light, not booming sort of voice. . . ." (as described by Dorothy L. Sayers in 1938). Disturbing grey eyes. Said once to look "like a melancholy adjutant stork." Dresses immaculately but "hates new clothes"; prefers Savile Row suits, matching socks and handkerchiefs, mauve silk pajamas, and a peacock-patterned bathrobe. Sometimes seen wearing a monocle (magnifying lens), carrying a malacca walking stick (concealed sword in the shaft and compass in the head) and a silver matchbox (flashlight). Extremely fit and can move "like a cat."

EDUCATION: Eton; Balliol College, Oxford University (First Class in modern history)

MILITARY SERVICE: Major in the Rifle Brigade, attached to military intelligence; active service, 1914–1918; wounded at Caudry in 1918; suffered shell shock after being buried in a bombed German "dugout."

RELIGION: Church of England, although "I don't claim . . . to be a Christian or anything of that kind."

OCCUPATION: None, except for frequent semiofficial diplomatic missions for the Foreign Office and brief stint as an advertising copywriter.

AVOCATION: Private detection ("I sleuth, you know, for a hobby."); well-known collector of first editions and incunabula (books printed before 1501).

MAGNUM OPUS: *The Murderer's Vade-Mecum or 101 Ways of Causing Sudden Death*

INTERESTS: Music (plays piano, flute, and church bells; sings tenor; whistles Bach when pleased with himself), art, wine, fast cars, fast women (before Harriet); detective stories and crosswords. Plays serious card games very well, builds houses of cards when stressed. Ace at cricket; swims like a fish; rides like the wind. Private clubs include Marlborough, Egotists', and Bellona.

FACTOTUM: Mervyn Bunter, who was Lord Peter's batman in the Great War and nursed him back to health. Valet, cook, nurse, photographer, chemist, undercover investigator. Very attractive to cooks and house-maids.

ROMANTIC HISTORY: Lord Peter received his sexual education at age seventeen, in Paris, under the tutelage of Uncle Paul Austin Dela-gardie. After leaving Oxford, engaged to Barbara, who dumped him in 1916. Long series of liaisons (e.g., a "spectacular Viennese singer"), close friendships (e.g., sculptress Marjorie Phelps), and professional entanglements (e.g., Dian de Momerie and Pamela Dean). Skilled lover ("I can produce testimonials") and one of England's most eligible bachelors. Forever faithful following 1935 marriage.

OTHER FRIENDS AND PROFESSIONAL ACQUAINTANCES: Miss Alexan-dra Katharine ("Kitty") Climpson of Pimlico (runs typing bureau-cum-investigation agency known as "the Cattery"); financial adviser, the Honorable Freddy Arbuthnot; attorney Jno. Murbles of Staple Inn; Sir Impey Biggs, England's most-feared defense barrister; foren-sic chemist Sir James Lubbock; Sir Andrew Mackenzie, chief of Scot-land Yard; Inspector Sugg; journalists Salcombe Hardy and Waffles Newton; "Blindfold Bill" Rhumm, safecracker turned evangelist; the cream of the aristocracy, including godmother, the Countess of Sev-ern and Thames, and the loftiest of British royalty; the Pope.

INDULGENCES: Fine wines (except champagne) and foods (except generic "cheese"); Villar y Villar cigars, Sobranie cigarettes, and a brier pipe; sleeping late; verbena-scented bathwater; Napoleon brandy. "Mrs. Merdle"—a custom-built Daimler. (In all, there are nine Mrs. Merdles, named for a character in Dickens's *Little Dorritt*.)

FIRST CASE: Unrecorded recovery of the Attenbury emeralds—or was it diamonds? (To be precise, Wimsey first appeared in an unfinished Sexton Blake short story Dorothy Sayers developed in 1920. She later used the storyline in "The Entertaining Episode of the Article in Question.")

FIRST PUBLISHED WORDS: "Oh, damn!"

THE LOQUACIOUS LORD PETER

There are reticent detectives; there are talkative detectives. Then there is Lord Peter Wimsey, the most voluble of fiction's classic sleuths. While not quite up to the standards of the greatest English aphorists, Lord Peter can always turn a clever phrase in a dicey situation, and he rarely stoops to puns. A sample of Wimsey wisdom:

> "Children are creatures of like passions with politicians and financiers."
>
> *Unnatural Death*

> "Time and trouble will train an advanced young woman, but an advanced old woman is uncontrollable by any earthly force."
>
> *Clouds of Witness*

> "You cannot trust these young women. No fixity of purpose. Except, of course, when you particularly want them to be yielding."
>
> *Murder Must Advertise*

> "Sex isn't a separate thing functioning away all by itself. It's usually found attached to a person of some sort."
>
> *Gaudy Night*

> "Sex is every man's loco spot . . . he'll take a disappointment, but not a humiliation."
>
> *Whose Body?*

> "Always distrust the man who looks you straight in the eyes. He wants to prevent you from seeing something. Look for it."
>
> *Strong Poison*

> "Even idiots occasionally speak the truth accidentally."
>
> *Whose Body?*

> "Nothing is so virtuous as a bicycle. You can't imagine a bicyclist committing a crime . . . except of course murder or attempted murder."
>
> *Five Red Herrings*

> "Nobody minds coarseness but one must draw the line at cruelty."
>
> "The Abominable History of the Man with Copper Fingers"

> ". . . after all, it isn't really difficult to write books. Especially if you either write a rotten story in good English or a good story in rotten English, which is as far as most people seem to get nowadays."
>
> *Unnatural Death*

DOROTHY'S TRAVELING MAN

Although Lord Peter Wimsey was her main man, Dorothy L. Sayers created another male crime-solver early in her career. Montague Egg proved quite popular with magazine readers in the early 1930s, possibly as an antidote to the affectations of Lord Peter. "Monty" Egg is a crack salesman for Plummet and Rose, Wines and Spirits of Piccadilly. His job takes him from city to town to hamlet, where crime is always afoot. A World War One veteran—"fair-haired, well-mannered," and chubby-faced—young Monty has a natural gift for commerce and a flair for detection. Like all good salesmen, he is "by nature persistent and inquisitive," excellent qualities when uncovering wrongdoing and unmasking murderers.

The Monty Egg stories are classic Golden Age detection; little puzzles that must be solved by carefully applied inductive reasoning. Dorothy created Monty Egg while she was working as an advertising copywriter in London, a job that put her in daily contact with the practical aspects of salesmanship. She invested Monty with the necessities of the trade: cheerful personality, natty attire and scrupulous hygiene, a reliable little Morris automobile, respect for his customers, and intense loyalty to his employers and their potable wares. Monty has a habit of speaking in rhymes echoing his bible of the road, *The Salesman's Handbook*. Even the most modern of marketers might do well to heed the mottoes of Monty Egg:

> "To serve the Public is the aim
> of every salesman worth the name."

> "Never miss a chance of learning
> for that word spells '£' plus 'earning.'"

> "The salesman who will use his brains
> will spare himself a world of pains."

> "Don't trust to luck, but be exact
> and verify the smallest fact."

. . . and Monty's favorite:

> "Speak the truth with cheerful ease
> if you would both convince and please."

The Montague Egg stories are included in two story collections: *In the Teeth of the Evidence and Other Mysteries* and *Hangman's Holiday*.

MISS CLIMPSON AND COMPANY

As a feminist, Dorothy Sayers called for education and opportunity rather than mandated equality. In a 1938 lecture titled "Are Women Human?" she argued, "When it comes to a *choice,* then every man or woman has to choose as an individual human being, and, like a human being, take the consequences." But Dorothy felt special sympathy for one group—the huge number of unmarried women left by the devastation of Britain's male population in World War One. These women, Dorothy wrote in *Strong Poison,* "were of the class unkindly known as 'superfluous.' There were spinsters with small fixed incomes, or no income at all; widows without family; women deserted by peripatetic husbands and living on a restricted alimony, who . . . had no resources but bridge and boardinghouse gossip. There were retired and disappointed school-teachers; out-of-work actresses; courageous people who had failed with hat-shops and tea-parlours; and even a few Bright Young Things, for whom the cocktail-party and the night-club had grown boring."

In *Unnatural Death* and *Strong Poison,* Dorothy deployed Miss Alexandra Katharine ("Kitty") Climpson—a "thin, middle-aged" Edwardian lady—to assist Lord Peter. He sets her up in a stenography and typing business (called the Cattery in jest) and employs her unique investigative services when needed. Initially Kitty Climpson is used only as a bright busybody who can gather information because no one suspects her of ulterior motives. But Dorothy Sayers had something more in mind. As the character develops, readers discover that Miss Climpson is tough and determined, intelligent and insightful, morally strong but not doctrinaire, realistic in her outlook, imaginative in her methods, and physically courageous when need be. Miss Climpson represents the kind of individualist feminism that Dorothy believed in: Kitty makes the most of the hand she has been dealt and gets on with her work without grumbling. Dorothy tells the reader that Kitty "was a spinster made and not born—a perfectly womanly woman." "I should have liked a good education," Kitty says without bitterness, "but my dear father didn't believe in it for women."

Appealing spinster ladies appear in a number of Dorothy's mysteries. In *Strong Poison,* thirty-eight-year-old Miss Murchison is "a business woman all her life" who joins the Cattery. Marjorie Phelps in *The Unpleasantness at the Bellona Club* is a self-supporting sculptress who holds her own with Lord Peter. In *Murder Must Advertise,* Miss Meteyard, an Oxford-educated ad writer who "makes the vulgarest limericks ever recited within these chaste walls," is a single career woman based on the author. Harriet Vane, until she weds Lord Peter, is a thirtyish spinster struggling to make her way with integrity.

Dorothy Sayers understood the vulnerabilities of the "superfluous" class because she had been a member in good standing. She had the example of her father's three sisters: ". . . brought up without education or training, thrown, at my grandfather's death, into a world that had no use for them," she wrote to a friend in 1941. "From all such frustrate unhappiness, God keep us," she declared. "Let us be able to write 'hoc feci' [I did this] on our tombstones, even if all we have done is to clean the 29 floors on the International Stores."

THAT'S DOROTHY WITH AN *L*. . . .

A guaranteed way to raise Dorothy Leigh Sayers's hackles was to call her "Dorothy Sayers." She insisted that, at least in print and public forums, she be Dorothy L. Sayers. Her name, she patiently explained to an official of Oxford University Press in a 1936 letter, "is part of the author's 'publicity.' " She didn't think she was demanding too much; other women writers—Charlotte M. Yonge and Ethel M. Dell, for example—asked for and got the same.

In speech, she said, the use of "Dorothy Sayers" invited a mispronunciation (Say-yers, instead of Sayers to rhyme with "stairs") that she hated: ". . . my old headmistress always pronounced it so, and gave me a distaste for the form that I cannot get over." Besides, she contended, reviewers and such who used her name ought to take the trouble to write it properly. To Sir Hugh Walpole, she once confessed her preference for the L. to be "a foolish fancy," but she followed her own dictates—signing correspondence to all but her intimates as Dorothy L. Sayers, D.L.S., or sometimes Dorothy L. Fleming.

BBC announcers had an infuriating tendency to drop her middle initial in their broadcasts, and she was sometimes confused with a guitar-playing variety performer also named Dorothy Sayers. This mix-up led Dorothy L. to wish fancifully that the other woman might die first. In that event, she reasoned, people would be confused, and she could read her own obituaries.

NGAIO MARSH

THE SECRET SELF

"What I have written turns out to be a straying recollection of places and people: I have been deflected by my own reticence."

Ngaio Marsh

℧ystery writers and critics Julian Symons and H. R. F. Keating have both told a story about a short, but tiring, book promotion tour they made with Ngaio Marsh to the English Midlands and North in the early 1970s.[*] Though she was nearing eighty and not in good health, Ngaio took the tour in stride, graciously greeting her many fans at a series of "literary luncheons" and signing countless copies of her novels without complaint. On the train back to London, Symons mentioned that he was working on a new mystery featuring an updated Sherlock Holmes character but was struggling to find a title. Immediately, Ngaio suggested "a three-pipe solution"—a phrase from "The Red-Headed League." Symons

---

[*] Reminiscences by Symons, Keating, John Dacres-Mannings, and others appear in *Ngaio Marsh: The Woman and Her Work*, a collection edited by B. J. Rahn and published in 1995, the centennial year of Ngaio's birth. Unless otherwise noted, quotations from Ngaio Marsh are from her autobiography, *Black Beech and Honeydew*, first published in 1965 and revised and extended shortly before her death in 1982, and from letters and diaries quoted by Margaret Lewis in *Ngaio Marsh: A Life*. London: Chatto & Windus (1991)

used the title and dedicated the finished book to his quick-witted traveling companion.

This pleasant anecdote illustrates the person Ngaio Marsh was to her public, her friends, and associates. When talking about her, people who knew her use a surprisingly similar list of adjectives: charming and gracious, poised and sophisticated, intelligent and perceptive, generous and self-effacing. Yet even close friends and family regretted not understanding her better. None of her biographers seems able to pin her down with certainty, and her own autobiography, *Black Beech and Honeydew*, raises more questions than it answers.

The only outsider among the grande dames of the English Golden Age, Ngaio Marsh wrote thirty-two detective novels between 1931 and 1981. Although she drew extensively from her own experiences in her novels, she dropped an iron curtain between incident and feelings. A gifted prose writer, she was often encouraged to expand beyond the limits of the detective genre, but she consistently refused to veer from her established pattern. She was generous with her talents, time, and money—especially through her work as a theatrical producer-director-teacher and arts advocate in her native New Zealand—yet she was always, in her word, "reticent" about her inner life and her emotions.

Biographer Margaret Lewis and others contend that Ngaio played roles throughout her life, but role-playing implies a degree of deception that doesn't quite fit what is known of her character. Ngaio Marsh concealed rather than contrived. Born at the end of the Victorian era, she was in many ways the most Victorian of the twentieth-century Women of Mystery—reserved and demure in a century that increasingly demanded self-exposure of its celebrities. One of her heirs, her second cousin John Dacres-Mannings, has commented on her ability to divide her life into compartments and to segment her relationships according to which department they fit: writing, theater, private life. To Dacres-Mannings, who, with his brother, was the closest Ngaio came to rearing children of her own, she was "a person ten feet tall, quite the most magical person I have ever known."

But Ngaio Marsh was not larger-than-life, though at 5'10" she stood tall. Rather, her extreme reluctance to reveal anything that was "messy" or "vulgar" about her feelings and her relationships created an aura of mystery and gave rise to extreme judgments by both her worshipers and her detractors. By peeking behind the curtain of reticence, however, we may get at least a sense of the flesh-and-bone woman.

". . . you must try to understand the life of a girl who
lives on the free hills goes without stockings in summer
and runs about all day."   —Ngaio Marsh's childhood diary

Edith Ngaio Marsh was born in a small house in the Fendalton section of Christchurch, New Zealand, on April 25, 1895. Her father accidentally registered his only child's birth year as 1899, and Ngaio never officially rectified the four-year error. Like Peter Pan, she clung to her youth with determination.

Her forgetful father, Henry Marsh, was the eldest son of a large English family that liked to claim descent from the pirate family of de Marisco (the lords of Lundy) and from Richard Stephen Marsh, a member of the seventeenth-century court of King Charles II. Henry's father was a London tea-broker who sent his older sons to Dulwich College, a private grammar school founded by the actor Edward Alleyn in 1613. But the family fortunes declined in the direction of genteel poverty, especially after the father's death.

Henry was trained for a banking career that was supposed to lead to success in the higher reaches of London finance. Hampered by illness and bad luck, however, Henry emigrated to New Zealand* in 1888 and found a position with the Bank of New Zealand in Christchurch. Ambition seems not to have been included in his makeup, and he remained a low-level bank clerk all his working days.

Henry, called "Lally" by his wife, was a funny and fun-loving man and a highly successful father—adored by his daughter even in his scrappy old age. In her autobiography, Ngaio wrote, "His rectitude was enormous: I have never known a man with higher principles. He was thrifty. He was devastatingly truthful. In many ways he was wise and he had a kind heart, and a nice sense of humour. He was never unhappy for

---

* New Zealand was among the youngest and farthest-flung colonies in the old British Empire. Located in the southern Pacific Ocean, New Zealand was "discovered" and named by Dutch seaman Abel Tasman in 1642, but claimed for Britain by James Cook in 1769. The first settlers, however, were not European: a Polynesian people, the Maori, arrived some six or seven hundred years before Tasman's voyage. New Zealand became a British colony in the 1840s. The colony achieved independence in 1907 and remains a part of the British Commonwealth. Geographically New Zealand comprises two main islands—North and South—and supports a population of approximately 3.5 million, most of British descent, although the Maori, who were displaced after a series of colonial wars, are now an important political and social segment. Two years before Ngaio Marsh's birth, New Zealand became one of the first modern nations to grant the vote to women. Christchurch is the largest city on the South Island.

long: perhaps, in his absent-mindedness, he forgot to be so. I liked him very much."

Ngaio's mother was a different sort. Rose Elizabeth Seager Marsh was, as Ngaio said, a woman of contradictions: talented, creative, attracted to the stage, daring in many ways, yet conventionally Victorian in her attitudes and morals. She clearly had a good mind that recognized her daughter's good mind early on, and she was ambitious for her child, though not the classic "stage mum" who pushes for shallow attainments. Her relationship with Ngaio was complex and often difficult for both.

Rose never underestimated her daughter's abilities, and she carefully structured Ngaio's young life to nurture her intellectual and creative talents. Though the family was never financially well-off, Ngaio seems not to have been denied much. Like many only children, she had extensive early contact with adults. (Rose had apparently been advised against another pregnancy after Ngaio's birth. When the doctor lifted this restriction some years later, Rose asked Ngaio if she would like a brother or sister. The response was a simple negative. Whether little Ngaio's preference was taken into account is unknown, but she remained the only child in the Marsh household.)

Rose was the disciplinarian, her rules a mix of permissiveness and strict attention to Victorian standards of conduct. Few chores were expected of her daughter; Ngaio was allowed to run and play almost at will. But both parents were sticklers for polite behavior: "Rude is Never Funny," shortened to "R is never F," was Rose's favorite platitude (later quoted by Marsh's fictional detective Roderick Alleyn), and instant obedience to a parental command was expected. While Ngaio often resented her mother's authority, she relied heavily upon it well past the age when most young women have untied the apron strings.

Ngaio believed that she came to understand her mother as she herself grew older, but she was never able to completely solve the puzzle. "Of one thing I am sure," Ngaio wrote some thirty years after her mother's death, "she had in her an element of creative art never fully realized. I think the intensity of devotion which might have been spent upon its development was poured out upon her only child. . . ."

Rose was a second-generation New Zealander. Her father, Edward Seager, was a well-known public official in Christchurch—an early member of the Colonial Police Force, rising to the rank of sergeant-major, and holder of a number of government posts including supervisor of the Sunnyside Asylum, where his enlightened management of mentally ill inmates included physical activity, art, music, and theater. He loved all aspects of theater and was an enthusiastic amateur magician who frequently employed his daughters as assistants.

Rose Seager was the fifth of eleven children and inherited her father's

theatrical gifts. As a young woman, she performed with several professional touring theater troupes (once traveling to Australia) and was offered the opportunity for a stage career in England. She did not go, and
Ngaio assumed that her mother's decision arose from a "natural fastidiousness" that was offended by the "easy emotionalism and 'bohemian'
habits of theatre people. . . ."* But after her marriage to Henry Marsh
in 1894 and the birth of her daughter a year later, Rose continued to act
in amateur theatricals.

The play was the thing in the Marsh household: Gramp Seager's tales
of the theater and famous actors and actresses entranced and delighted;
Rose's rehearsals were mesmerizing, though the image of her mother in
altered voice and appearance frightened Ngaio when she was small. Her
father also acted in amateur productions, and Ngaio's favorite among
her parents' friends was Dundas "James" Walker, who frequently indulged little Ngaio's imagination with his games and stories before he
became a professional actor in England.

One of the first plays Ngaio remembered seeing—and one she was to
produce almost twenty years later—was *Bluebell in Fairyland,* which she
attended in 1907 with her childhood pal Ned Bristed. Bristed remained
a friend until his death in World War One and was possibly more: Ngaio
once told an interviewer that she had been engaged to a young man
who had died, and she always treasured a small ruby ring Bristed may
have given her. But whatever their later relationship, Ngaio always remembered an afternoon in the dress-circle and "the shadows of a freck-
led boy and a small girl: ecstatic and feverishly wolfing chocolates."†

Ngaio's early years were carefree, aside from seemingly normal fears
and nightmares, including a terror of being poisoned and a "recurrent
dream in which everything Became Too Big." She taught herself to read
when she was four, and like both her parents, she was a devout consumer of fiction. But her first experience of formal education was "hell-
ish." At age six or seven, she was enrolled in a "select dame school"—an
elementary school known as "Miss Tib's" for the nickname of its mis-

---

* Rose Marsh's contention that the behavior of theater people was "messy" is echoed
  by Agatha Troy, the portrait artist who captivates Inspector Alleyn in *Artists in Crime*
  (1938). Lecturing a randy artist who attends classes in her home, Troy declares, "I
  won't have any bogus Bohemianism, or free love, or mere promiscuity. . . . It shocks
  the servants, and it's messy."
† Ngaio's claim that she was four years younger than her actual age causes persistent
  confusion in her autobiography, beginning on page one when she relates an incident
  that supposedly happened when she was fourteen but actually occurred several years
  later. The *Bluebell* story is told as if it happened to a very little child though she was,
  in fact, twelve. She got away with the deception, even on government documents and
  in *Who's Who,* in part because she looked younger than her years.

tress, Miss Sibella ("Tibby") Ross. Ngaio's height—well above that of her little classmates—deep voice, and shyness made her an easy target for teasing and playground bullies. She never told her parents about her unhappiness, but later concluded that her mother had known and chosen to let her child tough it out. That is precisely what Ngaio did, making friends and coming to enjoy most of the academic routines.

While Ngaio was still at Miss Tib's, her parents moved from their little house in Christchurch to the Port Hills (now the suburb of Cashmere), an area just a few miles south of the city. Volcanic in origin, the hills were sparsely populated and still grassy and wild. Henry Marsh bought a three-quarter-acre plot and set about having a house built near the top of a hill, but before construction was completed, the family set up tents and camped on the site. After a summer of roughing it, they finally moved into the new structure—a bungalow of native timber with a spacious, semicircular veranda. An adjacent cabin converted from a bicycle shed served as a guest room.

"From the beginning," Ngaio said, "we loved our house. It was the fourth member of our family. . . ." Over the years, this house on the hill, eventually named Marton Cottage, with its views of the growing city of Christchurch and the distant, snowcapped Southern Alps, became Ngaio's refuge, retreat, and the home she always came back to.

For a couple of years after the move, Ngaio lived every child's dream in her new environment: riding ponies, exploring hill and field, sneaking cigarettes with her friend Ned Bristed, and trying the patience of the governess her mother hired after Ngaio completed Miss Tib's in 1907. Rose had attempted to tutor her daughter but gave up the effort. Ngaio's memories of her governess, Miss Ffitch, were unremarkable save for the fact that the ladylike teacher provided her introduction to Shakespeare through an expurgated version of *King Lear.* "No lechery. No civit. No small gilded flies. Just torture, murder and madness." It was the beginning of a lifelong love affair.

Ngaio also studied piano, for which she may have had the aptitude but not the interest, and began drawing lessons at the Canterbury University College Art School. She once expressed her ambition to become an artist to Miss Tibby Ross, only to be assured by the headmistress that it was unlikely because her little hand trembled. But the drawing lessons apparently improved the hand, and by the time she entered St. Margaret's College (high school) in 1910, it was accepted that Ngaio would have her career in the arts.

"With us all was sweetness, tabards and tights."

St. Margaret was a new and expensive private girls' secondary school run by the Anglican order of Kilbern Sisters. Her parents, Ngaio later realized, endured considerable financial hardship to send their bright child to the school. St. Margaret's high-church theology could not have been the attraction: Rose was Anglican and a believer, though hardly dedicated, and Henry was a rationalist and vociferously "anti-religion." But St. Margaret's promised both quality academics and rigorous training in mannerly and moral behavior. Ngaio, now fifteen, loved it from the first minute.

She began making new friends and also fell under the spell of church ritual and rapture. "To say that I took to Divinity as a duck to water is a gross understatement," she later wrote with considerable amusement. "I took to it with a sort of spiritual whoop and went in . . . boots and all." In time, her religious passion was to focus on the headmistress, Sister Winifred, and her fervor was so intense that, to Ngaio's horror, the little nun assumed that her student intended to follow a religious vocation. (Ngaio's adolescent religiosity was not to last. She later rejected all forms of religious dogma, though she remained in the Church of England and struggled to her death to find a spiritual truth that she could accept. As John Dacres-Mannings has said, "She suffered much spiritual torment and greatly envied those who had a less difficult path on which to travel.")

Ngaio was not wholly holy in her teenage passions, admitting to exhilarating "onsets of love that were for some undefined object—the world, a flower . . ." and to storms of tears that her mother accepted as matters of course. Ngaio's first heartthrob was a retired church dean, a friend of her mother's. Teenaged Ngaio regarded the elderly churchman as a cross between the Duke of Wellington and Jane Eyre's Mr. Rochester. Alas, the dean, a widower, eventually married Miss Tibby Ross.

Ngaio did well at St. Margaret's. In Miss Hughes's English class, her fascination with Shakespeare was cemented. From Canon Jones, who lectured on church history, she learned the virtues of clarity and economy in writing. Her own writing was recognized: she was a coeditor of the school's literary magazine and won top honors in a national essay-writing contest, despite thirty-one spelling errors. Apparently, St. Margaret's behavioral standards made an impression too, for Ngaio was elected head prefect of the school.

Her love of theater was stoked by close friend Friede Burton and her sisters, Aileen, Helen, and Joan. These vicar's daughters, newly arrived from England, transformed their father's parish hall into a reasonable

facsimile of a theater, where they staged and played in "'costume' comedies, rather nebulous miracle plays and fairy pieces garnished with me-
diaeval songs and ballets of the gay flat-footed kind." Though Ngaio
played in these productions, it was not acting that lured her (possibly because her height and voice led to casting in the male roles), but "the living theatre." She recalled, "It was the whole ambiance of backstage that
I found so immensely satisfying: the forming and growth of a play and
its precipitation into its final shape."

There were also school plays, though not produced with the panache
of the Burton sisters. Ngaio wrote and directed a short piece called
"Bundles" for the Lower School girls, and then a full-length, blank-
verse play, *The Moon Princess,* which was staged by the Burtons and in
which Rose Marsh took the role of the witch. The play was nicely reviewed by the local newspaper. Gramp Seager attended and afterward
presented his granddaughter with two of his most cherished possessions:
a book titled *Actors of the Century,* annotated with his own observations,
and a worn jacket of velvet and silk that was reputed to have belonged
to the great early-nineteenth-century Shakespearean actor Edmund
Kean. (Many years later, Ngaio presented the coat to Sir Laurence
Olivier after seeing his *Richard III* in Christchurch.)

Still, the visual arts were Ngaio's apparent destiny when she completed St. Margaret's and entered the Canterbury College School of Art
in 1913. She'd been taking drawing and watercolor lessons for several
years, and now her training as a painter became full-time. Though the
college was coed, her classmates were mostly female, especially after the
outbreak of World War One in 1914, and Ngaio was to add many new
and close friends to her circle, including Evelyn Polson (Page), who became one of New Zealand's distinguished artists.

The war in Europe, which had the same devastating effect on the
young men of New Zealand and Australia as it did on their English
cousins, seems to have had little impact on the Marshes. But it may well
have been Ngaio's reticence that limited her autobiographical comments
on the Great War. She remarked that her mother was a Red Cross volunteer and her father trained with the Civilian Defense Corps, that
there was a shortage of male dance partners, and that the coming-out
balls were canceled. And she noted the death of Ned Bristed in Flanders, a few days after he had sent her a photograph.

The School of Art, modeled on England's Royal Academy, followed
a traditional, European-oriented curriculum that seemed to suit Ngaio.
She excelled at figure studies and won a number of prizes and scholarships that financed her tuition. She received special encouragement from
life-class teacher Richard Wallwork and his artist wife, who became
friends of all the Marshes. Ngaio particularly enjoyed her classes in nude

studies and made mention in her autobiography of the favored model, "a dictatorial but good-tempered girl who had come to us from show business." (Studio models were doomed to be immortalized in countless indifferent portraits, but Ngaio gave this one a more interesting fate; the "Miss Carter" of Christchurch seems to have been the model for Sonia Gluck, the nude poser with the vaudeville background who is skewered in *Artists in Crime*.)

There is no doubt that Ngaio had talent as a painter, and her artist's eye would translate into her descriptive power as a writer. But something was missing—the ingredient that separates the good from the inspired—and she seems to have suspected it. However, she stuck to her art for some time after completing her studies in 1919, and she stayed at home with her parents. During and after college, she cobbled together a small income from tutoring. She sold occasional pieces to local newspapers; her first sale was an account of an unchaperoned trip to the West Coast with her friend Phyllis Bethune, an amusing encounter with a raucous "company of gentlemen" aboard a train and a moonlight serenade. She visited a great deal with family and friends and took several camping and painting holidays. But she seems to have given little thought to finding either lucrative employment or a husband.

There were at least two serious suitors. The first was a thirty-five-year-old Russian lawyer of aristocratic heritage who had escaped the Bolshevik Revolution with dreams of returning to the land in New Zealand. Erratic and inclined to fight over perceived insults, "Sasha" studied agriculture, then art, then medicine. He met Rose when they costarred as mother and son in an amateur production, and she invited him to the house in the hills, where he met and fell in love with Ngaio. He declared his intentions, but she, though attracted, "was steered past this strange and, as I now see it, oddly lyrical encounter" by her parents. The Russian continued to visit the Marshes until he took offense at something, and several months later, the family learned that he had committed suicide.

The next experience, with an ardent "middle-aged Englishman," resulted in a muddle caused by Ngaio's inability to make her feelings clear. He was "violent" in his attachment, and she was equivocal. The man apparently got the impression that she returned his affections, until her father and mother extricated her from the sticky situation. But the man proved persistent, "haunting" (we would say "stalking") her for some time.

In her autobiography, Ngaio lays the blame for these fumbling encounters on her youth and inexperience. Certainly she was sheltered, but even her parents were surprised by her callow diffidence. "How could you be such an ass?" her mother demanded when told of the en-

tanglement with the Englishman. Ngaio was approaching her mid-
twenties and should have known better. But she had all her life been
perversely deaf to lessons in sex and romance, and it's hard to avoid the
supposition that she was either frightened of sex or, more likely, terrified by the implications of romance and marriage. It is just possible that
her aggressive naiveté was a means of clinging to her youth. At any rate,
Rose and Henry Marsh seemed unready to marry their daughter off,
and they were doubtless relieved when an opportunity came along to
get her out of town and away from the likes of "Sasha" and the Englishman.

The Allan Wilkie Shakespeare Company, one of the old-fashioned
professional touring repertory companies that brought culture to the
isolated Antipodes, played three times in Christchurch in 1919, and
Ngaio, her mother, and her friends were often in the audience. For
Ngaio, the troupe's performances of *Hamlet, Twelfth Night, As You Like
It,* and *A Midsummer Night's Dream* were a kind of epiphany, and she recalled the opening night of *Hamlet* as "the most enchanted I was ever to
spend in the theatre." She was inspired to write her own play, a melodramatic piece she called *The Medallion,* and with uncharacteristic
bravado, she delivered her manuscript to the theater when the Wilkie
players were making their third and final visit to Christchurch. She
wanted only criticism of her work, if Mr. Wilkie had the time, but she
was astounded when Wilkie wrote back, asking to see her. The meeting
at the Clarendon Hotel was attended by Ngaio, Rose, Wilkie, and his
wife and lead actress, Frediswyde Hunter-Watts. It must have gone well,
though Ngaio recalled few details, because a few weeks later, the
Wilkies tracked Ngaio down and made an even more astonishing offer.

The company would be returning to New Zealand with a new reper-
toire of modern plays, and because one of their actresses would be unavailable, they hoped Ngaio could fill in. Her parts would be small, but
as Wilkie pointed out, she could not ask for a better education in real
theater, on-stage and backstage. Ngaio was ready to go along, but feared
her mother would object. Rose, however, was agreeable, in part because
she liked the Wilkies and trusted them to be suitable guardians.

"I laid down a little cellar of experiences. . . ."

Ngaio made her professional acting debut in Christchurch playing "a
German maid masquerading as a French maid and up to no good" in
The Luck of the Navy. The tour, launched in April 1920, took the company up, down, and around the islands by ferry and train, carriage and
cart. Even in the worst of conditions (it was winter in New Zealand and

many a jerry-built, small-town playing hall was cold and damp), Ngaio soaked up the mechanics and traditions of English theater. She discovered "how actors work in consort, like musicians, how they shape the dialogue in its phrases, build to points of climax, mark the pauses and observe the tempi." She learned the manners of a tightly knit group and picked up backstage superstitions—never to "whistle in the dressing-room, look through the curtain on an opening night, speak the tag at rehearsals, or quote from *Macbeth*"—from the elderly character actress. And unconsciously, she said, "I laid down a little cellar of experiences which would one day be served up as the table wines of detective cookery."

When the tour ended and she returned to her home, a grateful Ngaio sent her Gramp's treasured book on *Actors of the Century* to Allan Wilkie; in return, he sent her a gold wishbone ring that she wore throughout her life. Eighteen years later, Ngaio saluted the Wilkies and their company in *Vintage Murder*—the first of her four mysteries set in New Zealand. As Inspector Alleyn rides a night train with actors of the fictional Caroline Dacres English Comedy Company, readers become acquainted with a cast of players lovingly drawn from Ngaio's memory. Ngaio dedicated *Vintage Murder* to the Wilkies, with whom she and her parents maintained a long friendship.

Few writers of detective fiction have ever made better or more loyal use of the theater. Five of Ngaio's mysteries are set in the professional theater (*Enter a Murderer, Vintage Murder, Opening Night, Death at the Dolphin,* and her last, *Light Thickens*). Three are plotted around the murders of flamboyant stage stars (*Final Curtain, False Scent,* and *Photo-Finish*), and others such as *Overture to Death* and *Death of a Fool* involve amateur theatrical productions. Even *The Nursing Home Murder* makes use of an operating theater for more than surgery. As *New York Times* critic Marilyn Stasio has written, ". . . no other writer evokes 'the incense of the playhouse' or describes the technical details of stage production with the degree of authenticity that Dame Ngaio achieved. . . ."

An atmosphere of theatricality permeates every Ngaio Marsh novel, from the actors, writers, producers, and promoters who appear so frequently among her main characters to Inspector Alleyn's habits of quoting Shakespeare and of staging crime reenactments in order to snare the killer. More telling is the structure of Ngaio's novels: each is to some degree a conventional three-act play. In the first act, a limited cast of characters is introduced and elaborated upon, and murder is committed. In the second, the great detective investigates, and a tangle of motives is uncovered. In the final act, suspicion narrows until the climactic revelation of the perpetrator. Of course, all good mystery writers follow Aristotle's basic narrative formula of beginning, middle, and end, but

Ngaio's divisions between the three phases of the drama are usually so distinct that the reader can almost see the curtain falling.

Plotting was the most difficult phase of her writing, while she excelled in character and dialog; following the rigid rules of the theater helped her construct intelligible plots and orchestrate the action. Even her methods of murdering tend to be theatrical—the most notorious being the jeroboam (oversize bottle) of champagne to the head in *Vintage Murder,* the gun in the upright piano in *Overture to Death,* and the suffocation by baling in *Died in the Wool.*★

But mysteries lay in her future. For eight years after the Wilkie tour, Ngaio was busy finding herself, painting and exhibiting with her "Group" of art school friends, writing articles for publication, trying short stories and starting a novel, acting in and producing amateur theatricals—all with careful steerage from her mother. There were little rebellions: soon after the Wilkie tour, Ngaio took an offer for a three months' touring stint with a comedy troupe. Rose declared, "It's not the right kind of thing for you." But Ngaio went anyway. When the little company failed, Ngaio and two friends from that tour took her own short play and other set pieces on the road. This time, Rose was supportive, possibly because the actors and the material were deemed suitable.

Rose pushed her daughter toward quality and development of her natural gifts. Ngaio remembered her mother as an "inverted snob," and it's pretty clear that Rose was more concerned with rectitude than riches. She wanted her daughter to do what was right and proper and to maintain focus on her talents. She was responsible for training Ngaio to speak the King's brand of English and banishing the dreaded New Zealand accent. She dressed her daughter appropriately for a Victorian-Edwardian child, cultivating Ngaio's taste for handsome but subdued fashion. Rose and Henry, in their different ways, promoted the family legends of noble blood and unfair reversals of fortune, and Rose seems to have evaluated Ngaio's friends and associates on their breeding as well as their behavior. And in a strange way, Rose protected her daughter's freedom by fostering dependence on herself.

Ngaio was undeniably under her mother's thumb, probably more

★ Despite her clever homicides and rich dialog and characterization, stage versions of Ngaio's mysteries, written by herself and others, never really worked. More-recent television adaptations have been only slightly more successful. Perhaps the reason is that Ngaio and her adapters didn't understand what Agatha Christie grasped instinctively—that even three-act novels cannot be transferred wholesale into a performance medium. Reverence for the novel, and the novelist, limits the ability to cut and chop, rearrange and eliminate, in order to bring the written word alive on stage.

than Rose intended or suspected. (When it was suggested that Ngaio, aged twenty-five, finally cut her long hair into a fashionable bob to play a male stage role, she adamantly refused, assuming her mother's displeasure, and wore a miserable wig instead.) It is hard to assess how controlling Rose actually was; at times Ngaio's guilty angst and self-effacement in regard to her mother seem both immature and calculated, a bit like the behavior of a coquettish girl feigning helplessness in order to gain the protection of a strong man. But it should be remembered that Ngaio was an only child and much loved by both her parents—a situation rife with opportunities for passive-aggressiveness on all sides.

A break had to come, and when it did, Rose pushed her daughter from the nest and sent her thirteen thousand miles away, to England. The catalyst was an invitation from friends to visit with them in Buckinghamshire. Ngaio was deeply attached to the Rhodes family—disguised as the Lampreys in her autobiography and her 1940 novel *Death of a Peer* (titled *A Surfeit of Lampreys* in England). Tahu Rhodes had been a friend from her childhood, the son of a wealthy and prominent landowning Christchurch family. Three or four years older than Ngaio, Tahu had married the daughter of Ireland's Lord Plunket during the war. He brought his bride, Helen ("Nelly"), and four lively children back to New Zealand—purchasing Meadowbank, a large sheep station near Christchurch.

During her 1924 production of *Bluebell in Fairyland* for a theater group's charity fund-raiser, Ngaio renewed her acquaintance with Tahu and met Nelly, who was her own age. For the next three years, Ngaio was a nearly permanent fixture in the Rhodes home. With her frequent escort, an Englishman named Toppy Blundell Hawkes who was a farmer-in-training at Meadowbank, she participated in the Rhodeses' exciting, boisterous, often outrageous, but ever-so-aristocratic social life. She became very close to Nelly and was godmother to the fifth Rhodes child. What amused and intrigued Ngaio was the family's "offbeat" way with wealth. When they had money and when they didn't, they lived lavishly: "All the [Rhodeses] made intermittent efforts to economize and then compensated for these bouts of abstinence by giving each other presents at the gold-cigarette-case level. 'After all,' they would say to each other, 'he [or she] must have *some* fun.'"

In 1927, however, the Rhodeses sold their estate and sailed first-class back to England. Financially strapped, Tahu had accepted less for his property than the amount he needed, and he tried gamely to win the difference at billiards. He lost, and, as was their custom, the family took it with a laugh. Their departure left Ngaio and their other friends feeling "rather as children do when the plug is pulled out of a swimming pool and summer goes down the drain."

The invitation from Nelly must have come like a rainbow after a storm. Ngaio had saved some money from her journalism and sales of paintings and arranged to write a series of travel articles that would be syndicated in New Zealand. Her father encouraged her to go, agreeing to pay for her passage and provide a modest income supplement. Unbelievably, Rose also consented. Whatever Rose's deepest feelings may have been, Ngaio insisted on seeing "anguish" in her mother's smile. Certainly, many tears were shed on both sides before Ngaio boarded the passenger-freight ship *Balranald* in September of 1928 for her first trip "home."

Ngaio took to shipboard life as she had once taken to religion—like a duck to water. Not even rough weather, seasickness, and a closet-sized cabin daunted her on the ten-week voyage. She relished each new port of call. Her first stop in Sydney (a "brash, handsome, cocky" city) brought a reunion with Allan Wilkie and Company. Durban was a "lovely interlude" brightened by the gallantry of a Zulu driver-cum-guide and by a night at the theater. Ngaio formed an intense dislike for the arrogant and crude Dutch Afrikaners who came on board in South Africa, though she was delighted to be met at Cape Town by her Uncle Freddie, one of her father's six brothers, with whom she corresponded for many years afterward.

But reaching the south coast of England—"a heraldic England in green and white"—swept everything else from her mind. She was, indeed, home. The ancestral land that had been only pictures and fantasies was now real. Met at the dock by one of the Rhodeses, Ngaio was whisked through London—a bewildering montage of sights, smells, and sounds—and driven to the family's Georgian manor in Buckinghamshire, which, in one of their endless practical jokes, the family had locked, shuttered, and plastered with For Sale signs for her arrival.

The reunion was sweet, and the Rhodeses were no less happy-go-lucky in prim and proper England than they had been in New Zealand. And so Ngaio began a five-year interlude that was to be spent mainly in the Rhodes ménage. Her old escort, Toppy Hawkes, was back in England, and the four—Nelly and Tahu, Ngaio and "Tops"—were frequent patrons of London's best restaurants and brightest nightclubs. They went to the theater—comedies and musicals for the most part. There were two Continental trips: the first via the famous Blue Train to Monte Carlo with Nelly and Betty Cotterill, a dear friend from Christchurch; the second to Paris. On her own, Ngaio explored the tourist sights of London, discovered the Old Vic, and saw John Gielgud in *Hamlet* (the same production that was to inspire Josephine Tey's career as a playwright).

Toward the end of 1929, Nelly and Ngaio got the idea to sell their handmade decorative items—lamp shades, lacquered trays, and other knickknacks for "my ladye's toilette." Calling their venture Touch and Go, they opened a little shop in London's Brompton Road, later moving to more spacious quarters in Beauchamp Place and adding interior design and specialty furniture to their line. Ngaio also did a brief stint as a fashion model for an exclusive Bond Street designer. She was still writing her travel articles for the New Zealand papers, but in the main she was living the life of a somewhat privileged shop girl when word came that her mother would be visiting.

At about the same time, Tahu and Nelly, in another financial crisis, moved from the country house to London. Their eleven-room, two-flat accommodation in Eaton Mansions (the setting for *Death of a Peer*) was cramped for the large family and their entourage, so Ngaio and her mother took a small basement apartment nearby, and Ngaio's routine began to change. Dundas Walker, now a successful actor, reentered their lives and introduced them to "another London: the London of the Caledonian Market and the Portobello Road, of junk stalls in Berwick Street and old print shops. . . ." An actor friend from New Zealand visited, and the little apartment was filled with theater talk. Rose, from her own preference, took Ngaio back to Shakespeare and serious drama instead of musicals and drawing room comedies. They saw Pirandello's *Six Characters in Search of an Author*, directed by Tyrone Guthrie, and Ngaio's old urges to produce and direct resurfaced. Out of the chaotic Rhodes household, she had more time to herself and began to write steadily. She tried her New Zealand novel, but gave it up for a genre she had considered before leaving Christchurch, and on a rainy weekend in 1931, she began her first detective story.

> *"There he was, waiting quietly in the background ready to make his entrance at Chapter IV, page 58, in the first edition."*
> —"Birth of a Sleuth," 1977

Ngaio picked up a detective novel, possibly an Agatha Christie, and decided she could do one of her own. She had already toyed with what she believed to be "a highly original idea" (it wasn't, but Ngaio was not a dedicated mystery reader and didn't know that others had beat her to the punch) for a crime committed during Murders—a popular party game in which participants must solve a pretend murder committed by one of the players. She set her mystery in a manor house during an English country weekend party, amid characters like the people she had met through the Rhodeses.

Over a number of nights and weekends, in little penny notebooks, she built a story that fulfilled the basic Golden Age formula. Judged by the standards of the day, *A Man Lay Dead* was only a so-so book with some troubling inconsistencies, but it was a *done* book. Ngaio achieved two things with her first effort: she completed a long-form story, and she invented the detective who would remain her companion for life.

Chief Inspector–Detective Roderick Alleyn of Scotland Yard makes his first appearance when he is assigned to investigate the stabbing death of a house-party guest. The basics are quickly established. Angela North, one of the guests at Frantock, describes him as "very tall, and lean," with dark hair and "grand" hands and voice. His grey eyes that turn down at the corners look "as if they would smile easily but his mouth didn't." Angela and everyone else sense immediately that Alleyn is not the average cop, but "the sort that they knew would 'do' for house-parties." The host of the party guesses an Oxford connection. Another suspect, after being questioned by the suave detective, says ruefully, "This man Alleyn, with his distinguished presence and his cultured voice and what-not, is in the Edwardian manner. He hectors me with such *haute noblesse* it is quite an honour to be tortured." Invited to Alleyn's home in "one of those curious little cul-de-sacs off Coventry Street," journalist Nigel Bathgate (who serves as Alleyn's Boswell and foil in eight novels) decides that the "unorthodox" C.I.D. man "must be a gent with private means who sleuths for sleuthing's sake."

There are other clues. Alleyn is fastidious: he is embarrassed to ask his suspects for their fingerprints. He is self-deprecating, constantly comparing the glamorous image from detective fiction to the real dirty work of crime-solving and disavowing any showing off as "impossibly vulgar." His humor is dry and facetious. He is intuitive but distrusts his feelings when not based on facts. He is fond of Sherlock Holmes and *Hamlet*. His lowest moments come when he must confront a killer of his own class.

In other words, Roderick Alleyn was created very much in the mold of Ngaio and her mother in temperament and attitude. Ngaio took his name from the founder of her father's English grammar school, actor Edward Alleyn. (She and Rose had visited Dulwich College on the day before Ngaio began her book.) His first name was chosen for its Scottish sound. Despite claims to the contrary, Roderick Alleyn was not unique as a gentleman-policeman; Josephine Tey had already created a more middle-class version of the financially independent Scotland Yard man in 1929, and Dorothy L. Sayers's Lord Peter Wimsey, though not an official policeman, had been suffering similar moral and social fastidiousness for some years. But Alleyn possessed a physical and emotional coolness that even in Ngaio's first effort made him mysterious and attractive; Ngaio would develop her detective considerably in her thirty-one ensuing novels, but she never stripped him of his fundamental reserve.

When Rose read the handwritten book, she pronounced it *"readable"* and then owned up that she "couldn't put it down." (As usual, Ngaio read meaning into her mother's words, sensing regret behind Rose's approval—presumably regret that Ngaio had written a mere detective fiction.) It was not much later that Rose returned to New Zealand, and after seeing her mother off, Ngaio went back to her empty flat and "was visited for the first and last time in my life by a complete emotional breakdown." It lasted about three hours, until she was rescued from her crying binge by the Rhodeses' no-nonsense nanny.

Ngaio fell back into the bosom of the Rhodes family, but she did submit *A Man Lay Dead* to an agent—the same Edmund Cork who was masterminding Agatha Christie's rising career. But in the summer of 1932, she received a cable from her father; her mother was seriously ill. Dropping everything, Ngaio booked passage and arrived in Christchurch at the end of August. Three months later, Rose died of cancer. Ngaio had known death before—her grandparents, Ned Bristed, "Sasha"—but holding watch over her mother's painful final months and days was excruciating. It marked, she said with typical understatement, "my own coming of age."

Ngaio and her father, now retired, settled down to life together in Marton Cottage. Word came that *A Man Lay Dead* would be published by Bles in 1934, and more books were wanted. Dundas Walker (always called "James" by Ngaio) returned to live with his brother and sister in their nearby Port Hills home. Ngaio began to resume old relationships and activities. She was painting again, though she had by now given up on making it her career. She was writing—*Enter a Murderer,* her first theater-set mystery, appeared in 1935, and *The Nursing Home Murder* later the same year. The latter novel, her only collaboration, came out of her own experience of gynecological surgery in 1934. Although the operation was not a complete hysterectomy, it did end her chances of having children. (One can't help wondering if this event, coming on the heels of her mother's death, wasn't the real end of childhood. Although almost forty, Ngaio had led an exceptionally untroubled life, protected by her parents and petted by her friends. Even her autobiography to this point is oddly girlish in tone.) During her recuperation, she got the idea for a hospital-based book and worked on it with one of her physicians, Dr. Henry Jellett. The duo also wrote a stage play, *Exit Sir Derek,* produced by the Canterbury University College Drama Society.

Ngaio was happy enough at home, but England was still her magnet. "On my return to New Zealand after five years," she later wrote, "I found myself looking at my own country, however superficially, from the outside, in." She needed England for inspiration, so in 1937—after completing her first New Zealand novel, *Vintage Death*—she left her father in the care of their housekeeper and returned to Europe with Betty Cotterill and another friend.

No one loved ship travel more than Ngaio, and it must have been heaven to be back at sea. She completed *Artists in Crime* on the voyage and presented it to Edmund Cork when she arrived in London. Her agent and her publisher were dubious about the book because in it Alleyn falls in love. The object of his passion is painter Agatha Troy,★ a woman who resembles Ngaio in many ways. Tall and thin with short dark hair, she is smudged with green paint when Alleyn encounters her on board a ship that has just departed the Fijian capital of Suva. He notes the fine bones of her face, her deep-set blue eyes and warm olive complexion, her "clear, rather cold voice." She is not beautiful but possesses "a kind of spare gallantry" and intelligence that appeals to the well-bred cop. Their meeting is abrasive, and Alleyn is smitten. The courtship, which is carried on between two murders and includes readers' introduction to Alleyn's widowed mother, the charming dowager duchess, comprises the principal subplot of *Artists in Crime*; Ngaio said that she should have titled the novel *The Siege of Troy*. In the end, however, the relationship is left unresolved, and it took another two novels to bring it to an engagement. Unlike Dorothy Sayers, Ngaio didn't marry off her sleuth in a public ceremony or take readers along on the honeymoon. The Alleyns' passion is so pristine and private that when, in *Spinsters in Jeopardy*, Ngaio was to supply them with a five-year-old son, the boy seems to have been found under a cabbage leaf.

Returning to New Zealand with a fresh palette of ideas for new stories, Ngaio found herself shipwrecked by World War Two. With Japan soon battling for control of the Pacific, New Zealanders edgily prepared for invasion, and everyone pitched into the war effort. Ngaio volunteered as an ambulance driver for the Red Cross, taking wounded to

---

★ Agatha Troy was *not* named for Agatha Christie. "I wanted her to have a plain, rather down-to-earth first name," Ngaio wrote in an article for Dilys Winn's 1979 compendium, *Murderess Ink,* and she selected Agatha over other "nice girl" names like Dulcie, Mona, and Gladys. Defending Troy's involvement in so many of Alleyn's cases, Ngaio said, "She is a reticent character and as sensitive as a sea-urchin, but she learns to assume and even feel a certain detachment." Ngaio might have been describing herself, and Troy is surely autobiographical to a degree. Ngaio insisted that she hadn't made Dorothy Sayers's mistake of falling for her fictional detective, but others have surmised that the Alleyn-Troy relationship may represent Ngaio's ideal of marriage—the strong, rational man matched with the strong, creative woman. Agatha Troy keeps her professional name after marrying, and Alleyn, who values her career above his own, always calls her Troy.

hospital and organizing entertainments for the soldiers. She left behind a novel fragment that may have been written around this time. Called *Money in the Morgue,* it comprises three chapters dealing with a Red Cross driver and a theft and murder in the hospital to which she is attached. A romance between the driver and a doctor is hinted at, but the fragment ends before the love story is developed.

Ngaio also began producing amateur theatricals again, and one of these productions was to lead her at last to her life's work. In 1941, she was asked by students of the Canterbury University College Drama Society—a nearly defunct group—to produce a play for them. She agreed and discovered that in spite of the lack of resources and experienced talent, she very much liked working with the young actors and stagehands. They came back for more in 1943, and Ngaio again signed on, with the condition that their play choice be *Hamlet.* This was her first production of Shakespeare, and despite predictions that New Zealanders would not be tempted by the musty old playwright, the play turned into a roaring success.

Ngaio hauled friends into her theater projects, relying on Dundas Walker for on- and off-stage help and even casting her father in bit parts. The student actors quickly found that Ngaio was a tough master, demanding professionalism of her young amateurs. She taught them the basics—be on time, learn lines and cues—and she goaded them to understand the meaning of the lines they were saying. It is interesting to compare her own teaching techniques, rigidly attentive to detail onstage yet warm and receptive off (her players called her "Mum" and often gathered at her home to hammer out their productions) to Agatha Troy's methods in *Artists in Crime.* Ngaio had a sharp eye for talent, and a number of her actors would go on to stage and film careers in London, New York, and Hollywood. But she was a traditionalist in her play choices and productions—solidly rooted in Shakespeare and English conventions, with a mostly tin ear for modern, experimental drama and the natural speech and nationalistic interests of her fellow countrymen.

In her later years, she would become the subject of resentment and ridicule among a younger generation of New Zealand writers, dramatists, and scholars for what they saw as her "essentially outdated colonial Anglophile sensibility."* By the 1960s and 1970s, when she was a potent figure in the arts in New Zealand, her seeming determination to impose Anglo-European standards on Antipodean tastes was roundly mocked by young New Zealand artists and writers who were struggling to find

---

* From an insightful essay by Terry Sturm in *The Oxford History of New Zealand Literature.* Oxford University Press, 1991.

their own distinctive vision and voice. But even her most antagonistic critics could not deny her role in reviving serious New Zealand theater during and after the war years.

Her writing provided the wherewithal to support herself, her father, and her theater work. Her first book after her return to New Zealand was *Death and the Dancing Footman,* an English country house murder that harked back to *A Man Lay Dead.* It is a rather dreary read now, though critics at the time loved it. Her next two novels, *Colour Scheme* in 1943 and *Died in the Wool* in 1945, are set in New Zealand, where Inspector Alleyn is trapped for the duration doing military intelligence. Researching *Colour Scheme* took Ngaio to the North Island thermal resort of Rotorua, and she stayed with her cousin Stella Mannings, a niece of Henry's, and her family in Hamilton. Ngaio formed strong attachments to the two Mannings sons, eight-year-old Roy (called "Bear") and his older brother John, though she was strangely indifferent to the third child, a girl. The boys were to remain close, particularly John, and Ngaio became intimately involved in their lives and education. As biographer Margaret Lewis has noted, this extended family relationship seems to have brought a "new dimension" to Ngaio's life and "added energy to her fiction. . . ."

Colour Scheme is certainly a more physical book than she had ever written before, with touches of thriller as Alleyn in one of his rare disguises chases through steaming geysers and mud pits. There is also a strong Maori presence, adding an exotic element that was new for the author. (Always liberal in her thinking about racial equality, she had included a Maori character in *Vintage Death,* but his ethnicity was perfunctory.) Ngaio believed that *Colour Scheme* was her best-written book, but *Died in the Wool,* set on a South Island sheep station, is almost as good. Alleyn's interrogations become tedious, but Ngaio's descriptions of the wild South Island landscapes (which she had often painted) and the routines of the Mount Moon ranch (reminiscent of the country estates of friends where she often visited) are vivid and evocative.

She finished *Died in the Wool* shortly before her second production of Shakespeare with the Drama Society. *Othello* was another success, prompting D. D. O'Connor, a professional theater manager, to arrange a national tour. More plays and tours followed—*A Midsummer Night's Dream, Henry V,* and *Macbeth*—and Ngaio was soon recognized as a leader in the movement to establish a permanent theater in New Zealand. Always a tireless publicist for her plays and young players, she was appointed an honorary lecturer in drama and launched a series of workshops at Canterbury University College. She also directed New Zealand's first residential drama school. In 1948 she was recognized in the King's Honours List with an O.B.E. (Order of the British Empire) for her contributions to New Zealand theater and literature. But the same year brought the death of her father, and at age fifty-three, Ngaio was on her own for the first time in her life.

"It was strange to be the only one of our little family."

"To begin with I was desolate," she said of the time after losing her father. But she was also free of responsibility, and hearing the siren's call, she shipped out for London, arriving in mid-July 1949. She found an apartment for herself and her secretary, student Pamela Mann, in Beauchamp Place, where she had run her Touch and Go shop with Nelly Rhodes twenty years earlier. Ngaio and Nelly picked up where they had left off (Tahu Rhodes had died in 1947), and Ngaio renewed her friendships with the now-grown Rhodes children and with a number of her former students who were living and working in Mother England. Her friends Evelyn Page with her husband and Sylvia Fox (from Miss Tib's) were in London, as was Allan Wilkie. Her apartment soon became a mecca for old acquaintances and new.

She was honored at a Marsh Millions party celebrating the reissue by Penguin (in association with William Collins, her publisher since 1940) of ten of her novels in quantities of 100,000 each. She was happily back in the world of the theater and was introduced to a new phenomenon: television. She began to dress expensively, and she bought the first of her Jaguars—a powerful sports convertible that she later shipped to New Zealand. She became a figure of some amusement in her Knightsbridge neighborhood, the slim lady in elegant dress who walked her Siamese cat on a jeweled leash.

There was a trip to Monte Carlo with Nelly. The Rhodeses had rented an old Saracen castle on the cliffs high above the casinos where Ngaio and Nelly stayed until the height drove them down to a hotel. Ngaio suffered from vertigo and hated high places, a weakness she shared with Inspector Alleyn and Agatha Troy, but the stay in the lofty fortress was long enough for Ngaio to draw inspiration for her next novel, the thriller-cum-mystery *Spinsters in Jeopardy*, in which she introduced the Alleyns' young son, Ricky.

Ngaio was busy, busy, busy with her writing, her guests, her frequent appearances on a number of BBC radio programs, and her plan to launch a British Commonwealth Theatre Company that would bring together young actors from England, New Zealand, and Australia and tour the Antipodes. She had also agreed to direct a stage version of her novel *A Surfeit of Lampreys*, adapted by Owen Howell, and struggled through a severe bout of flu and bronchitis during rehearsals. Though

Surfeit was coolly reviewed, its producer, Molly May, asked Ngaio to direct *Six Characters in Search of an Author,* the Pirandello play that she had
first seen with her mother in 1930 and later produced in New Zealand.
Ngaio faced a mostly English cast of professionals who looked down on
her New Zealand experience until, as her friend and former student
player Bruce Mason recalled, "She soon put them right, and made it
perfectly clear that first, she knew her job, and second, would stand no
indiscipline."★

Six *Characters* was well received, and Molly May made another offer,
that Ngaio direct a season of British comedies at the Embassy theater,
but Ngaio had to refuse. Her Commonwealth Theatre Company was
scheduled to leave for Australia and New Zealand in February of 1951,
and her time was fully occupied. Ngaio had given up the chance to
make her name in the British theater, and the Commonwealth tour,
which began with a disastrous staging of *The Devil's Disciple* in Sydney
and continued rockily along to fulfill its six-month commitment, was a
failure. Ngaio's dream was to set off a theatrical explosion throughout
the Antipodes, and she had, for one of the few times in her career, put
her own reputation on the line. She tended to blame the fiasco on poor
facilities, but even in her Christchurch, attendance was low. The tour
ended, the actors returned to England, and Ngaio remained in New
Zealand. She had taken a major risk and lost.

The failure of the British Commonwealth Company was followed by
another disaster, the destruction by fire of the Shelley Theatre, home of
the Canterbury Drama Society, in February 1953. But there was work
to be done—a scheduled production of *Julius Caesar* had to be mounted
in the University's Great Hall, a thousand-seat auditorium suited for lectures but not plays. Using techniques she had observed in England,
Ngaio and her student players pulled the rabbit from the hat, and their
Julius Caesar was a smash.

It would not be until 1967 that the Canterbury Student Players
would again have a home of their own. A new facility, built with
Ngaio's input though not exactly to her specifications, would be named
the Dame Ngaio Marsh Theatre. Ngaio would continue to produce
plays until 1972 and always remained one of New Zealand's strongest

---

★ From Bruce Mason's papers, which are held by Victoria University in Wellington,
New Zealand, and quoted in Margaret Lewis's biography *Ngaio Marsh: A Life.* Bruce
Mason first met Ngaio in 1941 when he was a member of the Victoria College drama
society. He went on to act and write in England and had a small part in Ngaio's production of *Six Characters in Search of an Author.* He returned to New Zealand to write
for and about the theater. Mason spoke movingly of his old friend at a memorial service held in Wellington soon after Ngaio's death in 1982, and he died the same year.

advocates for a serious national commitment to the arts and theater. Although she enjoyed the perks that came with her growing international fame as the creator of the Inspector Alleyn books, she never valued her mystery writing as more than a means to support her theatrical endeavors. In New Zealand, she rarely talked of her writing to friends, claiming, "Intellectual New Zealand friends tactfully avoid all mention of my published work, and if they like me, do so, I cannot but feel, in spite of it." The old concern about doing what was right and proper and her mother's teachings about worthy versus disreputable work combined with her own insecurities to deprive Ngaio of joy in a vital part of her career. She was often accused of snobbishness because her books seemed to exalt the British class system, but her real snobbery was toward the genre that paid her way. She never quite overcame her attitude that mystery writing was a necessary but demeaning chore, like mopping floors.

There was one exception to her rule about not discussing her books with her New Zealand crowd. Sometime after her return to Christchurch in 1951, she befriended a couple, Russian refugees Vladimir (Val) and Anita Muling. Though Val worked as a clerk for a machine company, his Old Russian sophistication charmed Ngaio, and his interest in her writing must have provided her a kind of escape valve to let off steam. He began to make regular Saturday visits to her house in the hills, and he and the writer would talk for hours about her books. Val was allowed to read her works in progress (something she had always dreaded), and friends began to suspect that Ngaio had fallen seriously in love. The "affair" was platonic: Ngaio liked and respected Anita Muling. There is also some evidence that Val Muling may have been homosexual or bisexual. But the friendship was important to Ngaio. As biographer Margaret Lewis says, "Val managed to overcome the subtle mental barriers erected by Ngaio to defend herself against intimacy. . . ." The relationship remained tight until Val's death in 1961. Ngaio arranged for his burial at Mount Peel, the estate of her friends Lord and Lady Acland, and planted roses on his grave. Anita was a doting friend for many years. But Ngaio's affection for Val Muling apparently never died; in the late 1970s, observant friends picked up echoes of the relationship in *Grave Mistake*. In this second-to-last of her mysteries, Ngaio created Verity Preston, a fiftyish spinster playwright who is attracted to a wealthy foreigner, Nikolas Markos—the only resident of their small village who is genuinely interested in her work and her life.

There were always rumors in Christchurch about Ngaio's sex life. An unmarried and mannishly elegant woman naturally attracted gossip. But Ngaio's "romances" were maternal rather than passionate. She cultivated the friendships of a number of her young male, often gay actors, providing nurture and shelter when needed, boosting their spirits and their careers, and basking in their admiration and companionship. Without evidence to the contrary, it seems clear that none of these relationships were physical; rather, they were like priestess and acolyte. Ngaio's men friends tended, like Bruce Mason, to be married to women she liked, or to be gay, or both; whatever their status and sexuality, they were safe. Ngaio's fear of intimacy was doubtless related both to her fear of losing her independence and her Victorian sense of propriety. Psychiatrists can delve into her hidden psyche (Ngaio herself wondered if she were not the victim of her mother's "daughter fixation"), but the upshot was that she lived a solitary life amid a mob of loyal and admiring friends.

The years between 1951 and 1974 were of a pattern—extended stays in England alternating with time at home in the hills. In England and on the world tours she took, she was ever the glamorous and accommodating mystery writer; in Christchurch, she was the hard-slogging theater producer who dressed down, puttered around her extensive garden, wrote her books at night, and rarely displayed her glamorous side except on official occasions and at her infrequent but famously large and boozy cocktail parties.

In 1954 she traveled to England via a Norwegian freight ship. She preferred these rough-and-tumble voyages to the posh luxury liners because both people and ports of call were more interesting. From her rented houses in London's Hans Street and Cliveden Place, shared with her old pal Sylvia Fox, she journeyed to Devonshire and Cornwall and to the Rhodes home in Kent. In the Kentish village of Birling, she found the model for *Death of a Fool,* a mystery centered around ancient winter solstice rites. The atmosphere in this book is literally chilling, a reflection of Ngaio's own distaste for cold weather, and many readers and critics regard *Death of a Fool* as one of her best works, in which plot rises to the level of her scene-setting and characterization.

Her social life on this English stay included drinks with Princess Margaret and dinners with the Laurence Oliviers and Anthony Quayles. She also enjoyed the company of John Dacres-Mannings, who was serving in the British Army. John was soon to need her help after her return to New Zealand in 1956; he contracted a serious illness while serving in Germany and went to his second home, Marton Cottage, to recuperate.

In February 1960, she again departed for England, this time via ship to Indonesia, Singapore, Hong Kong, Yokohama, Tokyo (where she visited with publishers and was wined and dined at the New Zealand Embassy), Honolulu, and San Francisco. Traveling by train—she detested flying—she crossed the country to New York, where she soaked up the atmosphere of the city and was toasted in the press. After meeting her American publisher in Boston, she left for the last leg of the exhausting trip, arriving in London in June. She found a house to rent in Knightsbridge and a new cat that was to be portrayed as Lucy Lockett, the very model of the feline sleuth in *Black as He's Painted*. She rented a room to one of her New Zealand students who was studying at the London Academy of Music and Dramatic Art; to stave off rumors, she told everyone that he was her godson. She also bought a new sports car—a sleek black Jaguar XK150—though her worried agent, Edmund Cork, opposed the purchase, fearing for her life and limb. She dosed on plays and began a project with Eileen Mackay, the eldest Rhodes daughter, to adapt her most recent novel, *False Scent,* for the theater. The play was staged by a provincial rep company but never reached its hoped-for place in the West End. It was during this trip that Ngaio received word of Val Muling's death. But she was also gathering details that would eventually be transported into one of her most popular books, *Black as He's Painted*.

Her next novel, *Dead Water,* completed with some difficulty after her return to Christchurch in 1962, was far below her standard. She redeemed herself, however, after a three-year hiatus. In *Death at the Dolphin* she returned to a theater setting, basing the book on a visit she had once paid with director Tyrone Guthrie to a bomb-damaged theater in Woolwich. Their hope was that the theater could be salvaged for a Shakespeare season during the 1951 Festival of Britain. The building was too far gone for repair, but Ngaio rebuilt it in her own way as the Dolphin Theatre, where murder is mixed with a valuable Shakespeare artifact.

Death at the Dolphin was published in 1966, around the time that Ngaio's autobiography, *Black Beech and Honeydew,* was released. She had undertaken a life story at the request of her publisher and friend, William Collins. It was not an easy assignment for the reticent writer; she was unhappy with the finished product and begged off attending a planned gala launch in the United States. Neither she nor her editors had faith in the project, and they were right. The book, which divulged few secrets and dealt only sparingly with her detective fiction, bombed with the public. She told a friend that she should have titled it *Other People* because she had given away so little of herself.

By April of 1966 she was back in London, and two months later came the announcement of her highest honor. She was to be named Dame Commander of the British Empire (D.B.E.) in the Queen's Birthday Honours. Friends and most of her countrymen were delighted. Her students cabled, "No man here but honours you and doth wish you had but that opinion of yourself which every member of the Canterbury University Drama Society bears of you."★

★ Quoted by Margaret Lewis in *Ngaio Marsh: A Life.*

For a time, however, it appeared that she might be forced to miss her investiture. Under Britain's tightening tax laws, she could stay in England only six months before becoming subject to the national income tax. The November ceremony at Buckingham Palace would fall beyond the time limit. She remedied the situation by taking an Aegean cruise and then visiting a friend, the daughter of her onetime collaborator Dr. Jellett, in Ireland. And so she became Dame Ngaio, but not without another kind of taxing experience. Denys Rhodes, who was part of the royal establishment, informed Queen Elizabeth that Miss Marsh was a cripple and that she preferred to be called Edith. So Her Majesty's minions thoughtfully arranged for "Edith" to be delivered to a side door of the palace, where a footman with a wheelchair awaited her. She missed her grand entrance with the rest of the honorees, but the Queen apparently enjoyed the practical joke.

The new Dame returned to New Zealand to produce *Twelfth Night* in the new University theater. To stage the first production in a theater bearing her own name was obviously satisfying. That the play made a profit was icing on her cake. She was working on a new novel, *Clutch of Constables,* in which she broke her formula somewhat to tell the story in flashback. Troy is the discoverer of the crime; on a lake cruise she looks down into the "idiotically bloated" face of a murder victim. Ngaio got the idea on a cruise on the river Trent during her last trip to England, and she enjoyed, she told *The Times,* "setting violence in such a tranquil scene."

Her next mystery was also drawn from her travels. Back in Europe, she paid an extended visit with the New Zealand ambassador to Italy, Alister McIntosh, and his wife at the embassy in Rome. The trip provided distraction from her grief at the news of Nelly Rhodes's sudden death in February 1968. It also inspired a new novel, *When in Rome.* As a number of critics have noted, this is the first novel in which she took square aim at corruption among the British elite, but *When in Rome* is equally notable for its sense of place. (Readers who visit Rome might stop in the basilica of San Clemente in Laterano, fictionalized as San Tommaso, the scene of the crime.)

Ngaio was now into her mid-seventies, and the deaths of old friends and colleagues were becoming all too commonplace. The passing of Allan Wilkie in his nineties could not have been a surprise, but the deaths of two young friends were shocks. Brigid Lanihan, the beautiful "bright star" of Ngaio's early days with the Student Players, was gone at age forty-one, a possible suicide. Then came word that Eileen Rhodes Mackay, the leading practical joker of the Rhodes clan, had died. Ngaio's 1971 trip to England was surely misted in sadness. So many friends were gone, and London itself had changed. For the first time, the night-owl writer was afraid to walk the streets alone after dark.

> *"One hesitates to speak of death to one's friends for fear of making them feel awkward."*

Ngaio, who had fought so hard to hang on to her youth, was coming to the end of many things. She produced her last Shakespeare play, a rousing treatment of *Henry V,* late in 1972. The work greatly sapped her strength. She suffered a fall at her home, and though not badly injured, she was shaken by her own frailty. She worried about her income and taxes, fearing she would not have funds for her old age. She perked up enough to entertain English novelist and essayist J. B. Priestley and his wife, whom she had known in England, and to start her new book, *Black as He's Painted.* But another fall in her steeply terraced hillside garden did cause injury, which she hid from most of her friends and her business associates.

Her 1974 trip to England was to be her last. Struggling to maintain a full social schedule, which included becoming a member of the famed Detection Club and taking her book tour with Julian Symons and Harry Keating, she at last had to admit that she was not well. Seeking treatment, she was diagnosed with cancer and immediately underwent a complete hysterectomy at London's King's College Hospital. Her convalescence was slow, but she was able to begin a new book (*Last Ditch*) in early 1975 during a holiday to the island of Jersey, and she also wrote a television play commissioned by Granada. She left London in August that year with every intention of returning, but for once the ocean voyage did not raise her spirits or improve her health, and it was with much relief that she finally reached her house in the hills above Christchurch.

Last Ditch was going badly and required a number of alterations. Her agents were well aware of the problems, but they concealed their doubts from Ngaio, hiding their honest judgments as so many of her friends did in order to protect her feelings. *Last Ditch* is in fact a silly book in which Ricky Alleyn, now grown, plays detective. Ngaio's next mystery, *Grave Mistake,* was an improvement and popular with readers. But her friends, whom she had come to rely on after the retirement of her longtime housekeeper, wondered how long the ailing writer could keep up the pace. She could easily have retired from writing; despite her worrying about money, she was quite well off. Her physical problems increased— gout, a hernia, deafness, and a cataract that forced her finally to stop driving her Jaguar. But the cancer had apparently been checked, and she was in rather good shape for a woman now in her eighties. She had a wide circle of friends of all ages and was still a strong voice in the New Zealand arts scene, continuing to speak and make public appearances.

One must wonder if she hadn't become attached to her mysteries and her famous characters. She often made odd, self-defensive excuses for her actions and inaction. (She said she couldn't write a New Zealand novel because the nature of the country would overwhelm any story. She said she couldn't write straight novels because her readers would be disappointed. Whenever a play failed, she usually blamed the facilities.) So it's possible she exaggerated her financial straits to justify her need to continue doing the one thing that gave her life structure—writing detective stories.

In May of 1977, she was hospitalized with heart trouble and a leg thrombosis. Unfortunately, word went out that she had died, and when an obituary appeared in London, she was amused to learn that "on the whole it was favourable." Another fall not long after she had come home from the hospital forced her to hire a live-in caretaker and be tended by visiting nurses, whom she nicknamed the "Daughters of Dracula" for their endless blood tests.

But still she thought about travel and England. She considered a trip to the United States, where she was to be honored, with Dorothy B. Hughes and Daphne du Maurier, with the Grand Master Award of the Mystery Writers of America. Wiser heads prevailed, and she stayed at home. But she did accept election to two annual terms as honorary president of the New Zealand branch of the international writers association PEN. Toward the end of 1978, she embarked on a new book, her fourth to be set in New Zealand. In *Photo-Finish,* dedicated to Ngaio's old friends Fred and Evelyn Page, Troy joins Alleyn for a command performance in a desolate South Island location. The plot owes much of its inspiration to the saga of Aristotle Onassis, Maria Callas, and Jacqueline Kennedy Onassis and to Mrs. Kennedy's much-publicized battles with the paparazzi. But the setting is pure Ngaio—the same Lake Brunner (Lake Waihoe in the book), "a looking-glass sunk in the mountains" that she had visited as a girl; the same steep road, full of zigzagging cutbacks, that descends into the Otira River Gorge and that had terrified young Ngaio as it terrifies Troy.

The mystery took some time to work out—Ngaio often compared her average eight-or-nine-month writing span to a pregnancy—and she was apparently suffering angina attacks. A major heart attack in June of 1980 put her back in the hospital. Again, a cascade of premature death notices appeared, but good reviews of *Photo-Finish* may have eased her irritation with the gun-jumping press. Convalescent now, with her social activities greatly curtailed, she started another book. (She had completed her revision of *Black Beech and Honeydew,* updating and adding a section about her mystery writing to appease fans disappointed by the first edition.) For the new mystery, her thirty-second, she revisited her two great loves: the theater and Shakespeare. *Light Thickens* involves a production of *Macbeth,* a play she had staged twice. It was a book she had long wanted to write. "It would be satisfactory to bring the two major interests of my life together for, as it were, a final fling. . . ." she said in her revised autobiography, adding, "I hope I have one more book in me and I hope too I'll have the sense to call it a day if it turns out to be below standard." While she was working on *Light Thickens,* her old friend Sylvia Fox, who lived nearby, broke her ankle and moved in with Ngaio to recover; the two invalids apparently had great fun recalling their girlhood.

Ngaio finally sent her completed manuscript to her agents just after Christmas in 1981. On February 3, she received word that *Light Thickens* had been accepted; again her agents spared her the news that extensive revisions were needed. On February 18, 1982, Ngaio died at home. The cause was a cerebral hemorrhage. She was two months shy of her eighty-eighth birthday, but her obituaries gave her age as eighty-three; she had kept her little secret from the public.

Agnostic to the end, she nevertheless had planned a full-scale Anglican funeral, and Christchurch Cathedral was packed on the day. Simon Acland, son of her old friends Lord and Lady Acland, officiated. An honor guard was formed by the girls of St. Margaret's school. The large funeral service, which was broadcast to the nation on radio, was followed by a small interment attended by friends. Her ashes, buried at the Church of the Holy Innocents at Mount Peel, lie not far from the final resting place of Val Muling. Ngaio left the bulk of her estate to the two cousins who had given her such pleasure in life, John Dacres-Mannings and "Bear" Mannings.

Light Thickens was released late in 1982, following extensive editing at Collins. The final appearance of Inspector Alleyn and his trusty team from the Yard sold extremely well. It was dedicated to the two actors who, as students, had played Macbeth and Lady Macbeth in Ngaio's last production of the play.

Evaluating the impact of Ngaio Marsh on detective fiction is difficult. Fervent fans contend that she was pivotal in elevating the genre from puzzle to novel of character and psychology. Less bedazzled readers find her mysteries well written but often dull and plodding after the murder is committed. Some contend that the popularity of her formula actually retarded modern developments in the mystery. But despite Ngaio's longevity and consistently good sales, she never achieved significant influence and couldn't have stopped progress if she had tried.

The criticism that really stung Ngaio came most succinctly from her companion on that 1974 book promotion tour, Julian Symons. In his critical history *Bloody Murder,* Symons cited the first half of *Opening Night* for its "brilliant picture of the intrigues taking place before the opening of a new play" and the reader's natural expectation that "after the murder the book will remain in the same key and that the problems will be resolved as they began, in terms of character." But no, Symons goes on: ". . . Marsh takes refuge from real emotional problems in the official investigation and interrogation of suspects. The temperature is lowered, the mood has been lost." This failing was not limited to a single book, Symons added.

Awkwardly, Ngaio had defended herself by blaming the intrinsic structure of the detective novel. Although she almost always began her books with characters in mind, she contended that the necessary "skulduggery" of finding and revealing the guilty party undercut characterization. A writer, she said, did her best by writing with "as good a style as he or she can command" within the "shamelessly contrived" conventions of the genre.

But she got closer to the truth when she talked about her lack of self-confidence, her fear with each new book "that I'm going to fall flat on my face and rise up with egg all over it." By contrast, she wrote in her revised autobiography, "as a director of Shakespeare productions, beset by the terrors of first nights and all the rest of the hazards of the game, I was persuaded, always, that what I wanted to achieve was on the right lines. . . ."

In her work—in her life—she trusted others and not herself. On the stage she felt free to interpret Shakespeare because he had done the hard part of the work, but she could never write a successful, mature play of her own. In her writing, she adapted but never expanded on the rules of the Golden Age puzzle mystery because she didn't trust her ability to break with convention. Few mystery writers have been so deft at drawing life sketches of instantly intriguing characters or making victims so interesting (the Boomer in *Black as He's Painted,* for example, or the opera star Isabella Sommita in *Photo-Finish*). But Ngaio never trusted herself to go beyond brilliant sketches to develop fully realized portraits that reach into the dark recesses of character. This is why the most satisfying part of her books is always the first act. (Agatha Troy Alleyn, on the other hand, is a gifted portrait painter whose true art lies in capturing the essence of her subjects on canvas. Is Troy the artist Ngaio wanted to be, fulfilling in fiction the promise that Ngaio could never bring herself to test in real life?)

In an exceedingly poignant little passage in the revised *Black Beech and Honeydew,* Ngaio wrote about the tricks of memory, and questioned why she could recall in every detail an incident that must have happened when she was a toddler—lying in bed "in a room with blue wallpaper and white flowers and, knowing my mother was resting on her own bed across the passage. . . ." Wondering if she could "stagger so far. . . ." Sliding down from her bed and making the perilous crossing to her mother's open door. "I see her, really and truly I do, as if it were days and not two-thirds of a century ago, turn and smile her astonishment and hold out her hands. Why did my brain choose to retain this moment and no other of my remote infancy?"

Throughout her long and busy life, Ngaio seemed always to have been seeking that approval. She stuck to the guidelines laid down in her youth and never strayed far from the professional and personal path that Rose Marsh had paved for her. The mother, who plainly wanted only the best for her daughter within the context of the early-twentieth-century mores of a still-colonial land, remained with Ngaio through all the social, cultural, political, and creative upheavals of the middle and late century. For almost fifty years after her death, Rose continued to hold out her arms to her tottering child.

Reticence is more than verbal uncommunicativeness. It is restraint, a conscious or unconscious holding back. One cannot help wondering what Ngaio Marsh might have been and done if she had not so totally embraced her mother's ideals, if she had ever let her guard down. That Ngaio so often referred to her reticence implies that she accepted it. She had opportunities most people only dream of to reach for the brass ring but chose only to ride the merry-go-round. Readers have little to complain of, however; her thirty-two detective novels may not be the best she was capable of, but they remain among the best of their kind.

BIBLIOGRAPHY

NGAIO MARSH
1895–1982
New Zealander (born: Christchurch)

"You certainly are the goods. I guess you've got British Manufacture stamped some place where it won't wear off. All this quiet deprecation—it's direct from a sure-fire British bestseller."

—Death in Ecstasy

All Ngaio Marsh's detective novels and collected short stories feature the fastidious Inspector Alleyn of Scotland Yard. Alleyn is sometimes joined by Agatha Troy, whom he meets in *Artists in Crime* and marries between

Death in a White Tie and *Overture to Death*. Marsh's first eight novels were published in England by Bles and in America by Sheridan, then Furman. Collins became her English publisher with *Death at the Bar* in 1940 and handled all her novels to her death in 1982. Little, Brown was her American publisher from 1940 on. Except where noted, dates are for first publication in England. Alternate titles are given. GB = Great Britain. US = United States.

Mystery Novels

1934	*A Man Lay Dead*
1935	*Enter a Murderer*
1935	*The Nursing Home Murder* (with Dr. Henry Jellett)
1936	*Death in Ecstasy*
1937	*Vintage Murder*
1938	*Artists in Crime*
1938	*Death in a White Tie*
1939	*Overture to Death*
1940	*Death at the Bar*
1940	US: *Death of a Peer*/GB: *A Surfeit of Lampreys*
1941	US: *Death and the Dancing Footman*
1943	*Colour Scheme*
1945	*Died in the Wool*
1947	*Final Curtain*
1949	*Swing, Brother, Swing*/US: *A Wreath for Rivera*
1951	*Opening Night*/ US: *A Night at the Vulcan*
1953	US: *Spinsters in Jeopardy*
1955	*Scales of Justice*
1956	US: *Death of a Fool*/GB: *Off with His Head*
1958	US: *Singing in the Shrouds*
1960	US: *False Scent*
1962	*Hand in Glove*
1963	US: *Dead Water*
1966	US: *Killer Dolphin*/GB: *Death at the Dolphin*
1968	*Clutch of Constables*
1970	*When in Rome*
1972	*Tied Up in Tinsel*
1974	*Black as He's Painted*
1977	*Last Ditch*
1978	*Grave Mistake*
1980	*Photo-Finish*
1982	*Light Thickens*

Short Stories

Alleyn and Others: the collected short fiction of Ngaio Marsh. Edited by Douglas G. Greene and published by The Library of Crime Classics, International Polygonics, Ltd., in 1989. Includes two Marsh essays, nine short stories, and the script of her TV play "Evil Liver."

Plays Dates are for first production or publication.

1922 *Little Housebound*

1935 *Exit Sir Derek* (with Dr. Henry Jellett)

1955 *The Wyvern and the Unicorn* (also the source for Marsh's libretto for the children's opera *A Unicorn for Christmas*)

1961 *False Scent* (with Eileen Mckay)

1962 *The Christmas Tree* (published)

1972 *Murder Sails at Midnight* (adapted from *Singing in the Shrouds*)

1975 "Evil Liver" (television play produced by Granada Television Ltd. for the *Crown Court* series)

1976 *Sweet Mr. Shakespeare* (with Jonathon Elsom)

Autobiography

Black Beech and Honeydew. US: Little, Brown, 1965/GB: Collins, 1966. Revised and expanded edition published in 1981.

Film and Video Adaptations

A theater person, Marsh seems to have had only passing interest in films, and no movies were made from her Inspector Alleyn mysteries. She did enjoy television and wrote one television play for broadcast. Her four New Zealand novels—*Vintage Murder, Colour Scheme, Died in the Wool,* and *Opening Night*—were produced for broadcast on New Zealand television in 1978 and starred British actor George Baker as Alleyn. Ngaio liked Baker's performance but felt the adaptations were slow and humorless.

The same could be said of a series of BBC adaptations made in the early 1990s with Patrick Malahide as Alleyn, Belinda Lang as Troy, and William Simons as Inspector Fox. This lushly produced series portrays Alleyn as more dour than facetious and stretches the early novels to include Troy for love interest but not much else. The BBC's Alleyn mysteries include *A Man Lay Dead, The Nursing Home Murder, Artists in Crime, Death in a White Tie, Death at the Bar,* and *Final Curtain.*

THE ALLEYN FILE

NAME: Roderick Alleyn (Rory)

ADDRESS: London: bachelor flat in a cul-de-sac off Coventry Street; marital home at 48 Regency Close, S.W. 1 ("near Montpelier Square"). Country cottage in the village of Little Copplestone, Kent. The Alleyns' ancestral estate is in Scotland and his mother's home, Danes Lodge, in Bassicote, Buckinghamshire.

OCCUPATION: Chief Detective-Inspector, C.I.D., Scotland Yard; promoted to Superintendent and Chief Superintendent.

AGE: Fortyish or fiftyish. (Alleyn's age, like his author's, is a matter of convenience. He's forty-two in *Vintage Death*, so would be eighty-seven—Ngaio's age—in his last appearance in *Light Thickens*. But real time isn't operative.)

MARITAL STATUS: Married to Agatha Troy Alleyn, R.A., well-known painter and portrait artist and daughter of Stephen and Harriet Baynton Troy.

CHILDREN: One son, Ricky

OTHER FAMILY: Roderick Alleyn is the second son of the late Lord Alleyn and the dowager duchess (née Blandish, Helena to her friends and "little mum" to her son). Elder brother George, the current duke, is an ambassadorial-level diplomat and "a bit of an ass." Sister-in-law is Grace. Niece Sarah is a debutante in *Death in a White Tie*. Sir George may also have twin sons. Cousin Christina Alleyn, a chemist, lends a helping hand in *A Man Lay Dead*.

PHYSICAL DESCRIPTION: 6'2", lean, athletic. Black hair and eyebrows. Gray-blue eyes that slant down at the corners. A "winged face" with deep depressions at corners of his mouth: "an attractive and fastidious face and, when nobody watched him, a very expressive one." "Albrecht Durer would have made a magnificent drawing of him. . . ." Known as "Handsome Alleyn" and "The Handsome Sleuth" in the popular press. Sometimes described as "faunish." Voice is deep and "resonant" with "Oxonian" accent. Good smile but rarely laughs. Smells, thinks Roberta Grey in *Death of a Peer*, "like a new book in a good binding."

OTHER DISTINGUISHING CHARACTERISTICS: Fastidious in style and temperament. Neat but not flashy dresser who likes to be "tidy" when making an arrest. Stickler for proper etiquette for self and his C.I.D. officers. Rubs his nose when concentrating (a quirk shared with his mother and Ngaio Marsh's mother). Requires little sleep and can wake self with the precision of an alarm clock. Speaks excellent French and good Italian. Hates heights. Likes cats. Often said to be ascetic and priestlike but can exhibit "indecent" charm when needed.

Has "what Kent recognized in Lear," i.e., authority. Tends to inspire hero-worship in subordinates. Carries a cheap Woolworth notebook and travels with his "professional homicide kit" and miniature camera. Favorite flower: lilac.

EDUCATION: Eton; Oxford (M.A.)

CAREER PATH: Three years soldiering in World War One; fought at Flanders. In the diplomatic service before and/or after World War One. Mysterious switch to police force ("before the days of Lord's Trenchard's scheme") never explained but may have been related to his brother's Foreign Service career. Worked his way up in the Metropolitan Police from constable to highest rank in the Criminal Investigation Division. Temporarily assigned to M.I.5 (military intelligence) in late 1930s.

MODUS OPERANDI: "I receive facts as a spider does flies." Finds the pattern, like fitting pieces in a jigsaw. Mistrusts hunches, intuition, and first impressions but follows them nonetheless. An "incurable nosey parker" and expert interrogator (could get "worked up over the life-story of a mollusc"). Particularly loathes blackmailers and drug dealers. Inclined to stage crime reenactments. Likes to characterize self as "simply a wheel in the machine" of justice and an "automaton." Enjoys "a dramatic close to a big case," inevitably followed by "beastly anti-climax depression." Regarded by the Yard as expert on actors and theater crimes.

ALIASES: Mr. Allen; C. J. Broderick (*Singing in the Shrouds*); Septimus Falls (*Colour Scheme*)

MAGNUM OPUS: *Principles and Practices of Criminal Investigation* (Sable & Murgatroyd, 21s.), a standard text with police forces internationally.

INTERESTS: Art; theater (frequent quoter of Shakespeare, partial to the first act of *Hamlet*). Well read in many subjects, including detective fiction—Conan Doyle, Edgar Wallace, R. Austin Freeman, Christie, Sayers, Freeman Wills Crofts, etc. Too urbane for ordinary hobbies? (His mamma raises dogs and weaves.)

FRIENDS AND ASSOCIATES: Nigel Bathgate, reporter for the London *Clarion,* and his wife Angela; Detective-Inspector Fox (Br'er Fox, Foxkins), Alleyn's "valued old one" and "the perfect embodiment, the last loveliest expression, of horse sense"; Detective-Sergeants Bailey (fingerprints) and Thompson (photography); Sir James Curtis, police surgeon and pathologist; lawyer Mr. Rattisbon of Knightley, Knightly and Rattisbon; Lord Robert (Bunchy) Gospell; Rangi Te Pokiha, Oxford-educated Maori physician; Reverend Walter Copeland and daughter Dinah of Wilton St. Giles; Bartholomew (Boomer) Opala, C.B.E., president of Ng'ombwana and Alleyn's roommate at Oxford; Samuel Whipplestone, retired Foreign Office;

young Nicola Maitland-Mayne, who calls Alleyn "Cid"; Lord Michael Lamprey, later Constable Mike Lamprey; law enforcers on several continents and innumerable individuals of high and low rank.

GREEN WITH MYSTERY

Before she became a mystery writer, Ngaio Marsh was a painter and erstwhile interior decorator with an eye for color. Was green her favorite hue? It pops out in many of her mysteries. The front door of Roderick Alleyn's bachelor flat is green in *A Man Lay Dead*. Agatha Troy's angular face is "disfigured" by a smear of green oil paint when she first meets Alleyn in *Artists in Crime*, and she again wears a streak of green paint across her nose when painting Reverend Copeland in *Death and the Dancing Footman*. In *Black as He's Painted*, Troy dresses in a green gown for a diplomatic party.

In *The Nursing Home Murder*, Dr. Roberts meets Alleyn in "a pleasant drawing room with apple-green walls. . . ." Murder is done in the green room at Marsdon House in *Death in a White Tie*, and Sir Daniel Davis's Harley Street office is "a charming room with apple-green walls, an Adams fireplace, and silver-starred curtains." Vicar Copeland's comfortable study has "faded apple-green walls" in *Overture to Death*. In *Killer Dolphin*, apple-green library walls seem to cast a pallor over the wealthy Mr. Conducis. The light green sitting room of Highfold Manor is decorated with nosegays in *Death and the Dancing Footman*, and apple-green watered silk hangs on the walls of the little boudoir at Halberds in *Tied Up in Tinsel*. The irritating Cedric Ancred chooses a pale green shirt and dark green sweater with an orange tie in *Last Curtain*, and an "emerald green cow with vermillion wings" drops a bombshell.

Is green a clue? Or a red herring? It tints the page more consistently than any other color in Ngaio's books. But readers searching for solutions to her mysteries will find better direction in the dialog than her color choice or other physical clues.

A MERRY MARSH CHRISTMAS

Scores of mystery writers have set their crimes to the sounds of jingling bells and "Ho, ho, ho." Arthur Conan Doyle chose Christmas for "The Blue Carbuncle"; Agatha Christie set several stories during Yuletide, including *Hercule Poirot's Christmas*. Ellery Queen sleuths over the holidays in *The Finishing Stroke;* Nick and Nora Charles indulge in Christmas shopping in *The Thin Man*. Nero Wolfe plays Santa in Rex Stout's "The

Christmas Party," and even the dour French cop Maigret is involved in a holiday caper in George Simenon's "Maigret's Christmas." There's something about the season of peace and goodwill that begs for a crime.

So Ngaio Marsh was not unique in the settings of her 1972 novel *Tied Up in Tinsel* or the Alleyn short story "Death on the Air." But in her private life, she made Christmas magic. A New Zealander of English heritage, Ngaio was raised on images of cold and snowy Victorian Christmases but celebrated the holiday in the middle of the hot Antipodean summer. The Christmas tree fascinated her as a little girl, and she collected presents for family and friends throughout each year. To contact Father Christmas, she put a letter in a little box tied to the top of a pine tree outdoors, and from age seven, she kept a secret Christmas Eve journal: "The last [entry] was made when I was thirty-five years old and unhappy. After that I burnt the book." In her teens, the Marshes went on summer camping trips and celebrated in the primal New Zealand woodland.

Her first English Christmas was in 1928. Ngaio, staying in a London hotel near her Brompton Road gift shop, never forgot the clear peal of an oratory bell when street sounds were muffled by falling snow or "Adeste Fideles" sung by a boy in the night—"not so much sound as vapour or perhaps a tingling vibration on frozen air."

In the 1950s, she inaugurated her own Christmas tradition—a gathering for her New Zealand friends and their children in her Christchurch home. After a meal on the best china, the youngsters were summoned by recorded sleigh bells and carols to an elaborate Christmas tree that sparkled in a darkened room. Decorated boxes of gifts gathered in her travels were distributed. After a few years, the children began rewarding Ngaio with plays, often pun-filled Shakespeare parodies such as *Macbath*. The tradition survived well into the 1970s, and later Christmas tree guests included the children of children who had attended earlier gatherings. Ngaio wrote her own seasonal play, *The Christmas Tree,* in the early 1950s, yet when she submitted *Tied Up in Tinsel* to her publishers in 1971, revisions were required to correct her romantic ideas about the typical English Christmas. She didn't like being told that the traditional pudding is made weeks in advance and not whipped up on Christmas morning. But the Christmas tree ceremony in *Tied Up in Tinsel,* with the local children agog, gives readers a close approximation of the magic Ngaio Marsh cooked up in her New Zealand home for a quarter of a century.

JOSEPHINE TEY

A SINGULAR SOUL

" 'I shall never write a book,' Grant said firmly. 'Not even My Twenty Years at the Yard.'
'What! Not even your autobiography?'
'Not even my autobiography. It is my considered opinion that far too many books are written as it is.'"

—The Daughter of Time

The centennial anniversary of a well-known author's birth usually brings forth new books and articles about that person's life and works. Nineteen-ninety was Agatha Christie's year; 1993 belonged to Dorothy L. Sayers; 1995 saw fresh tributes to Ngaio Marsh. But in 1996, a hundred years from the birth of a woman perennially ranked in the highest echelon of British mystery writers, there was hardly a peep—no new biographical revelations, no reminiscences by those who knew her when.

Josephine Tey

This peculiar oversight was no snub. Nor did it happen because no one cared. It happened because people simply do not know.

Of all the Women of Mystery, Elizabeth MacKintosh is the most deserving of the title. She never published under her own name, hiding her identity behind first the male pseudonym Gordon Daviot and then the pen name by which she is recognized today, Josephine Tey. She never submitted to press interviews, shunned all forms of personal publicity, and was guarded even with close colleagues. No one has yet collected her letters or edited her papers, if there are any around, and she never, so far as we know, chronicled her life beyond the most basic details. She left behind only the bare outline of a mystery whose clues must be extracted from her fiction.

For a long time, even her birth year was in doubt, but it has been determined that Elizabeth MacKintosh arrived in this world on June 25, 1896, in Inverness, Scotland. Both her parents were Scots-born. Her father, Colin, was reared in a small Gaelic farming and fishing community, and he learned English, his second language, in school. Moving to Inverness probably in the early 1890s, Colin set up as a greengrocer, and at age twenty-nine, he married.

Josephine Horne MacKintosh was six years younger than her husband. She was a teacher whose family tree included one Englishman—a grandfather named Robert Ellis who came originally from Suffolk. In *Deadlier than the Male,* a study of British women writers of detective fiction, Jessica Mann indicates that Josephine was raised in a strict Protestant sect and "had been a tomboy as a child." Not given to domesticity, she "was happiest when she could help her husband in the shop, or walk on the hills with her daughters. . . ." A woman of independent spirit, it seems.

Elizabeth was the first of the MacKintosh girls. She and her younger sisters, Jean and Mary, attended the local Inverness Academy, where Elizabeth must have been a good student; in a brief autobiographical sketch written late in her life, she said that she was "destined for a university. . . ." But, worn out by twelve years of rigorous Scottish academics, she chose instead a course in physical education, a serious and demanding field of study in those days. Turned down by a college in Scotland because of her eyesight—she wore glasses—she was accepted by the Anstey Physical Training College in Birmingham, England, and left her Scottish Highlands in 1914, the year that World War One began. Birmingham, one of England's major industrial centers, was hardly a safe location, subject to zeppelin raids and German shelling, but Elizabeth made it through her three years' training, which included teaching fitness classes for factory workers. In Inverness for school holidays, she worked as a VAD (Volunteer Aid Detachment) girl in a local convalescent home.

After her graduation from Anstey in 1917, her first job was as a physical therapist at a private clinic in Leeds. She moved on to teach at schools in Nottingham and in Oban, Scotland, where she was injured in a gymnasium accident that she was to recall, with fatal consequences, in her 1946 novel *Miss Pym Disposes.* Her career then took her to English schools in Eastbourne and finally Tunbridge Wells before she was called home in 1923 to care for her mother, who was dying of cancer. Now the only unmarried sister in the family, Elizabeth was back in Scotland to stay; following her mother's death, she remained with her father in Inverness.

> "... *the most delightful author I have ever worked with*
> *in the theatre.*"   —Sir John Gielgud in *Early Stages*

At some point, Elizabeth started writing for publication, and her poetry began to appear in newspapers and literary magazines in 1925. She adopted the name Gordon Daviot for public consumption. The source of "Gordon" isn't clear, but "Daviot" most likely came from the name of a small Scottish village, southeast of Inverness, where the MacKintosh family vacationed in Elizabeth's childhood.

Soon she was publishing short stories as well as poems, and in early 1929, her first novel, *Kif: An Unvarnished History,* appeared, garnering good reviews and American publication. A few months later, a second Daviot novel reached the bookstalls—the mystery of *The Man in the Queue,* which introduced Elizabeth's only serial detective, Inspector Alan Grant of Scotland Yard. Written for a mystery-fiction contest sponsored by English publisher Methuen, Elizabeth's winning novel was generally well received by the critics and was later awarded the Dutton Mystery Prize in the United States.

But mystery was not her chosen genre—she is said to have regarded the rules of detective fiction as too rigid for real imagination—and she would not repeat the form for another seven years. As Daviot, Elizabeth turned to the theater, although her first play was rejected for production and subsequently transformed into a romantic novel, *The Expensive Halo.* With her second play, however, Elizabeth hit pay dirt.

She wrote an historical drama, *Richard of Bordeaux,* apparently after a visit to London during which she saw John Gielgud performing *Hamlet.* She crafted *Richard* with the gifted, energetic young actor in mind, and through her agent submitted it in 1931 or early 1932. After reading the manuscript several times, Gielgud recalled thinking that "Richard was a gift from heaven. . . ." He saw problems with the play but quickly arranged to produce a two-weekend tryout at the Arts Theatre. Despite "enthusiastic audiences" for this trial run, Gielgud dropped plans to take the play to full-scale production, and *Richard of Bordeaux* was shelved while the actor completed his run in another play. But the project was revived later in the year, with Gielgud producing and starring. It proved to be a happy change of heart for the actor and the shadowy authoress.

From Gielgud's memoirs, we can get some idea of the type of professional Elizabeth MacKintosh was. "In spite of her innate shyness, and her dislike of staying in London for more than a few days at a time," he wrote, "Gordon is the most delightful author I have ever worked with in the theatre. She seems to have complete trust in everyone who is concerned in her plays, and does not interfere at all. She seldom comes near rehearsals until just before the first night, and her patience and consideration are limitless." This perfect author had conferred with Gielgud following the brief Arts Theatre production, discussing his serious worries about weaknesses in her play. Some weeks later, after the actor had pretty well decided not to take *Richard* further, he received a letter from "Gordon" that included rewrites for every one of his concerns. The much-improved play was back on; it opened at London's New Theatre to "enthusiastic" reviews and became what Gielgud described as a "smash hit." A subsequent road tour was equally popular.

Elizabeth attended the premiere performance at the New Theatre, and after the final curtain, she hurried to Gielgud's dressing room to offer her congratulations. But she slipped away before other well-wishers and the press arrived. Reporters, Gielgud remembered, were anxious to interview the author and pursued her for several days. "But Gordon is a most successful person at disappearing," Gielgud wrote of her. "There is no hint of false modesty in her attitude. She is kindly and thoughtful . . . but the idea of having to talk about herself to a stranger terrifies her."

The triumph of *Richard of Bordeaux* was followed by two more dramas: *The Laughing Woman,* one of Elizabeth's few nonhistorical stage plays, and *Queen of Scots,* both produced in 1934. *Queen of Scots,* focusing on the marriage of Mary Stuart to Lord Darnley, reunited Elizabeth, Gielgud, and actress Gwen Ffrangcon-Davies, with whom Elizabeth had become friends during the production of *Richard.* The two women had discussed Mary Stuart at some point, arguing about the doomed queen's real character, and Elizabeth then wrote the play for the actress. Could it have been Ffrangcon-Davies who provided a model for the theatrical women who make such frequent appearances in Elizabeth's mysteries?

Queen of Scots did not repeat the success of *Richard of Bordeaux* and must have disappointed Elizabeth. Something else occurred around this time, possibly something serious involving a charge of plagiarism (mentioned and rather airily dismissed by Gielgud in another set of his memoirs), and the shy playwright returned to the printed page. Another possible indication that whatever happened may have been traumatic is the fact that Elizabeth published her next book under the pen name Josephine Tey (a name she took from one of her English great-grandmothers). Although the new name may have represented Elizabeth's desire to separate her detective fiction from her theatrical writing, this is a not altogether satisfactory rationale since her Gordon Daviot identity was already associated with *The Man in the Queue.*

Whatever Elizabeth's reason, Josephine Tey made her debut in 1936 with *A Shilling for Candles,* a solidly crafted, Golden Age–style detective novel that is nevertheless almost a rewrite, in plot and development, of *The Man in the Queue.* But Elizabeth's style was more assured, and she added a new element in *Shilling*—a character type that was to become something of a staple in her novels. Though Alan Grant returns as the chief detective, his sleuthing is augmented by the determined legwork of a young girl named Erica Burgoyne, the daughter of an over-whelmed chief constable in the rural Kentish seacoast community where a movie star is found murdered, causing an international sensation.

Seventeen-year-old Erica is plucky and perceptive, sensing immediately a truth that Grant, the seasoned professional cop, cannot accept. She is given the lead role in a critical subplot and acquits herself splendidly as defender of the innocent, defying Grant and her father. The disarming girl-on-the-verge-of-womanhood crops up repeatedly in Tey novels (Elizabeth had created two similar, but older and less focused, characters in *The Man in the Queue*: Mrs. Everett and her niece Miss Dinmont); readers are wise to pay heed to her insights. The obvious source for Erica must be the schoolgirls whom Elizabeth MacKintosh had instructed in physical education at Oban and Eastbourne. But is it possible that Elizabeth put some of herself, her sisters, and even her mother into this tomboyish and appealingly self-reliant character?

Erica Burgoyne proved fascinating to an English movie director then building his reputation as a master of distinctly suspenseful films. Alfred Hitchcock's much-altered version of *A Shilling for Candles,* retitled *Young and Innocent,* centers on Erica's story★ and the action of the chase. When the film was released in 1937, its spirited and determined heroine surely must have appealed to a special group of British moviegoers—young men and women with another test of courage under fire looming in their future.

Elizabeth's next project was *Claverhouse,* a biography of John Graham, the first Viscount Dundee, a Scottish champion of James II, the seventeenth-century English king notorious for his persecutions of the rebellious Covenanter Scots. Her only nonfiction book, the scholarly

---

★ *Young and Innocent* is among Alfred Hitchcock's "Golden Six" films made in Great Britain between 1934 and 1938, before his move to the bright lights and big budgets of Hollywood. The screenplay by Charles Bennett and Alma Reville (Hitchcock's talented wife) provided a showcase for ingenue actress Nova Philbeam, who had appeared as the young kidnap victim in Hitchcock's 1934 version of *The Man Who Knew Too Much.* Regarded as lightweight, *Young and Innocent* is nonetheless satisfying for its ironic Hitchcockian vision and suspense techniques.

but one-sided *Claverhouse* was intended to correct Graham's image and also leveled a few well-aimed shots at the puritanical religion of her homeland. Elizabeth was never easy on Scots folk in general and the religious among them in particular.* The preacher-priest as ignorant and ineffectual at best, venal and predatory at worst, is a minor theme throughout her writing. But she was no pagan; her next play, *The Stars Bow Down,* drew on the biblical story of Joseph of the many-colored coat and Egyptian exile. Written several years earlier, *Stars* was produced in 1939.

From this point, Elizabeth, as Tey and Daviot, virtually disappeared for the duration of World War Two. No novels or plays appeared between 1939 and 1946, and how she occupied herself during these years is anyone's guess. John Gielgud later spoke about seeing her in 1942 and of her depression then, and he also speculated about some personal loss she may have suffered in World War One. Though she lived on in Inverness, Elizabeth apparently took "little or no interest" (in the words of an obituary) in her community. She is known, however, to have visited frequently in the south of England, where her English forebears had their roots. It is unlikely that she engaged in war work given her increasing reclusion.

She must have been writing, however, for 1946 brought the publication of a collection of eight one-act radio plays by Daviot. The same year, Josephine Tey resurfaced with a mystery that signaled a stunning shift in Elizabeth's approach. There is a mysterious death in *Miss Pym Disposes* and a detective of sorts, though a particularly inept one. But this novel is "straighter" than either of her two previous mysteries, much more forthrightly given over to characterization, and her best books would expand on the character-driven pattern she set in *Miss Pym Disposes.*

In this novel, Elizabeth took the reader into her own past, to the fictitious Leys Physical Training College, an all-female institution that harks back to her alma mater, Anstey College. The story centers on Miss Lucy Pym, a retired teacher of French who has written a volume criti-

---

* In *The Daughter of Time* (1951), Elizabeth allowed herself a full-scale rant against the Covenanter Scots, a Presbyterian sect that rebelled against England's crown and church in the seventeenth century. Contrary to conventional historical opinion that the Covenanters were a brutally persecuted lot, Elizabeth—in the voice of Inspector Grant—called them "the exact equivalent of the I.R.A. in Ireland. A small irreconcilable minority, and as bloodthirsty a crowd as ever disgraced a Christian nation." Elizabeth MacKintosh was not the only famous mystery writer who was affected by exposure to Covenanter thinking: Mary Roberts Rinehart, raised under the thumb of a Covenanter grandmother, found her childhood religion so oppressive and guilt-producing that she became an Episcopalian.

cal of popular psychological theories. To the little woman's astonishment, the book has hit a nerve with the public and become a bestseller. An unwitting celebrity, Miss Pym hits the lecture circuit and accepts the invitation of an old high school acquaintance to speak to the girls of Leys College, where the novel opens. A normally solitary creature with "the heart of a rabbit," Miss Pym finds herself lingering at the school, observing the little intrigues and jealousies of the teachers' common room, enjoying the campus in spring, and entertained by the pleasant company of its "nice, clean, healthy children."

Early in the book, Miss Pym meets a beautiful dancing student from Brazil, Teresa Desterro, known as the "Nut Tart" to her fellow students. Like Erica in *A Shilling for Candles,* Desterro is young, but full of instinctive insight and a worldly sophistication that Miss Pym envies. When Miss Pym declares that the Leys students are "too normal and too nice. Too much of a type" to be "psychologically interesting," Desterro disagrees. And in a sense, the entire book is about which woman will be proven correct.

In the gentlest possible manner—Miss Pym being in all respects a gentlewoman—*Miss Pym Disposes* is an angry book, and its ferocity is directed at the pecking order of the fictional Leys, a hierarchy of power based on wealth, middle-class values, and force of personality among the girls and reinforced by the deliberately oblivious faculty. (Any reasonably sensitive woman who ever attended an all-girls school will recognize the students of Leys not as stereotypes, but as girls they once knew or were.) Except for the "Nut Tart," who serves as disinterested observer, everyone at Leys seems to be in disguise. Leadership is really bullying, shallowness hides depths of feeling, friendship is either manipulative or stupidly self-sacrificing, loyalty is perverted. The undeserving succeed, the deserving are marginalized, and the guilty go scot-free. Though usually praised for its humor and deft characterization, *Miss Pym Disposes* is a harsh book that has a good deal in common with William Golding's *Lord of the Flies,* J. D. Salinger's *The Catcher in the Rye,* and even Maxwell Anderson's stage version of *The Bad Seed.*

Just how autobiographical *Miss Pym Disposes* is remains open to conjecture. The setting and certain events clearly come from Elizabeth's own student and teaching days: classes and dormitory life, the arduous curriculum and quirky faculty, the pressure on ambitious senior students. But does Miss Pym herself—the shy single woman thrust into the world of popular publishing and minor celebrity—express something of the author? After all, Miss Pym and Elizabeth MacKintosh were both self-appointed scholars, achieving popular recognition in esoteric fields (Miss Pym in psychology, Elizabeth in English history), but unsanctioned by academe. Both were loners by choice. The following passage, in which Miss Pym debates with herself whether to stay on for a time at Leys or return to her London flat, seems reflective of a writer who may have been ambivalent about the self-sufficient life she had chosen for herself:

> Why *should* she [Miss Pym] go back to London yet? What was there to take her back? Nothing and nobody. For the first time that fine, independent, cushioned, celebrated life of hers looked just a little bleak. A little narrow and inhuman. Could it be? Was there, perhaps, a lack of warmth in that existence she had been so content with? Not a lack of human contact, certainly. She had her fill of human contact. But it was a very all-of-a-piece contact, now that she thought of it. Except for . . . her daily help, and her Aunt Celia . . . and the tradespeople, she never talked to anyone who wasn't somehow connected with the publishing or the academic worlds.

One paragraph can hardly stand as evidence. But it indicates a questioning of the deliberately, even obsessively controlled existence, a theme that is consistent throughout Elizabeth's mysteries. All her main characters are in some manner shut off from the kind of warm and spontaneous human contact that Miss Pym seems to long for. Many, like Elizabeth's dapper Inspector Grant, live for their professions, amid but apart from the little niceties and niggling troubles that constitute the Average Joe's daily existence. For most of these characters, isolation is a choice, but one they are at times uncertain of. In the next two Tey novels—*The Franchise Affair* and *Brat Farrar*—Elizabeth continued to explore this theme of social isolation and its possible consequences.

> *"But once or twice lately an odd, alien thought had crossed his mind; irrelevant and unbidden. As nearly as it could be put into words it was: 'This is all you are ever going to have.' "*
>
> —lawyer Robert Blair in *The Franchise Affair*

Elizabeth returned to Alan Grant in *The Franchise Affair,* but his participation in the mystery is peripheral. The story is told from the point of view of Robert Blair, a self-satisfied, middle-aged bachelor who practices country law in a seemingly idyllic English village. In swift, sure strokes, the author painted a vivid picture of Robert and his environment in the opening pages: the reassuring regularity of tea at his office desk served precisely at 3:50 with "two biscuits; petit-beurre Mondays,

Wednesdays and Fridays, digestive Tuesdays, Thursdays and Saturdays";
the High Street of Milford, "a fine, gay, busy little street" along which
even the buildings seem polite to one another; acceptable village modes
of social interaction including dinners out by written invitation only
and immediate telephone access to the person one has called.

There is no likelihood that Robert's life will or should change, in
spite of his puzzling sense of disquietude—"a lost piece of childhood
crying for attention," he supposes. But this being a novel, change is at
hand: a late-afternoon phone call for help soon draws Robert into a
mystery that he is ill equipped to solve.

The crime in *The Franchise Affair* involves a charge of kidnapping
brought against the village eccentrics, Marion Sharpe and her intimidating elderly mother, by a fifteen-year-old girl named Betty Kane.
There is no murder, unless murder of reputation is considered. The plot
is drawn from two notorious eighteenth-century cases: the 1753 perjury
trial of Elizabeth Canning, a teenage girl who claimed to have been kidnapped, abused, and forced into an immoral life by an elderly woman;
and the 1787 murder trial of Mrs. Elizabeth Brownwigg, a London
midwife who brutalized a series of young women and was sentenced to
death for killing one of them.

At first glance, it would appear that Elizabeth dropped her strong, intuitive, adolescent heroine in *The Franchise Affair,* but on close examination, it's clear that she gave the role to Robert Blair and brought it front
and center. Fortyish and comfortably settled, Robert nevertheless possesses the naive idealism of adolescence and is willing to act on his faith
(initially contradicted by the evidence) in the innocence of his clients,
regardless of what the police, tabloid papers, and his own rational mind
have to say.

The Miss Pyms of this novel are the Sharpes. Wellborn but poor, the
women have inherited The Franchise, a large gated house set on its own
just outside Milford proper. Marion and her sharp-tongued mother take
no part in local society. Consequently, they are already the subjects of
outrageous local gossip: for starving a former maid, according to
Robert's Aunt Lin; for beating a dog "half to death," according to the
proprietress of the sportswear store; for being witches, according to rumors heard by another Milford lawyer. Old Mrs. Sharpe, a sardonic
woman of laudable intelligence, at least understands the villagers' reaction. "If you see a giraffe once a year it remains a spectacle," she informs
Robert, "if you see it daily it becomes part of the scenery." Her own
deliberate aloofness from Milford has made her and her daughter spectacular giraffes.

When pitted against a sympathetic schoolgirl victim whose virtue
and truthfulness are attested to by the sensational press and a bleeding-

heart bishop, the standoffish Sharpe women are instantly convicted by the village. Having spurned their neighbors, the women are in turn rejected, especially by other women.

The Sharpes are obvious loners, literally distancing themselves from the community. Robert Blair is solitary in his complaisance, too comfortable in placid Milford to look beneath the surface—involved but not engaged until his hand is called. Apart from the kidnapping, the mystery is whether isolated individuals can satisfactorily emerge into the broader society. Or will they retreat like poor, disillusioned Miss Pym? Tey's resolution is characteristically ironic.

In *Brat Farrar*, published in 1949, Elizabeth again addressed the subjects of misleading appearances and aloneness. There is an old murder mystery, but the story really deals with false identities and perceptions. A young man, abandoned as a baby and raised literally by himself, is tempted into a scheme of impersonation and fraud. Because of a striking resemblance to a long-dead child and that child's surviving twin, Brat Farrar becomes "Patrick Ashby" and is insinuated into the Ashby family, who maintain a horse farm in the southern English countrywide. A large inheritance is in the offing, and Brat is positioned to steal it, but he finds himself embraced by and reluctantly embracing the very family and community for whom his existence is a calculated lie.

There is no official detective in the book; the impostor is also the investigator of truth, including self-discovery. *Brat Farrar* is structured almost like a farce in which few characters are quite what they wish to appear. Double, even triple, identities must be untangled. Dangerous liaisons—such as the attraction between Brat and his "sister" Eleanor—are possible. And confusion reigns.

Brat Farrar is the work of a mature writer with full control of her themes and her style. It is often cited by other writers as the best Tey detective novel because it so completely meets the qualifications of a fine novel. Catherine Aird has called it "a real tour de force" that "epitomizes all that is good in detective fiction: excellent writing, the strictest fair play with the reader, sound plotting, characters that are well-drawn without being exaggerated, and a complete absence of tub-thumping for any class, creed or cause."*

In both *The Franchise Affair* and *Brat Farrar* (her best novels), Elizabeth MacKintosh advanced her theme of the solitary soul to a new level, in-

---

* Mystery writer Catherine Aird (whose real surname is McIntosh) is right to point out the "fair play" of *Brat Farrar*. Josephine Tey did not always follow the fairness rule of Golden Age detective fiction and provided so few clues to the identity of the real perpetrators in her early books that readers are justified in complaining. Ms. Aird's article "The Irreproachable Miss Tey" appears in Dilys Winn's 1979 collection, *Murderess Ink*.

troducing the possibility of integration for the isolated character into
family and community. The wise adolescent character is gone now
(though adolescent and prepubescent girls abound in *Brat Farrar*), possibly because the author in her fifties had accepted the notion that intuitive cognition of truth is not the province of the young alone. It is the
mother figure in *Brat Farrar*—Aunt Bee, the middle-aged spinster guardian
of her dead brother and sister-in-law's children—whose instinct, if not
wholly selfless, is correct.

> *"I expect this is what death is like when you meet it.*
> *Sort of wildly unfair but inevitable."*
>   —Robert Tisdall in *A Shilling for Candles*

In 1950, when Elizabeth was fifty-four, her father died. We have no way
to guess what kind of father he was or the relationship he had with his
eldest daughter because Elizabeth almost never developed father characters in her novels.* If Colin MacKintosh had been the tether that bound
her to Inverness, his death did not liberate her. We know that she would
have been financially capable of leaving home, but she stayed in Scotland, where she apparently worked best.

She was unquestionably prolific in the postwar years, writing plays as
well as detective fiction and doing historical research. A new Grant mystery, *To Love and Be Wise,* appeared in 1950, and although not one of her
more satisfying efforts, it includes a wryly unexpected mystery (another
case of impersonation), and as good a satire on literary celebrity as one
might find in the pages of *Punch* or *Spy*. Set in a writers and artists'
colony in Oxfordshire, the book neatly skewers the pretensions of artists
whose talents do not live up to their press releases.

To Love and Be Wise also brought a change in Inspector Grant. Probably the most introverted of Golden Age serial detectives, Grant in previous books seemed in a perpetual funk. Torn between the Yard's
demand for logically ordered evidence leading to quick arrests and his
own perverse instincts and conscience, he is a sucker for red herrings,

---

* Only three "good" fathers stand out in the Tey mysteries: Chief Constable Burgoyne
in *A Shilling for Candles*; Tommy Rankin, husband of Inspector Grant's cousin Laura,
in *The Singing Sands*; and Sergeant Williams, Grant's chief aide. But Burgoyne and
Rankin are minor players, and little is said of Williams's home life beyond his devotion to wife and children. No main character in a Tey mystery has a living, present father—though mothers and motherly aunts are common enough—and when fathers
are mentioned, they are dead like Marion Sharpe's in *The Franchise Affair,* abusive, or
frequently both.

worries himself into emotional sweats over clues that are just too pat, and is usually ready for extended sick leave at the end of each case. But in *To Love and Be Wise*, Grant finally puts logic at the service of his instinct and imagination and follows his first hunch. When all the threads of the mystery come together, Grant is euphoric: "Feeling ridiculously like a bubble—so help me, you could bounce me like a ball, he thought. . . ."

This is also the only Grant novel in which the laconic detective is given extended interplay with his salt-of-the-earth assistant, Sergeant Williams. The only novel in which Grant's private friendship with actress Marta Hallard is detailed. The only novel in which experience is explicitiy exalted over youth.

Elizabeth was at the peak of her form at the beginning of the new decade, producing a kind of mystery novel that was not bound to Golden Age conventions, nor overtly influenced by the shoot-'em-up school of American hard-boiled crime writing (though Grant, the lone wolf of Scotland Yard, would not be uncomfortable in the company of Sam Spade or Philip Marlowe). Plotting was difficult for her to the end; hence her frequent reliance on stories based on historical events and her focus on character. But she had found freedom by building her tales around crimes that are not necessarily fatal or in which the murder is a secondary interest, thereby enabling herself to explore the minds and motivations of people who do wrong but are not outside the circle of human understanding and sympathy. This was to be her gift to mystery fiction—a willingness to tackle complex characters who are, in the main, neither all good nor all evil. She was abandoning the restrictions of the Golden Age, but not abandoning the genre, as Dorothy Sayers had done. On her own, Elizabeth was forcing the form to grow.

We can only imagine where she might have taken the mystery had there been sufficient time. But late in 1950 or early 1951, she learned that she had an incurable illness. At the news, it is said that she retreated entirely and probably kept the illness secret from her family and few close friends. On February 13, 1952, during a trip to London, she died. The cause of her death was not revealed. She was fifty-five years old.

She had lived long enough, however, to see the publication of a novel that was a true labor of love, *The Daughter of Time*, in 1951. This time, she hadn't borrowed a mystery from the past; she had lifted it entirely. The plot has Inspector Grant in hospital, recovering from a broken leg, bored stiff and short-tempered. A stack of bestsellers supplied by friends has no appeal. "Was everyone nowadays thirled to a formula?" he wonders with growing irritation. "Authors today wrote so much to a pattern that their public expected it. The public talked about 'a new Silas Weekley' or 'a new Lavinia Fitch' [writers he had encountered in *To Love and*

Be Wise] exactly as they talked about 'a new brick' or 'a new hairbrush.'"
But not Grant—and not Elizabeth MacKintosh.

No reader of Josephine Tey could have predicted *The Daughter of Time,* a mystery that involves murder and detection in the fifteenth century. Attracted to a face in a picture, Grant is led to investigate the true story of Richard III, last of the Plantagenet kings and supposed perpetrator of one of the vilest crimes in English history—the assassinations of the "little princes," Edward V and his younger brother, in the Tower of London.

Elizabeth didn't write an historical romance or resort to flashbacks or time warps; she had her fictional Grant and his American assistant investigate the real record, using increasingly sophisticated research sources and building their conclusions on the evidence they accumulated. Grant follows what is first only a hunch, an instinctive response to the face in a portrait, and then plows through clues and red herrings, lies and alibis, to reach a logical solution. The conclusion is not surprising to those who know their English history, but *The Daughter of Time* is really about the investigative process—an historical police procedural. Elizabeth demonstrated through the popular form of a detective novel how history is also mystery and why no thinking person should simply accept historical "facts" without knowing the motivations of the fact-finders and the context of events.

The Daughter of Time (the title is from a French proverb: "Truth is the daughter of time") was an immediate success, much argued about by critics, reviewers, and historians. It remains her most famous book, loved or hated by readers but rarely failing to hold the interest of anyone who gets into it. Elizabeth's play *Dickon,* from the 1940s, had already dealt with what she believed to be the true story of Richard III, but it was the novel that achieved her objective of questioning public perceptions formed from schoolbook history and Shakespeare's play. She had successfully fused her serious interest in historical truth with the fiction form that was her bread and butter, and *The Daughter of Time* stands unique in the evolution of detective writing.

There were two novels published posthumously: *The Privateer,* an adventure based on the life of Sir Henry Morgan, the seventeenth-century British buccaneer; and *The Singing Sands.* Discovered in draft manuscript after her death, *The Singing Sands* is Grant's last mystery, but exactly when it was written is not clear. Although rough in places, the book was a fitting finale to the careers of the author and her detective.

The Singing Sands is the only Tey mystery set principally in Elizabeth's Scotland, ranging rather languidly from the country towns and lochs of the Highlands to the wild shores of the Hebrides. There is a murder and mistaken identity. Grant, recovering from a prolonged attack of claustrophobia and nervous exhaustion, is again inspired by the face of a dead man, though this corpse is contemporary. He follows his instinct and investigates a death that everyone else, including Scotland Yard, accepts as accidental. Not nearly so well constructed as *Brat Farrar, The Singing Sands* nonetheless captures the same sense of place and people—the rain-starved moors and shallow lakes, the desolate island seashore where the "whole world was one mad uproar of grey-green and white and wild noise," the quirky character and habits of the native Scots.

Elizabeth probably knew that she was dying when she drafted *The Singing Sands,* and a feeling of mortality hangs about Inspector Grant throughout. He seriously considers retirement and marriage, a kind of death for a man who lives to work. In his depression, he visualizes Hell not as "a nice cosy place where you fried," but "a great cold echoing cave where there was neither past nor future. . . . Hell was concentrated essence of a winter morning after a sleepless night of self-distaste."

He contemplates the myth of Tir nan Og, the Gaelic heaven where youth is eternal. In a cold bed in a cold room in a rundown island hotel, he recovers his equanimity through laughter: "Laughter must do untold things for one's endocrine glands, he thought. . . . More especially, perhaps, when it is laughter at oneself. At the fine, glorious absurdity of oneself in relation to the world." He philosophizes about the single characteristic shared by all true criminals: vanity that is "a frightening thing because it is incurable." He imagines a world in which England never existed. His solution of the murder hangs on another lost paradise, a mythic desert Shangri-La in the Arabian sands.

Most telling is the basic theme of the novel, that the dead can save the living: more specifically, that a commitment to recognition of and justice for the dead can rekindle passion in the living. And that only the living can make the dead immortal.

Whether Elizabeth died believing in an afterlife we do not know. It seems unlikely, if the existential bent of *The Singing Sands* is indicative of her state of mind. But she clearly believed in the duty of the living to serve timeless Truth. To the best of her ability, she fulfilled that duty in *The Daughter of Time,* repairing the reputation of a fallen idol as she had tried to do in her *Claverhouse* biography. She did it with her own final bequest, willing the copyrights of her novels to Britain's National Trust for Places of Historic Interest or Natural Beauty (a decision foreshadowed sixteen years earlier in *A Shilling for Candles* when a movie star puts her fortune in trust "for the preservation of the beauty of England").

Elizabeth MacKintosh then left it to posterity to determine the truth of her worth rather than her life. She may have regarded her mystery writing as a lesser achievement, hoping to be remembered for her plays.

But the outpouring of detective fiction in her last years (six of her eight mystery novels were written between 1946 and 1952) could also indicate that she had made peace with the genre, accepting it—as so many writers and critics were doing—as a legitimate avenue to literary destinations.

Despite her unwavering silence about her life, the careful reader can derive educated, if superficial, suppositions from her detective novels. She loved fishing and horses, and she seems to have been as comfortable with the natural world as she was uneasy with people, especially people in crowds. She relied on trains but may have flown toward the end of her life. She enjoyed movies, especially American gangster films, and read the glossy movie magazines on occasion. She was attracted to America and Americans but was not above other ethnic prejudices, though she saved her sharpest barbs for her own people, the Scots. She had little tolerance for the press and press agentry, and she despised the power of publicity to sway and corrupt the mass of people. She distrusted charismatic leaders and popular culture in general.

She was extremely conscious of the danger of judging by physical appearances, but probably did so herself. (Never trust a blue-eyed character in a Tey novel.) She was middle class but ever alert to bourgeois pretension and vulgarity. Excepting Lord Edward Champneis, pronounced "Chins," in *A Shilling for Candles* and Richard III in *The Daughter of Time,* she did not plumb the upper class for characters or crimes. She respected the theater as a medium and apparently enjoyed the company of theater people, but she could be devastatingly objective about the specious charms of actors.

There seem to be facets of her in all her major characters: shy Miss Pym, village-bound Robert Blair, loyal Erica Burgoyne, sexually ambivalent Leslie Searle in *To Love and Be Wise,* and especially Detective-Inspector Alan Grant—endlessly conflicted between instinct and reason, so private in a public profession, inclined to physical and mental depression, attracted to but fearful of human intimacy. But how much of these characters can be taken as self-portraiture is impossible to say.

Elizabeth MacKintosh, in the guises of Gordon Daviot and Josephine Tey, warned her readers again and again not to take anyone at face value, not to judge by appearances, and not to assume the validity of facts simply because they were written down in books. Perhaps we serve her best by heeding her warning and not speculating about her life. Then again, a woman who never hesitated to dig up, dissect, and reinvestigate history could scarcely have complained about our continuing curiosity.

BIBLIOGRAPHY

JOSEPHINE TEY (ELIZABETH MACKINTOSH)
1896–1952
British (born: Inverness, Scotland)

"Neither by nature nor by profession was he interested in mankind in the large. His bias, native and acquired, was towards the personal."
— *The Daughter of Time*

Elizabeth MacKintosh wrote under the pseudonyms Josephine Tey and Gordon Daviot. Her works now appear under the more famous Tey by-line. Her first four novels were published in Great Britain by Methuen and Benn. From 1936, her British publisher was Benn. Her first American publisher was Dutton, followed by Appleton, and, from 1936 on, Macmillan. Of her novels, the following chronology includes only her mysteries. Dates are for first publication; alternate titles are listed. Featured detective appears in ( ). US = United States.

Mystery Novels
1929   *The Man in the Queue,* first published under the pen name Gordon Daviot. (Republished in the US in 1954 as *Killer in the Crowd.*) (Inspector Grant)
1936   *A Shilling for Candles: The Story of a Crime* (Inspector Grant)
1946   *Miss Pym Disposes*
1948   *The Franchise Affair* (Inspector Grant)
1949   *Brat Farrar*/US: *Come and Kill Me*
1950   *To Love and Be Wise* (Inspector Grant)
1951   *The Daughter of Time* (Inspector Grant)
1952   *The Singing Sands* (Inspector Grant)

Stage Plays   All plays originally appeared under the name Daviot. Dates are for first major production or publication.
1932   *Richard of Bordeaux*
1934   *The Laughing Woman*
1934   *The Queen of Scots*
1939   *The Stars Bow Down*
1947   *The Little Dry Thorn* (published only)
1948   *Valerius* (published only)
1955   *Dickon* (published only)
1956   *Sweet Coz* (published only)

MacKintosh also wrote a number of one-act plays for radio, which were collected and published in *Leigh Sands and Other Short Plays* (1946) and in the three volumes of *Plays* (1953–1954).

Nonfiction
1937   *Claverhouse* (biography)

Film and Video Adaptations
Two of the Tey mysteries were adapted for the cinema. Alfred Hitchcock's 1937 version of *A Shilling for Candles* focused on the novel's main subplot. It was titled *Young and Innocent* in Great Britain and *A Girl Was Young* in the United States. The 1950 English adaptation of *The Franchise Affair* was truer to its source. This film has been characterized by British film critic Leslie Halliwell as an "unusual and absorbing mystery" given "rather too mild" production.

Brat Farrar and *The Franchise Affair* were dramatized for British television in the early 1990s. In *The Franchise Affair,* John Vine played Inspector Grant, and the central role of Robert Blair was taken by Patrick Malahide, the taciturn British actor who also portrayed Inspector Roderick Alleyn in the BBC's productions of Ngaio Marsh's mysteries.

THE GRANT FILE

NAME: Alan Grant
ADDRESS: London: 19 Tenby Court, S.W. 1
OCCUPATION: Detective-Inspector, C.I.D, Scotland Yard
BIRTHDATE: Born August 4, 1894 (Grant is thirty-five in his first published case, *The Man in the Queue.*)
BIRTHPLACE: A Midlands town much like Nottingham
FAMILY: Little known except that father was of Scots heritage; grandfather "belonged to the Strathspey." Mother must have been a principal influence, for Grant believes the second-best way to learn about a man is "to find out about his mother." Cousin Laura Grant Rankin lives with husband, Tommy, and children Patrick and Bridget in Scotland. At least one aunt (deceased) on his mother's side.
PHYSICAL DESCRIPTION: Of "medium height and slight in build." Dapper but not ostentatious dresser ("the last thing he looked like was a police officer"). "Army in plain clothes," says Sergeant Williams. Smile that cements the loyalty of his subordinates. A "slight twist" to his mouth when worrying a problem.
OTHER DISTINGUISHING CHARACTERISTICS: His "flair," an uncanny instinct for hidden agendas, secret motivations, and flawed conclu-

sions even when they fit the facts; related to his "overworked" conscience, the "looker-on in him" that constantly questions his motives and debates his decisions. He's "famous at the Yard for his good judgment of people. . . ." Has a "passion for faces" as mirrors of individual character. Stubborn to a fault ("a damned Juggernaut"). Unnaturally strong sense of geographic direction. Rarely cracks a joke and hates pickles. Weakness for good coffee served in large cups.

MILITARY SERVICE: Served "four years on the western front" in World War One; wounded at Contalmaison in France. Possibly served in World War Two in North Africa.

LIFESTYLE: A "legacy sufficient to permit him to retire into idle nonentity if such had been his desire." Despite this surprise inheritance from an aunt who married well in Australia, Grant lives middle class, probably on his salary, indulging only on his wardrobe, fine dining (though he insists on eggs and bacon for breakfast), and other small embroideries of life. Owns a two-seater sports car. Later in career, has own home and housekeeper. Uses legacy to invest in rehabilitation of ex-cons.

LOVE LIFE: Never married. Knows many attractive women, but few intimacies though "there's a woman in Amiens. . . ." Most of his loves classified as "romantic devotions." Close friendship with actress Marta Hallard. ("There was no room in his life for Marta, and none in her life for him; but it was a pity all the same.") As a youth, considered marriage to his cousin Laura. His head is briefly turned by Lady Zoe Kentallen—beautiful, intelligent, and a skilled fly-fisher—in *The Singing Sands.*

INTERESTS: Work, though he frequently calls it "a dog's life" and worse; fishing ("something between a sport and a religion") in the Highlands or Hampshire's Test River; golf, especially the satisfaction of a "clean smacking drive"; "scientific opinion on any subject" including handwriting analysis; America, which he knows well. Reads detective novels. Attends the theater regularly. (Saw Gordon Daviot's *Richard of Bordeaux* four times at the New Theatre.)

HEALTH: Physically fit but subject to mental exhaustion and periods of depression. Suffers a broken leg and concussed spine after falling through a trapdoor while chasing petty crook named Benny Skoll.

COLLEAGUES AND ACQUAINTANCES: Sergeant Williams (Grant's "opposite and his complement"); Superintendent Barker and Superintendent Bryce; Mrs. Field, first landlady; housekeeper Mrs. Tinker; Marcel, the head waiter at Laurent's; "Jammy" Hopkins, crime reporter for the *Clarion*; American researcher Brent Carradine. Grant has many acquaintances on both sides of the law, but few close friends and no confidants.

MAJOR ACCOMPLISHMENT: Always gets his man, or woman.

MARGERY ALLINGHAM

ODD WOMAN OUT

"There are hideous moments when I get the unhappy conviction that I'm a sort of demented beaver—a lunatic animal working itself to death to make something it not only doesn't need but doesn't particularly like."   —letter to a friend, 1937*

From the 1930s until her death in 1966, Margery Allingham was known to the public at large as the jovial fat lady who lived in the picture-perfect house in the quaint Essex village and wrote those wonderful Albert Campion mysteries with the support of her doting husband and her charmingly unconventional family and friends. Even some among her large circle of friends did not recognize until too late the seriously troubled woman who hid beneath the veneer of cheerfulness and contentment. Two decades after her death, however, biographers began to look closely at the facts, and a much

Margery Allingham

darker picture emerged. A picture of a woman battered for most of her sixty-two years by physical illness, emotional chaos, stunning insecurities, and self-doubts . . . a woman whose craving for love, reassurance, and security led her to virtually enslave herself, body and soul, to the

---

* Quotations, unless otherwise noted, are from Margery's published works and from unpublished manuscripts, diaries, letters, and other materials cited by biographers Julia Thorogood in *Margery Allingham: A Biography* (1991) and Richard Martin in *Ink in Her Blood: The Life and Crime Fiction of Margery Allingham* (1988).

whims of others . . . a woman who was, in her desire to please, her own worst enemy.

For all but two brief periods in her adulthood—the early years of her marriage and the World War Two years—she was engaged in a constant and enervating struggle for health and self-knowledge. Her temperamental highs and lows, combined with a variety of physical ailments (all hidden from public view) led those closest to her to dismiss her legitimate grievances, and she often feared that she would sink into madness. Only at the end of her life, too late for relief, was she diagnosed with a real mental illness, bipolar disorder, which explained her chaotic feelings.

In the 1920s, Margery and her husband were famous in a small way for their entertainments—boozy gatherings of Bright Young Things that invariably included a costume party. If there is a metaphor for her life, it is the masquerade party, superficially so gay and artful. But behind one of the masks was always the exhausted hostess who had orchestrated and financed the event for the pleasure of others and was left alone to clean up the mess and get on with her work.

> *"I was energetic, affectionate and lonely, and all the interesting people in the world appeared to be on the other side of the glass."*

Margery Louise Allingham was the only grande dame of the Golden Age to be born in the twentieth century, after the reign of Queen Victoria. The first child of Emily and Herbert Allingham, Margery arrived on May 20, 1904, at her parents' home in London's Ealing section. Her birth was not a welcome event.

According to biographer Julia Thorogood, Emily Hughes Allingham "was aggressively independent and despised the sexual relationship. . . ." Emily hadn't wanted children, and when they came (Margery was followed two years later by a brother, Phil, and in 1913 by her sister, Joyce), the young Allinghams were greeted more as inconvenient duties than bundles of joy. Margery was a large baby—who became a large woman—and her delivery was protracted and painful, which did not endear the infant to her mother. But "Marge" was not the particular target of her mother's indifference; Emily (usually called Em or Emmie) expended little affection on any of her children. Having birthed them, Em immediately turned their care over to nurses and her mother and got on with her own quixotic interests.

Parental love and encouragement were to be supplied by Margery's father. Herbert Allingham came from an extensive family with whom he maintained close ties. Educated at Cambridge, he was initially headed for a vocation in the Church of England, but after receiving his B.A. degree, he entered the family business—writing and editing. When Margery was born, he was editor of *The London Journal,* a Fleet Street weekly with a tradition of publishing the serialized stories of popular Victorian writers. By the time Herbert took the helm, however, the paper was in a steep decline, and when Margery was five, Herbert resigned and turned to freelancing his writing—a tumultuous trade by which he supported his family until his death.

Em, who had been a milliner before her marriage, also wrote for popular publication, though without the discipline of her husband. Em and Herbert were both rebels in a restricted sense. They flirted with socialism, traveling in London's Fabian circles in the early years of their marriage. Em experimented with religion, the more bizarre the better, and both Allinghams enjoyed the mildly Bohemian company of their many writer and artist friends. But Em's real rebellion, according to Julia Thorogood in her biography of Margery, was a near-absolute rejection of her own mother's principles and model, "which included the loving and cherishing of the very young."

"Granny" Emily Jane Allingham Hughes★ was a devout Christian who raised her four children and a stepdaughter alone after leaving her alcoholic husband, possibly to protect the children from violent abuse. Em's childhood, which she never discussed, had been marked by poverty and anxiety. The Hughes children grew up as the poor family relations, dependent on the charity of the other Allinghams, and this may explain Em's fierce independence and rejection of the traditional expectations of the Victorian wife and mother. Perhaps her behavior was the inevitable consequence of her deprived childhood coupled to a volatile temperament, but Em would have none of her mother's self-sacrificing ways and simple Christian humility. Em was, by most accounts, boorishly self-centered, verbally aggressive, controlling, and contentious to the point of hatefulness. But she was interesting as well as unpredictable; her opinions, however painful or crudely expressed, mattered to her family, and that gave her the power to hurt the people who loved her.

★ Margery's family ties were complicated. Her maternal grandmother, Emily Jane Allingham Hughes, was the sister of her paternal grandfather, William James Allingham. Thus Margery's parents, Em and Herbert, were first cousins. William Allingham ran an advertising agency and also published a Christian magazine. He had eight sons with his wife, Louise, and enjoyed a prosperous life. William and Louise both died in 1920. Herbert and Em's uncle John Allingham, though a poor manager and spendthrift, wrote popular boys' adventure series and published Herbert's first story.

In 1909, Herbert and Em Allingham made a move that was to profoundly affect Margery's life and later career. Leaving London, they rented a ramshackle old vicarage house in Layer Breton near Colchester in Essex. The isolated house near the sea lacked even basic conveniences, but five-year-old Margery soon filled its gardens and meadows with an imaginary population of fairies and other creatures. Though she later described her childhood as solitary, she was apparently an active child, given to practical jokes plotted with her brother, Phil, and to various forms of playacting. There were few other children for company, but the Old Rectory was often filled with family and grown-up friends (mostly writers who would come to Layer Breton to work on their projects), and there were servants aplenty. How much attention the adults gave to the children is another matter.

Perhaps to soothe their daughter's demands for inclusion in their adult world, Em and Herbert gave her an "office" for her seventh birthday—a room in the servants' wing that was outfitted with desk, chairs, and all the accoutrements of a writer's space. Here she began to write, under her father's direction. Although the office was apparently Em's doing, its result was the cementing of a bond between Herbert and Margery—a relationship that was as much master to apprentice as father to child. Margery's arguments with her mother were legendary, and Em was said to browbeat her husband mercilessly. It might be concluded that Margery and Herbert had a common interest in finding some sanctuary from Em's temper, but the basis for their alliance was writing.

The type of writing that Herbert, Em, and most of their friends did is commonly referred to as "hackwork." It is words for pay, writing to fill space and attract masses of readers. Because it is done quickly to meet tight deadlines, it is almost always writing to formula. As a freelancer, Herbert Allingham—who specialized in melodramatic fiction and adventure tales though he also wrote journalism and essays—would have received explicit assignments that included plot lines, character lists and profiles, and settings. There was little room for imaginative flights of fancy or verbal brilliance. The word *hack* is shorthand for hackneyed, and indeed hack writing is by its nature trite and clichéd. But to be successful the writer must be disciplined, dogged, and skilled at his craft; Herbert Allingham was all three. Within the narrow confines of his assignments, Herbert was a dedicated professional. (His diaries included careful accountings of his production of words written.) To him, any plot was available for the taking, like the simple plan of a house. Originality in story-writing came in the embellishment of the structure. Herbert believed that a professional writer was an observer who stored up every detail that came his way in life as material for later use. This was the lesson he taught his daughter.

For Margery's earliest writings, Herbert would set a plot, and she would develop a story to fit his outline. He was a taskmaster, though a kindly one, and he taught Margery to rewrite and polish every word. Her first story was a fairy tale, and soon after she occupied her little office, she produced a newspaper for the family, the *Wag-Tale,* complete with serials, poems, and advertisements.

Two of the Allinghams' closest friends from the Fleet Street days were also to influence Margery's development as a writer. William McFee, a seaman-turned-novelist and intellectual, enjoyed the young girl's "combative" spirit and later urged her to strive for a higher art than mere work for hire. Another writer friend was Irishman George Richard Mant Hearn, who promoted a middle ground between High Art and crass commercialism, and this was the road Margery eventually traveled.

But what mattered to seven-year-old Margery, her fingers and hands always smudged with ink as she struggled over stories in her little office, was that she had found an avenue into her father's affection. Through writing, she was able to create a place for herself in his busy life. As for Herbert, a fundamentally gentle soul, the company of his daughter and apt pupil must have compensated in some measure for the comfort and companionship that his difficult, mercurial wife could not offer.

"*. . . quick to rage or laughter, self-conscious, over-aware*
and altogether about as restful as an unbroken mule."

Sometime after her seventh birthday, Margery was sent to a weekday boarding school run by the Misses Dobson in Colchester, but after a year or so, she contracted a life-threatening case of typhoid fever. Nursed by her Granny Hughes, she recovered, but her doctor advised that she be allowed to remain at home and run free. Her education was continued by a series of governesses until 1915. The boarding school experience had been difficult, and Margery acquired a stutter that was to trouble her for many years. She was once publicly accused of cheating for submitting an essay that her teacher thought too good to be written by a child. Teased for her preoccupation with writing, she was dubbed "Inky" in disparagement. To be fair, Margery could be a handful, stubbornly refusing to do what she didn't want to do. She was also shy and probably made little concerted effort to find friends among her peers. In 1915, she returned to her Colchester boarding school, renamed Endsleigh House by its new owners, and was taken under the wings of two young teachers there. But still she resisted pressures to perform academically, and her impressions of formal education and schoolmistresses generally remained negative.

Margery was ten when World War One broke out. The British coastal regions were under the greatest threat of invasion during the early days of the conflict, so she, Phil, and their new little sister were shipped to London to live with Em's sister Maud. When the immediate threat passed, the children returned to their parents at Layer Breton and Margery reentered Endsleigh House school, but the whole family decamped back to London in 1917. The war had changed the publishing industry drastically, and a number of the formerly reliable outlets for Herbert's and Em's writings either folded or were merged with other publications. After a five-year period of relative affluence, the Allinghams could no longer afford their country idyll.

In a crowded Bayswater flat, under the stress of the war and financial worries, Herbert and Em found their relationship increasingly strained. The war, Margery later said, changed Herbert by diminishing his idealism: "My father believed in Tolerance. . . . and in his case I think it was probably this that the 1914 Germans had attacked, all but destroyed, and he hated them for that."

Another complication was Em's odd relationship with the doctor who treated the family in Essex—Dr. J. H. Salter, a vigorous octogenarian with a forceful personality to whom Em became devoted during the stay at Layer Breton. The friendship was properly chaste but, on Em's side, obsessive. She seemed to find in Dr. Salter her ideal man of action, without the threat of a sexual attachment; perhaps he was her father figure. Herbert certainly didn't protest when the doctor would arrive unexpectedly in London nor when Em would dash off to Salter's home in the village of Tolleshunt D'Arcy. But it must have been difficult for the gentle Herbert to see his wife give an opinionated, self-worshiping old man the attention she denied him. Em's interest also extended now to her son, and Phil often accompanied his mother on occasions that more correctly called for a husband. In turn, Herbert became even more reliant on Margery for companionship and conversation.

Help on the financial front came through Em's sister Maud, who was one of the founding editors of the *Woman's Weekly* magazine in 1916. One of her first commissions was for a series of detective stories from Emily Allingham, and Herbert also began writing for the new publication. *Woman's Weekly* spun off another magazine, *Mother and Home,* which published a fairy story by Margery in 1917. Other work for the elder Allinghams was forthcoming, but the family never did regain the financial stability they had enjoyed in Layer Breton.

Margery transferred from Endsleigh House to The Perse High School for Girls in Cambridge early in 1919, when she was fourteen. The Perse and the boardinghouse, called Sarum, where Margery lived with twenty-seven other girls, seemed to offer the reluctant scholar a chance at a genuinely classical education and serious preparation for university. She entered The Perse with optimism and later recalled the experience with some fondness, but in reality she found both the curriculum and the teachers dull. She never learned to spell (or bothered to try); her handwriting was atrocious; she balked at exams; and her response to any form of academic challenge ranged from bored to actively hostile. Classmates remembered her creativity, but amid young women who strove for academic excellence, Margery was the swine among pearls. Still, she made friends and while at The Perse wrote two plays that were produced by her classmates.

Her own recollections of her teenage self were of a "nervy, big-boned exciteable child . . . quick to rage or laughter, self-conscious, over-aware and altogether about as restful as an unbroken mule." She was growing taller, and with her new height came weight gain. Never athletic, she must have felt particularly ungainly on the playing fields of a proper girls' academy. She was perhaps more subject than most to adolescent highs and lows. More important, her time at The Perse convinced her that her gift for creativity counted for little compared to her failure as an intellectual, and she left the school in 1920, after barely more than a year. Back with her family in London, however, she continued her studies with a tutor, Barbara Harper, a fellow at Queen's College who somehow managed, over the next three years, to teach Margery a great deal of literature, language, and history. In 1920, Margery also began classes in drama and elocution as well as rhythmics and fencing at London's Regent Street Polytechnic. And she conceived an ambition that seems strange for an awkward and self-conscious girl—too tall and plump to be considered a beauty despite her lovely face— who still stuttered and was ill at ease in simple social situations. She wanted to become an actress and go on the stage.

Something remarkable had happened when she first auditioned for Miss Louie Bagley, principal of the Polytechnic's School of Speech and Drama. Margery recalled her terror as student after student rose to declaim and be critiqued under Miss Bagley's "bullet eyes." But when her turn came, Margery's voice "shot out naked and new and angry in a very cold and hostile world." The stutter had vanished. Although she retained minor problems in ordinary, unscripted conversation, her ability to recite was a revelation and the basis of a new self-confidence. Margery now found it easier to make friends, and for the first time, she threw herself wholeheartedly into a course of study. She continued her tutorials with Barbara Harper and was also writing steadily, plays as well as stories. The inevitable rejections came in, but a letter of encouragement from the great George Bernard Shaw was a boost for a seventeen-year-old's spirits.

Her free time was mostly spent in the company of family. It was on a family vacation in the summer of 1921 that she was inspired to write her first novel. During their years at Layer Breton, the Allinghams had become enamored of Mersea—an isolated island located off the Essex coast not far from Layer Breton—and it remained their favorite holiday retreat. Mersea Island had inspired other writers with its desolate landscape and medieval-like culture.* Margery loved the bleak setting and hints of violence under the dark humor and superstitions of the native population (a theme that was to pervade her mysteries).

The idea for her novel supposedly came from a night of playing "the glass" with her father, brother, and George Hearn. Spiritualism was the rage in the 1920s, and working "the glass"—akin to using a Ouija board—supposedly gave entrance to the spirit world. On this night and in twelve more sessions, Margery, according to her father's account, led the group through conversations with a two-hundred-year-old smuggler and other long-dead spirits who told the story of a Spanish pirate and the murder of the girl he loved. This exciting tale, which included witches as well as pirates, became the basis of *Blackerchief Dick,* published in 1923. The book, which probably owes more to Robert Louis Stevenson (one of Herbert's favorite authors) than to spirits, was reviewed more extensively than it deserved and later embarrassed Margery to the extent that she bought any used copies she ran across to get them out of circulation. But it made her a published novelist, and that she was to remain.

Her major interests were still the theater and the new group of friends she was acquiring. One was a young man named Philip Youngman Carter, known as "Pip," the brother of Margery's Polytechnic friend Betty Carter. Pip and Betty were the children of Lilian Robinson Carter, who had been close to Herbert during his Cambridge days, before he married Em. It was family tradition, though not fact, that Pip and Betty were cousins to the young Allinghams. Margery was not initially attracted to Pip, though they discovered mutual interests—he was studying art at the Polytechnic—and they became friendly.

But Margery's first romance was one of those sentimental attachments so common, and generally unremarkable, among schoolgirls of the period—a crush on the girl who played a lead role in Margery's student play, *Dido and Aeneas.* The attraction was mutual at first, but the relationship with Angela Doubleday, or "Charles" as Margery called her,

---

* Before Margery's *Mystery Mile,* the best-known story set on Mersea was Sabine Baring-Gould's *Mehalah.* Reverend Baring-Gould authored *Lives of the Saints,* hymns including "Onward Christian Soldiers," and Victorian romantic novels. *Mehalah* (1880) is a dark tale expressive of the reverend's distaste for the primitive island.

wore itself out after about a year, probably because "Charles" was too ardent and Margery lost interest. All the while, she had been seeing Pip more and more often, though barely conscious of him except as a companionable escort. So it came as a surprise when, in the late summer of 1923, he proposed marriage. After several rebuffs, she eventually "promised to marry him someday if [I] have not anyone else before" and let the issue drop. Pip, however, took the promise to heart and later said they were "secretly engaged" from this time.

Under pressure from her father, Margery began a new book, *Green Corn,* which was supposed to be a novel about the Bright Young Things—the footloose and, to their scandalized elders, morals-free postwar youths who were reaching their twenties in tandem with the century. Unfortunately for Margery the novelist, Margery the girl was not wild and debauched, nor were her friends (though her brother was on his way to meeting the qualifications). *Green Corn,* which was never published, became more autobiographical than Margery probably intended and is interesting for the portrait she paints of Pip, in a minor character named Noll, rather than for any literary merit.

By 1925, her twenty-first year, Margery had finished at the Polytechnic and given up the dream of a stage career (possibly because she was too large for leading-lady roles), had two unimpressive novels under her belt, was still living in her parents' contentious home, and needed to begin making her own way. Luckily, her aunt Maud had expanded her stable of women's magazines to include two devoted to the movies and one called *Joy* that was directed at the modern young working woman— the "flapper." Maud offered Margery regular work for these publications, and Margery took it. She was a feature writer for *Joy* and also became adept at writing movie stories, which were narrative versions of popular silent films. She would continue to churn out these assignments even after she began earning her fame as a mystery novelist.

She moved into a small studio apartment converted from an outbuilding in the garden of the block of flats where her parents resided. Here she worked, learned to cook, entertained friends, fell briefly in love with one of her brother's friends, Reggie Goode, a big, good-looking young man whose interest was motor mechanics. Though her feelings were reciprocated, she apparently ended the relationship in an emotional scene in the summer of 1926.

A year later, Margery's first novel-length detective story, *The White Cottage Mystery,* had been published in serial form by the *Daily Express,* and she was about to marry Pip Carter.

> *"I don't know if he is quite such a little beast as I
> thought . . ."*

Philip Youngman Carter was a pompous and opinionated young man—
a rock-ribbed Conservative who played at being Bohemian during his
Polytechnic days. Based on interviews with former schoolmates, Julia
Thorogood has described the youthful Pip as "hopelessly spotty and callow, tall, bending, a sort of second-rate Noel Coward and almost a joke
to some of their fellow-students." He did not impress Margery in their
first meeting. "Not much of a chap," she wrote in her diary. But he was
persistent, and when Margery's more romantic passions faded, Pip remained. It's tempting to think that she finally agreed to marry him out
of sheer exhaustion or was pushed by the fat girl's greatest enemy, desperation. In any case, she was very protective of him, even when he irritated her mightily with his "lordly" mannerisms. She portrayed Noll,
the character clearly based on Pip in *Green Corn,* as outwardly annoying
and ridiculous, but with inner strengths and goodness.

There doesn't seem to have been a strong sexual attraction. After
Margery's death, Pip wrote★ about their secret engagement: "It was a
curious courtship because we were both naturally shy and completely
inexperienced. We neither kissed nor held hands, but walked arm in
arm like children: yet between us there was that complete understanding that makes sex of minor importance and mutual interests so para-
mount that other considerations appear remote and mildly funny."
Hardly the kind of unfettered passion that might have been expected of
two twenty-somethings in the heyday of the Roaring Twenties. But
Margery had found in Pip qualities of intelligence, humor, companionship, and supportiveness that others ignored. Pip also provided the social
confidence, considered by many of their peers to be social-climbing, that
Margery lacked.

When the engagement was announced, Pip's mother, Lilian, wrote to
Herbert, expressing her serious concerns that Pip was too selfish and too
much burdened by his cynicism to be a good husband. Whatever doubts
Herbert may have had, he reassured Lilian that their children's match
would work. Perhaps as a consequence of his sentimental attachment to
his old college flame, the ever-tolerant Herbert quite liked his future
son-in-law and had promoted Pip's cause to Margery. What Em thought
is not known.

The wedding took place on September 29, 1927, the year both
Margery and Pip turned twenty-three. They honeymooned for a week

---

★ "A Profile of Margery Allingham," the preface to *The Allingham Case-Book.*

in the north of France, at Montreuil-sur-Mer, where the knowing French hotel proprietor assumed they were, in Pip's extravagant estimation, "pagans living in sin."

Before the wedding, they had found a three-room apartment off High Holburn street in London, adjacent to a printing plant, which shook them whenever the presses were rolling. Their place was soon cluttered with books and art materials and friends. One school pal and former roommate of Pip's, a sometime artist named Alan Joseph Gregory and called "Grog," came to visit and remained with the Carters for the next thirteen years. There were old friends from Pip's private school days and from the Polytechnic and many new friends, most gathered by Pip, who comprised a large circle known as the Gang. It was not a highbrow group, but intelligent and fun-loving young people associated with the arts and publishing, and many went on to outstanding careers.

Pip was earning intermittently, designing book covers but still working for recognition as a fine artist. Grog, talented but ambitionless, worked as little as possible. Margery, as the primary breadwinner in her household, kept up a steady flow of her hack writing. *The White Cottage Mystery* was published in novel form in 1928, and with Pip's help and encouragement, she began a new novel, *The Crime at Black Dudley*. Both Pip and Grog were intimately involved, and Margery recalled that "now I learned to work anywhere at any time with anything from a party to a dogfight going on in the same room. Better still I grew gay myself. For the first time I ventured to encourage the humour which until then I had always tried to keep out of my work. . . . "

The humor in *Black Dudley* is dated by today's standards (or perhaps not, since the Bright Young Things of the 1920s specialized in the kind of know-it-all irony so prevalent in the late twentieth and early twenty-first centuries). But the chief comic relief was supplied by the first public appearance of Albert Campion. Campion was intended as a foil and red herring, but his daft personality and style overwhelmed the main character, a love-struck pathologist and consultant to Scotland Yard named Abbershaw.

Who was the model for Campion? Based solely on the fiction of the time, Dorothy L. Sayers's Lord Peter Wimsey and P. G. Wodehouse's Bertie Wooster are obvious sources for Campion's "silly ass" manners and speech and upper-crust background. Some of the Carters' friends saw Pip in Campion; at least, they wore the same black, tortoiseshell-rimmed eyeglasses. Others thought Margery took her inspiration from Grog Gregory—an outwardly gentle young man whose quiet demeanor hid a sensitive lover of art and music with a robust gift for parody and dirty jokes. Julia Thorogood suggests that Margery's aristocratic detective owed to a character called Duffer, created many years earlier by her father in one of his serial adventures. Margery herself later joked to friends that Campion was the young George VI. Whatever the source— and Campion was probably drawn from a variety of influences—he rose above the pedestrian adventure of *Black Dudley*, particularly pleasing Margery's American publisher, Harry Maule of Doubleday Doran. Maule wanted more of Albert Campion, and Margery was glad to oblige.

She had written most of *Black Dudley* (dedicated to the Gang) at the Old Vicarage in Letheringham, a house in Suffolk that Herbert and Em had rented since 1926. She, Pip, and Grog, who served as typist, went back to Letheringham to put together a second novel, *Mystery Mile*. It was a much better book, with Campion now the focus. *Mystery Mile* also introduced a character who was to become almost as constant a presence as Campion himself—Magersfontein Lugg.★ He became one of the easiest characters for Margery to write, possibly because he expressed thoughts that Margery herself could not. It was Pip who later theorized that Lugg the manservant was an expression of Margery's "unconscious."

Mystery Mile sold well, particularly in the United States, where it was a recommended Book of the Month of the Doubleday Crime Club. Whether she realized it or not, Dorothy was now a mystery writer. And Pip had succeeded to the position of mentor and chief supporter so long held by her father. She credited her husband at this time as the chief plot-maker of her books and later said of *Mystery Mile* that "two-thirds of the ideas and half the jokes" originated with Pip.

Margery's early Campion adventures may not have been the kind of literature to which her old friend "Mac" McFee hoped she would aspire, but they gave her a degree of creative freedom that her hackwork never could offer. Within the general framework of the mystery-adventure story, she experimented, sometimes for better, sometimes for worse. (Her third Campion, *Look to the Lady,* was not nearly as good as *Mystery Mile*.) In her fourth Campion, *Police at the Funeral,* she showed her willingness and ability to adapt her central character. *Police at the Funeral* was consciously intended to attract the kind of readers who were snatching up the mysteries of Agatha Christie and Dorothy Sayers—"the higher-browed" reader in Margery's words—and so she adjusted Campion's role from lunatic thrill-seeker to professional private detective and plotted a

---

★ Criminal turned loyal factotum, Lugg is named for the Boer War battle of Magersfontein.

genuine murder puzzle. *Police at the Funeral* is set in Cambridge in the midst of a family under the bruising thumb of a Victorian matriarch. Beneath the well-constructed plot, there is an intriguing well of dark moodiness and psychological violence as Margery laid bare the lives of a family damaged by too much togetherness—a situation not unlike that of the various Allinghams.

"Where am I going? What am I getting?"

By 1932, Herbert and Em had moved to a smaller country house in Suffolk, The Dairy House, near Shelley. Phil, the wild brother, had tried writing and advertising but gone off on his own as a traveling fortune-teller and carnival pitchman. Young Joyce was away at school. When Margery and Pip stayed with her parents as she was completing *Police,* the mood was often tense. "Daddy rather snappy and Mother a disturbing element as usual," Margery wrote in her diary. "Pip complaining that he isn't fed enough. Mother very silly not to see to the housekeeping better." Returning to London, the Carters were thrown into more family disorder. Aunt Maud's husband, sportswriter Edward "Ted" Wood, was a heavy drinker and in constant need of rescue from one situation or another. Another uncle was seriously ill. And Margery and Pip's small London flat became a gathering point in these family crises. It could not have been easy to work, so the Carters, with Grog, moved out of the city to a rented Tudor farmhouse in Chappell, Essex. Located on the river Colne, Viaduct Farm was not far from her parents' house in Shelley, enabling Margery to see her father more consistently than she had since her marriage.

Although the record is slim for this period, biographer Julia Thorogood speculates that the move may have been motivated by a number of troubling events in addition to the family trials. Margery may have been ill; a doctor's prescription indicates that she was taking thyroid medication. From plump, she had grown fat; she was just twenty-seven, and the weight gain was surely depressing. In the country she could retreat from the constant partying of London and switch her attire from city fashions to loose and flowing garments. Country life also promised the level of domesticity she longed for.

Still, Pip and Grog, both underemployed, spent much of their time playing and drinking, adopting the freewheeling lifestyle of country gentlemen. Margery, the disciplined writer and financial mainstay of the ménage, mostly stayed at home while the men dallied. Is it any wonder she became resentful and jealous? She and Pip often quarreled, and there is some indication their fights may have been physical, but Margery tended to turn her anxieties back on herself. She wrote in her diary in 1934, "Feel put upon but have uncomfortable feeling that it's my fault. Have either taken on more than I can chew or else am trying to do a he-woman's job and . . . do it nicely and in a feminine fashion."

She was still writing film stories for her aunt's publications as well as working at her novels and serials. A new book was in progress—*Death of a Ghost*—when news of disappointing American sales of *Police at the Funeral* caused Margery to panic and crank out a Campion thriller, *Sweet Danger,* for publication in 1933. She also undertook a serial melodrama for *Answers* magazine; she eventually wrote three of these romantic thrillers—*Dangerous Secrets, Rogue's Holiday,* and *The Devil and Her Son*—which later underwent title changes and were published in book form under the pen name Maxwell March.

It was about this time that Em suffered a nervous breakdown, brought on by the death of her dear friend Dr. Salter in 1932. In his will, Salter bequeathed Em £500 but failed to make her his executor or to leave her his house, D'Arcy House at Tolleshunt D'Arcy, as he had promised. Em was crushed and became unstable. When neither Herbert nor Margery could cope, Em was committed to a private mental facility, where she remained for a month. She recovered, but her confinement was an omen. (Her medical records referred to Em's delusions and also indicated that she suffered from a thyroid deficiency.)

Sweet Danger, composed during this crisis, was a sweet release for Margery. There are dark elements, but the tone is decidedly light and the plot action filled. It is the best of her early quartet of adventure novels, and also marks the first appearance of Campion's future bride, Lady Amanda Fitton.

Promising writers attract publicity, and the emerging public image of the Carters of Viaduct Farm was that of a happy, slightly unconventional pair of artists working side by side amid the dogs and the clutter of creativity in their country home, entertaining rafts of interestingly arty friends at gay country weekends, always highlighted by a costume party, and at their annual cricket match. Margery was pictured by the publicity mill as an efficient female machine: writing, running the bustling household, entertaining, and indulging in her favorite domestic pastimes of cooking and sewing while Pip painted his book covers and engaged in the traditional manly pursuits. According to the press releases, Margery managed every aspect of her professional and personal lives with poise and confidence. It was a charming fiction. In truth, she was overworked and underappreciated by those closest to her. She was suffering from neck pains, and probably from the bronchitis and sinusitis that plagued her adult life. She was also drained by exhaustion and anxiety. There may have been trouble in her marriage—suspicions of other women. (Given Pip's reputation as a ladies' man and his later acknowledged infidelity, Margery's fears may not have been unfounded.)

Pip was no comfort and no help. He had basically given up his own artistic ambitions by the mid-1930s, did little commercial work, and devoted his time to his social life. Wherever there was a party with gin and pretty women, Pip was sure to be on hand.

> *"Feel disaster has overtaken me. One of the two sup-*
> *ports of my world is going."*

Late in 1934, D'Arcy House in Tolleshunt D'Arcy—the place where the obsessed Em had spent so many hours with her old idol, Dr. Salter—went up for sale. After visiting the house—complete with the flower gardens where Salter had once grown his prize-winning specimens, and two meadows used for local fetes and cricket matches—Pip was determined to own it. Margery balked at the cost; the asking price may have been as high as £3,500. The Carters argued, but Margery backed down when Pip received financial help from his mother. D'Arcy House had been inherited by Dr. Salter's medical partner, who was subsequently killed in an auto accident, and his executors clearly wanted to get the place off their hands. They accepted Pip's offer of £1,075 almost as soon as it was made.

Fatalistically, Margery accepted the move, though it would only increase her financial responsibilities. At thirty, whatever hopes she had for slowing her pace and perhaps for having children and taking on a more traditional, domestic role ended with the purchase of the large house and grounds in the center of Tolleshunt D'Arcy.

The move was accomplished in June 1935. Margery and Pip took along the inevitable Grog Gregory; Mary Orr, called "Cooee," an old friend from Polytechnic days who had joined the household in 1934; Christina Carter, their housekeeper; three horses; and a growing pack of dogs. They quickly added a cook and gardener. Margery supported the lot. She had come home, in essence, to the world of Layer Breton, where she had spent the happiest years of her childhood. Whether she was able to enjoy it is questionable.

She increased her output of serials and short stories, though she lost one regular source of income when her aunt Maud's movie magazine folded. *Death of a Ghost,* dedicated to her father, had done very well, and her new novel, *Flowers for the Judge*—whose conclusion may have been influenced by her brother's unusual lifestyle—was well received. But the cost of running and refurbishing the house was more than she could handle, and as soon as advances or royalty checks came in, the money went out to pay overdue bills. At one point Margery convinced Pip to sell D'Arcy House if they could make a reasonable profit, but it's doubtful he meant to do so.

Pip had settled into Tolleshunt D'Arcy as one to the manor born. He easily took on the role of squire and involved himself in local affairs. The entertaining traditions established at Viaduct Farm were quickly reinstated at D'Arcy, and Pip made friends with several businessmen and their wives who lived in the village and commuted to London. (Margery never had much fondness for these "suburban" types, especially the women.) Pip's intolerant brand of conservatism became even more pronounced, and he seemed to take pleasure in his prejudices against foreigners and homosexuals. As the new homeowner, he was too busy to provide the emotional support Margery needed. While Pip, Grog, and Cooee—whom Margery had dubbed the Kids—made the rounds of the local pubs and parties, the cricket matches and hunt balls, Margery stayed at home and worked. How much of this was Pip's fault, and how much was Margery's, is debatable. He may have neglected her, but she refused most of the Kids' invitations to join their fun. When she did attend social functions outside D'Arcy, she usually had a miserable time. She was jealous of Pip's women friends but did little to rein her husband in.

Margery's one port of safety in all her storms—her relationship with her father—had been renewed when she and Pip moved to Viaduct Farm. She had turned to Herbert increasingly with her writing, and they were in almost daily contact. Father and daughter could argue intensely, but they also shared the old faith in professional discipline and craftsmanship. It was Herbert, not Pip, who helped her with *Flowers for the Judge*. Surprisingly in light of what must have been unhappy memories of Dr. Salter's role in his wife's life, Herbert approved of the move to Tolleshunt D'Arcy.

Perhaps he knew that his own life was winding down. Just six months after the Carters took possession of D'Arcy House, Herbert died in a nursing home in Colchester. The cause of his final illness is obscure, but during his hospitalization, Em moved in with Margery and Pip and turned their lives on end. Em was erratic, made scenes, accused Margery of "sinfulness," and talked incessantly of Salter and of her own "destiny" to live in D'Arcy House. As her father was dying, Margery grew increasingly terrified of her mother's intentions, but she somehow managed to persuade Em to live with her cousin Grace at Pope's Hall in

Chappell. Granny Hughes was staying there as well, and Margery gladly agreed to assist with the expenses.★

With her mother apparently settled, Margery was left with the responsibility of sorting her father's affairs and dealing with her grief. She had lost Herbert, one of the two "supports" of her life, and the other, her husband, was wrapped up in his own interests. Not long after her father's death, she lost a member of her extended family: Cooee left. Although she eventually returned, the situation surrounding her departure had been highly emotional. Margery may have resented the burden of her permanent houseguests, but she resented it more when they deserted her.

Margery needed escape and found it in starting a new Campion, *Dancers in Mourning*. The story, which revolved around a family in chaos, was well received when published in 1937. Critics were quick to compare it to Dorothy Sayers's *Busman's Honeymoon,* with Margery's novel pronounced the clear victor. It is interesting that both these women† were making radical changes in the same year. *Busman's Honeymoon* was Dorothy's last completed mystery novel, and her career was to take an entirely new course. While Margery remained a mystery writer all her life, *Dancers in Mourning* was a major change for her as well. It won critical praise, sold more than any of her previous books, and established her as a success even in her own hypersensitive mind. She now entered the world of literary recognition, something she had always yearned for. She was invited to mingle with the greats of her trade—men like E. C. Bentley and Freeman Wills Crofts—and she began a beneficial friendship with the writer-critic Frank Swinnerton and his wife. She was asked by the influential literary magazine *Time and Tide* to write book reviews (quite a step up for the girl who had never finished high school).

★ "Aunt" Grace Allingham, eldest daughter of Herbert's flamboyant uncle John, had gone on the stage as a music hall performer in the 1890s and been one of the "Floradora" girls. She didn't make it out of the chorus but fell in love with a well-to-do businessman, Richard Cheffins, who purchased Pope's Hall for her. "Mr. and Mrs. Cheffins" lived there for a number of years without benefit of marriage. Grace later married another man, Steve Russell. It was Aunt Grace to whom all the Allinghams turned in times of trouble; she had managed Maud's husband and taken Em in after her nervous breakdown. The Beckoning Lady, the estate in Margery's 1955 novel of the same name, is based on Pope's Hall.

† Margery was unimpressed with Dorothy Sayers when they first met, thinking the better established and more intellectual writer too "headmistressy" for her taste. When they became better acquainted during the Second World War—Sayers's home in Witham was not far from Tolleshunt D'Arcy—Margery changed her mind and decided Dorothy was "quite a nice old duck. . . ."

Dancers in Mourning must have provided satisfaction in another way. Though she frequently used real people as the inspiration for her characters, she usually altered them out of easy recognizability. But in *Dancers,* the character of Dr. Bouverie is a nearly exact replication of old Dr. Salter, and Margery treated him not as the intrusive and dominating figure he had been in her own and her parents' lives, but as a poignantly out-of-date Victorian autocrat. A dismissive revenge.

Her next Campion novel won even greater praise. *The Fashion in Shrouds* was written with considerable difficulty, and its reception convinced Margery that she was quite capable, as her father's old friend George Hearn had advised her many years before, of writing serious novels of manners grafted onto the detective story formula, which she called "the box." The critics agreed. In the most often quoted review of *Shrouds,* the *Observer's* "Torquemada" wrote, "To Albert Campion has fallen the honour of being the first detective to figure in a story which is also, even when judged by the fixed stars of criticism, a distinguished novel." But Margery was not there yet, as her next book showed. *Black Plumes* (originally written as a serial and titled *Bring Out Your Rubber-Tyred Hearses*) dispensed with Campion in favor of an older, traditional detective, Inspector Bridie, and critics pointed out that it lacked both the energy and cohesion of *Shrouds.* Margery dismissed it as something done for money.

With the help of friends like Frank Swinnerton and Russell Meiggs, an old schoolmate of Pip's and a fellow in ancient history at Kebel College, Oxford, Margery was gaining some balance in her life. Pip and the Kids were now supplemented by serious conversation and correspondence with men who valued her intelligence. Writing to them (and there would be others, including the Archbishop of York and several other clerics), she was at last able to express her thinking on issues of more substance than the theme for the next costume party at D'Arcy House. Meiggs, whom she first met in 1934 and who attracted her (as he did most smart women who came his way) with his good looks and charm, was particularly important. Unlike Pip, Meiggs was willing and eager to seriously discuss serious issues, issues like Margery's concepts of Christianity, faith, and the purpose of human existence as well as her work and her personal anxieties. Margery confided to Russell Meiggs as she never could to Pip, and they kept in touch through frequent, long letters and his occasional visits to D'Arcy until 1941, when he married and she wrote a less than flattering portrait of him as Lee Aubrey in *Traitor's Purse.* Margery could be both nasty and insensitive when she felt betrayed. Whatever happened to cause the breach, when she learned that Meiggs had recognized himself in *Traitor's Purse* and been hurt by her portrayal, she didn't seem to care, expressing her hope in a letter to her sister that "it may have done him good."★

> *". . . so far the war has been my salvation . . . I've re-*
> *covered my health and equilibrium. I'm all right."*

What really saved Margery from total physical collapse and despondency was the second great tragedy of the twentieth century: World War Two. Perhaps it took a war to get Margery away from her work and into the real world, but for the first time since coming to Tolleshunt D'Arcy, she became involved with her fellow villagers, discovering that she both liked and respected them.

Long before the formal declaration of war, the people of England were preparing for the worst, and again it was anticipated that the southern and eastern coasts would bear the first brunt of any direct attack. Pip threw himself into defense work, with Margery not far behind. Pip was chief warden and deputy chief first aid officer for Tolleshunt D'Arcy, and D'Arcy House was soon transformed into command central for the local volunteers. The village was readying itself not only for bombardment and invasion by the Nazis, but also for the arrival of hundreds of London evacuees. When the local butcher resigned as billeting officer for the refugees, Margery took over. She eventually found accommodations for some three hundred evacuees in the village of 650 people and established a maternity home, called Mamas' House, for the large number of pregnant women.

By 1940, she was billeting troops at D'Arcy House, and the sight of the young soldiers touched her. In her wonderful nonfiction account of the village's preparation for war, *The Oaken Heart,* she wrote, "To blunder into the back hall to find a smooth-faced, fair-haired child sleeping sweetly in the camp-bed . . . his rifle clasped in his arms like a toy, was one of those things you could wish not to have seen until you remembered how lucky it was for you that there were children to do it, and that

---

★ Before *Traitor's Purse* was published in 1941, she sent Meiggs a nicely inscribed copy of her war book, *The Oaken Heart,* and she later agreed to be godmother to his daughter. But their last encounter in 1955, when Margery finally met his wife, was strange and strained. From remarks made after that occasion and in her private writings, it is likely that Margery always felt a strong emotional and physical attraction to Russell Meiggs. She once wrote to him that he went "through life in a rather affable charming fashion, promising people (women, I mean) much more than you are prepared to give them."

if you had had any sense there would be your children growing up to take their places."

(That Margery and Pip never had children was Pip's decision, according to their doctor. She was only in her mid-thirties when she wrote the passage above, and childbearing was not out of the realm of possibility. But in earlier diary entries, she had mentioned arguments over the question of children, Pip opting for material acquisitions instead. A 1934 diary note reads, "We ought to have some joint project. A kid? I'm afraid it's not in his line." But her acquiescence may also have been related to her own fears—of childbirth itself, of sacrificing her work to the demands of rearing children, of her abilities to be a good mother. Margery liked children and often wrote them into her novels, but she hadn't, after all, had the best role model in Em, and she was always more like her mother than she cared to admit.)

Margery was unhappy when her family began to break up. Phil and Joyce had already entered military service, but when Cooee decided to join, Margery threw a tantrum that created a permanent rupture in their relationship. On the other hand, Pip's decision to join the Army drew the couple closer, and until he shipped out to North Africa, they spent more time together than they had in years. Margery had Grog at home until 1941 when he joined the Royal Air Force. After that she lived in a house of women: her housekeeper, Chris Carter, who was more a companion and equal than a servant, and Granny Hughes (who remained a stalwart and comforting presence until her death in 1952, just before her hundredth birthday). For the first time since her marriage, Margery no longer had the responsibility of supporting her able-bodied husband and the rest of the Kids. She briefly considered some form of official service for herself, but decided that she served best by remaining at home and preparing for the day when her family would return.

Margery's contact with her fellow villagers during their war preparations had altered her attitudes and opened her vistas. She became convinced that victory over the Nazis depended on the people—ordinary people like her neighbors whose power lay not in the halls of government but in their simple determination to survive and endure. At the suggestion of her New York publisher, Margery undertook a book that would tell the world what the English were like in their time of deepest trial. It was *The Oaken Heart,* the story of Tolleshunt D'Arcy and the daily lives of ordinary country people at war. The title referred to the heart of England, "which is old and hard and true still, in spite of surface rot."

The book, which Malcolm Johnson had hoped would inspire his own countrymen, failed in the States when it was published in 1941. But in England, where it was handled by her old friend Robert Lusty of

Michael Joseph Ltd., the book struck a chord. Margery received congratulations from George Bernard Shaw and also from Dr. A. D. Lindsay, Master of Balliol College, Oxford, with whom she began another of her private, intellectual conversations on paper.

Margery was not having a crisis of faith at this time, but she was—helped by her letter-writing with people willing to accept her as a serious mind and also to challenge her thinking—clarifying her beliefs. She was Anglican all her life, but she had doubts about the Church, particularly the role it should play in wartime and after. Politically conservative and a devoted supporter of Winston Churchill, she nevertheless wrote to Dr. Lindsay that she was "pure socialist" in the old-fashioned sense. Christianity is brotherhood, she explained, and brotherhood is a kind of socialism. But she wanted the Church to address the great issues of Good and Evil, not fritter away its authority on social reform.

Margery did not believe in an individual soul or afterlife or a personal God. God, she had written to Russell Meiggs in 1937, is "a moving pattern of causes and effects, warnings and fulfilments, rewards and encouragements, all working together." Human existence, she thought, was part of and mirrored this design; humans were composed of elements and qualities that survived after death. In her version of reincarnation, human qualities were passed on to others through a kind of mystical inheritance. It was the similarities between people that mattered to her: "From one point of view we are all one person really." Brotherhood was achieved, she said, when people focused on their likenesses rather than their differences, as they did during times of great crisis.

This kind of thinking formed the blueprint of her next book—the book she hoped would lift her to the status of pure novelist. (She wrote to her sister that it was to be The Novel, "the 'Who-am-I?' one.") *Dance of the Years* is not a detective story but a family saga in which Margery intended to show how pattern is passed across generations of a family, from the Victorian age to the present. She drew inspiration from a family legend (disproved by Richard Martin's genealogical research for his literary biography *Ink in Her Blood*) of a great-grandfather who had married a gypsy, thereby accounting for the streak of wildness and independence in subsequent generations of Allinghams. Despite a strong opening section (on the basis of which Little, Brown eagerly contracted to publish *Dance of the Years* in the United States), the book fell apart in succeeding chapters, and Little, Brown regretted its commitment. Margery had, as she often said of herself, bit off more than she could chew, and the final section of the book, rushed to completion, was nearly incomprehensible. The idea she wished to convey, as Richard Martin has pointed out, was "too intrusive and too naively mystical to be able to carry the weight of the narrative."

Even though *Dance of the Years* was a failure, Margery felt that the effort had done her good, and she returned to Albert Campion with renewed energy. In *Coroner's Pidgin,* Campion has aged and matured, and within the confines of the detective story, the novel deals much more convincingly with the themes of change and continuation than the overblown *Dance of the Years* had.

Pip, meanwhile, was tasting his first real independent success. Stationed in the North African desert, he missed Margery and wrote loving letters home. But after seeing action with his supply unit at Tobruk, Captain Pip Carter was transferred to Baghdad shortly before the Battle of El Alamein. He was made a senior press officer, responsible for a variety of publications, broadcasts, and public relations—work that took him to Cairo, Teheran, and Damascus. He cut a trim figure, as one friend described him, in "his immaculate, ever resplendent dress, as fresh and well-cut as if every 24 hours there came to him on a magic carpet from Savile Row to Baghdad, a new uniform."[*] Never one to pass up an affectation, he had taken to wearing a monocle. He was working hard, however—writing, illustrating, editing—and with his new friend Sean Fielding, he founded *Soldier,* a magazine for the British forces.

When the war ended and Pip was released from the Army in 1946, with the rank of lieutenant colonel, he went back, not to D'Arcy House, but to London. He took an editing job with the *Daily Express* and lived in an apartment at 91, Great Russell Street that he and Margery had leased since the 1930s. Though he traveled to Tolleshunt D'Arcy some weekends, his life and livelihood were now in London. When Sean Fielding was named editor of *The Tatler,* Pip followed him and was soon working his way through London's new postwar society. He was intimately involved in the magazine's transition into the bright, clever chronicle of London's postwar high life, writing film and theater reviews and wine and food articles, drawing and writing sketches of theater personalities, and starting the popular "London Limelight" column. He was among the first members of The Thursday Club, a men's eating and drinking group dedicated to "Absolute Inconsequence." The early membership was mostly journalists and photographers, but the group soon included celebrities and even the husband of the future queen. (Pip was a guest at the wedding of Princess Elizabeth and Prince Philip in 1947.) His appearances in Tolleshunt D'Arcy were infrequent and usually involved cricket matches and country entertainments hosted for his new circle of friends.

---

[*] Jack Morpurgo, quoted by Julia Thorogood in *Margery Allingham: A Biography.*

For Margery, who had come to love and depend on D'Arcy House and the familiar comforts of Tolleshunt D'Arcy, the idea of joining Pip in London was hardly considered. Though the Kids had not reassembled after the war—Cooee was married, and Grog had been gently turned away—Margery had her Granny Hughes and her staff to care for, but they were excuses. Margery needed D'Arcy now; it was her support, her prop, her necessary environment. After a period of physical and emotional well-being during the war, when she underwent what was apparently successful thyroid treatment, she was ill again with neck pains, bronchitis, and sinusitis, and burdened by her weight. She was also having trouble with her British publisher, Heinemann, and considering a change.

More important, she was being hounded mercilessly by the tax authorities. Her tax problems, though not so dramatic as Agatha Christie's, were to plague her throughout the 1940s and 1950s, fan her hatred of the Labour Party, color her work, and eventually push her into a paranoid fear of the Inland Revenue Service. She had fallen behind on her tax payments during the war, and no matter what she tried to do, she could never bring her obligation up to date. Now that Pip had finally decided to take regular employment, his income was combined with his wife's, pushing them into the supertax bracket. Margery found herself in a Catch-22 situation: she would write something to pay taxes owed, then have nothing left to pay the taxes on her new earnings.

She might have eased her burden by selling D'Arcy House and moving to London or by giving up her career, but neither alternative was attractive. She hoped that she and Pip could be taxed separately, but the government made no such allowance for working couples. When she tried, at her lawyer's urging, to open a separate bank account so that she could better document her business expenses, the bank wouldn't talk with her unless her husband was present. Her accountant proved to be a conscientious number-cruncher but a tactless negotiator and eventually precipitated needless conflicts with tax officials. Pip, now the professional bon vivant, couldn't be bothered to worry about such trivialities.

> *"I think Minnie's mad and she thinks I'm dishonest,*
> *and we're both explosive personalities."*
> —Tonker Cassands on his marriage in *The Beckoning Lady*

There was a brief interlude with Pip in February 1949, a visit with her publishers, agents, and influential editors in New York, and a delightful stay with children's writer Lavinia Davis and her family in Connecticut. It was during this trip that Margery stoked the myth that Pip was her writing collaborator. In an article for *Town and Country* magazine, she heaped praise on Pip for contributions to her novels that even he never claimed. It is true that Pip had been the moving force behind *The Crime at Black Dudley,* greatly influenced Margery's early Campion thrillers, and designed most of the dust jackets for her first editions. But from *Death of a Ghost* forward, his contributions to the planning and writing were minimal to nonexistent. For Margery to go so far overboard in crediting Pip was not characteristic and may have revealed more about her desperation to ingratiate herself with him than any desire to set the public record straight.

She must have suspected that Pip was not being the good husband in London, but she had become adept at rationalizing his behavior during the prewar days in Chappell and Tolleshunt D'Arcy. In January 1951, however, reality smacked her hard. She learned that Pip was having an affair with a married woman, identified by Richard Martin in *Ink in Her Blood* as an actress named Diane. How Margery found out isn't clear—possibly from the aggrieved husband or his representative, though she later told friends several versions of catching Pip in bed with his mistress. At any rate, she talked first to her lawyer, then to Pip by telephone, and went to London the next day for a face-to-face confrontation. She headed her diary entry for that day "The Hour of the Angel" and wrote, "Most extraordinary day of my life—freedom." Whatever happened in London and then when Pip joined her at D'Arcy House for the weekend, she emerged from their meetings feeling exhilarated and ready to take the necessary steps for a separation. Her first move was to have the deed to D'Arcy House put in her name.

When Pip realized that she was serious, the wrangling began, and Margery uncovered something that was, for her, perhaps harder to take than Pip's infidelity. She had long disliked Sean Fielding, regarding him as a snob and a bad influence on Pip. But she invited him to D'Arcy and from things Fielding said, she realized that Pip had actually manipulated the bad feelings by implying to his editor and friend that Margery was "mental etc." Her anger increased when she decided that Pip had been reading her private diaries. What may have galled most was the realization that Pip was not only unfaithful, but that he was supporting his affair on her hard-earned income. At some point, according to Pip's sister as cited in Julia Thorogood's biography, Margery described Pip to his mistress as "an expensive luxury." (Did the two women meet? Pip continued the affair after its discovery, so openly that his friends referred to his "London wife.")

By Margery's birthday in May of 1951, Pip was trying mightily to effect a reconciliation. He courted her throughout the summer and fall, and on January 11, 1952, the first anniversary of "The Hour of the Angel," Pip escorted Margery to the opening night of *Much Ado about Nothing* with John Gielgud. Margery's diary entry for the day says, "A nice change from last year! Thank God all well."

During that awful year, Margery's solace had been her work, and she produced the novel that many regard as her finest, *The Tiger in the Smoke.* Set in London, it is a psychological mystery cloaked in fog and violence that demonstrates as well as anything she wrote Margery's ability to adapt to changing times. Campion is mature not just in age but attitude. The mood of postwar London is dark. Margery did not merely graft Golden Age conventions onto modern settings, as Agatha Christie and Ngaio Marsh were doing with a good deal of success. Margery, the acute observer of people and places, had observed change and, as her father had taught her to do so many years before, transformed her observations into fiction. But there is nostalgia, too: a major character in *Tiger* is Canon Avril, a "sort of portrait" of Herbert Allingham—a good man with Herbert's essential qualities of forbearance and forgiveness.

Since *More Work for the Undertaker* in 1949, Margery had slowed down her production, taking the time she never allowed herself in the 1930s and early 1940s. Chatto and Windus, her new publishers for *Tiger,* didn't pressure her for material as Heinemann had done. She was employing themes that were important to her, delving deeper into the psychology of her characters. She regarded her books literally as her "children" (and referred to her serial stories, written for money, as her "little bastards"). Margery was childless and now in her late forties, and her books were the only way she could pass on qualities—her pattern—to a new generation. In *The Tiger in the Smoke* and her succeeding five novels, she wrote for the present more successfully than any of her Golden Age peers.

Money remained a constant problem, chiefly because of her tax situation but also because Pip spent more than he earned and Margery still supported him. (Ironically, the quickest way for Margery to settle her problems with the tax authorities would have been to divorce her husband.) Her next novel, *The Beckoning Lady*—said by Pip to have been her favorite—did not solve her problems but did allow her to vent her frustration on all tax men and accountants. In it she paints thinly veiled portraits of herself and Pip as Minnie and Tonker Cassands, who are also up to their eyebrows in trouble with the Inland Revenue.

Set in rural Suffolk, *The Beckoning Lady* is light in tone where *The Tiger in the Smoke* was dark. A kind of retelling of Shakespeare's *A Midsummer's Night Dream,* the novel includes a murder or two but is really about romantic and marital love in their many forms. Minnie and Tonker Cassands (Margery and Pip) are cast as the middle-aged Titania and Oberon of a modern pastoral, and their story is the most direct portrait Margery ever painted of her complicated marriage, including not-too-subtle hints of physical violence. In one passage that will sound familiar to students of domestic abuse, Tonker Cassands rails, "What I did do when my wife told me of this latest and most monstrous demand was to lose my temper, black her eye, and break a window. That I was ashamed of. But this final piece of insanity . . . makes me want to do it again." In another passage, precocious Rupert Campion reports the choicest adult gossip to his parents by declaring that he will someday marry the "fattest" girl and "shout at her and put her across a bed and smack her until she cries, and then I shall kiss her until she laughs, and we shall go downstairs and pour out drinks for a lot of visitors." Margery, like any good novelist, may well have been exercising poetic license, but all of the Carters' friends recognized Pip in Tonker Cassands, a man who will not allow murder or his wife's troubles to impinge on his plans for a successful party.

In the spring of 1955, something extremely serious happened to Margery, possibly related to an overdose of thyroid medication or a massive injection of penicillin for her persistent sinusitis. Her behavior became bizarrely exuberant. Her mood shifts per se were nothing new; she had experienced sudden highs followed by depressions even in adolescence, and her household had grown used to them. But this was different. She seemed to visitors to be drinking champagne all the time, though she had never been a heavy drinker. She gave an interview to an Australian journalist that was out of character and sometimes barely lucid. In the midst of her euphoria, she decided she was about to die, and she began writing farewell letters and making disoriented late-night calls to old friends.

Chris Carter called in Dr. James Madden and the family's old friend Ronnie Reid, a noted surgeon in Colchester. Madden, the Carters' general physician for many years, tracked down Pip in London. Dogged by the memory of Em's severe breakdown after the death of Dr. Salter, the men decided that Margery needed immediate treatment. She was rushed off by ambulance to a nursing home in Chiswick, and within a day she received the first of four sessions of electroconvulsive therapy (ECT)—electric shock treatments. Little effort was made to determine if the cause of her illness was physical or mental, or even to take an accurate medical record. It was only after the treatments were completed that a doctor noticed something wrong with her neck—a goiter—and she at last pieced together her medical history.

The experience was terrifying. Her memory was addled, and one week was permanently lost to her. Ronnie Reid had objected to the shock therapy, but as a surgeon among psychiatrists, his opinion had little weight. Though Margery recovered and was able to resume working (her worst fear was of losing her ability to write), people who knew her well, Ronnie Reid and his daughter Sally among them, believed that she never fully recovered from the treatment.

Later that year, she saw a London specialist, Dr. Raymond Greene, and underwent a complete physical examination and tests in January 1956. During his exam, the doctor found a small lump in her breast and recommended exploratory surgery. Margery decided to seek another opinion. She was convinced that the lump was somehow related to her glandular problems, and no biopsy was done. Julia Thorogood theorizes that Margery's refusal was due to her longtime phobia about suffocation and fear of being anesthetized. She was also afraid of knives. Certainly her one hospitalization and the ECT treatments she received at Chiswick could not have built her confidence. She continued to seek alternative cures for her thyroid and sinus conditions, ignored Dr. Greene's warning, though she did quit smoking, and went back to work.

Her next Campion harked back to London and the mood of *The Tiger in the Smoke*. An exploration of the nature of Good and Evil, the story deals with a psychotic killer, based in part on Margery's study of real-life serial murderers John Reginald Christie and John George Haigh.* In *Hide My Eyes*, Gerry Hawker and Polly Tassie, the older woman who loves and protects Gerry as if he were her son, are not direct portraits of Margery and Pip; rather, the characters emerge, in greatly exaggerated form, as revealing comments on the Carters' worst failings. Gerry is a charming and self-confident sociopath, incapable of truth-telling or any emotional attachment. To Polly, Margery ascribed the quality of "Disinterested Love," so blind and forgiving of its object that Inspector Charles Luke calls it "a force like nuclear energy, it's absolute." When Polly is nearly killed, it is in the manner that most horrified Margery.

A major theme of the book is contained in the title (although Margery's working title was *Tether's End*). It is not only Polly Tassie who hides from the truth. Inspector Luke, in his affection for the old lady, refuses to believe Polly can have any involvement in the series of murders he is investigating: "I may be hiding my eyes but I just cannot see. . . ."

Did Margery recognize, as Polly does not, the power of Disinterested

---

* The case of Reginald Christie, the infamous "monster" of 10 Rillington Place, had been carefully studied by pathologist Sir Francis Camps, a friend and neighbor of the Carters. Christie murdered and raped at least seven women and was hanged for his crimes in 1953. John George Haigh, known as the Vampire Killer, killed six people for financial gain and disposed of the bodies in acid. Caught primarily because of his own overconfidence, Haigh feigned insanity to avoid the death penalty. He was convicted of murder and hanged in 1949. Although Margery used aspects of both cases for *Hide My Eyes*, Haigh is the obvious model for her villain.

Love to destroy? Was *Hide My Eyes* Margery's means of exorcising the enormous anger she must have felt toward Pip, who had allowed the indignities and horror of her shock treatments? She always regarded her work as an escape from real-world troubles, but she conceded that her writing reflected whatever was happening in her personal life, at least in terms of mood and tone. Certainly writing *Hide My Eyes* was a remarkable act of personal courage, for Margery was genuinely convinced that she had lost her writing ability, and she needed constant reassurance throughout the composition. The critics, especially the British, were mixed in their reaction to *Hide My Eyes,* but Margery had become used to that. She was working to write novels of ideas, but the critics, she believed, were unable or unwilling to evaluate her achievements outside the "box" of the detective story.

> *"The question of taste keeps cropping up. One hovers between titles like 'Old Age and How to Get Rid of It' and 'A Funny Thing Happened on the Way to the Cemetery' or, more simply, 'Euthanasia, Here I Come!'"*
> —January 1966 letter to Sir Allen Lane of the Penguin Press

In 1957, in an apparent dispute with the owners, Pip resigned as editor of *The Tatler,* the position he had taken when Sean Fielding left in 1954. He continued to live primarily in London, but he was Margery's responsibility once again. After some months, he found regular freelance employment as a gossip and society writer for the *Evening News* (reviving his "London Limelight" column) and began taking portrait commissions.

The Carters gained firmer control over their business affairs the next year, forming P. & M. Youngman Carter Ltd., a company that took over the available rights to Margery's works and paid its two shareholders salaries. (Margery had already assigned the principal rights to *The Beckoning Lady* to Joyce, hoping that her sister could protect the funds from high taxes and build a reserve for future family needs.) But the Inland Revenue was still bearing down. An official investigation of apparent discrepancies in past filings was in progress. Although the mistake, which concerned Margery's American earnings, was revealed in 1961 to be entirely the Inland Revenue's error, Margery was both frightened and deeply embarrassed to be investigated for what amounted to tax fraud. She became convinced that D'Arcy House was under surveillance, and she and Joyce, who now lived with her sister, moved into the Forge, a converted blacksmith's across the road from D'Arcy House. For a time in the late 1950s, D'Arcy House itself was treated strictly as a place of business.

Margery was spending more time with Pip in London, and she joined him on his rounds of the social scene. She didn't enjoy the high life and fled back to Tolleshunt D'Arcy on weekends, but at least she had her wandering husband under some restraint, and there is evidence that their relationship may have benefited. Margery busied herself with projects—interviews, talks, topical essays for popular publications—that indicated her status as one of the country's leading mystery writers. Pip had always basked in her celebrity; now he seemed to enjoy her company.

In a 1958 lecture titled "Crime for Our Delight," she considered the future of the murder mystery. The puzzle story, she said, was being transformed into "the novel of suspense," in which the theme was not the solution of a murder but explication of the "death of an aspect"— in other words, the psychology of human actions. "We seem to be catching up with the Greeks at last," she explained, as more and more modern writers concerned themselves with "the way one keeps on murdering one aspect of a person to give birth to another." In remarks on the novel, which applied as well to her personal life, she said, "We kill one relationship and another takes its place. We lose one of ourselves and find another."

Some losses, however, were not replaceable. Aunt Maud, who had saved little money during her long career, suffered a stroke in 1958, and Margery, who had little taste for institutionalization of the elderly, chose to bring Maud to D'Arcy. Em, who had bounced from pillar to post over the past decade,* supported by an allowance from Margery, followed early in 1960. The elderly sisters were installed in the Forge with a live-in nurse. Em, in her eighties, and Maud, not many years younger, were a challenge for Margery, Joyce, and the nurse. Though Margery described her mother and aunt as "naughty" and often found herself mediating their constant disputes, she enjoyed their vitality and managed to make some kind of peace with her mother before Em's death in June 1960.

Aunt Grace soon took Em's place, and at eighty-nine, she too was still lively, if no longer clear in memory. In a nonfiction book titled *The Relay* (never published), written after Grace and Maud had died, Margery recorded these caretaking days as she pondered the situation of the aged

---

* After a period of disorientation following Herbert's death, Em settled down as housekeeper and companion to the Reverend Marcus Lawrence on Foulness Island, near the mouth of the Thames. Pip had refused to take Em in, and after Margery met Lawrence (who disliked her intensely), she decided to let matters stand. Em remained happily in the rector's employ until 1950.

and their families. And she began thinking about her own old age, and Pip's.

Pip had helped her a great deal with her 1959 novel, *The China Governess,* the two working together almost in the same spirit that had guided *The Crime at Black Dudley* in the early days of their marriage. Margery's next book, begun in 1963, was also to return to an old interest, the extrasensory abilities that had once guided her to use the "glass" and uncover the story of *Blackerchief Dick.* But *The Mind Readers*—her last completed novel—was no story of ghosts and séances. *The Mind Readers* was a novel for the 1960s—the first, she said, of the new Allingham Adult Adventures concerned with the kind of contemporary ideas and action that had impressed her in John le Carré's novels of Cold War espionage, *The Spy Who Came in from the Cold* and *The Looking-Glass War.*

During the writing of *The Mind Readers* and after, Margery rarely left Tolleshunt D'Arcy. She and Pip had converted the old stables into a large and comfortable studio where they often worked together. Here she made plans for undertaking a biography of Dr. Salter and started her next novel, *A Cargo of Eagles.*

She had been tired and ill for some time, and her huge weight now made simple mobility difficult. When she came down with a viral infection early in 1966, the doctor who examined her found a large mass in her breast and called in Ronnie Reid. Reid immediately ordered radiation treatments and planned to do a biopsy. After the first treatment, Margery took to her bed and summoned her longtime secretary, Gloria Greci, to take dictation.

The tale Margery spun for Gloria was a strange and sometimes funny account of Margery herself as the Queen Beetle—a "large, white slug-like" insect who lies on her back, attended by her "swarm," and prepares herself for some mysterious change. The Queen Beetle reminisces and also attempts to explain the physical process of her metamorphosis, of her body coming apart and its pieces slipping away. It was, in a pathetic way, the type of story that the child Margery might have imagined for the fairies in the gardens of the Old Rectory in Layer Breton some sixty years earlier.

As Margery became increasingly depressed, a doctor from Severalls Hospital in Colchester was called in. Severalls specialized in treating mental patients, and psychiatrist Russell Barton, medical superintendent of the facility, examined Margery. Concluding that the breast mass was malignant and that Margery was in a state of denial about her illness, he had her legally committed to the hospital on his authority. Joyce approved of the action, and Pip basically stepped aside, incapable of accepting the seriousness of his wife's condition. (In Margery's Queen

Beetle story, the Queen's husband wants the metamorphosis to be stopped so that she will not die.)

Margery was furious at being taken to the local "loony-bin." She protested, begged to be released, and scribbled a plaintive plea to Pip on the back of a prescription: "Oh Tonker save poor Marge—Get Edward and if necessary Camps on to this and try try try again. I am ill, not at all balmy—all my love Marge."★

But gradually she accepted Dr. Barton's care, and by the end of February her emotional state was improving. In their sessions, the doctor seems to have broken down some of her inhibition, and she even spoke to him of her "cuckoo times." He came to the conclusion that, far from being insane (as she often feared), she was manic-depressive—her capricious and frightening mood swings caused by bipolar disorder. She continued radiation treatments at the hospital and by mid-March was able to return home, where Dr. Barton continued to see her. She wrote to friends in a hopeful mood, but also made final revisions to her will and had Joyce destroy a number of her papers, including Pip's love letters from their courtship days.

In June she began having panic attacks brought on by her fear of suffocation. Not long after her last social engagement, she suffered a stroke and was taken back to Severalls. X-rays revealed the cancer had spread to her heart and brain. Pip did not go to the hospital, though Joyce did and promised to come back with the priest Margery requested. There was not enough time. The next morning, Margery's heart stopped as she was being taken to an X-ray room.

Her last words to Pip, as she had been taken from D'Arcy House to the ambulance, were, "Forty years, forty years, not so bad, eh?"

She was buried in the churchyard at Tolleshunt D'Arcy. Several weeks later a community fete benefiting the local church school was held in her gardens, just as she had planned.

Pip, shattered by her death, took up the completion of her final novel, *Cargo of Eagles,* and then wrote two Campion mysteries of his own. He died of lung cancer in 1969.

Margery Allingham's life story, from her own words and the studies of others, was not a tragedy, but it was marked by extended and possibly preventable sadness. One cannot help asking what might have been her fate had those closest to her been more caring about her and less de-

---

★ "Tonker" had become Margery's favored nickname for Pip. Edward Terrell, Q.C., a friend and neighbor since the 1930s, was a barrister whom she frequently consulted on business matters. Dr. Francis Camps was the famed pathologist who had assisted her with *Hide My Eyes* and other novels.

pendent on her. What if Margery herself, so keen an observer of others, had trained a more objective eye on her own patterns of illness and volatile behavior? What if someone had paid closer attention to the warnings that are so obvious in hindsight—the persistent emotional escalations and depressions, the extreme fatigue and overwork of the 1930s, the instinct to sequester herself in the country and hide behind the cheerful facade of the jolly fat woman who, in her later life, reminded friends of someone from a Toulouse-Lautrec painting?

Margery was always protective of her husband, allowing him an extended adolescence well past the traditional growing-up point. What was also true is that the people who depended on Margery were just as protective of her. Few, it seems, dared to rock the gravy boat and give Margery bad news or straight talk. Those who tried were rejected cruelly, as Cooee Orr and Russell Meiggs had been, and did not persist. Not everyone thought Margery to be charming and cooperative (her professional image); Dwye Evans, a director and later chairman of Heinemann, found her to be difficult to work with, thin-skinned and conceited, and his refusal to kowtow eventually led Margery to leave her longtime publisher in 1950. But it was not until she was too weak to resist, in the months before her death, that someone—Dr. Russell Barton—simply took control and made her do what was in her own best interest.

What is remarkable is how much of herself she poured into her mysteries. Her revelations went beyond the obvious portraits of Minnie and Tonker in *The Beckoning Lady* and Russell Meiggs in *Traitor's Purse*. From the late 1930s, she used her books to express and explore dark questions and fears that haunted her—the meaning of Good and Evil, the nature of justice, the proper roles of women and men in a changing world, marital love in its many aspects, loyalty versus treachery, sanity versus insanity.

Though usually linked with Christie, Sayers, and Marsh, Margery always gave reviewers and critics a hard time. Her best books never quite fit the Golden Age mold. Her descriptive ability, her focus on character, and her interest in heavy themes meant that she could not be judged by the simple criteria of the Golden Age puzzle. She wanted to be a novelist who wrote within the mystery framework; too many critics faulted her for being a mystery writer who tried too hard to be a serious novelist. In part because of this critical ambivalence, Margery remains the most underrated of the Golden Age greats. Perhaps it is time for reevaluation.

In a 1998 interview, Minette Walters, one of today's best writers of crime fiction, bemoaned the fact that Allingham has not attained the recognition she deserves. "I think Margery Allingham was a brilliant writer." Walters said. "She was really remarkable, because her stories had a much more violent streak than Christie's or Marsh's."

Readers who haven't yet encountered the Campion novels are likely to be surprised by the quality of that violence. Under the graceful writing (too graceful and precious for some); the characterizations of the social elite and social climbers, the shopkeepers and petty "crims" and country rubes; the clever and nostalgic dialog; the development of Campion from silly ass to model moral man . . . under the Golden Age patina, there is a rich lode of psychological violence that is essentially modern.

In the mid-1920s, Margery wrote in *The White Cottage Mystery*: "The whole of our civilization is one network of little intrigues, some harmless, others serious, all going on in the dark just under the surface." A decade later, she wrote privately to Russell Meiggs, "I am of that type of woman who is three parts uncivilized (and who therefore feels everything intensely) and one part pure cold analyst who feels nothing at all and notes everything with intense interest." It was the rational analyst, trained to professional standards, who could stand apart from other people's lives and see clearly the "network of little intrigues" that lead to all manner of misunderstandings, miseries, and murders. But the "uncivilized" woman couldn't perform this task for herself. Plagued by her own illnesses, rioting emotions, and needs, and by the myopic selfishness of those closest to her, she was simply incapable of rewriting her own life plot.

BIBLIOGRAPHY

MARGERY ALLINGHAM
1904–1966
English (born: London)

"Mr. Campion . . . had cultivated the gentle art of unobtrusiveness until even his worst enemies were apt to overlook him until it was too late. He was known to a great many people but few were absolutely certain about what it was he actually did with his life."
—*Hide My Eyes*

Margery Allingham introduced her aristocratic detective, Albert Campion, as a secondary character and comic relief in *The Crime at Black Dudley*. While it is interesting to follow Campion's development from start to finish, readers can easily avoid *The Crime at Black Dudley, Mystery Mile,* and *Look to the Lady,* which are basically period thrillers and portray Campion at his silliest. *Sweet Danger* is also of the thriller school but more sophisticated and a good place to start the Campion saga. After Margery's adolescent adventure *Blackerchief Dick,* her British publisher was Jarrods, followed by Heinemann, then Chatto and Windus. In the United States, she was published by Doubleday until 1962, then by Morrow. Her three romantic mysteries under the pen name Maxwell March were published by William Collins. Unless noted, dates are for first publication in Britain. Alternate titles are given. US=United States. GB=Great Britain.

Mystery Novels

1928   *The White Cottage Mystery*

1929   *The Crime at Black Dudley*/US: *The Black Dudley Murder* (Campion)

1930   *Mystery Mile* (Campion)

1931   *Look to the Lady*/US: *The Gyrth Chalice Mystery* (Campion)

1931   *Police at the Funeral* (Campion)

1933   *Sweet Danger*/US: *Kingdom of Death* (reissued in the US in 1961 as *The Fear Sign*) (Campion)

1934   *Death of a Ghost* (Campion)

1936   *Flowers for the Judge* (abridged and reissued in the US in 1949 as *Legacy in Blood*) (Campion)

1937   *The Case of the Late Pig* (Campion)

1937   *Dancers in Mourning* (reissued in the US in 1943 as *Who Killed Chloe?*) (Campion)

1938   *The Fashion in Shrouds* (Campion)

1940   *Black Plumes*

1941   *Traitor's Purse* (reissued in the US in 1942 as *The Sabotage Murder Mystery*) (Campion)

1945   *Coroner's Pidgin*/US: *Pearls before Swine* (Campion)

1948   *More Work for the Undertaker* (Campion)

1952   *The Tiger in the Smoke* (Campion)

1955   *The Beckoning Lady*/US: *The Estate of the Beckoning Lady* (Campion)

1958   *Hide My Eyes*/US: *Tether's End* (reissued in the US in 1961 as *Ten Were Missing*) (Campion)

1962   US: *The China Governess* (Campion)

1965   *The Mind Readers* (Campion)

1968   *Cargo of Eagles* (completed by Philip Youngman Carter after Margery's death) (Campion)

Maxwell March Novels
1933   *Other Man's Danger*/US: *The Man of Dangerous Secrets*
1935   *Rogue's Holiday*
1936   *The Shadow in the House*

Short Story and Novella Collections
1937   US only: *Mr. Campion: Criminologist*
1939   *Mr. Campion and Others*
1946   *Wanted: Someone Innocent*
1947   *The Case Book of Mr. Campion*
1949   US: *Deadly Duo*/GB: *Take Two at Bedtime* (two novellas: *Wanted: Someone Innocent* and *Last Act*)
1954   *No Lost Love* (two novellas: *The Patient at Peacocks Hall* and *Safer than Love*)
1969   *The Allingham Case-book*
1972   *The Allingham Minibus*
1989   *The Return of Mr. Campion*

Other Writings
1923   *Blackerchief Dick: A Tale of Mersea Island* (juvenile adventure)
1941   *The Oaken Heart* (nonfiction published by Michael Joseph in GB and Doubleday in US)
1943   *Dance of the Years*/US: *The Galantrys* (novel published by Michael Joseph in GB and Little, Brown in US)

Campion Novels by Philip Youngman Carter
1969   *Mr. Campion's Farthing*
1970   *Mr. Campion's Falcon*

Plays   **Dates are for first performance and/or publication.**
1922   *Dido and Aeneas* (verse play, unpublished)
1924   *Water in a Sieve* (one-act play, published 1925)
1943   *Man at the Window* (BBC radio)
1947   *Room to Let* (BBC radio)

Film and Video Adaptations
In 1956, Rank produced *Tiger in the Smoke* without Campion. Adapted by Anthony Pelissier and directed by Roy Baker, this black-and-white film features a British cast and is described by Leslie Halliwell as "odd little melodrama with a complex plot and a different, Graham Greene–like atmosphere." Negotiations to film *Hide My Eyes* failed, thankfully. The film company wanted to turn the dark novel into a musical featuring pop singer Cliff Richard.

The BBC produced full-length adaptations of a number of the Campion mysteries in the late 1980s. Broadcast on American public television in 1989–1991, these nostalgia-laden versions included *Look to the Lady, Death of a Ghost, Police at the Funeral, The Case of the Late Pig, Flowers for the Judge, Dancers in Mourning, Mystery Mile,* and *Sweet Danger.*

THE CAMPION FILE

NAME: Rudolph K_____, but goes by Albert Campion (Bertie)

ALIASES: Too many to count but has been known as "Mornington Dodd," the "Honourable Tootles Ash," "Christopher Twelvetrees," "Eva Booth," etc.

BORN: 1900

OCCUPATION: In his early days, Campion, as "a sort of Universal Aunt," would take on "almost anything within reason—for a reasonable sum, but nothing sordid or vulgar. . . ." Later he's more selective in his cases and professional in his methods. Scotland Yard regards him as "an Expert, a chap we call in like a pathologist."

ADDRESS: 17A Bottle Street, Piccadilly, a cul-de-sac beside a police station and behind Rodriguez's restaurant.

DESCRIPTION: Campion is introduced as a "fresh-faced young man with tow-coloured hair and . . . foolish, pale-blue eyes beneath tortoiseshell-rimmed spectacles"; tall and very thin with "slightly receding chin and mouth so unnecessarily full of teeth." Hair turns white-blond with sun, and chin and protruding teeth become less noticeable as he ages; "falsetto" voice; deceptively "vacant" or "owlish" expression.

DISTINGUISHING CHARACTERISTICS: Polished liar who might have been a proficient criminal had he not been a gentleman. Adept at parlor magic and picking locks. Rarely carries a gun, other than a water pistol. Not an early riser. Dresses well but conservatively; suits by Jamieson and Fellowes ("so mercifully uninspired"). Horn-rimmed spectacles hide penetrating intellect. Drives a Lagonda, though he borrows his brother's Bentley on occasion. Drinks and smokes moderately.

WIFE: Lady Amanda Fitton of the heart-shaped face, honey-colored eyes, and red hair; a talented engineer and aeronautical designer.

CHILDREN: The precocious Rupert, born circa 1944

FAMILY: Campion is on the outs with his clan, one of the oldest and lordliest in the land. The rift isn't detailed, but he's apparently been disinherited numerous times. Younger sister Valentine (Val) Ferris also gets the heave-ho when she marries down. Big brother Herbert is heir to the family title and inheritor of Father's red hair. Mother

Emily is an aristocratic stiff: "She's living in the past, somewhere just before the Napoleonic Wars." Supportive grandmother Emily, the dowager duchess, is Campion's "partner in crime." Various uncles: the bishop of Devizes, Canon Avril, Uncles Henry and Edwin "from the outpost of empire."

FACTOTUM: Ex-con Magersfontein Lugg ("bull pup and *femme-de-chambre* combined"), who hooks Campion up with assorted helpful criminal types such as Thos. T. Knapp, skilled phone tapper.

EDUCATION: the best private schools (St. Agatha's and the Totham School); Cambridge

MILITARY SERVICE: In World War Two, serves "three years . . . at large on two warring continents employed on a mission . . . so secret that he had never found out quite what it was." Cold War missions for military intelligence.

INCOME: Campion apparently earns his own way. In *The Crime at Black Dudley,* he doesn't own a car, seemingly because he can't afford one.

FRIENDS AND COLLEAGUES: Margery Allingham kept secondary and even minor characters going through the body of her novels, so names pop up with frequency. Campion knows everyone sooner or later. Important connections at Scotland Yard including Detective Inspector Deadwood; Superintendent Stanislaus Oates (father of Campion's first godson); Superintendent Yeo; Inspector Charles Luke; and Sir Leo Pursuivant, chief constable of Kepesake. Scores of society and business types such as Lady Papendeik of the fashion house; Gilbert Whippet, chairman of the Mutual Ordered Life Endowment Insurance Company ("the Mole"); and Alan Dell of Alandel airplanes. Old pals: Giles and Biddy Paget of Mystery Mile; Guffy Randall, who marries Campion's sister-in-law; and Tonker and Minnie Cassands. Friends acquired during cases include William Farraday and Poppy Bellew (Pursuivant), and Harriet Huntingforest, "Aunt Hatt," of the Mill house, Pontisbright.

"IT'S CRACKERS TO SLIP A ROZZER THE DROPSY IN SNIDE."

(rough translation: It's crazy to bribe a cop with counterfeit money.)

—Magersfontein Lugg in *The Fashion in Shrouds*

Margery Allingham had an ear for dialog, dialects, and popular slang. Her main characters all have their distinctive speech patterns—Campion is given to using advertising slogans and non sequiturs in his early days but becomes increasingly reticent; Lady Amanda is charmingly direct; sister Val is languid and introspective. And Lugg speaks straight from the streets and his Cockney heart. In the Campion novels of the 1920s and 1930s, the patois can be rough going for modern readers, particularly Americans. The following brief lexicon may help:

barmy (from *barm* or yeast, the ingredient that gives beer its frothy head) exceedingly eccentric, light in the head, crazy (akin to *balmy* or somewhat mad)

blighter a contemptible man

bobbish well in health and good in spirits

bung-ho "au revoir," "be seeing you"

bunk leave hastily (". . . I nearly cut the whole job right out and bunked back to town."—*The Crime at Black Dudley*)

beak a magistrate (". . . if you 'ad to set in public court and 'ear a beak talkin' to 'im after the sentence . . ."—*The Fashion in Shrouds*). A *beaksman* is a constable, and to be *beaked* is to be hauled into court.

bokel a barmy yokel (a word coined by Margery and Pip Carter to denote eccentric rustic types)

to crack up to heap with praise

cove a fellow, a chap

dekko a look or glance, as in "take a dekko at those footprints."

knock up to exhaust or tire out

life preserver a stick or bludgeon heavily loaded on one end, usually used as a weapon of self-defense

moke a donkey

mutt a stupid person or a fool (from mutton, i.e., sheep)

natty neat or dainty

to nark to watch over or look after, even to spy on (A *nark* can be a police informer or a plain old spoilsport)

pigeon business, task, duty

to pip to beat or defeat (". . . those two losses to the criminal world, George Willsmore, and 'Anry, his brother—who pips him easily in the matter of duplicity, by the way."—*Mystery Mile*)

a parroty time a period of quarreling or verbal strife

quod prison

nob a person of high rank or great wealth, a VIP

to pink to detect or catch in the act. ("They pinked us the first evening you got down. . . ."—*Mystery Mile*)

spiv a worthless sort of chap, possibly a black-marketeer

sweep a scamp or disreputable person ("I'm afraid that Georgia woman's a sweep."—*The Fashion in Shrouds*)

stick a dull, awkward person, an incompetent or stupid soul

to tonk to strike or deliver a blow (from cricket jargon). A tonk is a hit or blow.

BREAD, CAKE, AND LOVE

The most consistent mystery in Margery Allingham's Campion novels is not a crime but the nature of men and women in love and in marriage. Like many of her generation, Margery mistrusted the emotional and physical power of romance. Fairly early on she came to believe that men and women are complementary, two halves of a single whole. "There is only one human entity and that is a man and a woman. The man is the silhouette, the woman is the detail," explains the wise old "Tante Marthe," Lady Papendeik, in *The Fashion in Shrouds.*

For a marriage to work, Margery believed, the partners had to recognize and support one another's true natures and callings. *The Fashion in Shrouds*—written in 1937–1938 and mistakenly read as antifeminist—is the novel that delves most deeply into this subject, particularly as it pertains to career women. Margery intended *Fashion* to be a novel of manners constructed around the detection format. The book is focused on two women: Georgia Wells, a famous and beautiful stage actress who lives in the moment, and Val Ferris, a famous fashion designer (and Campion's sister) who, having made one disastrous choice in the past, is trying for a better. Both women fall in love with the same man, and who gets him in the end is not so important as what each woman is willing to do for him.

Georgia, for all her earthy vulgarity, is a genuine artist. Val, for all her talent, is the more conventional and feminine. Georgia gives up nothing, for she considers herself a prize to be won. Val is willing to give up her success when the sacrifice is asked. A third woman, young Amanda Fitton, sees things with unnerving clarity, neatly dividing love into two categories: "cake love," or passion and lust, and "the bread-and-butter kind." All three women are intelligent, like their creator, and clearly represent conflicts that Margery—the committed artist and the feminine woman—struggled with.

At the time she was writing *Fashion,* Margery may have been debating cake versus bread and butter for herself. She was infatuated with an Oxford scholar named Russell Meiggs but deeply (some would say stupidly) loyal to her husband, Pip Carter. Margery opted for bread and butter and chose the same path for Amanda and Albert Campion.

Part
THREE

MODERN MOTIVES:
MYSTERIES OF THE MURDEROUS MIND

"Surely, an increasingly H. G. Wellsian universe will not fail to provide the crime novel with fresh and as yet unsuspected devices and situations." —Howard Haycraft in *Murder for Pleasure,* 1941

World War Two, like World War One, altered society and, with it, the novel of crime and detection. At times during the last half of the twentieth century, it appeared as if the traditional detective mystery might disappear altogether—killed off by sheer quaintness—as changes in society and politics effected changes in what people wanted to read.

In the immediate aftermath of the Second World War, the world found itself engaged in a less comprehensible, but even more dangerous, conflict—the Cold War, which pitted the industrialized democracies of the West against the Communist Soviet Union and its satellite states. The last acts of World War Two—the bombings of Hiroshima and Nagasaki—inaugurated the Atomic Age and the very real possibility of worldwide nuclear destruction. The Cold War and the Atomic Age combined to create an environment of fear and alienation that was pandemic. Postwar readers still needed and wanted escape, but the Golden Age British puzzle mystery and the American hard-boiled style seemed hardly relevant in a world that could literally blow itself sky-high.

The soldiers fighting the Cold War were diplomats, scientists, spies. And spies, those shadow sleuths behind the enemy's lines, offered whole new avenues of tactics and technologies for writers to explore. Lean, mean, and not burdened by the nitpicking ethics of the prewar detective, spies could do the most exciting and underhanded things, all in the name of God and country. When it came down to a choice between Sherlock Holmes and Hercule Poirot or Ian Fleming's licensed-to-kill superspy James Bond, how could the old fogies hope to compete?

A new generation of readers eagerly turned to novels of espionage—

the comic book macho romances of Fleming; Len Deighton's nameless hero in *The Ipcress File*; then the darkly cynical and depressing underworld of John le Carré (pseudonym of David Cornwell). In *The Spy Who Came in from the Cold* (1963), followed by *The Looking Glass War,* le Carré offered the kind of gritty realism that even the hard-boiled writers of the 1930s and 1940s never dreamed of. The kick of the popular spy story was that the reader could vicariously drop behind the lines of the Cold War, forget the traditional soldierly rules of conduct, deal with a godless enemy and a messy situation (in John Gardner's words, "a maze, a labyrinth, an unravelling, an equation of tension"), and, in the end, save Western Civilization for another day. Until the fall of the Soviet Union in the late 1980s, the spy novel and its offshoot, the technothriller (à la Tom Clancy), along with the films and television programs generated by the genre, provided cathartic adventure for the age of Mutually Assured Destruction.

Another genre emerged in the 1950s to challenge the mystery novel. After the atomic bomb, everyone seemed to accept the ascendance of science and its capacity to either save or annihilate humanity. Science fiction had been around for a long time, though taken none too seriously except when used by a writer of larger intentions as a framework for ideas (Aldous Huxley's *Brave New World,* for example, and George Orwell's *1984*). But the years following World War Two brought a boom in stories that fantasized on the threats and the promises of the sciences. A legion of good-to-very-good writers—Robert A. Heinlein, Arthur C. Clarke, Ray Bradbury, J. G. Ballard, Ursula K. Le Guin among them—turned to the form, producing works that were escapist, particularly in their futuristic visions, but also challenging in concept. By the 1960s, fantasy joined the mix; works such as J. R. R. Tolkein's *Lord of the Rings* trilogy and C. S. Lewis's *The Chronicles of Narnia*—swept on a wave of youthful utopianism (and not a few hallucinogens)—entered the mainstream of adult reading. A novelist like Kurt Vonnegut could easily straddle the lines between science fiction, fantasy, and straight writing and win readers as well as critical attention.

There were other influences working against the old-style detectives in fiction. In the last days of the war, the truth about Hitler's "final solution" had been laid bare, and the Nuremberg Trials revealed the human capacity for evil in a way that no mystery writer had ever contemplated. Golden Age writers often dealt with the basic conflict between Good and Evil but framed it as a contest between a great detective and a great villain that momentarily disrupted the general tranquility. But what was simple domestic murder compared to the Nazis' carefully and coldly plotted slaughter of millions? How could the desire to pop off dear Auntie for the inheritance hold interest in a world gone crazy? Readers were no longer satisfied with the usual cut-and-dried motives for criminal actions; they wanted to delve into the pits of the human psyche and explore the muck that fertilized depravity. Through the popularized theories of Sigmund Freud and his followers, interest in normal and abnormal behavior had turned inward. By the 1950s, words like *ego* and *id, neurosis* and *complex,* had become as commonplace as the canapés at swank cocktail parties and beer nuts down at the local bar. The mysteries of human psychology just did not fit the neat, fair rules of Golden Age mystery writing or the hard-boiled good-guy-versus-bad-guys mythology.

Police methods changed, and the day of the amateur detective or even private investigators of the Poirot school were over. Science and academic psychology had made their way into the squad room, and the new detective, to be believable, had to be educated at minimum in the arcana of forensics and criminal behavior. He or she would never, as had happened in Margery Allingham's *The Fashion in Shrouds,* allow a body to be removed to a soft bed before the police were called in. Television and movies familiarized the public with police methods, so it was no longer acceptable to find the corpse in Chapter 1, then jump to the inquest in Chapter 2.

Television arrived as a mass medium. Everyone was so worried that TV—cheap, immediate, and entertaining—would kill Hollywood that few noticed its real victims. Movies survived, but television virtually eliminated certain forms of escapist reading, particularly in the United States. The magazine market for short stories—an important outlet for mystery writers, especially newcomers struggling for an audience—all but dried up in the 1950s and 1960s. The old-fashioned knockabout adventure tale and the down-and-dirty detective story could be done far more excitingly on *Dragnet* or *Z Cars* and enjoyed with so little effort.

Finally, with younger writers lacking the training grounds of magazine short stories and serials and increasingly attracted to visual rather than written media, where was the next generation of crime and detective novelists to come from? Many of the Golden Age greats and a few hard-boilers were still hard at work—Christie, Creasey, Marsh, Ross Macdonald, etc.—some thriving on their reputations, others valiantly adapting to modern times. With the market for escapist novels being stretched to include the new genres and established writers still hanging on to their slots in the mystery section, the number of openings for new writers of detection shrank. New voices could barely be heard above old established ones. It is understandable that many in publishing, as well as a number of influential critics like Julian Symons, were ready to write off the detective story as a lost cause.

But the eulogies were premature. The 1950s and 1960s proved to be difficult but transitional. New writers, with new approaches, came forward on both sides of the Atlantic and in locations farther-flung than the dominant United States and Great Britain. By the time the 1970s arrived, memories of the Second World War were fading, and the Cold War had settled down to a kind of permanent irritation rather than an imminent threat of global annihilation. New dangers were in the headlines and on the nightly news: urban crime, youthful alienation that led to violence, drug use and trafficking on a massive scale, political assassinations, seemingly irreconcilable racial and cultural divisions, official corruption so extreme that an American president was forced to resign. If the whole world was not insane, the Boston Strangler, Charles Manson, and the University of Texas Tower massacre sent a message that one's next-door neighbor very well might be. As people began to take crime personally again, the old formula of rational detection leading to official justice looked a lot more attractive. The day of Hercule Poirot and Sam Spade had passed, but readers and writers gravitated once again to standards of detection and resolution at least as old as Sherlock Holmes. The mystery novel was back, adapted to include new forms and new faces for a new age:

- The police procedural now offers closely observed studies of official investigations by realistically portrayed policemen and policewomen. Police and other agents of the law are presented in their official and their private lives. They can be inept, corrupt, morally conflicted, arrogant, stupid, and just plain brutish, and in the hands of good writers, they become fascinating.

  Most students of the modern police procedural credit Lawrence Treat's *V as in Victim* (1945) as the first modern procedural and Hillary Waugh's *Last Seen Wearing . . .* (1952) as the first to arouse real public interest in the States. In Britain, veteran John Creasey (writing as J. J. Marric) started the trend with his Inspector Gideon series, beginning in 1955.

  The new procedural marked major shifts away from Golden Age and hard-boiled detection. Since real policemen work in teams, investigation is the province of at least two main protagonists and sometimes a full ensemble. The lone wolf, such as Ngaio Marsh's Roderick Alleyn or Michael Innes's Sir John Appleby, would be intolerable in any reality-based precinct station today. Seconds-in-command have been transformed from Watsonish foils into full-fledged partners. The crime scene team, medical examiners, lab scientists (characters who usually show up briefly, if at all, in a Golden Age novel, do their unexplained work, then vanish)—are now intimately involved in the investigation. And since real police work doesn't happen in a vacuum, procedurals normally include several active cases that may but normally don't link together by the end of the book. Although the central case is solved, others are often left dangling and may be picked up in subsequent novels.

The degree of realism demanded by the procedural requires intensive research by its writers, and the best—Ed McBain (pen name of Evan Hunter, creator of the 87th Precinct series), Elizabeth Linington (also known as Dell Shannon, Lesley Egan, and others), Elmore Leonard, Colin Wilcox, Lawrence Sanders, Reginald Hill (creator of the Dalziel and Pascoe series), Gwendoline Butler (author of the John Coffin series and under the pen name Jennie Melville, of the Charmian Daniels books)—immerse their readers in the sights, sounds, and smells of the homicide, vice, and narcotics divisions of their police forces. Real-life law enforcers such as Joseph Wambaugh (formerly of the Los Angeles Police Department), Dorothy Uhnak (retired New York transit cop and detective), and Janwillem van de Wetering (formerly of the Amsterdam Municipal Police) began to write popular crime novels from the viewpoint of seasoned professionals.

Opening the doors of the police department also broadened the range of characters available to the writer. Chester Himes created his Harlem cops Coffin Ed Johnson and Grave Digger Jones and paved the way for other African-American crime writers including Ed Lacy and Walter Mosley. Hispanic cops, Native American cops, Jewish cops, gay and lesbian cops—from the 1960s on, believable police characters have come in every size, color, and preference.

- The rational detective has been transformed from superman or superwoman to everyday Joe and Jane. Many work inside the police force, but private investigators have not disappeared, and in the 1970s, female professionals became believable as protagonists. In the United States, women writers—beginning in 1977 with Marcia Muller's *Edwin of the Iron Shoes* and followed in 1982 by Sara Paretsky's *Indemnity Only* and Sue Grafton's *"A" Is for Alibi*—make profitable use of the female private investigator. In England, P. D. James introduced her Cordelia Gray in *An Unsuitable Job for a Woman* in 1972; Liza Cody debuted Anna Lee of the Brierly Security Agency in 1980; and Val McDermid's highly regarded Kate Brannigan series was launched with *Dead Beat* in 1992.

The amateur detective has also survived in fine form, though he or she is more likely than a Miss Marple to possess specialized knowledge and investigate within the confines of a profession. In 1961, Mary Jane Latsis and Martha Henissart, writing as Emma Lathen, introduced a banker as their chief detective. Dick Francis's first racetrack novel appeared a year later.

In fact, by the 1980s, amateur investigators were moving through the new social order with the same ease as Lord Peter Wimsey still moves through the parlors of Mayfair. This trend has been a particular advantage to women writers who want to use women detectives in series books. Since even today the number of high-ranking female police is limited and the number of private eyes of either gender who might logically be involved in murder investigations is equally small, outsider status is still a viable career path to criminal investigation for women characters.

• Even felonious crime has its funny side, and sleuths need not be deadpan serious. Humor is not new to detective fiction, but since the 1950s, it has become a major element in the genre. Soft or snide, humor is now a perfectly acceptable format for mystery.

• Two other popular forms have supported and bred interest in crime and detection. First is the true crime story written novelistically. Edgar Allan Poe did it in his short story "The Mystery of Marie Rogêt," and other early writers, like Marie Belloc Lowndes, successfully fictionalized famous cases like the Jack the Ripper and Lizzie Borden murders. But the contemporary boom in true crime books can be dated almost exactly to Truman Capote's chilling, fact-based story of two thrill killers, *In Cold Blood*. Other straight novelists have turned to real crimes (notably Norman Mailer in *The Executioner's Song*). Perhaps the most unusual true crime story in the last decade is *My Dark Places* by James Ellroy (author of the acclaimed L.A. Quartet novels), which details the investigation of his own mother's murder.

The second popular trend is the legal novel, best exemplified in the United States by Scott Turow's *Presumed Innocent* and in England by John Mortimer's *Rumpole of the Bailey* series. The contemporary legal novel has become a virtual cottage industry for working lawyers with a yen for pen and ink.

• Most important, the psychological mystery has risen to dominance. As various critics have pointed out, virtually every serious crime novel written these days is psychological, whatever its form. But complex characterization that digs into the personal lives and private hells of detectives, perpetrators, and victims is now expected, especially in series novels.

Women of Mystery draws to its close with a look at the lives of three women who represent contemporary mystery writing at its finest. All three write psychological stories; all three write extremely well; all three exemplify what can be done with a mystery in the hands of intelligent thinkers who are determined to follow their own paths and their own visions. Each of these women has achieved significant commercial and critical success, but none is in the blockbuster league. Yet their influence on the genre is undeniable.

The first, Patricia Highsmith, was an American who never received the recognition she deserved in her own country. She was a true innovator who, from the late 1940s to her death in 1995, pushed the fictional limits of criminal pathology beyond all acceptable bounds. Her books can be difficult for readers looking for order and reassurance, for she relished turning comfortable moral expectations inside out. Yet if any writer merits the title of the mother of the modern psychological crime novel, it is she.

The second, the very English P. D. James, is a traditionalist. But within the confines of the conventional mystery story, she applies her elegant pen and sensitive mind to crafting plots and devising casts of characters that are modern, realistic, and perceptive. The situations she imagines are both tightly controlled and carefully observed, making her murders and her murderers all the more shocking and inexplicable.

The third, also British, is Ruth Rendell, who writes both traditional detective fiction and psychological novels. It is in the second category that, at her best, she has the power to stun and rivet her readers. No other established writer today has her ability to burrow inside the minds of ordinary people who, sometimes by design but most often by accident or by the convergence of the fates, violate society's most cherished rules and assumptions. Rendell may be unique in her ability to fascinate and terrify us by revealing the inner workings of characters who comprise the banal, anonymous bit players in most other fiction and in real life.

Women of Mystery concludes with eight examples of the myriad trends in contemporary mystery fiction. From the purely escapist suspense of Mary Higgins Clark and the light-as-a-soufflé cozies of Lilian Jackson Braun to the autopsy reports of Patricia Cornwell and the street savvy, kick-butt adventures of Sue Grafton—today's market serves up murder and mayhem in many flavors. The writers profiled here may not all be among the best, but they illustrate the rich variety in the genre today. Only one writer, Margaret Millar, began working in the Golden Age, but her still-potent mysteries—and those of many transitional writers who successfully broke with the past and helped create the present—should not be forgotten.

PATRICIA HIGHSMITH
MURDER WITH A TWIST

> *"It is skill that makes the reader care about characters. It must start with the writer caring. This is much of what that rather stuffy word 'integrity' is about."*★
>
> —*Plotting and Writing Suspense Fiction*

$\mathcal{B}$orn in Fort Worth, Texas, on January 19, 1921, Mary Patricia Highsmith was the only child of commercial artists Jay and Mary Coates Plangman, who separated before she was born. Mary Plangman later confessed to her daughter that she had drunk turpentine in a futile attempt to induce an abortion. Patricia did not meet her father until she was twelve years old.

As the unwelcome reminder of a failed relationship, Patricia spent a great deal of time alone during her early years, time that she filled with reading. Among the books that made an impression on her was a history of

Patricia Highsmith

World War One with black-and-white photographs of the trenches—an unusual choice for a young child. Much has been made of her interest in *The Human Mind* by Karl Menninger; her mother had a copy that Patricia purportedly read when she was eight. In a 1993 interview, the author herself discussed the influence of this particular book on her writing: "It was a book of case histories—kleptomaniacs, pyromaniacs,

---

★ Sources for quotations include Highsmith's published works and various interviews included in "References and Resources."

serial murderers—practically anything that could go wrong mentally. The very fact that it was real made it more interesting and more important than fairy tales. I saw that the people looked outwardly normal, and I realized there could be such people around me." One can make the case that a predilection for the macabre was encouraged by such early reading, and that the dark atmosphere that pervades her work had its genesis in the peculiar childhood reading of a lonely, unwanted child.

Following her parents' divorce, Patricia was cared for primarily by her grandmother, to whom she was quite close. Then, when Patricia was six, her mother married artist Stanley Highsmith, and the family moved to New York. About this marriage, she once said, "Basically everything goes back to my childhood. My parents' apartment was small, so I had to sleep in the living room. I would have had to be deaf not to have heard the cutting words with which my mother tormented my stepfather." Indeed, in a detailed criticism of Highsmith's work, Russell Harrison notes that Patricia rarely shows any relationship between a protagonist and his parents; her characters exist entirely on their own.

Patricia attended public schools in New York and got her "first push in the direction of writing" when she was nine. Assigned to write and recite a composition on the subject of "How I Spent My Summer Vacation" for English class, she recounted the visit made with her parents to the Endless Caverns. Describing how the caverns were discovered by boys who chased a rabbit into a crevice, she was amazed at her classmates' interest and attention: "This was my first experience of giving joy through a story. It was like a kind of magic, yet it could be done and had been done by me." Somewhat later, at age fifteen, she wrote her first piece for her own pleasure, "a fantastic epic poem."

Patricia went on to New York's prestigious Barnard College for women, graduating in 1942. As a college student, she was already writing near professional standard. One of her college short stories, "The Heroine," appeared in *Harper's Bazaar* in 1945; it was selected as one of the year's best magazine stories and reprinted in the O. Henry Awards anthology.

Following her graduation from Barnard, Patricia took a number of jobs, including one furnishing plots for comic books. She continued her writing and eventually achieved admission to Yaddo, a community of artists in Sarasota Springs, New York, in 1948. It was while at Yaddo that she wrote her first novel, *Strangers on a Train,* published by Harper and Row in 1950. The book did very well, but the film made from it really established Patricia Highsmith's reputation for offbeat psychological suspense. Adapted for the screen by Raymond Chandler and Czenzi Ormonde, *Strangers on a Train* was directed by Alfred Hitchcock and remains one of the classic suspense films of all time. Hitchcock—acting anonymously to save money—purchased the rights to Highsmith's novel in perpetuity for $6,800, a figure that still rankled many years later. But Patricia judged the performance delivered by Robert Walker, Sr., as Bruno—the demented mama's boy whose scheming included switching murders with a stranger—as outstanding; indeed, Walker's darkly disturbed characterization in this film promised great things for his future, but his career was cut short by his early death.

> *"There is no secret of success in writing except individuality, or call it personality."*

Her unique skill at drawing characters like the twisted, psychotic Bruno places the writings of Patricia Highsmith among the most important in the field of modern mystery and suspense fiction. Her work is dark and haunting; one searches in vain for happy endings. Often her novels begin with a protagonist who leads a predictable, if vaguely unsatisfying, life. This protagonist is ultimately driven, most often by his own shortcomings or mental illness, down a path that leads to his destruction, either literally or figuratively. Many of her novels follow the same pattern, in that the actual "plot" is the detailing of how the protagonist is ultimately undone by some major character flaw. For example, *The Blunderer* is just that—a man who is sabotaged by his own ineptitude. *This Sweet Sickness* is a study of obsession that leads to what is now called stalking behavior. *The Tremor of Forgery* is a story of the destructive effects of guilt. Thomas Ripley, the focus of five novels written between 1955 and 1991, is her only hero who is likable, and he is admittedly a psychopath. With one exception *(Edith's Diary),* all of Highsmith's suspense novels have male protagonists.

During an adulthood spent largely outside the United States—in Italy, England, France, and Switzerland—Patricia Highsmith produced twenty-four novels and several collections of short stories. She also published *Plotting and Writing Suspense Fiction* in 1966, yet she rigorously resisted being cast as only a writer of suspense novels. She always enjoyed far greater recognition in Europe—where she was regarded as a major novelist rather than a genre writer—than in her homeland, but her influence on crime and suspense writers has been international. Were it possible to credit any single writer with pushing the mystery novel to the dark side of criminal psychology, into the realm where all traditional moral precepts are twisted and turned on their heads, Patricia Highsmith would have to be the odds-on favorite.

About her approach to her craft, she said: "My book ideas begin with a situation of surprise or coincidence, some unusual circumstance, and around this, and forward and backward, I create a narrative with a beginning and an end. . . . I like to write three or four hours a day, taking a break frequently. . . . Under ideal conditions, I can write two thousand words a day. . . . I describe what is in the head of the protagonist, psychopath or not, because what is in his or her head must explain as well as advance the story. . . . For settings, I have to have seen the places I am using."

Strangely for a writer raised during the height of the Golden Age, Patricia owed virtually nothing to the great puzzle-makers or their detective heroes. The identity of the murderer is never a question in her work: "I am not an inventor of puzzles, nor do I like secrets." As for that which made her own work unique, she said, "There is no secret of success in writing except individuality, or call it personality. And since every person is different, it is only for the individual to express his difference from the next fellow. This is what I call the opening of the spirit. But it isn't mystic. It is merely a kind of freedom—freedom organized."

In his foreword to *Eleven,* a collection of Patricia's short stories, Graham Greene called her "the poet of apprehension rather than fear" who creates "a world without moral endings." With settings both abroad and in the United States, Highsmith always put her characters against a backdrop of oppressive sameness against which they play out the battle at hand, often a battle produced within their own minds. She was adept at creating an outwardly functioning character, and then peeling away the layers of the psyche to expose the tortured inner workings of the soul. In Greene's words, "Her characters are irrational, and they leap to life in their very lack of reason." Placing such characters within a suburban framework often lends a distinct twist to her tales.

She provided a blueprint for much of her work in *Plotting and Writing Suspense Fiction*: "The theme I have used over and over again in my novels is the relationship between two men, usually quite different in make-up, sometimes an obvious contrast in good and evil, sometimes merely ill-matched friends."

Her first novel, *Strangers on a Train,* remains the most widely recognized in the United States, probably because of the Hitchcock film. Guy Haines and Charles Bruno meet on a train and begin a conversation over drinks; Guy sees Bruno as "the stranger on the train who would listen, commiserate, and forget," but Bruno wants something more. The conversation ultimately turns to the problems each man faces: Guy's is a wife who will never consent to a divorce; Bruno's is his father. Bruno eventually comes up with the idea of "trading" murders and therefore committing the perfect crime: Bruno will rid Guy of his troublesome wife; Guy will return the favor by murdering Bruno's father. Since there is no way for anyone to know that the two men have ever met, each will avoid suspicion by establishing unbreakable alibis for the other's murder. The contrast between the two men is the foundation upon which the novel is laid: "All he despised, Guy thought, Bruno represented. All the things he would not want to be, Bruno was, or would become." Yet Highsmith proceeded to lock the two men in a *danse macabre* as their unholy alliance advances toward a predictably dark end.

Charles Bruno is a true psychopath; even Highsmith's physical description of him is repugnant. She gives the reader a glimpse at the extent of his madness in recounting Bruno's attitude toward Miriam Haines—"It was like killing a hot little rat, only she was a girl so that made it murder. . . . That night there had been the danger, the ache of his hands, the fear in case she made a sound, but the instant when he felt that life had left her, everything else had fallen away, and only the mysterious *fact* of the thing he did remained, the mystery and the miracle of stopping life." What a grotesque parallel to the mystery and miracle of the beginning of life.

Those who have seen the film of *Strangers on a Train* will find comparison with the novel intriguing; Hitchcock removed the menace from the character of Guy Haines and sanitized him into the classic hero. Hitchcock even changed Guy's occupation, from architect to professional tennis player; he is a "good guy" who literally wears white during a large portion of the film. Essential elements of the plot were altered for the film, yet the most striking change is the absence of the atmosphere of darkness that pervades the novel. No happy endings exist for Patricia Highsmith.

Her most widely recognized character is Thomas Ripley, introduced in 1955 in *The Talented Mr. Ripley.* Patricia said of her first Ripley novel, "No book was easier for me to write, and I often had the feeling Ripley was writing and I was merely typing." Although she seemingly abandoned her charming antihero for some fifteen years, Patricia returned to Ripley in 1970 with *Ripley Underground,* followed by *Ripley's Game* in 1974 and *The Boy Who Followed Ripley* in 1980. *The Boy Who Followed Ripley* is the fastest paced of the Highsmith novels, moving from one exciting scene to the next. The last of the series, *Ripley under Water,* appeared in 1991.

Tom Ripley is without question a psychopath;* indeed he is a refined version of Charles Bruno. Of her interest in psychopathic protagonists,

---

* Or is he? British mystery writer and critic Jessica Mann offered this alternative analysis in a 1982 essay in *Whodunit* (edited by H. R. F. Keating): "Commentators often describe [Tom Ripley] as a psychopath, that is, a person suffering from mental illness. But the fascination of Ripley both to his creator and to his readers, is that he is not mad, unless it is mad to be totally self centred [*sic*]. Tom Ripley's own good is his only good."

Highsmith wrote, "It depends on the writer's skill, whether he can have a frolic with the evil in his hero-psychopath. If he can, then the book is entertaining, and in that case there is no reason why the reader should have to 'like' the hero."

As the series begins, Tom Ripley is a young man living an unfocused life: "Something always turned up. That was Tom's philosophy." Always at a loss for funds, Tom aspires to luxury he cannot afford. He is an essentially likable character although he places his own interests first and has no hesitation to use friends and acquaintances to his own advantage. Down on his luck, he runs into the father of Dickie Greenleaf, an acquaintance who has moved to Italy and refused to return to the United States. At his wit's end, Mr. Greenleaf turns to this supposed friend for help. Greenleaf erroneously assumes that his son and Tom are very close, and Tom, always alert for an opportunity to convert any meeting to cash, does not correct this mistaken impression. Greenleaf easily talks Tom into traveling to Italy (at Mr. Greenleaf's expense, of course) to make one final effort to lure Dickie home, but Tom's arrival in Italy is an obviously unwelcome surprise, and Dickie makes no effort to conceal his irritation. Tom begins to imagine an ultimate solution to his problems; as in *Strangers on a Train,* the scene is set for murder. The remainder of this book, as well as the bulk of the four other Ripley novels, is devoted to Tom's efforts to outrun his past. Murders abound, and shocked but fascinated readers find themselves cheering for the amoral Mr. Ripley.

Patricia's creation of Thomas Ripley began with a chance encounter on a beach in Positano, Italy: she saw a solitary man walking along the beach at six one morning and found herself wondering what he had been doing there. It is in exploring the shadings of character that Highsmith excels, and one cannot but wonder if this skill was rooted in her early interest in Karl Menninger.

The Tremor of Forgery, considered by some critics her finest work, is a classic analysis of the effects of guilt. Howard Ingham is a young writer who travels to Tunisia, expecting to be joined by a friend from New York. As the weeks pass, Howard wonders what has become of his friend, and learns that the young man has committed suicide in Howard's apartment in the States. Howard is suddenly adrift in a world totally foreign to all he has known before. The title of the novel is the title that Ingham has chosen for the book he went to Tunisia to write: "Ingham had thought of a title for his book, *The Tremor of Forgery.* It was much better than two other ideas he had had. He had read somewhere, before he left America, that forgers' hands usually trembled very slightly at the beginning and end of their false signatures, sometimes so slightly the tremor could be seen only under a microscope."

Howard's new "home" is an uneasy place, with native workers who live in poverty and an atmosphere wherein petty crime flourishes. One night after retiring, Howard hears the unmistakable sounds of someone trying to enter his room. He hurls his typewriter at the intruder, and the tale of guilt begins: Howard believes that he has hit the intruder, and hit him hard. The man Abdullah is not seen again, yet his fate is unclear. Is Howard a murderer? The question is never answered. Howard's guilt and concern over what he may have done provide the psychological drama in this novel; as in much of Highsmith's work, the action is in the mind of the character himself.

(One of the most compelling aspects of Patricia Highsmith's work is that she didn't provide reassuring psychiatric, medical, or behavioral explanations for the actions of characters like Howard Ingham. Although she wrote primarily in the third person, she adopted the point of view of her protagonists so that bit by bit the reader learns what is in each character's mind. Highsmith does not judge the people she writes about; that is the discomforting chore left to the reader.)

In addition to the Ripley series and her other novels, Patricia published several volumes of short stories, many of which are among her best pieces. In her short stories, according to Graham Greene, "She is after the quick kill rather than the slow encirclement of the reader, and how admirably and with what field-craft she hunts us down." Two of her best stories are "The Terrapin" and "The Heroine"—her first published story—both of which appear in *Eleven*.

Several major themes pervade the body of Highsmith's work. Always accused of being a misogynist, she even wrote a book of short stories titled *Little Tales of Misogyny*. These stories are a litany of female "types" described in detailed vignettes. Early in her career, she responded to questions about her choice of male protagonists for her novels by saying, "I have a feeling which I suppose is quite unfounded that women are not so active as men, and not so daring. I realize that their activities need not be physical ones and that as motivating forces they may well be ahead of the men, but I tend to think of women as being pushed by people and circumstances instead of pushing, and more apt to say, 'I can't' than 'I will' or 'I'm going to.'"

There is no question that she viewed women not so much as the weaker sex, but more damningly as the more calculating and manipulative one. She described the wife of one character in *This Sweet Sickness* as "a female spider, every leg gripping a few web strands, keeping an eternal vigil for untoward vibrations and the threatening quiver of a breath of air. When Wes went to work, he went off with one of those strands attached to him, and he followed it back at night to the web and the spider." In the same novel, Patricia again took aim at the institution of marriage: "Women! Their prattling little minds and tongues, their so-far-and-no-furtherness, but please come so-far, and their tedious obsession with the idea that human bliss is based on getting a man and woman in the same house together!" (One can almost hear the fighting in the cramped New York apartment of Patricia's girlhood in a passage like this.)

Highsmith often portrayed women as the root of problems: Miriam in *Strangers on a Train* or the absent character Peggy, the wife whose suicide precipitates the events of *Those Who Walk Away*. The character Vic in *Deep Water* is a dedicated father and devoted husband driven to murder by his wife's cavalier infidelity. In each of these instances, the author's sympathy is clearly with the male.

Patricia Highsmith was an animal lover who confessed that she preferred the company of animals to that of people. During her later years in Locarno, Switzerland, she told an interviewer, "If I saw a kitten and a little human baby sitting on the curb starving, I would feed the kitten first." Animals figure prominently in much of her work, including a collection of short stories titled *The Animal-Lover's Book of Beastly Murder,* in which animals finally get the upper hand. Oddly enough, several of her stories in *Eleven* deal with snails; "The Snail-Watcher" and "The Quest for Blank Claverigni" are two delightfully twisted tales.

Thomas Ripley took part in no fewer than a dozen murders in the course of the five novels that bear his name; yet in the last book of the series, Highsmith describes his concern for two lobsters about to be served up for dinner by Mme Annette, his housekeeper and cook: "To Mme Annette, they [the lobsters] might be worthy of hardly more concern than haricots verts dumped into boiling water, Tom knew, but he imagined that he heard them screaming, wailing at least, as they were boiled to death. . . . There were people, Tom supposed, who could go about peeling potatoes while the lobsters got roasted to death—in how many seconds? Tom tried not to believe that Mme Annette was such a type." Later in the same book, Ripley listens with thinly concealed amusement as two of his enemies frantically try to escape death by drowning. His only discomfort comes from the presence of his colleague in crime: "Tom could feel Ed's tautness. Tom shifted his weight from left to right foot and back, as if weighing or debating something, yes or no. It was Ed's presence that made things different. The people in the pond were Tom's enemies. On his own, Tom wouldn't have hesitated, he would have walked away."

Another recurrent image in Highsmith's novels is water—used for concealment almost as often as a solution to problems. The plot of *Those Who Walk Away,* set in Venice, hinges on the pursuit of a young man by his father-in-law. The young man's wife has recently committed suicide by slashing her wrists in the bathtub; the gore diluted by water, she drowned in her own blood. Highsmith's description of Venice mirrors the image of life as fragile, transparent: "Coleman thought of the water that surrounded them, the deep water into which the whole city might one day slide." Drowning is a fairly neat way to commit murder, as in *Deep Water.* The protagonist is bound to a wife who continuously demeans him with her flagrant infidelity. Rather than take his anger and embarrassment out on his wife, Vic eradicates the problem by drowning one lover in a swimming pool and concealing the body of another in a watery quarry. In *Strangers on a Train,* the hero's problem is solved by an accidental drowning, and in *The Cry of the Owl,* one of the characters fakes his own drowning death.

Nowhere in Highsmith's work is the imagery of water found more frequently than in the Ripley series. Tom Ripley's parents had drowned when he was a young child, and Tom was left with a fear of water: "'Looks deep,' Tom said, for some reason suddenly thinking of drowning. He was afraid of deep water, hated swimming or trying to, and often thought that somehow his end might be watery" (*The Boy Who Followed Ripley).* In the case of Tom's first victim, water is both the instrument of murder and the means of hiding the crime. Tom murders by hitting his victim with an oar, and hides the body by sinking it. The image of the drowning is later repeated and romanticized.

Highsmith was ahead of her time in her presentation of characters of dubious sexuality. She vacillates between the old stereotypes—"Curiously enough for a ballet dancer, he wasn't queer" *(A Dog's Ransom)*—and depictions of homosexuality that show great sensitivity. A number of her male characters struggle with the issue of their own sexuality. In *Strangers on a Train,* Charles Bruno ponders his sexual identity: "Not only hadn't he ever fallen in love, but he didn't care too much about sleeping with women. He had never been able to stop thinking it was a silly business, that he was standing off somewhere and watching himself. Once, one terrible time, he had started giggling. Bruno squirmed. That was the most painful difference he felt separating him and Guy, that Guy could forget himself in women, had practically killed himself for Miriam."

Early in the Ripley series, Tom is presented with decidedly mixed feelings about his own sexuality. His attraction to Dickie Greenleaf has homosexual overtones; in fact, Tom even jokingly says to an acquaintance, "I can't make up my mind whether I like men or women, so I'm thinking of giving them both up." There is also a hint that Tom's father may have been slightly effeminate, even though his character is never directly referred to in the Ripley series.

Any analysis of Patricia Highsmith's work would be incomplete without mention of *The Price of Salt,* published under the pseudonym Claire Morgan by Coward McCann in 1952. The book was later retitled *Carol* and published under the author's real name.★ It is the story of a lesbian romance between a young girl and a married older woman— groundbreaking at the time of its publication. With great sensitivity, the novel presents a love story between two women without traditional ho- mosexual stereotyping. Interestingly, Highsmith's final book, *Small g: A Summer Idyll,* is also a novel of gay relationships. It was published after her death and has met with limited success.

> *". . . this is what makes writing a lively and exciting*
> *profession, the ever-present possibility of failure."*

Patricia Highsmith died of cancer at Locarno in 1995, and left her es- tate of several million dollars to Yaddo. Her life had come full circle, and in the end, she remembered the place that she credited with the nascence of her first novel.

A loner all her life, Highsmith is remembered as a reclusive soul who loved her pets and her solitude. She was a talented visual artist and con- tinued to sculpt after becoming a writer. She did not live the kind of life she wrote about so convincingly: "I am so law-abiding," she said, "I can tremble before a customs inspector with nothing contraband in my suit- cases." Even after she was an established author, she could be surpris- ingly short on self-confidence: once she completely rewrote a novel to satisfy her American publisher and after a second rejection put the man- uscript aside. Not until her British publisher requested to see the book—the award-winning *The Two Faces of January*—did it see the light of day. Faced with such rejection (and Highsmith experienced too much), she recommended, "A brief curse, perhaps, then tighten the belt a notch and on to something new. . . ."

She was honored with all the major mystery-writing awards during her career and recognized for her impeccable fusion of character and plot—"the most important crime novelist at present in practice" as critic Julian Symons said in 1985. In England and Europe, she found eager au- diences for her unique, some might say perverse, vision: the perception

---

★ There is still a good deal of speculation and rumor about Highsmith's personal pref- erence, but she has been welcomed into the gay and lesbian canon of writers, and her overtly lesbian *The Price of Salt/Carol* is often recognized as the first lesbian novel without a tragic or moralistic ending. More traditional feminists, however, have prob- lems with her seemingly antiwoman themes.

of the criminal as society's only truly free beings, and the moral dilemmas that amoral anarchists like Tom Ripley create for society and for the reader in particular. Her writing style, her themes, her characters, and her willingness to plumb the deepest, darkest reaches of their psyches have had enormous impact on writers to follow, both in and beyond the crime genre. Intentional or not, there are traces of Highsmith in the works of authors as diverse as Ruth Rendell/Barbara Vine and Thomas Harris. (What is a Hannibal Lecter, after all, but a Tom Ripley with a taste for flesh and blood?)

So why did she not earn her fair share of public and critical attention in her home country? She recognized the American publishing industry's determination to pigeonhole writers—in her case, with "the suspense label which America, American booksellers, and American reviewers are so fond of"—and the "handicap" this was to any writer who played outside the conventional rules. But it was not simply pigheaded marketers and book page editors who held her back. (Her books have always had a loyal, though relatively small, following in the States— readers unfairly dismissed as cultish.)

Patricia Highsmith was far ahead of her time in her understanding that evil exists in all people and that the potential for violence lives behind the most normal and often attractive facades. Her most successful novel in the United States was *Strangers on a Train,* in which the villain is both psychopathic and repulsive; in her more mature works, however, the central character is most likely to be an ordinary sort with whom it is frighteningly easy for the reader to identify. Patricia was too honest to provide pat and reassuring solutions to the crimes she dreamed up. In the Ripley books, the criminal not only escapes official justice; he suffers no remorse and no divine comeuppance. A Highsmith novel can be difficult, not because it is dense or especially erudite, but because it ranges so easily into the nightmare territory of willfulness, weakness, guilt, anger, fear, and what the law terms "depraved indifference." She takes us into the nightmare, and leaves us there to dream on.

The United States in the last half of the twentieth century was perhaps too smug and complacent to appreciate a writer who asked unsettling questions about evil and the meaning of guilt and innocence that are so difficult or impossible to answer. But a post–Oklahoma City, post–Columbine United States—willful, angry, fearful of its own children and neighbors—may just now be catching up to her.

—MCT

BIBLIOGRAPHY
⁂

PATRICIA HIGHSMITH
1921–1995
American (born: Fort Worth, Texas)

" 'There's no such thing as a perfect murder,' Tom said to Reeves.
'That's just a parlor game, trying to dream one up. Of course
you could say there are a lot of unsolved murders. That's differ-
ent.'"
                                                    —*Ripley's Game*

Highsmith's novels are not for every taste, but as *The Sunday Times* of London has put it, "In the geography of crime fiction the novels of the late Patricia Highsmith are one of the peaks. . . . She is a fastidiously honest, often uncomfortable writer who does not pass facile judgments on her characters." The bulk of her stories are one of a kind; however, her novels about the amoral Tom Ripley (listed separately) definitely should be read in order of publication. All her short story collections are included here, though many stories do not fit neatly into the mystery-suspense category. American publishers of her novels included Harper & Row, Coward McCann, Doubleday, Knopf, Simon and Schuster, and Lippincott. Her London publishers were Cresset, Heinemann, and Bloomsbury. Dates, except where indicated, are for first publication in the United States. GB=Great Britain

Mystery Novels and Story Collections
1950   *Strangers on a Train*
1954   *The Blunderer*
1957   *Deep Water*
1958   *A Game for the Living*
1960   *This Sweet Sickness*
1962   *The Cry of the Owl*
1964   *The Two Faces of January*
1964   *The Glass Cell*
1965   *The Story-Teller*/GB: *A Suspension of Mercy*
1967   *Those Who Walk Away*
1969   *The Tremor of Forgery*
1970   *The Snail-Watcher and Other Stories*/GB: *Eleven* (short stories)
1972   *A Dog's Ransom*
1975   GB: *The Animal-Lover's Book of Beastly Murder* (short stories)
1977   GB: *Little Tales of Misogyny* (short stories)

1977   *Edith's Diary*
1979   GB: *Slowly, Slowly in the Wind* (short stories)
1981   GB: *The Black House* (short stories)
1983   GB: *People Who Knock on the Door*
1985   GB: *Mermaids on the Golf Course* (short stories)
1986   GB: *Found in the Street*
1987   GB: *Tales of Natural and Unnatural Catastrophes* (short stories)

Ripley Novels
1955   *The Talented Mr. Ripley*
1970   *Ripley under Ground*
1974   *Ripley's Game*
1980   *The Boy Who Followed Ripley*
1991   GB: *Ripley under Water*

Other Fiction
1952   *The Taste of Salt* (lesbian romance published under the pen name Claire Morgan and later reissued as *Carol* under the author's name)
1958   *Miranda, the Panda Is on the Veranda* (children's book cowritten with Doris Sanders)
1995   *Small g: A Summer Idyll* (novel published posthumously)

Nonfiction
1966   *Plotting and Writing Suspense Fiction* (Published by The Writer, Inc., the book was expanded and revised for reissue in 1981.)

Film Adaptations
Patricia Highsmith's novels are probably too dark and morally clouded for translation to American commercial television (more's the pity), but they have inspired an impressive number of good-to-great film treatments as well as European TV adaptations. The most famous film is Alfred Hitchcock's 1951 version of *Strangers on a Train* for Warner Brothers. Starring Robert Walker, Sr., as Bruno and Farley Granger as Guy Haines, the film had a screenplay credited to Raymond Chandler, Whitfield Cook, and Czenzi Ormonde, though Ormonde apparently did the heavy lifting. Although Hitchcock never relinquished the rights to the book, a minor and forgettable Warner Brothers film, *Once You Kiss a Stranger* (1969)—in which the psycho is a girl, played by Carol Lynley—was clearly inspired by *Strangers*.

The first adaptation of *The Talented Mr. Ripley* was an excellent 1960 French-Italian version directed by René Clement and starring Alain Delon as Tom Ripley. Highsmith approved of Delon's portrayal. Titled

Plein Soleil in French and *Purple Noon* in English, this handsome film was rereleased by Miramax in 1996.

A more recent version of *The Talented Mr. Ripley* was released late in 1999. Adapted and directed by Anthony Minghella, this lavish production from Miramax/Paramount stars Matt Damon as Ripley and Jude Law as Dickie Greenleaf. An American production of *Ripley under Ground* is reported to be scheduled in 2000.

The 1977 German production of director Wim Wenders's *The American Friend,* based on *Ripley's Game,* starred Dennis Hopper as Ripley and received international attention, although Highsmith did not approve of Hopper's portrayal.

Other cinema adaptations include French director Claude Chabrol's *Le Cri du Hibou (The Cry of the Owl)* in 1987; a German film of *Edith's Diary* in 1986; and a 1985 German version of *The Two Faces of January.* French superstars Isabelle Hupert and Jean-Louis Trintignant took the lead roles in director Michel Deville's 1981 adaptation of *Deep Water (Eaux Profondes).* A German production of *The Glass Cell (Die Glaserne Zelle)* was released in 1978. A 1977 French version of *This Sweet Sickness (Dites-lui que je l'aime)* was directed by Claude Miller and starred Gerard Depardieu. A 1963 French-German-Italian version of *The Blunderer* (titled *Enough Rope* in English and *Le Meurtrier* in French) featured Gert Frobe and Robert Hossein.

P. D. JAMES

AN ARTFUL KIND OF ORDER

"If creativity is the successful resolution of internal conflict, the creative writer seeks out of this conflict to make sense of his experience of the world, to impose order on disorder and to construct a controlled pattern from his own internal chaos." ⋆

P. D. James

ℐn 1997, P. D. James undertook a project unlike any she had ever done: a "fragment of autobiography" written in the form of a year-long diary. She readily admitted that she was not a diarist nor even a very good letter-writer. And as interviewers long ago discovered, the very public James is a skillful miser when it comes to giving out the intimate details of her personal life. But plainly the author wished—as had Agatha Christie and Ngaio Marsh before her—to beat the biographers to the punch, characterizing herself before others had the chance.

Anyone who has read the body of her detective fiction will recognize the impulse behind her venture into memoir writing. P. D. James White, Baroness of Holland Park, is a woman who treasures order and control in her books and in her life. In her many interviews over the years, the words "structure," "control," and "order" are repeated like mantras. "I like structured fiction."

⋆ Unless noted, quotations are from P. D. James's 1999 memoir, *Time to Be in Earnest: A Fragment of Autobiography* (Faber and Faber), and from the various interviews listed in "References and Resources."

"You've got to control the plot." . . . "Well, you *can't* have them [the characters] running away with the book because you have to control the detective story." . . . "I hope that my books serve as small celebrations of order and reason in our increasingly disordered world." . . . "I put my faith, such faith as I have, in rationality and in order. . . ." Her favorite author is Jane Austen, whom James lauds for her "irony and control of structure." She quotes Tennyson: "Self-reverence, self-knowledge, self-control,/These three alone lead life to sovereign power."

When reviewing the public record of her life and career, it is very tempting to label her a "control freak." To read interviews she has given over three decades with all manner of reporters and scholars is to understand Yogi Berra's famous "déjà vu all over again" remark. James's responses to the usual questions are intelligent, even intellectual, and remarkably similar. It is as if, like a well-rehearsed politician, she were speaking from a script to avoid getting off-point. Such predictability is frankly suspicious, as James herself has admitted. "If I were reading myself," she once said, "I would feel that here was a woman with such a strong love of order and tradition that she is obviously covering in her own personality some basic turbulence and insecurity."

Her manner—she is almost universally described as gracious, kindly, soft-spoken, grandmotherly—abets her desire to keep private things private; few interviewers are willing to push this disarmingly courteous woman into uncomfortable personal revelations. But James is far too bright to expect to control her life story entirely. She herself has speculated about Jane Austen's life and bemoaned the fact that so many of Austen's private letters were destroyed by that revered writer's sister.

The author is mother to the tale, and in P. D. James's case, the tales she has woven in her fourteen novels are offspring deeply imprinted with the psychological, social, aesthetic, moral, and spiritual beliefs and interests of their creator. A little digging into her life and her thinking can, in fact, add another fascinating and illuminating layer to her multilayered fiction.

> "My mother used to tell me that I was a cynical child.
> Examining things seems to be in my genes."
> —1998 interview in *The Times* of London

Phyllis Dorothy James was born "a much wanted first child" on August 3, 1920, at home on Walton Street in Oxford. Her parents had experienced difficulty conceiving, and her mother, Dorothy May Hone James, had undergone some form of medical treatment to become pregnant. The birth itself was difficult, but the arrival of a healthy daughter was clearly a happy event. Phyllis was followed, at intervals of eighteen months, by her sister, Monica, and then her brother, Edward.

Phyllis's parents had met during World War One when her father, Sidney Victor, was a sergeant in the machine-gun corps. Sidney and Dorothy May married in 1917. Both their courtship and the early years of the marriage were apparently contented, but their children were relatively young when they sensed a change in their parents' relationship. The couple seem to have been opposites at every point: their daughter describes Sidney as "intelligent, reserved, sarcastic, deeply distrustful of sentimentality, fastidious and with little ability to show affection." Her mother was "sentimental, warm-hearted, vivacious, impulsive, and not intelligent. . . ." Sidney worked as middle-level civil servant in the Inland Revenue Service; apart from some nursing during the war, Dorothy May was never employed outside the home, although she became a popular speaker for church women's groups, sang in the choir, and was interested in (but had no opportunity for) amateur theater.

Phyllis's Hone and James grandparents were educators. Her grandfather Edward Hone had been appointed headmaster of the Choir School of Winchester Cathedral in 1887, and his wife ran the boarding school. Her father's father, Walter James, was a linguist who worked for the British and Foreign Bible Society and at some time served in India as the tutor to the children of a rajah. But money was a problem in the James family, and Sidney left school before he was sixteen, going to work for the Patents Office.

Many years later, Phyllis came to understand her father better—a man who gave little affection to his children because he had received so little when he was a child; a man who probably wanted to be a teacher but lacked the money for advanced education and so indentured himself for life to the civil service. Sidney became a difficult person, reserved and undemonstrative, restless and dissatisfied, solitary to the point of taking his meals alone, tightfisted, commanding respect and strict obedience, carrying Victorian notions of fatherhood into the modern, postwar world. He played golf, mastered a Boy Scout troop, and gardened obsessively—activities that further isolated him from his family. There is no suggestion he was abusive, but he terrified his family with his sternness, and his major failure as a father seems to have been his utter inability to express approval. His children later remembered that "our childhood had been lived on a plateau of apprehension with occasional peaks of acute anxiety or fear."

Phyllis was four or five when her parents moved from Oxford to Ludlow in the Shropshire countryside on the England-Wales border—"the ideal town for an imaginative child." Ludlow's gift to young Phyllis was its natural beauty. But Ludlow also introduced her to the face of rural poverty and honed her nascent sense of justice and injustice. She was an observant child with a knack for seeing the underlying meaning of the actions of her elders. It was not an altogether attractive trait: "From an early age I had this insight into adult motives and sometimes spoke uncomfortable truths aloud, a habit which caused my mother to describe me as a cynical child."

The James children played quite freely in both town and countryside, exploring the meadows, the river, and the rocky walks and caves that surrounded Ludlow Castle. Already a reader—she had learned to read from the comic books her mother bought weekly—Phyllis entered the local primary school at age five. She was escorted to and from school each day by an older boy whose favorite after-school activity was to go "down to the river in the hope of seeing drowned bodies. . . ." Phyllis didn't mind this morbid routine, except that it was invariably disappointing,★ but she enjoyed more the make-believe games played with her siblings, in which she took the superior role, the Saturday afternoons at the local cinema, and the family's long Sunday walks, which inspired a lifelong "love of walking." She was always an inventive storyteller, entertaining her sister and brother with her adventure tales, and as a child, occupying herself with ongoing narratives in which she cast herself as a third-person character (a mannerism she has retained in public references to herself as "one" and "the writer").

The Jameses were dedicated churchgoers, and in the Anglican services, Phyllis found herself enraptured by the language of the King James Bible and the Book of Common Prayer, even though she tended to be argumentative on matters theological.

Apart from arithmetic, she was an apt student, and at her second school, the British School, she discovered history and poetry. At around age ten, she sat for the examinations that would determine her future educational course. She was initially offered a scholarship to an academic high school, but it was rescinded when the public monies ran short, and she was sent to the local National School instead. But in 1931, her father transferred to Cambridge, and Phyllis "began the last and happiest stage of my formal education. . . ." Sidney James found the necessary £4 for his daughter's term fees, and she entered the Cambridge County High School for Girls. The education she received there was Victorian in approach and highly disciplined. "We were taught," James remembers, "as much by example as precept, to respect our minds and to use

---

★ In a 1975 article titled "First Love," written for *The London Sunday Times,* she wrote of seeing a drowned boy pulled from the river when she was ten and of a discussion with her first love, "Robert," about death and its aftermath. This incident is not related in her memoir.

them; to examine the evidence before rushing in with our opinions; to distinguish between fact and theory. . . ." (habits of mind familiar to any student of Adam Dalgliesh).

Phyllis's favorite subjects were English and history, and in English class—taught by Miss Scargill and Miss Maisie Dalgliesh, for whom James named her famous fictional detective—the young scholar was steeped in traditional literature. School also brought new friends and the usual adolescent escapades; James has described her schoolgirl self as "popular and gregarious . . . and yet at the same time essentially very private."

The curriculum, the comradeship, the intellectual discipline of the Cambridge High School provided a dramatic contrast to events occurring at home. The reticent author offers few details in her autobiographical writing, but at some point after the family's move to Cambridge, her mother was committed to Fulbourne Mental Hospital for an extended period. James says only that her mother "was finally compulsorily detained"—a phrase that indicates the trouble was not sudden. Only Phyllis was old enough to accompany her father on his weekly trips to the hospital: "The visits were always painful. My mother would sit clutching at her hospital dress with restless fingers, looking at us imploringly and constantly reiterating her wish to come home."

For months, apparently, the family coped alone, with much of the responsibility for her siblings falling on Phyllis. Then her father hired a jolly, Fascist housekeeper named Dusty. Despite her naive politics, Dusty brought a kind of "conscientious caring" into the home. It was some two years before Dorothy May returned to her family.

From earliest childhood, Phyllis had cultivated her ability to retreat from the insecurity of real life into her "private world." As a little girl in Ludlow, she had been able to fall sleep only after constructing in her imagination an immense building in which she and hundreds of children slept together under the constant protection of guards. "Even as a child," she has written, "I had a sense that I was two people; the one who experienced the trauma, the pain, the happiness, and the other who stood aside and watched with a disinterested ironic eye."

It is clear that Phyllis wanted and was fully qualified to go on to university studies, but because the family lacked the money to fund her education, she left Cambridge High School at sixteen. (It is often said that her father didn't believe in higher education for girls, but money was obviously the main issue.) So she took the civil service exam, and from a list of possible government positions, selected the Inland Revenue, "the worst possible choice" given her distaste for numbers. She was posted to Ely, and after a brief stay in a boardinghouse, commuted from her home in Cambridge. The work was dull, and, as a very young woman in an office of men, she was subject to a good deal of prejudice.

After eighteen months, she resigned and found more pleasing work as an assistant stage manager and all-around "go-fer" for the Festival Theatre in Cambridge. The experience fueled her vague ambition to become a playwright and provided the setting for her introduction to Connor Bantry White, the medical student whom she would marry on August 8, 1941, just five days after her twenty-first birthday.

> *"Charm is an odd word, but he had it. He was Anglo-Irish. He was fair. He had a very nice smile."*
>
> —1986 interview with *People Weekly*

Throughout her public career, P. D. James has conscientiously avoided discussion of her marriage. Her silence is understandable, for her husband's fate was both cruel and deeply sad.

Connor White, the son of a physician, had been a student at St. Catherine's College, Cambridge, when they married, and he continued his medical studies in London in the early days of World War Two. But as soon as he qualified to practice, Connor enlisted with the Royal Army Medical Corps. The Whites' first daughter, Clare, had been born in 1942, and Phyllis was pregnant when her husband was posted to India.

She was living in Essex but made the "somewhat perverse" decision to have her second child in London, at Queen Charlotte's Hospital, where a friend and colleague of Connor's practiced. In June 1944, baby Clare was sent to stay with Connor's parents, and Phyllis moved to the city. Even as she was giving birth, German V-1 rockets were exploding all around the hospital. The windows in the wards were kept open to avoid flying shards of glass, and the new mothers were instructed to hold pillows over their babies' cots during the bombardments. At night, the infants were sheltered in the hospital's basement, while the mothers were wheeled in their beds into the corridors. Phyllis remembers nightmares about losing her baby in the rubble when the hospital was hit. Fortunately, Queen Charlotte's withstood the German rockets, and mother and daughter—named Jane for Phyllis's favorite author—were released. After a brief stay with her in-laws, Phyllis took her two girls back to her rented flat in Essex.

Although White Hall, the house in Chigwell Row where she lived, was damaged in the V-2 bombing, James recalls the war years most vividly in terms of food—rationing and lining up for hours to buy fish and other scarce items that were not rationed; breaking all the established rules of child-rearing to breast-feed her hungry baby while huddled in a bomb shelter; eating rook pie made from birds shot in the garden. Phyllis had worked for a time for the Ministry of Food in Cambridge, so she understood the need for conservation and rationing. But when, near the end of the war, she received from her husband a package containing a tin of butter, she "couldn't resist one glorious splurge." She and her daughters were feasting on buttered toast when the bombing of Japan was announced on the radio: "I knew that for all of us the world had changed for ever."

Except for discussions of her civil service career and her writing, James is mostly silent about the period between her husband's return from the war and his death in 1964. But even the simplest of facts reveal the pain that she and her family suffered.

Connor White, the promising young doctor with the Irish charm, came back a different person. It soon became clear that he was suffering from serious mental illness—probably schizophrenia, although this diagnosis was never formally made—and that he would not be able to practice full-time or to support his family. He was to spend nearly twenty years in and out of mental hospitals, his commitments both voluntary and involuntary. Because his illness was never officially classified as war related, he was not entitled to a pension. If the family was to survive, Phyllis would have to become the breadwinner.

The Whites were living with Connor's parents in Ilford, Essex, and in 1949, Phyllis, answering a newspaper ad, applied for a clerical position under the newly formed National Health Service. This decision continues to reverberate in her fiction. She "found favour" with and was hired as a file clerk by the administrator of the London Skin Hospital, a small specialist service whose medical and operational plan and staff—down to the porter—is echoed in *A Mind to Murder*. For a time she was secretary to a committee on student nursing that provided vital background for *Shroud for a Nightingale*. And surely there is something of James's confident efficiency in the character of Mandy Price, the coolly observant temp secretary in *Original Sin*.

Following a minor promotion, Phyllis realized that advancement in the Health Service required better qualifications than she possessed, and she began night classes in hospital administration at the City of London College in Moorgate. The curriculum included classes in law, "taught by a vivacious, rotund and obviously excellent lawyer called Smitoff . . . with a penchant for the dramatic." The lecturer acted out the cases under discussion, illuminating arcane points of law and evidence that delighted the future mystery writer.

Phyllis passed her exams with honors and began her climb up the bureaucratic ladder, eventually going to the North West Metropolitan Regional Hospital Board. James makes it clear that her duties were always administrative and that her contact with patients was minimal. (When she describes corpses and their grievous wounds in her novels, it is the result of research rather than direct experience. She has never attended an autopsy, though the offer has been made, but on one occasion she did observe a patient being fed with a tube, an incident recalled to gruesome effect in *Shroud for a Nightingale*.)

That the family's situation was extremely difficult goes without saying. Those who knew Connor White in his youth describe him as highly literate, humorous, and sensitive—too sensitive, perhaps, for the cruelties he observed in war. Whatever caused his mental breakdown, his behavior became increasingly unpredictable and sometimes self-destructive. (He once threw himself from a window.) There were times when he didn't recognize his wife. He would prescribe medications for himself, probably exacerbating his illness, and would frequently check himself out of hospital (most often Goodmayes psychiatric hospital in Essex, where he adopted the name "Ted") with no notice to his wife. As Phyllis remembers with characteristic understatement, "I never knew quite what I would have to face when I returned home from the office." Her in-laws were loving caretakers for Clare and Jane; even so, the girls were sent to boarding school when Clare was five and Jane only three. Phyllis has said that her husband never directed his violence toward her or the children, whom he adored, but the atmosphere in their home was obviously volatile.

When Connor's father retired from his family practice and sold his house in Ilford, Phyllis found a small Victorian cottage in Kingston-on-Thames for her family. It was at this house on Richmond Park Road—not long after Clare's marriage and move to the United States—that Connor White, aged forty-four, died in August 1964. He had taken a fatal combination of alcohol and drugs. An inquest was held and returned an open verdict, but in a 1993 interview with Lynn Barber for *Vanity Fair* magazine, Phyllis conceded that her husband's death was "probably" suicide.

She believed that Connor "was glad to die," and she mourned not his going, but all that he had been deprived of by his illness. Asked once by a persistent interviewer for *People* magazine if she had ever considered divorce, James was vehement and uncharacteristically emotional: "No. Never. Never. Never. I loved my husband. I took him for better or worse, richer or poorer, in sickness and in health. . . . He was a very good father; he loved the children very much; he loved me. I was never the sort of woman who would throw over her husband because he proved to be mentally or physically ill. It wasn't his fault."

In her memoir, James makes a more dispassionate but no less poignant statement: "Only those who have lived with the mental illness of someone they love can understand what this entails. One suffers with the patient and for oneself. Another human being who was once a beloved companion can become not only a stranger, but occasionally a malevolent stranger." And in another passage, discussing poet Ted Hughes, who has been savaged by some feminists over the suicide of his first wife, poet Sylvia Plath, James writes that "no one who has never had to live with a partner who is mentally ill can possibly understand what this means. Two people are in separate hells, but each intensifies the other. Those who have not experienced this contaminating misery should keep silent."

When her father was elderly, Phyllis came to know him and to appreciate his strengths, particularly "the courage, huge courage. . . ." As an adult, she must finally have understood that Sidney James had endured, as she had endured, life with a mentally ill partner and that he had, like his daughter, kept his family together through sheer force of will. Dorothy May James, who died in 1966, suffered to the end with "Parkinson's disease and unrelievable mental anguish." Sidney survived his wife by thirteen years and perhaps enjoyed some peace before he died of an instantly fatal heart attack while cutting the lawn. Phyllis dedicated her 1999 memoir to both her parents "with gratitude and love."

> "*. . . I had an interest in death from an early age. It fascinated me. When I heard, 'Humpty Dumpty sat on a wall,' I thought, 'Did he fall or was he pushed?'*"
>
> —interview with *Paris Review*

James has said that she always knew she had a "gift" for writing and regrets her late start. She was in her late thirties when she experienced the moment, not uncommon to hopeful writers of a certain age, when she realized that she best get going. Not one to do things in a small way, she began a novel. She was working full-time, attending her evening classes at Moorgate, managing her family, dealing with her husband's hospitalizations; hours for writing were precious and few. She began what became the habit of rising at 6 A.M. and writing in longhand before leaving for her job.

"It didn't occur to me . . . to begin with anything other than a detective story," she has said. ". . . I was influenced in particular by the women writers: Dorothy L. Sayers, Margery Allingham, Ngaio Marsh and Josephine Tey." She was naturally attracted to her own favorite escapist genre and also to the structured nature of detective fiction. She absolutely rejected writing anything overtly autobiographical and assumed from the outset that a detective novel offered training for higher goals. In fact, she initially thought of detective fiction as a worthy "apprenticeship" for the straight novels she planned for her future. Her first effort was, she grudgingly admits, "in the mode of Agatha Christie even if it aspires to probe more deeply into the minds and motives of its characters."★

The detective form also allowed her to explore a lifelong fascination with death. As a child, she says, she "was always aware of the fragility of life"—not so much fearful of dying as sensitive to the fact that death may come at any moment. She followed newspaper coverage of sensational murder trails and was especially affected by the 1931 case of Vera Page, an eleven-year-old (Phyllis's age at the time) who was raped and strangled on the way home after visiting her grandmother. The chief suspect was released by a coroner's jury for insufficient evidence. "It is extraordinary how that child's face is imprinted on my imagination," James wrote more than sixty-five years later. "Perhaps there persists in the human psyche an atavistic belief that a murder must be solved if the dead are to rest in peace."

Cover Her Face took several years to complete. Then, through a series of fortuitous encounters, Phyllis acquired an agent—Elaine Greene— and a publisher—Charles Monteith at Faber and Faber. Faber, which happened to be on the lookout for new detective writers, accepted the novel and planned to publish it in 1961. The release was delayed for a year, but that disappointment seems hardly devastating for a first-time author who never received a rejection.

★ Like most new British female writers of traditional detective fiction, James was immediately compared to Agatha Christie when *Cover Her Face* was published. This, she has made clear, does not please, and her comments about Christie's work fall into the damning-with-faint-praise category. Those who accuse James of intellectual snobbery will recognize the condescension in this remark: "What's in her [Christie's] books is more like the smell of bad drains, but there's nothing wrong with that. Reading her provides a certain degree of comfort." James's view that Christie didn't write about or understand evil indicates either a serious misreading or, more likely, a determination to separate her own brand of detective writing as serious art from what Christie herself happily conceded was "lowbrow" entertainment. James most often identifies with Dorothy L. Sayers, another writer who tried to push the detective story into the serious novel field, and says that the four major influences on her own writing were Sayers, Jane Austen, Graham Greene, and Evelyn Waugh.

Cover Her Face hinges on the characters of a young unwed mother and the people who take her into their lives. Today, when babies born out of wedlock have become as unexceptional as tattoos and nose rings, the murderous events precipitated by Sally Rudd's disgrace may be difficult to take seriously. *Cover Her Face* is classically Golden Age in its mechanics: country house and small village setting, closed circle of suspects, upstairs-downstairs social order. Yet the book still has power, notably in characterization, and it is also the starting point for the public career of Adam Dalgliesh—the dark and dour man of many parts who has, over ten novels to date (eleven if one counts his brief appearance in James's first Cordelia Gray mystery), become both icon and literary heartthrob.

Much as Ngaio Marsh had done in her first Roderick Alleyn book, James allowed other characters to provide the first descriptions of her lead detective:

> Catherine Bowers thought, "Tall, dark and handsome. Not what I expected. Quite an interesting face really."
>
> Stephen Maxie thought, "Supercilious-looking devil. He's taken his time coming. . . ."
>
> Felix Hearne thought, "Well, here it comes. Adam Dalgliesh, I've heard of him. Ruthless, unorthodox, working always against time. I suppose he has his own private compulsions. At least they've thought us adversaries worthy of the best."
>
> Eleanor Maxie thought, "Where have I seen that head before. Of course. That Durer. In Munich was it? Portrait of an Unknown Man."

Readers would learn more about Dalgliesh in this and future novels—that he is a widower whose wife and son died in childbirth, that he is a published poet of some repute, that his father was a country vicar, that he is not musical but loves cats and keeps Jane Austen at his bedside—but James deftly laid down all the basics in the short passage above: the physical impact (James has said that she sees Dalgliesh as looking something like actor Gregory Peck), the vaguely arrogant demeanor, the professional toughness and discipline, even the hint of sensitivity that might attract the eye of a Renaissance master. As Norma Siebenheller noted in her 1981 study of the P. D. James novels, Dalgliesh ages and his relationships change as the series progresses: "Yet . . . he is today essentially the same man he was in *Cover Her Face*: introspective, compulsive, devoted to his work, sensitive to the feelings of others, yet withdrawn into himself." (In fact, Dalgliesh stopped aging in the 1980s—a necessary amendment since he would by now be past retirement.)

James wanted a detective who was credible to the modern reader—a character who was psychologically complex, imperfect, and not always likable. She has admitted lately that Dalgliesh shares characteristics with her. Some are obvious—his love of Austen, old churches, literary quotation, and so forth. But the psychological cross points are more interesting. In his official position, Dalgliesh is a demanding taskmaster who wields a velvet whip; he gets his way quietly and through the implicit threat of withholding approval (a management style similar to James's, according to former coworkers and committee colleagues). Dalgliesh has lost his spouse and is unwilling or unable to establish another lasting relationship. He has love affairs, conducted off-stage, but is solitary by choice. (James never remarried, though there were several proposals. She still misses her husband, and she told Lynn Barber that she has "certainly never wanted to make a great emotional commitment ever since.") Dalgliesh trusts facts, not theories or his occasional bright flashes of intuition.

"I made my detective a very private and detached man," James told interviewer Diana Cooper-Clark in 1983, "who uses his job to save himself from involvement with other human beings because of tragedies in his own life." Although many fans find Dalgliesh a romantic figure, this was not his creator's intention. The romantic aura comes not from what James reveals about him, but from what she hides.

When *Cover Her Face* was published in 1962, it received a good deal of critical attention and praise for a first novel, though most reviewers thought the author—P. D. James—was a man. Phyllis Dorothy James White declares that she had no intention of concealing her sex when she selected her authorial denotation; she had always intended to write under her maiden name and chose to use her initials because they were "enigmatic and would look best on the book spine."

The book made a little money and was soon followed by *A Mind to Murder,* released to more good reviews and reasonable sales in 1963. But Phyllis was in no position to give up her day job. She had considered looking for a new post or a promotion before her husband died; after his death, the need for change became intense. She applied for a supervisory position with the Home Office but was rejected because of her inadequate education credentials. When the same position—principal in the Home Civil Service—opened a year later with more flexible requirements, she got the job. In March of 1968, she went to work for the Home Office, where she remained for eleven years: "probably the most interesting and happiest part of my working life."

Her first posting was with the Police Department; her responsibilities included forensic science, forensic pathologists, and police vehicles (though she didn't and doesn't drive a car). One of her duties was preparing the Home Secretary for questioning by the opposition in Parliament, and she was also involved in public relations for her department—two roles that doubtless refined her ability to control and shape her own public image.*

She was later transferred to the Children's Department and finally the Criminal Policy Department, in which her area was juvenile law and justice. Her Home Office years proved invaluable to her fiction. *Death of an Expert Witness* (with its forensic laboratory setting) and *A Taste for Death* (in which a junior cabinet minister is murdered) depended heavily on her experience there, and her only nonfiction book prior to her memoir was cowritten with the Assistant Secretary of the Police Department, Thomas A. Critchley. *The Maul and the Pear Tree* (1971) examines a brief but brutal murder spree in 1811, the Ratcliffe Highway Murders. What attracted James to this historical case was the "extraordinarily incompetent" investigation and the guilt or innocence of a young seaman who was accused of the crime and subsequently died in suspicious circumstances.

During her stay in the Criminal Policy division, Phyllis was concerned with implementation of the 1969 Children and Young Persons' Act and then with aspects of the 1975 Children's Act relating to juvenile courts. But the part of the 1975 Act that inspired her breakthrough novel regarded changes in the adoption laws and the opening of previously confidential adoption records. The other source of inspiration was the execution, some years earlier, of Daniel Raven, who had murdered his parents-in-law shortly after visiting his wife and new baby in hospital. Listening to a radio report of Raven's hanging, James recalls, "I thought primarily not of him, nor of his victims, but of the young mother and her baby. How, if ever, could she break the news?" Later, as the Children's Bill was being debated in Parliament, James remembered the Raven incident. From these two strands came the idea for *Innocent Blood,* a novel about an adopted girl seeking her biological mother and the impact of her search on a closed circle of people.

Even before the publication of *Innocent Blood,* her eighth novel, Phyllis had decided to leave the Home Office six months in advance of her scheduled retirement, to write full-time. She had just enough savings to

---

* As a self-publicist, James is not always in control. In 1995 she sparked a vicious public debate among Britain's mystery writers. The cause was a radio interview in which James, asked about her consistent theme of moral choice, unwisely declared, "That's why my murderers, men and women, are intelligent, well-educated people." Moral choice, she added, was not possible in "the pits of the worst possible inner-city area, where crime is the norm and murder is commonplace. . . ." Crime writers of gritty urban fiction were outraged by her apparent class snobbery and took their complaints to the media. The dispute raged for some time, and James was roundly attacked.

support herself before receiving her government pension. But when *Innocent Blood* rose to the top of the bestseller list in the United States, followed by lucrative sales of paperback rights and film option, her financial future was secured. Some fifteen years later, she remembered the day she found out about the American sales, estimated at near $700,000. "I was rich!" she exclaimed, the sense of bemused disbelief still ringing in her words.

> *"No day is really without interest, being filled with thoughts, memories, plans, moments of particular hope and occasional moments of depression."*

Not that the respected and newly famous P. D. James, at sixty, disappeared into a placid retirement. Much of her best writing has been done since 1980, and her public responsibilities are myriad and time-intensive.

Not long after her retirement, she became a juvenile court magistrate. She has served on the Arts Council and the board of the British Council. She has been president of the Society of Authors, a governor of the BBC, chairman of the Booker Prize judging panel. She is a member of the Church of England's Liturgical Commission and an Honorary Fellow of St. Hilda's College, Oxford. She has at least six honorary university degrees and has taught creative writing classes both in England and the United States. She is a frequent lecturer, and a kind of traveling conversation show she does with good friend Ruth Rendell is in high demand.

In 1983, she was honored with the Order of the British Empire (O.B.E.) in the Queen's Birthday Honours List. In 1991, under the new Conservative government of her friend John Major, she was awarded a life peerage, becoming Baroness James of Holland Park and an independent member of the House of Lords. Her maiden speech in Parliament was on the subject of literature and language.

She has also been widely honored by her professional peers, and she accepts these plaudits with finely tuned self-deprecation and humor. The British Crime Writers Association awarded her its Diamond Dagger for lifetime achievement in 1987; she reciprocated by replicating the dagger as the murder weapon in *A Certain Justice*.

Today, she lives alone, except for a white cat named Polly-Hodge, in a tastefully unassuming and well-secured townhouse in London's Holland Park section. The city seems to provide her the perfect combination of human activity and solitude, as well as the concentration of church and public architecture to satisfy her aesthetic sense. James is an avid walker, and London's parks offer safe, expansive spaces: "When I walk, I'm often plotting my next novel. . . . I get so immersed in the world of the book that I'm hardly aware of my surroundings. But when I'm not plotting, I take in the beauty around me, and the sheer variety of people. . . ." London has been the most frequent setting for her novels, but she ventures rather widely outside its boundaries.

She bought a house in Oxford (setting of her futuristic novel *The Children of Men*) so that she could visit her daughter and family there. In 1995, she purchased and restored a seventeenth-century house in the village of Southwold (where her father had lived in his retirement) on the Suffolk coast, an area she first encountered as a child when her family spent summer holidays camping on the cliff top at Pakefield. A lover of London since first visiting it as a child (like Dalgliesh), James is not drawn to the countryside but to the seashores. She first used the wild Suffolk coast as setting in *Unnatural Causes* and then again in *Devices and Desires* (revamped as Norfolk with a mythical nuclear power plant); the rugged Dorset coastline provided the inspiration for *The Black Tower.*

New publications and lecture engagements give her the excuse for broader travel. She has a special fondness for North America, where her fans are eager to line up for hours to get a quick word and a signed copy of her latest book. Her crowded, multi-city 1998 publicity tour of the United States, promoting *A Certain Justice,* would have flattened many younger writers. Then there are always her daughters and sons-in-law, grandchildren, and friends to visit, official receptions to attend (though she hates the noise), and churches to inspect. Readers of *A Time to Be in Earnest* may at times find themselves thinking that they have mistakenly gotten hold of James's day planner.

Her books are published at intervals of two to four years. Unlike many mystery writers, she spends most of her writing time not writing but planning, allowing herself nine months or more for ideas to germinate. She is a dedicated researcher for facts. Her books are so meticulously planned before she sits down at her typewriter that she writes out of sequence, usually getting down the major incidents first, such as the discovery of the murder victim, and then filling in the gaps. Her inspiration is most often a place: for instance, the Thames River near Wapping, where the steamer *Alice* went down and more than six hundred passengers drowned in 1878, was her starting point for *Original Sin,* and Cambridge beckoned her back for *An Unsuitable Job for a Woman.* Setting suggests characters; characters have motivations; plot comes last. She likes to have her titles determined before beginning to write, and on the one occasion when her original title was already in use, she followed the suggestion of a Catholic friend and prayed to St. Anthony. She woke the next morning with *Innocent Blood.* So very orderly.

If all this sounds too pat, too neat and cozy, it is. There are other sides to P. D. James—darker and far more intriguingly human than the public persona. It is this woman in the shadows who crafts the books that are so frighteningly real in their examinations of human psychology.

> *"Death, after all, seldom comes when invited or by appointment."*

For all her independence and self-sufficiency, James is fearful. Violence, it seems, is an ever-present reality for her. As she told Marilyn Stasio in 1990, "I think I'm very frightened of violence. I hate it. I'm very worried by the fact that the world is a much more violent place than when I was a girl."

The little girl who could sleep only by imagining herself in a secure building surrounded by watchful guards is now the elderly novelist who keeps her house fortified with locks, sleeps with a policeman's club by her bed, and regards a night spent in the quiet of the country as "a demonstration of nature red in tooth and claw." Perhaps so many years in the Police Department exaggerated her instinctive anxieties, but she apparently regards violence as the norm. She has spoken of her need to be surrounded by people and human activity (hence her preference for cities), yet people hold the constant threat of unpredictable violence.

It is often asked how a woman afraid of physical violence can write such bloody good descriptions of murder. But James makes a distinction. She doesn't often describe the act of murder directly; she details its consequences. "The moment in a detective story when the body is discovered is one of horror and high drama, and the reader should experience both." The full horror, she believes, is most effectively achieved through the eyes of an innocent character.

Perhaps the fear of violence is linked to her attitudes toward death and her lifelong awareness of the swift passage of time. Death, she indicates in her writing, is natural because it is inevitable. But the timing of death is irrational, out of control, and that is what is so fearsome. Violent, premature death (including capital punishment, which, contrary to her conservative politics, she abhors) is the ultimate, unpardonable deprivation: ". . . however unpleasant a character may be," she told Diana Cooper-Clark in 1983, "however evil he may be, however disagreeable he may be, he still has the right to live his life to the last natural moment."

When she learned of the death of Princess Diana in August 1997, James's immediate reaction, she recalled, "was disbelief, as if the natural order had somehow been reversed. Death has power over lesser mortals but not this icon." Later she focused on the living and was plainly disgusted by the "self-indulgent, almost neurotic display of emotionalism" that marked the public grieving for the princess. She worried that "something has been released into the atmosphere and it isn't benign." P. D. James, who has so effectively shown the pervasive, corrosive effects of sudden and unnatural death on bystanders, reacted to the throngs of anonymous mourners with that duality—the empathetic fellow Englishwoman and the clear-eyed, ever so slightly judgmental observer—that is her second nature.

She is a religious person, active in the Anglican Church, but not predictably so. She believes in the Christian God, but not physical resurrection. Though she expresses her hope for an afterlife of the soul, she does not seem, in her references to other faiths and to nonbelievers, unduly anxious about it. She does, however, "believe in redemption through love. That is my religion. . . ." Her mysteries deal with moral realities and choices rather than specifically religious uncertainties. Her well-known attraction to churches (like Dalgliesh's) is born of a love of architecture, art, and solitude, and when churches appear in her novels (as in *A Taste for Death*), it is to provide contrast to the horror of murder— mankind's lofty aspirations versus its vilest deeds. In her fiction, churches and clergy rarely offer solace.

Critics often point to guilt and redemption as her major themes, but her central concern is more question than answer: what can be so terrible that it pushes basically sane people to commit what George Orwell called "the unique crime" of murder? It is interesting that her primary victims are usually unpleasant people. Often, like Gerald Etienne in *Original Sin* and Venetia Aldridge in *A Certain Justice,* they are people driven by ambition and power-lust to ride roughshod over the innocent and weak. James spends a great deal of time in her novels establishing the character of the unpleasant victim. By the time he or she is done in, the reader is wondering why it took so long for someone to do the deed. In part, this narrative format works to establish motivation among the circle of suspects. But more important, it sets up a moral dilemma for the reader. Did this patently noxious person deserve to die? Was there justification for the taking of this life? (James does blunt the question by including a second victim who may be unpleasant but is clearly an innocent.)

Though James allows no excuses for murder, some victims, she implies, make themselves targets. She does not blame the victim so much as hold even victims accountable for their actions. And she wants the reader to understand the murderer: "As a writer I find that the most credible motive and, perhaps, the one for which the reader can feel some sympathy, is the murderer's wish to advantage, protect or avenge someone he or she greatly loves."

More than anything else, this ambivalence, this blurring of the lines between guilt and innocence, sets her work apart from that of her Golden Age predecessors. Yes, she tells us, murder is the unique crime for which there can be no compensation. Yes, murderers must be identified and brought to justice. But no, the story is never so simple as an epic conflict between personifications of Good (detective) and Evil (killer). For order to emerge from chaos, we must recognize what has brought the guilty person to commit so horrible a crime and also how the victim has collaborated in his or her victimization.

James has said that she could not imagine writing, as Patricia Highsmith did, from the murderer's point of view. She has also said that everyone has the capacity to kill in self-defense or to protect a loved one from imminent danger. She has written about conscienceless psychopaths and characters who murder only to benefit themselves, but they are never so real as when she focuses on an ordinary soul driven by complex psychological forces to kill.

James has been least successful when she has veered away from the structure of the traditional detective novel. *Innocent Blood,* despite its popularity and its many good features, is an oddly unsatisfying book. Richard Gidez, in his 1986 study of James's novels, said of *Innocent Blood,* "Everything has been so carefully calculated and contrived, with no missteps or false starts possible, that the characters have no room in which to breathe, no chance to develop on their own, no opportunity to get off the treadmill James has put them on." James had conceded that the central character, young Phillipa Palfrey, is autobiographical to an extent. Though the novel deals primarily with James's familiar issues of sin and redemption, she seemed put off stride by the absence of a detective and the structure of an official investigation. Julian Symons wrote a negative review of the novel at the time, and though James was too gracious to comment directly on the review when she next saw him, she did say that *Innocent Blood* reflected "aspirations beyond my station."

But some years later, she tried another mainstream fiction with *The Children of Men.* This book got a good deal of attention for its dystopian story line (humankind in the near future has become infertile and faces extinction) and its spiritual themes. But again, without the rational structure of the mystery story, it is a cold novel and fails to engage readers.

James is not an innovator. What she has brought to traditional detective writing is seriousness of purpose, elegance of style, and realism in characterization. She has an exquisite eye for physical details and physiological nuances. One of her major accomplishments, rarely commented on, is her ability to capture the toxic nature of the modern work environment, whether professional or bureaucratic. With the exception of *Cover Her Face,* all her novels deal with some profession or trade. (Even *Unnatural Causes* is set in a colony of working writers.) The competent and the incompetent jockey for position, middle-management intrigues are rife, tensions boil with lunch in the company kitchen, and office gossip is served with biscuits at teatime. In *Original Sin,* for example, two of her most interesting and believable characters are Mandy, the temp typist, and Miss Blackett, the much-abused personal assistant to the chairman of Peverell Press.

Whether she has achieved her goal of producing genuine literature within the framework of the detective story is a question for future readers and scholars to decide, but she has unquestionably broadened the readership for contemporary detective fiction: people who don't read or won't admit to reading mysteries will blithely discuss the most minute detail of the latest P. D. James.

As a writer, she is both limited and enabled by the form she has chosen. Her two nonformula novels—*Innocent Blood* and *The Children of Men*—suffer from her need to impose order on complex and chaotic human passions and to find solutions for the insoluble. But within the structure and strictures of the detective story, she has much to say about society and the human condition: good people can do terrible things, and the terrible things they do inevitably have unintended and far-reaching consequences. Justice, however imperfect, is necessary for the modern psyche. Love is both destructive and redemptive. She deals in difficult dichotomies—reason versus passion, reality versus delusion, sanity versus insanity, self-interest versus social interest, personal responsibility versus dependence, commitment versus solitude, love versus hate, past versus present.

Of the detective story, James once said, "Here is a genre in which the problem is solved and solved by human beings; order and justice and morality are then restored." That is the practiced observer intellectualizing. But one hears in the remark, repeated with minor variations throughout her public career, the longing of the private woman for answers she knows are not available and for orderliness in heart and mind that she fears is not attainable. If only life were as sane as art.

P. D. JAMES
1920–
English (born: Oxford)

"It was at that moment that he sensed a warning, the unmistakable instinct for danger. It was as much part of his detective's equipment as his knowledge of firearms, his nose for an unnatural death. It had saved him time and time again and he acted on it instinctively. There was no time now for argument or analysis."
                                                              —*Unnatural Causes*

P. D. James has employed two serial detective—Adam Dalgliesh of Scotland Yard and private eye Cordelia Gray. For character and stylistic development, these books are best read in order, though reading them out of sequence is equally satisfying. The novel that cemented her career and won over the American market was not, strictly speaking, a detective fiction, but the psychological suspense story *Innocent Blood*. Her English publisher is Faber and Faber. American editions were published by Scribner's through 1980, and then by Knopf. Novels are listed chronologically, and dates are for first publication in Great Britain. Principal detectives appear in ( ).

Mystery Novels

1962   *Cover Her Face* (Dalgliesh)
1963   *A Mind to Murder* (Dalgliesh)
1967   *Unnatural Causes* (Dalgliesh)
1971   *Shroud for a Nightingale* (Dalgliesh)
1972   *An Unsuitable Job for a Woman* (Cordelia Gray)
1975   *The Black Tower* (Dalgliesh)
1977   *Death of an Expert Witness* (Dalgliesh)
1982   *The Skull beneath the Skin* (Cordelia Gray)
1986   *A Taste for Death* (Dalgliesh)
1989   *Devices and Desires* (Dalgliesh)
1994   *Original Sin* (Dalgliesh)
1997   *A Certain Justice* (Dalgliesh)

James has also written a small number of short stories that have not yet been collected for publication. Her only Dalgliesh short story, "Great-Aunt Allie's Flypapers," appears in *Verdict of Thirteen: A Detection Club*

Anthology (1978), published by Faber and Faber in Great Britain and Harper & Row in the United States.

Other Novels
1979   *Innocent Blood*
1992   *The Children of Men*

Nonfiction
1971   *The Maul and the Pear Tree: The Ratcliffe Highway Murders, 1811*
        (cowritten with Thomas A. Critchley)
1999   *Time to Be in Earnest: A Fragment of Autobiography*

Play
In the 1980s, James wrote a short play, *A Private Treason,* which had a very brief and unsuccessful production. It has not been published.

Video Adaptations
In 1983, the British launched a series of full-length television adaptations of the Dalgliesh novels with *Death of an Expert Witness.* The programs, which are produced by Anglia/United Film and Television and star Roy Marsden as the moody poet-detective, include all ten of the Dalgliesh titles issued to date and for the most part are true to James's stories. The author's favorite is *A Taste for Death.*

James's Cordelia Gray novel *An Unsuitable Job for a Woman* was the basis for a fine British film in 1981. This adaptation featured Pippa Guard as the young private eye heroine.

In the mid-1990s, Ecosse Films produced an updated version of *An Unsuitable Job for a Woman* for Anglia/United, and James assigned to Ecosse the video rights to her Cordelia Gray character for use in original stories. *An Unsuitable Job for a Woman,* the first in the series, is true to its source, and James was pleased with the performance of Helen Baxendale. But the next two installments, from pedestrian original scripts written with minimal input from James, have been less than satisfactory for the author or the many fans of Cordelia. James has distanced herself from the series and is attempting to force removal of the umbrella *An Unsuitable Job for a Woman* title.

Twentieth Century Fox purchased the option to film *Innocent Blood* (originally planning for playwright Tom Stoppard to do the screenplay), but the book proved to be a challenge, and the film was never made.

THAT GRAY GIRL

There is a subset of P. D. James fans who live in the perpetual hope that the author will bring back their favorite character—the appealing Cordelia Gray, private investigator. Cordelia arrived on the scene in 1972, well in advance of the American avalanche of female private investigators (McCone, Millhone, Warshawski, et al.) who came in with the 1980s. But there is something about Cordelia that captures hearts. In her first book, *An Unsuitable Job for a Woman,* she inherits a failing Cambridge detective agency from her boss, Bernie Pryde. Just about everyone agrees that private sleuthing is no job for this slip of a twenty-two-year-old with no experience or qualifications, but she is soon on the track of a killer. (Only later does Cordelia learn that she got the case *because* she was inexperienced and unqualified.) *An Unsuitable Job for a Woman* began with a setting: James wanted to wrap a mystery around beautiful Cambridge in summer. For her lead character, she decided on a woman and an amateur, unencumbered with the restrictions of official policing. Her model was her younger daughter, Jane: small, outgoing, intelligent, gutsy in a nicely bred way. Not that James intended to abandon her established star, Adam Dalgliesh; he is an unseen presence throughout the book until his cameo appearance in the final chapter.

As it turned out, Cordelia didn't need the Dalgliesh crutch. The tough little charmer with the difficult upbringing (dead mother, neglectful father, too many foster homes, and a bureaucratic bungle that landed her for six happy years in a convent school) proves perfectly capable of making it on her own and solving five deaths, past and present. The real mystery was why James waited nine years to resume Cordelia's story in *The Skull beneath the Skin* (1982) and why she has not revived it since. Fans haven't given up begging that Cordelia return or that she find her true love (namely, the aforementioned Superintendent Dalgliesh). James teased the issue for awhile. In a short essay titled "Ought Adam to Marry Cordelia?" (in Dilys Winn's *Murder Ink,* 1977), she totted up the disadvantages—the differences in age, temperament, career, and worldliness, plus the whopping big lie that Cordelia told on first meeting Adam—then left the door ajar. But after *The Skull beneath the Skin,* Cordelia vanished.

In the mid-1990s, James assigned video rights to the Gray character to a British production company and effectively gave away control over Cordelia's future. When a program was produced in which Cordelia becomes an unwed mother, James concluded, ". . . the damage, as far as I am concerned, can't be repaired, since Cordelia with an illegitimate child is no longer my character." Hope springs eternal . . . but perhaps it is fitting that the original Cordelia Gray (who would now be in her fifties) remain in the land of what-was: a long-ago summer flirtation still youthful in memory.

RUTH RENDELL

TRIPLE THREATENING

*". . . I feel very strongly this situation of the fork in the road, whether you take left or right, and I'm conscious of that in my daily life."** —1991 interview with Julian Symons

There is a story often told about Ruth Rendell . . . about the time when, as a journalist, she was assigned to cover the annual dinner of a local tennis club. Like many a newspaper reporter faced with a deadline and yet another predictable social event, she wrote her story from the advance copy of the guest speaker's text. What Ruth didn't know was that the speaker had dropped dead in the middle of the speech. The reporter turned in her resignation the next day.

This incident, apart from its anecdotal value, is like a capsule version of the themes that have dominated Ruth

Ruth Rendell

Rendell's mystery novels for almost forty years: the unexceptional situation, the decision to do something just a little different, the intervention of fate or coincidence or bad luck, the unexpected consequences. What fascinates Ruth Rendell (Baroness Rendell of Babergh since 1997) and her loyal readers is the inexplicable interplay of chance and coincidence with violence. In a 1983 interview with John C. Carr, she

---

* Quotations of Ruth Rendell are taken from various interviews listed in "References and Resources" and from her published works.

said, "I collect coincidences in people's lives. So, yes, I like to write about chance, the kind of chance that makes you go left instead of right and the whole course of things is changed."

In her mystery and psychological suspense novels and stories, the choice of one way over another generally means her main characters are heading straight for disaster; that fundamental premise is what makes her writing so compelling and, at bottom, terrifying. Rendell excels at presenting the seemingly ordinary person who becomes violent because chance presents the opportunity and the equally ordinary people who are victimized by accident.

She is a writer for our paranoid times, focusing her observant eye and mind on situations that exemplify life in modern, industrialized societies. If her villains were always crazy, her books would be less unsettling. But as often as not, her murderers couldn't pass the insanity test. They may be weird, neurotic, obsessive, repressed, stupid, vain, one-brick-shy-of-a-load types—just like the folks next door or down the street. But killers?

At the end of a Rendell mystery, one can almost imagine what might follow as TV reporters gather at the scene and question the bystanders to get sound bites for the late-night news. "He seemed a nice enough boy," the neighbors would say, "and devoted to his mother." Or, "She was a quiet type. Never caused any trouble." Or, "He was always pleasant when we passed on the street."

If only someone had noticed the glazed eye or the angry stare, the solitary habits, the absence of commonplace reactions—what might have been prevented? But then, no one does take notice, except the omnipresent author.

Rendell's writings have sometimes been criticized as cold, lacking in editorial passion. But it is her objectivity—her reporter's eye—that makes her writings so chilling. She has the almost unique ability to move viewpoint back and forth between victim and victimizer, building up layer upon layer of information about their lives, weaving an intricate web of physical and psychological detail in which the reader, like her characters, becomes entangled until the final, inevitable conclusion. Yet when the end comes, she gives it one last twist.

> *"Am I extrovert or introvert? I'd have to say introvert. I live inside me, although I've struggled a lot not to do so."*

Rendell was born Ruth Barbara Grasemann in London on February 17, 1930. Both her parents were teachers. Her mother, Ebba Elise, was

Swedish, though raised in Denmark. Her father, Arthur, was English. Arthur Grasemann had come to his profession with difficulty, from a childhood of extreme poverty. Raised in Plymouth, he had left school at fourteen and completed an apprenticeship in the dockyard, only to find that no job was available for him. Ruth credits her grandmother with somehow getting Arthur into a university. He became a teacher of mathematics and science. He was also a great reader, given to quoting frequently from his favorite authors, and an amateur painter.

Ebba Elise Kruse Grasemann, whom Ruth has characterized as "a very vague strange woman," contracted multiple sclerosis—a debilitating disease that includes progressively more visible tremors and other symptoms—soon after her only child's birth. Little was known about multiple sclerosis at the time, and Mrs. Grasemann likely suffered from the general ignorance about the condition; Ruth has said simply that her mother was "misunderstood." Her father displayed a strongly pessimistic attitude, though Ruth remembers him as "a very good, sweet and caring father" who taught her the importance of self-discipline. (It was only after writing a number of her Wexford mysteries that Ruth realized how much her primary detective was like Arthur Grasemann. The similarity was pointed out by her son, Simon, who was studying psychology.)

The Grasemanns didn't suffer in silence, however, and the atmosphere in the household was often heated. Ruth remembers her "rather unrepressed childhood with highly emotional parents who were always fighting and generally expressing their feelings, bursting into tears and so on, which, though hazardous at the time, I think didn't do me any harm." But it was not easy to hear the discord over which she had no control, and her childhood did, she believes, imbue her "from a very early age with a sense of doom" (a comment accompanied by laughter when she made it to Julian Symons, one of the mystery writers she admires).

Ruth grew up in South Woodford in Essex, on the northeast fringes of London, and attended Loughton High School during World War Two. After leaving school, she took a job as a junior reporter for her local newspaper, the *Chigwell Times*. She moved on to become a reporter and copy editor for the *Essex Express and Independent* in 1948. It was at this paper that she meet Donald Rendell, also a reporter. They married, and when their only son was born, Ruth settled down at home. But the housewife and mother was also writing, testing fictional genres, and turning out novels and short stories that were repeatedly rejected.

She doesn't remember being particularly drawn to mystery fiction as a girl, saying that she probably read Christie and Sayers but doesn't recall much about them. But in the early 1960s, she tried a mystery as the most likely type of story to find a publisher. Through a connection of her husband's—Don was by then working for London's *Daily Mail*—the book was sent to an editor at Hutchinson. *From Doon with Death,* with "a lot of rewriting," was accepted for publication in 1964. "The classic Rendell hallmarks were all there right from the beginning—" writer Val McDermid has observed, "the sense of place, the delicate filleting of the characters' psyches, the avoidance of the prosaic both in character and in motivation."

From Doon with Death might be called the start of the first phase of Ruth's writing career. In form, at least, it follows the classic detective novel lines. The murder of a woman is investigated by a police detective, Chief Inspector Reginald ("Reg") Wexford, and his able if unimaginative second-in-command, Michael Burden. The story is set in the mythical market town of Kingsmarkham (based on Midhurst where Rendell lived for a time in her childhood) in Sussex.

At first introduction, Reg Wexford is described as "taller than Burden, thick-set without being fat, fifty-two years old, the very prototype of an actor playing a top-brass policeman." He is a local boy and a country cop, so people, especially suspects, often underestimate both his intelligence and his shrewdness. He likes an "untidy" desk. He has a temper and a sarcastic tongue, frequently directed at the uptight Burden. He is well-read, "always intuitive, sometimes even lyrical," but with the tendency to be "coarse" when discussing sexual motivations. In spite of the gruff exterior, Wexford is also sensitive: "He had seen too many men's souls stripped to relish an unnecessary spiritual skinning." His investigations are intellectual rather than forensic. (Rendell has indicated that she doesn't put much faith in criminology and deliberately avoids procedural-like descriptions of police work.)

Ruth had no idea that *From Doon with Death* would spawn a long-lasting series when she invented Wexford. His initial character was not distinctive, drawing on both Hillary Waugh's Fred Fellows and Georges Simenon's Maigret. Wexford's name came from the Irish coastal town where she had recently spent a holiday (". . . it might easily have been Waterford").

Like Agatha Christie, with whom she hates being compared, Ruth was surprised when people wanted more of her detective, and she eventually came to regret starting him out at a relatively advanced age for a serial detective. Although his aging is distorted—if Rendell were absolutely accurate, Wexford would now be approaching his nineties—he is not a static character. Rather, he works much like the patriarch of an ongoing soap opera that provides the continuing subplots of each new book. As the series progresses, Rendell adds to the personal stories of Wexford, Burden, and their families. Readers come to know the ever-patient Dora Wexford and her two daughters; suffer with Burden when personal tragedy almost shatters his career; watch as Kingsmarkham grows, becoming more urban and crime ridden; and even diet with the hypertensive Wexford.

The year after *From Doon with Death* appeared, her first psychological crime novel, *To Fear a Painted Devil,* was published, launching the second phase of the Rendell oeuvre. For the next twenty years, the prolific Mrs. Rendell would follow something of a pattern, alternating her Wexford books with these self-contained, disturbing, and often brilliant novels that dig into the psychological underpinnings of madness and murder. The closest comparison is to the works of Patricia Highsmith, although Rendell is in no way derivative.

Not all of these novels work. Ruth personally hates *In Sickness and in Health,* which she has dismissed as "a silly book" about "a stupid woman," and is not fond of *One Across, Two Down.* In a few others, the piling on of chance and coincidence sometimes gets out of hand. But for the most part, these singular novels succeed beautifully. They are not for the squeamish: Rendell has no qualms about exploring the motivations behind unspeakable crimes and exposing the inner workings of the most obsessive and abnormal minds.

What is often amazing is her ability to reveal the crime and the criminal at the outset and still keep the reader enthralled to the final sentence of a book. Witness the opening line of *A Judgement in Stone*: "Eunice Parchman killed the Coverdale family because she could not read or write." The murders, we learn in the next paragraph, were without motive and unpremeditated, and accomplished "nothing but disaster. . . ." But Eunice Parchman was not mad. From this opening unravels a tightly woven tale of unexceptional decisions (the Coverdales simply want to hire a competent maid to clean their book-littered house), chance encounters (Eunice simply wants a chocolate bar when she walks into the village store), misunderstandings, and missed opportunities that lead to the horrific murders of four innocent people.

Or are they? Rendell is perfectly comfortable with the theory that there are people who unconsciously invite victimization. Some victims, like Maud Kinway in *One Across, Two Down,* just plain ask for trouble. Others are random, like the women strangled in *A Demon in My View.* But her most effective victims are those selected by some accident of fate that nevertheless reflects their own choices and weaknesses. No other writer has so successfully exploited the "wrong time, wrong place" theme.

"You are what you are," Ruth told John Carr. "So I do believe in determinism and I believe in destiny and I believe in fate, but I also believe in choice and chance. They go together." Can people change their natures? Ruth says some can, but not quickly. In *Judgement in Stone,* for instance, young Melinda Coverdale—a loving, generous, ebullient girl—simply cannot comprehend that another person may not want her help. She, like her father and stepmother, is an "interferer"—"afraid of being selfish." If Melinda had lived longer, she might have learned; then again. . . . Rendell makes it clear that although no victim deserves to die, victimhood arises partly from the victim's pattern of behavior.

One of few concessions she makes to the traditional detective story is an insistence that justice be done, whether by man or the gods. Ruth says that she has always written what she would enjoy reading and never caters to popular tastes. Indeed, her books don't end happily, but they do satisfy the reader's natural instinct for some form of retributive resolution. (It is hard to imagine Ruth Rendell writing anything like Patricia Highsmith's Tom Ripley series, in which the psychopath moves unscathed from book to book, success to success. Teddy Brex in *A Sight for Sore Eyes* is a character not unlike Highsmith's Ripley, but Teddy's fate is far more fitting for a moral universe.)

It may seem that Ruth Rendell is preoccupied with abnormal psychology and the depredations of social misfits, but two of the strongest currents running through all her books are as old as humankind itself: love and family. In particular, she explores the nature and consequences of love between husbands and wives and between parents and children. As in life, even the healthiest relationships (Reg and Dora Wexford, for instance, or George and Jacqueline Coverdale in *A Judgement in Stone*) have their blind spots. But where the author really reveals her understanding of human nature is in her depictions of unhealthy marriages and family relationships in which people are bound together by their miseries and weaknesses. Rendell has said that as a matter of her faith she believes in an ideal love. But there is nothing idealistic about her portrayals of the earthbound varieties.

As a number of critics have pointed out, there's also a lot of sex in Ruth's writing. Nothing is graphic; she says she doesn't have any interest in that kind of writing. But sex permeates the lives and motivations of many of her villains and victims. Good, bad, impotent, perverted, angry, manipulative, furtive, repressed, obsessive, abusive, brutal, incestuous—Rendell knows that sex, however it is practiced or fantasized about, is intrinsic: "I'm very interested in sex. I think it's a fascinating subject and I've never been able to come to terms with people who think that it isn't very nice to be interested in sex." She is also mistrustful of white-hot passion, untempered by time and, yes, marriage: ". . . I think that if people have very fraught, intense, passionate relationships, they do lead to a lot of grief."

Ruth Rendell doesn't talk much about her own marriage and home life, but it wasn't always a bed of roses. (Unlike P. D. James, Rendell gives relatively few interviews, but she is equally guarded in her personal comments and has a reputation for becoming irritable with unprepared reporters.) Ruth and Don Rendell were divorced in the mid-1970s, though they remarried several years later. Don has since retired from newspapering, and their son, a psychotherapist, lives in the United States with his family. For many years, the Rendells lived principally in the Suffolk countryside—first in a thatched cottage and then a comfortable, shrimp-colored house of fifteenth-century origins on wooded acreage not far from Colchester—though they also maintained houses in London and at Aldeburgh on the Suffolk coast. As anyone who reads Rendell knows, place is almost as significant as character in her fiction,★ and until recently her most productive writing place was in pastoral isolation.

> *"It is the suspense and the build-up of fear that has always interested me most. There's also a lot about obsession in my books. I have an obsessive nature and I observe."*

In 1986, to a good deal of publishing fanfare, Ruth Rendell adopted a pen name, Barbara Vine, for *A Dark-Adapted Eye.* The pseudonym, combining her own middle name and her grandmother's maiden name, was never intended to conceal her true identity. It marked the third phase in her development as a writer. The Vine books, which only tangentially involve elements of the murder mystery, allow Rendell greater range to roam through her characters' psychological landscapes. The stories explore past acts (sins, some would say) that have long arms, reaching across time and attaching to future lives and generations. *The Chimney Sweeper's Boy,* published in 1999, begins with the death of Gerald Candless, a British novelist (good enough to have been nominated for Britain's prestigious Booker Prize but not good enough to win), and the commissioning of his elder daughter to write her father's biography. There is nothing untoward about Candless's death, but his life is not so straightforward. As the adoring daughter searches the past, it becomes clear that Candless's identity (in the literal and psychological senses) has

---

★ For an interesting look at Rendell's mysteries as seen through the eyes of a geographer, try to find Lisa Kadonaga's article "Strange Countries and Secret Worlds in Ruth Rendell's Crime Novels," published in the July 1998 issue of *The Geographical Review.*

been a complex lie shaping her own life, her mother's, and her sister's. Such a simplistic summary is misleading. *The Chimney Sweeper's Boy,* like *A Dark-Adapted Eye* and the other Vine novels, shows that the obsessions of the past are never simple and never separable from the present.

One of the advantages of the Vine name is that it clearly distinguishes this aspect of Rendell's writing from the others; readers who love murder mysteries are less likely to pick up a Vine by mistake, while readers and reviewers who are not attracted to the mystery-detection genre, with which Ruth Rendell is so closely associated, may be willing to try a Barbara Vine novel without prejudice.

The Vine novels also free Rendell from the restrictions of plotting that the Wexford and the psychological mysteries require. Rendell readily admits that she doesn't enjoy plotting. Plot is the weakest element in her mysteries, propelled too often by too many coincidences that require too many suspensions of disbelief, though the characterization is usually more than sufficient compensation. But the Vine novels do not need such staples as clues, red herrings, forensics, witness interrogations, or even external investigations.

By the beginning of the new century, Ruth had published more than fifty novels and collections of short stories. She has also written a couple of nonfiction books (both concerned with Suffolk) and edited several anthologies. She is involved as consultant for the long-running *The Ruth Rendell Mysteries* series for Britain's ITV television. She even participated, with American author John Updike, in a 1997 Internet project called Web of Intrigue, which involved writing an on-line story with collaborative contributions from readers. When she is not writing, she is reading—as many as five books a week.

Her own book production seems to have slowed marginally in the last few years, and some complain that she is now inclined—perhaps under pressure for the "big" books the public craves—to pad her once tight writing. It may be the demands of her new political life. Always a liberal with a strong social conscience, her novels have from the beginning reflected her understanding of the inequities of Britain's still-class-ridden society and included a far from subtle contempt for both old and new rich. In 1996, Rendell was named Commander of the British Empire (C.B.E.) in the Queen's New Year's Honours. A year later, under the Labour government of Tony Blair, she was elevated to a life peerage. Now Baroness Rendell of Babergh, she sits as an active member of the House of Lords. Her good friend P. D. James, Baroness James of Holland Park, is a member of the same body, though at the opposite side of the political spectrum.

With this new political outlet for her lifelong interest in social justice, her writing has also taken a turn that even some of her most ardent admirers say is for the worse. Social injustice has always been an underlying issue in her fiction, and she has never been afraid to tackle what she sees as foolishness in a good cause. Her 1985 Wexford mystery, *An Unkindness of Ravens,* skewered feminist extremism, prompting an outraged response from feminist extremists. But recent novels in the Wexford series particularly have become increasingly polemical; 1995's *Simisola, Road Rage* in 1997, and *Harm Done,* released in 1999, all seem to some readers more concerned with the sociological consequences of racism, environmental abuse, and domestic violence than murderous psychology and crime-solving.

For a writer who "collects coincidences" and obsessively adapts what she observes to the needs of her fiction, this development shouldn't be too surprising. She once explained how her ideas came together for *A Demon in My View*: she was sharing a flat with a cousin whose last name was the same as that of another person in her building, causing mix-ups in the mail. The building also had a garden shed where Ruth found part of an old mannequin. These two minor and unrelated incidents jelled with her intention to write about a psychopath. Ruth Rendell doesn't simply draw on her own experiences; she mines them for every usable nugget.

Now she lives in London again—having sold the shrimp-washed country house near Colchester. She is a member of Parliament, a public figure identified with the ruling party, no longer just one of the crowd of protesters but a part of the powers-that-be. If the voice for social and political change is raised louder in her latest works, it is because her life and presumably her obsessions have altered. Fate or chance has dealt her another hand, and she is playing it. She seems to be a little like Wexford that way . . . adapting with the times, not necessarily liking change but making the best of it, participating yet always observing. If the political explicitness continues in her novels and if she links it to her psychological insights, who knows what new horrors Ruth Rendell may reveal?

RUTH RENDELL
1930–

English (born: London)

*"From long experience Burden knew that whatever may happen
in detective fiction, coincidence is more common than conspiracy
in real life."*
—From Doon with Death

Ruth Rendell, under her own name, writes the Inspector Wexford series and stand-alone psychological crime novels. She is also a gifted short
story writer with several collections. As Barbara Vine—an identity
launched in 1986 with *A Dark-Adapted Eye*—she writes intense novels
that may involve murder but are primarily studies in the psychological
consequences of past acts. To follow the private lives of Rendell's Kingsmarkham characters, the Wexford books should be read in order of
publication. Her British publisher is Hutchinson. Viking publishes her
Barbara Vine titles. Her American publishers include Doubleday, Pantheon, The Mysterious Press, and others. Novels and collections are
listed here by date of first publication in Great Britain. Alternate titles
are given. US = United States.

Mystery Novels and Short Story Collections
1965   *To Fear a Painted Devil*
1965   *Vanity Dies Hard*/US: *In Sickness and in Health*
1968   *The Secret House of Death*
1971   *One Across, Two Down*
1974   *The Face of Trespass*
1976   *A Demon in My View*
1976   *The Fallen Curtain* (short stories)
1977   *A Judgement in Stone*
1979   *Make Death Love Me*
1980   *The Lake of Darkness*
1982   *Master of the Moor*
1982   *The Fever Tree* (short stories)
1984   *The Killing Doll*
1984   *The Tree of Hands*
1986   *The New Girlfriend* (short stories)
1986   *Live Flesh*
1987   *Talking to Strange Men*

1988   *The Veiled One*
1989   *The Bridesmaid*
1990   *Going Wrong*
1991   *The Copper Peacock* (short stories)
1993   *The Crocodile Bird*
1996   *The Keys to the Street*
1998   *A Sight for Sore Eyes*
2000   *Piranha to Scurfy and Other Stories* (short stories)

Inspector Wexford Series
1964   *From Doon with Death*
1967   *A New Lease of Death*/US: *Sins of the Fathers*
1967   *Wolf to the Slaughter*
1969   *The Best Man to Die*
1970   *A Guilty Thing Surprised*
1971   *No More Dying Then*
1972   *Murder Being Once Done*
1973   *Some Lie and Some Die*
1975   *Shake Hands Forever*
1978   *A Sleeping Life*
1979   *Means of Evil* (Wexford short stories)
1981   *Put on by Cunning*/US: *Death Notes*
1983   *The Speaker of Mandarin*
1985   *An Unkindness of Ravens*
1992   *Kissing the Gunner's Daughter*
1995   *Simisola*
1997   *Road Rage*
1999   *Harm Done*

Barbara Vine Novels
1986   *A Dark-Adapted Eye*
1987   *A Fatal Inversion*
1988   *The House of Stairs*
1990   *Gallowglass*
1992   *King Solomon's Carpet*
1993   *Asta's Book*/US: *Anna's Book*
1994   *No Night Is Too Long*
1996   *The Brimstone Wedding*
1998   *The Chimney Sweeper's Boy*
2000   *Grasshopper*

Other Works

Rendell has edited and/or provided introductions to a number of works, including *The Reason Why: An Anthology of the Murderous Mind* (published by Jonathon Cape, Ltd., in 1995).

Her nonfiction works include *Ruth Rendell's Suffolk* and *Undermining the Central Line* (a political tract cowritten with Colin Ward in 1989).

Film and Video Adaptations

Several theatrical films have been based on Rendell novels. In 1989, *Tree of Hands* (U.S. title: *Innocent Victim*) received a not especially successful British treatment, starring Lauren Bacall and Helen Shaver. *A Judgement in Stone* has been filmed twice: the first was a 1986 Canadian production (alternate title: *The Housekeeper*) starring Rita Tushingham. A recent French version, *La Cérémonie,* was cowritten and directed by the noted Claude Chabrol and featured chilling performances by Sandrine Bonnaire, Isabelle Huppert, and Jacqueline Bisset. Spanish director Pedro Almodovar adapted *Live Flesh* for a 1997 Spanish-French film, changing the location to Madrid. Though well-made, neither of these European adaptations have been true to the spirit of their sources.

British television, however, has proven the most effective medium for Rendell's essentially British mysteries. In 1987, ITV began broadcasting the Wexford stories and others under the banner title *The Ruth Rendell Mysteries.* Produced by Meridian Broadcasting Ltd. for ITV, this ongoing series features George Baker as Wexford, Christopher Ravenscroft as Burden, and Louise Ramsey (who is married to Baker) as Dora Wexford.

The BBC has produced a number of the Barbara Vine novels, including *A Fatal Inversion* and *A Dark-Adapted Eye.* The lushly made and handsomely cast Vine adaptations have been broadcast on public television and on BBC America in the United States.

MARY HIGGINS CLARK

DAMSELS IN DISTRESS

"You begin with a sense of apprehension. You are involved from the get-go. . . . If it's a particularly good story, you start to hear noises in your own house—the staircase creaking, the wind outside, the furnace settling." —"Suppose? And What If?"

There's this woman, you see, and basically she's an ordinary sort. She might have a job that's more exciting than most. Or she might not. Chances are, she's a mom, though she could be uneasily single. She has a homely name like Nancy or Maggie or Jenny. And she is just going about her business, not bothering anyone, when all of a sudden . . . wham! Some psycho is out to get her.

Mary Higgins Clark has made a fortune writing novel after novel to this simple formula. Her first mystery, *Where Are the Children?*, was turned down by two publishers who were

Mary Higgins Clark

squeamish about its kiddies-at-risk theme, but the public took the book to their hearts when it appeared in 1975 and made it a bestseller. And the seemingly ageless author has never looked back.

Given that her formula is not new—damsels in distress are as old as storytelling—and that her writing style is plain vanilla at best, Mary Higgins Clark's extraordinary success can be confounding. Critics and scholars have a hard time with her books, not knowing exactly where they belong or how seriously to take them. Are they mysteries or romances or both? But her readers have no problems at all. The millions of devoted Mary Higgins Clark fans care not a jot or tittle about her status among contemporary mystery and crime writers nor about a proper definition for her genre. All they need to know is that every new Mary Higgins Clark will be a page-turner.

That few have attempted in-depth analysis of Clark's work is indicative of both critical snobbery (of the kind that likes to dismiss Agatha Christie as merely a popular writer) and bewilderment. But Mary is part of a long and proud literary tradition that survives despite efforts to ignore it to death. Just as the all-but-forgotten Mrs. Henry Wood and Mary Elizabeth Braddon did in the nineteenth century, Mary Higgins Clark writes sensationalist fiction in which all stops are pulled out to deliver certified thrills and chills. Though a notable holdout against explicit sex and violence, she happily takes on the darkest subject matter—kidnapping, child abuse, infanticide, insanity, serial murder, pedophilia, necrophilia—and exploits the worst, most paranoid of modern-day fears. And she does it with such innocent gleefulness and simplicity that the reader doesn't mind being manipulated. Of all the Women of Mystery at work today, Mary Higgins Clark produces the most purely recreational novels; like a sunny day at the beach, her books offer a degree of satisfaction that far exceeds the reader's investment of money, time, or mental effort.

> *"From the time I was a little girl, I loved to tell stories.*
> *It was part of my Irish heritage."*
>
> —1993 speech, Fordham University

Mary Higgins was born in New York City on December 24, 1929, and grew up in the Bronx, where her father, Luke, a hardworking Irish immigrant, owned the Higgins Bar and Grille. Her mother, Nora Durkin Higgins, who was second-generation Irish-American, had worked her way up from messenger girl to buyer for Manhattan's B. Altman department store before her marriage. Luke and Nora were both nearing forty when they tied the knot and quickly had three children; Mary was the middle child, between Joseph and John. In addition to her parents and two brothers, Mary was very much a part of her large, extended family, in which the gift of gab was prized and attention was paid to those who could spin the best tales at the dinner table.

There was also a strong streak of toughness in the family, the kind that faces tragedy head-on and overcomes. Prohibition and the Depression struck the family hard, and when Mary was ten, her father died unexpectedly. Her mother was left to support her daughter and two sons, taking in boarders to keep her family going. Everyone pitched in, although the family eventually had to give up their house and move into a tiny apartment. Tragedy seemed to cling to the family; Mary's brother Joe contracted spinal meningitis after joining the Navy in 1944. The Higginses' parish priest provided funds for Nora to travel to her son's bedside in the Long Beach Naval Hospital in California, and she was with him when he died. But the stalwart mother refused to allow grief to cloud her daughter's high school graduation a few months later.

Mary had worked as a baby-sitter and operated a telephone switchboard during her school years at Villa Maria Academy, the local parochial school for girls. Instead of going on to college as she wanted, she trained at a secretarial school and settled into a safe job as an advertising assistant with Remington Rand. But the dependable path was also the dull one, and responding to an offhand remark by a friend who was an airline stewardess, Mary applied to Pan American Airways and was soon serving passengers on international routes that took her to exotic locales and even into danger zones—Syria during a revolution, Czechoslovakia on the verge of Soviet domination. She flew for Pan Am for a year, but at Christmas in 1949, two days after her twentieth birthday, she married the man on whom she had set her eye several years earlier: Warren F. Clark (the F, he told her on their first date, was for "Fascinating"), a friend of one of her brothers.

The young couple settled down to raise a family in the New Jersey suburbs. Three daughters and two sons later, Mary was ready for something more. While Warren worked at a series of sales jobs, eventually becoming regional manager for a charter airline company, she enrolled in a creative writing course at New York University. Following her instructor's advice that students write about what they know, she used her experience in Czechoslovakia for inspiration and wrote her first short story for the class, "Stowaway." It took six years and forty rejections to sell the story, but when *Extension* magazine finally took it for $100, Mary was ecstatic.

(To be accurate, her first "sale" was not a story but a "twenty-five-words-or-less" entry in a contest sponsored by a Manhattan bakery in 1955. Mary, dispirited by a particularly direct rejection note, entered the competition, telling why she would choose a dress by one of four high fashion designers. On the entry blank she wrote, "I choose the Givenchy creation because I have three young children and it's a long time since I've felt irresistible. I am sure that in that gown I could feel irresistible plus." She won the dress—"swirling black silk, layers of crinoline, puffed sleeves, and a tiny waist"—and wore it for years.)

The sale of her short story attracted an agent and began a moderately successful run of story sales to national magazines But the closing of several major publications in 1963, she knew, signaled the end of the short story market, and Mary began freelancing for radio. It was important that she develop her earning power. Her husband had already suffered three heart attacks, and the specter of becoming the family's main support (as her mother had done) must have weighed on Mary. Warren's death in 1964—at age forty-five—left her with five children aged five to thirteen, a mortgage, and very little money. With her mother as babysitter, she turned to full-time radio scripting that included researching and writing historical sketches for a short, daily segment called *Portrait of a Patriot.* The research she did became the basis of a biographical fiction she titled *Aspire to the Heavens,* based on the life of George Washington. *Aspire* fell flat when it appeared in 1969—in part because the title led booksellers to shelve it in the religious section—but the experience proved to Mary that she could write a full-length novel and get a publisher.

She stayed in radio, however, forming her own production company with a partner and continuing to write and produce scripts on an eclectic list of subjects. Radio, she later said, taught her the virtues of succinctness and swift pacing and how to craft believable dialog. But it was not where she wanted to be. In the late 1960s and early 1970s, radio was rapidly turning to straight music formats, and Mary must have known that the market for writers of her type was drying up.

She wanted to write another book, and deciding what kind led her to examine her own reading. She was surprised to discover that what she enjoyed most was mysteries. Her favorite writers, she realized, were Mary Roberts Rinehart, Agatha Christie, Josephine Tey, and Charlotte Armstrong.★ She had always loved stories full of mystery and suspense. As a child, she'd been fascinated by the kidnapping of the Lindbergh baby, especially when her father pointed out the cemetery where the ransom note had been left, located near the Higginses' summer cottage. As a little girl, she had suffered from asthma and was frequently confined to bed, spending many solitary hours listening to the exciting dramas and serials that filled the radio airwaves in the 1930s. From age seven, she had written poems—much praised and prompted by her mother—and adventure plays, forcing her brothers to act in her garage productions

---

★ Charlotte Armstrong (1905–1969), Michigan born and Barnard College educated, wrote novels of crime and suspense that were very popular from the 1940s to the 1960s (and still deserve attention). Like Mary Higgins Clark, Armstrong often revealed the villains in the opening pages of her books, featured heroines who are ordinary women cast into extraordinary situations, and included children among the main characters. A number of her mysteries were adapted to film; *Mischief,* the source of 1952's *Don't Bother to Knock,* offered Marilyn Monroe her first major role, as a psychopathic baby-sitter.

and saving the star roles for herself. But most important, she had always been a storyteller. Perhaps it was the Irish in her, but young Mary Higgins could always weave a tale that kept her friends and relatives spellbound to the end.

Suspense it would be, and Mary began *Where Are the Children?* by playing, as her creative writing teacher once advised, a game of "what if?" Beginning with the actual case of Alice Crimmins, a New York cocktail waitress who was convicted of murdering her own children,★ and her vivid memory of the Lindbergh kidnapping, Mary imagined what might happen to a woman accused of just such crimes. Mary worked on the book for three years—writing in the early morning hours, as is still her habit—and after two rejections, the story of a young mother with a terrible secret in her past was bought by Simon and Schuster. Mary received a $3,000 advance. The author who had once persisted for six years to sell a short story soon found her name among the bestsellers of 1975. The advance rose to six figures for her second novel, *A Stranger Is Watching,* and by the time it was published in 1977, Mary was able to give up her production company and to support her family on her earnings as a writer. She had also fulfilled an old ambition for herself, returning to college in 1974. In 1979, she received her bachelor's degree, summa cum laude, from New York's Fordham University. She was almost fifty years old.

The bandwagon was rolling. Each new novel attracted more dedicated readers. Print orders increased, and the author's name grew larger and larger on book covers. Mary was very soon to rank in the multimillion-dollar class. In 1988, she was guaranteed $10 million for her next five books; her 1992 contract stipulated $35 million for six books. By 1996, she had risen to very near the top of the pay scale, signing a $36 million contract with Simon and Schuster/Pocket Books for the world book and audio rights to her next three publications. In April 2000—twenty-five years after signing her first contract with Simon and Schuster—Mary put her name to a new deal for the astronomical sum of $64 million. Her obligation comprises four suspense novels ($15 million each) and her memoir ($4 million). Will success spoil Mary Higgins Clark? It's doubtful.

In her introductory editorial for the *Mary Higgins Clark Mystery Magazine,* Mary wrote, "By the time I was in third grade I knew that my book of choice would always be a mystery. Creaking doors, footsteps in the night, whispering voices from a dark corner. . . ." Even with her

---

★ The Crimmins murder also inspired, among others, Dorothy Uhnak's novel *The Investigation.* The case was sensational in its day, principally because it involved infanticide.

phenomenal success, she never seems to have lost that initial joy and her own delight in a suspenseful tale. Yes, her stories are formulaic. And yes, they are derivative, owing particularly to Mary Roberts Rinehart and the Had-I-But-Known school of the 1930s and 1940s and to the romantic thrillers of writers such as Daphne du Maurier and Vera Caspary.* But Mary takes such enormous pleasure in telling a ripping good yarn, and her belief in her stories is infectious. She has compared suspense fiction to a roller coaster ride, and in that metaphor lies the essence of her approach. She goes straight for the gut, bypassing all the impedimenta of traditional crime writing like complex clues, evidence, and the rational detective. Readers can slip into her novels and barely disturb a brain cell because there is no puzzle to work out. The action is usually compressed into a period of hours or days to enhance the tension. In many of her novels, the bad guy is known from the start. The question is not whodunit, but will the plucky heroine survive it. Mary has admitted, "I love the idea that the reader is one step ahead of the main character and worried about her. 'Don't get in the car with him, he's a killer.'"

Her stories are visceral, grown-up versions of ghost stories told around the campfire at a Girl Scouts' overnight. Like Mary Roberts Rinehart, Mary relies on coincidence, often employs sixth-sense-type intuition, and sometimes includes a supernatural element in her mysteries—the dead mother in *A Cry in the Night,* for example, and the long-dead Lady Margaret Carew in *The Anastasia Syndrome*—then leaves it unresolved as a kind of bonus aftershock. Motivation is rarely complicated or even logical, and in contrast to the work of her Golden Age predecessors, official justice is of little concern. When there is a madman behind the door or under the bed, what matters is survival.

> *"I want the woman to be in jeopardy."*
> —"Suspense" in *The Crown Crime Companion*

The fundamental appeal of a Mary Higgins Clark novel is always the heroine, who is so very like the women who make up the vast majority

---

* Britain's Dame Daphne du Maurier (1907–1989) was very popular in her day and remains so for her moody, sexually charged Gothic and historical romances, including *Rebecca, Jamaica Inn,* and *My Cousin Rachel.* Despite her disclaimer that she was not a crime writer, du Maurier was named a Grand Master of the genre by the Mystery Writers of America in 1954. The fame of Chicago-born Vera Caspary (1904–1987), however, rests on *Laura,* the first of her fifteen novels, which is best known from the 1944 film version directed by Otto Preminger.

of Clark's audience. If the women Mary writes about were contestants for the Miss America title, they would probably be second runners-up—smarter than average, beautiful but not stunning, and always trying harder. Even when her job is in a glamour field, a Mary Higgins Clark heroine is not yet at the top of the heap. For instance, Elizabeth Lange in *Weep No More, My Lady* is a struggling actress, though her dead sister was a movie star. Pat Traymore in *Stillwatch* and Meghan Collins in *I'll Be Seeing You* are both TV reporters on the rise but nowhere near the Barbara Walters level. Lady lawyers tend to be assistant district attorneys. Only in her 1996 *My Gal Sunday* short stories about a former president and his congresswoman wife can the female protagonist be called a genuine celebrity. (Sunday Britland is like the balancing side of the scales for Alvirah Meehan, a character introduced in *Weep No More, My Lady* and carried on in *The Lottery Winner* and *All through the Night*. Alvirah, a cleaning lady, hits the jackpot in the New York State Lottery, and she and her plumber husband Willy retire to a life of comfort and amateur detection. The Meehans and the Britlands are Mary's only continuing characters.)

Clearly, the prototype for Mary Higgins Clark's heroines is Mary Higgins Clark. From humble working-class or middle-class origins and often orphaned, these women make their way on intelligence, hard work, and willpower. Whether dead, divorced, or just plain jerks, the first men in their lives have deserted them. Alone and often the sole support of young children, they must fight a daily battle to balance work with family and social life. There may have been some early trauma in their lives—the loss of a parent or parents, sibling, or child—but the heroine has come through stable if not unscathed. (An exception is the psychologically damaged Laurie Kenyon in *All about the Town,* and she is one of Mary's least successful heroines because Laurie's mental state, on which the plot turns, makes her weak, dependent, and pitiable.) These early traumas, in addition to explaining the heroine's strength of character, become, like the death of dress designer Neeve Kearney's mother in *While My Pretty One Sleeps,* central to the mystery.

Despite her hectic life, the typical Mary Higgins Clark heroine is lonely but not desperate. If Mr. Right comes along, she will greet him with open arms, as soon as she puts away the groceries and tidies up the messy corpse in the living room. Although Mary includes strong men in her novels and they may even rescue the heroines from physical danger in the end, these heroes are secondary characters, just as Mary's brothers were in her childhood plays. They are useful as plot devices but never given center stage for long.

Above all else, the heroine is just so darn normal, if overachieving, and so likable that when she gets into trouble, never of her own making, the reader cannot resist wanting to help her through to safety. Mix this attractive and resourceful woman, who could easily be your best friend, your daughter or granddaughter,* with Mary's imaginative storytelling and skillful pacing; toss in a hot tabloid topic (radio psychology, plastic surgery, infertility, in vitro fertilization, dating via the personal ads, repressed memory, political chicanery, witness-protection programs); and flavor with lots of women's magazine–style details about room furnishings and fashions and easy-to-digest factoid history and reportage. It is a recipe for commercial success.

While other writers can imitate the formula fairly well, Mary Higgins Clark has mastered it, filling out the basic structure with elements that are almost entirely her own. Older characters are significant and sometimes more interesting than the heroines, even when they are dead. The elderly Newport ladies of *Moonlight Becomes You;* Ethel Lamston, the murder victim in *While My Pretty One Sleeps*; and Jane Clausen, the bereaved mother in *You Belong to Me*—all share a kind of spirit and determination that is really heroine spunk aged in oak. Older characters are also allowed love, and their romances (beginning with lawyer Jonathan Knowles and office manager Dorothy Prentiss in *Where Are the Children?*) are often woven through the plot as counterpoint to the rocky love lives of the heroines. Parent-child relationships are always crucial to motivation, both good and evil. Sexual desire, when perverted, is presented as a powerful first cause for mayhem and murder and as contrast to the heroine's pure heart.

Mary, ever the good Catholic schoolgirl, works within a strict moral framework: good is really Good, bad is really Evil and often insane. There are few shadings in her characters, though her good people have a tendency to be either secretive or pigheadedly obtuse and her villains can be charmers. Her best stories have the same compelling power to raise goose bumps as the scariest fairy stories—"Snow White," "Hansel and Gretel"—because they evolve from the premise that evil lurks in the banal details of everyday activity.

Mary Higgins Clark's own life story certainly has a fairy-tale quality to it, but there was no Prince Charming to rescue her from the ashes. She accomplished her transformation from New Jersey housewife and widowed mom to celebrity writer on her own. And people who know her well agree that she has remained solidly grounded despite her success. Although her name on a cover is sufficient to sell millions of copies, she has been a tireless traveler, happily promoting her books and

---

* Since the 1989 publication of *While My Pretty One Sleeps,* most of Mary's books have been published in May to take advantage of Mother's Day buying.

meeting her throngs of devoted readers. She reads and enjoys her fan mail with the relish of a first-time novelist. She is actively involved in a number of professional organizations and private causes: she has served as president and board member of the Mystery Writers of America and chair of the International Crime Writers Congress, and is a strong supporter of adult literacy programs, libraries, and Catholic charities. With fellow writers including Thomas Chastain and Dorothy Salisbury Davis, Mary was a founding member of the Adams Round Table—a group that meets monthly to talk about their craft. (The group has produced several joint volumes, including *The Case of the Caribbean Blues, Missing in Manhattan,* and *Murder on the Run.*)

Until 2000, she had received few awards for her writing—the 1980 French Grand Prix de Littérature Policière and another French literary prize at Deauville in 1998 being the notable exceptions. Yet she has been heaped with tributes from other directions: an honorary doctorate from her alma mater, Fordham University, and honorary degrees from at least a dozen other colleges and universities, the first Gold Medal in Education from the National Arts Club, Irish Woman of the Year. In the spring of 2000, however, she at last got the recognition of her peers when she was named Grand Master by the Mystery Writers of America.

But when asked in an interview by Jan Grape to name her greatest success, Mary replied simply, "My family." The attentive reader need only note the dedications to her novels to understand the central role of her five children—Marilyn and Warren, both lawyers and judges; David; Carol, also a published mystery writer; and Patricia—her eight grandchildren, and many close relatives and friends. Her first mystery was dedicated to her mother, that staunch supporter whose encouragement never wavered. Her 1997 *Pretend You Don't See Her* honors her new husband and their children and stepchildren.

After more than three decades of widowhood, Mary told *People* magazine in May 1996 that she was content with her life as "an aging debutante" and had no intention of remarrying. Eight months later, exercising the female prerogative, she had changed her mind. Her second marriage, in November 1996, to retired Merrill Lynch executive John Conheeny resulted from a meeting arranged by her daughter Patty. A fairy-tale ending perhaps, but more appropriately a classic Mary Higgins Clark wrap-up. The Conheenys divide their time between homes in New Jersey and Manhattan, where Mary does no housework but still cooks for guests, and world travel. At the time of her marriage, Mary told reporters that she intended to slow down and smell the roses; whether she can give up her rigorous work habits or her dedication to her readers remains to be seen. She published fifteen novels and short story collections between 1991 and 2000—an Agatha Christie–like pace that may partly account for the increased predictability and diminishing suspense in her latest books. Her heroines, too, have become more upper class (and proportionately less engaging), possibly reflecting Mary's own escalating financial status. Even *Publishers Weekly,* the influential trade publication that tends to treat major authors with kid gloves, accused her of writing in her sleep in a 1998 review of *You Belong to Me.*

But Mary has said that she works for neither money nor fame, and while cynics can scoff, there is the ring of truth to this statement. That she enjoys the limelight of celebrity is obvious; in interviews she never complains about her rigorous touring schedule, her doting fans, or even witless interviewers. Though she is unlikely to win many prizes for literary merit, she is a constant proselytizer for the *craft* of writing, urging the young to study the basics, hone, and persist. Her own novels have a rare quality in the modern world of blockbuster fiction: each seems written for the pleasure of the author as much as the audience.

Barring future revelations of some deep, dark secret, Mary Higgins Clark seems to be exactly as she appears: a pleasant middle-class matron with a history of personal loss who hit the jackpot by writing clean, scary suspense stories suitable for and beloved by readers of all ages past third grade. In her own words, "I'm as open as apple pie." An American success story in the nicest way.

BIBLIOGRAPHY

MARY HIGGINS CLARK
1929–
American (born: New York City)

"We all ignored facts today in a way that might have contributed to disaster." —Jonathan Knowles in *Where Are the Children?*

Except in two recent short story collections and her 1998 holiday book, *All through the Night,* Mary Higgins Clark does not employ series characters. All of her novels are self-contained, and they can be read in any order. Simon and Schuster, with its Pocket Books paperback imprimatur, is her American publisher. British publishers have included Talmy Franklin, Collins, Century, and Chivers. Dates are for first publication.

Novels
1975   *Where Are the Children?*
1977   *A Stranger Is Watching*

1980 *The Cradle Will Fall*
1982 *A Cry in the Night*
1984 *Stillwatch*
1987 *Weep No More, My Lady*
1989 *While My Pretty One Sleeps*
1989 *The Anastasia Syndrome and Other Stories* (novella and short stories)
1991 *Loves Music, Loves to Dance*
1992 *All around the Town*
1993 *I'll Be Seeing You*
1994 *Remember Me*
1994 *The Lottery Winner* (short stories with Alvirah and Willy Meehan)
1995 *Let Me Call You Sweetheart*
1995 *Silent Night*
1996 *Moonlight Becomes You*
1996 *My Gal Sunday* (short stories with Henry and Sunday Britland)
1997 *Pretend You Don't See Her*
1998 *You Belong to Me*
1998 *All through the Night* (Alvirah and Willy Meehan)
1999 *We'll Meet Again*
2000 *Before I Say Good-bye*
2000 *Deck the Halls* (with daughter Carol Higgins Clarke)

In addition to her own works, Mary Higgins Clark has edited and/or contributed to several collections, including:

1986 *Murder in Manhattan* (Adams Round Table)
1987 *Murder on the Aisle; 1987 Mystery Writers of American Anthology*
1988 *Caribbean Blues* (Adams Round Table)
1992 *Missing in Manhattan* (Adams Round Table)
1995 *The International Association of Crime Writers Presents Bad Behavior*
1997 *The Plot Thickens*
1998 *Murder on the Run* (Adams Round Table)
1999 *The Night Awakens* (Mystery Writers of America)

Film and Video Adaptations

A number of Mary Higgins Clark's novels have been adapted for film and television, though none has managed to convey fully the pacing or suspense of the originals.

A film version of *Where Are the Children?* was produced in 1986 with Jill Clayburg as the beleaguered mother. *A Stranger Is Watching* (MGM-UA) was released in 1982; Kate Mulgrew starred. Both are R-rated and unpleasantly un-Clark.

   Television adaptations have fared better. Grosso-Jacobson Productions
has produced video versions for CBS and the cable networks The Family Channel and USA Network. *While My Pretty One Sleeps* with Connie
Sellecca and *Let Me Call You Sweetheart* with Meredith Baxter can be recommended for Clark fans. Despite her broadcast background, the author has taken little part in these adaptations.

SUE GRAFTON

AN "ORNERY" ORIGINAL

"Everything I own, everything I am, goes into these books."★

Simply put, Sue Grafton is a delight. She is one of the best-selling authors in the world: more than 12 million copies of her "alphabet" books have been sold, published in twenty-eight countries and twenty-six languages. Yet she remains remarkably unchanged by her success, willing to be interviewed and always attentive to her fans. She worked for years as a screenwriter in Hollywood and was good at it, but two early novels went largely unnoticed. Her success came from doing what new writers are told to do: write about what you know best. Sue crafted her main character as

Sue Grafton

a younger, thinner version of herself, and plunged into a life of crime.

Sue Grafton is the creator of Kinsey Millhone, a private investigator who works in the fictional city of Santa Teresa (the name given to Santa Barbara by Ross Macdonald in his Lew Archer books). Millhone made her debut in *"A" Is for Alibi* in 1983, and with a couple of brief breaks, her author has since delivered a book a year (never soon enough for her panting fans). The "alphabet" series is widely credited with giving respectability to the hard-boiled female private eye. Millhone—like Mar-

---

★ Sue Grafton's quotes are from an interview conducted for *Women of Mystery* in January 2000, and from other interviews cited in "References and Resources."

cia Muller's Sharon McCone and Sara Paretsky's V. I. Warshawski—was not the first female private investigator, but she has become an icon of the "new woman" who lives out, rather than preaches, her feminism. There are plenty of male followers of Grafton's novels, but the stories have their most devoted readership among women. "I think women are looking for a mirror rather than an escape," Grafton told *Newsweek* in 1990. In Kinsey Millhone, she has reflected the complicated lives of women at the turn of the new century: Kinsey is tough but not lacking in sentiment, independent, often stressed but never incapacitated, conflicted by the demands of her job and personal life, coping by means of common sense and a wealth of offbeat humor. She isn't Sue Grafton, but she is close.

Sue Grafton was born in Louisville, Kentucky, the second daughter of parents who were themselves the children of Presbyterian missionaries in China. Sue's parents were alcoholics, and as a child she had more freedom than most in the Highlands area of her hometown. Her father was an attorney; Cornelius Warren "Chip" Grafton wrote four mystery novels during a career cut short by his death from a heart attack. The senior Grafton's first novel won the Mary Roberts Rinehart Award in 1943. Though she has considered republishing her father's books, Sue admits that the passage of time has dated them somewhat. Changes in the industry would make publishing the books herself the only realistic option, so in all likelihood her own work will serve as monument to the creative ability inherited from her father.

Sue remains grateful for the influence of both her mother, Vivian—a high school teacher—and her father: "My parents, for all their failings, were very intellectual and they were into books, and part of the escape in our family was into reading. So all of us did a ton of reading . . . my father, who was a full-time municipal bond attorney, wrote mystery fiction in his spare time. So there was always great value set on the language and on reading and on the imagination. I consider that I had the perfect childhood. And I would not change one minute of it."

The "ornery" streak so endearing in Kinsey Millhone has its roots in her creator: "On my report card where it says 'cooperates with others,' I used to get an exact zero. It took a lot of time to discover this about myself." Sue graduated from Atherton High School in 1957 and went on to earn a degree in English from the University of Louisville in 1961. Her absolute unwillingness to be seduced by ego is evident in Sue's attitude toward her alma mater: "I had to do this gig for the University of Louisville where I graduated, I must say, as a rather mediocre student. But now that I've got this high profile, they're acting as though I'm their favorite. They keep doing me these honors." Recently she was named

Alumna of the Year. "It's quite clear they didn't go back and look at my grade-point-average."

For more than twenty years, Sue has been married to philosophy professor Steve Humphrey—her third husband. Unlike Kinsey Millhone, who is childless, Sue is the mother of three grown children (from her previous marriages) and is a grandmother; a granddaughter is named Kinsey. Sue currently divides her time between homes in Montecito, California, and Louisville.

Her early first marriage ended in divorce. Kinsey Millhone may well be the product of Sue's second marriage, which also ended in divorce after ten years. Sue readily admits that she looked for an outlet for her anger with her second husband during the divorce and subsequent bitter custody battle. She found catharsis by imagining his demise, and these thoughts eventually led to *"A" Is for Alibi.* Having worked as a Hollywood screenwriter, Sue understood the craft of mystery writing: "I learned how to write a dialogue scene, how to get into a scene and get out of it. I learned how to write an action scene. I learned how to structure a story, which is critical." There is no question that Kinsey Millhone was Grafton's ticket out of Tinsel Town, but she will never sell her character to the same system: "I invented Kinsey Millhone as my way out; I would never sell her back to them. I would have to be nuts to do that. I don't want them to have any power in my life."

Kinsey Millhone leads a simple life: she lives in a small apartment, drives an ancient VW bug, owns one dress—a black one, serviceable for all occasions (Grafton still has the original in her closet), and cuts her own hair (badly). Sue is used to suggestions from readers that Kinsey get a makeover, but she vows to resist. Kinsey's parents died in an automobile accident when she was five, and she was raised by her mother's sister. As the books progress, readers come to know Kinsey as she opens up to her past and learns about herself, and to understand the fear of abandonment that plagues her. Sue likes to refer to her own subconscious as her Shadow, and she said recently, "In many ways, I don't consider that I'm inventing the facts [about Kinsey] so much as bringing them to light. I operate in the belief that Shadow knows everything about Kinsey's life and that I'm given the information on an 'as needed' basis."

With each new novel, Sue adds more details about Kinsey, to the obvious delight of her readers. In *"J" Is for Judgment,* she introduced Kinsey's cousins and was almost overwhelmed with requests from readers for more about her character's personal history.

Fans of the series know that Kinsey has been divorced twice; her first husband is a central character in *"O" Is for Outlaw.* The Millhone books are also peopled with an engaging entourage of continuing characters. Henry Pitts (born February 14, 1901) is a retired baker in his eighties who is also Kinsey's landlord. He is by far the most popular secondary character in the series, and readers have been introduced to members of his Michigan family. At one time Sue contemplated a minor heart attack for Henry. She does extensive research while working on every book and decided to visit a California hospital to learn more about the care of heart patients. But when nurses on the cardiac unit learned the reason for her visit, they refused to cooperate; faced with fans so protective of Henry, Sue reluctantly returned him to good health.

Kinsey gets her only exposure to home cooking through periodic visits to Rosie's Tavern. Rosie is the most colorful series character and a sometime antagonist for Kinsey. A reluctant cook at best, Kinsey is (unlike her creator) a devotee of fast food. Her two failed marriages have left her somewhat gun-shy in dealing with the opposite sex. Pressed by readers for more information about Kinsey's family, Sue somewhat reluctantly plans to explore her character's past in more detail in coming volumes. She is committed to working her way through the alphabet and, if she keeps up her pace, will be just seventy when she gets to Z. But for hardcore fans who must have a Millhone fix between books, Kinsey's life and habits have been chronicled in *"G" Is for Grafton* by North Carolina academics Natalie Hevener Kaufman and Carol McGinnis Kay. The authors were granted access to Sue's journals, in which she plans plot and character development, so this book is the literal guide to every nook and cranny of the works of Sue Grafton.

As a writer, she is also an organized and exhaustive researcher. She begins with a journal for each book, in which she records her feelings about the book, ideas for the plot, and her struggles to create. She also draws charts of the locale in every book, visiting the "scene of the crime" to ensure the accuracy of each detail. To illustrate how comprehensive her background work is, the completed manuscript of *"O" Is for Outlaw* was 425 pages, double-spaced; the journal for the same book was almost 400 single-spaced pages. Asked where she gets ideas for new books, Sue explains that she often looks through journals for earlier books: an idea jotted in the margin may provide the seed for the next installment in the series.

Like Kinsey, Sue is fit and exercises daily; she jogged for twenty-five years, but now hitting sixty, she has begun to walk three miles a day in deference to aging knees. She also lifts weights on a regular basis and swims. But she abhors violence and has made a decision never to write from the point of view of the criminal. No paranoid, Sue is nonetheless conscious of the threat of danger in everyday life; she lives with caution and expresses concern about the access to private information on each of us. Her take on the distinction between real and fictional murder is matter-of-fact: "Real homicide is often alcohol-related; it's impulsive;

it's ugly; it's dirty; it's stupid. . . . In a murder mystery, the first conceit is
that if you are murdered it is because someone devious and cunning
with much to be gained has plotted for weeks and come up with terribly clever schemes to do you in. . . . The second conceit of mystery fiction is, if you are murdered, there is a detective who is equally cunning
and equally dedicated who will move heaven and earth to see that justice is done."

Influenced by both Raymond Chandler and Ross Macdonald, Sue
also enjoys contemporary mysteries, particularly those by Elmore
Leonard (her favorite), Ruth Rendell writing as Barbara Vine, and
Michael Connelly. About detective novels, Sue Grafton has said, "If
they told me as of tomorrow the hard-boiled female private eye was going out of fashion, I'd write them anyway because it isn't about trends,
it's about what I want to do for my life. Even if none of them sold again,
I would still write them." The work of the detective, as described by
Sue Grafton, is nine-tenths hard work—following up on leads, inter-
viewing witnesses, processing myriad seemingly useless details until a
pattern emerges—and one-tenth excitement. At some point in each
book, Kinsey begins to pull the threads of the solution together, and her
real gift as a detective becomes apparent. Although her fictive fathers are
clearly the street-hardened tough guys of Chandler and Macdonald,
Kinsey is also an ex-cop who solves her cases—many involving past injustices—with diligence and solid reasoning worthy of the Golden Age.

Sue Grafton has always been most generous and helpful to aspiring
writers. She seems never to have forgotten her own origins, the girl with
few boundaries who grew to discipline herself as a demanding and
meticulous author. Her books are not always even in quality. ("N" Is for
Noose was generally considered below standard, but "O" Is for Outlaw
was well received and allayed fears that Grafton might be slipping.) Yet a
large part of what makes each book so enjoyable—in addition to the
strengths of plot and characterization and the crackling dialog—is the
reader's strong sense of the writer's genuine personality. Fans identify
with Kinsey to be sure, but they also have a feeling of kinship with
Grafton. Of her own life since "A" Is for Alibi first caught the public's
attention, Sue Grafton says that "the smartest move I ever made was to
invent somebody who now supports me."

—MCT

SUE GRAFTON
1940–
American (born: Louisville, Kentucky)

> *"I feel compelled to report that at the moment of death, my entire life did not pass before my eyes in a flash. . . . Mostly, I regretted I hadn't tidied my chest of drawers. . . . It's painful to realize that those who mourn your untimely demise will also carry with them the indelible image of all your tatty underpants."*
>
> — *"I" Is for Innocent*

Sue Grafton has one detective—the memorable Ms. Millhone—who features in all her mystery novels. To follow Kinsey's life and career, the "alphabet" series is best when read in sequence. Grafton has been published by Henry Holt and Company in the United States since the beginning of the series. Macmillan has published the series in England.

Kinsey Millhone Mystery Novels
1983   *"A" Is for Alibi*
1985   *"B" Is for Burglar*
1986   *"C" Is for Corpse*
1987   *"D" Is for Deadbeat*
1988   *"E" Is for Evidence*
1989   *"F" Is for Fugitive*
1990   *"G" Is for Gumshoe*
1991   *"H" Is for Homicide*
1992   *"I" Is for Innocent*
1993   *"J" Is for Judgment*
1994   *"K" Is for Killer*
1995   *"L" Is for Lawless*
1996   *"M" Is for Malice*
1998   *"N" Is for Noose*
1999   *"O" Is for Outlaw*

(Grafton's "P" novel is scheduled for release in January 2001.)

Other Works
Sue Grafton has edited several collections as well as a mystery-writing guide for the Mystery Writers of America. She also produced, through

Bench Press, a very limited edition of *Kinsey and Me,* a collection that includes eight Millhone short stories and eight personal stories.

Before beginning the "alphabet" books, she wrote two nonmysteries, *Keziah Dane* (1967) and *The Lolly-Madonna Wars* (1969). The latter was adapted into a 1973 MGM film titled *Lolly Madonna XXX* in the United States, with Grafton dividing the screenwriting credits. Despite a cast including Rod Steiger, Robert Ryan, and Jeff Bridges, this tale of a hillbilly feud is best forgotten.

Grafton's Hollywood experiences—she wrote for several popular TV series, including *Rhoda*, and also adapted two of Agatha Christie's Miss Marple novels for television—have led the author to refuse all offers to film the Millhone novels.

PATRICIA CORNWELL

DANGEROUS DISSECTION

*"I have this real cagey way of worming myself in. I'm an infec-
tion. You try to pacify me, and before you know it, you can't get
me out of your system."*★

𝒫atricia Cornwell is one Woman of Mystery whose personal life is
in many ways more fantastic than that of her main character, Dr. Kay
Scarpetta—the fictional Virginia coroner in the series of novels that
have made Cornwell one of the highest-paid female novelists working
today.

Cornwell is a crime writer, and the niche she works in—the forensic
procedural—is neither new nor unique to her, though no one would
ever confuse Scarpetta with a Quincy. But partly through riveting characterization and partly through her extraordinary skill at detailing the
scientific and intellectual processes of forensic investigation, she is the
clear pacesetter in this field. Her novels are knee-deep in the consequences of violence, often random multiple murders, yet she does not
present either the interior mental machinations or the homicidal acts of
her murderers. The sheer horror of murder comes on the medical examiner's table as a physician (who is also a lawyer) trained to save lives
dissects the dead. Cornwell's readers experience the brutality of murder
through the clinical indignities a victim suffers even after death. Cornwell herself expressed it, in a 1994 interview with Rosemary Herbert,
as the "fearful symmetry of having this humane, civilized, physician,
who is sworn by the Hippocratic Oath to do no harm, be the one who
is going to these scenes and dealing with the spoils of this hideous irra-
tionality and cruelty."

★ Patricia Cornwell's quotes are from various interviews listed in "References and Resources" and from her published works.

This duality is intrinsic to the design and impact of the Scarpetta books, as is the particular kind of irrational, often motiveless violence she presents. Cornwell is admittedly terrified of violence and gore: ". . . I couldn't even dissect worms in the ninth grade!" To write of it, she says that she practices a kind of detachment, a form of role-playing, that she learned in her childhood.

Born Patricia Carroll Daniels on June 9, 1956, little "Patsy" was the middle child between two brothers. Her father, Sam, who died in 1996, was a lawyer. The family lived in Miami, Florida, until the Danielses' marriage collapsed when Patricia was five. Two years later, she moved with her mother, Marilyn, and brothers to Montreat, North Carolina. A victim of severe depression, Marilyn Daniels was eventually hospitalized several times. Before one breakdown, knowing that she was in deep emotional trouble, Mrs. Daniels took her children to the home of Billy and Ruth Graham. Mrs. Graham, wife of one of the world's best-known Christian evangelists, placed the children with missionaries who had recently returned from the Congo. In so doing, Ruth Graham entered the life of a young child who needed a mentor and began what would be a long and sometimes tumultuous relationship with the future author.

Cornwell has described the missionary couple who cared for her as very Victorian in their attitudes and determined to teach her to be a "lady." For a tomboyish little girl who wanted to play with her brothers, the experience prompted a great deal of anger. To deal with her anger and her fears that her mother might not return, Patricia remembers, "I just escaped in my head."

For a time, Patricia hoped for a career in professional tennis. She did well in early competition: in four years on the boys' tennis team in high school, she never lost a match (an achievement shared with Deputy Chief Virginia West of the Charlotte Police in Cornwell's new crime series). She briefly attended King College in Tennessee, then transferred to Davidson College—one of the South's cadre of elite liberal arts schools—on a tennis scholarship. But realizing that she was not in the pro league, she gave up her scholarship for other goals.

During her freshman year at Davidson, she suffered from anorexia and bulimia, which resulted in her hospitalization in the same mental health facility where her mother had been a patient. She wrote a novel, which she says was highly autobiographical, as her thesis for an English degree, and graduated from Davidson in 1979. Along the way she became infatuated with Charles Cornwell, a never-married English professor seventeen years older than she. The two married, and in 1981 they moved to Richmond, Virginia, where Charles entered Union Theological Seminary. Patricia began work on a biography of Ruth Bell Graham, published as *A Time for Remembering* in 1983. Years earlier, at Mrs. Graham's suggestion, Patricia had begun the habit of keeping a journal, and she credits Ruth Graham with encouraging her to pursue her writing.

Before moving to Richmond, Patricia had won an award for crime reporting for the *Charlotte Observer*. In Richmond, she went to work in the office of the state's medical examiner, first as a technical writer, then as a computer analyst. (Her skills at the computer were later mirrored in the character of Kay Scarpetta's niece Lucy.) She also joined the volunteer police force, which gave her direct experience with crime in an urban setting. While working in the medical examiner's office, Patricia wrote three books whose main character was a male detective, "a kind of poor man's Adam Dalgliesh." The books were rejected for publication, but in the course of her correspondence with publishing houses, Cornwell was encouraged by Sara Ann Fried, a sympathetic editor with Mysterious Press, to write about what she knew. Fried also suggested that Cornwell promote a minor character named Kay Scarpetta to a leading role. Cornwell's first Scarpetta novel, *Postmortem,* was purchased for around $7,000 and published by Scribner's in 1990.

By this time, she and Charles Cornwell had divorced, but she kept his name, and *Postmortem* was released under the byline "Patricia Daniels Cornwell."

Cornwell's ascent in the world of publishing has been swift and stunning—she now commands a reported $8 million for each new mystery—but not without conflict and controversy. Indeed, she seems to have had more than her share of trouble, including an estrangement of several years' duration with Ruth Bell Graham over Cornwell's biography.

A more public scandal had serious legal ramifications. Cornwell had met with Robert Ressler, a former F.B.I. agent, about possible collaboration on his memoirs. Before their professional association was over, Ressler was involved in a lawsuit with his former agency over his supposed disclosure of secret information to Cornwell. The case, which was settled with no damage to Ressler's character or reputation, was not only time-consuming and distressing; it was also highly expensive in legal fees. Ressler and his wife both feel that the trouble had basically begun with the first meeting with Cornwell.

Cornwell has sued and has been sued on several occasions. She sued Cynthia Stevens, a former employee, claiming that Stevens had not returned company property; Stevens countersued and accused Cornwell of sexual harassment. Both actions were dismissed.

Cornwell has also been sued by William and Jewell Phelps of Richmond, who claimed that details in the 1992 novel *All That Remains* were taken from the autopsy of their daughter, whose murder is still unsolved.

Because the case has not been closed, autopsy details are supposed to be known only to the police and the family of the victim. Mr. and Mrs. Phelps claim that Cornwell had access to this information because of her position as an employee in the medical examiner's office.

There have been other incidents. In 1991, a Florida man named John Benson Waterman was accused of strangling a neighbor using techniques described in *Postmortem*. (Imitation has been an unhappy consequence of fame for other writers in the crime and mystery field, including Agatha Christie.)

In another publicized episode, Cornwell was supposedly rebuffed when she tried to set up a meeting with the actress Jodie Foster to discuss working on a film together. Cornwell allegedly tried to establish a friendship with Irene Brafstein, a former tutor with whom Foster had remained close. Foster has not commented on reported allegations that Cornwell was pursuing her through the tutor, and no film project ever materialized.

By far the most spectacular publicity, however, came from Cornwell's alleged liaison with a female F.B.I. agent named Marguerite "Margo" Bennett. Bennett's estranged husband, Eugene, kidnapped the Bennetts' minister and threatened to blow up his church unless the minister called Marguerite to arrange a meeting. Marguerite came to the meeting armed and took a shot at her soon-to-be-ex-husband. Eugene Bennett, who was subsequently charged with four counts of criminal behavior and convicted of attempted murder, insisted that his former wife had been sexually involved with Cornwell.

Whatever the cause of her actions, Cornwell is viewed by most of the press as a hard-living, driven woman virtually obsessed with personal security. She bought her first gun while writing *Postmortem* and is reported to travel with personal bodyguards in what is widely regarded as a fast-paced and expensive lifestyle. It's hard to think of a writer other than Stephen King who works so hard for visibility. She now has her own company, her own helicopter, and her own "Cornwell Crest," which emblazons T-shirts and other items offered for sale amid the many pictures of herself on her own Internet Web site. But she is also intensely involved with several charitable causes, especially related to literacy, and has endowed a writing scholarship at Davidson, her North Carolina alma mater.

Regardless of her flamboyant personal life and the often overblown publicity that she has received, Patricia Cornwell is a talented author whose every publication is anxiously awaited by critics and the buying public. Her most popular character, Dr. Kay Scarpetta, is the chief medical examiner of the state of Virginia, based in Richmond. Divorced after a brief marriage, Kay has forged a place for herself in the formerly male-dominated medical examiner's office. Although many have focused on Dr. Marcella Fierro, deputy chief medical examiner in Virginia and Cornwell's acknowledged mentor, as the model for Scarpetta, Cornwell insists that the character is not based on any one individual. The character of Lucy Farinelli seems to mirror Cornwell in a number of ways. Scarpetta's niece, who grows from young girl to difficult adolescent to F.B.I. agent in the course of the novels, is intelligent and gifted with computers. She is also a lesbian, and her struggle to hide her sexual identity is constant.

The police officer Pete Marino is a tremendously credible character: he tries to lose weight and quit smoking, and cannot understand why his relationships never work out, all the while plugging away at a job that can be both frustrating and life-threatening. Cornwell has said that Scarpetta and Marino both reflect competing aspects of herself: his sloppiness and lack of discipline, her discipline and objectivity.

What makes the Scarpetta books so popular with readers is a combination of strengths. Cornwell has managed to create an ensemble of characters—Scarpetta, Lucy, and Marino (plus Kay's on-again-off-again married lover, F.B.I. agent Benton Wesley)—who are believable and likable in their own special ways. Scarpetta has made a success in a man's world through hard work and determination, yet her relationships with her family are difficult. Kay finds herself struggling to understand the motivations of her mother, her sister, and her niece, often with no success. Her love life is equally troubled, and in the modern way, she never seems to hit that right balance between career and personal life.

Cornwell's books have been cited for their controlled violence. Asked why she has never turned her talent to writing about true crime, Cornwell says, ". . . I could not bring myself to victimize people all over again." She has no sympathy for the psychopathology of crime, saving her feelings for the people who are left behind in the wake of terrible violence.

Cornwell was never a reader of mystery novels, which may explain why her first books were so well received. (*Postmortem* is the only crime novel ever to win the Edgar, Creasey, Anthony, and Macavity Awards in the same year.) Despite her dark subject matter, there is a freshness of approach in the early novels that has very broad appeal, and she is one of the few women writers today who is reported to have more male than female readers.

But some would say that in her first decade of novel writing she has burned her candle too close at both ends. Between 1990 and 2000, she has produced eleven Scarpetta novels, two Charlotte police procedurals (*Hornet's Nest* and *Southern Cross*), a 1997 revised version of her Ruth

Graham biography, a 1999 children's book called *Life's Little Fable* (dedicated to her mother), and *Scarpetta's Winter Table* (1998), an odd cross between a cookbook and a Mary Higgins Clark–like Christmas fable.

Although the Cornwell name could probably sell floor polish to her devoted readers, there is grumbling in the ranks. *Hornet's Nest* and *Southern Cross,* in which she employs another three-person ensemble cast reminiscent of the Kay-Lucy-Marino ménage, has not been especially well received, and readers and reviewers alike have complained that several recent Scarpetta mysteries dip too deeply into the espionage–foreign intrigue genre. (In *Black Notice,* for instance, Kay Scarpetta gets involved with foreign criminals and Interpol, which seems, at least in fiction, to be a bit of a stretch for a medical examiner from Virginia.) Others point out that Cornwell may be allowing her own conservative biases to overwhelm her stories.

It remains to be seen if Patricia Cornwell can maintain her extraordinarily successful career. It would be a shame if this bold voice in crime writing were to be damaged by the disease of fame.

—MCT

BIBLIOGRAPHY

PATRICIA CORNWELL
1956–
American (born: Miami, Florida)

"A reporter came up to me. 'Excuse me, Dr. Scarpetta? So what brings you out this night? You waiting for someone to die?'"
—From *Potter's Field*

Cornwell's bestselling series features Dr. Kay Scarpetta and her family and colleagues. Because their stories develop as the novels progress, the series is best read in sequence. Cornwell has also written two police procedurals set in Charlotte, North Carolina, and also including continuing characters. Her books were published by Scribner's to 1995; her current publisher is G. P. Putnam's Sons. Dates are for first U.S. publication.

Kay Scarpetta Mystery Novels
1990   *Postmortem*
1991   *Body of Evidence*
1992   *All That Remains*
1993   *Cruel and Unusual*

1994 *Body Farm*
1995 *From Potter's Field*
1996 *Cause of Death*
1997 *Unnatural Exposure*
1998 *Point of Origin*
1999 *Black Notice*
2000 *The Last Precinct*

Charlotte Mystery Novels (featuring Police Chief Judy Hammer)
1996 *Hornet's Nest*
1999 *Southern Cross*

Other Works
1983 *A Time for Remembering* (biography, revised and released by Doubleday in 1997 as *Ruth, A Portrait: The Ruth Bell Graham Story*)
1998 *Scarpetta's Winter Table* (a "novelette" with a Christmas setting)
1999 *Life's Little Fable* (children's book illustrated by Barbara Leonard Gibson)

MINETTE WALTERS

DARK SHADOWS

*"What intrigues me is why there is this incredibly small minority
of people who see the killing of another as a solution to a problem rather than . . . the beginning of an entirely different set of
new problems. And that, in a nutshell, is what I write about."*

—1999 interview with *Maclean's* magazine*

On first glance, Minette Walters's résumé is a press agent's dream. Out
of nowhere, housewife and mother of two emerges on the writing
scene in 1992. First novel wins the John Creasey Award from Britain's
Crime Writers' Association (CWA). Second novel picks up the 1993
Edgar from the Mystery Writers of America. Third novel wins CWA's
Gold Dagger for best of 1994. Fourth novel is a hit with public and critics. Fifth novel opens at the top of British bestseller lists. BBC produces
popular TV adaptations of everything she writes. Overnight sensation!

But since this is real life, the story behind the headline is more complicated. Minette Walters was forty-three when *The Ice House* was published in 1992, and she had spent a long and demanding apprenticeship
toiling in the fields of magazine journalism and romance novels (not to
mention having and raising two sons). Inevitably, she has been compared
to Agatha Christie, P. D. James, and Ruth Rendell, but in Minette's case,
the comparisons are apt. If she sustains both the quality and ingenuity of
her first half-dozen mysteries, there is a very good chance she may earn
her place in the modern pantheon of first-tier mystery novelists.

The author was born Minette Caroline Mary Jebb in 1949 in Bishop's
Stortford, Hertfordshire, to the north of London on the road to Cambridge. Her mother, Colleen, became sole support for her daughter and

---

* Quotations are taken from various interviews in a number of publications that are
listed in "References and Resources."

two sons when Minette's father, a professional military officer, died in 1958. To stretch a small pension, Mrs. Jebb, an artist, advertised in London's *Times* and began to earn extra income by painting miniature portraits from photos. Life was a struggle for the family, but the mother was determined, and her children were bright and studious; all three young Jebbs won scholarships to boarding schools. Minette's five years of university prep were spent at the Godolphin School for girls in Salisbury—an institution that has educated its fair share of Women of Mystery, including Dorothy L. Sayers and Josephine Bell.

After her graduation, Minette participated in a volunteer service program called The Bridge, which took her to Israel. This experience, "the most formative time" of her life, offered a degree of independence she had not known before. It also confirmed her "hatred" for prejudice in all its forms—a theme that runs like a strong undercurrent through her mysteries.

Returning to England, she entered Durham University, where she majored in French and German literature but spent most of her time writing stories she describes as "weird, surreal . . . very postmodernist." The stories were not published, but after completing her degree and working briefly as a bartender, she moved into the publishing world—taking a position as a journalist and copy editor with IPC, a conglomerate that included the popular *Woman's Weekly* magazine and books. She soon found herself responsible for editing the company's hospital romance fiction and complaining endlessly to her office mate, writer Patrick Cunningham, about the quality of the hundreds of manuscripts she received each month. Tired of her carping, Cunningham challenged her to write one of her own. She met the test, producing the first of some thirty romance novelettes ("thirty thousand words maximum, no sex, no strong drink, and only chaste kissing") penned under pseudonyms that she has never revealed.

In 1978, after leaving IPC to freelance, she married businessman Alec Walters. The arrival of their two children temporarily shoved writing to the back burner—"Babies and writing don't mix." But when her younger son entered boarding school, she returned to her craft, though not to the pleasantly gauzy world of popular romance.

A reader of mysteries since childhood, she turned instead to her "favorite fiction genre." Minette's first encounter had been with Agatha Christie, and she is a great admirer of Patricia Highsmith. But the most important influence came from her reading of Graham Greene, whom she calls her "total hero": "His characters struggle with eternal truths and, as I tend to do the same myself, I always empathise with them." From Greene she learned that it is possible to write fiction that is both literary in quality and highly readable. She also admits to reading "vast quantities of true crime books," which reflects her interests in criminology and psychology.

From the outset, Minette's novels have veered from the traditional whodunit pattern. There is grisly murder done for certain—with the victim always revealed within the first four pages—but it is the *why* of murder that fascinates the author and ensnares her readers. She has deliberately avoided the use of a serial detective (though she hints that she may reprise a character in a later novel), and police procedures and forensics, though accurately observed, are secondary. She isn't particularly devoted to neat or just endings. Her focus is always character, the victims' as well as the suspects'.

In what may seem a concession to traditional detective format, Minette tends to build her stories around a closed circle of characters, usually a family. Her definition of "family" is decidedly unconventional, however. In *The Ice House,* it comprises three women friends who seclude themselves in a country mansion. In *The Sculptress,* it is a seemingly normal, middle-class, suburban nuclear family in which the elder daughter is imprisoned for killing and dismembering her mother and sister in the kitchen. *The Scold's Bridle* involves three generations of bitter, repressed women, and *The Dark Room* centers on a literal kind of repression, a cosseted young woman's traumatic amnesia. In *The Echo,* Minette gives the devil his due and creates a "family" of men, an odd quartet of amiable investigators, each to some degree socially outcast. Minette has said that in *The Echo,* she particularly wanted to address current attitudes about men: "The idea that society is flooded by rampaging pedophiles is absolutely absurd," she told an interviewer. "In *The Echo* I wanted to show that most men are extremely pleasant, dependable, and perfectly trustworthy, and long may it be so!"

The primary investigator in *The Echo,* journalist Michael Deacon, like other Walters protagonists, is encumbered with his own family problems, and Minette makes very effective use of contrasting domestic situations in her novels. What is it, she asks repeatedly, that breeds murder in one family and not in other, equally troubled homes? What is the trigger that launches some people over the edge into violence and murder while others repress the impulse? "Where," she asks, "does the level of anger and dysfunction, which must exist in order for this most traumatic of acts to occur, come from?"

Minette contends that she never knows who the murderer is when she starts a book. In a "claustrophobic environment," she assembles a small group of people with motive and then moves the action forward (or backward as motivation is uncovered) in the manner dictated by the characters' true natures. The challenge for the reader is to discover not which suspect has the best motive, but who has been pushed past the limits of reason and common morality. That committing murder is possible, even desirable, for many people is a given. That so few resort to it is the real mystery.

What makes Minette's mysteries novelistic (in the same sense that P. D. James and Ruth Rendell write novels that are also about crimes) is the degree to which she dwells on the consequences of the act. Her subplots may function as red herrings, but more important, they draw the reader into the complicated and often illogical reactions and behaviors that follow from the commission of a crime. Why, for instance, do people immediately accept the guilt of an accused suspect when that acceptance goes against everything they had believed about the suspect? What motivates a person to persist in lying when the truth will literally set her or him free? In a 1999 review, *New York Times* critic Marilyn Stasio wrote, "Ambiguity is an art, and Minette Walters has perfected it in *The Breaker.* . . ." Ambiguity is the heart and soul of every Walters novel (not that the reader is left without a solution); in love as much as in hate, motivation is never simple or predictable.

So many mystery writers have resented having to include a love interest; Minette seems to relish it, perhaps because on the verge of a new millennium it is no longer necessary for love to end in marriage or the prospect of "happily ever after." Her love stories are gritty and problematic; love at first sight, that staple of the romance writer, is nowhere to be found. Men and women must struggle for their relationships, and the fragility of love of all kinds is a constant. Roz Leigh, the journalist-protagonist of *The Sculptress,* for example, has experienced the worst fates of love—the accidental death of her child, the infidelity of her husband, and the resultant devastation of her marriage. Jinx Kingsley, the central character of *The Dark Room,* must cope not only with betrayal of romantic love but also with the corrupting power of a self-absorbed parent. Maggie Jenner in *The Breaker* has isolated herself from human emotion after a disastrous marriage to a bigamist and con artist.

Love portrayed realistically, however, is not always bleak. "I have great faith in the redeeming properties of love," Minette says. "However black a situation may be, where there is even the smallest spark of affection, tolerance, or kindness, then there is hope." But the key to love, especially between men and women, is mutual respect and open communication, which Minette repeatedly reminds her readers are not achieved or maintained easily. Asked by readers of *The Ice House* if she thinks the odd couple in the novel will eventually marry, Minette frequently disappoints expectations with a negative prediction. But even when love, or friendship, in her novels is unlikely to last, it can be curative.

Sex, on the other hand, is often destructive. Being a modern, Minette is not hesitant to deal with the myriad permutations of sexual behavior and dysfunction. The act itself is not her focus; rather, she deals with the power of sex to twist lives and lead to acts that are anything but loving.

Readers often wonder where Minette gets her ideas. One obvious source has been an interest that predates her mystery writing—her volunteer work as a prison visitor. Visiting with convicts, which she likens to hospital visiting, convinced Minette that contrary to the popular press, the worst criminals cannot be identified by appearance or manner and that it is entirely possible to like a person who is guilty of the most heinous acts. The inspiration for *The Sculptress* came directly from a prisoner Minette visited—"a mountain of a man" accused of rape, who initially terrified the petite Mrs. Walters but turned out to be "completely and utterly charming, one of the nicest people I've ever met." Though this story had a happy ending—the man's innocence was established, and he was released before the case came to trial—it led Minette to consider what might have happened. *The Sculptress,* she says, is the most conventional of her novels. It also deals most obviously with the theme of prejudice, in this case bias based on physical appearance. In the novel, the mountainous man becomes "a grotesque parody of a woman," and all the world is ready to believe the worst of her.

Another idea was retrieved from a childhood memory of a relic seen in a Reading museum. The scold's bridle, a medieval device for harnessing the runaway tongues of female gossips and nags, became symbolic of abusiveness in a household of three disappointed and vitriolic women in the novel that takes its name from the torturous implement.

The murders in her novels are gruesome and graphically depicted, and Minette admits to a fascination with dead bodies. The effect, however, is not voyeuristic (as it always threatens to become in Patricia Cornwell's Kay Scarpetta novels). By detailing the savagery with which her victims are done in, Minette achieves her goal of giving the victim a voice and arousing the reader's sense of injustice. Not that her victims are necessarily undeserving of their deaths, but Minette does not allow them to become simple plot devices to be killed off and forgotten as the detection proceeds. No one, she seems to be telling us, deserves this kind of brutality. And if she must rub our shock-resistant noses in the injustice of it all, she will.

The gruesome murders and moldering bodies of her stories contrast sharply with the comfortable real life of this self-professed pacifist who now lives with her family in the Dorset countryside not far from Dorchester. Her forty-five-acre estate includes a number of eighteenth-century stone buildings in an area closely associated with Thomas Hardy and more recently known as the setting for Minette's *The Breaker.*

The cozy image of the writer as mistress of the country manor is somewhat at odds with the shadow world of her fiction. But it's fair to say that she has earned her current success and thus far lived up to her promise and her press. As a representative of the new generation of Women of Mystery, Minette Walters is carving out for herself a space in the dark and fascinating field of psychological crime fiction, and if she sustains her creativity and her vision, hers may well be the name that resides deservedly alongside Highsmith, James, and Rendell. A happy ending that would be for a writer who traded the wedding-cake world of romance for bloody murder.

BIBLIOGRAPHY

MINETTE WALTERS
1949–
English (born: Bishop's Stortford, Hertfordshire)

" 'You can be loved too much as well as too little, you know, and
I'd be hard-pushed to say which was the more dangerous.' "
—Detective Inspector Galbraith in *The Breaker*

Minette Walters's mysteries do not feature serial characters and can be read in any order. Her British publisher is Macmillan. In the United States, her first three mysteries were published by St. Martin's Press, succeeded by Putnam. Dates are for first publication.

Novels
1992 *The Ice House*
1993 *The Sculptress*
1994 *The Scold's Bridle*
1996 *The Dark Room*
1997 *The Echo*
1999 *The Breaker*
2000 *The Shape of Snakes*

Video Adaptations
Walters's first five novels have all been adapted by the British Broadcast Corporation (BBC), and several have appeared on American television. *The Sculptress* was the first to be produced and broadcast and features a remarkable performance by Pauline Quirke as the convicted murderess Olive Martin.

EMMA LATHEN

FATAL GREED

"Wall Street is the greatest financial market in the world, and the function of a market is to provide an arena for smooth and orderly transactions. . . . Reality from the Battery to Maiden Lane is less tidy."
　　　　　　　　　　　　　　　　　　　—The Longer the Thread

*W*all Street is paved in avarice, and some of its three-piece-suited citizens are not (if you believe the crime novels of Emma Lathen) above a touch of homicide to achieve their rapacious ends. In two dozen smart and witty mysteries, Emma Lathen transformed the boardrooms and executive suites of American commerce and industry into crime scenes where the most unexpected people do the most dastardly things to one another in the name of business.

But Emma Lathen's longest-running mystery was not contained between book covers. For more than a decade following the publication of her first novel, *Banking on Death,* in 1961, everyone who read her mysteries was left to wonder who she might be. Who was this woman who seemed so well versed not only in the complex workings of investment banking and stock exchanges but also in the operations of enterprises from computers to vegetable seeds? Could she even be a woman and know so much?

The truth came out in the 1970s: Emma Lathen was not a woman; she was *two* women, who were more than qualified to know whereof they spoke.

Mary Jane Latsis and Martha Henissart met in 1952 at Harvard University when both were in their early thirties and pursuing postgraduate degrees: Latsis in agricultural economics and Henissart in law. They soon discovered a mutual addiction to literature in general and classic Golden Age detective fiction in particular. Their friendship endured after the women left Harvard's hallowed halls to pursue their separate careers. But like most serious mystery fans, they eventually ran out of new books to read and discuss. Their solution was to write their own.

By the time they began their first novel in 1960, both Latsis and Henissart were employed full-time, which accounted for their unusual writing strategy. Together they developed plot and characters and outlined the novel completely; then they went their separate ways to write alternate chapters simultaneously. "That is," Henissart explained in an interview, "I'll be writing chapter 5 somewhere and Mary Jane will be writing chapter 6 somewhere." They worked out the inevitable conflicts (as when Latsis once bumped off her partner's favorite character) until, according to Latsis, "I can no longer tell, in some of our earlier books . . . who wrote what."★ Latsis, however, always did the first chapter, and Henissart the last.

Their famous pen name, combining the first three letters of their last names, was selected because they thought a single and pronounceable name easier to remember than their own.

For a detective, they needed someone who could plausibly be knowledgeable about and have access to any business or institution that interested the writers. They picked an investment banker: mature, intelligent, and patrician John Putnam Thatcher is an institutional man, a vice president of the world's third largest bank, the Sloan Guaranty Trust. He is a detective by chance rather than choice. The institutions of capitalism—international corporations to family-owned companies, profit-making and not-for-profit—are what intrigued the writers. "In America most people go to work. . . . and they do not go out to a field to dig up radishes: they go into a big, big institution of some sort or another, and we try to catch the flavor of that kind of life," Latsis said.

Latsis and Henissart surrounded their detective with a delightful cast of supporting players (bankers with the best and worst characteristics of the trade) and gave him one of the most efficient secretaries in detective fiction, Miss Rose Theresa Corso, "a young woman clearly designed by nature for the motto: *We are not amused*." Critics with a feminist bent have sometimes questioned why the authors created a male detective with mostly male workmates, but Thatcher et al. were born in 1960, after all, and anyone other than a WASP male would have been unthinkable. Until well into the 1980s, banking (above the level of cashier) was a man's world, and the men at the desks and in the boardrooms were

---

★ Quotations from Latsis and Henissart are from a lengthy interview conducted by John C. Carr that appears in his 1983 collection *The Craft of Crime*. Other sources are listed in "References and Resources."

predominantly white, Anglo–Saxon, and Protestant. (So suitable for admission to the country clubs.)

The New York Times once called Emma Lathen "Wall Street's Agatha Christie," but the beauty of Latsis and Henissart's novels is that the reader need not know the Big Board from Big Bird to enjoy Thatcher's eminently accessible adventures. In the classic tale of detection, there are three primary motives for murder—passion, self-protection, and greed; the material world created by Latsis and Henissart is ripe for all three. In fact, their thirty-two books (twenty-four by Emma Lathen and another eight written under the pseudonym R. B. Dominic and featuring Ohio congressman Ben Safford) are as good a lesson in late-twentieth-century white-collar crime and political cupidity as any economics text—and a heck of a lot more fun.

Mary Jane Latsis (1927–1997), the daughter of Greek immigrants, was born in the Chicago suburb of Oak Park and was educated at Wellesley College. Latsis worked for the Central Intelligence Agency and then the United Nations Food and Agricultural Organization in Rome before returning to the United States to study public administration and earn a Ph.D. in economics at Harvard. She then taught her subject at Wellesley.

Martha Henissart was born in New York in 1929. A physics major in college, she switched to law at Harvard and went on to practice in New York. She took a corporate position in Boston in 1960 and naturally stayed with her friend Mary Jane while house-hunting. Neither woman remembered who suggested collaborating on a book, but the proximate cause was a writing contest sponsored by the Macmillan publishing company. They didn't win the contest, but Macmillan took their book. Latsis and Henissart had a rough time getting attention from a constantly changing series of editors in the frenetic publishing business of the 1960s, but things settled down in the next decade, and Emma Lathen began to acquire a devoted following in the United States and Great Britain. (The Lathen books have also been translated into a number of foreign languages.)

In a 1970 review in London's *Financial Times,* scientist and novelist C. P. Snow paid Lathen the highest compliment, comparing "her" to Balzac and declaring "her" writing good enough to be English. "She is probably the best living writer of American detective stories . . . ," Lord Snow opined. Lathen had already received a Silver Dagger award from the British Crime Writers in 1967 for *Murder against the Grain.* By 1983, Americans were in full agreement, and the Mystery Writers of America Awards Committee presented their first Ellery Queen Award (a distinction named for another writing duo) to Emma Lathen.

The women remained in Massachusetts and eventually turned full-time to their novels. In addition to their separate homes in the Boston area, they bought a vacation cottage in Warren, New Hampshire, where they would retreat to plot and complete their novels in the solitude of the White Mountains. Neither married; Latsis, who was said to have an aversion to marriage, nevertheless maintained a forty-year relationship with a Boston investment executive. Mary Jane Latsis died in Warren of a heart attack and stroke at the end of October 1997. Emma Lathen's twenty-fourth novel, *A Shark out of Water*, was published the following month.

Another Lathen novel, with a Gulf War setting, was nearly completed at the time of Latsis's death and is scheduled for publication in 2000. Although Henissart has indicated that she will probably not continue the series after this book, Emma Lathen has created an impressive portfolio. Latsis and Henissart's work demonstrates that there can be as much mystery in stock futures, junk bonds, leveraged buyouts, and corporate takeovers as in any quaint English village. They had, wrote Marilyn Stasio in *The New York Times Book Review,* "a wonderful knack for turning the driest, most complicated corporate maneuvers into high drama, and occasionally burlesque."

The Thatcher books fall neatly into the novel-of-manners category, revealing as they do the behind-the-scenes workings of the financial world and the people who inhabit it. Latsis once whimsically said, "I like to believe, when I'm having delusions of grandeur, that we are Trollopean more than anything else just in trying to give a picture of a complex society." But unlike the Victorian novels of Anthony Trollope, Latsis and Henissart's works are eminently accessible to modern readers. Moreover, the stylishness of the Lathen and Dominic books is a pleasure for all who value language well used. Clean, sophisticated, and grammatical—the women took pride in their use of complex sentences correctly punctuated—the novels proceed with a buttery smoothness that never betrays the fact they are composite works.

Their subjects and outlook are thoroughly modern (which may explain why the novels, unlike today's stock quotes, age well). Yet Latsis and Henissart maintained the best traditions of Golden Age puzzle writing, right down to their amateur detective. John Putnam Thatcher—old New England "leading family" background, well educated, highly placed in the world of finance, and cool under pressure—is in many ways like an Americanized Peter Wimsey or Albert Campion stripped of British fustiness and "silly ass" habits. The mysteries he solves in classic style involve the stuff of daily life, now that even the most ordinary daily activities revolve around the vagaries of international commerce and the decisions made in distant boardrooms.

Always wryly skeptical and inclined to deflate the pomposities of the self-important, Latsis and Henissart took their readers behind the oaken doors and brass nameplates and into the arcane culture of the men and women who churn money. While real-world financiers and tycoons are not as inclined to murder as the Lathen books require, Latsis and Henissart can never be accused of exaggerating the seductiveness of the Almighty Dollar and the deadly consequences of greed.

BIBLIOGRAPHY

EMMA LATHEN
Mary Jane Latsis   1927–1997
(born: Oak Park, Illinois)

Martha Henissart   1929–
(born: New York City)

"It is not publicly admitted, but behind every chaste earnings statement reported in the financial press lies a human drama."
—Accounting for Murder

Emma Lathen is the pen name of the writing team of Latsis and Henissart. As R. B. Dominic, the women also wrote political mysteries. In the United States, Lathen's Wall Street novels were published by Macmillan until 1968, and then by Simon and Schuster, and most recently by St. Martin's Press; in England, by Gollancz. Original publishers of the R. B. Dominic mysteries include Abelard Schuman, Macmillan, Doubleday, Harper & Row, and St. Martin's Press. Dates are for first publication in the United States. GB = Great Britain.

Emma Lathen Novels (featuring John Putnam Thatcher)
1961   *Banking on Death*
1963   *A Place for Murder*
1964   *Accounting for Murder*
1966   *Death Shall Overcome*
1966   *Murder Makes the Wheels Go Round*
1967   *Murder against the Grain*
1968   *A Stitch in Time*
1968   *Come to Dust*
1969   *When in Greece*
1969   *Murder to Go*
1970   *Pick Up Sticks*

1971   *Ashes to Ashes*
1971   *The Longer the Thread*
1972   *Murder without Icing*
1974   *Sweet and Low*
1975   *By Hook or by Crook*
1978   *Double, Double, Oil and Trouble*
1981   *Going for the Gold*
1982   *Green Grow the Dollars*
1988   *Something in the Air*
1991   *East Is East*
1993   *Right on the Money*
1996   *Brewing Up a Storm*
1997   *A Shark out of Water*

R. B. Dominic Novels (featuring Congressman Ben Safford)
1968   *Murder Sunny Side Up*
1969   *Murder in High Place*
1971   *There Is No Justice*/GB: *Murder out of Court*
1974   *Epitaph for a Lobbyist*
1976   *Murder out of Commission*
1980   *The Attending Physician*
1983   *A Flaw in the System*
1984   *Unexpected Developments*

MARGARET MILLAR

LEST WE FORGET

"I never write about real people.
Real people are duller than my people. . . .
I do see humor in the most tragic things, and vice versa."
—interview, 1986*

In the headline to a 1979 article, the late Dilys Winn, mystery connoisseur, credited Margaret Millar with "the greatest opening lines since 'In the beginning. . . .'"

Ms. Winn exaggerated, of course, but Margaret Millar did have a way of grabbing the reader on page one and not letting go. For those who haven't yet experienced one of her openers, here's a small sample:

In *The Listening Walls*: "From her resting place in the broom closet Consuela could hear the two American ladies in 404 arguing."

Or this first sentence of *Fire Will Freeze*: "Miss Isobel Seton settled her chin into the collar of her sable coat and, as was her custom in moments of stress, mentally composed an abusive letter."

Margaret Millar paid off opening lines like these in a total of twenty-one sly and crisply economical mystery novels that are guaranteed to warm the cockles of a true mystery lover's heart. She was particularly praised in her heyday for her head-snapping surprise endings, which still supply their punches.

Why Mrs. Millar—who was the wife of Kenneth Millar, also known as Ross Macdonald, creator of the hard-boiled Lew Archer series—never achieved the level of popularity her books merit is the real mystery of her career. Perhaps she was outshined by her husband's success. Perhaps because she did her best work in the 1950s and 1960s, when the

---

* Quotations are taken from various interviews in a number of publications that are listed in "References and Resources."

mystery novel was under a cloud, her books did not receive significant recognition. Perhaps she was handicapped by her tendency to tackle (and take seriously) "delicate subjects"—pedophilia, transvestism, personality disorders and madness, race relations—before they entered the public domain. Or perhaps she was, as scholar John M. Reilly has suggested, a victim of supply and demand, lost in the shuffle of too many skilled writers in general and too many women writers in particular.

She earned the respect of her fellow craftsmen and of the critics, however. Will Cuppy, the respected reviewer for the *New York Herald-Tribune,* once called her a "humdinger" of a mystery writer. Julian Symons wrote, "Among the crime writers who have come into prominence since the war [World War Two] she has few peers, and no superior, in the art of bamboozlement"—a view he reaffirmed years later. Three of her books were nominated for Edgar Awards by the Mystery Writers of America (MWA): *Beast in View,* which took top honors in 1956 and also was selected by the group as one of its "Top 100 Mysteries of All Time" in 1995; *The Fiend* in 1965; and *Beyond This Point Are Monsters* in 1971. The MWA, of which she served as president, honored her entire body of work by naming her a Grand Master in 1983.

Yet it is like pulling teeth to find a Millar title even in libraries today, and her name (pronounced as "Miller") is not widely known. Her dedicated readers have always been fierce, if not legion, and many claim her talent was superior to her famous husband's. "Mrs. Millar doesn't attract fans," declared Dilys Winn, a devotee. "She creates addicts. When her new hardcover comes out, they rush home to devour it. Dinner can wait. The dog can wait. They tell friends they'll call them back. That book gets finished in one sitting. And quoted from for months after." But there have been no new hardcovers to devour since *Spider Webs* was released in 1986. And no groundswell of interest in Margaret Millar since her death in 1994. More's the pity, because most of her mysteries stand up as strongly today as when the words were fresh ink on a page. In a world of literary cubic zirconiums, Margaret Millar still provides gems.

She began life as Margaret Ellis Sturm, the daughter of the mayor of Kitchener, Ontario. Born on February 5, 1915, she was a bright and apparently precocious little girl who read detective magazines and started writing when she was eight. Her first story involved four sisters who were only three months apart in age, a biologically remarkable feat that she didn't understand to be funny until she was in her teens. She also studied music, beginning piano lessons at age four and progressing to perform on local radio while in high school. Seemingly headed for a career in music, she won a scholarship to the University of Toronto, but she switched to classical studies and became interested in psychiatry. She intended to become an analyst, but circumstances intervened, and she didn't finish her degree. With a world war looming, she left school and married her childhood sweetheart, Kenneth Millar, in 1938. The couple moved to Michigan, where Ken completed his doctorate and taught at the University of Michigan in Ann Arbor; then he enlisted in the United States Navy, and Margaret moved to Santa Barbara, California.

Her first mystery was completed during a period when she was bedridden for a heart condition. She passed the time by reading detective novels, and against her doctor's orders set about writing one of her own. This book, *The Invisible Worm,* and her next two featured her version of the Golden Age detective—a psychiatrist named Parker Prye. (Margaret was familiar with the British expression "nosey parker," which refers to one who pokes and pries into other people's business.) Prye is an amateur sleuth in the Lord Peter Wimsey mold, and his investigations are solidly classical with a light touch. But in her fourth and sixth books, the mood turned darker, and Margaret put aside her psychiatrist for a professional detective as lead character, Inspector Sands of the Toronto Police.

Sands lasted for two novels only, and in the postwar years, Margaret took on "straight" fiction, writing three novels between 1946 and 1949. Though sales of her detective fiction had been modestly profitable, it was the autobiographical *It's All in the Family* that earned her only stay on the bestseller lists. But Margaret went back to the mystery, and over the next decade—a time of enormous upheaval as the detective genre adapted to post–World War Two reality—her writings revealed her to be a perceptive mistress of the psychological drama. Her interest was increasingly murder as a behavior, admittedly extreme yet with its roots running deep in the inner lives of villains and victims alike. Margaret observed the conventions of classic detection as needed, but the mystery and the fear, as well as her characteristic ironies, lay in character. Socrates said that the unexamined life is not worth living. Margaret Millar, however, was using her fiction to show that the examined life can scare you to death.

By this time, her husband had also picked up the yen for mystery fiction, and though he wrote at first under his own name, Ken switched to the pen name John Ross Macdonald (later shortened to Ross Macdonald to avoid confusion with John D. MacDonald) in order not to infringe on his wife's career. With the introduction of tough-guy private eye Lew Archer in 1949, Ken's star soared, and both the public and critics hailed him as the direct lineal descendant of Dashiell Hammett and Raymond Chandler. (As it turned out, Archer was to be the last of the original hard-boiled private investigators, and even Ken changed his approach dramatically at the end of the 1950s, moving away from sheer grit and gunplay to more subtly psychological studies, perhaps influenced by his own time in analysis.)

The Millars never collaborated, but they worked with a teamlike closeness. They wrote at different times of day—she in the morning, he the afternoon—in their Santa Barbara beachfront home. But they critiqued each other's work, and Margaret deeply missed Ken's finely tuned editing after his death. By all accounts, they were very close—a shy pair who admired and supported each other's work. They had one child, Linda, who died in 1970.

Both Millars were deeply attached to California, featuring it frequently in their novels and giving their time to protect its natural beauty. (Ken was actually born in the state but moved to Canada as a small child.) They cofounded a chapter of the National Audubon Society in Santa Barbara and worked tirelessly for environmental causes. It was as much for her service to the state as for her career in mystery that the *Los Angeles Times* honored Margaret Millar as their Woman of the Year in 1965.

But in the early 1950s, Margaret was approaching the apex of her form, and her best works, beginning with *Beast in View* in 1955, "show the full scope of her skill as a novelist whose chosen theme," according to Julian Symons, "is almost always a mystery with roots deeply hidden in the past." She began writing in the dog days of the Golden Age and had great respect for writers like Agatha Christie, but Margaret broke the mold early and went her own way. She was not a puzzler, though her mysteries are puzzling and her surprise endings are fairly achieved. She was an analyst, her earlier ambition, who created her own patients from her own fertile brain. In his study of detective and crime fiction, *Bloody Murder,* Symons contrasts the use of a religious cult in Millar's *How Like an Angel* to similar situations in novels by Ngaio Marsh and Margery Allingham. Where the Golden Age grande dames merely sketched in unrealistic cults for the sake of their plots, Margaret delved deeply into her fictional True Believers, presenting the members and their activities and beliefs "with a powerful sense of pathos and absurdity, joined to respect for a way of life." Marsh and Allingham were old school; Millar was new.

Women are central to most of Margaret's mysteries, and children often play key roles, but she was by no means a "woman's writer" of the Mary Roberts Rinehart–Mary Higgins Clark school. Her characters and their relationships are too complex for the damsel-in-distress formula. But her women are not feminist icons either; they can be shallow, vain, manipulative, nasty, homicidal, and just plain nuts in the most interesting of ways. Just as Margaret's sense of the absurd, her penchant for black comedy, and her interest in the psychological underpinnings of her characters' actions separated her early from the Golden Age focus on the puzzle, they also distinguish her from the modern mania for maggoty corpses and maniacs.

Though she created three male serial characters—psychiatrist Prye and cop Sands in the 1940s, and Los Angeles lawyer Tom Aragon three decades later—her best works are each one-of-a-kind, self-contained and satisfying on their own. But they are not easily categorized, and it's hard not to believe that her unfair ranking as a second-tier writer owes in part to the publishing industry's inability to promote what it cannot easily label. In the 1970s, for example, Avon Books planned a reissue of a number of her titles in paperback editions. The publisher commissioned covers that clearly conveyed a Gothic impression—women in jeopardy, surrounded by symbols of danger and isolation and drenched in pretty pastels. But Margaret Millar mysteries as Gothic romances? Hardly. Though psychological terror, and terrorism, is intrinsic to even her lighthearted writing, there is little else of the Gothic about her stories.

The appeal of Margaret Millar and her mysteries is that they are unconventional, unpredictable, rebellious. She did it her way, and her way was, for the most part, riveting.

Her own life was less novelistic—outwardly conventional and happy and sad in turns. The blurb to a 1986 study of mystery writers described her as an "ex–family woman" as if she put aside her family at some point to write. But her marriage to Ken Millar lasted for forty-five years, until his death from Alzheimer's disease in 1983. She lost her only child and experienced her own share of illness, including a serious battle with lung cancer in the late 1970s and the loss of most of her sight to glaucoma. Though severely visually impaired, she coped, switching from writing by hand to typing. She was always a careful craftsman with language, sometimes spending as much as a day on a single sentence, and though she can be called prolific, each of her novels has the feel of being carefully nurtured.

Margaret Millar died of a heart attack at her Santa Barbara home—the condominium near the water and the beach club where she and her husband spent so many good times with friends—in March 1994. *The New York Times* marked her passing with a lead obituary: "Mrs. Millar earned a reputation as a master of the suspense novel with her carefully constructed, literate mysteries populated by complex, sometimes disturbed characters and rooted in her belief that psychological terror achieved an effectively chilling 'violence by implication.'"

Some might say her death was the end of an era—a time when a murder novel could be terrifying, mystifying, and satisfying without resort to buckets of bloody mayhem. Because she began writing in the early 1940s, Margaret Millar is sometimes classed as a transitional author, but even her early books in classical detective form were concerned with internal motivation more than external investigation. She might well be compared to Josephine Tey, the solitary Scotswoman who also took her own route. But Margaret dug more deeply and more comfortably into the hidden sources of crimes. She abandoned the tradition that goes back to Poe of the "great detective" who is a pure reasoning machine. John M. Reilly has called her a revisionist, one who does not violate the rules of a form for effect, as Agatha Christie did, but who re-creates the form to reflect a different kind of vision. It was not enough to discover whodunit or even whydunit. Margaret Millar asked how the devil someone's life could get to the point where committing murder becomes, for that person at least, a rational activity. The answer to that question, as she knew, could be creepier and scarier than a room full of monsters.

BIBLIOGRAPHY

Margaret Millar
1915–1994
Canadian (born: Kitchener, Ontario)

"The insane and the sane kill for the same motives, to make life easier for themselves. If the insane person appears to kill without reason, it is because we don't know enough of his history."
—Parker Prye in *The Weak-Eyed Bat*

Margaret Millar used several series detectives, but the bulk of her mysteries stand on their own and can be read in any order. Her mysteries were first published in the United States by Doubleday, followed by Random House. Her later books were handled by Morrow. Dates are for first publication. Featured detectives appear in ( ). Alternate titles are given. GB=Great Britain.

Mystery Novels
1941   *The Invisible Worm* (Parker Prye)
1942   *The Devil Loves Me* (Parker Prye)
1942   *The Weak-Eyed Bat* (Parker Prye)
1943   *Wall of Eyes* (Inspector Sands)
1944   *Fire Will Freeze*
1945   *The Iron Gates*/GB: *Taste of Fears* (Inspector Sands)
1950   *Do Evil in Return*

1952   *Rose's Last Summer* (later published by Dell paperback as *The Lively Corpse*)

1952   *Vanish in an Instant*

1955   *Beast in View*

1957   *An Air That Kills*/GB: *The Soft Talkers*

1959   *The Listening Walls*

1960   *A Stranger in My Grave*

1962   *How Like an Angel*

1964   *The Fiend*

1970   *Beyond This Point Are Monsters*

1976   *Ask Me for Tomorrow* (Tom Aragon)

1979   *The Murder of Miranda* (Tom Aragon)

1982   *Mermaid* (Tom Aragon)

1983   *Banshee*

1986   *Spider Webs*

Other Novels

1947   *Experiment in Springtime*

1948   *It's All in the Family*

1949   *The Cannibal Heart*

Nonfiction

1968   *The Birds and the Beasts Were There*

Film and Video Adaptations

Millar's *The Iron Gates* was bought by Warner Brothers as a star vehicle for actress Bette Davis but was never filmed, apparently because Miss Davis refused to play a character who would die halfway into the movie. But *Rose's Last Summer* was adapted for Alfred Hitchcock's television series in the 1950s and starred Mary Astor.

LILIAN JACKSON BRAUN

PURR-FECTLY PLEASANT

*"I tell people that psychologically I'm 35, physically I'm about
55, and chronological age I don't believe in."*★

One does not have to be an ailurophile to enjoy the writings of Lilian
Jackson Braun. A lover of cats may be naturally drawn to her books, yet
the author takes great care to see that her work appeals to the general
public. And appeal they do. . . . Braun currently produces at least a book
a year, is published in some fifteen countries, and delights readers with a
continuing cast of characters who revolve around newsman Jim
Qwilleran and his feline sleuths Koko and Yum Yum.

The old advice to fledgling writers to stick with what they know best
has certainly proven valid for Lilian Jackson Braun. Although she currently lives with her second husband at the foot of the Blue Ridge
Mountains in North Carolina, Braun spent the bulk of her life in
Michigan—the setting of her books in the fictional town of Pickax in
Moose County, "four hundred miles north of everywhere." Lilian was
born around 1916† and was an only child for nine years, until the arrival
of her brother and sister. Taught by her mother, she began reading and
writing at the precocious age of three. Storytelling was an everyday pastime in her household, and her mother's lively dinner table tales of the
day's events taught Lilian valuable lessons in making the ordinary into
something humorous or exciting. At age twelve, Lilian tried writing her

---

★ Lilian Jackson Braun quotations are taken from her own writings, from *The Cat
Who . . . Companion* by Sharon A. Fester (revised edition, 1999), and from various interviews listed in "References and Resources."

† Lilian is cagey about her birth date, sometime in or around 1916, and birthplace,
somewhere in Massachusetts. Her family moved to the Detroit area when she was a
child.

first book, "a French historical novel" in which everyone died tragically. Her mother advised her to take a different approach and write what made her laugh—advice Lilian has followed throughout her career.

She continued to write during high school, and under the pseudonym Ward Jackson (Ward was her mother's maiden name) sold a number of pieces to national sports magazines. She was "crazy about baseball," composing what she called "spoems"—sports poems that caught the attention of the *Detroit Times.* The Great Depression made it impossible for her to attend college, so after high school, she briefly tried freelance writing but found it too solitary. She went to work writing advertising for several department stores, rising to the position of director of public relations. But after eighteen years, she returned to newspapering and began a thirty-year stint editing special sections and writing about art and antiques, home decoration, architecture, and preservation for the *Detroit Free Press* (the inspiration for Jim Qwilleran's "Gracious Abodes" column for the *Daily Fluxion.*)

It was during this time that she saw and was overwhelmed by a Goldscheider porcelain figure of a Siamese cat. In a 1991 interview in *The Armchair Detective,* Lilian told of the origins of her series: for her fortieth birthday, her first husband (to whom she was married for twenty-four years) gave her a Siamese kitten. Always a fan of light opera and of Gilbert and Sullivan in particular, Lilian named the kitten Koko, after a character in *The Mikado.* "I adored him and he adored me," she said.

Lilian was devastated when Koko was killed at age two in a fall from a tenth-story window. Some of her neighbors speculated that the cat had been pushed, and anger was added to Lilian's sense of loss. The extent to which an owner can feel the death of a pet has, until recently, been overlooked by laymen and psychologists alike. Surely during the 1960s, Lilian Jackson Braun's grief at the death of Koko would have been dismissed by many of her peers. Her need to come to grips with her loss led her to write "The Sin of Madame Phloi," a short story inspired by her experience and written, she admits, for revenge. The story, sold to *Ellery Queen's Mystery Magazine,* was selected by Dutton as one of the best of its year. After the publication of a handful of short stories with cats as main characters, Braun was asked by Dutton to produce a book-length tale, and so she wrote *The Cat Who Could Read Backwards* in 1966.

(On the theory that it's best to get back on a horse after a fall, Lilian's first Koko was quickly replaced by two Siamese kittens—Koko the Great and Yum Yum. Koko the Great, who inspired many of the traits and habits of his fictional counterpart, lived for a happy eighteen years and was succeeded by Koko III, who now shares his home with another Siamese, Pitti Sing.)

Lilian's first three novels met with some success, yet her fourth attempt was refused by her own publisher and a number of others to whom it was submitted. The market, she remembered, had changed: "They wanted sex and violence, not kitty-cat stories." Busy at the *Detroit Free Press,* she had plenty to occupy her time. Perhaps with some disappointment, she put the manuscript away for what turned out to be sixteen years. In the meantime, her first husband died, and she retired from her job at the newspaper.

Widowed for twelve years, Lilian married former actor Earl Bettinger in 1979. A year after their marriage, he read her discarded manuscript and encouraged her to resubmit it. Published by Putnam in 1986, *The Cat Who Saw Red* was nominated for an Edgar Award, and Lilian's life of quiet retirement came to an abrupt end.

More than twenty novels later, Lilian Jackson Braun is both widely recognized and extremely popular. Her popularity transcends her subject matter: the main character in all her books is Jim Qwilleran, a bachelor, recovered alcoholic, and survivor of a divorce, who initially works in the big city "Down Below" but eventually accepts a job at a small-town newspaper as a feature writer. Readers learn in the fourth book of the series that Qwill, a large man with salt-and-pepper hair and a luxuriant mustache, had been unemployed for some time before joining the staff of the *Daily Fluxion* and that he had been deserted by an ambitious wife. In the first book of the series, Qwilleran "inherits" Koko, a male Siamese whose owner meets an unfortunate end and leaves the cat an orphan. Lilian established a trusting relationship between man and cat that is sustained throughout her novels. Yum Yum, a young female Siamese, joins the family in *The Cat Who Ate Danish Modern.* The reader follows Qwill from the border of poverty to vast wealth as the series progresses; Qwill and the cats move to upper Michigan and settle in the fictitious Pickax ("population 3000") in order to collect a tremendous inheritance. Along the way several characters move in and out of the main narrative, with the relationship of man and cats always at the center of each novel.

It is important to note that there is nothing of the supernatural in Koko; although the cat might appropriately be called the "detective" in these books, he is indeed a cat. (Lilian has called Koko her Sherlock Holmes and Qwill the Watson.) In addition to feline curiosity and Siamese intelligence, he possesses an intuition that can put him on the scent of a crime. With a sniff here and a scratch there, he can dig up information that astounds humans, who must rely on brainpower alone. Koko was a legend among newsmen Down Below—the only cat in the history of journalism to be an honorary member of the Press Club. But with the exception of his editor, Arch Riker, Qwill alone is aware of

Koko's important role in solving the mysteries. It is Koko who frees Qwill's own imagination to work out the solution of each crime. More than once, Koko leads the way into a highly revealing situation, but if the cat has a sixth sense about suspicious behavior, Qwilleran's sensitive mustache—which twitches (reminiscent of the green glow in Poirot's eyes) as the mystery begins to unravel—possesses an equal awareness. Many a time it alerts him to bad news, hidden danger, and even unsuspected crime.

In addition to newspaper journalism, Lilian includes her other interests from time to time. Her husband Earl's theatrical experience has influenced several of the plots; her own knowledge of Scotland is explored in *The Cat Who Wasn't There.* "Aunt Fanny" Klingenschoen's Michigan retreat, featured in *The Cat Who Played Brahms,* is modeled on a cabin Lilian once had, minus the Jacuzzi. She also includes ideas from her devoted fans: in *The Cat Who Tailed a Thief,* she gave Polly Duncan a sister in Cincinnati in response to a comment in a letter from one of her avid readers.

Although crime is afoot in each book of the series, the tone of Lilian's writing has been accurately described as comfortable; the reader is spared the gory details of the murders that occur. Romance is decidedly cast in a supporting role, with Qwill most recently enamored of the town librarian, Polly Duncan, but the books contain little sexual reference. There is an *Our Town* quality about Lilian's characters and settings. The atmosphere of Pickax and Moose County is apparently simple and uncomplicated. But as in Agatha Christie's St. Mary Mead, there is an undercurrent of evil that bubbles to the surface in each book.

Humor is consistent throughout Lilian's mysteries. In a good-spirited jab at her own career, she has named the newspapers the *Daily Fluxion,* the *Morning Rampage,* and the *Moose County Something.* While Qwill worries as his weight increases, Koko and Yum Yum refuse ordinary cat food and dine on salmon, king crab, and béarnaise sauce. A great deal of action takes place near the Itibitiwassee River—you get the picture.

Lilian Jackson Braun has said that her writing is easy for her; after "working from nine to five for fifty years," she adheres to no rigid schedule of hours or pages per day. She shares writing habits with her main human character: both she and Qwill prefer composing in longhand on legal pads. Lilian produces one or two books per year and genuinely likes doing it. She is one of those increasingly rare people who sincerely enjoy every minute of what they do, and it shows in her work.

The underlying tone of humor and simplicity makes her novels relaxing to read; a vacation in Pickax is a delightful way to escape the stress of everyday life. One critic has written that her books provide comfort to readers, who return again and again to her reliable, reassuring patterns. Her work fits, to a degree, in the lighthearted "cozy" tradition—small town or village setting, recurring characters with their distinctive eccentricities, murder as the exceptional event and not the rule. (There are no mean streets in Pickax.) Though set in the present, *The Cat Who . . .* books have a nostalgic quality owing to the fundamental decency and humor of its main human and feline characters. Even when the good folks of Pickax and Moose County have murder thrust upon them, for the most part they react as all good people hope they might in a crisis.

Despite Lilian's bestseller status, critics these days generally ignore her books, probably because they are both formulaic and difficult to categorize. No great truths about the criminal mind are explored, nor does anyone worry overly about the meaning of life or death. But even with the clever cats, the cute names, and the folksiness, each new addition to the series manages to stay several steps ahead of cloying sweetness. Murder, instead of being the focus of each story, works as the anchor that weighs down what might otherwise become just so much cotton candy. Lilian herself has said that she regards her books not as mysteries so much as "character stories." So for those who enjoy their escapist reading thick with people and locales that will become as comfortable as a well-broken-in set of walking shoes, start with book one of *The Cat Who. . . .*

—MCT

BIBLIOGRAPHY

LILIAN JACKSON BRAUN
ca. 1916–
American (born: Massachusetts)

"If the scientists Down Below ever found out about the psychic cat, they would charter flights to Pickax to test Koko's brain and count his whiskers. . . . No way! Qwilleran thought."
—*The Cat Who Said Cheese*

Braun's *The Cat Who . . .* books were first published in the United States by E. P. Dutton. Putnam has been her American publisher since 1986. In Great Britain her books have been published by Collins, Chivers, Headline, and others. All the novels feature newsman-cum-philanthropist James Qwilleran ("a respectable Scottish spelling") and his Siamese cat Koko. To follow their adventures, the books are best savored when read in order of publication. The earlier books are stronger on mystery, the latter on Pickax personalities.

Mystery Novels

1966	*The Cat Who Could Read Backwards*
1967	*The Cat Who Ate Danish Modern*
1968	*The Cat Who Turned On and Off*
1986	*The Cat Who Saw Red*
1987	*The Cat Who Played Brahms*
1987	*The Cat Who Played Post Office*
1988	*The Cat Who Knew Shakespeare*
1988	*The Cat Who Sniffed Glue*
1989	*The Cat Who Went Underground*
1990	*The Cat Who Talked to Ghosts*
1990	*The Cat Who Lived High*
1991	*The Cat Who Knew a Cardinal*
1992	*The Cat Who Moved a Mountain*
1992	*The Cat Who Wasn't There*
1993	*The Cat Who Went into the Closet*
1994	*The Cat Who Came to Breakfast*
1995	*The Cat Who Blew the Whistle*
1996	*The Cat Who Said Cheese*
1997	*The Cat Who Tailed a Thief*
1998	*The Cat Who Sang for the Birds*
1999	*The Cat Who Saw Stars*
2000	*The Cat Who Robbed a Bank*
	(*The Cat Who Smelled a Rat* is scheduled for release in early 2000.)

Short Story Collection

1988	*The Cat Who Had 14 Tales*

ANNE PERRY

PAST IMPERFECT

". . . there are no monsters, there are only people. We don't nec-
essarily like all of ourselves, but bit by bit, we learn to under-
stand and then, when you understand yourself, one hopes you
can transfer that understanding to other people." ★

—1998 interview in *Speaking of Murder:*
Interviews with Masters of Mystery and Suspense

In 1983 Anne Perry granted her first interview ever to scholar Diana
Cooper-Clark. In the course of their lengthy conversation, Perry said,
"I think that the Victorian period is ideal for a mystery writer because
so many things are not what they seem." When Cooper-Clark asked if
Perry would be capable of killing, the author replied, "I don't know. I
would think probably, if I felt that it was the only answer. Almost certainly, yes, if I was defending somebody else."

Within ten years of the interview, the truth and the irony of these
seemingly innocuous statements became glaringly obvious.

Early in the 1990s, a journalist researching a 1954 New Zealand murder trial contacted Meg Davis of MBA Literary Agents in London with
a question: was Anne Perry in fact Juliet Marion Hulme, who had been
born in London in 1938? Davis got in touch with her client, expecting
the confusion to be immediately resolved. Anne Perry then admitted
that she was indeed Juliet Hulme, one of the two young girls convicted
for the 1954 murder. Though she has never denied her true identity,
Perry had kept it well hidden for thirty years.

★ Anne Perry's quotations are from this interview, conducted by Adrian Muller, other
  interviews listed in "References and Resources," and her published writings. Quotes
  from trial reports are taken from materials assembled by the Christchurch Library in
  New Zealand and listed in "References and Resources."

The crime was re-created in the film *Heavenly Creatures,* cowritten and directed by New Zealand–born Peter Jackson. The discovery of Perry's true identity was made in connection with publicity surrounding the 1994 release of the film by Miramax—forty years after the brutal murder that shook a nation. Perry was terrified that the revelation of her past and the release of *Heavenly Creatures* would destroy her career, but as it turned out, the ensuing wave of interest actually increased her sales, confirming the old wisdom that there is no such thing as bad publicity.

Perry had a lot to lose. By 1994, she was well on her way to becoming a formidable name in the mystery-fiction industry. As Anne Perry, she had entered the field with the 1979 publication of *The Cater Street Hangman.* She is the author of two popular series of novels set in England during the period of Queen Victoria, who reigned from 1837 until her death in 1901.

From the middle of the eighteenth century until the middle of the nineteenth, the population of England virtually exploded, with the resultant problems of overcrowding and poverty. According to one historian, ". . . the greater part of social legislation throughout the nineteenth century was concerned with ameliorating the lot of the poor, often amidst a great deal of class hatred or rancor." This conflict of rich and poor—the chasm between the lives of the upper and lower classes and the thin veneer of respectability covering seething health and social issues—is the background against which Perry has set all her mystery novels.

Perry began writing historical fiction while in her mid-twenties but was unpublished until her stepfather suggested a story about Jack the Ripper. "I wasn't curious about who the Ripper was," she told interviewer Adrian Muller in 1998, ". . . but through that suggestion, I became interested as to what might happen to a group of people when they find themselves under an enormous pressure by the investigation of murder."

In *The Cater Street Hangman,* she introduced Thomas Pitt and Charlotte Ellison. Pitt is a policeman whose parents were a cook and a gamekeeper. His father, accused of something he did not do, had been forced out of his position and sent to Australia for ten years. This experience left Thomas with a strong sense of justice and the frustration of trying in vain to clear his father's name. A series of murders in Cater Street lead Pitt to Charlotte Ellison, a young woman of respectability whose upper-class family is drawn into the case when one of their maids falls victim to the Hangman. Later in this first volume, crime invades the heart of the Ellison family, and Thomas and Charlotte fall in love while working to solve the mystery.

Policemen of the Victorian period were regarded as lower-class. Thus

Thomas is in love with a woman to whom he is socially inferior, and the conversations between police officer and gentlewoman allow Perry to shift her perspective between the social classes. But despite the differences in their social stations, Thomas and Charlotte marry, and as the series progresses, they become the "Tommy and Tuppence" of the Victorian Age as Perry often uses Charlotte to ferret out the motives that will help her husband.

Anne Perry's work is filled with social commentary, and she seems to delight in piercing the facade of the upper class with the dark dagger of crime. Prominent secondary characters include Charlotte's sister Emily, Aunt Vespacia, and brother-in-law Dominic. Yet the world of Thomas and Charlotte Pitt is peopled with the masses of the middle and lower classes, whose lives of poverty and frustration are a striking contrast to those of the upper classes, bound by often-ridiculous social mores. The role of Victorian women is a recurring theme in Perry's work; Charlotte Pitt is an intelligent woman whose only way to lead an exciting life is through her husband. Perry addresses the social injustices of the period, and no crime is too sordid. The Pitt books have included adultery, pedophilia, homosexuality (a serious crime in Victorian times), and blackmail as well as murder. Although criticized for sometimes ponderous details, the Pitt series has gained a loyal following and propelled Anne Perry to a position of prominence among historical-mystery novelists.

Shortly after leaving her original publisher, St. Martin's Press, and signing with Ballantine in 1990, Perry introduced a new series with *The Face of a Stranger*. When this book opens, a police detective, William Monk, has lost his memory as the result of a carriage accident. Monk returns to the force after his accident, and tries to hide his amnesia. He learns that he was almost universally disliked before the accident. In the course of the series, Monk has flashes of recall about his earlier life. Set in the mid-1800s, about forty years earlier than the Pitt books, the Monk volumes are darker in tone, usually with legal, medical, or military backgrounds. While the Pitt novels generally focus on crime in the upper class, the Monk books deal more with the lower classes and often include trials. William Monk meets Hester Latterly, a nurse with Florence Nightingale during the Crimean War, in *The Face of a Stranger*. Barrister Oliver Rathbone is the third recurring character in this series, introduced in *Defend and Betray*. For a long time Perry left open the question of whether two of this triangle would ever marry.

Anne Perry makes every attempt to ground her work in the Victorian period, relying on extensive research for historical accuracy. She currently publishes two books per year, one in each series. Writing in longhand, she works for six days each week and is often helped creatively by her next-door neighbor and friend, Meg MacDonald, who works with her two mornings per week. Perry has also written an historical novel set during the French Revolution, which has not yet been published. A recently published fantasy novel titled *Tathea,* about a woman's quest to find God, has been described as a religious allegory with strong Mormon overtones.

> *"A purity of heart is not being unblemished, it's learning to understand your faults so that you can erase them yourself. It's purity of intent."*
>
> —1998 interview in *Speaking of Murder*

Juliet Marion Hulme was the first child of Henry Rainsford Hulme, an up-and-coming scientific mathematician, and his wife Hilda Marion (née Reavley), the daughter of a prominent Anglican clergyman. They married in 1937, and the following year, Henry was appointed chief assistant at the Royal Observatory in Greenwich, where Juliet was born on October 28, 1938. Her brother, Jonathon, was born four years later. Henry, who had earned his Ph.D. at Cambridge in 1932, worked for the British Admiralty during World War Two—an "on loan" arrangement common among Britain's finest young scientists—and became a scientific adviser to the Air Ministry at war's end.

As a child, the precocious Juliet Hulme (pronounced "Hume") suffered from respiratory illness and nearly died of pneumonia when she was six. Advised that their daughter would not survive another London winter, her parents sent her to live with friends in the Bahamas. Separated from her family at such an early age, Juliet had trouble making friends and felt isolated from most of her peers even after the family was reunited in Christchurch, New Zealand, in 1948. Juliet's father, a man of keen intelligence who had risen from a working-class background in England's manufacturing city of Manchester, had been appointed rector of Canterbury University College—a position equivalent to chancellor or president. Apparently his scientific colleagues were astonished by this move, the equivalent of storing his rising career in mothballs, but it is speculated that the motivation for Henry Hulme's decision was his concern for his daughter's health.

While a student at Christchurch Girls High School, Juliet was hospitalized for three months with tuberculosis. She could have no visitors, but received daily letters from Pauline Yvonne Parker, a classmate to whom she became increasingly close. Early in 1954 the two girls learned that Juliet's parents planned to separate; her mother, Hilda, had fallen in love with a man named Walter Perry, called "Bill." Life in the Hulme home could not have been easy, especially after Bill Perry, an engineer, moved in with the family and the affair became the subject of common gossip. Dr. Hulme had not endeared himself to the faculty of Canterbury College, and in March 1954, he resigned under pressure. His plan was to leave his wife and take Juliet and her younger brother back to England.

Among his worries at this time was the unusually close friendship between his daughter and Pauline Parker, a concern shared by Pauline's mother. Together, the girls had created a rich and bizarre fantasy world for themselves, and both girls hoped that Pauline would be allowed to accompany Juliet to England, but Honora Parker refused to allow her daughter to leave Christchurch. As Pauline's diary chillingly revealed, the two girls decided that the death of Pauline's mother was their only hope of remaining together. The girls planned an outing for themselves and Mrs. Parker to Christchurch's lovely Victoria Park on June 22, 1954—ostensibly a farewell for Juliet. They had planted a bright object on a path and waited for Mrs. Parker to investigate it. When she bent over, the girls killed her by bashing her head in with a brick placed in a stocking. According to the evidence, Mrs. Parker was struck more than forty times.

The next day, police investigating the murder found Pauline's diary, in which she had written extensively about the plans the two girls had made, and she and Juliet were arrested. Pauline at first attempted to take full responsibility, but the police found a note she had written: "I am taking the blame for everything." Under police questioning, Juliet finally admitted to being part of the plot and said, "I took the stocking and hit her too." Pauline's diary indicated that the murder was premeditated by both girls.

The pair were convicted of murder in a sensational August trial that lasted only six days. Juliet's mother and Bill Perry were among the witnesses, but her father did not attend any of the legal proceedings and left the country before the trial began.* The defense of insanity—based on the concept of folie à deux, or shared madness, and paranoia—had been rejected. Juliet had not been allowed to testify by her defense team. She was sentenced to an indefinite term in a women's prison. She was not quite sixteen.

---

* When Henry Hulme left New Zealand, he virtually disappeared from public view for a time. But he went on to an extraordinary career: he was one of the physicists responsible for the development of Britain's first hydrogen bomb. In 1959, he became chief of nuclear research for the Atomic Weapons Research Establishment at Aldermaston—a position that involved him directly in most of the major crises of the Cold War. He also remarried, choosing the daughter of a peer. Although he had denounced his daughter's crime in 1954, they reconciled at some point. Henry Hulme, who died in 1991, is the model for Oliver Rathbone's father in the Monk novels.

The two girls were sent to different institutions; after five and a half years, upon reaching twenty-one, they were released with new identities, on the condition that they never see each other again. In 1997 Pauline Parker was discovered living in anonymity in a small English village. She and Juliet Hulme have presumably not met for almost fifty years.

When released from prison, Juliet left New Zealand for England with a passport in the name of Anne Stuart (Stuart was her grandmother's maiden name), and Juliet Hulme was effectively laid to rest. She later assumed the last name of her stepfather, Bill Perry. After several years in England, during which she worked as an airline hostess, Perry moved to the United States, and it was during her residence in northern California that she became a convert to the Mormon Church. She had experimented with a number of Christian churches, but found in the Church of the Latter-Day Saints a spiritual philosophy that matched her own, particularly in the Church's doctrines of forgiveness and free agency.

She returned to England in early 1972 and moved to Scotland in 1989. "I'm the woman who lives up the hill and converted the stone barn," she says of her life in the village of Portmahomack overlooking the Dornoch Firth on the northeast coast of Scotland.

In interviews she has given since the news of her past became public, Perry has said that she remembers very little about the murder of Honora Parker. She has also claimed that she believed Pauline would commit suicide if they were separated. At the time of the murder, she was taking a respiratory medication that has since been taken off the market because of its judgment-altering side effects: "I think my judgment was considerably distorted because I was still being treated, experimentally, with drugs for my illness." In interview after interview, she resolutely avoids discussion of the murder, saying little more than that she has forgiven herself and gotten past it.

Although she never saw *Heavenly Creatures,* Perry was devastated by the film's release and the resultant publicity. She was particularly disturbed by the suggestion (in the film and a book published about the case in 1991) that her relationship with Pauline Parker was a lesbian one. She also realized that her life of comparative anonymity was at an end and feared that she might lose both her home and her career as a result. A major factor in Perry's ability to withstand this difficulty was her faith. She has said, "I think, honestly, once you have offended your own conscience, mortally, you are desperately careful, forever afterwards, not to do it again."

If anything, disclosures about her past seem to have increased the popularity of Anne Perry's writings. The evil lurking beneath the surface is a recurrent theme in the Thomas and Charlotte Pitt series; loss of memory is important in the William Monk books. Both themes are obvious in the life of Anne Perry, who went on from a disastrous adolescence to a productive career. Whatever remorse she may feel, she has not shared it with her public. But in a twist that can only be called ironic, the fifteen-year-old who once plotted with her closest friend to escape to the United States where they would have their "novels" published has found her most adoring audience among Americans. She routinely embarks on gala publicity tours of the States, promoting her most recent book, speaking, greeting her fans, giving interviews, and shunting aside questions about her past.

—MCT

BIBLIOGRAPHY

ANNE PERRY
1938–
British (born: Greenwich)

"He waved aside the necessity for recalling the name of a mere policeman. They were anonymous, like servants."
—*Bluegate Fields*

Anne Perry's mystery novels were first published in the United States— where her popularity has always been wider than in her native England—by St. Martin's Press, followed after 1990 by Ballantine/Fawcett. Her British publishers have included Hale, Souvenir Press, HarperCollins, and Headline. Her books are listed by first publication date in the United States. Featured detectives appear in ( ).

Mystery Novels
1979 *The Cater Street Hangman* (Pitt)
1980 *Callander Square* (Pitt)
1981 *Paragon Walk* (Pitt)
1981 *Resurrection Row* (Pitt)
1983 *Rutland Place* (Pitt)
1984 *Bluegate Fields* (Pitt)
1985 *Death in the Devil's Acre* (Pitt)
1987 *Cardington Crescent* (Pitt)
1988 *Silence in Hanover Close* (Pitt)
1990 *Bethlehem Road* (Pitt)

1990   *The Face of a Stranger* (Monk)
1991   *Highgate Rise* (Pitt)
1991   *A Dangerous Mourning* (Monk)
1992   *Belgrave Square* (Pitt)
1992   *Defend and Betray* (Monk)
1993   *Farrier's Lane* (Pitt)
1993   *A Sudden, Fearful Death* (Monk)
1994   *The Hyde Park Headsman* (Pitt)
1994   *The Sins of the Wolf* (Monk)
1995   *Traitor's Gate* (Pitt)
1995   *Cain His Brother* (Monk)
1996   *Pentecost Alley* (Pitt)
1996   *Weighed in the Balance* (Monk)
1997   *Ashworth Hall* (Pitt)
1997   *The Silent Cry* (Monk)
1998   *Brunswick Gardens* (Pitt)
1998   *A Breach of Promise* (Monk)
1999   *Bedford Square* (Pitt)
1999   *The Twisted Root* (Monk)
2000   *Half Moon Street* (Pitt)
2000   *Slaves of Obsession* (Monk)

Nonmystery Novel
1999   *Tathea,* a religious fantasy published by Shadow Mountain

Video Adaptation
In 1998, Yorkshire Television aired the first adaptation of a Perry mystery—*The Cater Street Hangman*—which was subsequently shown on the Arts and Entertainment Network in the United States. Produced by Ardent, which is owned by Prince Edward (Perry enjoys the royal connection), the two-hour production stars Eoin McCarthy as Thomas Pitt and Keeley Hawes as Charlotte. Perry herself makes an appearance in the graveyard scene.

SOME OF THE BEST OF THE REST

SO MANY MYSTERIES; SO LITTLE TIME

*M*ystery-crime-detective fiction is a crowded field, and new writers are coming to the bookshelves almost daily. *Women of Mystery* has spotlighted the leaders, past and present, but there are so many more. The following authors—all but one active today—represent just some of the best reading available to mystery lovers. There are a few veterans, but most entered the mystery game in the 1980s and 1990s.

CATHERINE AIRD (British: born 1930)

Born in Yorkshire, Aird has been publishing since 1966. Her bright, intelligent mysteries are firmly located in Agatha Christie country—the mythical county of Calleshire, where villages, towns, and countryside provide plenty of opportunities for murder. Her continuing cast of police is headed by Inspector C. D. "Seedy" Sloan. Aird's novels reflect her interest in history and her sharp eye for English eccentrics.

LINDA BARNES (American: born 1949)

Barnes, a Detroit native, lives in and writes about Boston, where her Carlotta Carlyle and Michael Spraggue series are set. The stronger series features private eye Carlyle, a Jewish-Irish divorcée who drives a cab to earn money between clients. Barnes's plots can be violent, but her focus is on character and contemporary issues.

GWENDOLINE BUTLER (British: born 1922)

Under her own name and as Jennie Melville, Butler has written more than fifty novels. She taught history at Oxford before writing her first mystery in the mid-1950s. Her working cops in two series—Inspector John Coffin (Butler) and Charmian Daniels (Melville)—solve traditional mysteries and deal with personal and professional dilemmas, and her London is a special place. Butler has also written a number of nonseries mysteries under both names. Her books may be hard to find but are worth the search.

SARAH CAUDWELL (English: 1939–2000)

Sarah Caudwell (Cockburn) graduated in law from St. Anne's College, Oxford, where she was famed for her pipe-smoking and her schemes to open the Oxford Union to women. She lectured in law, spent several years as a barrister, then became a tax specialist for Lloyd's Bank. She wrote only four mysteries before her death at age sixty. Her witty, erudite books feature a team of young Lincoln's Inn lawyers and their mentor, Hilary Tamar, an Oxford specialist in medieval law whose gender is never revealed.

DEBORAH CROMBIE (American)

A Texan by birth and education, Crombie sets her novels in England, where she has lived and now visits regularly. Her investigative team are Superintendent Duncan Kincaid and Sergeant Gemma James. Her form is traditional, but *Dreaming of Bones* and others demonstrate a rare talent. She lives in Texas and has published six books since 1993.

LINDSEY DAVIS (British)

A very popular English writer of historical mysteries, Davis is also very good at what she does. Her lively mysteries are set in ancient Rome, where Marcus Didius Falco, a kind of backdated Sam Spade or Philip Marlowe, deals with evil villains and the seamy side of the empire. Beginning with *The Silver Pigs,* Davis's novels have become surefire bestsellers with a devoted following.

LINDA FAIRSTEIN (American)

A graduate of Vassar College and the University of Virginia Law School, Linda Fairstein is currently challenging the male stranglehold on the legal crime novel in the United States. With her background in prosecution—for more than two decades she has headed the Sex Crimes Unit of the New York County District Attorney's office—she brings both knowledge and verisimilitude to her Alex Cooper series.

FRANCES FYFIELD (British: born in 1948)

Frances Fyfield (Frances Hegarty) is a criminal attorney who served for some time in England's Crown Prosecution Service. Her series investigators, debuted in 1988, are an unlikely pair: Crown Prosecutor Helen West and Detective Superintendent Geoffrey Bailey, whose intense relationship is both personal and professional. Often compared to her friend P. D. James, Fyfield writes fine psychological mysteries, strong on characterization. Another Fyfield series features lawyer Sarah Fortune.

ELIZABETH GEORGE (American: born 1949)

Born in Ohio and now a resident of California, George is one of a cluster of audacious American women who choose to write *veddy* English novels. Her protagonists, aristocrat Thomas Lynley and his working-class partner Barbara Havers, must be Scotland Yard's least compatible couple. They solve crimes, aided by an ensemble of friends, and all the characters develop as the series progresses. British critics have complained that George isn't always spot-on in her presentation of English manners and mores, but her books are still tense and well-told tales.

ALLISON JOSEPH (British)

A graduate of Leeds University, Joseph worked in radio and television production and founded her own documentary company. Then she wrote her first mystery, *Sacred Hearts,* featuring Sister Agnes. The sister was once married, disastrously, and then chose to get herself to a nunnery. A woman of independent spirit and decidedly upscale tastes, Sister Agnes belongs to an open Catholic order in London, and her work takes her among the young and the poor. She has solved crimes in six mysteries since 1994.

LAURIE KING (American)

King's first mystery, *A Grave Talent,* which picked up top awards in the United States and England in 1993, features contemporary San Francisco homicide detective Kate Martinelli. King's second series goes back to the great detective tradition—to Sherlock Holmes no less—but the focus is Mary Russell, a young late-Victorian feminist every bit as smart and clever at solving mysteries as her teacher and friend, the mighty Holmes, and the Russell mysteries focus on *her* detection. King, who has an advanced degree in theology (a background that inspires topics for her novels), is married to a professor of religious studies and lives in her native California.

VAL McDERMID (Scots: born 1955)

Reared in Scotland, McDermid studied English at Oxford and went on to a career in journalism before turning to mystery writing. She uses several series characters: Lindsay Gordan, "cynical socialist lesbian feminist journalist"; Kate Brannigan, private eye; Dr. Tony Hill, head of the National Profiling Task Force, whose handling of his shocking cases earned McDermid the title of "Manchester's answer to Thomas Harris" from the *Guardian*.

MARGARET MARON (American)

Maron, born and educated in North Carolina, worked at the Pentagon for a time, where she met her husband, and lived in Italy and Brooklyn before returning to Southern soil. Her first love was poetry, but her New York days inspired a series of mysteries about New York Police Department homicide investigator Sigrid Harald, whose outward severity hides inner feminine turmoil. Maron went back to her roots for *Bloody Kin* in 1985, followed by a new series with lawyer Deborah Knott, set in North Carolina.

CAROL O'CONNELL (American: born 1947)

When O'Connell's first mystery, *Mallory's Oracle,* appeared in 1994, *Time* magazine called it "wild-eyed nonsense and good fun" but with a "cleverly built foundation. . . ." Critics find her books hard to classify—especially since her lead character, NYPD cop Kathleen Mallory, is beautiful, smart, computer-savvy, and possibly a sociopath. But in her first and subsequent books, O'Connell has succeeded in making her heroine more than a two-dimensional freak: Mallory has a modern mind perfectly suited for our morally ambiguous times.

DOROTHY SIMPSON (Welsh: born 1933)

Simpson began writing psychological thrillers in the mid-1970s. Though her first novel, *Harbingers of Fear,* was quite successful, her next books were rejected. So she turned to the more traditional mystery, launching her Inspector Luke Thanet series with *The Night She Died* in 1981. The psychological elements remain—Simpson, a former teacher, also worked as a marriage counselor—in her presentations of complex personal relationships. Though Simpson's mood is more positive than Ruth Rendell's, the Thanet series is similar to the Wexfords in the intermingling of regional police work and the ongoing development of a cast of characters.

JOAN SMITH (British: born 1953)

Smith updates the amateur detective with her lead character, London University professor Loretta Lawson. The Lawson books have increasingly moved away from tradition, however, as her protagonist—a feminist looking for a middle road—encounters institutional corruption that leads to murder. Smith's writing has a sharp, cynical edge that fits a society in which the cover-up has become an art form and powerful people are rarely brought to account.

MARGARET YORKE (British: born 1924)

Yorke is a plot-maker who turns the cozy, country house murder on its ear. In her Dr. Patrick Grant (Oxford dean) series and her many stand-alone novels, she explores the ills and evils that hide beneath the neat surfaces of contemporary England. Her central characters are often middle-class women, and she has been compared to Barbara Pym in her interest in characters whose outward respectability covers frustration and desperation. As investigations unfurl, "why?" is the dominant question.

A CRIMINOUS CHRONOLOGY I

HIGHLIGHTS IN THE HISTORY OF
MYSTERY FICTION, START TO GOLDEN AGE

1794   *Caleb Williams* by William Godwin (English): not quite detection, but close.

1828–1829   *Mémoires de Vidocq* by Eugène Françoise Vidocq (French): the autobiographical exaggerations of the criminal who, in 1811, became the first chief of the Paris Sûreté and later founded the first detective agency.

1841   "The Murders in the Rue Morgue" by Edgar Allan Poe (American): the first true detective short story; French mystery and French detective, by an American genius.

1853   *Bleak House* by Charles Dickens (English) and first literary use of a working-class detective, Inspector Bucket.

1861   *East Lynne* by Mrs. Henry Wood (English) and *Lady Audley's Secret* by Miss Mary Elizabeth Braddon (English) in 1866: Two sensational romance novels that influenced the future of detection.

1865   *The Notting Hill Mystery* by Charles Felix (English): first detective novel; the investigator is an insurance man.

1866   *The Dead Letter* by Seeley Regester (American): first, but forgettable, detective novel written by a woman.

1868   *The Moonstone* by Wilkie Collins (English): classic detection by Sergeant Cuff.

1869   *Monsieur Lecoq* by Émile Gaboriau (French): "roman policier" series starring the vain but honest French detective Lecoq.

1878   *The Leavenworth Case* by Anna Katharine Green (American): wildly successful first book by the "Mother of the Detective Novel" introduced Inspector Ebenezer Gryce.

1887   "A Study in Scarlet" by Arthur Conan Doyle (English): Sherlock Holmes is born.

1893   First Sexton Blake story by Hal Meredith published.

1899   *The Amateur Cracksman* by E. W. Hornung (English): Arthur Conan Doyle's brother-in-law creates Raffles, the gentleman thief.

1906   *The Triumphs of Eugene Valmont* by Robert Barr (English): French detective in English hands.

1907   *Arsène Lupin: Gentleman-Cambrioleur* by Maurice Leblanc (French): collected stories of a master disguise artist who, in a later novel, actually arrests himself!

1907   *Le Mystère de la Chambre Jaune (The Mystery of the Yellow Room)* by Gaston Leroux (French): famous locked-room mystery by *The Phantom of the Opera* author.

1907   *The Red Thumb Mark* by R. Austin Freeman (English): first appearance of forensic scientist Dr. John Thorndyke.

1907   *The Thinking Machine* by Jacques Futrelle (American): short story collection featuring Professor Augustus S. F. X. Van Dusen, Ph.D., LL.D., F.R.S., M.D., M.D.S. A Georgia native, Futrelle died at age thirty-seven aboard the *Titanic*.

1908   *The Circular Staircase* by Mary Roberts Rinehart (American): the start of a long and profitable Had-I-But-Known career.

1909   *The Old Man in the Corner* by Baroness Orczy (Hungarian-English), featuring the model of armchair detectives.

1910   *At the Villa Rose* by A. E. W. Mason (English): debut of Inspector Hanaud of the Sûreté and his sidekick, Ricardo.

1911   *The Innocence of Father Brown* by G. K. Chesterton (English): first collection of Father Brown stories—the "metaphysical" priest-detective.

1913   *The Lodger* by Mrs. Belloc Lowndes (English): novel retelling of the Jack the Ripper murders, with speculative solution.

1913   *The Mystery of Dr. Fu-Manchu* by Sax Rohmer (English): racist series, awfully popular in its day.

1913   *Trent's Last Case* by E. C. Bentley (English): influential "modern" detection.

1914   *Max Carrados* by Ernest Bramah Smith (English): literature's first blind detective.

1915   *The Thirty-Nine Steps* by John Buchan (Scots): influential thriller by a well-known British politician, introduced secret agent Richard Hannay.

1918   *Uncle Abner, Master of Mysteries* by Melville Davisson Post (American): the collected stories of a Virginia detective in the Jeffersonian mold.

A CRIMONOUS CHRONOLOGY II

HIGHLIGHTS IN THE HISTORY OF MYSTERY FICTION, 1920 TO 1950

1920 *The Mysterious Affair at Styles* by Agatha Christie (English): first appearance of the egg-headed Belgian detective Hercule Poirot and his "cher ami" Hastings.

1920 *The Cask* by Freeman Wills Crofts (Irish): first and excellent novel by the writer whose next creation was the popular Inspector French of Scotland Yard.

1920 *Call Mr. Fortune* by H. C. Bailey (English), introducing doctor-detective Reggie Fortune.

1920 *Bull-Dog Drummond: The Adventures of a Demobilized Officer Who Found Peace Dull* by "Sapper" (H. Cyril McNeile, English): popular adventure series between the wars.

1922 *The Red House Mystery* by A. A. Milne (English): Winnie-the-Pooh's creator crafts his only detective novel.

1923 *Whose Body?* by Dorothy L. Sayers (English): first murder for Lord Peter Wimsey.

1924 *The Rasp* by Philip MacDonald (English): first Colonel Anthony Gethryn novel.

1925 *The House without a Key* by Earl Derr Biggers (American): the birth of Charlie Chan.

1925 *The Layton Court Mystery* by Anthony Berkeley (Anthony Berkeley Cox, English): first Roger Sheringham novel by the prolific author also known as "Francis Iles."

1925 *The Viaduct Murder* by Ronald Knox (English): first novel by the monsignor who developed the ten rules of detective writing.

1926 *The Benson Murder Case* by S. S. Van Dine (Willard Huntington Wright, American): first in the popular series featuring the erudite snob Philo Vance.

1926 *The Murder of Roger Ackroyd* by Agatha Christie: controversial Poirot novel established Christie as the "Queen of Crime."

1928 Patricia Wentworth's (English) Miss Maud Silver is born in *Grey Mask*.

1929   *The Man in the Queue* by Josephine Tey (pseudonym of Scotland's Elizabeth MacKintosh): first of the reclusive writer's mystery novels features Inspector Alan Grant.

1929   Margery Allingham (English) introduces the "silly ass" Albert Campion as a supporting character in *The Crime at Black Dudley.*

1929   Ellery Queen (Americans Frederic Dannay and Manfred B. Lee) begins long and influential career with *The Roman Hat Mystery.*

1929   First Dashiell Hammett (American) novel, *Red Harvest,* features the investigation of the Continental Op. *The Dain Curse* appears the same year.

1929   Gladys Mitchell's (English) consulting psychiatrist Mrs. Beatrice Lestrange Bradley has her first outing in *Speedy Death.*

1930   *The Diamond Feather.* Helen Reilly (American) launches her Inspector McKee mysteries.

1931   Anthony Berkeley Cox writing as Francis Iles reveals the killer on page one of *Malice Aforethought.* One of the great "inverted" mysteries.

1931   *The Death of Monsieur Gallet* by Georges Simenon (Belgian): begins the worthy career of Inspector Maigret of the French Sûreté.

1934   Erle Stanley Gardner (American) starts his Perry Mason series with *The Case of the Velvet Claws.*

1934   *A Man Lay Dead* by New Zealand's Ngaio Marsh: first case for Roderick Alleyn, fastidious gentleman-cop.

1934   Rex Stout (American) conjures up Nero Wolfe, the ultimate armchair detective, and his legman Archie Goodwin in *Fer-de-Lance.*

1935   *Gaudy Night* by Dorothy L. Sayers: Oxford romance stirs heated debate among critics.

1935   John Dickson Carr's (American) *The Hollow Man,* considered the best locked-room mystery by many.

1939   Raymond Chandler (English-educated American) moves private investigator Philip Marlowe from pulps to novel in *The Big Sleep.*

1940   Elizabeth Daly (American) debuts her literate expert in rare books and murder, Henry Gamadge, in *Unexpected Night* and *Deadly Nightshade.*

1941   Founding of *Ellery Queen's Mystery Magazine.*

1941   *The Invisible Worm,* first mystery novel by Margaret Millar (Canadian). Millar's husband Kenneth—Ross Macdonald—will publish his first novel in 1944.

1949   Hard-boiled Lew Archer makes first appearance in Ross Macdonald's *The Moving Target.*

1950   Patricia Highsmith (American) breaks the mystery mold with *Strangers on a Train.*

A Criminous Chronology III

HIGHLIGHTS IN THE HISTORY OF MYSTERY FICTION, 1951 TO PRESENT

1952   Agatha Christie's *The Mousetrap* opens on the London stage.

1952   Hillary Waugh publishes what is credited as the first popular American police procedural novel, *Last Seen Wearing.*

1953   British writers found the Crime Writers Association, with John Creasey as chairman.

1954   Mystery Writers of America award first Edgar for Best Novel to *Beat Not the Bones* by Charlotte Jay.

1954   *Casino Royale* by Britain's Ian Fleming: introduces the world to "Bond. James Bond."

1955   Patricia Highsmith's first Tom Ripley novel, *The Talented Mr. Ripley.*

1955   The prolific John Creasey (English) as J. J. Marric creates Commander George Gideon of Scotland Yard in *Gideon's Day,* the first modern British police procedural.

1955   The Mystery Writers of America name Agatha Christie as their first Grand Master, honoring the entire body of her work.

1956   American Ed McBain's first 87th Precinct novel, *Cop Hater.*

1961   Emma Lathen (Americans Mary Jane Latsis and Martha Henissart) takes crime to Wall Street in *Banking on Death,* the first John Putnam Thatcher novel.

1962   Poetic Adam Dalgliesh of Scotland Yard debuts in P. D. James's (English) *Cover Her Face.*

1962   First Dick Francis (English) novel, *Dead Cert.*

1963   John le Carré's (English) *The Spy Who Came in from the Cold,* influential on crime as well as espionage writing.

1964   Ruth Rendell (English) begins Inspector Wexford series with *From Doon with Death.*

1964   Chester Himes's (American) *Cotton Comes to Harlem,* featuring detectives Coffin Ed Johnson and Grave Digger Jones, achieves wide audience, opening doors for later African–American detectives, including Walter Mosley's Easy Rawlings.

1965   From Sweden, Maj Sjöwall and Per Wahlöo's first Martin Beck mystery, *Roseanna,* breaks the Anglo–American hold on international success in the genre. The team's 1968 *The Man on the Balcony* is often called the first philosophical mystery.

1969   Elmore Leonard (American) debuts with *The Big Bounce.*

1975   Mary Higgins Clark (American) begins her multimillion-dollar career with *Where Are the Children?*

1975   Colin Dexter's (English) soulful Inspector Morse makes first appearance in *Last Bus to Woodstock.*

1977   Ellis Peters's (Edith Pargeter, English) *A Morbid Taste for Bones*: digging for mystery in the Middle Ages with the first Brother Cadfael novel.

1977   Marcia Muller (American) starts the ball rolling for American women private investigators with her first Sharon McCone mystery, *Edwin of the Iron Shoes.*

1982   Sara Paretsky's V. I. Warshawski in *Indemnity Only* and Sue Grafton's Kinsey Milhone in *"A" Is for Alibi*: American authors push tough female private investigators in Chicago and California settings.

1986   Ruth Rendell adopts pen name Barbara Vine for intensely psychological novels, starting with *A Dark-Adapted Eye.*

1986   British Crime Writers Association awards first Diamond Dagger for lifetime contribution to Eric Ambler (American).

1988   Debut of Detective Inspector Lynley series with Elizabeth George's (American) *A Great Deliverance.*

1990   *Postmortem* by Patricia Cornwell (American): Virginia coroner Kay Scarpetta makes first appearance.

1990   Walter Mosley (American) introduces private investigator Easy Rawlings in *Devil in a Blue Dress.*

1992   *The Ice House* launches Minette Walters's (English) mystery-writing career.

REFERENCES AND RESOURCES

Primary works (fiction and autobiography) by the *Women of Mystery* are listed in the bibliography section at the end of each chapter. The following list includes other sources that have been quoted and/or from which authors' quotations have been taken or which served as major resources in the preparation of this book. For the reader who wishes to learn more about an author or the history and criticism of detective/mystery fiction, recommended titles are marked with an ★.

———— *Merriam-Webster's Encyclopedia of Literature*. Springfield, Massachusetts: Merriam-Webster, Incorporated, Publishers. 1995.

———— "One Hundred Masters of Crime," *The Sunday Times*. April 18, 1998. (Special section.)

★Auden, W. H. "The Guilty Vicarage" from *The Dyer's Hand and Other Essays*. 1948.

Bakerman, Jane S. (ed.) *And Then There Were Nine . . . More Women of Mystery*. Bowling Green, Ohio: Bowling Green State University Popular Press. 1985.

Barzun, Jacques, and Wendell Hertig Taylor. *A Catalogue of Crime*. New York: Harper & Row, Publishers.

Bell, Ian, and Graham Daltry (eds.). *Watching the Detectives: Essays on Crime Fiction*. New York: St. Martin's Press. 1990.

Benstock, Bernard (ed.). *Art in Crime Writing: Essays on Detective Fiction*. New York: St. Martin's Press. 1983.

Bloom, Harold (ed.). *Classic Mystery Writers*. New York, Philadelphia: Chelsea House Publishers. 1995.

Budd, Elaine. *13 Mistresses of Murder*. New York: Frederick Ungar Publishing Co. 1986.

★Carr, John C. *The Craft of Crime: Conversations with Crime Writers*. Boston: Houghton Mifflin Company. 1983.

★Chandler, Raymond. "The Simple Art of Murder." *Atlantic Monthly*. December 1944.

Cooper-Clark, Diana. *Designs of Darkness: Interviews with Detective Novelists*. Bowling Green, Ohio: Bowling Green State University Popular Press. 1983.

Cox, Michael (ed.). *Victorian Detective Stories*. Oxford and New York: Oxford University Press. 1993.

★Craig, Patricia, and Mary Cadogan. *The Lady Investigates: Women Detectives and Spies in Fiction*. New York: St. Martin's Press. 1981.

Craig, Patricia (ed.). *The Oxford Book of English Detective Stories*. Oxford and New York: Oxford University Press. 1990.

Doyle, Arthur Conan. *Sherlock Holmes Reader.* Philadelphia, London: Courage Books. 1994.

Doyle, Arthur Conan. *The Complete Sherlock Holmes.* Garden City, New York: Garden City Books.

Friedman, Mickey (ed.). *The Crown Crime Companion: The Top 100 Mystery Writers of All Time, Selected by the Mystery Writers of America.* New York: Crown Trade Paperbacks. 1995.

Gardner, John. "The Espionage Novel" in *Whodunit?* (See Keating, below.)

Gorman, Ed, and Martin H. Greenberg (eds.). *Speaking of Murder: Interviews with the Masters of Mystery and Suspense.* New York: Berkley Prime Crime. 1998.

★Gorman, Ed, and Martin H. Greenberg, Larry Segriff, and Jon L. Breen (eds.). *The Fine Art of Murder: The Mystery Reader's Indispensable Companion.* New York: Carroll & Graf Publishers, Inc. 1993.

Grape, Jan, and Dean James and Ellen Nehr (eds.). *Deadly Women: The Woman Mystery Reader's Indispensable Companion.* New York: Carroll & Graf Publishers, Inc. 1998.

Halliwell, Leslie. *Halliwell's Film Guide.* New York: Charles Scribner's Sons. Fourth edition, 1985.

★Haycraft, Howard (ed.). *The Art of the Mystery Story: A Collection of Critical Essays.* New York: Carroll & Graf Publishers, Inc. 1992. (First published in 1946.)

Haycraft, Howard. *Murder for Pleasure: The Life and Times of the Detective Story.* New York: Carroll & Graf Publishers, Inc. 1984. (First published in 1941.)

★Herbert, Rosemary. *The Fatal Art of Entertainment: Interviews with Mystery Writers.* New York: G. K. Hall & Co. 1994.

Hubin, Allen J. *Crime Fiction 1749–1980: A Comprehensive Bibliography.* New York and London: Garland Publisher, Inc. 1984. (*1981–1985 Supplement.* 1988.)

Hughes, Winifred. *The Maniac in the Cellar: Sensation Novels of the 1860s.* Princeton, New Jersey: Princeton University Press. 1980.

Keating, H. R. F. *Whodunit?: A Guide to Crime, Suspense and Spy Fiction.* New York: Van Nostrand Reinhold Company. 1982.

Klein, Kathleen Gregory (ed.). *Great Women Mystery Writers: Classic to Contemporary.* Westport, Connecticut, and London: Greenwood Press. 1994.

Lambert, Gavin. *The Dangerous Edge.* New York: Grossman Publishers. 1976.

Light, Allison. *Forever England: Femininity, Literature and Conservatism between the Wars.* London & New York: Routledge, Chapman and Hall, Inc. 1991.

Mann, Jessica. *Deadlier than the Male: Why Are Respectable English Women So Good at Murder?* New York: Macmillan Publishing Co., Inc. 1981.

★Murch, A. E. *The Development of the Detective Novel.* Port Washington, N.Y.: Kennikat Press. 1968.

Nash, Ogden. *Verses from 1929 On.* New York: The Modern Library. 1959.

Orczy, Baroness (Emmuska). *The Man in the Corner.* Introduction by Vincent Starrett. New York: W. W. Norton & Company, Inc. (The Seagull Library of Mystery and Suspense.) 1966.

Ousby, Ian. *Guilty Parties: A Mystery Lover's Companion.* New York: Thames and Hudson. 1997.

Panek, LeRoy. *Watteau's Shepherds: The Detective Novel in Britain 1914–1940.* Bowling Green, Ohio: Bowling Green University Popular Press. 1979.

Partridge, Eric. *A Dictionary of Slang and Unconventional English.* New York: The Macmillan Company. Sixth Edition, 1967.

Paul, Robert S. *Whatever Happened to Sherlock Holmes: Detective Fiction, Popular Theology, and Society.* Carbondale and Edwardsville: Southern Illinois University Press, 1991.

Peterson, Audrey. *Victorian Masters of Mystery: From Wilkie Collins to Conan Doyle.* New York: Frederick Ungar Publishing Co. 1984.

Reynolds, William, and Elizabeth A. Trembley (eds.). *It's a Print!: Detective Fiction from Page to Screen.* Bowling Green, Ohio: Bowling Green State University Popular Press. 1994.

★Sayers, Dorothy L. Introduction to *The Omnibus of Crime.* New York: Payson & Clarke. 1929. (*Great Short Stories of Detection, Mystery, and Horror.* London: Gollancz. 1928.)

Skow, John. "Cops with Machisma," *Time.* October 3, 1994.

★Slung, Michele B. (ed.) *Crime on Her Mind: Fifteen Stories of Female Sleuths from the Victorian Era to the Forties.* Penguin Books. 1975.

Steinbrunner, Chris, and Otto Penzler (eds.). *Encyclopedia of Mystery and Detection.* New York: McGraw-Hill Book Company. 1976.

Stern, Madeleine. Introduction to *Behind a Mask: The Unknown Thrillers of Louisa May Alcott.* Madeleine Stern (ed.). New York: William Morrow & Company, Inc. 1975.

Symons, Julian. *Criminal Practices: Symons on Crime Writing 60s to 90s.* London: Macmillan. 1994.

Symons, Julian. Introduction to *Verdict of Thirteen: A Detective Club Anthology.* New York: Harper & Row, Publishers. 1978.

★Symons, Julian. *Mortal Consequences: A History from the Detective Story to the Crime Novel.* New York: Harper & Row, Publishers. 1972. (Published in the United States as *Bloody Murder.* The Mysterious Press. Third revised edition, 1992.)

★Watson, Colin. *Snobbery with Violence.* London: Eyre and Spottiswode. 1971.

Wilson, Edmund. "Why Do People Read Detective Stories?"; "Who Cares Who Killed Roger Ackroyd?"; and "Mr. Holmes, They Were the Footprints of a Gigantic Hound!" *New Yorker* magazine articles reprinted in *Classics and Commentaries: A Literary Chronicle of the 1940s.* New York: Farrar, Straus and Giroux. 1950.

★Winks, Robin W. (ed.) *Detective Fiction: A Collection of Critical Essays.* Englewood, N.J.: Prentice-Hall, Inc. 1980.

Winn, Dilys. *Murder Ink: The Mystery Reader's Companion.* New York: Workman Publishing. 1977.

★Winn, Dilys. *Murderess Ink: The Better Half of the Mystery.* New York: Bell Publishing Company. 1981.

Anna Katharine Green

Maida, Patricia D. *Mother of Detective Fiction: The Life and Works of Anna Katharine Green.* Bowling Green, Ohio: Bowling Green State University Popular Press. 1989.

Hayne, Barrie. "Anna Katharine Green" in *10 Women of Mystery.*

Ross, Cheri Louise. "Anna Katharine Green" in *Great Women Mystery Writers.*

Mary Roberts Rinehart

★Cohn, Jan. *Improbable Fiction: The Life of Mary Roberts Rinehart.* Pittsburgh: University of Pittsburgh Press. 1980.

Cohn, Jan. "Mary Roberts Rinehart" in *10 Women of Mystery.*

★MacLeod, Charlotte. *Had She But Known: A Biography of Mary Roberts Rinehart.* New York: The Mysterious Press. 1994.

MacLeod, Charlotte. "Murder Most Cozy," *The Armchair Detective.* Summer 1993.

Rinehart, Mary Roberts. "If I Had a Daughter," *Forum and Century.* March 1932.

Rinehart, Mary Roberts. "My Experience in the Movies," *The American Magazine.* October 1920.

Rinehart, Mary Roberts. "My Public," *The Bookman.* December 1920.

Rinehart, Mary Roberts. "The Repute of the Crime Story," *The Publishers' Weekly.* February 1, 1930.

Rinehart, Mary Roberts. "The Unreality of Modern Realism," *The Bookman.* December 1922.

Rinehart, Mary Roberts. (Uncredited.) "Up and Down with the Drama," *The Saturday Evening Post.* July 6, 1912.

Rinehart, Mary Roberts. "A Woman Goes to Market," *The Saturday Evening Post.* January 31, 1931.

Rinehart, Mary Roberts. "Writing Is Work," *The Saturday Evening Post.* March 11, 1939.

Agatha Christie

——— "A Mysterious Affair of Style," *The Economist.* September 29, 1990.

——— "Commentary," *Times Literary Supplement.* September 18, 1970.

Barnard, Robert. *A Talent to Deceive: An Appreciation of Agatha Christie.* New York: Dodd, Mead & Company. 1980.

Christie, Agatha. *The Mousetrap and Other Plays.* New York: Harper Paperbacks. 1978. Introduction by Ira Levin.

★Gill, Gillian. *Agatha Christie: The Woman and Her Mysteries.* New York: The Free Press. 1990.

Grant, Ellsworth. "A Tribute to Agatha Christie," *Horizon.* Autumn 1976.

Grossvogel, David I. *Mystery and Its Fictions: From Oedipus to Agatha Christie.* Baltimore, London: The Johns Hopkins University Press. 1979.

Hart, Ann. *The Life and Times of Miss Jane Marple.* New York: Dodd, Mead & Company. 1985.

Hart, Caroline G. *The Christie Caper.* New York: Bantam Books. 1991. (Fiction.)

★Keating, H. R. F. (ed.) *Agatha Christie: First Lady of Crime.* New York: Holt Rinehart & Winston. 1977.

Kitchin, C. H. B. "Five Writers in One: The Versatility of Agatha Christie," *Times Literary Supplement.* February 15, 1955.

Knepper, Marty S. "Agatha Christie—Feminist," *The Armchair Detective.* August 1983.

Lowenthal, Max. "Agatha Christie, Creator of Poirot, Dies," *New York Times.* January 13, 1976.

Maida, Patricia D., and Nicholas B. Spornick. *Murder She Wrote: A Study of Agatha Christie's Detective Fiction.* Bowling Green, Ohio: Bowling Green State University Popular Press. 1982.

★Mallowan, Max. *Mallowan's Memoirs: The Autobiography of Max Mallowan.* New York: Dodd, Mead & Company. 1977.

★Morgan, Janet. *Agatha Christie: A Biography.* New York: Alfred A. Knopf. 1985.

Mortimer, John. "Murder Most Tidy," *The New York Times Book Review.* October 14, 1990.

Ramsey, G. C. *Agatha Christie: Mistress of Mystery.* New York: Dodd, Mead & Company. 1967.

Riley, Dick, and Pam McAllister (eds.). *The New Bedside Bathtub and Armchair Companion to Agatha Christie.* New York: Ungar Publishing Company. Second edition, 1986.

Robyns, Gwen. *The Mystery of Agatha Christie.* Penguin Books, 1979.

Rowse, A. L. "Ah, Sweet Mystery! The Agatha I Knew," *The New York Times Book Review.* October 14, 1990.

Rowse, A. L. *Memories of Men and Women.* London: Eyre Methuen. 1980.

Sanders, Dennis, and Len Lovallo. *The Agatha Christie Companion.* New York: Berkley Books. 1989.

Shenker, Israel. "The Past Master of Mysteries, She Built a Better Mousetrap," *Smithsonian.* September 1990.

Toye, Randall. *The Agatha Christie Who's Who.* New York: Holt, Rinehart and Winston. 1980.

Tynan, Kathleen. *Agatha.* New York: Ballentine Books. 1978. (Fiction.)

Wagoner, Mary S. *Agatha Christie.* Boston: Twayne Publishers. 1986.

Waugh, Auberon. "Letter from Europe: Murder at Newlands Corner," *Esquire.* July 1976.

Dorothy L. Sayers

★Brabazon, James. *Dorothy L. Sayers.* New York: Charles Scribner's Sons. 1981. (Preface by Anthony Fleming; Foreword by P. D. James.)

Christopher, Joe R. "The Mystery of Robert Eustace," *The Armchair Detective.* Fall 1980.

Cournos, John. *The Devil Is an English Gentleman.* (Two volumes.) New York: Farrar & Rinehart Incorporated. 1932.

Dale, Alzina Stone (ed.). *Dorothy L. Sayers: The Centenary Celebration.* New York: Walker and Co. 1993.

Durkin, Mary Brian. *Dorothy L. Sayers.* Boston: Twayne Publishers. 1980.

Freeling, Nicholas. "Dorothy Sayers," *The Armchair Detective.* Summer 1994.

Hall, Trevor H. *Dorothy L. Sayers: Nine Literary Studies.* Hamden, Connecticut: Archon Books. 1980.

Hannay, Margaret P. *As Her Wimsey Took Her: Critical Essays on the Work of Dorothy L. Sayers.* Kent, Ohio: The Kent State University Press. 1979.

Hitchman, Janet. *Such a Strange Lady: An Introduction to Dorothy L. Sayers (1893–1957).* London: The New English Library. 1975.

Klein, Kathleen Gregory. "Dorothy Sayers" in *10 Women of Mystery.*

Panek, LeRoy. "Dorothy Sayers" in *Watteau's Shepherds.*

★Reynolds, Barbara. *Dorothy L. Sayers: Her Life and Soul.* New York: St. Martin's Press. 1993.

Reynolds, William. "The Patriarchy Restored: BBC Television's Adaptation of Dorothy L. Sayers's *Strong Poison, Have His Carcase,* and *Gaudy Night*" in *It's a Print!*

★Sayers, Dorothy L. *The Letters of Dorothy L. Sayers: 1899–1936, the Making of a Detective Novelist.* Barbara Reynolds (ed.). New York: St. Martin's Press. 1996.

★Sayers, Dorothy L. *The Letters of Dorothy L. Sayers: 1937–1943, from Novelist to Playwright.* Barbara Reynolds (ed.). New York: St. Martin's Press. 1998.

Sayers, Dorothy L. *Unpopular Opinions: Twenty-one Essays.* New York: Harcourt, Brace and Company. 1947.

Whelpton, Eric. *The Making of a European.* London: Johnson. 1974.

Ngaio Marsh

Bargainnier, Earl F. "Ngaio Marsh" in *10 Women of Mystery.*

Dacres-Manning. "Thoughts on the Life of a Marvelous Woman" in *Ngaio Marsh: The Woman and Her Work.* (See Rahn, below.)

Dooley, Allan C., and Linda J. "Rereading Ngaio Marsh" in *Art in Crime Writing.*

Keating, H. R. F. "Outsold and Outsmarted, But . . ." in *Ngaio Marsh: The Woman and Her Work.* (See Rahn, below.)

★Lewis, Margaret. *Ngaio Marsh: A Life.* London: Chatto & Windus. 1991.

McDorman, Katherine Slate. *Ngaio Marsh.* Boston: Twayne Publishers. 1991.

★Marsh, Ngaio. "Birth of a Sleuth," *The Writer.* March 1977.

★Marsh, Ngaio. "Portrait of Troy" in *Murderess Ink.*

Mitgang, Herbert. "Ngaio Marsh," *The New York Times Book Review.* (Book Ends.) November 9, 1980.

Panek, LeRoy. "Ngaio Marsh" in *Watteau's Shepherds.*

Rahn, B. J. "Ngaio Marsh: The Detective Novelist of Manners." *The Armchair Detective.* Spring 1994.

★Rahn, B. J. (ed.) *Ngaio Marsh: The Woman and Her Work.* Metuchen, New Jersey, and London: The Scarecrow Press, Inc. 1995.

Stasio, Marilyn. "Another Body, Another Show: Bravo for the Backstage Mystery," *The New York Times Book Review.* October 17, 1993.

Strum, Terry (ed.). *The Oxford History of New Zealand Literature in English.* Auckland: Oxford University Press. 1991.

Symons, Julian. "Random Recollections" in *Ngaio Marsh: The Woman and Her Work.*

Josephine Tey

Gielgud, John. *Early Stages.* London: Macmillan & Co., Ltd. 1939.

MacKintosh, Elizabeth (as Gordon Daviot). *Dickon.* London: Heinemann Educational Books Ltd. 1966. (Introduction and Historical Commentary by Elizabeth Haddon.)

Roy, Sandra. *Josephine Tey.* Boston: Twayne Publishers. 1980.

Talburt, Nancy Ellen. "Josephine Tey" in *10 Women of Mystery.*

Margery Allingham

Gaskill, Rex W. "Margery Allingham" in *And Then There Were Nine . . . More Women of Mystery.*

★Martin, Richard. *Ink in Her Blood: The Life and Crime Fiction of Margery Allingham.* Ann Arbor and London: UMI Research Press. 1988.

Pike, B. A. *Campion's Career: A Study of the Novels of Margery Allingham.* Bowling Green, Ohio: Bowling Green State University Popular Press. 1987.

★Thorogood, Julia. *Margery Allingham: A Biography.* London: Heinemann. 1991.

Patricia Highsmith

Adams, Susan. "A Dark View," *Forbes.* June 15, 1998.

Becker, Mary Helen. "Highsmith, Patricia—Biography," *Collier's Encyclopedia, 1997 Edition.*

Chin, Paula. "Through a Mind, Darkly," *People Weekly.* November 1, 1993.

Dupont, Joan. "Criminal Pursuits," *The New York Times Magazine.* June 12, 1988.

Dupont, Joan. "The Poet of Apprehension," *Village Voice.* May 30, 1995.

Harrison, Russell. *Patricia Highsmith.* Twayne Publishers. 1997.

Highsmith, Patricia. "Not-Thinking with the Dishes" in *Whodunit?*

★Highsmith, Patricia. *Plotting and Writing Suspense Fiction.* Boston: The Writer, Inc. 1981. (Revised edition.)

Hilfer, Tony. *The Crime Novel—A Deviant Genre.* Austin: University of Texas Press. 1990.

Klein, Kathleen Gregory. "Patricia Highsmith" in *And Then There Were Nine . . . More Women of Mystery.*

Little, Craig. "Patricia Highsmith: The Reclusive Writer Has Another Book about Antihero Ripley," *Publishers Weekly.* November 2, 1992.

Mahoney, Mary Kay. "A Train Running on Two Sets of Tracks: Highsmith's and Hitchcock's *Strangers on a Train*" in *It's a Print!.*

Mawr, Noel Dorman. "From Villain to Vigilante," *The Armchair Detective.* Winter 1991.

Pappas, Ben. "Ripley—Believe It or Not," *Forbes.* June 15, 1998.

Pearlman, Jill. "A Terrifying Talent: Mistress of Fright," *Harper's Bazaar.* February 1989.

Wheelwright, Julie. "Small g: A Summer Idyll," *New Statesman and Society.* March 17, 1995.

P. D. James

————."Murder in Mind," *The Economist.* December 16, 1995.

★Barber, Lynn. "The Cautious Heart of P. D. James," *Vanity Fair.* March 1993.

Budd, Elaine. *13 Mistresses of Murder.*

Frumkes, Lewis Burke. "A Conversation with . . . P. D. James," *The Writer.* June 1998.

Gidez, Richard B. *P. D. James.* Boston: Twayne Publishers. 1986.

Guppy, Shusha. "P. D. James: The Art of Fiction CXLI," *Paris Review.* Summer 1995.

Gussow, Mel. "Murder, She Wrote, and Why She Did," *The New York Times.* February 3, 1998.

Harkness, Bruce. "P. D. James" in *Art in Crime Writing.*

Herbert, Rosemary. "A Mind to Write," *The Armchair Detective.* Fall 1986.

James, P. D. "A Series of Scenes" in *Whodunit?*

James, P. D. "My Bit of London," *In Britain.* December 1995. (Transcribed conversation with Suzanne Askham.)

Perrick, Penny. "Taking the Old Order and Shaking It Up," *The Sunday Times.* April 18, 1998. (Special section.)

Siebenheller, Norma. *P. D. James.* New York: Frederick Ungar Publishing Co. 1981.

Stasio, Marilyn. "No Gore, Please—They're British: An Interview with P. D. James," *The Writer.* March 1990.

Wadler, Joyce. "P. D. James: She's the Soul of Cozy Gentility, Yet Many Have Died by Her Hand," *People Weekly.* December 8, 1986.

Ruth Rendell

Alexander, Lynn M. "Ruth Rendell" in *Great Women Mystery Writers.*

Bakerman, Jane. S. "Barbara Vine: Great Expectations Generously Fulfilled," *The Armchair Detective.* Summer 1993.

Bakerman, Jane S. "Ruth Rendell" in *10 Women of Mystery.*

Barnard, Robert. "A Talent to Disturb: An Appreciation of Ruth Rendell," *The Armchair Detective.* Spring 1983.

Clark, Susan L. "A Fearful Symmetry," *The Armchair Detective.* Summer 1989.

Green, Ruth. "Author Fact File: Ruth Rendell." BBC Education: www.bbc.co.uk.

Guttridge, Peter. "Writers at War." BBC Education: www.bbc.co.uk.

★Kadonaga, Lisa. "Strange Countries and Secret Worlds in Ruth Rendell's Crime Novels," *The Geographical Review.* July 1998.

McDermid, Val. "Val McDermid on Ruth Rendell." The Tangled Web: www.twbooks.co.uk.

Rendell, Ruth and Colin Ward. *Undermining the Central Line.* London: Chatto & Windus (Chatto Counter Blasts series). 1989.

Mary Higgins Clark

Clark, Mary Higgins. "A Husband Beyond Compare," *Reader's Digest.* December 1989.

Clark, Mary Higgins. "In Defense of Suspense," *Mary Higgins Clark Mystery Magazine.* Premier issue, 1996.

Clark, Mary Higgins. Online interview with the Book Report: BookPage@aol.com. April 15, 1997.

Clark, Mary Higgins. "My Wild Irish Mother," *Reader's Digest.* July 1991.

Clark, Mary Higgins. "Suppose? And What If?" *The Writer.* March 1996.

Clark, Mary Higgins. "Taking the Plunge," *The Writer.* July 1992.

Donohue, John W. "Of Many Things," *America.* May 1, 1993.

Fakih, Kimberly Olson. "The Reassuring Triumph of the Good: An Interview with Mary Higgins Clark," *Library Journal.* March 15, 1990.

Fisher, Rachel. "French Toast Pulp Fiction Queen," *Variety.* August 31, 1998.

★Grape, Jan. "A Conversation with Mary Higgins Clark" in *Deadly Women.*

Pelzer, Linda C. *Mary Higgins Clark: A Critical Companion.* Westport, Connecticut, and London: Greenwood Press. 1995.

Sue Grafton

————— *The Voice-Tribune Newspaper.* October 10, 1999.

Ames, Katrine with Ray Sawhill. "Murder Most Fair and Foul," *Newsweek.* May 14, 1990.

Goodman, Susan. "Interview: Sue Grafton and Tony Hillerman," *Modern Maturity.* July–August 1995.

Morgan, Sue. "Female Dick," *Interview.* May 1990.

Silet, Charles L. P. "Sue Grafton" in *Speaking of Murder.*

Thomas, Margaret Caldwell. Interview with Sue Grafton. January 18, 2000.

West, J. Alec. "An Interview with Sue Grafton," *Murderous Intent.* Spring 1998.

Patricia Cornwell

————— "A Tale Too True," *People Weekly.* September 8, 1997.

★Bachrach, Judy. "Death Becomes Her," *Vanity Fair.* May 1997.

Duncan, Paul. "Patricia Cornwell" in *Speaking of Murder.*

Miller, Mark and Katrine Ames. "A League of Her Own: Patricia Cornwell Mines Her Dark Side." *Newsweek.* July 22, 1996.

Reid, Calvin. "Books in Court: Libel, Copyright, Privacy Disputes," *Publishers Weekly.* August 18, 1997.

Tangora, Joanne. "Patricia D. Cornwell: Life Imitates Art in the Career of Mystery/Thriller Author," *Publishers Weekly.* February 15, 1991.

Tresniowski, Alex. "Stranger than Fiction: Novelist Patricia Cornwell Gets Caught up in a Real-life Crime," *People Weekly.* July 22, 1996.

Walls, Jeanette. "Jodie, Jodie, Jodie," *Esquire.* January 1997.

Minette Walters

Came, Barry. "Literary Autopsies: Minette Walters Spares Few Murderous Details," *Maclean's.* March 8, 1999.

James, Dean. "Interview with Minette Walters" in *Deadly Women.*

Ludbrook, Peter. "Thrillers to Die For." BBC Education Archive: The Bookworm.www.bbc.co.uk.

*Muller, Adrian. "Minette Walters" in *Speaking of Murder.*

Silet, Charles L. P. "An Interview with Minette Walters," *The Armchair Detective.* Spring 1994.

Stasio, Marilyn. "Crime," *The New York Times Book Review.* June 27, 1999.

Emma Lathen

Bedell, Jeanne F. "Emma Lathen" in *10 Women of Mystery.*

Boys, Peter, "Emma Lathen on Accounting," *CPA Journal.* May 1995.

Kleinfield, N. R. "Wall Street's Agatha Christie," *The New York Times.* February 22, 1981.

Lathen, Emma. "The Great American Bank Robbery," *The New York Times Book Review.* November 21, 1993.

Sarjeant, William A. S. "Crime on Wall Street," *The Armchair Detective.* Spring 1988.

Stasio, Marilyn. "Crime," *The New York Times Book Review.* December 8, 1991.

Storhoff, Gary. "Emma Lathen" in *Great Women Mystery Writers.*

Thomas, Robert McG., Jr. "M. J. Latsis, 70, Emma Lathen Writing Team Collaborator," *The New York Times.* October 31, 1997. (Obituary.)

Margaret Millar

Grimes, William. "Margaret Millar Is Dead at 79; Wrote Psychological Mysteries." *The New York Times.* March 29, 1994.

Hale, Virginia S. "Margaret Millar" in *Great Women Mystery Writers.*

Reilly, John M. "Margaret Millar" in *10 Women of Mystery.*

Winn, Dilys. "Margaret Millar and the Greatest Opening Lines since 'In the Beginning'" in *Murderess Ink.*

Lilian Jackson Braun

———— "The Bumbler and the Silken Sleuths: 'The Cat Who' Mysteries of Lilian Jackson Braun." *The North Carolina Literary Review* 5. 1996.

———— Article in *People Weekly.* February 17, 1997.

Braun, Lilian Jackson. Transcript of on-line interview. www.barnesandnoble.com. February 2, 1998.

Braun, Lilian Jackson. "Why Cats?" *Mystery Readers Journal.* Winter 1990.

*Feaster, Sharon A. *The Cat Who . . . Companion.* New York: Berkley Prime Crime. Revised edition, 1999.

Nelson, Catherine. "The Lady Who." *Armchair Detective.* Fall 1991.

Anne Perry

———— The Canterbury Public Library/Christchurch City Council Project Resource Pack: a collection of materials related to the Parker-Hulme case and Juliet Hulme/Anne Perry; includes ten contemporaneous accounts of the murder, trial (with direct testimony), subsequent events, and later publications gatherred from New Zealand newspapers. The article "The New Zealand Girl Murderers" by Rupert Furneaux in *Famous Criminal Cases V2* (London: Wingate. 1955) is also included. www.ccc.govt.nz/Library/Kete/ParkerHulme/document.html.

———— Interview with Anne Perry. *20/20* (ABC television) February 10, 1995. (Steve Schnee, *20/20* correspondent.)

Brainard, Dulcy. "Anne Perry: A Structure in Which to Grow," *Publishers Weekly.* March 27, 1995.

Darnton, John. "Author Faces Up to a Long, Dark Secret," *The New York Times.* February 14, 1995.

Lambert, Pam. "Blood Memory," *People Weekly.* September 26, 1994.

LeJeune, Anthony. "Cain His Brother," *National Review.* May 6, 1996.

Lyall, Sarah. "Mystery Writer's Hidden Mystery," *The New York Times.* August 17, 1994.

*Muller, Adrian. "Anne Perry" in *Speaking of Murder.*

Porter, John Douglas. Biographical information on Henry Rainsford Hulme including *Who's Who* entry and obituaries. www.geocities.com/Hollywood/Studio/2194.

Weintraub, Bernard. "Making a Film out of the Horror of Mother Murder," *The New York Times.* November 24, 1994.

White, R. J. *England.* American Heritage Publishing Co., Inc. 1971.

Wickens, Barbara. "Haunted by Homicide, *Maclean's.* March 27, 1995.

Others

———— "Mulled Murder, with Spice," *Time.* January 28, 1946. (Craig Rice.)

———— "Sarah Caudwell," *The Times.* February 4, 2000. (Obituary.)

———— "Wuxtry! Read All About It," *Time.* July 29, 1946. (Craig Rice.)

Marks, Jeffrey. "Craig Rice & *Time* Magazine," *The Armchair Detective.* Spring 1994.

Moran, Peggy. "Craig Rice" in *And Then There Were Nine . . . More Women of Mystery.*

INDEX